# The Best Of Paris
## Gault/Millau

Written by
**HENRI GAULT & CHRISTIAN MILLAU**

Translated by
**MARGOT DUXLER, JOHN HULL,
EDOUARD MULLER**

Edited by
**MICHAEL DEMAREST**

Contributing Editors
**JACQUES BRUNEL, MARIANNE RUFENACHT,
CHARLOTTE RUFENACHT**

Designed by
**BORDNICK & ASSOCIATES**

Crown Publishers & The Knapp Press

Published in the United States of America in 1982
Crown Publishers/The Knapp Press
Copyright© 1982 by Knapp Communications Corporation
5900 Wilshire Boulevard, Los Angeles, California 90036

Published by Crown Publishers, Inc.,
One Park Avenue, New York, New York 10016
(simultaneously in Canada by General Publishing Company Limited).

Printed in the United States of America

Library of Congress Cataloging in Publication data

Translation of: Le guide de Paris.
Includes index.
1. Paris (France)—Description—1975 — Guide-books.
I. Millau, Christian.   II. Title.
DC708.G3313      1982b      914.4'3604838      82-13064

ISBN:  0-517-547740
0-517-547759 (paperback)

10 9 8 7 6 5 4 3 2 1

First Edition

# CONTENTS

# PARIS

## CITY LIGHTS

**E**veryone knows the story of the tourist who arrives before Notre Dame, glances at his watch and says to his wife, "We have ten minutes. You do the inside, I'll do the outside." If you are getting ready for this kind of trip to Paris, we regret to inform you that this book is a very bad buy. You will be justified in writing us a cranky letter and perhaps even in demanding an invitation to lunch in retribution.

It is not for visitors hurrying to get home nor for those who let themselves be hustled about like their baggage that we have written this guide, but for those, happily numerous, who love the unexpected, the chance encounter, the surprises of the streets, and who insist on traveling like grown-ups. We even have the wild hope that after you have plunged into this thick tome, you'll no longer want to go home.

We are, obviously, not so naive as to suppose that you will sample all the thousands of addresses that we have collected for you. A whole lifetime would be too short for that. The justification of this abundance is that it opens the door to adventure. A successful trip, an intelligent trip, is always a kind of adventure: a marvelous chance to meet people, to venture into unknown shops, to visit little-known places, and to be, in a sense, a thief in a vast cavern full of treasures, rather than a lock-stepping tourist whose hours are numbered and whose freedom does not exist.

**I**n truth, Paris is an inexhaustible territory. We have combed her systematically for nearly thirty years without even coming close to discovering all her resources. You will find, for example, one of the densest concentrations of artisans in the world; and, although it is unlikely that you will have to have a Louis XVI pendulum clock repaired or to buy a fan, we promise you that if you go strolling in the old neighborhoods of the Marais and investigate the interior courts where these artisans proliferate and resist the assault of modern civilization, you will spend some of the best hours of your life. Too bad if this doesn't leave you time to go up the Eiffel Tower, climb to the top of Notre Dame, or get in line to see Napoleon's tomb. Keep in mind that there is nowhere in Paris that you *absolutely* have to visit, no restaurant where you *absolutely* must have lunch, no museum in which you *absolutely* must shuffle about. It is not a dozen "musts" that make Paris incomparable; it is her diversity: her quais of the Seine which beckon to strollers; her cafe terraces; her seemingly idle throngs which, under any pretext at all, saunter along her boulevards; her bistros whose shirt-sleeved proprietors serve you the wine of the house. And if, by chance, you can discover a little of all of this, you will have the impression, not of being a stranger in Paris at all, but of being a Parisian in his own hometown.

*Henri Gault and Christian Millau*

P.S. We do not claim to have said everything in this guide, which is, after all, a list of addresses. To visit Paris, you should also have a tourist guide, and the best, in our opinion, is *Michelin's Guide Vert,* which describes interesting streets, quarters and monuments. Each guide complements the other.

P.P.S. We welcome your comments. Please feel free to contact us at Gault Millau America, 5900 Wilshire Boulevard, Los Angeles, California 90036

# THE RESTAURANTS

# Dining Out

For centuries France was like the Seal Woman displayed in circus sideshows: a huge head on an almost nonexistent body. The huge head was Paris—Paris, where everything happened and all decisions were made: in politics and economics, literature and entertainment, social life and gastronomy. People in the provinces ate well and abundantly, but the ultimate refinement was cultivated in Paris. The great chefs worked for the Court, for the nobility and old families who staked their honor on the excellence of their table. This was the origin of the French fine art of cooking: skillful, incredibly complicated, insanely taxing and at least as concerned with how things looked as with how they actually tasted. This rather crazy way of life (no one would have dared serve fewer than ten dishes in the course of a supper) was the monopoly of a certain class of society. Under the Ancien Régime, restaurant meals were much less refined and Parisians ate at home or at friends'. But with the Revolution, and especially after 1792, these great chefs found themselves out of jobs, since their masters had either emigrated or lost all taste for food on the gallows. The chefs took their savings (they were experts at padding bills) and opened restaurants. After the Revolution, under the Directoire, these restaurants were such a hit that new ones kept opening right and left: at the beginning of the nineteenth century Paris had more than two thousand restaurants. Some of them were of unimaginable luxury and refinement. Amid the sumptuous décor at Méot's, owned by a former chef to the Duc d'Orléans, ecstatic customers selected their food from a list of a hundred dishes and could even take baths in Champagne. Beauvilliers, who had been the chef of the king's brother, the Comte de Provence, strolled among tables loaded with silver dishes and crystal, his sword at his side and his jabot unfurled on his chest. Later, under Napoleon I, Véry was to offer, in a setting of staggering richness, thirty-one poultry dishes, twenty-eight of veal and lamb, fifteen kinds of roast meat and forty-four varieties of entremets (side dishes). Under such conditions it is easy to see how Grimod de la Reynière (one of the greatest French gourmets) never spent less than four hours at the table.

Parisian restaurants kept up a rather heady pace throughout the entire nineteenth century. Balzac has given a magnificent account of the feasts at the Rocher de Cancale, where he himself would down twelve dozen oysters just to whet his appetite. Veritable fortunes—in the form of truffles à la serviette, lobster, woodcock, pheasants à la Sainte Alliance—were consumed every day at the Café de Paris and at the Café

Anglais, presided over by the great chef Dugléré. Bills of the time make one's head spin: In 1875 the Duke of Brunswick paid 2,250 francs (about $2,000) for a dinner for four at the Petit Moulin Rouge. Restaurateurs didn't give a fig for costs. Why should they, when their customers were willing to pay any price to sample one of the first melons of the year?

These eating orgies continued to some extent until World War II, but four years of German occupation, plus a 52% income tax (practically unknown in 1900) and, finally, a radical change in living habits (the discovery of dietetics and new ways of spending money, such as on automobiles, vacations, travel and weekend homes) all dealt a terrible blow to the luxury restaurants. Larue, Voisin and Le Café de Paris were forced to close down in the face of almost total indifference. A few of the great establishments—La Tour d'Argent, Lasserre, Lucas-Carton, Le Grand Véfour, Maxim's, Lapérouse—are still holding out, but neither the menus nor the service are anything like they were in the old days. They still look quite impressive, all the more so since the public—continually less refined and demanding—is easily dazzled. But there as elsewhere, things are simplified, reduced, replaced. If, for example, truffles and foie gras were to be served as generously as they were forty or fifty years ago, no luxury restaurant would be able to survive.

In the end, the cuisine in the great restaurants is becoming less and less distinguishable from the food served in less luxurious but much better establishments. The finest restaurants used to be temples where a great religion was celebrated with wildly complicated rites. Nowadays, they must strive for wide appeal in order to survive, and tend to lose their spectacular originality. They do their best to live up to their image; it's not their fault if this is becoming more and more difficult. Such as they are, they are as indispensable to Paris as the Vendôme Column or the quais along the Seine. The memory of duck at La Tour d'Argent or a bottle of Perrier-Jouët Belle Epoque at Maxim's is one of the most precious souvenirs that a man of taste can take with him from Paris.

# SMALL TREASURES LITTLE FINDS

We think that, as gastronomy now stands in Paris, the places run by an owner-chef are, with certain exceptions, in the best position to preserve fine culinary traditions. It is easier for them to foster the cult of sincere cooking; decorating and service costs are reduced to a minimum, the menu revolves around a few specialties (often good home-style dishes like braised beef, pot au feu, that are not harmed by being prepared in advance; indeed, they often benefit by it). Finally, there is a limited number of tables and the clientele is usually more knowledgeable and more demanding than in luxury establishments. Prices generally run just as high, sometimes even higher, as, for example, at L'Archestrate. At least you have the satisfaction of knowing that your bill covers only what's on your plate and not what's on the walls.

The little places, with their strong provincial flavor, are unaffected by the fads and fashions that blow now hot, now cold. Their one weak point is that they rarely survive the loss of their owner, except when he has had the wisdom to start molding his successor far in advance.

# THE PRICE MYTH

We're not telling you anything new when we say that Paris is an expensive city. But is it fair to claim that its restaurants are more expensive than those in New York or London? Knowing both sides, this assertion strikes us as most unjust. Then how does this notion come to be so widespread among visitors?

We see three explanations. The first is that inhabitants of a rich country always have a hard time accepting the fact that prices in poorer country can be just as high as at home. This feeling goes so deep that when French people go to Spain, where life is rather inexpensive for them, they spend their time arguing about prices.

The second reason, which is a corollary of the first, is that a considerable number of visitors live on a higher level than usual when they come to Paris. They head straight for the most famous restaurants, these being the only ones they have ever heard of. Do they really think that Parisians have their every meal at La Tour d'Argent or Taillevent? Of course not. In Paris, as in New York or London, dinner in a great restaurant is for most people a rather rare occassion, out of the ordinary feast.

The last reason is that people still drink relatively little wine outside of France. Here, on the contrary, a visitor doesn't dare refuse wine, either out of curiosity or because he is somewhat dazzled by his surroundings. Sommeliers in the great restaurants say that most of their prestigious (and therefore extremely costly) bottles are ordered by foreigners, and by Anglo-Saxons in particular.

You mustn't forget that a single bottle can easily double your bill. So if you want to compare the price of a first-rate meal in Paris with that of a dinner in New York or London, you should do it honestly and not compare a bottle of Haut-Brion with a dry martini. You'll then see that a great meal costs just as much on either side of the Atlantic or of the channel.

To wind up the topic of prices, here's a little trick to enable you to calculate the price of your meal quickly, as you read the menu. If you triple the price of the entrée, you'll get a figure close to your total bill, including the wine (if it's a reasonable vintage).

If this is your first visit to Paris, it is obviously preferable to go to the great restaurants in the evening. With the exception perhaps of La Tour d'Argent, because of its striking view of the Seine and Notre Dame. In the other restaurants and bistros, lunch attracts an overwhelming proportion of men. Women stay at home or nibble a sandwich as they shop, while their husbands gorge themselves, building a better world on a foundation of beef and Beaujolais.

# WHAT TIME

For lunch, from twelve-thirty to two o'clock. Dinner, around eight-thirty; later (between nine and nine-thirty) in luxury restaurants. In any case, and perhaps due to Spanish influence, Parisians are getting into the habit of dining later and later. Opening and closing times of restaurants, bars and nightclubs are subject to changes, and we suggest that you verify these with a telephone call.

# RESERVATIONS

As a general rule, reservations are necessary. Even when a restaurant isn't full, a reservation assures you of a better table. If you are alone and want to dine in a large restaurant, our advice is to fib a little and reserve a table for two! Single diners are a thorn in the side of restaurateurs, who often seat them at any odd place.

# WHAT TO ORDER

**A** good rule to follow is: Trust the owner or maître d'hôtel and let him make suggestions. If the menu includes a plat du jour (daily special), you generally can't go wrong by ordering it. As a rule it is guaranteed not to have languished in the kitchen or refrigerator. This is especially true at lunch. If the dinner special is, for example, a leg of lamb that is already three-fourths gone, pass it over, it's had more than enough time to dry out since lunchtime.

It is wise to take the time of year, and even the time of day, into account. If you are offered game out of season, it will be domestically raised or imported but frozen and of abysmal quality. You should know, for example, that it is extremely difficult to get freshly killed native hare in Paris after the month of October, and that when Christmas is past, young partridge becomes old partridge, and can only be eaten stewed with cabbage. Once the season is over, why bother ordering cèpes, which are marvelous when they're fresh, and mediocre when they come from a can or, dried, from a bag?

Since you can't possibly know the right season for everything, the simplest solution is to ask the waiter or owner whether or not something is a produit de saison (in season). There is a world of difference between a stringbean picked that morning or the day before and a bean that comes out of a can. And if you can't tell the difference, rush this book back to the store this very minute . . . .

The day of the week is important too. Fish is the freshest on Fridays (when the demand is greatest), whereas meat and shellfish are sometimes not as fresh on Mondays, when restaurants use up their odds and ends and the markets are closed.

Take your time reading the menu and ordering. If the waiter tries to rush you, complain, call the owner, if necessary walk out. Waiters are there to serve you, not vice versa. And don't let yourself be cowed by surly bistro waiters. Tell them, with a smile, to stop bugging you. Once they know who's boss, they'll bend over backward for you.

Don't be afraid to order a single dish for two if you're not particularly hungry. After the hors d'oeuvres, for example, share one fish and one meat course. You won't be overeating, and your meal will have a pleasant note of variety. Some restaurants, like the Ami Louis, serve such enormous portions that sharing is essential, even if it isn't suggested to you.

Gourmet restaurants always have two or three spécialités de la maison, usually underlined in red on the menu. These are often worth looking into. Not always. We therefore take the liberty of advising you to make careful note of the dishes we recommend at each of the restaurants mentioned in this book.

For some years now, a number of quality restaurants have been offering a *menu-dégustation,* or sampling menu. This allows you to taste seven or eight different dishes, all served in tiny quantities. It's a good idea when the cuisine is really worth the trouble.

# WHAT TO DRINK

If you dare drink martinis or whiskey before a fine meal, we'll kill you! How do you expect to appreciate good cooking when your palate has been numbed by alcohol? It might even be all right if people were satisfied with one drink, but they have to have two, three, four. They get to the table with a heavy head and coated tongue, incapable of discerning the flavor of a dish or a wine. If you absolutely must drink something, order a goblet of Champagne, a glass of port, a kir (red or white wine with a dash of black currant liqueur) or simply open the nice cool Beaujolais, Muscadet or fine Sauternes which you will be drinking with your meal.

# HOW TO SELECT WINE

We are not about to review all the wines of France. The subject has been covered many times in many volumes. Our more modest aim is to call your attention to a few points that authors generally forget to mention.

If you are in a restaurant that has a wine sommelier, remember: his role is to advise, to help you profit from his knowledge, not to bring you a piece of cardboard. You should therefore tell him what you are having (and in what order) and ask what he suggests. Some sommeliers, spoiled by the ignorance of their customers, have a tendency to be remiss. If, for example, the wine steward can't make a more intelligent suggestion than Champagne or rosé, on the pretext that you are having both fish and meat, you have a perfect right to ask him to be a little more imaginative. A dinner accompanied by Champagne, although undoubtedly pleasant in hot weather, is debatable gastronomically. Champagne is very good with light meals, but is not at all suited to rich dishes like flamed woodcock or hare à la royale. As for those rosés that "go with everything," they actually go with nothing.

This holy fear of mixing wines is absurd: No one has ever died from starting off with a Corton-Charlemagne or a Meursault and following it with a Chambertin or a good Pomerol. The essential, as in everything, is not overdo it.

A number of good restaurants have a "house wine," generally served in a carafe. It comes directly from the barrel, is reasonably priced and, without being a great wine, is more often than not a good, honest one. For several years Beaujolais has been "the" wine. Beaujolais (Beaujolais-Villages, Morgon, Chiroubles, Juliénas, Fleurie, Brouilly, Côte-de-Brouilly, Moulin-à-Vente, Chénas, Saint-Amour) is full-bodied and delicious. It is best when young and cool. The trouble is that some are very bad. The good bistros serve authentic Beaujolais (we'll point them out as we go along). If the name on the label is followed by the words viticulteur (winegrower) or propriétaire-récoltant (owner-producer), the wine stands a good chance of being honest and pure. Origin is important for all wines. In Burgundy, the vineyards (with the exception of the Romanée-Conti estate) belong to a multitude of owners. There is not any one particular kind of Gevrey-Chambertin or Pommard (whereas in the Bordeaux region there is only one Château Lafite-Rothschild, one Château Pétrus, etc.) so that the same name may apply to two very different wines. This is why the dealer and estate are so important. At present, the list of dealers one can trust almost blindfolded (which doesn't preclude an occasional unpleasant surprise) is headed by Louis Latour, Leroy, Louis Jadot, Drouhin-Laroze, Drouhin, who handle almost all the Burgundies, followed by estates of varying importance but uniformly high quality, such as Comte de Moucheron, Marquis d'Angerville, Comte de Vogué, Bouchard père et fils, Ropiteau, Paul Rouleau, Grivellet père et fils, Moingeon and Lupé-Cholé.

If you are determined to treat yourself to a prestigious bottle, try to act like a true connoisseur. Ideally, you should telephone a few hours in advance so that your bottle can be uncorked and the wine become thoroughly aerated while it waits. This may be difficult to do; in that case, select your wine as soon as you get to the restaurant and don't hesitate to postpone sitting down at the table. In an hour the wine will have rounded out and recaptured its full fragrance.

Since we are on the subject of old wines, it's a good time to warn you about the excessive idolatry from which they often benefit. Aging a wine for thirty, fifty or sixty years doesn't necessarily make it wonderful; on the contrary, it risks getting the wine past its prime. It can be sublime, but it's often disappointing. So don't have any misgivings about drinking a great Burgundy which is under twelve years old (much less for the whites, since, with some exceptions, these keep very badly). Bordeaux, however, improves with age, since it loses its harshness, but it is perfectly drinkable four, five or seven years after bottling.

One final word, do not allow anyone to serve you a red wine that is too warm. This may mean that the bottle was chambréed by being put near a hot stove or, who knows, even in a basin of hot water, which is guaranteed to "break" it. An old wine should be drunk at room temperature, which implies that it should be a few degrees below that when it is brought out, since contact with your hand will warm it up very quickly in the glass. On the other hand, a young red wine should be drunk at the temperature of the wine cellar.

# HOW MUCH TO TIP

The service is almost always shown on the menu, and can be 12, 15 or 18 percent, depending on the class of the establishment. If you are very pleased with your meal and the way it was served, it is an elegant touch to leave a few franc pieces on the table, but nothing obliges you to do so. Leave five or ten francs for the sommelier if you have had a fine bottle of wine, but you can be sure that his behavior will in no way indicate that he expects something from you.

# SYMBOL SYSTEMS

Restaurants are marked on a scale of 0 to 20, and are judged only on their cooking. Decor, welcome, atmosphere and service do not influence the rating, but are otherwise commented upon quite explicitly within the reviews. Restaurants that score 13 and above are distinguished with toques (chef's hats), according to the following table:

| | | |
|---|---|---|
| Exceptional | ⚜ | 4 toques, for 19 or 20/20 |
| Excellent | ⚜ | 3 toques, for 17 or 18/20 |
| Very good | ⚜ | 2 toques, for 15 or 16/20 |
| Good | ⚜ | 1 toque, for 13 or 14/20 |

Toques in yellow indicate nouvelle or, at least, creative cuisine; the others for classical cuisine.

We should point out that these marks are *relative.* One toque for 13/20, when awarded to a highly reputed restaurant, is not a very good mark, whereas it is for a small restaurant without much culinary pretention.

Except when otherwise indicated, the restaurant prices listed are for an average meal comprising an appetizer, a main course, a dessert, and a half-bottle of wine. The prices are obviously only approximate, and unfortunately, many will have changed by the time you read these lines.

Many chefs have the bad habit of changing restaurants, and thus a good restaurant can turn mediocre or even bad in just a few days. Restaurants where the chef is also the owner are, in theory, more stable, but even they are liable to deteriorate: Success can turn an owner's head, and he may be tempted to accept too many diners, and quality generally suffers for it. Should this have occurred, please be indulgent with us. Our profession is not an easy one—we can't be held responsible!

And one last word: menus can change often. The dishes we have described were available pre-publication. We apologize if what we reviewed is no longer available; it's out of our control!

## 12/20
### *L'Absinthe*
**24 place du Marché-St-Honoré**
**260.02.45**
*M. Malabard*
*Open until 11:30 P.M. Closed Sat. (at lunch) and Sun. Pay parking at Saint-Honoré.*
*DC, V.*

M. Malabard's small turn-of-the-century bistro is always filled with young, pretty customers, especially during the evening. It's not surprising that this has been going on for years: the decor is charming, the prices are not too high, the welcome is friendly, and the cuisine is fashionable, but intelligent. Magret of duck with fruit, farci of poultry with cabbage, fricassée of sole with lime, escalope of lotte with purée of bell pepper. In spring and summer, a few tables are set on the sidewalk on the square.
Carte: 150F.

## 11/20
### *Joe Allen*
**30 rue Pierre Lescot**
**236.70.13**
*M. Lesueur.*
*Open until 1:00 A.M.*

A reasonably faithful copy of the Los Angeles and New York restaurant-bar we have so often seen in Hollywood movies: dark walls covered with theater posters, friendly waiters, an amusing mixture of clientele, and "exotic" cuisine (chile con carne, American mixed salads, apple pie). This is Joe Allen's, which, after several years of operation, remains one of the sincerest and busiest restaurants of the new Halles. Carte: 130F.

## 11/20
### *Chez Armand*
**6 rue du Beaujolais**
**260.05.11**
*M. Bandeira*
*Open until 2:00 A.M. Closed Sun. (during summer), 10 days at Christmas and 2 weeks during August.*

It's not only the salads that are gay in this small, cozy cellar with a vaulted ceiling—although the candlelight does make the ladies look prettier, whenever there are any to be found. Expect an amusing clientele drawn from show business and the gay element of Paris high society, and a somewhat less amusing cuisine based on salads ("from field and sea"): Harlequin salad, lotte en brochette and steamed turbot. A disastrous liver soufflé with écrevisses, good fresh fruit salads and inflated prices.
Carte: About 160F.

## 11/20
### *Auberge des Trois Bonheurs*
**280 rue Saint-Honoré**
**260.43.24**
*M. Chong*
*Open until 11:15 P.M. Pay parking on rue des Pyramides.*
*AE, DC, V.*

An elegant, old Chinese restaurant whose latest chef came straight from Hong Kong (specifically, the Golden Crown in Kowloon), bringing with him a whole load of delicacies. These include rice, of course, and it is some of the best in Paris. The two other delights to be discovered in this inn of happiness are the steamed turbot and braised gambas à la cantonaise. Prices are a little too high.
Carte: 120F–150F.

15

## Barrière Poquelin

**17 rue Molière**
**296.22.19**

*M. Dard.*
*Open until 11:00 P.M., Fri. and*
*Sat. until midnight; Closed Sat.*
*(lunch) and Sun.*
*AE, DC, V.*

Some thirty place settings, a bit tight, in a small dining room with an intimate and banal décor, everything in yellow, and fading before your eyes (the green plants too, with their garnishing of plastic hydrangeas). An elegant and alert clientele in the evening—noticeably quieter at lunch (retired executives and old frumps for the most part)—who take their time studying the lovely seasonal menus of the very young, new chef, Stéphane Lagorce, a fresh twenty-year-old who shows the sure signs of a born performer. Even if it happens that a vegetable ragoût turns out to be neither under-cooked nor frankly raw. Or when the Sauternes sauce accompanying the (perfectly roasted) calf's kidney extends over the spinach garnish—the most unlikely sauce to bring out its smoothness. But we'll overlook the blurry regions of a menu conceived essentially to highlight the precocious mastery of Patrick Dard's protégé, the great Frédéric, the eldest son. Instead, we'll emphasize the dishes that seemed to us to dominate the last meals: that is, the salad de bouquet with walnut oil, the fricassée of fish of the day (steamed with mushrooms), the salmon en escalopine, the roast game in general (including the Scottish grouse not listed on the menu), the young rabbit with ginger, and then the Roquefort served with old port—just as Talleyrand liked it. To finish, a curious charlotte à l'orange covered in a pear purée with red wine.
Carte: 170F to 200F. Menu: 120F + 15% serv.

## 10/20
## Les Bateleurs du Pont-Neuf

**14-16 rue du**
**Pont-Neuf**
**233.38.47**

*Mme Benain*
*Open until 12:30 A.M. Pay*
*parking at Louvre.*
*AE, DC, V.*

Evelyne Benain never tires of her unchanging repertory: grilled meats, fondue bourguignonne, and, once in a while, a good special of the day. The result is that our latest impression of this large, neo-medieval pub is exactly the same as our earliest: a nice, friendly place for the night owls who haunt the area between the Samaritaine and Saint-Eustache.
Carte: 120F. Menus: 36F (wine incl.) + 15% serv., 47F (wine and serv. incl.).

13

## Baumann-Baltard

**9 rue Coquillière**
**236.22.00**

*Mme. Moreau.*
*Open until 2:00 A.M.*
*Open terrace.*
*V.*

An Alsatian restaurant without foie gras? That's right. Guy-Pierre Baumann directs this operation with the help of a computer, and banishes all products that are too expensive. The exception always is fish, his choucroute with fish is sacrosanct, and there is no question of sacrificing it. But if he loses on the swings, he wins on the round abouts with typical bistro offerings that do not cost too much to prepare and stick to the ribs, such as salad of tripe with chives; calf's head, stuffed pig's tail (too fat), and the whole gamut of choucroutes, in which he is the leading specialist in Paris. Try the latest, cooked in red

wine with preserved pork; you must have a cast-iron stomach for this, but it is delicious. The decor is by Slavik—mirrors everywhere, with frilly, checked shades, and the atmosphere is as warm as the excellent house Riesling is cold. On the plant-enclosed terrace it's almost like dining in the country.
Carte: 110F–135F.

15

## Gérard Besson
**5 rue Coq-Héron**
**233.14.74**
*M. Besson.*
*Open until 10:30 P.M.;Closed Sat.*
*(at lunch) and Sun.*
*V.*

It's not surprising that this small restaurant has a faithful clientele. The decor is not wildly inspiring, but it is comfortable; the welcome is warm; the service is particularly friendly; and the cooking of Gérard Besson (Meilleur Ouvrier; formerly with Gavin and Chapel) perfectly executed, with a dash of fantasty and real a interest in natural flavors. Each day he offers, depending upon availability, a half-dozen ably cooked fish dishes, (turbot with eggplant, roast bass en papillote and appealing items such as fricassée of veal with vinegar, entrecôte Bercy with a celery mousseline, or a rarity in restaurants these days—a succulent roast Bresse chicken with mushrooms fricassée, followed by several good desserts, notably a prélat d'Alexandre Dumaine or the small cream puffs with melted chocolate or pistachio nuts. The bill is a bit steep, but take note of the several entrées between 30F and 35F.
Carte: 150F–250F. Menus (at lunch only): 140F (wine, coffee and serv. incl.), 190F (dégustation) + 15% serv.

16

## Le Bistro d'Hubert
**36 place du Marché-Saint-Honoré**
**260.03.00**
*M. Hubert.*
*Open until 10:30 P.M. Closed*
*Sun. and Mon.*
*Open terrace. Air cond. Parking.*
*V.*

For those who are not tempted at lunch by the superb menu (prices superb also) on the second-floor dining room, Hubert had the good idea of putting a dozen tables on the ground floor of his attractive bistro. This back room is a little dark, but not disagreeable, and he serves several entrées and plats du jour, such as a good leg of lamb with gratin dauphinois, roast chicken with mashed potatoes, followed by simple and very good desserts with good regional wines by the glass or carafe (around 50F–70F for an honest meal). Or, if you are in a hurry, Hubert's shop next door serves sandwiches and prepares meals to take out. But the upstairs dining room is the gem of Hubert's empire. There, aided by a first-rate team, (his assistant Gérard Chotard, has worked with Senderens, and Menau, a helper, was formerly with Troisgros) he prepares a modern, imaginative, polished cuisine. Delicious raw salmon with oil and ginger, braised bass with white Cadène, chicken with basil and pastis, veal sweetbreads with prawns and chevril butter, braised kidneys with mint and mustard. The list of delicious dishes is long and often changed, and they are never weighted with heavy sauces,

Hubert rightly preferring the juices in which the meats are cooked. His desserts are always a delight, and his wines perfect, even the most modest ones such as the Pierre Coste Bordeaux at 45F or the Testut Côtes-du-Rhône at 40F. Another innovation: cooking classes for small groups on Tuesdays and Fridays.

Carte: 180F–250F (at lunch, a fixed-price meal at 120F).

**12/20**

## Le Boeuf du Palais Royal

**18 rue Thérèse**
**296.04.29**
*Open until 9:00 P.M. Closed Sun.*
*AE, DC, V.*

A cozy decor, but the comforts are rudimentary—especially lunch, when it's elbow to elbow. Dinner is usually quieter. The fries and fillet of beef with poivre vert are still tops, as are the confit of duck sarladaise and côte de boeuf à la moelle. Duboeuf Beaujolais and increasingly unreasonable prices outside of the minuscule list of specials.

Carte: 130F. Menu: 36F + 15% serv.

**11/20**

## Les Bouchons

**19 rue des Halles**
**233.28.73**
*Messieurs Eclache and Rosine*
*Open until 1:00 A.M. Pay parking*
*at Forum des Halles.*
*AE, V.*

Behind a triumphal facade supported by two monumental caryatids stands what was once the old establishment of M. Brun, king of the Parisian café. With a surface of nearly 10,000 square feet, there is more than enough breathing room. The decor is imitation marble, bistro tables, and green plants. The cuisine, half Lyonnaise and half exotic, is quite well prepared: stuffed crab, lamb curry, cervelles Lyonnaise. The pastry chef (formerly of the Hôtel Crillon) creates some remarkable tartes. Modest wines starting at 25F. In the late evening, you can hear good jazz in the cellar piano bar.

Carte: about 100F.

**13**

## Caveau du Palais

**19 place Dauphine**
**326.04.28**
*M. Dieuleveut.*
*Open until 10:00 P.M. Closed Sat.*
*evening and Sun.*
*Open Terrace. Pay parking at*
*rue de Harley.*
*Card: V.*

The two levels of this likeable restaurant between the quai des Orfèvres and the quai Dauphine are enjoying a growing success since the installation of a young team which is parlaying a sincere welcome, smiling service, and a good, unpretentious cuisine into a good, unpretentious eating place. The kitchen is presided over by Pascal Loué, formerly saucier at the Sofitel in Sèvres. You will enjoy his terrine of veal sweetbread with pistachios, his fricassée of calf's kidneys and sweetbreads with honey, the sole and lotte with fresh mint, and his chocolate marquise. There is a choice of good modest wines around 30F per bottle including Bordeaux.

Carte: 150F–170F.

**10/20**

## Le Centre Ville

**9 rue de la**
**Grande-Truanderie**

Yes, it is a restaurant (amusing pine nut salad, somewhat heavy tagliatelli, not-too-exciting desserts), but above all, it is an old tripe shop renovated and attractively decorated (bricks, carmine-red lacquer, black-lacquered shades)

**260.50.96**
*M. Brezinski.*
*Open until 2:00 A.M. Closed Sun.*
*Dinner only.*
*V.*

which attracts a diversified spectrum of the latest Parisian fashions. Chic teenagers, funkies from well-to-do families, prancing rockers, very pretty girls more or less accompanied, and, later in the evening, members of the "in" crowd. Blaring "mood" music.
Carte: 120F. Menu: 70F (serv. incl.).

**11/20**

### Chez Clovis
**33 rue Berger**
**233.97.07**
*M. Cornut*
*Open until midnight. Closed Sun.*
*and during August. Pay parking*
*at Forum des Halles.*
*V.*

A Merovingian relic from the era of the old Halles. Even in the second-floor dining room, with its superb view of Saint-Eustache and Sacred Real Estate, you are immersed in the auroch-like atmosphere, carefully maintained by the owner and his staunch cuisine. It's solid (if not light) eating: homemade headcheese, haricot of lamb, boeuf à la ficelle with four vegetables, tête de veau in sauce gribiche, and clafoutis. You'll go away comfortably stuffed.
Carte: 120F.

**12/20**

### Au Cochon d'Or
**31 rue du Jour**
**236.38.31**
*Mme Ayral*
*Open until 10:15 P.M. Closed Sun.*
*Pay parking at Forum des Halles.*
*AE, V.*

This little piggy is the baby brother of the famous Cochon d'Or at the Hotel Villette. Its keeper is the exacting restaurateur, Jean Ayral, or, to be more exact, his daughter–procurator, Beatrice. Under her guidance, this old, restored bistro is rising out of its torpor. The exquisite meats from Jouanno are no longer mistreated, and the new chef isn't afraid to experiment: leeks with smoked salmon, warm gulf terrine with two sauces, minced calf's kidneys in Roquefort sauce. We are also happy to discover a slightly more relaxed note in the welcome and service. Reasonable prices.
Carte: 130F–150F.

**10/20**

### Conway's
**73 rue Saint-Denis**
**508.07.70**
*Mme. Conway.*
*Open until 1:00 A.M. Closed Mon.*

Our pretty Avia loves spareribs and banana cake (judge for yourself if this retired fashion model resists temptation). We adore our pretty Avia, and somewhat less her barbecued chicken, her hamburgers, or, on Sundays between noon and 4:00 P.M., her brunch, solid and banal chow for lazy late-risers.
Carte: 70F.

**11/20**

### Côté Jardin
**22 rue Mondétour**
**508.11.35**
*M. Devey.*
*Open until 1:00 A.M. Dinner only.*
*AE.*

There is so much greenery, palms, bamboo, brilliant lacquer, and freshness in this attractive retro setting that one has the impression that the salads (côté jardin), the artichokes (à la Tsarine), the eggplant (Sicilienne), the chives (with young rabbit), the avocados (in pâté with green pepper) are growing under the chef's feet in the kitchen. The simplicity and freshness of these dishes, served year in and year out, make for their own charm—not to mention a reasonable bill as well as a sympathetic welcome.
Carte: 100F.

**10/20**

### Au Diable des Lombards

**64 rue des Lombards**
**233.81.84**
*M. Eclache*
*Open until 1:00 A.M.*
*AE, V.*

Alain Eclache loves the restaurant business, especially when he's successful. So, he very wisely sees to it that his business is nothing but successful, both here and in his new bistro in the rue des Halles, Les Bouchons. In other words, he tries never to disappoint the beautiful people who come to enjoy his cuisine: grilled meats, hamburgers and cheeseburgers, country-fresh chicken and rabbit, and good ice cream made on the premises with raw milk straight from a farm in the province of Berry.
Carte: 100F–120F.

**12/20**

### Escargot Montorgueil

**38 rue Montorgueil**
**236.83.51**
*Mme. Terrail.*
*Open until 10:30 P.M. Closed*
*Mon. and the wk. of August 15.*
*AE, DC, V.*

Along with le Véfour, Lucas-Carton and Maxim's, this old post house possesses one of the most attractive and authentic décors in Paris. It is essentially Restoration (with touching up in 1880) the painted ceiling, of the most exquisite Romanticism, with cut-glass mirrors, dark paneling, crimson velvets, and bronze tulipped chandeliers. The cuisine is under the rule of Mme Saladin-Terrail, nicknamed Kouikette, sister of Claude Terrail (of the Tour d'Argent). Snails are still the principal attraction: à la bourguignonne, with fennel, mint, or curry; with some good fish dishes, notably the turbot Montorgueil stuffed with salmon, and some interesting fritters with seasonal fruits. Over-run at midday by the prosperous neighborhood merchants, the Escargot is much more charming in the evening. The female clientele likes its flattering lighting, its old-fashioned service, and the Champagne in carafes; it tends to like the bill a lot less.
Carte: 180F–200F.

**10/20**

### André Faure

**40 rue du Mont-Thabor**
**260.74.28**
*M. Faure*
*Open until 10:00 P.M. Closed Sun.*
*and during August.*

At lunch, you'll find models from Chanel, IBM employees, and upper echelon civil servants who've come to enjoy the special of the day and the grilled meats. In the evening, you'll find foreigners and visitors from the provinces, young couples out on a tight budget, and unpretentious folks who appreciate good value for their money. Fair enough: the owner's motto is "Boire et manger à gogo" (Eat and drink as much as you like), and he is true to his word. The country–style meals—although not terribly delicate and served with excessive haste—are bountiful: a selection of fifteen hors d'oeuvres, a country special (sautéed rabbit, stewed chicken), cheese and fromage blanc, dessert and all the wine you can drink.
Carte: 40F. Menu (dinner only): 50F (including wine) + 15% serv.

**12/20**

### La Ferme Irlandaise

**30 place du**

The ownership has just changed, as has the decor (simple and fresh, discreet and appealing), and the charming Colleens, who will certainly find some helpful French men to teach them our own language, unabashedly serve

**Marché-Saint-Honoré**
**296.02.99**
*M. Whelan.*
*Open until 11:00 P.M. Closed Sun.*
*evenings, Mon., and*
*December 20 to 30.*
*No dogs.*
*AE, DC, V.*

**11/20**

## Chez Gabriel
**123 rue Saint-Honoré**
**233.02.99**
*M. Chasselay.*
*Open until 9:30 P.M. Closed Sun.*
*evening, Mon. and during August.*
*Pay parking at rue Bailleul.*
*AE, DC, V.*

**12/20**

## Le Globe d'Or
**158 rue St. Honoré**
**260.23.37**
*M. Clement.*
*Open until 11:00 P.M.*
*Closed Sat. and Sun.*
*AE, DC, V.*

14

## Goumard
**17 rue Duphot**
**260.36.07**
*M. Goumard.*
*Open until 10:30 P.M.*
*Closed 20 days in August.*
*AE, DC, V.*

16

## Le Grand Véfour
**17 rue du Beaujolais**
**296.56.27**
*M. Oliver.*
*Open until 9:30 P.M. Closed Sat.,*
*Sun. and during August. No dogs.*

country dishes—we are informed by a sign—whose ingredients come directly from the coasts and hills of the Emerald Isle. Exquisite smoked salmon cut in thick slices, superb "black" sole, an interesting chicken stuffed with spices with very crisp cabbage, Irish stew (the national dish), Irish cheeses (among them the admirable Wexford blue), fresh raw fruit tartes, an agreeable homemade soda bread, and, to be sure, Guinness—but also some good little French wines. Pleasant clientele—especially if you like pretty young people. For around 100F you can have a pleasant meal, provided you specify that the meat or fish not be overcooked.
Menu: 90F, 130F. (serv. incl.).

No change this year in this pleasant bistro located in the old Halles. If that surprises you, then you don't know M. Chasselay. He would rather be drawn and quartered than add the slightest invention to his immovable menu printed in violet ink. A menu where, since time eternal, the rosette de Lyon, cervelle of lamb and skate in brown butter have held their sacred places.
Carte: 150F–170F.

A short journey through France's Southwest: a Castelnaudary cassoulet on Thursdays and, every day, preserved duck with sautéed potatoes, cèpes à la bordelaise, daube of beef with carrots, braised andouillettes with Sauternes and prunes, a sprightly little Lot-et-Garonne Pinot. Newly redecorated, and a farily fashionable clientele.
Carte: 130F.

In an attractive decor of old faïence tile, you will be served delicate and inventive dishes such as feuilleté with fresh frog legs, sea trout with watercress, bouillabaisse or on Fridays, excellent shellfish, and sherbet from Lenôtre. Healthful and honest, all the dishes are prepared by the family, with all fresh foodstuffs. Expensive wines.
Carte: about 160F.

Our Raymond Oliver has been very sick lately, but we know that he is now back on his feet. Let us first thank heaven for that, for there are few chefs so dear to our hearts and dear to the hearts of millions throughout the world. He is the symbol of the French cuisine and its most zealous proponent. And thank heavens also, because a good and strong constitution is necessary to support the loss of a toque—and, even more, to win it back. We hesitated for a long time before taking it away because by doing so we are attacking one of France's most prestigious establishments. But if we are to maintain credibility and if our judgment is to be followed when we crown with three toques some breathtaking young chef or some reborn old master, it is necessary that we adhere to our criteria, even when it concerns a mecca as charming and ravishing and rich in gastronomical memories as the Grand Véfour. Our rankings are based only on the cuisine. And this restaurant, with its banal sauces, frequent overcooking, flavors masked or dulled, and a general lack of inspiration, is no longer worthy of three toques (even though simply prepared dishes such as fresh goose foie gras, salad with artichoke bottoms and brochette of prawns border on perfection). As for the rest—the welcome of François Mesnage, the friendly and princely service, the décor (a bit worn but so purely and beautifully authentic), the distinguished and worldly clientele—the Véfour remains the Grand Véfour. Carte: 300–400F.

## 11/20
### *Guyomard*
**5 rue du Jour**
**236.94.81**
*M. Hyvonnet*
*Open until midnight. Closed Sun.*
*and 3 weeks July–August.*
*AE, DC, V.*

A visit to Guyomard (located alongside the church of Saint-Eustache in les Halles) is rather like taking a trip to pre-war Normandy. On the ground floor is the bistro. On the second floor, a quiet dining room, which has retained the flavor of the old province with its beamed ceiling, chests of drawers and ironwork. The lovely owner takes such kind care of her customers that you want to hug her. The cuisine, on the other hand, inspires a somewhat cooler reaction. By and large, the seafood is acceptable, but the scallops antiboise with tomatoes and mushrooms are overcooked and the sauce is too greasy. The fresh salmon en papillote and barbue with aubergines, too, have stayed too long on the fire. The choice of desserts is limited, and the wines are rather ordinary. Nevertheless, we must give Guyomard credit for its staunch cuisine and reasonable prices.
Carte: about 150F. Menu: 100F (incl. wine and serv.).

## 12/20
### *Louis XIV*
**1 bis place des**
**Victoires**
**261.39.44**
*M. Delory*
*Open until 10:00 P.M. Closed Sat.,*
*Sun., and August. Open terrace.*

During good weather you must try by all means to obtain a table on the terrace facing the majestic equestrian statue of Louis XIV, Charles X version but of good pedigree nevertheless. The dining rooms are bustling and cramped in the aging bistro style, but not enough to discourage the faithful throng, who come for a breath of the disappearing past and to comfort themselves with massive portions of entrecôte beaujolaise, beef bourguignon, quenelles Nantua, hot sausages with potatoes, all washed down with the Beaujolais of the year.
Carte: 120F–140F.

## 10/20
## Le Lyonnais du Forum

**Forum des Halles-Niveau-2, 27 passage de la Réale**
**297.40.44**
*M. Klein*
*Open until 10:00 P.M. Closed Sun. Pay parking (5F) at Forum des Halles.*
*V.*

Finally, a real Lyonnais restaurant in Paris! The event was so great that, last year, we invited you to celebrate with us by partaking of the tablier de sapeur, frisée with bacon, and chicken au gros sel. Located in the Halles Forum, this bistro extends onto a large and pleasant outdoor terrace. Since last year's celebration, we've had a rather ordinary meal, and now wonder if quality cooking can actually survive in the busy hole-in-the-ground known as the Forum.
Carte: about 110F. Menu: 69F + 15% serv.

## 14
## La Main à la Pâte

**35 rue Saint-Honoré**
**508.85.73**
*M. Bassano*
*Open until midnight. Closed Sat. (at lunch) and Sun.*
*A, E, DC.*

While waiting for the old market area of Les Halles to be transformed into the "extraordinary garden" promised by the mayor of Paris, Silvio Baridon and his manager, Livio Bassano, have thought it more expedient to plant a vine on the second floor of their Main à la Pâte overlooking the "great hole"—a vine that has nothing to fear from the cold weather: it and all the other decorations are genuine imitations guaranteed to fool the eye. Anyway, the result is not without charm, and with a little imagination you can believe you're in Tuscany or Umbria. A visit is your chance to try the latest creation of Mme Bassano: an exquisite spider crab with fresh pasta in a highly-spiced sauce that is served in the crab's shell and presented on a bed of seaweed. Ask also for her bread dough galettes stuffed with fresh herbs and deep-fried in olive oil, her Parma ham cut in very thin slices, her authentic and delicious coppa, her stuffed veal with tuna, her daurade with preserved lemon, and her freshly made pasta, which she prepares as no one else can. On the other hand, we will leave to others her "elephant ear" and her flambée chicken Nero with citronella, dishes which have never much appealed to us. A very Parisian clientele, a choice of the best Italian wines, and quick lunches based upon an entrée and a pastry.
Carte: about 150F–170F. Menu 48F (serv. incl.).

## 11/20
## Le Mandarin du Forum

**17 rue de l'Arc-en-Ciel Forum des Halles, niveau-3**
**297.52.46**
*M. Chow*
*Open until 11:00 P.M. Pay parking at the Forum.*
*AE, DC, V.*

Just as in Hong Kong, where the most popular restaurants display all of the intimacy of a railway station, this Mandarin restaurant can hardly be singled out for the charm of its decor or warmth of its atmosphere. But this doesn't seem to bother the 150–customers–per–sitting who come here to enjoy some 50 delicious varieties of dim sum, at prices perfectly suited to the clientele of the Forum. The fine menu has its high points (duck à la cantonese) and low points (steamed salted fish); both are directly related to the chef's mood that day.
Carte: 100F–120F. Menus: 42.50F, 44.50F, 56.50F.

## 14

## Mercure Galant
**15 rue des Petits-Champs**
**297.53.85**
*M. Caille*
*Open until 10:30 P.M. Closed Sat.*
*(at lunch) and Sun.*

The elegant, turn-of-the-century decor of this attractive house is less severe in the evening under soft lighting. It is, moreover, at dinner that you see the regular clientele, doubtless because of the remarkable fixed-price meal that is proposed: gâteau of Bresse foie blonds with vegetables (or homemade duck foie gras), crayfish feuilleté (or a mousse of red mullet), roast rack of lamb (or fricassée of chicken with Champagne), and homemade desserts, among which is the mille et une feuilles, which one would swear comes from Lenôtre's (the prawn feuilleté on the full menu is no less astonishing). The service is excellent, and the wines are good. Very attractive second-floor dining room for business lunches.
Carte: 200F. Menu (dinner only): 130F + 15% serv.

## 12/20

## Le Monastère
**60 rue de l'Arbre-Sec**
**(261.63.50)**
*M. Harrosch*
*Open until 1:30 A.M. Closed Sun.*
*V.*

The news might even have made the parish bulletin: "Canon Michel Derbane has joined the Monastery after completing his training at the Jouteux seminar (les Semailles), and has created a small sensation on rue de l'Arbre-Sec beneath the beautiful vaulted ceiling of this restaurant which dives three levels deep into the belly of Paris." No matter how crowded it is, you will always receive a warm welcome and attentive service, and in the glow of the candlelight, the ladies often look strikingly beautiful. But the real story is told in the sacristy, where Derbane prepares his fresh and unpretentious cuisine, using only the best materials. At present, two different menus are offered; one of these, the "grande faim" (hearty appetite) includes such dishes as scalloped foie gras on a bed of lettuce, or fresh salmon with (perfectly cooked) baby vegetables. Then there is the fillet of beef with chervil, followed by crottin de Chavignol on mixed salad. Finally, there are half a dozen excellent desserts. Hurrah for the cloister!
Menus: 54F, 112F + 15% serv.

## 11/20

## Les Noailles
**6 rue du 29-Julliet**
**296.57.11**
*M. Lagrange*
*Open until 11:00 P.M. Closed Sun.*
*AE, DC, V.*

If you're looking for an elegant, discreet place for a quiet lunch here in one of the noisiest sections of Paris, you could not make a better selection than Les Noailles. The restaurant opens onto a small inside court, where tables are laid in good weather. Among its other attributes are attentive service and reasonable prices. If we understand correctly, the owner of the excellent Cochon d'Or, René Ayral, has left Les Noailles. In any case, the chef has remained, and offers a rather unoriginal cuisine, lacking in distinctive taste. He would do well to come to his senses in a hurry. The vegetable terrine en gelée is insipid, the salade de mesclun aux gésiers badly seasoned, and the calf's liver with purée of leeks overcooked. But the fish is beautiful and very fresh, and the strawberry charlotte is delicious.
Carte: 160–170F. Menu: 120F + 15% serv.

## 14
### Chez Pauline
**5 rue Villedo**
**296.20.70 and**
**261.79.01**
*M. Génin*
*Open until 10:30 P.M. Closed Sat.*
*evenings and Sun.*

Blessed be the house where you know each day what awaits you. . . . In a corner of our appointment book is scribbled "Chez Pauline: Mondays, calf's-head sauce gribiche, streaky bacon with lentils or cabbage; Tuesdays, truffled Bresse chicken comme à Lyon; Wednesdays, blanquette of veal à l'ancienne; Thursdays, beef au gros sel; Fridays, navarin of lamb, or a cassoulet with preserved goose." In addition, there are the classical dishes firmly ensconced on the menu: beef bourguignon, stuffed cabbage, roast andouillette, and, finally crème caramel, rice pudding, and chocolate mousse. Genin, father and son, stick to tradition. A good, intimate, old-time bistro. Carte: 160F to 180F.

## 13
### Pharamond
**24 rue de la**
**Grande-Truanderie**
**233.06.72**
*M. Hyvonnet*
*Open until 10:15 P.M. Closed Sun.,*
*Mon. (at lunch), and during July.*
*Open terrace. Paid parking at*
*Forum des Halles.*
*AE, DC, V.*

It is not possible to think of tripe without thinking of Pharamond—and vice-versa—nevertheless, one comes here today to order the admirable tripe à la mode de Caen, prepared in this restaurant since the days of Louis-Philippe, rather than to dine in a ravishing decor of ceramic tiles and cut-glass mirrors, circa 1900, much admired by the habitués of the new Halles. One also comes for the foie gras and the more modern dishes prepared by chef Gérard Endot: turbot with chive sauce, veal sweetbreads with spinach, knuckle of veal with mushrooms. There is delicious Auge Valley apple cider and the even rarer pear cider. Carte: 150F.

## 11/20
### Au Pied de Cochon
**6 rue Coquillière**
**236.11.75**
*M. Blanc*
*Open 24 hours, year-round.*
*AE, DC, V.*

Nostalgic pleasure-seekers and sentimental night owls have never forgotten this address. Along with the locals, provincials, foreigners and die-hards on a tour of Gai Paris, they continue to lend a hint of impudence and a great deal of warmth to this sanctuary of a once-great district. Fine etchings of the old Halles decorate the walls of the refurbished dining room and evoke the wonderful memories of this ancient establishment. As do the superb assorted grilled plate Saint-Antoine (pig's nose, tail and feet), the andouillette, the suckling pig, and the beef steaks which have been served 8784 hours out of 8784 by the indestructible Blanc family. Carte: 120F. Menu: 98.90F (serv. incl.).

## 15

### Pierre Traiteur
**10 rue de Richelieu**
**296.09.17**
*M. Nouyrigat*
*Open until 10:15 P.M. Closed Sat.,*
*Sun. and during August*
*AE, V.*

The death of the good Mother Nouyrigat does not keep us away from this sanctuary of bourgeois virtues. The greeting of her son Guy, the warm provincial atmosphere, and the solid dishes of the Southwest are as exquisite as ever. With the young Marc Faucheux in the kitchen, the cooking is a bit lighter but remains faithful to the four corners of France. There are still green cabbages with preserves, the stuffed breast of lamb, the beef à la ficelle, oeufs à la neige, and the magnificent estofinade rouergate in which the cod puts all the sea bass and lobsters in creation to shame. Excellent wines, both famous and obscure. The bill is almost reasonable. Carte: about 170F.

**11/20**

## Porte du Bonheur

**8 rue du Mont-Thabor 260.55.99**
*M. Chong*
*Open until 11:00 P.M.*
*AE, DC, V.*

In the olden days, people used to come here to watch Mme Chong smoke her pipe while she added up the checks, listen to the tales of Mandarin banquets told by discreet, esthetic Felix Chong, and enjoy some of the best Chinese food in Paris. Gone are those happy days, and all that remain are the excellent ingredients, ably shaped to Western tastes. The litany of the dishes may sound enchanting, but what lies behind is everyday, depersonalized cooking served in a distinguished Oriental atmosphere crowded with tourists. Recently, some Malayan specialties have been added. Carte: 150–170F. Menu: 48F (serv. incl.).

13

## Les Potiers

**49 rue de l'Arbre-Sec 261.26.19**
*M. Deslot*
*Open until 10:30 P.M. Closed Sat. (at lunch), Sun. and during August*
*AE, V.*

In this simple and warm bare brick setting you will taste cooking full of freshness and ideas: salad with smoked magret with red cabbage; sander with saffron and whites of leeks; mixed grill; exquisite rhubarb tarte and impeccable sherbets. The wines, principally from the Loire, are of the best (red Sancerre, Champigny, Bourgeuil). A charming reception from Mme. Deslot and prompt service from waitresses. Carte: 150F. Menu: 79F (serv. incl.).

16

## Prunier-Madeleine

**9 rue Duphot 260.36.04**
*M. Funaro*
*Open until 10:30 P.M. Closed in August. Parking in place de la Madeleine.*
*AE, DC, V.*

All alone and with dedication, Aldo Funaro has taken the reins of this old house, shaken up the kitchen, redecorated all the rooms in style—in short, restored its varnished luster to a restaurant that, along with Maxim's and La Tour d'Argent, was once the most celebrated in the world. The clientele remain international but with a fine injection of youth and beauty. The nouvelle cuisine is applied principally to seafood: lotte with watercress, aspic of prawns with vegetables, crayfish with dill, salad of salmon with asparagus, jellied bouillabaisse, red mullet with basil, John Dory with leeks, beef fillet with oysters, and all shellfish, even in summer. With a good white wine, you can expect a hefty bill. Service is in the grand style. Carte: 230F to 260F.

**12/20**

## Rôtisserie Rivoli

**3 rue de Castiglione 260.37.80**
*Open until 11:00 P.M. Open*

You will lunch, according to the season and the prevailing winds, either on the splendid, flowery terrace with the murmurings of the fountains (it is one of the most elegant and best situated interior courts among those of Parisian hotels), or else in the intimacy of the Rôtisserie; in either

terrace. No dogs.
AE, DC, V.

place, at eminently reasonable prices (salad with lamb fillets and tabbouleh, mousseline of young rabbit dijonnaise). Or, if you wish, more simply and at a lower price, you may lunch at the Café Tuileries, where a gâteau of carrots with chervil cream, a roast young chicken with sage, and a good pastry will not cost more than 100F, a small Côtes-de-Bourg included. Service is irreproachable at each place.
Carte: 100F to 200 F. Menu: 60F (at the Cafe Tuileries), 140F, 160F. (serv. incl.).

**11/20**

## Au Roy Gourmet

**4 place des Victoires**
**508.10.16**
M. Constant
Open until 10:00 P.M. Closed Sat., Sun. and holidays.
AE, V.

The aptly-named Constant family has been here for four generations. That gives you some idea of the number of miles of andouillette (sausage specialty of the house— not terribly memorable) that have traveled under the chandeliers of this delightful, old-fashioned restaurant with its amusing murals. However deprived of genius, the cuisine remains reliably good, exemplified by the navarin and the calf's kidneys. When the weather is good, dinner is served on a charming, small terrace.
Carte: 160F.

**10/20**

## Royal Mondétour

**14 rue Mondétour**
**236.85.50**
M. Bonnenfant
Open until 11:00 P.M. Closed Sun. and during August. Pay parking at Forum des Halles. Open terrace.

A rather small address for such a large bistro! One that has remained unwavering in its loyalty to morue à l'auvergnate and boeuf gros sel. The venerable decor evokes the pre-war period, and the Bonnenfant family (father, mother and son) show the tenderest of care for their amiable clients. Now isn't that worth a royal detour?
Carte: 80F–100F.

**11/20**

## Le Samovar

**14 rue Sauval**
**261.77.79**
M. Siew
Open until midnight. Closed Sun. and during August.
V.

A splash of white paint, a few bread boards hung on the walls like icons, and there you have it: the little Samovar rejuvenated and ready to welcome the Russians (whether they be pink or white) and all those Parisians who love the guitar and balalaika. They come every evening to share a beef Stroganoff with two house musicians. Tasty, authentic cuisine: herring, salmon, tarama, blinis, Caucasian chachlik, pelmenis (Siberian ravioli), and blintchikis (crêpes with jam). And lots of vodka late into the night . . . inspiring dreams of adventure.
Carte: 120F. Menu: 78F + 15% serv.

**12/20**

## La Sardegna

**23 place du Marché-Saint-Honoré**
**260.54.69**
M. Gilardino

Many of our readers under 7 years of age are simply delighted by Mme Gilardino's standing invitation to enjoy a free lunch on Saturday in her refreshing, vaguely-Italian dining room. Of course, they have to bring their parents with them. But, the latter don't seem to mind, since they pay only for themselves. In fact, it's a rather

*Open until 11:00 P.M. Closed Sun.*
*AE, DC, V.*

moderate sum, considering the good quality of the cullingiones (plump stuffed ravioli), the tagliarini à la matriciana, the spaghetti in oil and garlic, and the ravioli with pumpkin. Charming, peninsular wines, with excellent selections by the glass.
Carte: 120F. Menu: 90F + 15% serv.

## 11/20
## Saüdade

**34 rue des**
**Bourdonnais**
**236.30.71**
*M. Hémart*
*Open until midnight. Closed Sat.*
*(at lunch) and Sun.*
*AE, DC.*

Saüdade is a key word in the language of the Portuguese poet Camoëns. It's something like the nostalgia and langor we've come to recognize in the soft, sad expressions of crane operators and concierges. Those who come here with an adventurous appetite will discover a frank, country-style cuisine which sticks to the ribs and which is essentially devoted to celebrating the joys of "bacalao" (cod): oven-baked, fried, poached, or beignets. On the menu you can also find good tripes à la mode de Porto and a curious pork dish à l'alentejana. A small room, almost elegant, with attractively set tables. Take this opportunity to discover some of the robust Portuguese red wines.
Carte: 120F. Menu: 60F (serv. incl.).

## 11/20
## Ta Yen
**32 bis rue**
**Sainte-Anne**
**296.37.10**
*M. Payen*
*Open until 11:30 P.M. Closed Sat.*
*and Sun. (at lunch).*
*V.*

From the approximately 30 Cantonese steam-cooked specialties which will be brought to you in delightful, small baskets, select 8–10 (for two people) without really trying to find out what they are. Ravioli with shrimp, shrimp en papillotte, sautéed rice noodles with beef, lacquered pork dumplings . . . all served by a courteous, pleasant staff. An aviary and aquarium liven up the otherwise sombre decor of the three or four consecutive rooms. Prices are easily affordable.
Carte: 70F. Menu: 28F + 15% serv.

## 11/20
## La Tour de Montlhéry
**5 rue des Prouvaires**
**236.21.82**
*Mme. Benariac*
*Open day and night, except Sun.*
*and July 14 to August 15.*

A blessed refuge when, at about three in the morning or five in the evening, one is doing the rounds. The good Jacques will greet you with open arms and seat you next to a tramp perhaps, or perhaps an attractive woman, beneath the garlands of hams smoked in the bluish haze of tobacco, in the best tradition of the postcard bistro of Les Halles. His equatorial moustache twitching over his paunch, tightly belted in by a three-tiered apron, Jacques will lose no time in serving you the heavy artillery: mutton with beans, steak with shallots, stuffed cabbage, all of it washed down with great pitchers of Brouilly.
Carte: 100F–120F.

## 13
## Vendôme
## (Hôtel Ritz)
**15 Place Vendôme**

When awaiting the reopening of the Espadon, one was installed in the ornate Louis XV–III Republic dining room (at Hôtel Ritz) surrounded by mementos of Marcel Proust

**260.38.30**

*M. Klein*
*Open until 10:30 P.M.*
*Open terrace. Pay parking 36 F*
*underground at place Vendôme*
*All major credit cards*

and Escoffier and redolent of tournedos Rossini and of quail Trois Empereurs. In such a setting did it really matter what one ate? Yes, replied the new owners of the Ritz two years ago, feeling that in a world grown painfully prosaic people should go to the restaurant—let it be the Ritz—to experience gastronomic emotions in a surrounding where elaborate sconces and gilt moldings evoke the nostalgia of yesterday. They also enlisted the talents of Guy Legay, who was chef for more than ten years at Ledoyen, with predictable results. Having swept away the pretentious dishes that had been the mainstay of the Ritz for the past eighty years, he developed a menu that is both traditional without being boring and modern without being precious—a menu so long and impressive that it contains many hazards and dishes of uneven quality. But, overlooking these, let us sample with joy the three fish marinated with fennel, the mullet with pistou, the sole soufflé Vendôme, the veal kidneys with wine vinegar and chives. The checks also seem to have been heartily reinvigorated; the great wines are ruinous; an old Chartreuse at an unspeakable 300F the glass.
Carte: 350F–plus.

## Vert Galant
**42 quai des Orfèvres**
**326.83.68**

*M. Bos*
*Open until 10:15 P.M. Closed Sat.*
*Pay parking.*
*AE, DC, V.*

For years, this lovely, old establishment has lent comfort to the more or less fortuitous visitors to the nearby headquarters of the Paris police, as well as to judges, attorneys, and their clients. It continues peacefully along its unchanging path: you won't find innovative dishes here, but rather, reliable, classic fare, elegantly served in a charmingly old-fashioned decor. The stewed chicken is still the best in Paris, and the selection of wines is outstanding.
Carte: about 200F.

## Chez la Vieille
**37 rue de l'Arbre-Sec**
**260.15.78**

*Mme Biasin.*
*Closed Sat., Sun., and*
*during Aug. Lunches only.*

The most generous of cuisines prepared by women is that prepared by Adrienne at Chez la Vieille, who for more than twenty years has been making all those dishes that we remember eating at Grandmother's when we were kids. But the pot-au-feu, the aiguilette of beef en cocotte, the sautéed lamb, the veal Marengo are really delicious dishes for grownups. Adrienne will also prepare, if it is ordered in advance and if your party is to be six or more, a splendid hachis Parmentier baked in the oven, a creamy beef miroton, or an impressive peasant pot-au-feu with four different meats (beef, veal, pork, and poularde. Prices rise regularly; Adrienne Biasin never lets the cost-of-living index sneak up on her.
Carte: 140F. Menu: 59.90F (serv. incl.).

## Chez Vong aux Halles

It was in this very attractive and authentic Chinese restaurant that we rehearsed our demonstration of the

**10 rue de la
Grande-Truanderie
296.29.89**

*M. Vong Vai Lam.
Open until 1:00 A.M. Pay parking
at Forum des Halles. Open terrace.*

marriage of French wines with the cuisine of Peking, Canton and Szechwan prior to the enactment of the real thing in Hong Kong. You could not find a more appropriate place for this in France, perhaps in all of Europe: M. Vong's intelligence and savoir-faire, the virtuosity and refinement of his cooking, the precision of the service—all closely approached that of a great Hong Kong restaurant. You, too, can play this game, for M. Vong's wines are excellent; and you can gorge yourself on marvelous and unusual dim-sum, lacquered pigeon, beef with oyster sauce, shrimp in a "nest of happiness," and all his dishes of the day, proposed according to their availability on the market. More expensive than some other Chinese bistros in Paris but much less so than a French restaurant would be in China.
Carte: 120F–180F. Menus: 68F, 88F (serv. incl.).

# 2ème Arr.

**12/20
A l'Abbé
Constantin
13 rue du
4-Septembre
297.50.93**

*M. Trompesauce
Open until 10:15 P.M. Closed Sat.
(at lunch) and Sun.
AE, DC, V.*

Who would have guessed that the terribly serious M. Trompesauce would one day flee his sweet little bistro in Montparnasse (La Guérite du Saint-Amour), and set out on a new adventure under the sign of l'Abbé Constantin—this ecclesiastical setting fairly buzzing with innuendo? But so things go in this dangerous world, and we find our two fugitives beneath the fake beams of this exalted place: the little lady out with the customers, and the nice gentleman in the kitchen. At its best, this cuisine is sincere and faithfully regional: cabbage salad with bacon, salad of baby rabbit, confit aux cèpes, terrine of suckling pig, roast rabbit with mousserons, flognarde Limousine, and douillon Normand. At the other end of the spectrum, the intrepid M. Trompesauce has indulged in several well-intentioned creative culinary exercises, probably aimed at satisfying his new clientele, made up largely of businessmen. One of these is an incomprehensible oyster gratin with melted cheese (that's right!). The service is good, though a little overworked. Keep an eye on the prices.
Carte: 160F–180F.

**11/20
L'Aman-
guier
110 rue de Richelieu**

A fresh, exotic setting, management by a young businessman on the go (he has just opened a "central laboratory" where all the pastries are prepared for his

**296.37.79**
*M. Derderian.*
*Open until midnight.*
*Open terrace.*
*AE, DC, V.*

three restaurants), low prices, always an hors d'oeuvre and a hot entrée (quiche, navarin, salad of chicken livers and escalope of salmon), and a light dessert with wine if you wish it. Quick, intelligent, and well-served, proof that the French can create and profitably operate a good popular (fast-service) restaurant.
Carte: about 80F. Menu: 63F (wine and serv. incl.)

13
## Auberge Perraudin
**164 rue Montmartre**
**236.71.09**
*M. Perraudin*
*Open until 11:00 P.M. Closed Sat.*
*(at lunch) and Sun.*
*AE, DC, V.*

Ironic providence has entrusted the kitchen of this intensely ugly neo-kitsch restaurant to a 24-year-old chef who studied his art with Orsi at Lyon, and who works here under the wing of Claude Perraudin, a "disciple of Paul Bocuse." The result is that some excellent ideas (which have been at the root of the success of some of the "greats") have found their place here, at the right price. The hors d'oeuvres are complimentary. You pay only for the main course. Among the entrees are a delicious fish paté, vegetable gâteau in a fine sorrell sauce, fish salad, and aiguillettes of duck with peaches. All of this augurs well, in spite of the fact that the desserts are excessively sweet and the sherbets rather flavorless. Remarkable little menu. Competent, friendly service.
Carte: 130F–150F. Menus: 57.50F, 95F (serv. incl.).

13
## Le Canotier
**19-20 passage des Panoramas**
**508.89.19**
*Mme. Marotta*
*Open until 10:30 P.M. Closed Sun.*
*and July 20 to August 20.*
*AE, DC, V.*

The Canotier, almost hidden in a corner of the passage des Panoramas, is one of our recent discoveries. Two charming young ladies offer an à la carte menu, bourgeois style, featuring navarin of lamb with fresh vegetables, estouffade of beef à la provençale, daube of mutton "des demoiselles d'Avignon," knuckle of ham with Puy lentils, mutton chops Champvallon, a fricandeau of veal, guinea fowl with cabbage, shoulder of lamb stuffed à la provençale, stuffed cabbage à la ballottine—all cooked with a skilled hand. Music and charming French folk songs upstairs in the evenings.
Carte: 160F. Menu: 95F (lunch), 120F (dinner) + 15% serv.

13
## La Corbeille
**152 rue Montmartre**
**261.30.87**
*M. Viot*
*Open until 10:30 P.M. Closed Sat.,*
*Sun. and during end-of-year*
*holidays.*
*AE, DC, V.*

In this vaguely modern setting, Christian Viot addresses a light hand and an inventive mind to nouvelle cuisine. There are two menus, both with a Bordeaux accent: you can have a meal that is resolutely modern (raw scallops with spinach, leg of wild boar with figs), or regional dishes such as his astonishing veal kidneys with mustard, his Rocamadour, goat cheese with walnut oil, and other dishes that make up his "Bordeaux menu" at 110F. The wine list on the other hand still lacks balance.
Carte: 160F. Menu: 75F (lunch) + 15% serv., 110F (dinner–wine incl.) + 15% serv.

14 🍴

## Delmonico
**39 ave. de l'Opera**
**261.44.26**
*Mme Corbel*
*Open until 10:30 P.M. Closed Sun.*
*AE, DC, V.*

Gone is the era of the Prince of Wales: with its lovely, modern decor and Christian Simon's intelligent, delicate, contemporary cuisine, this venerable establishment has entered the modern age with marinated salmon in juniper, artichokes with écrevisses, pike with fennel, lamb in thyme sauce, duck in honey, and candied lime soufflé. Also with stiff prices and a clientele of equally stiff businessmen, we might add.
Carte: 220F–250F. Menu: 120F + 15% serv.

12/20
## Drouant
**Place Gaillon**
**742.56.61**
*M. Pascal*
*Open until 1:00 A.M. Valet*
*parking.*
*AE, DC, V.*

The art deco splendors of the dining room (a symphony in brown and gold by Ruhlmann), the extreme amiability of the waiters, the nice wines, and the moderate prices are almost enough to compensate for the weakness of these "new dinners from the grill" so sought after by the black tie and evening gown opera crowd. But the 150F menu (including service) is uneven. Nothing catastrophic ( a decent seafood plate and nice fish). But why should the beautiful magret of duck with blueberries be served with reheated potatoes? And why toss canned peaches into the honey dessert? What a pity that such an attractive decor, as dramatically lit in the evening as a stage, cannot inspire a more appealing, more carefully-prepared cuisine.
Carte: 250F. Menu (dinner only): 150F (serv. incl.), 195F + 15% serv.

10/20
## Gallopin
**40 rue N.-D.**
**des-Victoires**
**236.45.38**
*M. Wagrez*
*Open until 11:00 P.M. Closed Sat.*
*and Sun.*
*V.*

We had almost forgotten the way to the old Gallopin, where young journalists from the *Journal* or *Paris-Presse l'Intran* had gathered since time immemorial to gulp down an onglet à l'échalote or a lentil salad. All cleaned and freshly polished, this wonderful "stock-exchange lunch bar," with its turn-of-the-century stained glass and Victorian wood paneling, sends us back to the London of George Bernard Shaw. And the young brokers dressed in their Savile Row suits once again rush to the bar or the dining room to fight it out with a green bean salad, hot saucisson, cold roast pork, or a new generation of journalists from A.F.P. or *France Soir,* exchanging the latest prices and the hottest scoops over a couple of glasses of good Beaujolais.
Carte: 100F–120F. Menu: (dinner only) 85F (serv. incl.).

11/20
## Gérard
**4 rue du Mail**
**296.24.36**
*M. Léonetti*
*Open until 11:30 P.M. Closed Sun.*
*and July 25 to September 2.*

Your basic local bistro, but with depth and sparkle. Members of the press ( *Le Figaro* ) and the world of fashion (place des Victoires) set the tone for the clientele. The menu: salad frisée with garlic or bacon, beef salad, hot saucisson, pot-au-feu, calf's liver with vinegar. The enjoyment you might derive from your visit depends entirely on the mood of Gérard (Léonetti).
Carte: 120F.

**10/20**
## La Grille
**50 rue Montorgueil**
**236.24.64**
*M. Lenoble*
*Open until 10:30 P.M. Closed Sun.*
*and during August.*
*DC.*

Still one of the most beautiful bars in Paris and still serving (with a few slight modifications) the same cuisine which has reigned supreme since 1913, and which reached its zenith during the '60s under the hand of père Lenoble. Now it's up to the younger members of the family to perpetuate the entrecôte marchand de vin, and the veal kidney flambé, and to serve a typically Parisian Beaujolais. To be truthful, each year the atmosphere and the cuisine take on a stronger taste of ash—to which we are less and less inclined.
Carte: about 150F.

**12/20**
## La Locomotive
**6 rue Chabanais**
**296.52.90**
*M. Purgato*
*Open until 10:00 P.M. Closed Sat.*
*(at lunch) and during August.*
*AE, DC, V.*

This little train that could is operating at full steam on a street which was once fast asleep. M. Purgato's restaurant is located just behind Molière's house, but rest assured, he takes better care of his customers than Dr. Purgon did of his patients: he installs them comfortably in the attractive, flowered decor and serves them all sorts of treats, such as mussel salad, fresh pasta with basil, and gambas in onion jelly. Charming candlelight dinners in the evening.
Carte: 200F. Menu: 50F, 100F + 15% serv.

**11/20**
## Aux Lyonnais
**32 rue Saint-Marc**
**296.65.04**
*M. Schoulner*
*Open until 10:00 P.M. Closed Sun.*
*and during August.*
*AE, DC, V.*

This was the classic casual bistro, with muskets on the wall, good Beaujolais on the tables, and a tab that caused no pain. They may have a few gray hairs, but père Viollet's sweet little waitresses are still there. So is the decor, as magnificent and sad as a dinosaur. Unchanged, too, is the menu, which carries on the tradition of salad of lamb's feet, scallops à la nage, chicken au gros sel or calf's livers à la Lyonnaise . . . just like the good old days. Alas, the ladies who once ruled the kitchen of this honest bistro, mellowed by the scent of andouillette, are no longer there, and the chef who has succeeded them is incapable of maintaining the smoothness and grace which we so appreciated. The flavors are just not put together right and the sauces are sometimes unfortunate. Nostalgia is the order of the day.
Carte: 130F–150F.

**13**
## Palais Impérial
**6 rue d'Antin**
**261.25.52**
*M. Chiu*
*Open until 11:00 P.M., Closed Sun.*
*and during August. Pay parking at*
*marché Saint-Honoré.*
*AE, DC, V.*

One of the most serious and elegant Chinese restaurants in Paris. The decor is roomy and well-lit, and the waiters are attentive and if you wish, will explain to you the subtleties of a menu that is not lacking in them: delicious slivers of Peking beef with leeks, breaded crab claws and steamed turbot. A good Côtes-du-Rhône and an even better Châteauneuf-du-Pape.
Carte: 120F–150F. Menu: 39.50F (serv. incl.).

**11/20**
## Saint-Amour

This elegant restaurant, with its comfortable English decor (lovely, private booths for business lunches or

### 8 rue de Port-Mahon
*M. Marancy*
*Open until 10:00 P.M. Closed Sat.,*
*Sun. and holidays.*
*V.*

romantic dinners) is trying to attract a larger evening clientele, but people seem to steer clear of this iceberg after 9:00 P.M. In the end, Jean and Chantal Marancy will surely win them over with their remarkable menu priced at 100F (everything included), offering, for example, fresh homemade foie gras of duck, mousseline of fish, Brie de Meaux, and sherbet. Fascinating Duboeuf Côtes du Rhône served by the carafe.
Carte: 130F–150F. Menu: 69F (serv. incl.), 100F (wine and serv. incl.).

### 11/20
## *Tannhauser*
### 16 rue Saint-Augustin
### 296.82.70
*M. Guillot*
*Open until midnight. Closed Sat.*
*(at lunch), Sun. and during*
*August.*
*V.*

The six varieties of sauerkraut (the one with beef hocks is rather interesting) go beautifully with the good German charcuterie. With a little imagination and some help from the Munich beers—served in quantities ranging from the "baron" (half-a-pint) to the "chevalier" (a gallon)—you can lose yourself in the Wagnerian atmosphere of this classic Bavarian meeting place. (Note, however, that they don't hesitate to serve cervelle grenobloise or lotte with poivre vert). We've also been told that the welcome has become considerably warmer, and we are delighted for your sake. Note also that M. Guillot may have left the restaurant by the time these lines are published.
Carte: 130F–150F. Menu: 59F (serv. incl.).

### 13
## *La Tour de Jade*
### 20 rue de la Michodière
### 742.07.56
*Mme Nguyen Van Nhung*
*Open until 10:00 P.M.*

One of our readers couldn't believe that they hadn't held his table for him when he showed up half an hour late. Is that really so surprising? Two others complained bitterly about the food—something which we frankly can't understand. We have patronized La Tour de Jade for the past 20 years, and, while some meals have certainly been less brilliant than others, we have always considered this to be one of the most respectable representatives of Chinese-Vietnamese cuisine in Paris. It's true that we take the trouble to place an advance order for meals featuring specialties such as tête de porc grillée, fresh breast of pork marinated in coconut milk, fish in tamarind sauce, shrimp and rice crêpes, and pork ribs à la citronnelle. We assure you that chef Tchang, a 15-year veteran of this restaurant, has certainly earned his toque.
Carte: 80F–130F. Menu: 38F (wine and serv. incl.).

### 12/20
## *Le Vaudeville*
### 29 rue Vivienne
### 233.39.31
*M. Bucher*
*Open until 2:00 A.M. Pay parking*
*at place de la Bourse*
*V.*

This is all that remains of the old theater of the same name, the theater where *La Dame aux Camélias* first played. Jean-Paul Bucher, who collects old brasseries (Flo, Terminus-Nord, Julien), has rescued this wreck from oblivion near the place de la Bourse. A good scrubbing was enough to restore the walls and the marble floors, which are of the purest "bleu d'Auvergne" style, circa 1930. As for the rest, it sufficed to install his efficient team and to tap as customers the neighborhood businessmen (stock market, Club Méditerranée) for lunch and the theater crowd in the evenings. The bill of fare is straightforward (blanquette of rabbit with basil, parsleyed rack of lamb à la provençale, and reasonably priced oysters all year long). As well, grilled meats, fish and shellfish can be recommended. There is an excellent selection of wines in carafe at rock-bottom prices (Riesling at 39F per bottle) Carte: 120F.

### 12/20
### *Au Vieux Saumur*
**1 rue de la Banque**
**260.90.66**
*M. Viguié*
*Open until 10:00 P.M.; Closed Sat. and Sun. Open terrace.*

This very old bar was drowning in Beaujolais, wines of the Loire Valley, and obscurity. It has now been redone from top to bottom by its owner, Roland Viguié, in a style reminiscent of the 1930s—not too subtle but winning. The cuisine combines the traditional with the fashionable in some interesting dishes, such as the blanquette of veal tourangelle, blanquette of lotte with small onions, stuffed cabbages à la rouergate, a salad of preserved gizzards with sherry vinegar. There are occasional lapses in cooking and seasoning, but these are not hanging offences. Nice choice of good little wines that are not too expensive. Carte: 110F. Menu: 50F (serv. incl.).

### 12/20
### *Vishnou*
**11 bis rue Volney**
**297.56.54**
*M. Gupta*
*Open until 11:30 P.M. Closed Sun. AE, DC, V.*

One of four restaurants owned by the Gupta brothers, who also happen to own half of the Indian restaurants in Paris (including the Indra). The reception is friendly, and local color is provided by the Indian wood paneling, etchings and attentive personnel. Be sure to sample the Punjab tandoori cooked in a clay oven (with shrimp, breast of chicken and boulettes of veal). Also try the fish in spicy sauces, the curries from various regions of India, the consommé of mutton with yogurt, the Bengali beef, and, to complement this exotic meal, a delicious iced tea from the Nihgiri region. Carte: 130F–150F. Menu: 58F (serv. incl.).

# *3ème Arr.*

14
### *Ambassade d'Auvergne*
**22 rue du Grenier-St-Lazare**
**272.31.22**
*M. Petrucci*
*Open until 11:00 P.M., Closed Sun., Pay parking at 25 rue Beaubourg. All major credit cards.*

With Roman stoicism Joseph Petrucci has pledged himself to the celebration of mountain ham, tripe, stuffed cabbage, pig's trotters with aligoté, estofinado, boudin with chestnuts, and other massive specialties from the Massif Central. These he treats with the brio, the conjugal tenderness and patriotic self-sacrifice that only an Italian married to a woman from Auvergne can show. The table d'hôte before the fire, beneath festoons of cured meats

and beautiful heavy beams, as well as the warm, simple welcome, show how well a rustic setting goes with the magisterial Auvergnian cuisine. The young chef, Emmanuel Moulier, the owner's son-in-law, seems made for his job. Tempting desserts and interesting Auvergne wines.
Carte: about 160F.

**15**

## L'Ami Louis
**32 rue du Vertbois**
**887.77.48**
*M. Magnin*
*Open until 10:30 P.M., Closed Tues,*
*during July and August.*
*AE, DC, V.*

This year good Father Magnin will blow out 82 candles on his birthday cake, but the flame that has lit this curious old bistro for fifty-one years is not ready to be extinguished—not for another 100 years. Stewing in the juice of a bygone era—the 1930s—L'Ami Louis wildly and heroically resists the great inventions of the century—including detergents. If you have not yet stepped across the threshold of this sanctuary, your sin is unpardonable. Fast for several days prior to your visit, fill your wallet, and you will be ready for a giant's feast, an immutable ritual (Landes foie gras, sublime leg of lamb, gigantic beef rib, young partridge, cèpes, fine Burgundy wines) garnished with a bill whose likes you have never seen before.
Carte: 250F–280F.

**10/20**

## L'Enclos du Marais
**3 rue**
**N.-D.-de-Nazareth**
**887.77.91**
*M. Gorin*
*Lunch only. Closed Sun. and*
*during August.*

André Gorin's unpretentious, slowly-simmered dishes are as nice as can be: haricot of mutton, beef bourguignon, duck cassoulet, tarte tatin, and strawberry charlotte. Nice, but not exactly cheap.
Carte: 100F. Menu: 38F (serv. incl.).

**12/20**

## Chez Jenny
**39 blvd. du Temple**
**272.32.50**
*M. Chrétiennot*
*Open until 1:00 A.M.*
*DC, V.*

It would be doubly wrong to pass up this old brasserie perched on the upper end of the boulevard where the labor unions begin their marches between the République and the Bastille. First, because this is one of the most remarkable restaurant interiors in all of Paris: there is a great expanse of marquetry work in the manner of Hansi located in the huge second floor dining room . . . sweet land of storks and choucroute. (These treasures have survived the extensive, recently-completed renovation work). And second, because the choucroute (offered in two varieties, "special" and "country style") is some of the best that one could hope to find in this sort of huge brasserie. The cabbage is well-cooked and not acidic; the charcuterie (which is available for takeout in the adjoining deli) is extremely well-prepared under the supervision of new owner Christian Chrétiennot, a professional "brasseur." And the new management has just opened an amusing weinstübe where patrons can savor delicious grilled sausage and pitchers of Alsacian wine far into the night.
Carte: 100F–120F. Menu: 58F (wine incl.) + 15% serv.

13

## Les Roseaux

**14 rue Portefoin**
**887.61.03**

*M. Lefour*
*Open until 11:00 P.M., Closed Sat.*
*(at lunch), Sun., holidays.*
*AE.*

He is so alone and forgotten in this lost street of the Marais quarter, especially at lunchtime, that this hermit is often tempted to throw up his hands. All the same, we've never seen Pierre-Jean Lefour with idle hands as he served us his menu of "15 flavors," a true litany of tastes, all balanced and measured. One after another they came: fillet of raw daurade with lemon; mousseline of red mullet; terrine of artichoke; a surprising soufflé of sea urchins with vegetables; delicate crayfish feuilletés; gougeonnettes of sole with avocado; fricassée of calf's sweetbreads and kidneys with pistachios, and some exquisite desserts. We were seduced and overwhelmed by all of this as well as by an attractive special hypocaloric menu developed with a dietician, which will permit you to feast upon a light, fine meal of from 500–860 calories; for example, salad with truffles, saffron-spiced seafood pot-au-feu, green-tea sherbet: 511 calories with fresh grapefruit juice. We were somewhat less impressed by the colonial decor and by the bill.
Carte: 200F–plus. Menus: 100F, 130F and 180F + 15% serv.

13

## Taverne des Templiers

**106 rue**
**Vieille-du-Temple**
**278.74.67**

*M. Bertrand*
*Open until 10:00 P.M. Closed Sat.,*
*Sun. and during August.*
*V.*

The pompous decor of the first floor (which didn't really need all that) is the handiwork of a decorator infatuated with neo-medieval frippery. All things being equal, in this atmosphere one should dine on such ultra-traditional fare as canapé of quail and lobster Bellevue. Well, almost! Chef Laurent Elhuin does lean toward truly classic cuisine. But make no mistake, his chartreuse of partridge, filets de barbue soufflés Crécy, and flambéed calf's kidneys with shallots are not imitation antiques. This is beautiful, original work. Try the magnificent ice creams (with nougat or massepain), and while you empty your glass of Côtes du Rhône La Tour Lirac (45F), take a moment to admire the beautiful seventeenth-century beamed ceiling.
Carte: 180F–200F.

13

## Daniel Tuboeuf

**26 rue de**
**Montmorency**
**272.31.04**

*M. Tuboeuf*
*Open until 10:00 P.M. Closed Sat.*
*(at lunch), Sun. and during*
*August. Pay parking at*
*Beaubourg.*
*V.*

Daniel Tuboeuf has succeeded Daniel Bouche, and given his own name to the restaurant which used to be the Petit Montmorency. But his range and ambition are more limited than his predecessor's, and he has his work cut out for him. Tuboeuf has been known to go completely off the track, as evidenced by a miserable dinner reported by a member of our team last year. Fortunately, that experience was later eclipsed by a pleasant one, and we are inclined to encourage this young chef and hope that he'll soon find the funds necessary to refurbish his restaurant. A la carte, you will find such fare as oysters with fresh mango and caviar, bar in crème of smoked salmon, and duck with fruit, Tuboeuf also offers a handsome menu which includes feuilleté of salmon, duck with blueberries, Brie de Meaux, and chocolate gâteau fondant.
Carte: 150F–170F. Menu: 100F (wine and serv. incl.).

# 4ème Arr.

## 10/20
### Auberge de Jarente
**7 rue de Jarente**
**277.49.35**
*M. Charriton*
*Open until 10:00 P.M. Closed Sun.,*
*Mon. and during August.*
*AE, DC, V.*

An amusing little place, only a short way from the attractive marketplace of Sainte-Catherine, offering bérnaise-Basque products honestly prepared, the owner's smile, and a modest check. Fish soup, beefsteak, preserved goose with garlicked potatoes. At all costs avoid the scallops (mercilessly overcooked), but do taste the little regional wines, such as Irouléguy, Côte-de-Buzet and Cahors, while thanking heaven that the Marais, in becoming more and more modern, has left intact this small plot of yesterday.
Carte: about 100F. Menu: 62F (serv. incl.) and 68F (wine and serv. incl.).

## 12/20
### Le Beau-bourgeois
**19 rue Sainte-Croix-de-la-Bretonnerie**
**272.08.51**
*Messieurs Proslier and Reyes*
*Open until 12:30 A.M. Pay*
*parking.*

What an exquisite dining room (it used to be part of a theater restaurant), and what a delightful decor with its hues of blue and pink, shimmering white tablecloths and the discreet twinkling of the lamps that illuminate the Gavarni etchings and family portraits (they belong to the owner, Jean-Marie Proslier). But the cuisine is indecisive, weak in its execution, and no doubt the victim of a menu which is too extensive and too diverse. After our almost-frozen melon with "Danish" salmon and a rather mediocre feuilleté of mussels sucarelle, we wished we had tried our luck with the baby mackerel en gelée, the salad of artichoke hearts with foie gras, or the salmon with cream of chives. But we'll leave that for next time. Very good, tangy wines, including an excellent Saumur-Champigny.
Carte: 160F–180F. Menu: 80F + 15% serv.

## 13
### Benoît
**20 rue Saint-Martin**
**272.25.76**
*M. Petit*
*Open until 10:00 P.M.*
*Closed Sat., Sun. and*
*during August.*

Here you take one step toward bourgeois cuisine and two toward that of Lyon. Do you prefer mussel soup or a salad of beef and brawn, hot sausage with a bacon salad or homemade boudin with apples, calf's tongue with herbed sauce or veal kidneys en cocotte, duckling with turnips or sauté of lamb, beef mode or steak with shallots? This restaurant dates from 1912, the era of long-simmering dishes, and we should note that these are more successful than the attempts that M. Petit sometimes makes at nouvelle cuisine. The decor is endearing and attractively fresh.
Carte: 150F–170F.

**11/20**

## Bofinger
**5 rue de la Bastille**
**272.87.82**
*M. Urtizvéréa*
*Open until midnight.*
*Open terrace.*
*Cards: AE, V.*

This old and illustrious restaurant was saved from oblivion and refurbished at great expense about ten years ago. Its slightly naughty turn-of-the-century decor is surely one of the most attractive to be found in Paris, with its flower and fruit motifs and its woodwork of naive inlaid medallions. The mirrors which softly reflect the copper pots and the buttoned leather of the seats also reflect the somewhat discontented faces of the guests of M. Urtizvéréa, who expected something a bit better. But let's not dramatize: One can find perfect happiness in the plat du jour (cassoulet of beans with mutton, preserved duck) or a fish plate such as the cod pot-au-feu. Prices are agreeably stable.
Carte: 130F–150F.

**11/20**

## Brasserie de l'Ile Saint-Louis
**55 quai de Bourbon**
**354.02.59**
*M. Guepratte*
*Open until 1:30 A.M. Closed Wed.*
*and during August.*

The Ile Saint-Louis may change, but this old brasserie remains the same. In an attractive wine cellar setting, sausages, hams, beer steins and other reminders of Alsatian folklore hang from the ceiling, and several hundred meals are served each day to the clientele of sometime students, pseudo-artists, real tourists, and its gruff waiters. One feels like a sardine in a can while dining on ceruelas, curly lettuce salad with lardoons knuckle of ham, an undistinguished sauerkraut, welsh rarebit, damson plum tartes; and, in the winter, a delicious onion tart, all washed down by rivers of beer served in mugs.
Carte: 80F–100F.

**11/20**

## Le Brise-Miche
**10 rue Brise-Miche**
**278.44.11**
*M. Sabatier*
*Open until 1:00 A.M. Closed Sat.*
*and Sun. (at lunch). Open*
*terrace.*

Brick walls, small tables, a massive bar, lots of guys and dolls, a few couples on a strict budget, and students who have heard of the grilled andouillette, the Corrèze hams, or the preserved duck. Nice little wines, nice little desserts, nice little prices.
Carte: 100F–120F.

**17**

## La Ciboulette
**141 rue Saint-Martin**
**271.72.34**
*M. Coffe*
*Open until 1:00 A.M. Closed Sat.*
*and Sun.*
*DC, V*

The ordeal is over. Surviving the expenditure of millions of francs, the bills of gold-hungry decorators, chefs with heads too big for their toques, the extravagant advice of friends, Jean Pierre Coffe, in silken blouse, holds his head high. And with good reason. His Ciboulette is one of the most beautiful restaurants in the world and certainly one of the best. The cuisine of Francis Pointevin, the new chef, bursts with inventiveness, with refinement, with balance. It is good above all, even exquisite, and were it not for our inveterate reserve we would award 18/20 for his preparations, which are as much a treat for the eye as for the palate: mussels with ginger, cold lamb fillets with mint, salad of bitter figs and

raw cèpes, soft-boiled eggs with crayfish, stuffed sole with garlic cream, daurade with salt, roast pigeon with preserved thighs, beef fillets en croûte . . . But let's wait to make sure we're not dreaming. In the ground-floor dining room, businesswomen's lunches and dinners for the tweedy set are becoming institutions. Sitting at plain wooden tables in the extraordinary garden, eating the elegantly home-like cooking with a glass of Côtes-du-Rhône, is at once the most snobbish and the most charming experience imaginable.
Carte 220F–280F.

## 12/20
### Coconnas
**2 bis place des Vosges**
**278.58.16**
*Mme Gorge and M. Terrail*
*Open until 10:00 P.M. Closed Mon. and Tues. Open terrace.*
*Card: DC.*

After a very long period of uncertainty, this old house has finally set a straight course under the guidance of a young chef who practices a polished and consistent cuisine, highlighting a unique, all-inclusive menu with inventions that are sometimes inspired: terrine of skate with fresh mint, leek feuilleté, salad of stuffed cabbage with turbot, preserved rabbit, and amusing desserts. The service is in tune with the cuisine—serious and obliging. On the other hand, the wines offered on this menu are inferior—a quite ordinary Côtes-du-Rhône and a banal Muscadet.
Menu: 120F. (wine and serv. incl.).

## 13
### Aux Délices de Chine
**26 rue des Lombards**
**278.38.62**
*Mme. Chau Kit Wan*
*Open until 10:45 P.M. Closed Sun. Pay parking at Centre Pompidou or Forum des Halles. V.*

The banal decor will not tire your eyes; only a few knickknacks remind you of its orientation. The cuisine is everything: done by Victor Chau, it's served with gentleness, love and care worthy of the best burgeois family. Suzanne Chau, Victor's wife, oversees the dining room and—if you try anything beyond the light, delicious steamed dim-sum or the classic specialties of Peking, Canton or Shanghai—she strongly advises you to order your meal 48 hours ahead of time. For example, the lacquered duck, the Chinese "hot pot" with a dozen dishes (meats, fish, vegetables), the marvelous decorated appetizers and, above all, the delicious stuffed pigeon with swallows' nest, steamed and served in its broth.
Carte: 100F–120F. Menu: 30F (serv. incl), 34F + 15% serv.

## 11/20
### L'Excuse
**14 rue Charles-V**
**277.98.97**
*M. Barbet*
*Open until midnight. Closed Sat. (at lunch) and Sun.*
*AE, DC, V.*

This was once the Falcatula, which achieved near-greatness under the hand of M. Aulibé. Before that, it was an outbuilding of the neighboring mansion where the famous Mme Brinvilliers concocted her poisons. Today, this new little restaurant is run by Jean-Denis Barbet (formerly of the Napoléon-Baumann). The decor is very modern: blond wood paneling, high mirrors, and sleek table accessories. The cuisine offered by young Chef Alain Rouvière (formerly with the Paris in Lille) is of a similar vein and is reasonably priced: terrine of vegetables, ragoût of lotte with leeks, magret with (exquisite) fresh pasta, and a very trendy classic, pan-cooked fillet of beef with blue cheese. Desserts are also fashionable, but quite successful (for example, lemon mousse with rhubarb). Reception and service are youthful and light.

Carte: about 120F. Menu: 85F (serv. incl.).

## Au Franc Pinot

**1 quai de Bourbon**
**329.46.98**
*M. Meyruey*
*Open until 11:30 P.M. Closed Sun. evening and Mon. AE, DC, V.*

One of the most attractive cellars in Paris: two underground levels, clean and whitewashed, descending all the way to the Seine, which flows by just the other side of the wall. A very interesting and extensive choice of wines, served by glass, by bottle or, by golly, to take out. Furthermore, M. Meyruey, the new boss of this delightful place (with remarkable service and welcome), has hired two very young chefs, both of whom served their apprenticeships in excellent kitchens. The result is that never before in the more than three centuries that the house has been in business has it been possible to eat so well: dried duck's wing, médaillon of smoked fish; escalope of sea bass with honey and grapefruit; preserved tuna with olive oil, wine granité.

Carte: 170F. Menu: 85F + 15% serv., 100F-only during the week at lunch (wine and service incl.).

## 11/20
## Galan

**36 blvd. Henri-IV**
**272.17.09**
*Mme Bourgue-Chambrette*
*Open until 9:30 P.M. Closed Sat. May through October. Open for lunch only Sat. during winter months. Closed during August. V.*

Not exactly a monument to revolution, this quiet, country-style restaurant near the Bastille features the mandatory bouillabaisse and cassoulet every day. Other dishes from the sea include mussels marinière, skate in black butter, tendron of veal with fresh noodles, and so on. In short, the kind of cuisine from the heart that you can fall in love with when it's properly prepared (which is sometimes the case here).

Carte: 150F.

## Gaspard de la Nuit

**6 rue des Tournelles**
**277.90.53**
*Mme Haïm*
*Open until 11:00 P.M. Pay parking. AE, DC, V.*

Alone now in the little bistro where Marc Lauger used to set the tone with a light, inventive cuisine, Suzy Haïm, while following the culinary style of her predecessor, has happily seen fit to brighten up his bland decor: new glasses, a few flowers, and some etchings here and there. This refurbishing seems to attract an evening clientele of artists who come to feast upon aiguillettes of duck with pears, seafood fricassée, turbot with red berries, and the fabulous chocolate quatre-quats. The preciousness of the dishes (avocado mousse with kiwi) does not mean an astronomical check. There is a nice choice of good little wines (Coteaux du Lyonnais and Gamay from Oisly). Suzy Haïm also offers an attractive luncheon fixed-price meal: fish soup, preserved duck, and sherbets—that should—we hope—soon be filling the dining room at midday.

Carte: 150F. Menu: 85F (serv. incl.).

**10/20**

## Jo Goldenberg
**7 rue des Rosiers**
**887.20.16**
*M. Goldenberg*
*Open until 2:00 A.M.*
*Card: V.*

"People come to my place and weep for joy," proclaims Jo Goldenberg. True, some people come here to feel at home and to breathe the nostalgic atmosphere of the schtettl, although that is not necessarily the motive of all the habitués of this picturesque Yiddish pub. (Late Sunday afternoons are particularly animated.) Happiness here is being served (at the bar) chopped liver, delicious pickelfleisch, Cracovian sausages, Romanian mittite, exquisite cheese feuilletés, and king strudel, while drinking a good Pilsen and never risking bankruptcy. Carte: 100F. Menu: 45F, 50F (serv. incl.).

**12/20**

## Au Gourmet de l'Isle

**42 rue Saint-Louis-en-l'Ile**
**326.79.27**
*M. Bourdeau*
*Open until 9:45 P.M. Closed Mon., Thurs., and during August.*

Jules Bourdeau, nearly eighty, white moustache bristling, always overflowing with good humor, continues his fight against inflation by serving the most generous meal on the island. A beamed ceiling, tapestries, an attractively arched cellar add to the personality of this bistro always as full as an egg, so that jostling is inevitable. But no one can complain about the breaded tripe or the melt-in-your-mouth andouillettes with red beans, or the cock's kidneys, or the fruit tartes. Carte: 90F. Menu: 60F (wine and service incl.).

**11/20**

## Le Grenier sur l'Eau
**14 rue du Pont-Louis-Philippe**
**277.80.96**
*M. Mauget*
*Open until 11:30 P.M. Closed Sun. and 1 week beginning August 15.*
*Pay parking.*
*AE, DC.*

Outside of the respectable, fixed-price menu, forget it! The a la carte prices are fearsome for a cuisine which can be categorized only as quite nice and carefully-prepared. We must admit, though, that the decor is charming and intimate, perfectly suited to a quiet tête-à-tête. And anyway, why not stick with the menu? Portions are generous, and the selection is vast. For example: eggplant custard with coulis of tomatoes, confit of duck with vegetable ratatouille, and mousse of fromage blac with coulis of strawberries. Good service. Carte: 170F. Menu: 90F (serv. incl.).

**13**

## La Guirlande de Julie
**25 place des Vosges**
**887.94.07**
*Mme Rasanen*
*Closed Wed. Open terrace.*

She is beautiful, she is Finnish, she is named Jaria; and she is one of the most seductive attributes of this Guirlande de Julie, located on the ground floor of a glorious old house in the Marais quarter. Fresh and charming atmosphere redolent of the eighteenth century with eight splendid chandeliers lighting the dining room. If the mousse of smoked salmon with caviar proclaims a Scandinavian origin, the little menu, which changes often enough, is thoroughly French and permits you to eat well without a dictionary. It includes such delicacies as skilfully prepared navarin of lamb and pochouse with Saint-Véran. Carte: 120F–140F.

**12/20**

## Chez Julien
**1 rue du Pont-Louis-**

Squeezed in between the church of Saint-Gervais (the small island has been superbly restored) and the

## Phillippe
**278.31.64**

*M. Riault*
*Open until 11:00 P.M. Closed Sun.*
*and Mon. (at lunch). Pay parking*
*at Pont-Marie.*

entrance to a vast underground parking garage, this restaurant has been converted from an old bakery shop. It is now attractively dedicated to the country-style cooking of our grandmothers—which is making a comeback. Steak with purée of leek, feuilleté of veal sweetbreads with Sauvignon, lotte à la bourguignonne, and chocolate charlotte that the new owner, like the old one, makes a point of preparing with care and serving generously.
Carte: 150F.

## 12/20
# La Lieu-tenance
**24 rue Chanoinesse**
**354.91.36**

*M. Devigne*
*Open until 11:30 P.M. Closed*
*Mon. Parking.*
*V.*

Pierre Devigne used to run a fashionable little restaurant in Honfleur called La Lieutenance. Its preciosity is recreated in the decor of this ivy-covered sixteenth-century residence, located only a short distance from Notre-Dame. In a dining room abundant with flowers, its walls covered with etchings and faience, you'll taste a cuisine characterized by great finesse and just a hint of mannerism, served by charming young men with hair as curly as a poodle's. The raw, marinated tuna, salad of calf's sweetbreads, and bar duchesse with watercress are so beautifully arranged on the plate that you will hate to disturb them. In his affinity for cutting everything into slices, chef Patrick Roucoules (formerly of the Trois Marches and Grand Vefour) sometimes spoils his work. An example was our magret of duck with figs, which was rather tasteless. Will they be able to overcome these little vices? In any case, nothing seems to displease the very fashionable, very show-biz clientele which flocks to this isle of charm every evening. But at noon, it's almost deserted. Take advantage of it to enjoy an intimate lunch, accompanied by one of the exquisite wines from Aix. The bill is less affable than the service.
Carte: 200F.

## 13
# M
**14 rue des Lombards**
**278.44.68**

*M. Le Bret*
*Open until 10:30 P.M. Closed Sat.*
*(at lunch) and Sun. Pay parking*
*3F at rue Beaubourg. AE, V.*

The M stands for nothing—simply the 13th letter of the alphabet, which is supposed to be lucky. François Le Bret himself turned out to be the lucky one, for, after finding on the bottom level of his cellars the graceful pointed arches that are the remains of the Saint-Merri chapel, he engaged Christian Thuillart, previously a sous-chef at La Ciboulette, who finally gives this restaurant, one of Paris's most elegant, the kind of cuisine that it deserves. It is cooking done intelligently in a modified modern style. We particularly liked the lamb's tongue with capers; the fricassée of guinea-hen with lardoons, mushrooms, artichoke and small onions; the sautéed prawns with cream; and a millefeuille with caramelized pineapple. A good sommelier has charge of a wine list that is still too brief.
Carte: 200F-plus. Menu: 120F (lunch only, serv. incl.), 170F + 15% serv.

## Le Monde des Chimères
**10/20**

**69 rue Saint-Louis-en-l'Ile**
**354.45.27**
*Mme Coureau*
*Open until 10:30 P.M. Closed Sun.*
*and during September.*

Our experiences in this pretty stone-and-beam bistro decorated with enchanting paintings have always left us feeling, at best, dissatisfied, and, at worst, disappointed and annoyed—as was the case the other day after a bitter-tasting, inadequately cleaned and poorly prepared crab salad, overcooked daurade in an invasive, over-floured wine sauce, a fatty bavette with shallots, and oeufs à la neige worthy of a company cafeteria. The ice cream, served directly from the freezer, was as hard as a rock. We think we know what the trouble is: when they started out, friends and co-owners Jeanine Coureau and Françoise Matheron took lessons from a star chef, but these proved too difficult to be successfully applied. We thought that Jeanine and Françoise would have had the wisdom to embark on a simpler, more personal course . . . but they haven't done that yet. In the meantime, theirs is just one more pretty restaurant on the Ile where the reception is less friendly and the service less efficient than in days gone by. Well?
Carte: 160F–180F.

## Montecristo
**13**

**81 rue Saint-Louis-en-l'Ile**
**633.35.46**
*M. Cese*
*Open until 10:30 P.M. Closed Sun.*
*and during August.*
*AE, DC.*

Fernando Cese and Filippo Liberatore, a stout-hearted pair of Abruzzians transplanted to the Ile Saint-Louis, were previously in the service first of Karim Aga Khan and later that of Italy's ambassador to UNESCO. They run this small restaurant with gusto. The setting is immaculate and subtle, and a faithful clientele comes to taste by candlelight a cuisine one might call Italian-bourgeois, rarely found in Paris. Here and there on the menu you'll find a few disappointing dishes, but there are also some delicious rarities, such as the artichoke tarte à la piémontaise; fresh pasta with chanterelles or with duck; squab à la toscane; escalopes of veal sweetbreads, seasoned with a drop of vinegar and married with sublime spinach; ice cream with Amaretto; or that crême brûlée which one feasts on in Italy or in Catalonia but which is still, incredibly, unknown to Parisian chefs.
Carte: about 150F. Menu: 80F (serv. incl.)

## Le P'tit Gavroche
**10/20**

**15 rue Sainte-Croix-de-la-Bretonnerie**
**887.74.26**
*M. Dickmann*
*Open until 11:30 P.M. Closed*
*Sun., holidays and during August.*

A precious address for all those who do not know that a meal for 22F can still be had in Paris. Le P'tit Gavroche is not a cafeteria but a real little restaurant in turn-of-the-century bistro style where one is well-received, well-served, and well-surrounded by a well-enough-off, well-spirited clientele that for 22F finds honest food such as céléri rémoulade, daube and chocolate mousse.
Menu: 22F + 15% serv.

## Les Philosophes
**10/20**

**28 rue**

More in the epicurean vein, although the menu is sprinkled with illustrations drawn from Descartes' *Metaphysical Meditations,* and a few major eggheads have

**Vieille-du-Temple**
**887.49.64**
*M. Spindel*
*Open until midnight. Closed Sun.*
*and during August.*
*AE, DC, V.*

been conscripted to endorse the salads (Plato), gésiers (Bergson), and cutlets (Spinoza). Attributable to living geniuses are the andouillette (Duval), the charcuterie (Drancy), the sherbets (Berthillon), and the scrumptuous struedels that you'd swear came from the Rue des Rosiers. Handsome decor of white stone. A well-chosen, small wine list.
Carte: 100F. Menu: 69F (serv. incl.).

16

# Au Quai des Ormes
**72 quai de l'Hôtel-de-Ville**
**274.72.22**
*M. Masraff*
*Open until 10:30 P.M.*
*Closed Sat. (at lunch), Sun.*
*and during August.*
*V.*

Many Parisian restaurateurs dream idly of fresh country air and little birds. Georges Masraff, on the other hand, has left this bucolic ideal where a cook spends long winter months gazing at an almost empty dining room. Giving up his beautiful manor in Brittany, he has come to Paris with his attractive wife Marianne to breathe the exhaust fumes of the Parisian quais. He could not have found a better site: this end of the quai de Hôtel-de-Ville, with its village-like square and its delightful old houses in the shadow of Saint-Gervais' steeple, is in the process of rejuvenation, much to the delight of pedestrians. His decor suffers a few faults attributable to youth (they will be quickly remedied), but the façade is very attractive, the country scene painted on the back wall is graceful. M. Masraff, a young Armenian from Cairo who dropped out of medical school to learn cooking (Taillevent, Haeberlin, Bernard Loiseau, Troisgros, and, finally, in his own kitchen), is surrounded by cookbooks, which he devours like a neophyte, and produces a subtle cuisine that is (discretely) modern and (openly) light. He stumbles a few times along the way, but a delicious dish of pan-fried artichokes and prawns with tomato butter, braised John Dory with a clove of garlic, an émincé of veal sweetbreads on a bed of sensational spinach, a beautiful rabbit with morels, and intoxicating desserts have made of the Quai des Ormes a gastronomic event— and this without too much strain on your wallet.
Carte: 160F–180F. Menus: 100F, 110F + 15% serv.

**12/20**

# Le Tourtour
**20 rue Quincampoix**
**887.82.48**
*M. Dumas*
*Open until 1:00 A.M.*
*AE, DC, V.*

This remarkable old restaurant on the rue Quincampoix has held fast to all of its good habits, never giving in to the temptations created by the cultural activity and heavy tourist traffic in and around Beaubourg. Here, you can still find some of the most respectable food in the area, served on pretty tablecloths in an extensively (finally!) renovated decor. (In fact, they plan to open a piano bar later this year in the wonderful, newly-restored cellar.) A shrewd affair, as we might expect from former marketing student Jean-Pierre Dumas. Try the poached salmon with fennel, the rack of lamb with three vegetables, and, of course, the superb, thin apple tart.
Carte: 110F. Menus: 59.50F, 64.50F (serv. incl.).

**10/20**
## Le Trumilou
**84 quai de l'Hôtel-de-Ville**
**277.63.98**
*M. Rouby*
*Open until 9:30 P.M. Closed Mon.*
*and during September.*
*Open terrace. Pay parking*
*at rue Laban.*

An old bistro of the quais across from the Ile-Saint-Louis; a little tired but charming, with habitués whose like you'll hardly see anywhere else. The friendly service is "personalized." Roast chicken, ratatouille, leg of lamb with haricot beans, sole meunière, and a Gamay at 16F per bottle.
Carte: About 80F. Menu: 28F, 40F (serv. incl.).

**13**
## Les Ursins dans le Caviar
**3 rue de la Colombe**
**329.54.20**
*M. de Tougarinoff*
*Open until 1:00 A.M. Closed Sun.*
*Dinner only.*
*AE, DC, V.*

The kitchen of this ravishing combination of restaurant and antique shop, located in one of the oldest structures on the Ile de la Cité, has changed hands three times during the past three years. We certainly don't blame Igor de Tougarinoff for trying to install a cuisine worthy of his decor. But we do regret that on such short notice, we were unable to sample the alluring offerings of his newcomer, Nilo Roginas, a young chef who was number two for two years at L'Archestrate. With such references, we don't expect any unpleasant surprises. Salad of smoked magret au gros sel, fricassée of chicken with candied leeks, fillet of daurade with watercress
Carte: 170F–200F. Menu: 95F + 15% serv.

**13**

## Wally Saharien
**16-18 rue Le Regrattier**
**325.01.39**
*M. Wally*
*Open until 11:00 P.M. Closed Sat.*
*(at lunch), Sun. and Mon. No*
*dogs. Pay parking at Pont-Marie,*
*La Cité.*
*AE, DC, V.*

A subtle, intimate decor filled with beautiful Arabic objects that no man of the desert would even dare to dream about; well-spaced tables harmoniously distributed among small dining rooms; quietly efficient service and soft music of the south. The aristocratic Wally has overlooked nothing to receive you according to the Sahara's rigorous rules of hospitality. His cuisine is simplicity itself—one central dish, a light and subtle couscous accompanied by spit-roasted lamb; or chorba, pastilla, stuffed sardines (his desserts are less convincing). Assuredly the most unusual and by far the most elegant couscous restaurant around. Also the most expensive . . . Tajines and paella if ordered in advance.
Menu: 150F (wine incl.) + 15% serv.

# 5ème Arr.

**15**
## L'Ambroisie
**65 quai de la Tournelle**
**633.18.65**
*M. Pacaud*
*Open until 10:00 P.M., closed Sun.*
*and Mon. No dogs.*

This minuscule restaurant of only nine tables, on the ground floor of a seventeenth-century mansion which is undergoing renovation, was *the* discovery of 1980. Bernard Pacaud, who for four years was Claude Peyrot's chef at the Vivarois, has had to reduce his menu to a minimum because of the smallness of his dining room. Even so, the finesse of his preparations, the clarity of flavors in his cooking, reveal a true talent. Only a few—too

few even—entrées: four fish dishes, three of meat; certainly, the list is short, even though the items change each day. Comfortably seated in a chrome and black leather armchair, taste the remarkably seasoned dodine of duck with foie gras; the sensational skate with sliced green cabbage, covered with a sauce courte with sherry vinegar; the veal sweetbreads with shallots and parsley accompanied by the best fresh pasta on earth; or the succulent oxtail in sauce; and, finally, an admirable chocolate cake. Then you, too, will have the urge to award Pacaud two toques. To these we add one small reproach: sauces and butter are Pacaud's pet sins, and he should not over-indulge them. A good menu with artichoke hearts and foie gras, a nage with three different fish, cheeses and dessert.
Carte: 160F–190F. Menu: 115F (serv. incl.).

## 13 🍸
## *Atelier Maître- Albert*
**1, rue Maître-Albert**
**633.13.78**
*M. Caille*
*Open until midnight. Dinner only.*
*Closed Sun.*

This Left Bank outpost of the Mercure Galant, at the mouth of one of the more picturesque small streets of the Maubert quarter (already being enviously eyed by developers, alas), has for years been able to maintain an abundant, painstaking cuisine at virtually unbeatable prices. It is without competitors if you add the friendliness of the reception and the service, the majestic setting with its old beams and great chimney, and the attractive table service. A half-dozen possibilities at each meal: for example, an exquisite terrine of pigs' tails; a thick calf's liver with basil, very well prepared; Meaux Brie cheese, and a frozen strawberry soufflé. And after dinner when you leave, there is Notre-Dame illuminated before your eyes.
Menu: 100F (wine incl.) + 15% serv.

## 13 🍸
## *Auberge des Deux Signes*
**46 rue Galande**
**325.46.56**
*M. Dhulster*
*Open until 11:00 P.M. Closed Sun.,*
*holidays, and during August.*
*Pay parking at rue Lagrange*
*and Notre-Dame.*
*All major credit cards.*

The charming M. Dhulster, who spends his early mornings at the Rungis market choosing and collecting the freshest foodstuffs and his afternoons in his medieval restaurant to make it even more welcoming and comfortable, is from the Auvergne; therefore he is a perfectionist. His customers have no cause for complaint as they sit in this exceptionally attractive inn with the gardens of Saint-Julien-le-Pauvre before them and Notre-Dame framed by the trees in the evening. In addition to the solid food of the Cantal and the Puy-de-Dôme (the pounti, the talmouse, the lait lardé, the tripous), Chef Guittonneau (who spent three years at Maxim's) prepares a mousse of pike with purée of lobster, fillets of sole meunière, a lobster feuilleté, and several other well-composed and classic dishes. M. Dhulster has just invented his own version of Irish coffee, the whiskey being replaced by the prune liqueur of Souillac. He deserves a statue. Note: You can rent the magnificent arched cellars for group lunches or dinners.
Carte: about 180F.

## 11/20
## Le Balzar
**49 rue des Écoles**
**354.13.67**
*M. Marolleau*
*Open until 12:30 A.M. Closed*
*Tues. and during August. No dogs.*

As we once again travel the path we took as starving students, we sometimes take our rest on the naugahide benches of the Balzar (not without some emotion, we might add) between some bilious university professor nursing his beer and a future poet madly scribbling iambic verse, a plate of cervelas rémoulade at his side. At lunch, it's sometimes a little sad, a little forsaken, but still touching. The old paneling, the mirrors, the waiters who've been there since day one, the pigs' feet Sainte-Menehould and the calf's liver Niçoise all strive to divert the mind. But in the evening, everything cheers up. The clientele is brighter (pretty girls, intellectuals, actors), and the old brasserie of the Rue des Écoles becomes one of the liveliest places on the Left Bank. Well, almost. Carte: 110F.

## 10/20
## Le Baptiste
**11 rue des Boulangers**
**325.57.24**
*M. Pelizza*
*Open until 10:30 P.M. Closed*
*Mon. No dogs.*

Located half way up this steep, irregular street, Le Baptiste is a restaurant for customers of modest means and bourgeois tastes: beams and more beams, from floor to ceiling, waiters who lack only the straw in their hair, and crowded bistro-type tables. A good, three-meat pot-au-feu, grilled specialties (onglet with shallots), and a daily special (daurade au four), preceded by respectable country salads and terrines, and followed by disastrous desserts. Bearing all that in mind, the meals are pleasant and bountiful, especially in light of the moderate prices. Opened a little less than a year ago, Le Baptiste is always filled with amiable, noisy customers largely representing the university set and the bourgeoisie. The Touraine Marionnet gamay is charming, fruity and so inexpensive. Carte: 70F–80F. Menu: 40F (wine and serv. incl.).

## 15
## La Bûcherie
**41 rue de la Bûcherie**
**354.78.06**
*M. Bosque*
*Open until 1:00 A.M.*
*AE, DC.*

The atmosphere of this restaurant (located across from Notre Dame) is still delightful, Bernard Bosque's cuisine remains at the same high level, and the value for one's money is still quite remarkable. But, although we are always delighted to rediscover the stuffed cabbage with crab, ocean salmon with chives, sander with rhubarb, fillet of pork with rosemary, and navarin of sweetbreads, we *would* like to see the menu change a little, and the sweet breeze of inspiration blow through the kitchens. It is true that Bernard Bosque has recently undergone a long and trying ordeal. He has every excuse, and we know that he will apply himself wholeheartedly to the task of renewing his restaurant. Carte: 160F

## 11/20
## Le Buisson Ardent
**25 rue Jussieu**
**354.93.02**
*M. Héligon*

It used to be a rather tight squeeze in this estimable bistro located across from the University. Bernard Héligon has improved the situation some by removing a few tables to the dining room extension. Now it will be even easier to enjoy the cuisine served with a certain graciousness by his

*Open until 9:30 P.M. Closed Sat. (at lunch), Sun. and during August.*

bustling wife: frisée with goat cheese, confit of duck, leg of lamb with gratin dauphinois (Fri. and Sat.), and clafoutis. Bordeaux wines served by the carafe, and very low prices.
Carte: 80F–100F. Menu (lunch only): 46F (serv. incl.).

## 11/20
## Le Coupe-Chou

**11 rue de Lanneau
633.68.69 and
354.36.54**

*MM. Azzopardi, Lemonnier et Nani. Open until 1:00 A.M. Closed Sun. (at lunch). Parking at Maubert-Mutualité.*

The sign refers to the evil deeds that once occurred in this very place, the Parisian version of Sweeney Todd: the barber who slit his clients' throats and the butcher next door who transformed the cadavers into pâté. But have no fear; the three actor-owners—mild-mannered and charming—transformed a ruined house about a dozen years ago into one of the most seductive inns of the Left Bank. The style is Louis XIII, with arches, chimneys, soft lights, obscure corners. Within the last few years, they have evolved a cuisine very much up to date in style and in price. You will eat, on an attractively set table, a fish soup with vegetables, lamb with fresh mint, magrets of duck with prunes and apples, the hot homemade millefeuille, with a young Burgundy served chilled (26F), and you will be flushed with happiness.
Carte: 170F–180F.

## 17
## Dodin Bouffant

**25-27 rue
Frédéric-Sauton
325.25.14**

*Mme Cartier
Open until 12:45 A.M. Closed Sat., Sun., during August, 15 days at year's end. DC.*

Now it is only rarely that we are greeted by the warm smile of Jacques Manière, for he has retired to the country. No one will ever replace him, but the Manière spirit lives on in this very special restaurant which is neither bistro nor brasserie yet a little of both, in the warm if somewhat disorganized style that characterized this exceptional man. In truth, Maurice Cartier, his wife Danièle, and their chef Jean-Marie Clément have worked with Jacques Manière for more than ten years during which time—though they may have acquired some of his faults—they became imbued with his enthusiasm and integrity. One can have confidence in this team not the least of whose merits is to have made of the Dodin Bouffant one of the most reliable restaurants in Paris for high quality at a fair price. It is the only one of our "3 Toques" in the capital where it is still possible to dine really well for 170F–180F and also to drink excellent wine for less than 40F, choosing from an enticing and often-revised menu such Manière-inspired dishes as steamed scallops with fresh pasta; daube with oysters and pig's trotters; curried sole with squash fondue; calf's head with rosemary, to say nothing of one of Paris's most delectable selections of seafood and shellfish directly from saltwater fish tanks. Only the service, entrusted to youngsters of limited experience, is sometimes to be criticized.
Carte 170F–180F.

**12/20**

### Aux Iles Philippines
**17 rue Laplace**
**633.18.59**

*Mme Daza*
*Open until midnight. Closed Mon.*
*and December 15 to January 15.*
*No dogs.*

Both the setting—a courtyard garden behind the Panthéon—and the cooking—agreeably exotic—make you return here. There is an air of authenticity about the restaurant and the food, which is watched over by Mme Daza Nora Bong, who also owns a French restaurant . . . in Manila. Contrasts of tastes dominate the cuisine of the Filipino chef, and you will pass some agreeable moments as you savor the kuhol bicol (snails with coconut milk), the alimange (crab meat with cream), or the Kawali, the plat de résistance at any Philippina festival and consisting of crispy pork served with a liver sauce. The service is exotic, smiling, but a bit sluggish.
Carte: 120F. Menu: 80F (wine and serv. incl.).

**11/20**

### Le Mange-Tout
**30 rue Lacépède**
**535.53.93**

*M. Simon*
*Open until 10:30 P.M. Closed Sun.*
*evening, Mon., 1 week at Easter*
*and August 15 to September 8.*
*Parking.*
*DC.*

Don't draw any hasty conclusions from the name of this restaurant (literally, the Eat-Everything). It doesn't mean that there's a culinary deviant in the kitchen who will serve you just anything, it means that you'll finish every bite of the simple, moderately-garnished meal set before you. Credit for this goes to M. Simon, the owner who hails from Aveyron (in the central region of France known as Rouergue), and all sorts of good products from that area, purchased at the nearby shop of the Villefranchois in the Place Monge. Gésiers d'oie confits, Rouergue plate, potatoes sarladaise with walnuts, rabbit in mustard sauce. A good and varied selection of Cahors wines.
Carte: 120F–150F.

**12/20**

### La Marée Verte
**9 rue de Pontoise**
**325.89.41**

*Messieurs Bouroumeau et*
*Gibergues*
*Open until 10:00 P.M. Closed Sun.,*
*Mon. and during August. Pay*
*parking.*
*V.*

New owners, new chef (formerly with the Galant Verre and Bistrot de Paris) but, it's rumored, still under the watchful eye of its famous neighbor, Jacques Manière. Whatever the case, let us note the much-improved reception and service, and the cuisine, which seems to have settled comfortably into the small, seafood-oriented range of the menu: a bountiful, exquisitely fresh fisherman's plate, turbot soufflé almost worthy of the Dodin-Bouffant, and exquisite meringue tarte with citrus fruits. Good, lesser wines that are not too expensive. Lots of people in the evenings, but the lunches are quiet. Excellent value for the money.
Menu: 115F (incl. wine and serv.).

**11/20**

### Mario
**7 rue des Ecoles**
**326.83.59**

*M. Vernocchi*
*Open until 11:00 P.M. Closed Mon.*
*and August 5 to September 10.*
*DC.*

At 70, Mario is one of the oldest and sprightliest Italians in Paris. He has just repainted the faded interior of his restaurant in tones of blue, and has equipped the kitchen with one of the most modern pasta machines in the world. This may be why the pasta has never been better and why the customers of this little corner restaurant are all regulars, and even fanatics: cappelletti, pasticciata, cannelloni, and tagliatelle . . . these alone would be worth

the visit. But you'll also find a wide range of antipasti, a good selection of Chianti, and Mario—who's blessed with the gift of gab.
Carte: 170F. Menu: (lunch only) about 120F.

13

## Moissonnier
**28 rue des**
**Fossés-Saint-Bernard**
**329.87.65**
*M. Moissonnier*
*Open until 9:30 P.M. Closed Sun.*
*evening, Mon. and during August.*

Sturdy as the Pont Neuf, honest, bourgeois and tasty: just as you remember the cuisine of Moissonnier from three, five or ten years ago, so you will find it today. Beige walls and white tablecloths, a zinc bar just inside the entrance, and a basket of grapes and vines in the middle of a folkloristic dining room. Nothing has changed, and if you have not made a reservation you'll be lucky to find a table in this bistro of faithful clients—professors, provincial politicians, wine merchants—who come to breathe the restorative air of Lyon and the Jura. You will find that the brézi of the Franche-Comté is even better than the viande des Grisons, the tripe as well sautéed as at Fourvières, and that the salads (sheep's trotters, cervelas remoulade, beef brawn), the gratins of potatoes, the Morbier cheeses, the jugs of Beaujolais and the bill are just right to console you for so many mediocre meals and steep checks that you have put up with elsewhere.
Carte: 110F.

16

## Au Pactole
**44 blvd.**
**Saint-Germain**
**633.31.31**
*M. Magne*
*Open until 11:00 P.M. Closed Sat.*
*(at lunch) and Sun. Pay parking.*
*V.*

When Jacques Manière first opened au Pactole, he had no trouble at all filling his restaurant in the evenings, but for years he had a good problem convincing customers that he also sets a great table at lunch. Roland Magne, his successor, is having the same difficulty and, despite a fine menu at 125F, perfect for business lunches, there are days when his heart is heavy between 12:00 and 2:00. Doesn't the evening crowd know that there is easy parking a stone's throw away? And that a new parking lot is being built even closer? Therefore, courage, Roland Magne, and profit from the lull to vary your menu a little more often. We like your salmon with Chartreuse, the bass Cravache d'Or, and the pavé of steamed calf's liver, and we adore your fricassée of kid with fresh mint; but we wouldn't be upset to discover some new facets of your talents. The dining room is still unchanged (should we complain?). The charming Mme Magne welcomes you with unfailing grace, and, with an excellent Chez Paul Maitre Bourgueil, the bill will not go beyond 170F–180F.
Menu: 125F (serv. incl.).

**11/20**

## Le Petit Navire
**14 rue des**
**Fossés-St.-Bernard**

The motor which powers this little boat is its owner-chef, M. Cousty, who putts over to Les Halles every morning to buy what he needs to prepare his seafood cuisine—whose only real defect is the excessively nautical decor in which it is served. And so they go, from one year to the next:

**354.22.52**

*M. Cousty*
*Open until 10:00 P.M. Closed Sun.,*
*Mon. (at lunch), holidays, March 1*
*to March 17, and September 1 to*
*September 17.*
*DC.*

bourride, tapenade, and turbot en cassolette. Honest food at high prices.
Carte: 130F. Menu: 45F (serv. incl.).

**11/20**

## Le Petit Prince

**12 rue Lanneau**
**354.77.26**

*Messieurs Gobe and Floux*
*Open until midnight. Closed 2*
*weeks in August.*
*AE.*

Messieurs Floux and Gobe persist in maintaining the mysteries of their menu, whose secret compartments and master code are known only to the regulars. But don't be afraid to ask; without fear of bankruptcy, you'll discover rather good terrines, salad frisée with bacon, bavette with shallots, magrets and confits which make for pleasant (but—alas!—not quick) little after-theater meals.
Carte: 120F.

**10/20**

## Le Raccard

**20 rue Descartes**
**325.27.27**

*M. Rennard*
*Open until 12:30 A.M. Dinner only.*
*AE, DC, V.*

Once upon a time, there was a Swiss chalet, high atop Mont Saint-Geneviève. . . . In this tiny restaurant you can sample the specialties of the canton of Valais (including raclette, mountain ham and dried meats), while enjoying a bottle of Fendant. Be sure to have a look at the authentic raccard—a typically Swiss apparatus used for storing hay.
Carte: 100F. Menu: 65F (serv. incl.).

**12/20**

## Chez René

**14 blvd.**
**Saint-Germain**
**354.30.23**

*M. Cinquin*
*Open until 10:15 P.M. Closed Sat.,*
*Sun. and during August. Pay*
*parking at*
*St.-Nicolas-du-*
*Chardonnet.*

Despite our inclination to stand in defense of the few remaining authentic Parisian bistros, our latest visit here was a definite disappointment. Could this be the result of too much success? The hot saucisson was greasy and too salty, the andouillette heavy, the steak tough, and the boeuf bourguignon a disappointing imitation of the real thing. Unchanged are the good, minor wines, amusing owner and waiters, the between-two-wars decor, reliable specials of the day, and reasonable tab.
Carte: 100F–120F.

**14**

## Le Senonnes

**9 rue Royer-Collard**
**326.13.13**

*M. Fajolles-Villeneuve*
*Open until 10:00 P.M. Closed Mon.*
*(at lunch), Sun. and during*
*August. Pay parking*
*at rue Soufflot.*
*Card: V.*

Michel and Anita Fajolles-Villeneuve—he at the reception, she at the stove—have transported from Brittany to this old sloping street in the Latin Quarter their gracious hospitality, their insistence upon the season's best ingredients, and their strict belief in limited cooking time and copious portions. Although the summer and winter menus are not the same, certain staples appear on both: fish and lobster simply grilled, salad of prawn or sole with pasta. In addition, happy surprises such as grilled turbot au gros sel; stuffed artichokes with crab, and rack of lamb with mint. There is a nice choice of Loire Valley wines, certain of them (Muscadet, Sauvignon) at very interesting prices and served by the pitcher.
Carte: 170F. Menu: 55F, 100F + 15% serv.

## 10/20
### La Taverne Descartes
**35 rue Descartes**
**325.67.77**
*Messieurs Vellu*
*Open until 11:30 P.M. Closed Sat.*
*(at lunch).*
*AE, V.*

The Vellu boys, Pierre and Claude, come to us from Switzerland. They've climbed to great heights here in Paris, but not without the help of their daddy, Roland Vellu, who, far below in the valley near the church of Saint-Médard, keeps a watchful eye on their progress. And you have to admit that these boys are anything but lazy—they work like dogs to prepare a fine, inexpensive menu, based on fish (lotte in red wine) and solid bourgeois dishes (sauté of lamb with eggplant).
Carte: 90F–100F. Menus: 40F + 15% serv., 55F (wine and serv. incl.).

## 11/20
### Tong Shin
**21 Quai Saint-Michel**
**354.74.76**
*Mme Louie*
*Open until 1:45 A.M.*
*AE.*

The great number of Oriental customers here implies a certain authenticity about this fine Chinese restaurant. With a predominately Cantonese influence, you'll find a good deal of dim sum. But you can also enjoy the fresh crab in ginger and a potée of fish. Good coconut pastries and a flamboyant new decor.
Carte: 70F.

## 17
### La Tour d'Argent
**15-17 quai de la Tourelle**
**354.23.31**
*M. Terrail*
*Open until 10:00 P.M. Closed Mon.*
*Attendant parking.*
*AE, DC.*

This is no longer the world's best restaurant. Nor is it any longer Paris's best restaurant. But it is the restaurant which, throughout the world, symbolizes the luxury of la vie et la cuisine françaises. The Tour d'Argent this year celebrates its four-hundredth anniversary, and it is always a feast for the eyes and the spirit to enter these exquisite salons where Claude Terrail has installed his little museum of cooking (recently half-destroyed by vandals protesting the consumer society), to take the elevator, which reminds you of a sedan chair of the eighteenth century, and to debark finally into this dining room which could have been decorated by Louis XIV himself, and where the director and the maîtres d'hôtel never confuse civility with obsequiousness in showing you to your table. Here you are seated high in the sky of Paris, with Notre Dame just across the way and the barges slipping by on the Seine below. Always a flower in his lapel, Claude Terrail, with the bearing of an ambassador, receives you with a kiss of the ladies' hands, and moves from table to table while the six hundred thousandth (plus) Tour d'Argent duckling—yours will be presented with a card bearing its number—is being prepared. (The first of these was to Edward VII in 1890, then Prince of Wales). Brought to you in two services—first, aiguillettes of magret; next, the roast legs and wings—this world-renowned duckling is not, however, our favorite among the eight different preparations that are suggested. Personally, we prefer the duckling Bourdaloue with lemon, or the "Marco Polo" with four peppers, but it is, after all, a matter of taste. Some of the plates do not live up to the promise of their pompous names, but the cold lobster, served with a

herbed mayonnaise (called—Lagardère), the patties André Terrail, the flambéed peaches, and, above all, the always marvelous wines, will not disappoint you. These wines are brought up from an extraordinary cellar (120,000 bottles down there) which, if you ask, you will be shown after dessert and where by candlelight you can sip a vintage cognac while watching a miniature *son et lumière* that will recreate for you the history of this privileged place. And, why do people neglect the Tour d'Argent for lunch? The atmosphere is less touristy, and you are offered (except on Sundays) the very attractive menu at 180F. In the evening, however, you will spend with no difficulty at all 500F. per person.
Carte: 350F–500F. Menu: 180F + 15% s. (at lunch weekdays.).

## 12/20
## Chez Toutoune
**5 rue de Pontoise**
**326.56.81**
*Mme Dejean*
*Open until 10:30 P.M. Closed Sun.,*
*Mon. and August 15 to September*
*15. Pay parking at blvd.*
*Saint-Germain.*

The soup tureen, or, rather, its contents—cream of watercress, pumpkin, haricot beans—dominates the table of blond Toutoune (a.k.a. Colette Dejean). It is a cuisine devoted almost exclusively to traditional dishes, with perhaps a nod here and there to those of the Midi: pot-au-feu of three meats (beef, veal, stuffed chicken); braised guinea fowl with cabbage; kidneys with preserved baby onions; tendron of veal bourgeoise; haricot mutton; leg of lamb with scalloped potatoes (or Swiss chard); poteé of pig's tail. Simple, honest, and copious: (entrée, main dish, salad or cheese, dessert).
Menu: 70F + 15% serv.

## 12/20
## Les Trabou-cayres
**12 rue de**
**l'Hôtel-Colbert**
**354.61.99**
*M. Excoffier*
*Open until 11:00 P.M. Closed Mon.*
*(at lunch).*
*AE, DC.*

The décor is medieval, and the cuisine, prepared by the owner, is generous and of a high standard. The carte-menu at 48F (service, wine and dessert not included) permits a choice among eight appetizers and as many main dishes. This is an extraordinary price-quality ratio. Specialties such as marinated fish with lime, green salad with warm fins, preserved duck with vegetables, blanquette of suckling pig with coconut milk are generally without fault, and if the service improved a bit this would be one of the best little addresses in the quarter. The wines of the house (Menetou Salon, Coteaux-du-Giennois) are excellent.
Carte 100F. Menu: 48F + 15% serv.

## 12/20
## La Truffière
**4 rue Blainville**
**633.29.82**
*Messieurs Bouleau and Gaussot*
*Open until midnight. Closed Mon.*
*and during July. Dinner only.*
*AE, DC, V.*

Just a step away from the Place de la Contrescarpe (which is trying to put on a new face, but still hasn't managed to rid itself of its bums), but leagues away from the usual greasy fare which serves as the fodder for this night district. You'll be admitted only after ringing the bell, and you'll eat only goose and duck, their by-products, and their most traditional accompaniments, prepared without

a trace of culinary exoticism. You'll enjoy a warm reception in the cozy sitting room near the fireplace, genial service by witty young waiters, and a candlelight dinner under the beamed ceiling. What could you possibly complain about . . . the prices are reasonable, the Cahors wines delicious, and the cuisine robust, sincere and generous. Well, maybe the desserts, which are a little weak (especially the tarte Tatin).
Carte: 160F. Menu: 100F (wine and serv. incl.).

**12/20**

## La Vallée des Bambous

**35 rue Gay-Lussac**
**354.99.47**
*M. Tchao*
*Open until 10:30 P.M. Closed Tues.*
*and during August.*

Here they prepare the famous full-moon cake (made with cream of lotus and candied egg yolk) two months in advance, to be served only in September. But you can enjoy other treats all year long: the delicious and subtle dim sum, lacquered meats, and grilled shrimp with pepper. A good many Oriental customers come here—not a bad sign in this type of restaurant—to enjoy life on the bamboo side and forget this valley of tears.
Carte: 70F–90F. Menu: 30F (serv. incl.).

13

## Le Villars Palace

**8 rue Descartes**
**326.39.08**
*M. Fargeau*
*Open until midnight. Closed Sat.*
*(at lunch) and Sun. Pay parking*
*at rue Soufflot.*
*AE, DC, V.*

A chic young businessman versed in gastronomy, Bernard Fargeau, latched onto Chef Michel Taillois, who had worked for nine years at the Bistrot 121. The result of this alliance is a surprising modern decor of unfathomable sea green, a bit cold but attractive, stylish place settings from Villars Palace in Villars-sur-Olon (hence the restaurant's name), and some cleverly inventive dishes: hot oysters with a sabayon of chives; raw fish in a white sauce (marinated with coconut); salmon "cooked on one side only," brochette of scallops and prawns with beurre blanc; John Dory with foie gras and truffles; and all sorts of other seafood. A few errors of execution: a ruined beurre blanc; some careless seasoning. But otherwise it is very well done and amounts to a "happening" here on this hill of Sainte-Geneviève, where until now one has found only kebabs and pomme frites stands. Pretty expensive too, unless one sticks with the excellent all-inclusive menu.
Carte: 180F–200F. Menu: 120F (wine and serv. incl.).

# 6ème Arr.

15

## Allard

**41 rue Saint-André-dés-Arts**
**326.48.23**
*M. Allard*

When all is said, this is one of the last and most honest of the great Parisian bistros. Neither Fernande Allard, who is forever busy at her ovens, nor André, who continues to discover in the vineyards the best Burgundies in the world, is ready to throw in the towel. Life flows happily in

*Open until 10:30 P.M. Closed Sat.,
Sun. and during August
DC, V.*

this sanctuary with sawdust-covered floors, where the waiters recite the gospel according to Allard by heart: cassoulet on Monday; veal à la berrichonne on Tuesday; leg of lamb and coq au vin on Wednesday; navarin on Thursday, and beef with carrots on Friday—to which we add our own testimony: a delicious turbot with beurre blanc, incomparable pheasant hen with cabbage, duck with small spring turnips, and a chocolate charlotte so good you would sell your soul to the devil for a slice. Carte: 160F–200F.

14
## Les Arêtes
**165 blvd. du
Montparnasse
326.23.98**
*Mme Loison
Open until 10:45 P.M. Closed Sat.
(at lunch) and Mon. Parking at
145 blvd. du Montparnasse.
AE.*

How could we have so long neglected this fine intimate restaurant, with its varnished wood decor, its smiling hostess, and its wise and clever chef (her son)? Yet it is in this very place that, ten years ago, we chanced upon the incredible sole "rose à l'arête" (pink at the bone) which was one of the vanguards of nouvelle cuisine. Let us do justice to the freshness and quality of the fish and oysters—always superb, summer or winter—and the simplicity of the preparations, which are nonetheless touched with imagination and cooked to perfection: whiting with basil, skate with tarragon (a questionable marriage), a lobster salad with baby vegetables, salmon à la nage, haddock à l'irlandaise, cotriade, and some fine white wines. The a la carte prices are quite stiff, but the "business lunch" at 135F, including wine and service, is intelligent, straightforward, and generous. Carte: 200F. Menus: 135F, 175 F (wine and serv. incl.).

**11/20**
## Athènes
**13 rue Serpente
354.52.76**
*M. Dedeyan-Kyriakides
Open until 11:00 P.M. Closed
Mon., Tues. (at lunch), and the
weekend of August 15.
V.*

Alex perseveres, without the slightest deviation, in the preparation of an honest authentic Hellenic cuisine. This old rugby player puts together very well some lesser-known specialties, such as doner-kebab (lamb cooked on a vertical skewer), gambas à la turkolimano, and a fried langoustes. Discreetly folkloristic decor, appealing atmosphere and a relatively light check. Carte: 100F. Menu: 115F (wine and serv. incl.).

**12/20**
## L'Attrape-Coeur
**9 rue Christine
354.43.42**
*M. Philiponet
Open until 1:00 A.M. Closed Sun.,
15 days in February and 3 wks. in
August. Dinner only.
AE, V.*

Attractive 1930s decor, attractive chic clientele, and a cuisine that little by little is becoming attractive: salmon terrine, gratin of mushrooms with paprika, daube of pork with eggplant. Carte: 130F. Menu: 69F + serv.

**11/20**
## Le Bélier
**13 rue des Beaux-Arts**

This is the restaurant in L'Hôtel, the charming edifice where Oscar Wilde "died beyond his means." Perhaps

**325.27.22**

*M. Duboucheron*
*Dinner only. Open until 1:30 A.M.*
*Closed during August. Pay parking*
*at 22 rue Mazarine.*
*DC.*

yours will allow you to accede its winter garden, transformed into a ravishing piano bar and restaurant. We hope so, because if you are in love, you will spend the most exquisite evening here—lost in the perpetual sigh of the fountain tumbling beneath the flowers, gazing at the palms and listening to the piano player's interpretation of Scott Joplin. Tables are exquisitely laid, the service discreet and attentive, and the limited menu offers a well-prepared, interesting selection: Oscar Wilde salad, crab tournedos with coulis of langoustine, aiguillettes of candied duck with broccoli. (If you pay by check, you'll need some identification: blame Oscar, he destroyed their faith with his rubber checks.)
Carte: 180F.

## 11/20

**Le Bilboquet**

**13 rue Saint-Benoit**
**548.81.84**

*M. Chavière*
*Open until 1:00 A.M. Closed Sun.*
*Pay parking on blvd.*
*Saint-Germain.*

Still slightly tumultuous and a trifle snobbish, with lots of pretty girls to watch from atop the mezzanine while listening to some good jazz and enjoying the new menu of classic grilled selections (rack of lamb, côte de boeuf) offered by the new chef.
Carte: 150F. Menu (lunch only): 70F (serv. incl.).

## 12/20

**Bistro d'Isa**

**3 rue Saint-Benoit**
**260.80.83**

*Mme Canto*
*Open until 1:00 A.M. Closed Sun.*
*AE, DC, V.*

The menu of this charming bistro, decorated in the manner of a winter garden, is making a noticeable return to traditional, good bourgeois cuisine: salade de boeuf with potatoes, veal sauté with carrots, and blanquette de volaille. The reason given by Isabelle Canto (no, she's not a character out of Alphonse Allais) is most commendable: this simpler cuisine allows her to use less costly products which are easier to work with, so she can lower her prices—a major concern for most restaurant owners during this inflationary time. That's all well and good, but the oeufs à la Mornay, the trout in Port wine, and braised ham in Madeira, among others, are as incongruous in this program as the daffodils in Lent.
Carte: about 130F.

## 12/20

**Brasserie Lutétia**

**23 rue de Sèvres**
**544.38.10**

*M. Astier*
*Open until 1:00 A.M.*
*AE, DC, V.*

The hearty round bread from chez Poilâne pitches in like a good neighbor to serve as the bed for the house rillettes of sardine, which, among several other amusing specialties (culotte of rabbit in honey and pea soup with bacon) have made this large, fairly new establishment deserving of a spot on our list of favorite brasseries. The massive bar which is the focal point of the brasserie is the work of the prolific designer, Slavik, and it is one of the most successful pieces of restaurant decor anywhere. Sauerkraut is a worthy dish here, the tête de veau is not a vain sacrifice to brasserie cooking, and the Sonia Rykiel tablesettings are very pretty.
Carte: 120F. Menus: 39F, 64F (serv. incl.).

16

## Jacques Cagna
**14 rue des Grands-Augustins**
**326.49.39**
*M. Cagna*
*Open until 10:30 P.M. Closed Sat.,*
*Sun. (except for 1 Sat. per month ),*
*holidays, 10 days at Christmas and*
*during August Pay parking at 27*
*rue Mazarine.*
*AE, DC, V.*

This young chef took over a difficult spot seven years ago, and he has been working at it like mad ever since. You can dine "à la Cagna" at home, either by ordering his dishes or by having one of his chefs come to take care of everything. But it's simpler to go and eat in the elegant setting of this rejuvenated old inn: oysters cassolette with Brittany lobster; excellent asparagus feuilleté; bass steamed with seaweed and tomato fondue with basil; steamed lotte with mushrooms; mallard with zests of lemon and orange; braised veal sweetbreads with oysters and truffles; and some delicious desserts—in all, a very tempting arrary in which invention is never lacking and flavor never faked. Much steam cooking, many light sauces using cooking juices, vegetables prepared at the last minute; in short, the modern cuisine that we like and reward this year with an additional point. The cuisine has recently been complemented by the superb addition to the cellar of 45,000 bottles of 380 different wines. Always full in the evenings, but Jacques Cagna cannot understand why his clients forget that he serves lunch too. We can't either. There is parking (in the Ile de la Cité) only five minutes walk away, so leaving your car somewhere is not an insurmountable problem.
Carte: 300F. Menu (dégustation): 230F + 15% serv.

**11/20**
## Calvet
**165 blvd. Saint-Germain**
**222.85.03**
*M. Cramois*
*Open until 12:30 A.M. Parking on*
*blvd. Saint-Germain.*
*AE, DC, V.*

Calvet's new formula (more in the bistro style) still retains the curious Hungarian decor it inherited from an earlier experiment. Between the red velvet seats, private nooks, split levels, and prepossessing service, you can't help but feel out of place here. Perhaps that's why the local publishers complain that they miss the old haunt. But they would be wrong to abandon this Calvet, which serves up an agreeable assortment of dishes, including a good fish terrine and an irreproachable seafood sauerkraut. Some more expensive dishes top off this panoply of seafood delights: fillet of lotte on a bed of spinach, sautéed écrevisses with herbs, bouillabaisse, and the seafood platter. A la carte, you can easily spend 200F. A nice Muscadet and a rather expensive minor Gewurztraminer. Menus: 47F, 58F + 15% serv.

13

## La Cannelle
**53 quai des Grands-Augustins**
**325.00.53**
*Mme Oliver*
*Open until midnight. Dinner only.*

When you have two or three generations of cooks behind you and a brother who teaches you to tend the stove, it is difficult to resist the temptation to try for yourself. Stéphane Oliver, daughter of Raymond and sister of Michel, has just taken over this quay-side bistro which had been lost in tranquil anonymity. If the decor is still the same—a perfectly agreeable monochrome beige and brown, the tables squeezed in a bit here and there—the cuisine has undergone a radical change with the advent of a Japanese chef, a graduate of Gérard Besson and Jacques Cagna. This cook is not without talent. You will discover an intelligent marriage of precise tastes in his remarkable

pâté of chicken livers with a purée of peppers; his gratin of oysters and lotte; his roast fillet of lamb with vanilla; and thin wild rice crêpes, an audacious combination that succeeds.
Carte: 160F.

**11/20**

### Au Charbon de Bois
**16 rue du Dragon**
**548.57.04**
*Mme Chalvet*
*Open until 10:30 P.M. Closed Sun.*
*and during August. Pay parking*
*(4F per hour) at 156 blvd.*
*St-Germain.*
*DC, V.*

Nothing about the atmosphere has changed since the recent arrival of the new owners: the ground floor, with its view of the kitchen, is still tumultuous, while the loggia is often a bit more calm. The once-excellent fries are a little less so now, and we did well by straying no further than the fried éperlans and the simple grilled meat dishes (steak, leg of lamb with tarragon). With a rather commonplace charlotte of apples and a good Duboeuf Beaujolais, our bill was rather out of line with the modest pleasure we derived here.
Carte: 130F–150F. Menu: 60F + 15% serv.

**12/20**

### Aux Charpen-tiers
**10 rue Mabillon**
**326.30.05**
*M. Bardèche*
*Open until midnight. Closed Sun.*
*Open terrace. Pay parking at rue*
*Lobineau.*

This site was once the home of the Compagnons Charpentiers du Devoir et Liberté, an eighteenth-century carpenters guild. It is now presided over by its owner Pierre Bardèche, who divides his time between kitchen and dining room. His dishes are prepared in copper cookware, his sauces without flour or starch; he prefers using crème fleurette to butter. There's good news every day: Monday, sautéed veal; Tuesday, beef stew with carrots; Wednesday, streaky bacon with lentils . . . Friday, ailloli with vegetables. And every day an exquisite andouillette and a sturdy estouffade of beef with basil. This is work worthy of a good journeyman. For the price this is one of the best little bistros in Paris.
Carte: 90F. Menu: 17.30F (serv. incl.).

**13**

### Le Chat Grippé
**87 rue d'Assas**
**354.70.00**
*M. Guilhaudin*
*Open until 10:30 P.M. Closed Sat.*
*and Sun.*
*V.*

A onetime chef in a private home has taken over this former butcher shop. His switch to public "restauration" has been easily accomplished: Bernard Guilhaudin was trained at Chapel's and at the Vivarois. For the moment, his aims are limited—so much the better—and his menu is short, intelligent and well planned; one senses a chef who does not lack talent, as shown, by his excellent warm salad with breast of chicken and preserved liver and gizzards, his haddock poached with chive butter; his fillets of sea trout with basil; his feuilleté of lamb sweetbreads; and his admirable chocolate cake. The wine list is still scanty.
Carte: 120F. Menu (at lunch only): 43F + 15% serv.

**12/20**

### Le Cherche-Midi
**22 rue du Cherche-Midi**
**548.27.44**

Donatello Di Méo, a "still practicing" art dealer, is doing a landslide business with the young executives who crowd his long, rather banal dining room in search of Italian-style food. The selection is limited but well-chosen and nicely varied. Prices are relatively low and the appetizing cuisine

*M. Di Méo*
*Open until 12:30 A.M.*

is still dominated by an excellent soup of the day, rather unextraordinary pasta (we are told that it's made on the premises, and we believe it), and a remarkable kidney with gorgonzola, among other cheese dishes. Uninteresting Chiantis. Success has brought out a tendency toward condescension in both management and personnel.
Carte: 120F.

**11/20**

## La Chope d'Alsace
**4 carrefour de l'Odéon**
**326.67.76**
*M. Dorin*
*Open until 2:00 A.M.*
*V.*

In geography as in choucroute, the Rhine has its highs and lows. . . . but here, you'll hardly notice. The kind reception and service are quite the opposite of what you might expect (and dread) in this sort of combination German weinstübe-French dance hall. The decor consists of a forest of beams and a relentless pictoral evocation of Alsacian folklore. Six different kinds of choucroute are served by the ton to hundreds of customers every day. If you don't like choucroute, you might select a good onion tarte, a baeckeoffe or the rindfleischuppe (old Alsacian pot-au-feu). Decent Alsacian wines served in glass pitchers.
Carte: 80F. Menus: 37.50F (wine and serv. incl.), 58F + 15% serv.

**10/20**

## La Closerie des Lilas
**171 blvd. du Montparnasse**
**326.70.50**
*Mme Milan*
*Open until 1:30 A.M. Open terrace.*
*Pay parking at 120-141 blvd. du Montparnasse.*
*AE, DC, V.*

What would remain of this brasserie without its charming aura of literary associations (Gide, Trotsky, Verlaine, Hemingway); without its bar, which is still one of the most Parisian in Paris; without a shadowy pianist; without the pretty young ladies in the evening; or without the occasional movie star or writer? On the restaurant side, nothing but an inconsistent cuisine that is both pretentious and frightfully expensive; an attractive terrace with its greenery and the statue of Marshall Ney just outside. On its boulevard side, some sound plats du jour (andouillette, haddock, steak tartare) served until very late in the evening. But all with such languor, such indolence and such lack of charm that even the staunchest habitués admit they are fatigued. And so are we.
Carte: 230F–250F.

**12/20**

## Dominique
**19 rue Bréa**
**327.08.80**
*M. Aronson*
*Open until 10:00 P.M. Closed during July. Pay parking at 122 blvd. du Montparnasse.*
*All major credit cards.*

The nicest things about this old Dodo (52 years) is still, for us, the small annex with a small boutique where Paris's best smoked salmon and caviar can be bought, and its long bar with its stools always crowded, where one eats cheese tartes on the run, blinis with sour cream or pressed caviar, zakouski, smoked salmon of course, and in winter an unctuous burning hot borscht. Dodo's unhappiest feature is the red dining room of worn silk where the clientele tries valiantly to relive old Petersburg soirées while dining upon a mockery of côtelette Pojarski.
Carte: about 100F at the bar. Menu: 105F (serv. incl.).

### 10/20
## Le Dragon
**14 rue du Dragon**
**548.75.58**
*M. Dumouchel*
*Open until 10:00 P.M. Closed Sat.,*
*Sun. and August 15 to*
*September*
*15.*

Drunk with wine, the quails au porto lay languid on the soggy canapé set down for them by Jacques Dumochel. . . . This former waiter (no less proud for his humble beginnings) places his quails on the menu alongside other, more alluring dishes: cassoulets, navarins, and confits which give no cause for complaint. It is obvious that the chef knows his part well, because he has been playing it faultlessly for the past 20 years. A pleasant cafe-style decor probably from the period, just like the amiable clientele.
Carte: about 80F. Menus: 28F (wine and serv. incl.), 35F (serv. incl.).

### 11/20

## Drugstore Saint-Germain
**149 blvd.**
**Saint-Germain**
**222.92.50**
*M. Boutersky*
*Open until 1:30 A.M. Open terrace.*
*Pay parking.*
*AE, DC, V.*

If you can get your nose out of the mixed salad and the ice creams stacked with crème Chantilly long enough to try a plat du jour, you will realize that the Drugstore is far from the worst eatery in Saint-Germain-des Prés. Excellent sandwiches, good country wines (in carafe, as in all the Publicis Drugstores) and Slavik's decor that's a total mess.
Carte: 100F–120F.

### 13 🍲
## L'Échaudé Saint-Germain
**21 rue de l'Échaudé**
**354.79.02**
*MM. Layrac*
*Open until 1:00 A.M.*
*All major credit cards.*

With its lace, little mirrors and plump banquettes, L'Échaudé is heaven-sent for that intimate little dinner. You may spend more time gazing into your companion's eyes than at your plate, but the chef has not taken advantage of this to serve just anything. The Layrac brothers (who also own the Muniche and Le Petit Zinc) keep their eyes on everything, and Jean-Paul Chossat is a serious cook. One might reproach him for lack of innovation, but this is perhaps unfair, for his boudin of rascasse with purée of prawns, his feuilleté of snails, and the duck with raspberries are all excellent. Good and even very good small and medium wines.
Carte: 160F. Menu: (at lunch only): 100F (wine and serv. incl.).

### 13 🍲
## L'Epicurien
**11 rue de Nesles**
**329.55.78**
*M. Díaz*
*Open until 11:00 P.M. Closed Mon.*
*(at lunch) and Sun. Pay parking*
*at rue Mazarine.*
*All major credit cards.*

This narrow old lane is not exactly the busiest in Paris, so this very elegant little restaurant hidden away on it is not filled each evening by casual strollers; rather by those who come to find a refined calm in one of the three little white dining rooms that open onto a tiny verdant patio and to dine by candle light on a highly civilized cuisine. Jean Diaz, a former Sorbonne student of Spanish descent, is a charming, warm man who seems to know everyone but does not for a moment forget to be a real chef. Last year we led him to hope for a first toque, and this we now award him without hesitation for his crab feuilleté, for his haddock with cream, for his delicious bitter chocolate charlotte, which really is made by his mother; and for all those robust dishes of the southwest: cassoulet; sautéed mutton with haricot beans; fricassée of chicken with cèpes; preserved duck with potatoes sarladaise; and thin slices of smoked magret, as tender as a baby's cheek. Carte: 140F–160F.

---

**12/20**

## La Fourchette en Habit

**75 rue du Cherche-Midi**
**548.82.74**

*M. Dufeu*
*Open until 11:00 P.M. (until 1:00 A.M. Fri. and Sat.). Closed Sat. (at lunch), Mon. and during August.*
*AE, V.*

It was in this minuscule and uncomfortable bistro that, during the '60s, papa Chataignier introduced Parisian society to the pleasures of the then very fashionable beurre blanc Nantais. Under new owner and chef, Jean-Marc Dufeu, the avant-guerre decor has become almost elegant (after a frivolous interlude with the fisherman's net). The butter is still white in some cases (loup, turbot, scallops), black in others, (skate), melted in still others (haddock, sole, etc.), and sometimes—but not often enough—pleasantly absent (grilled rougets and sardines, overcooked turbot with kelp). The menu of this pleasant restaurant is devoted almost entirely to seafood, and for a reasonable price, you can enjoy beautiful fresh oysters and shellfish with a bottle of Gros-Plant or the house Quincy. The desserts are largely uninteresting.
Carte: 150F. Menu: 80F (wine incl.) + 15% serv.

---

**12/20**

## La Foux

**2 rue Clément**
**325.77.66**

*M. Guini*
*Open until 11:00 P.M. Closed Sun.*
*AE, DC.*

Though it's no longer young, the setting is resolutely contemporary, comfortable, bright and a treat for your eyes. The jovial Alexandre Guini isn't young any longer, either, but he has lost none of his enthusiasm . . . or his girth. The Lyon-style cuisine remains his cup of tea (tripe, tablier de sapeur, hot sausage), but here and there he allows a seductive ray of Mediterranean sunshine to shine upon his menu (cannelloni, soupe au pistou). Moreover, not one of his clients (whether senator, journalist, or publisher) is unaware that Wednesday is the day that Alex has set aside to serve his remarkable pot-au-feu.
Carte: 130F–150F. Menu (except Sat. and holidays): 55F, 87F (serv. incl.).

---

**12/20**

## Chez Gramond

**5 rue de Fleurus**
**222.28.89**

*M. Gramond*
*Open until 9:45 P.M. Closed Sun. and July 14 to August 20.*
*AE, DC, V.*

Only about ten tables in a narrow, very meticulous pink room. Mme Gramond is adept at those discreet acts of courtesy and esteem to which her customers and neighbors from the Senate and the Académie Française are not insensitive. She seats them comfortably on tufted benches and helps make their selections from the small menu of delicious, traditional dishes so carefully prepared by her husband Jean-Claude: salad of aiguillettes of duck, terrine of trout sauce Ricard, pan-cooked partridge with fresh noodles, salmon with chives, and good family desserts. The only shortcoming of this remarkably executed cuisine is the price, dealt a fatal blow by the Bordeaux and Bourgogne wines from the cellar.
Carte: over 200F.

**12/20**
### La Grosse Horloge
**22 rue Saint-Benoît**
**222.22.63**
*M. Masurier*
*Open until 11:30 P.M.*
*AE, DE, V.*

The big hand of this clock is set on fish and seafood, and the new owner, Pierre Masurier, is in his element—he is a professional fish specialist. The only problem is that he has no notion of how to prepare the superb fish he purchases at Les Halles in any way other than with beurre blanc, mayonnaise, sauce meunière or sauce Américaine. This accounts for the uninspiring nature of the short menu, and the paradoxical relative interest of the meat dishes (a fair magret of duck, good grilled meats). The decor has been renovated to create more atmosphere: old floor, old beams, pretty lighting. With just a little adjustment, this clock will be fine.
Carte: 160F. Menu: 58F + 15% serv.

**12/20**
### Guy
**6 rue Mabillon**
**354.87.61**
*M. Leroux*
*Open until 1:00 A.M. Closed for lunch (except Sat.), Sun. and during August.*

Be it chez Guy (where it is carefully prepared and quite genuine) or chez anyone else, Brazilian cuisine simply does not inspire delicate emotions or great enthusiasm. This being said, the shrimp with pepper, feijoada, churrascos, civet of chicken, and empajadas de camarao served here are generous, well-prepared, and spicy from every point of view. You'll enjoy a batida de limao (Brazilian punch) before dinner, and, just like the regulars, beer or mineral water with your meal. The pretty clientele is made up largely of members of the Brazilian colony in Paris (fully gathered on Saturdays for lunch) and the show-biz community. They flock here to enjoy the charming music of a young Brazilian quartet in the delightful tri-level decor. In short, a fun place, full of charm, exquisite music, pretty girls and gaiety.
Carte: 150F.

**12/20**
### La Hulotte
**29 rue Dauphine**
**633.75.92**
*M. Güys*
*Open until 10:30 P.M. Closed Sun., Mon. and during August. Pay parking at 29 rue Mazarine.*
*AE, DC, V.*

But yes, of course you're right, dear, patient Bernard Güys—what attention and love you've brought to the long and careful preparation of your traditional plats du jour since 1968: sautéed lamb with parsley, aiguillette of beef with carrots, York ham with spinach, tourte of duck, pot-au-feu of cod. . . . Don't be upset with us because we say the same thing year after year with our poor words. And thank you for making us love this type of cuisine . . . for making it lighter by steam cooking the vegetables and using egg yolks and vegetables for thickening. And bravo for the little Bourgueil at 30F a bottle.
Carte: 80F. Menu: 60F + 15% serv.

14
### Joséphine (Chez Dumonet)
**117 rue du Cherche-Midi**

We've tended somewhat to overlook the good old bistros in recent years. Without reneging on our passion for the new cuisine, let's admit that a little calf's trotters with vinaigrette or a navarin printanier can sometimes be worthy of just as much praise as raw langoustine antennae steamed with kiwis. A green light, then, for this old (1898)

**548.52.40**

*M. Dumonet*
*Open until 11:00 P.M. Closed Sat.,*
*Sun. and during July. Open*
*terrace.*
*V.*

house run by this veteran sea wolf (Dumonet has sailed in the trans-Atlantic race), with his omelet with truffles, his leeks vinaigrette, his simmered andouillette, his rabbit in mustard. (We were so carried away that we almost wrote "for his tournedos Rossini," but let's not get carried away.) Friendly service, clientele of old pals who dabble in the big and little wines, all admirable, served here.
Carte: 170F. Menu: 90F, 120F + 15% serv.

**11/20**
## *Korean*
## *Barbecue*
**1 rue du Dragon**
**222.26.63**
*M. Lee*
*Open until 10:45 P.M. Closed Mon.*

The only cooking here you will do yourself on a gas stove that occupies the center of your table. The emincés of beef (rib, fillet, tongue) from the fixed-price meal is served finely cut and bathed in a light marinade, accompanied by rice or vegetables, you grill to taste, holding the meat with chopsticks, before seasoning it with a dip into a delicate soy sauce. Altogether an unusual and not at all unpleasant experience, for the meat is good, the appetizers are full of surprises (seaweed soup, meat and vegetable crêpes salad of shrimp and cucumber with vinegar). Moreover, the bill will hardly pass 70F. A bare but not chilly setting.
Carte 70F–80F. Menu: 40F, 71F + 15% serv.

**11/20**
## *Au Lac De*
## *Côme*
**129 blvd. du**
**Montparnasse**
**322.52.35**
*M. Franciosa*
*Open until 11:00 P.M. Closed Sun.,*
*Mon. and during August. Pay*
*parking.*

The gruff old cook has been succeeded by a new, much more amiable owner who learned his art in "various restaurants in Picardie" (well-known as a source of the best Italian cooks). And so tradition will be carried on in this slightly cramped, country-style restaurant with its rather ordinary decor: you'll be served agreeable Italian-style cuisine, totally dominated by pasta and good charcuterie imported directly from Venice. Let us mention the mixed pasta plate with spaghetti, tomato sauce and smoked bacon, the fettucini lombard, and fresh noodles in cream and brandy. A few attempts at creativity in the sauces and pretty wines from Piémont.
Carte: 120F.

**13**
## *Lapérouse*
**51 quai des**
**Grands-Augustins**
**326.68.04**
*M. Bicheron*
*Open until 11:00 P.M. Closed Sun.*
*Pay parking at rue Mazarine.*
*AE, DC, V.*

Maxim's and Laurent have had the luck to find silent partners, but most restaurants surviving from the nineteenth century—either because they are sunk in lethargy or because they cannot live eternally outside their own century—are finding life difficult these days. All the more reason then, to admire a man like Lucien Bicheron who started out knowing nothing about restauration and was possessed of very limited resources, but nonetheless successfully resuscitated the delapidated Lapérouse. Devoting night and day to this resurrection, working by trial and error, he has brought back, if not the chic Tout-

Paris, at least French and foreign clients to this restaurant which offers eloquent testimony to a vanished art of living. Obviously, with additional millions one could give incomparable sparkle to this old jewel, but what has already been done is enough of a miracle. The kitchens are clean at last, the ceiling paint no longer flakes off into the dishes, and, little by little, the small private dining rooms where courtesans once scratched their names on the mirrors with their diamonds are finding fresh life—a prudent, bourgeois life, perhaps, but a life nevertheless. And this thanks to the touching enthusiasm and good will of Lucien Bicheron and team—as well as to a completely honest cuisine that is half-modern, half-classic, and deftly prepared by Chef Gérard Gravier, 30, who learned his trade in two excellent houses: the Comte de Gascogne and Julius. His feuilleté of asparagus with chervil, soupe de coques, stewed lobster with fennel, his ragoût of fresh pasta and foie gras, his duck with green pepper and his superb Bresse poularde in a bladder make up, along with some excellent desserts (notably a hot apple tarte and a millefeuille with red fruit), a well-balanced menu whose price has been carefully restrained (you can find appetizers at less than 25F). Add to this a respectable menu and you can understand why this once deserted place is now full.
Carte: 200F–250F. Menu: 11F (service incl.).

## 13
## Lipp
**151 blvd. Saint-Germain**
**548.53.91**
*M. Cazes*
*Open until 12:45 A.M. Closed Mon., Easter, during July and Nov. 1 and Christmas. Pay parking across the blvd.*

In 1920, when Marcelin Cazes bought from the Alsatian Lippmann the "Brasserie from the Banks of the Rhine," his menu was cervelat remoulade, sauerkraut, and Munster cheese. In 1926, he added Baltic herring; a little later beef gros sel (this, still served after 55 years on Saturdays and Sundays, is exemplary). A blanquette of veal on Tuesday? Perfect. Boeuf à la mode on Wednesday? Just like home. Cassoulet on Thursday? Delicious. Calf's head on Friday, and choucroute every day? Not bad at all. Certainly we have no hesitation in reciting this honest and immutable menu—this makes 15 years that we've been doing it and until recently smack against the current—because for a long time it was considered smart, especially by its habituées, to hold all of Lipp's food in contempt. Today they are more apt to be raving about the virtues of the pig's trotters, the fruit tartes and even the french fries. Should we let ourselves be coerced into crowning Roger Cazes with two toques? No, for his head is not swollen enough to accommodate them, and ours is still squarely on our shoulders.
Carte: 140F.

## 10/20
## La Lozère
**4 rue Hautefeuille**

Opened a few years ago on the initiative of the tourist office of the department of Lozère, this friendly establishment is dedicated to the celebration of the robust

**354.26.64**
*Open until 10:00 P.M. Closed Sun., Mon. and during August.*

cuisine of that area. Between the charcutailles and the goat cheese, young chef Charmaillac will offer you an onion omelette, pouteille and herb sausage, just like down on the farm.
Carte: 70F. Menus: 43F (wine and serv. incl.), 49F, 59F + 15% serv.

**11/20**

## Chez Maître Paul

**12 rue Monsieur-le-Prince**
**354.74.59**
*M. Gaugain*
*Open until 10:30 P.M. Closed Sun., Mon. and during August. Pay parking at l'Ecole de Médecine.*
*AE, DC, V.*

Don't be confused—the waitresses are not barebreasted Polynesian beauties in grass skirts. For the simple reason that this Monsieur Gaugain is named Armand, not Paul, and the exoticism of his small, rather confined restaurant is that of the region of Franche-Comté: its wines, its cheeses, its sauces, its sauces. . . . and its sauces. It's been like this for twenty years, without a hint of deviation from the matelote (in a sauce based on Arbois wine), the sweetbreads (in a sauce based on Château-Chalon), the chicken (in yellow-wine sauce), the calf's liver (in a sauce based on Paille wine), the fillet of veal (in a sauce of Jura wine): did we miss any of the sauces? There is one exquisite pastry: the walnut cake, with which you must drink the house Pupillin blanc.
Carte: 130F–150F.

**12/20**

## La Marlotte

**55 rue du Cherche-Midi**
**548.86.79**
*Mme Agaud and M. Bouvier*
*Open until 10:30 P.M., Fri. until 11:00 P.M. No dogs.*
*DC.*

The cuisine of the Marlotte is old-fashioned, with here and there a touch of modernism. The menu you read by candle light is a list of simple joys offered by this agreeable house. It will lead you from beef stew au gros sel through sautéed veal, rabbit paysanne, potée auvergnate, to the navarin of lamb. All this is well and good gently punctuated by the smiling advice of M. Bouvier as he helps you choose. And it is not too ruinous with a friendly Bourgeuil.
Carte: 120F.

**11/20**

## Les Mas- careignes

**8 rue du Dragon**
**544.12.53**
*M. Hoareau*
*Open until 11:00 P.M. Closed Mon.*
*AE.*

A few big pictures of palm trees lend a rather suffering air of exoticism to the stone interior of this bistro where, for ages, M. Hoareau has served his specialties from the isles of Madagascar and Réunion. Some of these are not deprived of interest or spice. For example, the Achards, samboss, rougail with eighteen spices, and whiting with lime.
Carte: about 120F. Menu: 40F + 15% serv.

**11/20**

## Le Montagnard

**24 rue des Canettes**

We love to come here when it's cold and gray, sit beneath the beamed ceiling and breathe in the warm smell of the fondue, shared in the noisy après-ski atmosphere. The excellent cuts of Charolais beef help make this some of

**326.47.15**
*Mme Bruneau*
*Open until 11:30 P.M. Closed*
*Monday and from December 23*
*until January 5. Pay parking at the*
*Place St.-Sulpice.*
*AE, DC.*

the best fondue bourguignonne in the city, and the house
tarte is honesty incarnate.
Carte: 100F.

**12/20**
## Le Muniche
**27 rue de Buci**
**633.62.09**
*MM. Layrac*
*Open until 3:00 A.M. Open terrace.*
*All major credit cards.*

The cuisine is identical here to that next door at le Petit
Zinc, which is to say, it's good, except that at the Muniche
four different choucroute are served. We regret that the
three Layrac brothers take advantage of the fact that their
two restaurants are contiguous to impose on the guests of
both restaurants a uniform cuisine prepared by the same
chefs in a common kitchen, Give thanks at least for a very
successful decor by Slavik that helps to create the liveliest,
gayest, and most agreeably overcrowded atmosphere of
the Saint-Germain brasseries.
Carte: 120F.

13
## Le Palanquin
**12 rue Princesse**
**329.77.66**
*Mme Tran Kim Quang*
*Open until 10:30 P.M., Closed Sun.*
*and last 3 wks. of August. Pay*
*parking at place Saint-Sulpice.*

The Tran sisters—the ravishing Kim Quang at the
reception and her twin Vân Ngô in the kitchen—
admirably resist the temptation to copy the greasy spoons
that are the plague of this quarter. In a decor lighter than
the usual polyurethane-pagoda, they prepare a Far Eastern
cuisine in which the flavors are well-defined and owe
nothing to monosodium glutamate, the taste-numbing
additive that is the basis for most Chinese restaurants in
Paris. You feel immediately that sensation of lightness,
without tingling or burning, in their stuffed seasoned
mushrooms with shrimp, in their magret of duck with
sesame seed (exquisite, but must be ordered in advance),
or in their pork spareribs seasoned with citronella. There
is always a pleasant little luncheon menu.
Carte: 90F–100F. Menus: 42F (at lunch), 70F (serv. incl.).

13
## Pascal
**12 rue de l'Eperon**
**634.13.34**
*M. Lebleu*
*Open until 12:00 A.M. Closed Sun.*
*and Mon. (lunch). Pay park rue de*
*l'Ecole de Médecine.*
*AE, DC, V.*

This Pascal has also made a bet, and definitely won it! In
this very old establishment (formerly the Relais de
Porquerolles and the Ménaudière), he has created an
elaborate little tri-color candy box, and the fire which
nearly turned his hopes to ashes is nothing but a bad
memory. With his young chef, Michel Bourdet (previously
with some top restaurants: Le Lion d'Or in Liffré, La
Coquille, Louis Landès), Pascal Lebleu has developed a
menu which is a bit too long, but definitely interesting
despite its penchant for sauces. Such a menu, along with
the charming decor and the delightful district, should
bring him quick and pretty success. Also because, in
addition to a few clever dishes, such as the pigonneau in
pink grapefruit and the sole with soufflé of smoked
salmon, he offers some very handsome and solid classics
for lunch: blanquette, navarin, and bourguigon, and so on,
all for the single price of 42F, including service.
Carte: 180F.

## 10/20
### Le Petit Saint-Benoît
**4 rue Saint-Benoît**
**260.23.91**
*M. Gervais*
*Open until 10:00 P.M. Closed Sat.,*
*Sun. and July 14 to August 15. No*
*dogs.*

Even if it were not located on the most hokey street of Saint-Germain-des-Prés, this old coach-house bistro would deserve mention for its prices, its rabbit chasseur, its veal blanquette, and the roast veal with mashed potatoes, served for the last 125 years to the impecunious intellectuals of the quarter. There are several terrace tables which, in summer, are the most hotly fought over in Paris. Carte: about 40F–50F.

## 12/20
### Le Petit Zinc
**25 rue de Buci**
**354.79.34**
*MM. Layrac*
*Open until 3:00 A.M. Open terrace.*
*All major credit cards.*

A dozen years ago this was one of the first bistros to convert to fin-de-siècle decor. It is also one of the only ones in the intervening years to have maintained the openness and honesty of its kitchen. The clientele of Saint-Germain-des-Prés are not deceived, whether at the squeezed together tables downstairs, those upstairs or those out on the sidewalk (this street is now converted into a pedestrian's paradise), and the Petit Zinc is mobbed every night until two in the morning (oysters year-round, sauerkraut with fish, homemade preserved duck, chicken au pot, and always an agreeable little red Haut-Poitou). Carte: 150F. Menu 100F (wine and serv. incl.).

## 13
### La Photo-galerie
**2 rue Christine**
**329.01.76**
*M. Bardawil*
*Open until 11:00 P.M. Closed Sat.*
*(evening) and Sun.*
*Card: V.*

Georges Bardawil, editor of a photography magazine, is a remarkable young man who has transformed his bookstore-gallery into a very chic restaurant-tea room without forgetting his first love: pretty women—press attachés, fashion models—who at the stroke of three come in to nibble his tarte with vegetables and hot York ham with spinach. In the evenings a real meal, both delicate and simple, is proposed: hot terrine of fish with sorrel; effilochade of skate with tomato purée (although the lettuce sometimes is drowning in olive oil); turbot with cèleri-rave; exquisite homemade pastries and fresh quincy, all of which assures a clientele mainly of the "intellocrates" of the quarter, who bring their families to dine in good spirits for 100 F (without wine). Menu (dinner only): 95F (serv. incl.).

## 11/20
### Polidor
**41 rue Monsieur-le-Prince**
**326.95.34**
*Mme Ker Vella*
*Open until 10:00 P.M. Closed Sun.*
*and during August.*

The place is subtitled "Home Cooking" and who would deny it? Streaky bacon with lentils, blanquette of veal, beef bourguignon, tendron of veal with green peas, rabbit with mustard, rice gateau . . . we could go on and on. Mme Ker Vella, a former law student, is the present owner of this legendary old house whose guest book mentions Joyce, Paul Valéry, and Hemingway, and, more modestly, today, Fallet, Sabatier, Wolinski. It is the vocation of this restaurant to competently and quickly feed a clientele temporarily embarrassed, chronically impecunious, or philosophically hostile to spending much money for food. Carte: 40F–60F.

## La Porte Fausse

12/20

**72 rue du Cherche-Midi**
**220.20.17**

*Mme Louis*
*Open until 11:30 P.M. Closed Sun.,*
*Mon., one week during Easter and*
*August.*

A good, new restaurant devoted to the traditional cuisine of the county of Nice. The large, comfortable dining room is decorated in rustic style, the feminine reception has a natural charm, and the prices are gentle for the salad of mesclun, delicious tian de courgettes, well-seasoned ratatouille, slightly oily sausages à la polenta, and, on Fridays, the good aïlloli. A few nice wines in pitchers and desserts which, unfortunately, are terribly weak.
Carte: 80F–100F.

15

## Princesse (Castel)

**15 rue Princesse**
**326.90.22**

*M. Castel*
*"La Véranda" is open for lunch only, dining room on the second floor. Closed Sun. and during August.*
*AE.*

The news of the year on the rue Princesse is that Castel no longer sleeps chez Castel. He has moved his wife, his bed and his toothbrush to another part of Paris, and, under the glass roof of the winter garden of his ravishing suite on the top floor of his building, opened an ultra-refined restaurant where the lunches might even outdo those at Maxim's. There are 40 place settings, reserved for some of the 2000 happy few who can be proud that they own the card to the club St.-Germain (and that they've paid their dues). The chef is Bernard Chirent, a very talented young man who learned his art at the Troisgros. While he works in the kitchen, Jean and Yolande Castel take care of the day people by arranging small salons for them where they can play cards or billiards, watch video films, and even take a sauna. The night owls will continue to dine in the Belle Époque dining room, where the mussel soup with flower of thyme, salmon with sorrel, calf's kidney with three mustards, the great wines from Nicolas, the high style of Michel, the manager, the chitchat in the booths, the superficial smiles, the civilized back-biting, and, on every face, that special look which comes from belonging to a golden world, make Castel the most civilized domain in Paris.
Carte: 250F–300F.

## Le Procope

10/20

**13 rue de l'Ancienne-Comédie**
**326.99.20**

*M. Deroussent*
*Open until 1:30 A.M. Closed during July.*
*AE.*

Founded in 1686, this is the world's oldest operating cafe, and there's always a crowd at the old bistro. It is full of evocative mementos, and recent renovation has resulted in an exquisite decor of red walls bathed in the soft glow of crystal chandeliers. Always a crowd, but not crowded, for the tables are comfortable and the service is not frantic. Guinea fowl with cabbage, civet of duck with pasta, and shoulder with lentils will keep you gentle (but not sparkling) company while you reflect upon Voltaire, Diderot, Rousseau, Bonaparte, Robespierre, George Sand and other celebrated clients who have preceded you on these same banquettes.
Carte: 90F. Menu: 53F + 15% serv.

10/20
## Pub Saint-Germain-des-Prés
**17 rue de l'Ancienne-Comédie**
**329.38.70**
*M. Cassagnes*
*Open day and evening.*
*AE, DC, V.*

M. Cassagnes—founder, active member and award winner of France's arch-fraternity of beer specialists—claims to have the largest selection of beers in Europe (sixteen kinds on draft and 300 in bottles). We can also attest to the fact that he owns a rather friendly, extremely lively pub, capable of holding 600 people in all of its nooks and crannies, and simultaneously feeding them with basic, honest specialties of the day and other, more unusual specials made with beer: mussels grande cervoise, escalope of veal Gambrinus.
Carte: 120F. Menus: 32F, 50F (wine and serv. incl.).

13
## Relais Louis XIII
**1 rue du Pont-de-Lodi**
**326.75.96**
*M. Poindessault*
*Open until 10:15 P.M. Closed Sun. and during August. Pay parking at 27 rue Mazarine.*
*All major credit cards.*

All is beautiful and harmonious, and the profusion of attractive old paintings hanging beneath the original Louis XIII beams give this old restaurant in this very old neighborhood an inimitable charm. A modern kitchen is at the service of the generally remarkable chefs, who produce meals of quality, freshness and spontaneity: salad of spinach with shrimp and crayfish; fillet of John Dory with preserved leeks; wing of duckling with green cabbage stuffed with foie gras. The prices are formidable.
Carte: 220F–250F.

10/20
## Restaurant des Saints-Pères
**175 blvd. Saint-Germain**
**548.56.85**
*M. Audin*
*Open until 10:00 P.M. Closed Wed. eve., Thurs., and August 15– September 15. Pay parking across the street at 169 blvd. St.-Germain.*

The decor is one hundred years old, the owners have been there for at least fifty, and the chef, Linot, just retired after a quarter of a century with the restaurant. Eternity stands both behind and before the cuisine, as the current chef still holds fast to the coq au vin, petit salé, sauté of beef, and some 120 other dishes which comprise the great inventory of old style cuisine (correctly prepared, but nothing more).
Carte: 100F.

10/20
## La Rose des Prés
**54 rue de Seine**
**325.25.54**
*M. Thai Ton Truong*
*Open until 10:30 P.M. Closed Sun. and in August.*
*AE, DC, V.*

This is one of the oldest Vietnamese restaurants in the district. It has survived through periods of modest highs and some lows (nothing catastrophic). For the time being, the crab claws with shrimp paste, Vietnamese shrimp with pepper, and tamarind soup contribute to what are honest meals, served in a sober, restful decor. Prices are still quite reasonable.
Menu: 36F and 46F, serv. incl.

**12/20**

### La Rôtisserie (Chez Dumonet)

**117 rue du Cherche-Midi**
**222.81.19**
*M. Dumonet*
*Open until 10:30 P.M. Closed Mon.,*
*Tues. and during August.*
*V.*

The friendly annex of Joséphine, where the grills and skewered meats (superb lamb) and country-style appetizers, have that quality and simplicity that Jean Dumonet gives to everything he touches. The menu is a real pleasure, as are the little wines.
Carte: about 125F. Menu: 90F (wine and serv. incl.).

**10/20**

### Claude Sainlouis

**27 rue du Dragon**
**548.29.68**
*M. Piau*
*Open until 11:00 P.M. Closed Sun.,*
*in August, 15 days during*
*Christmas and Easter.*

We are without a doubt the oldest hagiographers of Sainlouis (alias Claude Piau) and his carte-menu, carved indelibly in stone for the past 25 years: special salad with nuts, faux fillets or lamb chops, wine, chocolate mousse, service not included. Nothing else to say again this year— only that we're a year older, just like Claude Piau and his sturdy, unchanging chow.
Carte: 70F.

**11/20**

### Saint-Germain-de-la-Mer

**2 rue du Sabot**
**222.84.90**
*Open until 10:00 P.M. Closed 2*
*days at Christmas.*
*AE, DC, V.*

Oysters straight from the boat contribute to some very nice seafood platters (crab, mussels, shrimp, clams, Bélon oysters), and the fish that you will be served here in a maritime atmosphere is equally fresh and is served with admirable simplicity: moules marinière, grilled sardines, skate with leeks. Several bourgeois-style plates, such as beef bourguignon, and good little wines at prices that are as reasonable as the food.
Carte: about 130F. Menu: 40F (at lunch only), 58F (wine and serv. incl.).

**12/20**

### Le Sybarite

**6 rue du Sabot**
**222.21.56**
*M. Salas*
*Open until 11:00 P.M. Closed Sun.*
*and August. Pay parking on the pl.*
*St.-Sulpice.*
*DC, V.*

After one overly-ambitious false start, the chef and owner (both from Lot-et-Garonne in the Southwest of France) are returning to the pleasures of a simple, robust, straightforward cuisine, made almost entirely with products from the family farm: bean soup with rouzoles (small sausages), salad with duck skins, fricassée of poultry liver with cèpes, an exquisite tarte feuilleté. Not everything is perfect yet, but they're traveling in the right direction. This is a reasonable, pleasant discovery in this district, where good food is so hard to find. Always a warm, smiling welcome; the decor is beamed ceilings and white stones.
Menus: 49F, 95F (wine and serv. incl.).

**13**

### Chez Tante Madée

**11 rue Dupin**

Mme Trama, who for a long time was one of the best cooks in Paris, has retired from the kitchen and for the past two years has left the stove to her offspring Alain, who

**222.64.56**

*M. Trama*
*Open until 10:00 P.M. Closed Sun.*

is following well in Tante Madée's footsteps. But she still greets her clients in this warm, intimate little restaurant, guides them in their ordering, and supervises the provisioning of the kitchen. Without a doubt, though, Alain Trama is responsible for all the rest, which is to say the hot clams with tomato and basil; Scottish salmon steamed, to perfection, with mint; a delicate veal mignon with vegetables and shellfish; and the imponderable strawberry feuilleté. An ingenious, balanced, assured cuisine. Tante Madée's teaching was not in vain.
Carte: 180F. Menu: 90F (serv. incl.).

### 13 ⌂
## *Yakijapo Mitsuko*
**8 rue du Sabot**
**222.17.74**

*M. Nakano*
*Open until 11:00 P.M.*
*AE, V.*

This wise little Japanese restaurant, one of the oldest in Paris, seems to have waited for the very moment we were compiling this guide to add Yakijapo to its name, break up its decor and announce a new, more specifically Japanese formula (charcoal barbecue). However, the chef will stay and the menu will retain its raw fish (sashimi) specialties at reasonable prices. All reasons to continue to trust this restaurant, just as in the past.
Menu: 40F (serv. incl.).

# *7ème Arr.*

**12/20**
## *Annexe du Quai*
**3 rue Surcouf**
**551.48.48**

*M. Bigeard*
*Open until midnight. Closed Sat. and Sun. Open terrace.*
*AE, EC, V.*

Here's a bit of luck for our television colleagues who've been competing for tables in the local restaurants around the Maison de la Radio. Etienne Bigeard last year opened a charming bistro just a few yards from the quay and is already enjoying success with its long bar, at which meals can be served, and some twenty tables. Its walls are covered with etchings and caricatures from the nineteenth century and, although the cuisine is strictly French, one is reminded of an English club. There is an all-inclusive menu offering a choice from among seven or eight traditional specialties (miroton of beef brawn, papillote of plaice with herbs, pieds et paquets à l'ancienne, four desserts, among which is a very good crème brûlée with pears, all of this accompanied by a good appellation red or white wine.
Carte: 120F. Menu: 75F (wine and serv. incl.).

### 14 ⌂
## *Chez les Anges*
**54 blvd.**
**Latour-Maubourg**

The young chef of Les Anges, Bernard Labrosse, is not best inspired by modern cuisine; he lacks precision and adroitness in handling the proportions of ingredients and flavor combinations. So it is not the bar in vinegar and

**705.89.86**
*M. Benoist*
*Open until 10:30 P.M. Closed Sun.*
*evenings, Mon. and August 8–31.*
*AE, DC, V.*

pink peppercorns, the perch in creamed sorrel, or his sweet and sour veal kidneys that are the attraction for us, but the good old-fashioned ham with parsley, the eggs en meurette, the thick slice of pink calf's liver and the goat's cheeses which had our mouths watering as far back as twenty years ago in the days of good old Armand Monassier. The establishment is always full of flowers, always welcoming, and run to perfection by François Benoist.
Carte: 180F–200F.

## L'Archestrate
19
**84 rue de Varenne**
**551.47.33**
*M. Senderens*
*Open until 10:30 P.M. Closed Sat.,*
*Sun., 3 wks. beginning of August*
*and 10 days at year's end.*
*AE.*

Bearded, moustached, with an eye as black as a pirate's, Alain Senderens is today, at the age of 42, at the summit of his glory. When we discovered him for the first time in 1968, he had just opened a small, extraordinarily uncomfortable restaurant with the bizarre name of an ancient Greek chef, Archestrate pronounced Arkestrate. Since then, he has moved to the Invalides neighborhood, into somewhat more attractive quarters that, despite the elegance of his Limoges dishes and his silver service, are still not on the same level as his talent. In several years, Senderens has, in sum, become one of the foremost prophets of the new cuisine, one of those who, with Michel Guérard and several others have sought to invent and not to be satisfied with the indolent philosophy of a Paul Bocuse, according to whom "There is never anything new as concerns cooking." If you are ready to spend 400 to 500 francs per person, you will see which of the two is right. Some of Senderens generally fabulous plates: prawn en papillotte with leek, lobster with vanilla, bass with beans, red mullet with celery, the fabulous "Appicius" duck, roast pigeon with ginger, and many others, for Senderens is not one of those chefs who roasts on his laurels. He sometimes commits errors; it is also true that the helpings are not always generous, the service is confused, and the reception lacks warmth. And it is certain, also, that a meal taken here, accompanied by a great Bordeaux or Burgundy, is a severe trial for your wallet. But what a meal!
Carte: 400 F and over. Menu: 280F, 320F + 15% s.

**10/20**
## Babkine (Chez Germaine)
**30 rue Pierre-Leroux**
**273.28.34**
*M. Babkine*
*Open until 9:00 P.M. Closed Sat.*
*evening, Sun., holidays and during*
*August*

There's always competition for the few tables spread with oilcloth where one sits elbow to elbow while appreciating the joys of an inexpensive meal in this authentic neighborhood bistro. For example, streaky bacon with lentils (14F), zéphir of chicken livers (6.50F), rabbit à la savoyarde (15F), or the clafoutis of seasonal fruits (6.50F), nimbly prepared by Chef Charbonnier, a 15-year veteran of this kitchen.
Carte: 35F–40F.

**10/20**

### Le Babylone

**13 rue de Babylone**
**548.72.13**

*M. Garavana*
*Closed Sun. and during August*
*Lunch only.*

Ah, Byzantium! Beef gros sel is only 16F. Osso buco, navarin, and sautéed veal Marengo are all about the same price. If, in this old family bistro, M. Garavana and his chef of eighteen years provided us with a Babylonian hanging garden one of these days, we wouldn't be a bit surprised; after all, they did repaint the walls only last year.
Carte: about 50F.

**13**

### Le Bellecour

**22 rue Surcouf**
**551.46.93**

*M. Goutagny*
*Open until 10:30 P.M. Closed Sat.*
*evening from October 1 to June 1,*
*Sat. and Sun. from June 1 to*
*October 1. Pay parking.*
*All major credit cards.*

This little restaurant, with its rather gloomy decor that is enlivened at midday by television people, has decided, after a fruitless go at nouvelle cuisine, to stick to the tried and true dishes like those that the famed grandmothers of Lyon used to make. And we must say that, aside from the unfortunate tablier de sapeur, one does not complain—about the hot sausage with gratin of potatoes, the salad with sheep's trotters, the rabbit terrine, hare with fresh pasta, or the superb fruit tartes. Nor about the kindness of the invariably excellent reception.
Carte: 150F–180F. Menu (lunch only): 100F (wine and serv. incl.).

**15**

### Bistrot de Paris

**33 rue de Lilla**
**261.16.83**

*M. Oliver*
*Open until 11:30 P.M. Closed Sat.,*
*Sun., holidays. Pay parking at*
*Bac-Montalembert.*
*V.*

One of our readers complains, "They serve Christian Millau a marvelous Troplong-Mondot 1970 in a carafe, but not me!" He adds, "These little favors amount to nothing, since they cannot influence the judgment of Gault and Millau who don't need them." He's right. We were enchanted by our last meal at the Bistrot de Paris, and we tell Michel Oliver so loud and clear. He has a superb young chef, Jean-Pierre Frelet, and because Michel Oliver has been able to hang onto him for more than two years now, we can hope for the best. In fact, we have always eaten well at Oliver's, but sometimes it has come close to pot-luck, according to the mood of the moment. Now, however, there are no unpleasant surprises; the cuisine is of consistently high quality, light, intelligent, with an oft-revised carte. We cannot swear that on any given day you will find the remarkable fresh marinated salmon with dill, the delicious chartreuse of prawn brought to perfection with a pinch of curry, the chicken with coriander or the rosy calf's liver with raspberry vinegar (the real thing, applied with such a delicate hand!). But you will find other dishes just as good, unpretentious and turned out with equal skill. My God! We almost forgot the desserts! They are always marvelous (ah! that cake of bitter chocolate on a thin round of meringue). And so is the decor which now, almost twenty years old, is still attractive. Need we add that even the least expensive (50F–60F.) of the wines is chosen with incomparable flair? Try a Marques de Caceres Rioja. For 48F it is a giveaway.
Carte: about 180F.

**12/20**

## La Boule d'Or

**13 blvd.**
**Latour-Maubourg**
**705.50.18**

*Mme Guinot*
*Open until 10:00 P.M. Closed Mon.*
*and during August.*
*AE, V.*

The affluent, conservative clientele of the Tour Eiffel district is unlikely to suddenly run wild after sampling this cuisine . . . Patrick Dubois learned his trade at Taillevent and the Pavillon Royal, but he sticks to an essentially bourgeois range, spiced here and there with a few more fashionable dishes, such as suprême of sea bass with écumée of fennel, or with something modern such as barbue with chives. His work is not entirely faultless, but we found nothing wrong with the tête de veau ravigote, the magnificent sole meunière which was cooked to perfection, or the hot apple tarte Normande.
Carte: 160F–180F, Menu: 95F + 15% serv.

**15**

## Le Bour-donnais

**113 ave. de La**
**Bourdonnais**
**705.47.96**

*Mme. Coat*
*Open until 11:30 P.M. Closed Sun.*
*and Mon. (at lunch). Open*
*terrace. Pay parking at place de*
*l'Ecole-Militaire.*
*V.*

You can always count on an attractive French smile from Micheline Coat and attractive cuisine à la française from Chef Hiro Nakamura. It must be said of this Japanese that he attended good schools (the Oasis in Napoule and the Marée and Laurent in Paris) before installing himself in the kitchen of this small, charming restaurant where he is free to cook as his heart dictates. A cuisine that is modern without being showy, and light without being affected will impress you with a mousse of red mullet with red pepper, fricassée of crayfish with chevril butter, papillote of sea trout, a ragoût of calf's kidneys and sweetbreads with mushrooms—and delicious desserts. Micheline Coat, who takes her charm and good advice from table to table, dreams of a larger and more comfortable restaurant where she can spoil her innumerable faithful clients. Let us reassure this perfectionist: the Bourdonnais is one of the most sympathetic and attractive little restaurants in Paris, elegant in the evening and animated at midday by businessmen who are attracted by an excellent menu.
Carte: about 160F. Menu: 130F (wine and serv. incl.).

**13**

## La Bourgogne

**6 ave. Bosquet**
**705.96.78**

*Messieurs Julien*
*Open until 10:30 P.M. Closed Sat.*
*(at lunch), Sun. and during*
*August. Valet parking.*
*AE, DC, V.*

Unquestionably, this is the truly Burgundian cuisine in the true tradition of Robert Monassier, who originally brought fame to this beautiful, opulent and ultra-conventional restaurant with its diplomas and its waxed woodwork. A dizzying array of dishes presented by the maître d' precedes a cuisine that is unabashedly grandiose, consisting of well-filled plates of rich foods with a festival of sauces, just like in the old days. The kidney des Ducs, the mousseline of brochet Nantua, the sweetbreads or côte with morilles, the estouffade of beef are not really our favorite style of cuisine. This does not prevent Christian Julien (formerly of Bougnat de la Chambre, now with the Ferme Saint Simon) from doing quite well with them (this is probably due largely to the quality and the freshness of his ingredients). However, there is also the fact that he is an expert, exacting and extremely painstaking. His biscuit of lobster, his shrimp salad Fer and Point, a lovely magret of duck with Meix-Pile (with a splash of Mercurey Burgundy) go down as smoothly as a

letter (or a big fat package) through the mails. They contribute, in any case, to sensational old-time luncheons, especially with the great Burgundy wines to wash them down. There is actually hardly anything else to choose from, because the lesser red wine here is a Santenay Gravières 1974 at 85F a bottle. The service is traditional, the clientele (straight out of the diplomatic pouch and the television studios), bravely indifferent to the prodigious bills and the prospect of a hazy afternoon.
Carte: about 250F.

**13**

## Le Champ de Mars
**17 ave. de la Motte-Picquet 705.57.99**
*Open until 10:15 P.M. Closed Mon. and July 14 to August 15.*
*Open terrace.*
*DC, V.*

The rustic decor of this large restaurant marks the private domain of a traditional cuisine prepared without surprises—although a good cuisine always prepared intelligently and generously served is a surprise in itself. Fillets of mackerel with Pouilly, turbot with sorrel, calf's liver à l'ancienne, calf's head sauce gribiche. Good fresh fruit sherbets.
Carte: 150F. Menu: 60F (serv. incl.).

**14**

## Les Champs d'Or
**22 rue du Champs-de-Mars 551.52.69**
*M. Cloet*
*Open until 10:00 P.M. Closed Sun. and Mon.*
*DC, V.*

About five years ago, Georges Cloet arrived from Brussels with the intention of reinventing seafood for Parisians. Now Georges Cloet is no simpleton. He is one of the rare restaurateurs who spends his very early mornings at the Rungis central market, and he delivers these marvelous products in all the natural freshness that only perfect cooking with the right juices, light sauces and vegetables of the season can preserve. There's a fabulous salad of lobster on a bed of fresh macédoine; crab feuilleté (his pastries are in general admirable, notably the delicious millefeuille with fruit), braised lotte with cooking juice of calf, very delicate brawn of skate en blanquette. All of this is prepared with such skill that as soon as you finish your meal, you want to start all over again, beginning with the waterzoi, (a Flemish dish), eel au vert. And even more so because the portions served in this very comfortable setting are too often insufficient. A less mild criticism is that you don't often find a new dish on the menu. The attractive Mme Cloet welcomes you with charm, and the service is marred only by slowness. Very good Savennières 1979, Clos du Papillon from Chez Baumard.
Carte: 200F. Menu: 116F (serv. incl.).

**11/20**

## La Chaumière
**35 rue de Beaune 261.26.09**
*M. Richard*
*Open until 10:15 P.M. Closed Sat.*

How could you be unhappy here? It has everything, including André Richard's big, warm heart. We have known André for more than ten years and he has always offered one of the most honest, modest cuisines in the neighborhood. Many antique dealers and quite a few of their clients come here regularly to spend a fat 100F note to eat the grenadin of veal in peaches, the fillet of barbue

*evenings, Sun. and during August.*
*Pay parking at Montalembert.*

with fresh pasta or the steak antiquaire with pink peppercorns.
Carte: about 100F.

**10/20**
## Le Chiroubles
**23 ave. Duquesne**
**705.59.17**
*M. Guyard*
*Open until 10:00 P.M. Closed Sun.,*
*holidays, and December 15 to*
*January 15.*
*AE, DC, V.*

Capucine always provides the same personalized welcome in her cutesy-pie style using such terms of endearment as "my little lambs," which her clients from the nearby government offices adore. As for the rest, there is fish soup (bad!), grilled loup (worse!), but a good pan-fried andouillette and tarte Tatin.
Carte: 130F–150F.

**13**
## La Chope d'Orsay
**10 rue du Bac**
**261.21.89**
*M. Cosnard*
*Open until 10:30 P.M. Closed Sat.*
*and Sun. No dogs.*

Discreet, with a touch of refinement and an elegant clientele, this "chope" (beer mug) does not forget its bistro origins in offering some old-fashioned dishes. But little by little the intelligent menu of Jacques Cosnard is becoming modern: small platter of raw fish, vegetable terrine, creamy gâteau of asparagus, marinated white of chicken with red peppers, bass with rhubarb. A la carte, the bill rises quickly, but a good fixed-price meal will bring you back to this estimable house frequented by writers both well-known and on their way. Cool Chinon and good Cahors.
Carte: 150F. Menu (only at lunch): 80F (serv. incl.).

**14**
## Conticini
**4 rue Pierre-Leroux**
**306.99.39**
*M. Conticini*
*Open until 10:30 P.M. Closed Sun.*
*and during August. Air cond.*
*Cards: EC, V.*

The cuisine of Roger Conticini is the very essence of freshness and simplicity. A meal taken in this flowery setting, served by a warmly attentive staff, amounts to an unexpected, subdued festival. This ardent defender of the "cuisine of the marketplace" seems to manifest in all of his preparations a rejection of formula and convention, and this glimmer of fantasy never goes wrong in execution. The cooking is done with remarkable precision, the sauces are balanced, and the blending of flavors is always just right: salad of melon and prawns with honey, minute of red mullet with aniseed and fresh fennel, escalope of bass with young cabbage, papillotes of truffle, drumstick of cockerel. An attractive wine list on which appear some excellent and inexpensive little wines (a delicious Aude red, for example) accompanies an exemplary fixed-price meal: salad of seafood en chiffonade, aiguillette of chicken with lemon and coriander, cheese of the day, and a choice of desserts.
Carte: about 160F. Menu: 85F + 15% serv.

**12/20**
## La Croque au Sel

This was one of those places which, about 15 years ago, started the 1900's bistro fashion in Paris. The charming little square (could one imagine anything as quaint with

**131 rue
Saint-Dominique
705.23.53**
*Open until 11:00 P.M. Closed Sun.
Pay parking.
AE, V.*

its fountain and arcades) became a rendez-vous for
Parisian high society, before it reverted to obscurity. Today
the distinctive decor and rather elegant clientele have re-
emerged and the Croque au Sel is back on the right side of
the tracks with a relaxing, well-prepared cuisine by the
young chef Georges Bermond, examples of which are pot-
au-feu à l'ancienne, seafood pot-au-feu, magret of duck,
and daily specials.
Carte: 120F. Menu: 53F + 13% serv.

13
## Le Dauphin
**32 rue
Saint-Dominique
555.91.80**
*M. Potier
Open until 10:00 P.M. Parking
garage (30F).
AE, DC, V.*

Monsieur Fezau comes from Pau, and he brings his good
meat confits from Saint-Sever and his good clientele from
the neighboring publishing houses of Gallimard and the
Table Ronde. The minute terrace offers an impregnable
vantage point from which to observe passers-by and the
fascinating bustle of the publishing world. For about 100F
or a little more, charming and capricious ladies will serve
decent provincial fare, such as cucumber salad in cream,
magret, leg of lamb, gratin dauphinois, and prune sherbet.
Could you dare ask for more? Very expensive carte and a
delicious Tursan red wine.
Carte: 200F. Menu: 95F (serv. incl.).

12/20
## Aux Délices Saint-André
**2 rue Sédillot
551.95.82**
*M. Marchal
Open until 10:00 P.M. Closed Sat.
(at lunch), Sun., August 1–21 and
1 week in December.
AE, DC.*

Jacques Marchal, the owner of this formal, elegant
restaurant in the Champ-de-Mars, makes no secret of his
ardent knowledge of excellent fresh fish, acquired when
he was maître d'hôtel at Charlot the King of Shellfish, at
the Place Clichy. So, for your own sake, choose from his
long but rather wordy menu of classic dishes only: the
marinated fresh sardines, the mussels, the rougets
meunière, the barbue with sorrel and the other fresh fish
of the day, diligently prepared by the chef, Gilles
Marchand, who also trained at the school of seafood in
Nantes. Good game in season.
Carte: 150F.

## Aux Délices de Szechuen
**40 ave. Duquesne
306.22.55**
*Mme Lau
Open until 10:30 P.M. Closed Mon.
AE, V.*

Not many of the famous dishes of the Szechuen
province—the largest and most populated in China—
although there are pork tripes, frogs legs with
peppercorns or duck with camphor. However, this
recently opened restaurant run by Mme Lau, the daughter
of Uncle Yang, will compensate for this with its meticulous
and typical—that is, not too westernized—cuisine.
Outstanding dishes are: the exquisitely light chicken with
celery, spicy Shanghai soup, crab claws with soy beans,
and glazed duck—a stereotyped dish in three operations
which is particularly well done in this elegant
establishment.
Carte: 120F–130F. Menu: 67F (serv. incl.).

## La Ferme Saint-Simon

**6 rue de Saint-Simon**
**548.35.74**

*M. Vandenhende*
*Open until 10:30 P.M. Closed Sat.*
*(at lunch), Sun. and August 1 to*
*15.*
*V.*

The young chef Patrick Buret, who has worked with Lenôtre, Bocuse and Haeberlin, prepares a very fine half-traditional, half-modern cuisine made even more attractive by a good price-quality ratio. Each day a few plates of what is freshest on the market complement the bavarois of mussels with tarragon, a navarin of fish with crayfish, stuffed feuilleté of sea trout, pigeon en bacasse, fricassée of calf's kidneys and sweetbreads with juniper berries, not to mention a dessert list that brings to mind the days when Francis, the owner, was first assistant to Gaston Lenôtre. At lunch there is a good menu, but even à la carte the bill is not too steep, thanks to a good choice of pleasant little owner's wines from 30F–50F.
Carte: about 170F. Menu (at lunch): 100F. (wine incl.)
+ 15% serv.

## 11/20

## Aux Fins Gourmets

**213 blvd.**
**Saint-Germain**
**222.06.57**

*Mme Dupleix*
*Open until 10:00 P.M. Closed Sun.,*
*holidays and during August.*
*AE.*

A traditional bistro, with its mirrored walls, wooden bar, naugahide-upholstered booths, and its owner, a genuine old "mama," who grumbles and shouts when the clients refuse to sit on the terrace facing the Bac-Saint-Germain intersection on the absurd pretext that it is raining. Very plain and very good home cooking: leeks in vinaigrette, petit salé with cabbage, duck with turnips, and an exquisite leg of lamb, accompanied by pleasant wines from the Southwest.
Carte: 130F–150F.

## La Flamberge

**12 ave. Rapp**
**705.91.37**

*M. Albistur*
*Open until 10:00 P.M. Closed Sun.*
*and August 10 to September 10.*
*AE, DC, V.*

Like a big boy, all alone in his luxurious, plush dining room, Louis Albistur ignores culinary fashions and trends, and prepares his own truly inspired cuisine, whose inventiveness is not confined to the descriptions on the menu (as is so often the case in certain fashionable establishments). His salad of oak leaves, fennel, artichokes and warm langoustine with a hint of raspberry is a miracle of lightness. His raw salmon (not marinated, but flavored with a little lemon juice) has true finesse and blends perfectly with the chopped artichoke. His sweetbreads with horn of plenty mushrooms, his young wild boar with lime zest, his escalopes of magret and duck liver with bilberries, his baron of rabbit with mint, and fresh pasta with a trace of honey flavor are true examples of a successful, if unusual, combination of inventiveness and shrewdness. Sometimes rediscovering an old recipe proves to be a marvelous idea, as is the case of the delicious oyster salad with chipolatas à la Charentaise, and the delicious, traditional desserts. Louis Albistur was trained as a pastry chef, as he proves in his puff pastry, wonderful petits-fours and hot tartes with orange peel, and noteworthy langoustine canapés served as appetizers. Attentive service, beautiful clientele, and a very expensive wine list (but a good Château La Pelleterie, grand cru Saint-Emilion for 86F).
Carte: about 200F.

14

## A la Fontaine aux Carmes
**124 rue de Grenelle**
**551.77.23**
*M. Lausecker*
*Open until 10:00 P.M. Closed Fri.*
*evenings, Sat. and during August.*
*Pay parking at place des Invalides.*
*V.*

Alsace remains dear to the heart of Clément Lausecker, who does the province honor, according to the season, with his superb sauerkraut, baeckeoffe, chicken in Riesling with fresh noodles or foie gras in Gewürztraminer. But these are only incidental, hidden deep within an excellent menu of classic dishes enlivened with newer, lighter and more subtle preparations. The latter tend to gain with each passing year, pushing out the sweetbreads in morilles and the tournedos Ambassadeur. So on your next visit to this redecorated establishment, taste the barbue in fresh mint garnished with saxifrage, the feuilleté of snails with anise, the river salmon with sorrel, or the écrevisses salad. Delightful Alsatian-style welcome. Carte: about 160F.

**11/20**

## La Fontaine de Mars
**129 rue**
**Saint-Dominique**
**705.46.44**
*M. Launay*
*Open until 9:30 P.M. Closed Sat.*
*evenings, Sun. and during August.*

A good bistro with a stable clientele, although not as good as it was a short while ago. When a cuisine never has a new idea, it never displays a fault. Unfortunately, the unchanging estouffade of beef, boudin with apple and leeks in vinaigrette have not aged as gracefully as the old decor, checkered tablecloths or the red and violet duplicated menu. The atmosphere is still exquisitely home-style, and the prices are very affordable. Carte: 75F. Menu: 49.50F (serv. incl.).

**12/20**

## Chez Francoise
**Aérogare des**
**Invalides**
**705.49.03**
*M. Demessence*
*Open until 10:15 P.M. Closed Mon.*
*and August 16 to September 1.*
*Parking.*
*DC, V.*

There is always a lively holiday atmosphere in this airport terminal, with its train whistles and the revving of bus engines. Departing passengers cross the concourse with their suitcases, but those who have arrived, by making it to the National Assembly, the embassies, or the nearby government offices, take their places with their briefcases in this vast basement room, generously lit by a skylight adorned with climbing plants. They are served with food that is also worth a short trip: not so light that it will fly off the plate, but always decent and generous. Fish mousse with tomato coulis, barbue with spring vegetables, aiguillette of beef à la mode. Pleasant little wines. Carte: 150F. Menu: 80F + 15% serv.

14

## Le Galant Verre
**12 rue de Verneuil**
**260.84.56**
*M. Cohen*
*Open until 10:30 P.M. Closed Sat.*
*(at lunch), Sun. and during*
*August. Parking.*
*DC, V.*

Three fine meals in three visits prove that the cuisine of young chef Pascal Daguet is today mature, and has taken off in a manner worthy of Guy Girard, who created this restaurant's reputation and whose influence is still noticeable here and there, from the extraordinary just-pink duck liver (perhaps the best in Paris) or the exquisite marinated raw mackerel with green pepper, to the charlotte with peaches, pears, and raspberry purée. But the new departure finally manifests itself in the preparation—until now a little hesitant—of plates such as hure of chicken with leeks, skate with salmon roe, turbot with periwinkles, mignon of veal with leeks, bass with

beurre rouge and a mousse of squash, well-cooked game in season, and a kiwi charlotte. Pascal Daguet seems determined to leave the traditional cooking, where we thought he was perfectly at home. The sublety of his sauces, the intelligence of his preparations, and his choice of accompanying vegetable indicate that he is on the right road. All that is necessary now is to make it known along the rue de Verneuil that the Galant Verre, along with the Bistrot of Paris, is the best table in the quarter. If some faithful clients, publishers from the neighborhood who like the small varnished and English tapestried dining room were not there to fill it up, a diner might feel pretty lonely, were it not for the attentive personnel. Let's point out that the prices have barely risen during the past year and that a remarkable fixed-price menu-dégustation is offered at 130F.
Carte: about 180F.

## Les Glénan
**54 rue de Bourgogne**
**551.61.09**
*M. Yvonnou*
*Open until 10:00 P.M. Closed Sat. (at lunch), Sun. and during August.*

Les Glénan is named for the little islands where one learns how to tack a sailboat off Concarneau. The sea there around Morbihan in Brittany is directly responsible for most of the ingredients needed to produce the cotriade de Belle-Ile (Mon., Wed. and Fri.), the panaché of island fish, the skate fish bouclée au beurre blanc, the langoustines du Guilvinec, etc. The new chef, Michel Gras, previously with Jamin and the Petit Riche, manages all this effortlessly. His cooking times are right, his sauces light, and he is creative (barbue fillets braised with three salads, civet of lotte in red Macon, marinade of oranges with walnut liqueur and limes). The prices have become reasonable.
Carte: 150F. Menus: 69F, 120F (wine and serv. incl.).

## Lefèbvre
**Port de la Bourdon-nais, quai Branly**
**556.11.23**
*M. Lefèbvre*
*Open until 10:30 P.M. Closed Sun. and during February. Parking. AE, DC, V.*

Aside from overcooked lamb brains in overjelled aspic, we have recently eaten meals here that confirm unequivocally the sure talents of Bernard Dupuy, who used to be a chef at Faugeron's. In this luxurious barge moored at the foot of the Chaillot hill, he offers a short, intelligently conceived menu based on the products of the season. The buisson of vegetables, the salad of shellfish, the roast lotte with sauce meurette, bass with curry, the three sautéed meats. You will have an excellent dinner in a comfortable and spacious floating setting with efficient and smiling waiters. The good red house Sancerre (40F), plucked from the extensive wine list, keeps your bill very reasonable.

**10/20**
## Lucie (Lou Mino)
**15 rue Augereau**
**555.08.74**

All alone in her little kitchen, the good Lucie has captured some of the rays of her native Martinique sun, with her warm salad of gambas, macadam of cod, gratin of christophines, and the rest of the good food served with

*Mme Manyri*
*Open until 10:30 P.M. Closed Sun.,*
*Mon. and during August.*
*Reservations required.*
*V.*

more than enough friendliness to compensate for the lack of amenities.
Carte: 100F–120F.

13
## Chez Marius
**5 rue de Bourgogne**
**551.79.42**
*M. Aküstapas*
*Open until 10:00 P.M. Closed Sat.*
*and during August. Parking.*
*DC, V.*

The bearded members of the new National Assembly do not appear to scorn this establishment, which for such a long time served almost as a cafeteria to their predecessors, even at almost 200F per person. The new management no longer feels obliged to serve bouillabaisse (special order), but offers, in redecorated surroundings, excellent, very fresh shellfish and seafood prepared in a more contemporary style than that which prevailed in the days of good old père Pommerol.
Carte: 180F–200F.

**10/20**

## L'Oeillade
**10 rue de Saint-Simon**
**222.01.60**
*Mesdames Kornicki and*
*Papadopoulos*
*Open until 10:00 P.M. Closed Sun.*
*and the week of August 15.*
*AE, V.*

Reading the menu is not too great an intellectual exercise: terrine of poultry livers, taboulleh, lamb chops with mint, duck à l'orange, sherbet. . . . But the two women who run this intimate and feminine little bistro probably did the best they could in this neighborhood where top restaurants abound and they are almost next door to Francis and Denise Vandenhende's La Ferme Saint-Simon. However, for what it is, this family cuisine prepared just the way they learned it at home is providential for the large appetites of the thrifty locals. Delicious Gamay de Touraine (28F a bottle).
Carte: 90F.

**10/20**

## L'Oeno-thèque
**37 rue de Lille**
**261.23.40**
*M. Ambert*
*Open until 11:00 P.M. Closed Sun.*
*and July 1–15. Pay parking rue*
*Montalembert.*
*AE.*

The wine and spirits list looks a bit like the Trois Suisses mail order catalogue. There are some 500 items—that is more than one decent vintage per day for those crazy enough to eat daily at this peasant-style inn, frequented by the publishing trade. In fact, the cuisine lapses a little further each year into the commonplace. There are a few broiled meats served with reheated potatoes, a rather tough magret of duck drowned in its own sauce, a good small dried sausage . . . Rather lacking for it to remain long in the most prestigious of gastronomic guides.
Carte: 130F–150F. Menu: 60F (serv. incl.).

14
## Pantagruel
**20 rue de l'Exposition**
**551.79.96**
*M. Israël*
*Open until 10:30 P.M. Closed Sun.*
*and during August.*
*AE, DC.*

How nice to be completely idle, seated in the attractive dining room of the Pantagruel, while all around you the busy world whirls on! Especially when Alfred Israël is at his oven engaged in the delicate and perilous preparation of a sole soufflé with a mousse of scallops or salmon. Mme Israël, the most charming of hostesses, will explain to you her husband's preparations while taking your order. The chef demonstrates sureness and finesse in the preparation of his sauces and plates, which are finished

with a marvelous clarity. Taste his hot duck liver with bilberries, the mousse of scallops, the saddle of hare and the remarkable desserts.
Carte: 200F–plus.

10/20
## La Petite Chaise

**36-38 rue de Grenelle**
**222.13.35**
*M. Jessel*
*Open until 11:00 P.M.*
*V.*

If you can't find a petite chaise, grab yourself a folding stool to come dine in this very old inn (serving since 1680), which is packed with graduate students and personnel of every echelon from the neighboring publishing houses. A bit calmer in the evenings if you wish to eat hot sausages en croûte, tripe provençale, and whatever fresh fruit salad appears on the always inspired and varied single menu. The owner's reception is always warm.
Menu: 48F (wine incl.) + 15% serv.

10/20
## Le Petit Niçois

**10 rue Amélie**
**551.83.65**
*M. Ruols*
*Open until 10:15 P.M. Closed Sun.,*
*Mon. (at lunch) and during*
*August.*
*V.*

The bouillabaisse at the Petit Niçois is among our oldest and fairly good gastronomic memories. We were several half-dozen years younger, and so was the (less and less) temperamental Roland Ruols. Today, however, his bouillabaisse is not nearly good enough to bring back all our memories. It still has its moments, such as the paella on Thursday and Saturday, or the seafood gratinée on Friday—all pretty good in the long run.
Carte: 120F.

11/20
## Aux Petits Oignons

**20 rue de Bellechasse**
**705.48.77**
*Mme Andremont*
*Open until 11:30 P.M. Closed Sat.*
*(at lunch), Sun. and from*
*Christmas day until January 3.*
*No large dogs.*
*V.*

Edith Andremont and an American friend transformed a local dive into this friendly, stylish little address. It's modishly furnished with bistro tables with flowered tablecloths and fruit bowls. It's also a happy place, always full of smart people, and despite a fresh cuisine of the rustic school (lamb with preserved lemons, genoese of eggplant with foie gras, fricassée of veal with garlic sauce, poached chicken with fennel), the prices remain quite reasonable.
Carte: 90F-110F. Menu: 49.50F (serv. incl.).

10/20
## Au Pied de Fouet
**45 rue de Babylone**
**705.12.27**
*M. Persoons*
*Open until 9:00 P.M. Closed*
*during August and 1st wk. of*
*September*

We discovered this old coach house a dozen years ago. Aside from a telephone, installed several years after our first visit, success has changed nothing: neither the number (a dozen) of tables, nor the menu—chicken with cream, beef miroton, rabbit with lemon—nor the prices, so easy on your wallet. The clientèle consists of hard-up publishers and authors of succès d'estime.
Carte: 50F. Menu: 24.70F (wine and serv. incl.).

14

## Au Quai d'Orsay
**49 quai d'Orsay**
**551.58.58**
*M. Bigeard*
*Open until 10:45 P.M. Closed Sun.*
*and during August. Air cond. Open*
*terrace.*
*AE, EC, V.*

Last year the cuisine of the Quai d'Orsay, which previously had been a bit heavy, appeared to us more subtle and light. The impression was confirmed this year. Returning to this charming, very Parisian old bistro where the reception is unfailingly friendly, we tasted the mushrooms with cream, compote of duck, small fried sole, lotte with curry of fresh fruit, John Dory with caramelized vegetables and ginger, leg of rabbit with girolles (they're mad about mushrooms in this restaurant), the éminicé of cold confit with peaches, and the chocolate charlotte of Étienne Bigeard and his chef Antoine Bouterin. No one could say that the portions are stingy; on the contrary, the pretty waitresses attend to big appetites with particular attention, a contrast to the midget-sized servings in some restaurants where you pay just as much. In fact, with a half-bottle of Cahors, the check should not exceed 170F.
Carte: 150F–180F.

## 12/20
## Que Huong
**66 ave. Bosquet**
**551.93.36**
*Mme Nguyen-Van-Day*
*Open until 10:30 P.M. Closed Sun.*
*and during August.*

Huge flowers paper the walls of this cozy but gaudy establishment. However, as far as the cuisine is concerned, the exoticism is more original, with delicate dumplings, shrimp with almonds, and a very good caramelized breast of pork.
Carte: 80F–100F. Menu: 28F (serv. incl.).

15

## Le Récamier
**4, rue Récamier**
**548.86.58**
*M. Cantegrit*
*Open until 10:30 P.M. Closed Sun.*
*Open terrace. Air cond. Pay*
*parking at Boucicaut.*
*AE, DC, EC.*

No use crying over spilled cream—even though too much of the stuff has ruined a couple of dishes we've eaten here. Despite certain small imperfections, the Récamier is one of the restaurants we return to with the greatest of pleasure. Above all, on pretty days when the tables are lined up on the sidewalk of this flowery dead-end which opens onto one of the most delicious and unknown gardens of the Left Bank. A clientele of editors, writers and familiar faces. A warm reception from Martin Cantegrit, who brings from his cellars some great Burgundies and some astonishing Côtes-du-Rhone. A well-filled, eclectic menu: tartare of salmon, a remarkable lobster à la nage, a platter of raw fish, terrine of veal, delicious fricassée of cèpes or of girolles, calf's liver à l'auvergnate, one of Paris's best strawberry sherbets, and succulent apple tarte.
Carte 170F–200F.

13

## Relais Saint-Germain
**190 blvd.**
**Saint-Germain**
**548.11.73**

Jean-Marie Frugier brings all his considerable talents to a simple and light cuisine characterized by an exceptional price-quality ratio. The menu, which has not gone up in price this year, offers a very fine choice of dishes, such as raw wild salmon or terrine of fish sauce lyonnaise for starters; aiguillettes of beef with Meaux mustard or piccata

*M. Frugier*
*Open until 10:30 P.M. Closed Sun.*
*evening and Mon. Parking at 169-*
*171 blvd. Saint-Germain.*
*AE, DC, V.*

of brains as the main dish. This sort of food makes you want to hurry right over, but don't forget to call first for a reservation.
Menu: 90F (wine incl.) + 15% serv.

14
## Chez Ribe
**15 ave. de Suffren**
**566.53.79**
*M. Pérès*
*Open until 10:00 P.M. Closed Sat.*
*evening, Sun., during August and*
*1 wk. from Christmas and New*
*Year's Day. Open terrace.*
*All major credit cards.*

A long, split-level dining room in the comfortable, classic bistro style. The cuisine of owner-chef Jean-Antoine Pérès is as meticulous in preparation as in presentation. One sees this in the duck pâté served with preserved onion, poached egg with warm artichokes covered with a light béarnaise sauce, as well as in the lotte with fresh tomato and basil, or in the mignon of veal with lime and fresh tomato. It's really a shame, particularly in view of the high prices, that the portions seem rationed (one cassolette of snails with croutons, and a seafood pot-au-feu, although perfectly cooked, were in this respect only barely acceptable). Among the wines, a very good light Côtes-du-Rhône, drunk chilled. The staff is young, diligent, and exceedingly friendly.
Carte: 200F–plus. Menu: 62F, 70F, 130F (wine incl.) + 15% serv.

14
## La Sologne
**8 rue de Bellechasse**
**705.98.66**
*M. Guillerand*
*Open until 10:00 P.M. Closed Sat.,*
*Sun., and during August. Parking*
*at Deligny.*
*AE, DC, V.*

The chef of this pretty, rustic house had virtues and talents—but also faults. So owner Christian Guillerand took over and has produced a remarkable cuisine by applying new ideas to recipes hundreds of years old: calf's kidneys "de sept heures," sautéed turkey with ginger, grilled veal sweetbreads with raspberries, beautiful butcher's-choice meats—and game. The result is a happy one, refined and enticing. Prices are affordable with an agreeable Loire Valley wine.
Carte: about 150F. Menu: 100F, 110F, 115F, 160F (wine and serv. incl.).

14
## Tan Dinh
**60 rue de Verneuil**
**544.04.84**
*M. Vifian*
*Open until 10:00 P.M. Closed Sun.*
*and during August. Parking at*
*corner of rue du Bac and*
*Montalembert.*

M. and Mme Vifian and their two sons, who rank among the world's foremost experts on French and foreign wines, continue to offer a Vietnamese nouvelle cuisine; it is inventive, often very successful, showing that Oriental flavors mix admirably with the best wines (there are several hundred wines on their list, among which are 150 Pomerols, some of the very best vintages). In the pleasing surroundings, very floral downstairs, you can choose the new crab and basil soup, the scallops with black soybeans, frog's legs soup, won ton with coriander, a portefeuille of oysters with asparagus, the fresh pasta with small shrimp.
Carte: about 120F.

**12/20**

# Than

**42 rue des Saints-Pères 548.36.97**

*M. Than*
*Open until 11:00 P.M. Closed Mon. (at lunch), Sun. and August 8–25. AE, DC, V.*

Mr. Truong Van Than has long displayed his rather exuberent qualities as a host in this narrow bistro, where moderately affluent medical students like to gather. He himself initiated Marie Ta into the mysteries of a Vietnamese housewife's cooking, and we must admit that, aside from a few blind spots, the results are excellent. For instance, the caramelized pork spare ribs, the sweet and sour pork, the fried mixao noodles and the chicken with citronella.
Carte: 90F. Menu (lunch only): 35F (wine and serv. incl.).

**12/20**

# Au Vert Bocage

**96 blvd. de Latour-Maubourg 551.48.64**

*M. Baudry*
*Open until 10:00 P.M. Closed Sat. evenings, Sun. and during August. AE, DC, V.*

Since there are now gardens around the Invalides—although they wouldn't qualify as groves (bocages)—they have given the name of this quiet little restaurant some justification. The cuisine of the chef, Michel Deleplanque, however, is not particularly rustic. His sweetbreads immersed in cream and flambéed in Calvados remain the star attraction alongside calf's kidney, whose mustard and Madeira sauce has, to coin a phrase, seen better days. However, the cooking is rescued from imbecility by the noteworthy accuracy of the cooking times, the impeccable quality of the ingredients and also by some less formidable dishes such as a good tart with fresh tomatoes, the grilled scallops, and the turbot or barbue with delicate beurre blanc. Pleasant wines from the Loire.
Carte: 170F.

# 8ème Arr.

**12/20**

# L'Alsace

**39 Champs-Elysées 359.44.24**

*M. Blanc*
*Open 24 hours, year round. Pay parking at George V. AE, DC, V.*

This large corner brasserie, which we have often scorned in the past for its boisterousness, has changed considerably. The place has been improving steadily for the past two years. The choucroute is especially noteworthy. It is cooked in a special vacuum-sealed vessel that requires very little fat, and leaves the cabbage agreeably crisp; indeed, it is now among the best in Paris. The delicatessen from Kirn's in Strasbourg which accompanies it is also distinguished. But read on through the menu of this embassy of sweet Alsace which also lists oysters and shellfish of remarkable freshness (the owner, Jacques Blanc, sells a ton of them each weekend). There is the suckling pig Colmar-style, cream cheese tarte, and Alsatian great wines from Lorentz and Léon Beyer. The rustic decor is not too enchanting but the service is efficient. All the dishes on the menu may be purchased at the small adjoining shop, which like the restaurant, is open day and night.
Carte: 120F. Menu: 95.45F (serv. incl.).

## 12/20
### Chez André
**12 rue Marbeuf**
**720.59.57**
*M. Méthivier*
*Open until 11:40 P.M. Closed Tues.*
*and during August.*

André's has become an awful restaurant. Could this outright lie be enough to get us a table in one of the most crowded establishments in Paris? Alas, no, because everyone knows enough to praise the roast leg of lamb, the poached skate, the small fresh mackerel, the shoulder of lamb with cabbage. There is the entire range of André's conscientious cuisine, which, in truth, we are bound to admit hasn't changed one iota. No change either in its active owner, its mixed clientele, its acrobatic service and, consequently, in the length of the daily line stretching out to the sidewalk. Too bad for us!
Carte: 110F–120F.

## 11/20
### Androuet
**41 rue d'Amsterdam**
**874.26.93**
*M. Androuet*
*Open until 10:00 P.M. Closed Sun.*
*AE, DC.*

Lots of vaulted ceilings, stonework, wooden beams and mullioned windows in a style which varies from Renaissance to Gothic. There is a pre-war flavor in the decor, exacerbated by the fake coats of arms and their pretentious mottos. The long menu of this huge vault is a long homage to the heavily-sauced style of yesteryear. (Examples: chicken Vallée d'Auge, three fillets Beaugency). So one would do well to remember—you are persistently reminded of the fact here—that Pierre Androuet is the most knowledgeable cheese expert in France and that hundreds of his cheeses, in perfect condition, reign supreme here, either in their natural state or ready for endless tastings, or "cooked up" as an ingredient in puff pastries, soufflés and tarts. That is really all that is needed to provide the occasional amusing and original meal.
Carte: 120F. Menus: 85F, 120F + 15% serv.

## 12/20
### L'Artois
**13 rue d'Artois**
**225.01.10**
*M. Rouzeyrol*
*Open until 11:30 P.M. Closed Sat.,*
*Sun., and from July 14 to*
*September 14.*

It is in this very place some 15 years ago (a commemorative plaque is being struck even as we speak) that we began our first tour of the restaurants of Paris with a boudin de Corrèze and tripous d'Aurillac. That is why we have a soft spot for this small Auvergne restaurant, which is never empty. But we are far from complacent when we can still, to this very day, recommend the charcuterie, the ham gratin, the sautéed rabbit, the hot tart, and finally, just about all of the reliable cooking of the Rouzeyrol family.
Carte: 150F.

## 11/20
### L'Assiette au Boeuf

**123 Champs-Élysées**
**720.01.13**
*Open until 1:00 A.M. No dogs.*

Jammed every day and a line on the sidewalk. Nonetheless, you get a civil if cursory reception, speedy and efficient service, and an elementary but well-prepared cuisine. The success of the Assiettes (there are four of them in Paris) continues to grow, and with good reason: a

decor that is always immaculate (in this Assiette the style is somewhat eclectic: baroque chairs, Tiffany lamps, which illuminate a seemingly endless jungle of gilt bamboo, lots of mirrors), clean white table linen, steaks of good quality, french fries and some lovely desserts. Prices are relatively reasonable, despite extras (for service, for wine, for cheese, for dessert; best to figure about double the base price). All of which gives you the illusion of eating in a real restaurant without paying real restaurant prices, especially with the new after-midnight formula of an all-inclusive menu for less than 50F.
Carte: 80F–100F. Menu: 39F + 15% serv.

## 12/20
## L'Aubergade
**122 rue La Bôtie**
**225.10.60**
*M. Uzan*
*Open until 11:30 P.M. (midnight on Fri. and Sat.) Closed Sun. and in August.*

Recently-opened L'Aubergade is entirely devoted to seafood. This is a good idea, because there were no fish restaurants in the neighborhood of the Champs-Elysées. The oysters of varying sizes are the Marennes type from the isle of Oléron, and, by selecting the fixed-price menu (which does not include service or wine), you may eat as many as you like. Some customers can eat more than a hundred, but the average is 3 or 4 dozen per person. The menu is extensive and quite varied. Examples are stuffed crab, grilled salmon "à l'unilatérale," the bourride, bouillabaisse, the mouclade (no brandade), the rouget Niçois, and the raw scallops with chives. All of this is very nicely prepared. The cheese platter is rather poor, but there is a good choice of desserts; very poor coffee. Bourgogne Aligoté is served by the pitcher. The decor is discreetly nautical.
Carte: 160F. Menu: 105F + 15% serv.

## 10/20
## L'Auvergnat
**11 rue Jean-Mermoz**
**359.21.47**
*M. Charrié*
*Open until 10:30 P.M. Closed Sat. and Sun.*

Suffice it to say that this 1900s Auvergne restaurant was rather a disappointment, and its prices rather disconcerting, considering we had a very uninteresting stuffed neck of duck, and a greasy, salty potée Auvergnate. The rumpsteak with Roquefort cheese was good. Marcel Charrié swears that all this was merely unfortunate, and that he once again has an excellent chef. Let us hope so, for we had been accustomed to eating much better in this little establishment. The reception is charming and the decor is in the chocolate-boxy Belle Époque style.
Carte: about 130F.

## 11/20
## Bistro de la Gare
**73 Champs-Elysées**
**359.67.83**
*Open until 1:00 A.M. No dogs.*

The decor succeeds admirably: an old bistro imaginatively restored by Slavick. As for the cuisine, it is the Assiette au Boeuf formula: a stock menu including a salad of pinon nuts and strips of sirloin and several suggested plates in a distinguished country style, followed by excellent

desserts. Reception breathless, service sometimes pleasant, sometimes odious. Less than 50F all-inclusive after midnight.
Carte: 80F–100F. Menu: 39.90F + 15% serv.

### 13
### Le Bonaventure
**35 rue Jean-Goujon**
**225.02.58**
*MM. Chabannes and Gutrin*
*Open until 10:30 P.M. Closed Sat.*
*(lunch) and Sun.*
*V.*

Opened only two years ago on the ground floor of a hotel near the Alma, Le Bonaventure has become a very sympathetic rendezvous, comfortable and discreet, for business lunches. The small interior garden makes up for the otherwise drab decor, and Chef Noël Gutrin is making heroic efforts to suppress his Burgundian tendency to over-sauce, with the result that the cuisine is classic and precise without being fussy: effiloché of duck en salade with sherry, fricassée of chicken livers with meadow mushrooms, and several more imaginative dishes with well-defined flavors, such as the fattened oysters with leeks or the fillets of red mullet with steamed chicken livers.
Carte: 180F.

### 12/20
### Boulangerie Saint-Philippe
**73 ave. Franklin-Roosevelt**
**358.78.76**
*M. Chaumontet*
*Open for lunch only. Closed Sat.*
*and Sun.*
*V.*

There is a vast dining room behind this bakery, decorated in a difficult-to-define style that is both peasant and modern, and as far removed as possible from the baker's trade. This is borne out by the fact that the patron has installed a real cook from the Lyon region, who learned his trade at the famous La Mère Guy in Lyon, and who worked in the bake house right alongside the dough boy. His talent certainly contributes to those long lines outside of the restaurant during the lunch hour. The prices must also have quite a lot to do with this craze for beef sirloin with shallots, the civet of lotte in Muscadet wine, the leg of lamb with fresh mint, not to mention the traditional daily specials, and the delicious pastries made with butter, the primary avocation of the house. The bread, incidentally, is delicious.
Carte: about 100F.

### 11/20
### La Boutique à Sandwiches
**12 rue du Colisée**
**359.56.69**
*MM. Schick*
*Open until 1:00 A.M. Closed Sun.*
*and during August*

Every day the tiny elevator zips up and down filled with compressed humanity hurrying to compete for the crowded tables on the mezzanine. As for the consumption it is ultra-rapid: a dish of Valais raclette, pickelfleisch (beef brisket à l'alsacienne), and Welsh rarebit—the bill should not come to more than about 50F–60F. A large choice of cold plates and good sandwiches on the ground floor.
Carte: 80F.

### 11/20
## *Brasserie Löwenbraü*
**84 Champs-Elysées**
**562.78.63**
*M. Rath*
*Open until 2:00 A.M.*
*AE, DC, V.*

The dynamic little Mme Rath seats her customers in much the same way a junior master directs students in the college cafeteria. But she knows her job, and nobody complains, especially when the Alsatian white sausage, the vast array of sauerkraut dishes, the suckling pig with spätzle noodles, and the variety of beers from the biggest brewery in Bavaria are paraded before them. In the evening, a Bavarian orchestra, presided over by a costumed Fritz in an Alpine hat, makes this cozy Munich-style beer-cellar vibrate until 1:00 A.M.
Carte: 150F.

### 15
## *Le Bristol*
**112 rue du**
**Faubourg-Saint-**
**Honoré**
**266.91.45**
*M. Spaeth*
*Open until 10:30 P.M. Parking.*
*No dogs.*
*AE, DC, EC.*

If others must sometimes question German taste, we can only admire the exceptional talent with which the Baden-Baden group, the proprietors of this luxury hotel, has beautified Le Bristol. On the top floor is a swimming pool overlooking the roofs of Paris; about 30 rooms and apartments with terraces have been furnished with perfect taste, and the sumptuous dining room, dressed in Regency paneling, has just been given an attractive garden restaurant seating 120, surrounded by a magnificent colonnade. One might have worried that Emile Tabourdiau, trained as he was in the old school (Le Doyen, La Grande Cascade), would have been awed by such surroundings and that, as a result, his cuisine would become finicky. Not at all; he has had to work a bit on the presentation, but he is on the right road, for his inventive spirit manifests itself every day in the production of some weighty fixed-price meals on which no item is programmed for any special day (there are 60 different dishes per month) and a menu where we would be hard put to find a single conventional offering. It is certainly not a simple cuisine, but the flavors are distinct and the cooking precise, and, attended by princely waiters, one eats a sumptuous meal amid a field of mink and chinchilla: hot oysters with a purée of sea urchin; biscuits of prawn with caviar; turbot with Sauternes; mousseline of carp; braised veal liver with the lees of wine; mignonnettes of lamb with a fumet of truffles; an iced lime wafer; gratin of peaches with caramelized zabaglione; and superb wines which fatten the bill.
Carte: 300F–500F. Menus: 160F, 180F, 190F, 200F, 210F, 220F (serv. incl.).

### 12/20
## *Café Terminus*
**108 rue Saint-Lazare**
**522.34.16**
*M. Navarre*
*Open until 11:00 P.M.*
*AE, DC, V.*

Who would ever miss the defunct Rôtisserie Normande—that apalling gastronomic leftover from the days of the old Chemins de Fer de l'Ouest railway company—now replaced by this delightful Café Terminus, with its wall-to-wall carpeting, booths, mirrors and wood paneling. These rather too-careful touches of the late nineteenth century

and the Eiffel Tower era may not quite match the enchanting and absolutely authentic decor of the vast adjoining hotel lobby. Nonetheless they make a pleasant contribution to the atmosphere around a well-prepared brasserie-style cuisine: salad of shrimp and langoustine, magret of duck, broiled meats, sauerkraut. Service is slower in the restaurant lobby, which has been christened a bistro for the occasion.
Carte: 130F–150F.

**12/20**
### *Les Champs-Zé*
**1 bis, rue Jean-Mermoz**
**359.84.85**
*M. Dard*
*Open until 1:00 A.M.*
*AE, DC, V.*

The Champs-Zé is the amusing if slightly crazy idea of Patrick Dard, who also owns the remarkable Barrière-Poquelin. The originality of the formula is that, aside from some pleasant hors d'oeuvres and, an attractive list of desserts, nothing but beef is served: various French cuts and also those from Scotland, Argentina, Brazil, the U.S. and even from Madagascar (of the Zébu is not at all bad). With these we must be patient while awaiting the meat par excellence (but wildly expensive) of Kobe, from Japanese beasts nourished on beer and massaged by hand. The pretty waitresses and the bucolic charm of the place (the chairs, however, must have been designed for six-year-olds), the reasonable prices, and the generosity of the portions of meat (two sizes) should very quickly establish the Champs-Zé as a popular restaurant. Good choice of minor regional wines, from 35F.
Carte: about 100F.

**12/20**
### *Château de Chine*
**9 rue de la Trémoille**
**723.80.90**
*Mme Ting*
*Open until 11:00 P.M.*
*AE, DC.*

Mme Ting, originally from Shanghai, is the kindliest of restaurateurs. Attentive to the smallest detail, she is always smiling and gay. For a long time her husband, an excellent cook, toiled alone in the sparkling little kitchen, but now he has hired a helper, and—is it coincidence?—we noted in the absence of M. Ting several shortcomings: a Peking soup too watery, fairly tasteless chicken fritters with lemon, and a duck of five flavors whose skin was not crispy. But the fried won ton, the Shanghai shrimp, the scallops in hot sauce, and, above all, the Peking duck (must be ordered ahead of time) attract a sizable following to this comfortable and elegant restaurant.
Carte: 90F–120F.

**16**
### *Chiberta*
**3 rue Arsène-Houssaye**
**563.77.90**
*M. Richard*
*Open until 10:30 P.M. Closed Sat., Sun., during February and August*
*AE, DC, V.*

Chiberta was an immediate hit when it opened six years ago. This luxurious restaurant has prospered ever since, and is certainly in the forefront of Parisian restaurants. This despite a risky location only a couple of steps from the vulgarity of the Champs-Elysées. But it is notable for a decor which to our eyes is perfect, an uncompromisingly modern cuisine, and astronomical bills. The public was not wrong. The extreme elegance and comfort of this restaurant in both the principal and the smaller dining rooms, the beauty of the floral arrangements, the sublety of the lighting, the quality of the reception and service, the perfection of the wines (in particular the Burgundies), and, finally, the talent of chef Jean-Michel Bédier, whose every plate is a small masterpiece of presentation, have conquered that certain category of Parisians more appreciative of taste than of ostentation. From time to time we regret that Chef Bédier fails to emphasize the flavor of such and such a plate, but far more often we are enchanted—even awed—by such dishes as the salad of Brittany lobster with basil, the chartreuse of salmon, the fricassée of lamb sweetbreads with beans and basil, and his white meat of chicken with a purée of truffles. Carte: 240F–300F.

**12/20**
## China Town
**6 rue de la Pépinière**
**522.86.90**
*M. Quach*
*Open until 11:30 P.M. Pay parking*
*(square Bergson).*
*AE, DC, V.*

Built on the ruins of the Reine Pédauque, the decor of the second floor is fearsome, almost painful in its unbridled surrender to fake Chinese and karate western style. However, nothing prevents you from sitting on the first floor (the restaurant seats 450 on the two levels), where the decor is far less aggressive. You will be served (better, since the unexplained departure of the previous owner, Monsieur Tsé, and arrival of Monsieur Quach) a medley of dim sum, and more than 150 dishes prepared by a team of ten chefs made in Hong Kong. This year there is also whole fried quail, soft or crunchy deep-fried morsels with red beans, duck feet in oyster sauce, and provided there are at least ten of you, the eleven-course banquet. Carte: 120F, Menus: 49F + 15% serv., 58F (serv. incl.).

**14**
## Clovis
**14 rue Beaujon**
**563.04.04**
*M. Bonnetot*
*Open until 10:30 P.M. Closed Sat.,*
*Sun., and in August.*
*AE, DC, V.*

The new team which has taken over Clovis' slightly faltering affairs comes from the hotel Frantel at Orly. Monsieur Bonnetot, who now manages this great, modern dining room decorated with greenery and a metallic ceiling, has great authority. Both the reception and the service are once again perfect. His chef, Pierre Larapide, is returning Clovis to the circuit of the good Paris hotel restaurants, following several years of uncertainty. Formerly a supervisory chef for the Hilton chain, where he was put in charge of installing nouvelle cuisine, this virtuoso performer appears to us to have to beware of his inclination toward dishes which are too complicated or too close to unnecessary virtuosity. He definitely succeeds in avoiding a confusion of flavors in the most sophisticated dishes—such as the cassoulet of poached eggs with haddock in puff pastry accompanied by spinach with pears and kelp butter, or the gigotin of lotte with shellfish served with exquisite hollandaise sauce flavored

with green peppercorns. However, even he cannot rescue from the commonplace the veal fillet stuffed with prosciutto, nor avoid the dangerous over-elaboration of a bavarois in Alsatian wine. These temptations are not so strong in the section of the menu which recognizes modestly priced dishes, where we recently discovered a very fine baked cauliflower custard over artichoke hearts and a delicious heart of fillet au gros sel cooked à la ficelle. An interesting businessman's lunch menu and an excellent wine list.
Carte: 220F–250F. Menu: 145F ( serv. incl. ).

## 12/20
### Colisée Pagode
**22 rue du Colisée**
**359.43.09**
*M. Chan Tak Ping*
*Open until 11:00 P.M. Closed at luncheon Sat. and Sun. Pay parking.*
*V.*

An increasingly gallicized version of Chinese cuisine. There is hot scallop pâté, portefeuille of oysters with asparagus, fresh Tan Dinh noodles, and braised veal with Ginko nuts. The cuisine of this pagoda is decent and reliable, which serves as a substitute for genius, and invites us to take a charming stroll into the Far East. Pleasant decor.
Carte: 100F, Menu: 29F + 15% serv.

## 13
### Copenhague et Flora Danica
**142 Champs-Elysées**
**359.20.41**
*M. Engström et M. Tönnesen*
*Open until 10:30 P.M. Closed Sat. at lunch in summer, Sun., holidays and during August (Copenhague).*
*All major credit cards.*

The Flora Danica—a small dining room decorated in blue tile, with an attractive patio far from the rumble of the avenue—and the Copenhague—the large restaurant on the second floor with a marvelously comfortable though a bit somber decor—are the Parisian branches of the Plaza in Copenhagen. In the former you take lunch, snacks, and tea ( smörgasbord, smoked eels, plat du jour, good pastries ), and go upstairs to dine upon the elegant cuisine of Chef Guillot, trained in France and in the intricacies of Danish cooking at the above-mentioned Plaza. Choose from among its fifteen varieties of salmon ( marvelously tasty when grilled on one side only, in the purest "unilateral" fashion) without forgetting an abundance of other plates with a strangely exotic sweet and sour quality: the saddle of reindeer with a ragoût of turnips, presalted duck with mousseline of leeks, fish marinated in beer. Polished service and high prices.
Carte: 180F. Menu ( in Flora Danica ): 85F + 15% serv.

## 16
### Le Crillon
**10 place de la Concorde**
**296.10.81**
*M. Roche*
*Open until 10:30 P.M.*
*AE, DC, V.*

Thanks to the determination of its director, Philippe Roche, and the skill of its remarkably gifted chef, Jean-Paul Bonin, the venerable Crillon grill has become one of the best tables in Paris. And one of the most elegant as well, since the restaurant, taking leave of the old grill, moved into the sumptuous Ambassador Room whose windows overlook the place de la Concorde. The choices vary too often for us to cite them with accuracy, but it is

impossible to forget a fabulous soup of rock fish with a fillet of red mullet, turbot covered with a marvelous saffron sauce, duck with preserved turnips and a wonderful sauce with sherry, truffled poularde in a sabayon of carrots, and some of the most delicious desserts in Paris, prepared by Jean-Claude Allard. Jean-Claude Maître, whom we first met at Lucas-Carton and later at Maxim's, is putting together an extensive cellar. You can have complete confidence in his guidance; he is a charming and intelligent young man who will immediately find the bottle to suit you.
Carte: about 250F. Menu: 250F (wine and serv. incl.).

15 ⟨⟩
## La Dariole de Paris
**49 rue du Colisée**
**225.66.76**
*M. Drouelle*
*Closed Sat. (at lunch), Sun. and holidays.*

A new two-toque restaurant, on the Champs. We gave it one toque in the *Guide de France*, 1981, saying, "Let's wait and see." Well, now we've seen, and Gilbert Drouelle, who opened the Dariole de Paris only last year, deserves two of them today. Here is a charming little second-floor restaurant, decorated with taste in an early nineteenth-century style; once you've been there, you'll want to be a regular. There is no bravado, no creative delirium in the cuisine; just the opposite: it is precise with taste and personality, both traditional and modern at the same time and without ever plagiarizing other chefs. Gilbert Drouelle is an enormous moustachioed man who trained in the U.S. before returning to the P.L.M. Hotel in Paris, then opened his own restaurant in Viry-Châtillon (run at present by his wife). He possesses that particular gift of turning the simplest dish into a feast by a precise blending of ingredients that produces a sauce that neither dominates the food nor is dominated by it. Like us, Gilbert Drouelle is crazy about tripe, brains, trotters, and other such parts that are sometimes held in contempt by those who consider them too heavy. He treats these in such a way as to render calf's trotters ravigotés en lanières, a dariole of brain or pigs' trotters with white of chicken so light as to disprove this notion. But if you do not share this passion, don't fret; on the menu each day there is a selection of fish so fresh they are still breathing, and among the meats you will find something to please you: fried loin of veal with pepper, a fricassée of lamb with sorrel, or fillet of beef sautéed with its juices. And some excellent desserts, such as the chestnut charlotte or a chilled cake with pears.
Carte: 160F–200F.

11/20
## Drugstore des Champs-Elysées

In tacky surroundings and a deluge of decibels, you are making a pilgrimage to the grandaddy of all Parisian drugstores. Do not be too severe in your judgment; after all, the Drugstore serves a purpose. Perhaps you will drop in after the movies to down a few oysters, beautifully

**133 Champs-Elysées**
**723.54.34**
*M. Silvere*
*Open until 1:30 A.M.*
*AE, DC, V.*

opened, before attacking a good grilled steak; cross your fingers that the french fries are properly cooked, for sometimes they are not. And if the children are with you, watch their eyes pop when the strawberry sundaes or the Coca-Cola floats are set before them: mountains of ice cream with a little flag at the summit.
Carte: 100F.

**12/20**
# Le Drugstorien
**(Drugstore Matignon)**
**1 ave. Matignon**
**359.38.70**
*M. Guivarch*
*Open until 1:30 A.M.*
*Pay parking.*
*AE, DC, V.*

The cuisine adopted by the Drugstorien, in a decor all shiny and bright, long ago abandoned the sandwiches dripping with mayonnaise and the horsemeat hamburgers. It is now an agreeable, classic and, on the whole, successful cuisine, offering calf's head ravigote, scallops en papillote, saddle of young rabbit with herbed butter, and an attractive, really fresh grilled sole. In short, it is a true restaurant, except for the bill which, thanks to an "hors d'oeuvre included" (in the price of the main dish), is fairly low.
Carte: 110F.

**12/20**
# L'Écluse
**64 rue Francois-Ier**
**359.77.09**
*M. Bardawil*
*Open until 1:00 A.M. Closed Sun.*
*Pay parking at George-V. Open terrace.*
*V.*

This is the best news to hit the Champs-Elysées in a long time. Georges Bardawil has opened a little sister to his marvelous Écluse on the quai des Grands-Augustins. Here you'll find the same formula as at the Left Bank restaurant: a genuine old-time bistro where you drink good wines served by the glass to wash down rustic cooking of unsurpassed quality, such as the house foie gras, San Daniele ham, fillets of smoked goose, Roquefort à la cuillère and a chocolate cake like grandmother used to make.
Carte: 70F–100F.

14
# Chez Edgard
**4 rue Marbeuf**
**720.51.15**
*M. Benmussa*
*Open until 1:00 A.M. Closed Sun.*
*Open terrace.*
*AE, DC, V.*

*"Nil novi sub' sole,"* replies M. Paul Benmussa to our questionnaire. We must be forgetting our Latin: recent visits and a study of his menu indicate that there is something new under the Paris sun after all; we have to add a point to his score. Some clever, light, novel dishes are delighting his brilliant (and noisy) clientele: brochette of preserved duck hearts and gizzards, a sautéed lotte with squash, turbot grilled with asparagus, curried duck, and sumptuous pastries. The house rolls smoothly on, and there are still enough politicians and businessmen to fill the charming little dining rooms. Excellent small Bordeaux. An affordable bill.
Carte: about 160F.

13 ☖
## L'Elyséum
**19 rue Bayard**
**723.51.25**
*M. Herbert*
*Open until 11:30 P.M.*
*AE, DC, V.*

Despite the uncertain and already somewhat shabby decor of this new establishment (crowded at lunchtime by our colleagues from Radio Luxembourg) we have only praise for this establishment. The reception is friendly, the service quick, though not silent, and, above all, the chef knows his job. The confit of eggplant and grapes makes a delicious starter; the scallops with endives are worthy of a famous restaurant; the fillet of bar with sea urchin sauce is also perfect; the oeufs à la neige are exquisite. We were only fairly disappointed by one dish—the young rabbit in blanquette with spring vegetables, not as good a choice as it seemed: the meat was dry instead of being moist and tender. In any case, this is one of the excellent and new small restaurants in the Champs-Elysées neighborhood, and among the best value for your money.
Carte: 150F.

13 ☖

## La Fermette Marbeuf
**5 rue Marbeuf**
**720.63.53**
*M. Laurent*
*Open until 11:30 P.M. Open terrace.*
*AE, DC, V.*

A restaurant open on Sundays in the Champs-Elysées area is news enough. But when, in addition, you are offered every day of the week an all-inclusive (service, wine, coffee) menu at 115F with, for example, fresh house foie gras, followed by ham with Chablis, or fillets of rascasse with fresh pasta and basil butter, a Meaux Brie, and, finally, a bitter chocolate cake which melts in your mouth, it is not difficult to reconcile yourself to the neighborhood—especially if you can get a table in the exquisite and authentic 1900s winter garden, hidden at the end of the less attractive rustic dining room. The garden was discovered by the proprietor Jean Laurent entirely by accident as he was renovating the restaurant. A la carte you will spend about 120F–130F for a mousseline of rascasse, lamb's tongue with Sauternes, a dessert, and a half-bottle of good Beaujolais.
Menu (dinner and Sun. only): 115F (wine and serv. incl.).

13 ☖

## Le Fouquet's
**99 Champs-Élysées**
**723.70.60**
*M. Casanova*
*Open until 1:00 A.M. Open terrace.*
*AE, DC, V.*

Pay no attention to the pompous dining rooms on the second floor, the site of a disquieting incident we shall generously overlook. Instead, turn around and go back down to the ground floor, where we enjoyed a completely agreeable and perfectly served meal, consisting of a fondant of eggplant with purée of tomatoes, which wouldn't have suffered from a little more seasoning; a solid domestic pot-au-feu, very smooth with clear-cut flavors (the noix of veal sweetbreads with endives was, on the other hand, overcooked and boring); and delicious little pots of crème au chocolat, of which you can gobble up as many as you like—all for 210F per person, plus 95F for a Crozes-Hermitage—that's no gift. But at least there's the decor, the unblemished service and the illusion (quickly dispelled) that you are going to meet, on this historic ground floor, the most Parisian of Parisians and

the most beautiful women in the world. We'll leave a toque behind, a very small one, because after all we mustn't drive Fouquet's to despair.
Carte: 200F–250F. Menu: 140F (serv. incl.).

**12/20**

### Chez Francis

**7 place de l'Alma**
**720.86.83**
*M. Richard*
*Open until midnight. Open terrace.*
*All major credit cards.*

The decor is ridiculous, the cuisine lamentable, the personnel odious—that was the verdict on Chez Francis before it was closed last year by M. Richard, who decided to start all over again from scratch. Slavik's new setting, spanning everything from Louis XV to 1900 and including dragonflies, is a phenomenal success and plays an important role in this renaissance. But the charms of the terrace to which the interesting clientele has returned, the superb display of oysters, the beautifully simple cuisine (terrine of vegetables, sole with pasta, scallops with ginger) and the honest prices have done the rest. Let us hope the new chef can maintain his high standard.
Carte: about 150F. Menu: 90F (serv. incl.).

**12/20**

### Garnier

**111 rue Saint-Lazare**
**387.50.40**
*M. Menut*
*Open until 12:30 A.M. Closed in*
*August. Pay parking (107, rue*
*St.-Lazare).*
*AE, DC, V.*

Anchored at two cable lengths from the great hall of the Gare Saint-Lazare, this dual-level brasserie is decorated in a nautical style so trite that it borders on bad taste. But this is of absolutely no importance if you come to eat oysters—because it's here that you will find some of the best in Paris. The superb Cadoret No. 4 Belons and those from the Marennes-Oléron beds are all perfectly fresh and open. The same perfection applies to the generous seafood platter which has great variety. But stray no further until you hear differently . . . the fish are generally overcooked. Excellent Loire wines.
Carte: about 170F.

**11/20**

### Germain

**19 rue Jean-Mermoz**
**359.29.24**
*M. Claude*
*Open until 10:30 P.M. Closed Sun.*
*and during August*

Germain, whose name is really Claude, needs no publicity to fill this charming, old-fashioned bistro. With its antique bar, imitation leather settees and a few posters from neighboring galleries, the decor sets you quickly at ease. You can easily understand why the tables are all full when you consider that for 60 francs or so you are served fresh crudités, a good grill or a plat du jour before finishing with damson plum tart. The cuisine is straightforward without any unpleasant surprises.
Carte: about 60F.

**12/20**

### Hippo-potamus

**6 ave.**

This remains the best of a chain of fast-food restaurants, mainly because of the quality of the meat, but also because of the reception and the service. Much attention is paid to detail: popular wines served at exactly the right

**Franklin-Roosevelt**
**225.77.96**
*M. Guignard*
*Open until 1:00 A.M.*
*V.*

temperature, cheese from the same house that supplies Maxim's and Taillevent. From the grill you can choose from sirloin, butcher's choice, slaughterhouse cut, filet mignon—all accompanied by good pommes allumettes. Smiling, rapid service.
Carte: 80F. Menu: 36.50F + 15% serv.

**12/20**
## Impérial Sélect
**23 rue Vignon**
**742.69.14**
*M. Tsai*
*Open until 10:30 P.M. Closed Sun.*
*AE.*

"Satisfaction or your money back"—assures Monsieur Tsai, the owner of this Chinese restaurant where the decor is neither Imperial nor select, but seems rather to have been designed by a conclave of manic depressive Buddhist monks. (Perhaps we've gotten too accustomed to the exotic decors of the Far East.) In short, we would not hesitate to ask for our money back on that basis. However, it's a different story as far as the cuisine is concerned: Chef Hong Bong from Hong Kong does rather well, both in the North Vietnamese and Cantonese style. Just sample his Hanoi soup, his whole bream à la cantonaise, and his butterfly shrimp.
Carte: 90F–100F. Menus: 31F, 50F (serv. incl.).

**13**
## Indra
**10 rue du Cdt-Rivière**
**359.46.40**
*Mme. Gupta*
*Open until 11:00 P.M. Closed Sat.*
*(at lunch) and Sun. Pay parking*
*at 87 rue La Boétie.*
*All major credit cards*

If you've eaten real Indian cooking and thus have a basis for judgment, you will be surprised by the finesse, the quality, and authenticity (a bit less highly seasoned than is usual in French restaurants serving Indian food) of the dishes served in a chill, confused setting. If not, well, you have everything to learn, and this without any help on initiation from the nonetheless charming waiters. Try your luck with a Goa fish with onions and spices, tandoor shrimp, lamb curry, the tandooris (meat or fowl baked in a clay-lined oven), the succulent mixed vegetables, some startling chutneys, or the delicious sweet carrot pastry.
Carte: 130F – 150F. Menu: 59F (serv. incl.).

**12/20**
## Les Jardins d'Edgard
**92 rue La Boétie**
**359.08.20**
*M. Feutré*
*Open until 11:30 P.M. Closed Sat.,*
*Sun. and in August. Pay parking.*
*AE, DC, V.*

Edgard left, the gardens remained. A comfortable and refreshing reminder of the gardens can be found in the pretty little flowery courtyard and in some of the dining rooms in the 1925 or colonial style that Guy-Louis Duboucheron, one of the idols of Paris high society, has been wise enough to retain. In the kitchen, Guy-Louis has installed Alain Velazco, a chef who is loaded with honors and medals, and who is also the boss at the kitchen at the restaurant of his hotel on rue des Beaux-Arts. Compare the two menus, and you will find them extremely similar. Our judgement concerning both cuisines is also similar: very successful cuisine adapted to contemporary taste. You will enjoy tasting the salade de gésiers with confit of vegetables, the émincé de veau with tarragon, and the

duck jambonnette with peppercorns.
Carte: 150F. Menus: 85F and 120F (wine and serv. incl.).

14
## Au Jardin du Printemps
**32 rue de Penthièvre**
**359.32.91**
*M. Tan*
*Open until 11:30 P.M. Closed Sun.*
*and August 8 to 31. Pay parking*
*at the Champs-Elysées.*
*AE, DC, V.*

The Tan family continues its inexorable ascent, enlarging this attractive restaurant, modernizing the decor and wisely choosing to direct the cooking, not toward the classic Chinese, but rather toward a sort of nouvelle Foukien and Tchao-Tchao cuisine . . ." Thus, you find Fou-Hen shrimp, calf's liver with hot sauce, "drunken" chicken, grilled pork spareribs, and brochettes of beef with saté. Fine food and not too expensive, served with the eternal smile. As always, one of Paris's best Chinese restaurants and very much in vogue with sophisticated clientele.
Carte: about 150F.

11/20
## Joseph
**56 rue Pierre-Charron**
**723.41.06**
*M. Rapp*
*Open until 10:30 P.M. Closed Sat.*
*(lunch) and Sun.*
*AE, DC, V.*

The corner frontage retains its ecological parity; green climbing plants cover paintings of greenery, green upon green. And as always there is the slightly out-of-date atmosphere inside, in spite of the major renovations undertaken in the last few years. The cuisine seems to have exactly the same difficulty in breaking away from its old style, based upon the most debatable and costly traditional dishes of French bourgeois cuisine. However, it is gradually modernizing its fare with fresh Scotch salmon cutlet, feuilleté of aiguillettes of duck, and fillet of beef in poivrade. Unfortunately, these efforts are not always convincing.
Carte 180F–200F.

15
## Lamazère
**23 rue de Ponthieu**
**359.66.66**
*M. Lamazère*
*Open until 12:30 A.M. Closed Sun.*
*and July 13 to August 17. No dogs.*
*Pay parking at 25, rue de*
*Ponthieu.*
*All major credit cards.*

Noticing that his clients were avoiding the fixed-price meals (not wanting to look like cheapskates in the eyes of their guests), Roger Lamazère, who has not forgotten his magic, pulled this rabbit out of his hat: At lunch he offers a grand menu of sixteen entrées and 25 main dishes which, with cheese and dessert, comes to 180F. This is an elegant solution, and in any case the diner can ask for the other menu with the heavier prices, if he is interested in allaying his hunger for truffles à la croque; cèpes which he manages to serve "like fresh" year-round; fresh duck liver with grapes which, with his marvelous preserves, his civet of goose with cèpes, his goose heart with morels, and his incomparable cassoulet. This menu makes Lamazère one of the Southwest's most influential ambassadors in Paris. Furthermore, while retaining several popular offerings—lobster gratin, steak with green pepper—Lamazère is at present filling our hearts' desire by restoring to his menu the marvelous Gascony accent that it should never have lost. To conquer us completely,

all that now remains to be done is to offer these fantastic goose tripe such as one eats only in a few establishments in Landes and Gers. Leaving no detail overlooked, he has redecorated the dining room, changing from one that appeared fussy to us, to a more elegant and agreeable setting. And with a simple telephone call you can dine at home on some of the specialties that have made this restaurant glorious.
Carte: 250F–350F. Menu: 180F + 15% serv.

## 12/20
## *Lancaster*
**7 rue de Berri**
**359.90.43**
*M. Sinclair*
*Open until 10:00 P.M. Closed Sat. and Sun. evenings. Pay parking at 6 rue de Berri.*
*AE.*

The small dining room, which opens up into a tiny yard, is decorated in a style which is as conventional as it is patchwork. Yet, it is snug and intimate, which is convenient if you need to discuss secrets of state or of the heart. A former chef from Maxim's offers a menu which is rather small and fairly conventional. This might not be bad because originality is not his strong point (why serve the barbue with a violent pink berry sauce, which kills the taste of the fish?). The remaining items (scallops with saffron, pink and juicy lamb cutlets, reasonable desserts) may not arouse enthusiasm, but would be perfectly acceptable if one didn't have to pay a bill of 200F or more. Under the circumstances, it might be far more sensible to pay just a few francs more and go to Chiberta or to the nearby Taillevent.
Carte: 200F. Menu: 100F + 15% serv.

## 17
## *Lasserre*
**17 ave.**
**Franklin-Roosevelt**
**359.53.43**
*M. Lasserre*
*Open until 10:30 P.M. Closed Sun., Mon. and during August.*
*No dogs.*

Should we pretend that nothing has changed . . . or shall we tell the truth and draw conclusions from it? It is not with a light heart that we take a point away from Lasserre. We have known René Laserre for twenty years and have never missed a chance to celebrate his personal success, his immense organizational talents, and the merits of his cuisine. Last year, it even seemed to us that a new wave of inspiration was beginning to stir the cuisine, which we never faulted for remaining classic. Several experiences since then have left us puzzled; the last one was favorable, we admit, even if our pleasure derived from one dish (admirable marinated salmon with dill) that was not prepared in the kitchen and from another (delicious leg of duck stuffed with mushrooms) that was. This said, we know of at least twenty houses in France where one can eat better than at Lasserre. Is it truly fair, then, under the pretext that it is an institution or that we are fond of René Lasserre, that only one point should separate this cuisine from that of Girardet or of Guérard? Evidently not, for we searched this year in vain for that spark, that little something, which makes the difference between the very good and the sublime.
Carte: 450F–500F.

16

## Laurent
**41 ave. Gabriel**
**225.00.39**
*M. Ehrlich*
*Open until 11:00 P.M. (until midnight in summer). Closed Sat. and Sun. Open terrace. Pianist in evening. No dogs. Attendant parking.*
*AE, DC, V.*

Just after the 1981 elections, when a cold breath was blowing on deluxe restaurants, Edmond Ehrlich, Laurent's director, pulled a wry face, and told us his reservation book had never been so full! To be sure, the sun had been shining and there is no other terrace in the heart of Paris as seductive as that of Laurent. Indeed, this restaurant, whose future was for so long in doubt, is now beginning to reap the fruits of its efforts. If Laurent has once again become a favorite of financiers, politicians and society, it's not solely because of its ravishing nineteenth-century decor or its sumptuous little salons, impeccable service or its exceptional cellar (directed by the master, M. Bourguignon), but also because of the progress of its cuisine. The cooking is at times needlessly fussy; it has not yet quite liberated itself from the constraints of the "grand style." But you will be won over, as we were, by that marvelous salad of lobster prepared at your table, the paillard of wild salmon with sea fennel, the exquisite fried red mullet with a purée of fresh herbs, aiguillettes of duckling with black currants, the lamb chops prepared with thyme blossoms and squash with mint, chocolate fondant with coffee syrup, or the two Laurent soufflés. Carte: 300F–350F. Menus: 200F, 230F, 250F, 290F + 15% serv.

14

## La Ligne
**30 rue Jean-Mermoz**
**225.52.65**
*M. Speyer*
*Open until 11:00 P.M. Closed Sat., Sun. and August 8 to 31.*
*AE, V.*

Jean and Nicole Speyer—he at the stove, she in the downstairs dining room, which is somewhat New Yorkish in its understated elegance—are progressing with an ardor that is not always rewarded. In the evenings they serve charming suppers, and it is easy to forget that their place is only a hundred yards from the Champs-Elysées. Jean Speyer and his lieutenant, Jean-Pierre Beghin (ex-Lenôtre and Troisgros), continually revise their modern and attractive menu, and you will find on it, for example, salad of brain with currants, fricassée of scallops with mushrooms, blanquette of veal sweetbreads with spinach, steamed bass with ginger, aiguillettes of duck with the zest of preserved lemon, and desserts that are always exquisite, all accompanied by some excellent house wines, whose prices, which were always reasonable, have not risen this year. This, in fact, is true also of the prices of dishes, which have miraculously remained steady. Carte: 130F–150F. Menu: 100F (serv. incl.).

15

## Le Lord Gourmand
**9 rue Lord-Byron**
**562.66.06**
*MM. Météry, and Rabaudy*
*Open until 10:30 P.M. Closed Sat., Sun., during August and 1 wk. at*

Although the eating factories just outside the movie houses are packed, Daniel Météry, only a hundred meters away, gazes on empty tables. He has no trouble filling his Lord Gourmand to overflowing at midday, but in the evenings his modern little dining room, tastefully decorated with soft lighting, fresh flowers, and attractive paintings, remains half-empty. As for the cuisine of Daniel

*Christmas.*
*AE.*

Météry, who was a chef at Bocuse, it has assumed a perfect rhythm without relinquishing its personality. Some of the dishes are marvelous, like the gâteau of vegetables with tomato purée, the bavarois of lobster, the fried kidneys with parsley, or the veal sweetbreads with marrow, not to mention some very good desserts (a very tasty warm tart of apples and apricots) or the excellent price-pleasure ratio of the fixed-price meal. Daniel Météry also prepares some dishes to go.
Carte: 190F. Menu: 130F (serv. incl.).

## Lucas-Carton
**9 place de la Madeleine**
**265.22.90**
*Mme Allégrier-Carton*
*Open until 10:00 P.M. Parking at*
*25 place de la Madeleine.*
*All major credit cards.*

Our old readers will surely remember: twenty years ago, in our first Paris guide, we raised this old monument of Parisian "restauration" out of the semi-oblivion into which it had unjustly fallen. At the time, it was endowed with an admirable chef, Mars Soustelle, whose grand, traditional cuisine used to enchant us, and whose merits we would espouse at length to anyone willing to listen. Lucas-Carton again joined the ranks of fashionable restaurants, and, without exaggerating our own role, we were rather proud of this rediscovery. Unfortunately, Soustelle went his way, and the second childhood we cherished showed signs of succumbing to senility. From guide to guide, our frustration was matched only by our disappointment, and finally this year, in the French version of this guide, after a last, badly served, entirely regrettable meal, we chose not to award it any mark at all. Upon which the owner, Mme Allégrier-Carton, thought it best to address us the following letter: "Not being able to tolerate any longer your excessive remarks, which constitute a veritable assault on my establishment and its staff, I hereby forbid you to make in the future any reference whatsoever to the Lucas-Carton, be it only to mention its name. This prohibition being absolute, I will consider myself justified in submitting this matter to the courts should I find that it has been infringed upon in any way, even by a mere allusion in any of your publications." As Mme Allégrier has "forbidden" us to exercise our rights as critics, it seems to us only fair that we should "forbid" her to serve any meals . . . That way, neither side will have any complaints about the other.

## 12/20
## La Maison du Caviar
**21 rue Quentin-Bauchart**
**723.53.43**
*Open until 2:00 A.M.*

Order the Sevruga caviar from Iran in the first flush of enthusiastic hunger . . . then, upon reflection, switch to the creamy herring, which will give your palate just as much pleasure and will be far easier on your pocketbook when the check comes. Nothing as appetizing and light as the salmon (Scottish, Danish, Norwegian) plates, the "smoked plates" (eel, sturgeon, salmon) or the delicious Alaskan crab, cold with mayonnaise or hot with tarragon sauce, served late into the night to an always full house, sometimes brilliant but always very uncomfortably seated. Carte: about 120F without caviar.

**12/20**

## La Maison du Valais
**20 rue Royale**
**260.22.72**
*Mme Le Duc*
*Open until 10:30 P.M. Closed Sun.*
*Pay parking at Concorde ou*
*Madeleine.*
*AE, DC, V.*

This Swiss chalet situated between the church of the Madeleine and the Place de la Concorde is devoted to cementing Franco-Swiss friendship, and obviously feels an obligation to satisfy the majority of its customers who patronize it for this purpose. It therefore serves fillet of perch "rue Royale," raclette, fondue, émincé de veau with morels, Graubündenfleisch, and gâteau du Cervin. But this doesn't mean that the young chef, Pierre Lemerle, is unable to make anything else; for instance, as specials of the day, he offers a well-prepared calf's kidney in Pinot Noir, fillet of barbue with tarragon, or charlotte in fresh mint. The Fendant in pitchers is pleasant, and there are all the Valais wines.
Carte: 150F. Menu: 118F (wine and serv. incl.).

**16**

## Le Marcande
**52 rue Miromesnil**
**265.76.85**
*M. Ferrero*
*Open until 10:30 P.M. Closed Sat.,*
*Sun., holidays and August 7 to 23*
*and December 20 to January 1.*
*Open terrace.*
*AE, DC, V.*

With fabulous cold crayfish—called "Monsieur le Préfet" —a brouillade with girolles, and fillets of red mullet, we had, in the shaded court of the Marcande, one of the most exquisite and balanced meals we have eaten all year. Installed for the last two years in this large and inviting dining room, with white walls and a wooden ceiling that opens onto a flowery patio, Jean-Claude Ferrero is a now happy fellow, and the cuisine reflects his happiness, as if a ray of sunshine had transfigured both of them. It is the spirit of Provence, much more than the traditional recipes, that inspires him: joyous flavors, its subtle seasonings of herbs and spices. The most jaded appetite responds immediately to the warm salad of langoustes with a mixture of olive, walnut and hazelnut oils; to the bouillabaisse with green peas; artichokes with lardoons; fillets of raw daurade with lemon; the sauté of leg of lamb with fresh vegetables; the grilled heads of cèpe with foie gras; and the fried John Dory with melon. Faithful to the marketplace, Ferrero presents each day a dozen entrées and different main dishes; for him, cuisine is a permanent creation which he can transform into a feast. A remarkable choice of wines (what happiness to accompany one's meal with a white Château Rayas, followed by a red Rayas), attentive service, and the warm smile of Mme Ferrero, one of the most charming hostesses in Paris. Carte: about 250F.

**18**

## La Marée
**1 rue Daru**
**227.59.32**
*M. Trompier*
*Open until 10:45 P.M. Closed Sat.,*

No one ever says anything bad about La Marée. In fact, we believe we've never received a letter of complaint from our readers about this restaurant. And God knows they are not reluctant to vent their spleen: the arrogance of this chef; the conceit of another; the culinary disasters they

*Sun., and during August.*
*Attendant parking.*
*AE, DC.*

were subjected to at Pierre's or Paul's; and, of course, the size of the bill anywhere. Lord knows, La Marée and the good Marcel Trompier certainly are not immune to complaints on this last score, but how is it that his clients accept his majestic checks without batting an eye? Perhaps because Trompier is a true commander, always on the bridge, always alert, particularly when it comes to tracking down the finest materials. There's nothing routine in the traditional cooking of Chef Rouillard: the admirable Belon oysters with Champagne; ballotine of eel with lime aspic; the assortment of steamed fish with basil; Scottish salmon with rhubarb; and for dessert notable pastries such as, for example, a millefeuille of red fruit. The service is exemplary, the wine list exceptional. Do not overlook an excellent Muscadet at 65F and a Sancerre at 75F.
Carte: 280F–320F.

### 14
## Marius et Janette
**4 ave. George V**
**723.41.88**
*M. de Saintdo*
*Open until 10:00 P.M. Closed Sun.*
*and during August. Reservations*
*required.*
*V.*

This old establishment, with its post-war decor, enjoys more fame abroad than it does in Paris. This is unfair, since under the superb management of M. de Saintdo, it offers the fish and seafood lover one of the best selections in France. Just one piece of advice: ask specially for the cooking time to be short; then you will discover that traditional cooking has its merits, whether it concerns the deep-fried baby squid and rougets, plain poached turbot, sole meunière, bourride, bouillabaisse or aïlloli. Make reservations, the place is always full. Remarkable Chablis and a big check.
Carte: 200F–250F.

### 11/20
## Martin Alma
**44 rue Jean-Goujon**
**359.28.25**
*M. Boullenger*
*Open until 10:15 P.M. Closed Sun.*
*evenings, Mon. and during August.*

Very old, pre-war decor as untypically North African as possible. Any exotica is strictly gastronomical. The fare is modest but decent: Moroccan pastilla, baby squid Oran-style, lamb or chicken couscous, kebobs. Delightful service.
Carte: 120F.

### 16
## Maxim's
**3 rue Royale**
**265.27.94**
*M. Vaudable*
*Open until 1:00 A.M. Closed Sun.*
*AE, DC, V.*

Take away the magic of the fin-de-siècle decor, the shivers at recognizing well-known faces, the ethereal ballet of the maîtres d'hôtel, the great Champagnes, and the memories of legends from this bastion of the Belle Époque . . . and what have you got? Astronomical bills ($80–100 a head at least) for a meal surpassed by dozens of other restaurants in France where the past ten years have seen an explosion of culinary talents and ideas. You will eat far better at Taillevent or l'Archestrate—but does one truly go to eat at Maxim's? Evidently not. One goes here as one goes on a pilgrimage, to a shrine that reflects an extravagant past and an inimitable epoch—in the hope, perhaps of meeting the

ghost of the turn-of-the-century gallant who, to celebrate his birthday, was served on a silver platter a beautiful woman au naturel; or that of another who buried his bachelorhood by drinking Champagne in a coffin. Maxim's is perhaps the last restaurant in the world where one dines among dreams and phantasmagoria. In any case, it is the only restaurant in Paris to which no woman will refuse an invitation. In the old days it was Albert, a kind of stout high-priest and despot who received guests and, with an almost imperceptible expression sized up and categorized each new arrival. Roger, who superseded him, was no less haughty and quickly consigned the unknown to the least desirable tables, the best tables being the settee to the right of the entrance to the large dining room; at the rear, beneath the incomparable glass roof; or, better yet, to the left where, from Edward VII to Onassis and La Callas to Princess Grace of Monaco, the world's best-known celebrities have had the privilege of placing their august bottoms. The service around you is constant and so well disciplined that you do not even notice it, especially since your eyes are so busy devouring the neighboring tables. The scenery is such, in fact, that you probably also do not notice that the table linen is not of the best quality or that the alcohol burners of the chafing dishes emit a nauseating odor. Avoid the over-elaborate plates. Order, rather, smoked salmon or caviar, lobster à la nage (it is always marvelous); let the Champagne take hold of you, distribute hundred-franc bills to the orchestra (which has the remarkable talent of rendering rock as if it were a Viennese waltz); and tell yourself that you are having the greatest evening of your life. It is almost true. But avoid Saturday evenings; fashionable types will assure you that they let just anyone in on Saturdays. Even though it is not necessary to dress for them, Tuesday and Wednesday evenings are the most elegant. And for some time now lunches have been served in the Omnibus, a kind of winter garden that is closed in the evening; the cream of the business world and also some attractive women gather there.
Carte: about 400F.

## 10/20
### *Mignonnette du Caviar*
**13 rue du Colisée**
**225.30.35**
*Mme Polkonikoff*
*Open until 11:00 P.M. Closed Sat. (at lunch), Sun. and July 13 to beginning of September.*

Just the place for a nice little dinner composed mainly of piroshki, borscht and blinis with cream, Baltic herring, and hot apple tart. In the evenings the owner lights candles on the tables, and one's meal is accompanied by gypsy violins (on tape): This is the moment to resist ordering caviar and Polish vodka, which will do no good at all to the wallet. An insignificant Paris-Isba decor.
Carte: 80F.

## 14
### *Napoléon*
**38 ave. de Friedland**

Under the régime of Guy-Pierre Baumann, choucroute reigns supreme. Whether in Les Halles, or at Ternes or at

**227.99.50**

*M. Baumann*
*Open until 10:00 P.M.*
*All major credit cards.*

the Étoile, choucroute serves as the bed for confits, oxtail, guinea fowl, fish, and even for the oysters. This, quite coincidentally, makes the fortune of the Alsatian who invented a stainless steel washing machine for the choucroute, which is the whole secret of its incomparable quality. At any rate, for the clients in this elegant Napoleonic setting, who do not wish to stuff themselves on this vegetable, Baumann has encouraged Chef Philippe Vallée to develop some original recipes gleaned from old gourmet cookbooks. These have yielded a potage with herbs Carême, a plaice à la façon d'Alexandre Dumas, a beef mode Pierre de Luna (1656) and thighs of duck Menon (1742). These and other dishes are prepared with a light, sure hand, without needless frills, proving that each century has its own nouvelle cuisine. A very agreeable atmosphere in the evenings.
Carte: 200F.

**10/20**

## Le Pecheur
**27 blvd. des Batignolles**
**387.56.87**
*M. Mondor*
*Open until 9:45 P.M. Closed Sat., Sun. and during August.*

Odette Mondor goes to the market every morning and devises her bill of fare according to availability, the season, and, above all, the good deals which allow her to keep her prices down (or as she says, reasonable). However, certain dishes can always be found on her menu, no matter what the season or the week: haddock in melted butter, the whiting meunière, tongue in vinaigrette, and cold petit salé. The surroundings are pleasantly rose-colored, high-lighted with greenery. Rest assured, this good bourgeois cuisine, served by Monsieur Mondor (Henri to the regulars), will not make you a pauper.
Carte: 80F.

16

## Au Petit Mont- morency
**5 rue Rabelais**
**225.11.19**
*M. Bouché*
*Open until 10:00 P.M. Closed Sat., Sun. and during August. No dogs.*
*V.*

Daniel Bouché's talents include an ingenuity and grace far removed from that "restaurant cuisine" of which you grow tired so quickly. In his cooking, virtuosity never masks the authenticity of tastes. One appreciates this in dining at the Petit Montmorency, only a short distance from the Rond-Point, a small restaurant in his own image, which is to say without flashiness, and without false notes. Here, among the utensils of the old kitchen, the etchings, the bistro tables,the untiring smile of his wife Nicole, he serves his latest creations, too numerous to list completely: roast lotte with cream and bacon, stuffed lettuce with wild rice; tuna bouillabaisse with young vegetables; rabbit with sea urchins; or chicken with tarragon cream and spaghetti with lobster purée sauce, to name only a few of the most recent. But we should also mention among our favorites the stalwarts of the menu, notably veal with pasta, truffles and duck foie gras, a daube with beef bream, navarin printanier, admirable pot-au-feu with three meats, a warm seafood platter, caramelized ice cream with honey, Chinese tea-flavored

ice cream, and the chaud-froid of cheeses.
Carte: 180F–250F.

**12/20**

## La Poularde Landaise

**4 rue Saint-Philippe-du-Roule**
**359.20.25**
Mme Herbomel
Open until 10:30 P.M. Closed Sat.,
Sun. and holidays.
AE, V.

At lunch it is always overcrowded, and rather deserted in the evening. A pity, because that is just the time when charming Mme Herbomel lights the fire in the hearth, and that's when it is really most comfortable to take one's ease in these rustic but intimate surroundings. There is even a special, inexpensive menu to reward those shrewd enough to brave the nocturnal isolation of rue St.-Philippe-du-Roule, because they enjoy easy parking and a calm atmosphere in which to enjoy the unpretentious, reliable cuisine inspired by the Southwest of France: rillettes of goose, eggplant caviar, magret of duck, escargots simmered in butter. Good wines from the same region (Madiran, Cahors), and delightful feminine service. Carte: 160F–180F. Menus: 90F (incl. serv.) 120F (eves., incl. aperitif, wine and coffee).

**12/20**

## La Poêle d'Or

**37 rue de Miromesnil**
**265.78.60**
Mme Pettinati
Closed Sat. and Sun.
V.

An appealing little pillar of traditional cuisine. You have to jostle for a table there at lunchtime every day, but you're sure to be greeted with a smile, served gently, and have your plate filled with excellent products carefully prepared: a trolley of hors d'oeuvres without much originality but magnificently fresh, a nice leg of lamb cooked just right, and some delicious old-fashioned desserts. Wines by the pitcher at reasonable prices. Carte: 180F.

**13**

## Les Princes

**31 ave. George-V**
**723.54.00**
M. Falcucci
Open until 11:00 P.M. Open
terrace. Pay parking.
All major credit cards.

Thirty or so years ago Chef Carrat prepared dinners for princes in this restaurant, which is dedicated to their memory. To say that the cuisine has not evolved since then would be misleading. You'll find the lightest of sauces, the most audacious preparations, the marriage of the most adventurous tastes in certain dishes on this long, prewar-style menu; for example, bouchée of skate with an herbed salad; raw salmon with two peppers; Challans duck, lightly cooked and served with delicious new turnips. But for the rest, only dated dishes. This does not prevent our liking the large, well-lit and comfortable dining room or, even more, the interior garden where, in fine weather, one dines among the flowers and the fountains, and the bubbling good humor with which M. Frison, the director, receives his clients and watches over their needs.
Carte: 300F-plus.

**13**

## Régence-Plaza

**25, ave. Montaigne**
**723.78.33**
M. Cozzo
Open until 10:15 P.M. Open
terrace. No dogs. Attendant

Although the prices go up, no one here really cares, and the cuisine continues to awe the South Americans and emirs on holiday. There's the mousseline of scampi with caviar; the veal sweetbreads with tarragon quenelles; the sole Reine Astrid; and always the exquisite aiguillette baronne in aspic. The dining room in Regency paneling can stand up to any clientele, as can the marvelous flowery

*parking.*
*DC, EC.*

## 10/20
### Relais Boccador
**20 rue du Boccador**
**723.31.98**
*M. Nicolo*
*Open until 10:30 P.M.*
*AE.*

## 12/20
### Relais-Plaza
**21 ave. Montaigne**
**723.46.36**
*M. Cozzo*
*Open until 1:00 A.M. Closed during August. No large dogs. Attendant parking.*
*AE, DC, EC.*

## 11/20
### Le Righi (Aux Trois Frères)
**11 rue de la Trémoille**
**723.37.32**
*Messieurs Righi*
*Open until 10:45 P.M. Closed Sat. and during August.*
*DC, V.*

## 11/20
### La Rose des Sables
**19 rue Washington**
**563.36.73**
*M. Tessier*
*Open until 11:00 P.M. Closed Sun. and during August.*

## 14
### Royal Monceau
**35 ave. Hoche**
**561.98.00**
*M. Serre*
*Open until 10:00 P.M.*
*AE, DC, V.*

patio where one dines in the summer.
Carte: about 350F.

You might wonder why this small restaurant has been consistently crowded for the past three years. It's very simple: the owner, Mario, has worked for a Parisian name who sends his friends to him. They may not all be exacting gourmets, but they mainly enjoy meeting their pals in the neighborhood, and then spending only 100F or so (including a carafe of Italian red wine)—even if the carpaccio is poorly seasoned, the meats rather commonplace, and the lemon tarte lacking in finesse. (Good fresh pasta and delicious chocolate gâteau).
Carte: about 100F.

No one but the modish here in this air-conditioned, circa 1930 ocean liner decor, where, at any time between 11:00 P.M. and 1:30 A.M. one is allowed to nibble such fare as a gratin of John Dory with spinach, a cold charlotte with eggplant, an escalope of salmon with mint, all for the insignificant sum of 200F. Even so, it is one of the rare and at the same time elegant places where one can take supper after the theater (Studio or Comédie).
Carte: 150F–250F.

The three Righi brothers immigrated 31 years ago to open this corner restaurant which has become the unofficial embassy of the powerful republic of San Marino. The brothers continue to sing the praises of their little homeland, as well as of the large country which surrounds it, in the form of innumerable kinds of fresh pasta., porchetta, Sicilian eggplant, and the potée of cabbage (in winter only). As soon as the warm weather comes, try to reserve a sidewalk table on rue de la Renaissance. It's much more fun, no more expensive than inside, and a lot less cramped.
Carte: 100F–120F.

Although the establishment was redecorated a couple of years ago, it still refelects the taste of those who like it . . . Personally, we prefer the cuisine offered by Hamed Mernissi, who for sixteen years has been in the service of the owner, Roger Tessier (a former bodyguard for General De Gaulle). He is also in the service of pastilla, tajines, sweet couscous with raisins, and the whole range of Moroccan cuisine which he used to practice at the Mamounia Hotel in Marrakesh.
Carte: 100F–120F.

It's important to keep you up to date with the Royal Monceau, so you are aware that marvelously varied English business breakfasts are served each morning; that Sunday is the day for the buffet brunch; that Thursday evening is the day for the fisherman's buffet, where you can eat raw or smoked oysters, shellfish and fish to your

heart's content; and finally that every midday for the fashionable clientele of brokers and politicians from the Champs-Élysées, the extraordinary "garlands of the royal buffet," is offered, comprising about 60 hot and cold hors d'oeuvres, a choice of dishes (grills, tendron of veal with prunes), cheeses, and a wide variety of desserts and attractive wines by the pitcher (Gamay) or the bottle (Bordeaux, white Bergerac). To this is added the charm of the garden-patio beneath its striped canopy, with its cheerful Asian service; there one immediately forgets the great columned dining room with its ruinous prices where, however, are served some very attractive, modern and light dishes: fillet of veal with sorrel, Barbary duck in green sauce.
Carte: 250F–300F. Menu (buffet): 175F.

**12/20**

## Le Saint-Germain
**74 Champs-Elysées**
**563.55.45**
*M. Hasegawa*
*Open until 10:15 P.M. Closed Sat. and Sun. Pay parking at 60 rue de Ponthieu.*
*AE, DC, V.*

Located near the escalator on the lower floor of the Claridge complex, the Saint-Germain looks as though it were put in the corner as a punishment. And yet, its cuisine is one of the most interesting by comparison with those served in the shopping center in the same area. The chef, formerly with Jamin and Gérard Besson, prepares a very skillful sauté of veal, skate à la bohémienne (with an excellent, well-flavored sauce), barbue in cream of celery, and a pleasant fricassée of young rabbit with spring vegetables. On the whole, this is a good establishment, which has avoided the surrounding vulgarity, where one is not served carelessly, and where the value for the money is excellent. The pale pink decor with green plants is attractive, and the tables are comfortable.
Carte: 150F. Menus: 80F, 100F (wine and serv. incl.).

**11/20**

## La Saladière
**77 rue La Boétie**
**723.56.18**
*M. de Beaurepaire*
*Open until 11:15 P.M. Open terrace. Pay parking at 87 rue La Boétie.*
*V.*

Tarzan lived in the jungle and ate roots and vines. He stayed young lithe, and muscular. Do as Tarzan did while lunching at the Saladière, with its bamboo seats, palms on the walls and ceilings on a beige background, green plants, and pink lights. If there were a fan suspended from the ceiling you could easily imagine yourself in St. Louis (Missouri or Senegal). The Saladière offers six salads; they are fresh, crispy, bursting with sunshine, and not too expensive (for example, the Riveraine: fillet of lotte, broccoli, curly lettuce, tomato, and mayonnaise for 30F). Afterwards, you will be just hungry enough for a dessert (tartes and charlottes). Like Tarzan, you will skip the main dishes (rabbit with a few mushrooms and a slightly bitter sauce). About 100F at most with a friendly little country wine.
Carte: 80F–100F. Menu: 49F (wine and serv. incl.).

**13**

## Savy
**23 rue Bayard**
**723.46.98**
*M. Savy*

Monday, navarin of lamb; Tuesday, stuffed cabbage; Wednesday, knuckle of ham with lentils; Thursday, blanquette of veal; Friday, calf's brains, grenobloise. And there is the whole week wrapped up in a neat package.

*Open until 11:00 P.M. Closed Sat., Sun. and during August.*

Yes, but you have not tasted the divine calf's liver with a purée of green peas or the shoulder of roast lamb. Well, if the jostle of the midday crowd (the Radio Luxembourg studios are just across the street) is too much for you, come in the evening when a provincial calm reigns at Savy's.
Carte: 150F.

## 13
## Le Séoul
**13, rue Montalivet**
**266.14.10**
*Mme Kang*
*Open until 10:00 P.M. Closed Sat. (at lunch), Sun. and during August.*
*AE, DC.*

One of us lives only a few steps from this charming Korean restaurant and practically has a napkin-ring waiting for him. There are beautiful raw daurade, fried shrimp, breaded squash, warm tripe à l'orange, caramelized chicken, and a multitude of attractive salted vegetables. You are received by a sort of princess in a billowy sequined robe. You can begin immediately on the koujolpan (delicate hors d'oeuvres), the boulgogui (marinated meats) and all the mysterious dishes offered from a cuisine that is a cross between Chinese and Japanese. Service is friendly and energetic. Good little Rully white, and Saint-Emilion.

## 10/20
## Show Gourmet
**66 Champs-Elysées**
**225.75.79**
*M. Teyssendiè*
*Open until midnight. Closed Sun. Pay parking at 49 rue de Ponthieu. DC, V.*

A somewhat futuristic decor extending over two levels, impossibly overcrowded at lunchtime, but quieter in the evening. The owner is a nice guy from the region of Lot who was formerly with the Western in the Hilton Hotel. The menu has some amusing starters, such as the vegetable terrine with bell pepper purée, which precede the classic broiled meats which are far too heavily herbed. A few cheeses, including warm goat cheese on toast with curly endive salad. Nice selection of pastries and delectable ices. In fact, the worst showing of the Show Gourmet comes from an appalling Côtes du Rhône and a "Parisian" Cahors which is hardly better.
Carte: 90F. Menus: 19.50F (incl. serv.), 29.95F, 34.50F + 15% serv.

## 11/20
## Soma
**10 rue du Cdt-Rivière**
**359.46.40**
*Mme Gupta*
*Lunch only. Closed Sat. and Sun. Pay parking at 87 rue La Boétie.*

Open only at lunchtime, this Indian snack bar is actually an annex of its prestigious neighbor, the Indra. The prices at this pleasant little restaurant are so soothing that it has become quite hard to find a seat in the comfortable leather-upholstered booths. If you are successful, you will taste the raitas (vegetable yogurts), pakora (various deep-fried morsels), curry (egg, fish, chicken, etc.), and the disgusting Indian sweets (gulab jamun: rosewater delicacies). Delicious teas.
Carte: 60F. Menu: 35F (serv. incl.).

## 11/20
## Stresa
**7 rue de Chambiges**
**723.51.62**
*M. Mazzucato*
*Open until 9:45 P.M. Closed Sat. evenings, Sun., month of August,*

All is simplicity and peace, in the calm of the most traditional Italian cuisine and the tranquility of the rue de Chambiges, lost somewhere between the Champs-Elysées and the Pont d'Alma. But, to return to practical matters, it must be said that all of the fresh pasta is made à la casa,

*and December 18–January 3.*
*AE, DC.*

with ten fresh eggs per kilogram of flour, and it is very thinly rolled, as it ought to be everywhere. The family Mazzucato will welcome you most charmingly in their ancient modern surroundings.
Carte: 130F.

19

## Taillevent
**15 rue Lamennais**
**563.39.94**
*M. Vrinat*
*Open until 10:30 P.M. Closed Sat.;*
*and Sun. and during August.*
*No large dogs.*

"I prefer salmon with mint to cold salmon with mayonnaise, turbot with a cream of leek to turbot Dugleré . . . and our clients do, too. Even if I were one of the last faithful, I would still cry aloud, 'Vive la nouvelle cuisine!' " Jean-Claude Vrinat, the author of this proclamation of faith, has made his choice once and for all, knowing perfectly well that if Taillevent has become what it is today it is because it was he himself who decided to break with tradition and to give his cuisine a transfusion of new blood. And if we congratulate him unreservedly it is because neither he nor his chef, Claude Deligne, has ever allowed himself to ride a fad. A taste for proportion and a sense of nuance inspire that which might be christened the "new classicism," by which we mean a cuisine always steady, always light, always intelligent. The finesse of the mousse of foies blonds with walnut oil, the warm escalopes of veal sweetbreads en salade, the aiguillettes of bass with lime, the pot-au-feu of Bresse guinea hen, the Barbary duckling in black currant vinegar, the cassolette of lobster with tarragon; the elegance of the woodwork, of the lighting and of the old paintings; the perfection of the reception and of the service; the intelligent choice of wines which, from the humblest (84F to under 100F) to the noblest, are always perfect, make of Taillevent the foremost, the best, the surest of the great Parisian restaurants.
Carte 300F–400F.

## 12/20
## Chez Tante Louise
**41 rue**
**Boissy-d'Anglas**
**265.06.85**
*M. Fiorito*
*Open until 10:30 P.M. Closed Sun.*
*and during August. Pay parking at*
*Madeleine.*
*AE, DC, V.*

Aunt Louise was from Franche-Comté. For over 30 years (until the 60s), she presided over this rather somber decor with its stained glass and wrought iron windows in the art deco style. Her memory lives on in the uninteresting fillets of sole Normande which bear her name, but what a pity that her ghostly influence has not extended to the coq à la Jurassienne, which helped to make her famous. The new owner, Christian Fiorito, fired his chef, and tends the stove himself. Whatever he does, he is truly most successful with the feminine cooking inherited from Aunt Louise (such as the sauté of young rabbit with cèpes, the navarin of milk-fed lamb with thyme) than with dishes from his native Southwest (foie gras, confits). From the little we know about him, he appears to be unquestionably professional, but with a range that is still a bit dull. Good wines.
Carte: 180F.

**12/20**
## Tong Yen
**1 bis rue**
**Jean-Mermoz**
**225.04.23**
*Mme Luong*
*Open until 11:30 P.M. Closed*
*during August.*
*AE, DC, V.*

Tong Yen used to be the Brasserie Lipp of the Far East—the Chinese restaurant favored by Paris high society. It is still one of the most elegant with the most fashionable clientele. And it is one of the few Chinese restaurants where, even if your meal is not staggeringly original, you will never be disappointed. Nor will you be disappointed by the charming welcome extended to you by Paul Luong's daughter, Thérèse, nor by the refined decor and Parisian atmosphere, nor by the scallops in oyster sauce, the barbequed spareribs, or the shrimp saté.
Carte: 130F–150F.

**12/20**
## Les Trois Limousins
**8 rue de Berri**
**562.35.97**
*M. Gamberini*
*Open until 12:30 A.M. Pay parking*
*at 1 rue de Berri.*
*AE, DC, V.*

In spite of a change in ownership, the formula remains the same: You choose your meat course (anything from a civet of beef to the butcher's bourride, including steak tartare and T-bone steak), then, just as in heaven, the rest is provided to you. The rest consists of hors d'oeuvres, salad, cheese, desert, coffee, and wine—as much as you can eat and drink. It is not exactly a giveaway, but you get your money's worth, not only in terms of quantity (almost too much), but also in terms of quality (the meat is quite decent). Besides, the service is always charming.
Menus: 152F, 157F, 160F, 164F, 167F, 175F (wine and serv. incl.).

**12/20**
## Les Trois Moutons
**63 ave.**
**Franklin-Roosevelt**
**225.26.95**
*M. Méric*
*Open until 12:30 A.M. Closed Sun.*
*AE, DC, V.*

The price of the meat you select (and garnish)—épigramme, clou, guidon, slice of lamb; steak, pavé, onglet of beef—determines the price of your meal. You begin with a beautiful starter (assorted crudités, mussel salad), continue with salad and cheese, and finish with sorbet and coffee. The house red is served in a pitcher—as much as you can drink. Extremely busy at lunchtime, but in the evening, you can dine intimately in one of the cozy little rooms.
Menus: 154F, 157F, 165F, 167F, 168F, 175F (wine and serv. incl.).

**11/20**
## Le Verger
**Galerie des Champs-Elysées, 84 Champs-Elysées**
**562.00.10**
*M. Cousinard*
*Open until 10:00 P.M. Closed Sun.*
*V.*

This is the big brother of the Verger in the Forum des Halles. An agreeable decor with a sky-blue ceiling dotted here and there with small white clouds, and with large posters representing quiet pastoral scenes. Charming reception. The meat or fish dish (grilled steak, sautéed rabbit, fillet of bass) determines the price of the meal, and your choice gives you access to the long hors d'oeuvres table where you can serve yourself as you will. Also included is a limited choice of cheeses (of modest quality), a dessert (better) of your choice, and as much wine as you want (in pitchers).
Menus: 49F, 52F, 55F, 58F (wine and serv. incl.).

### 13
## Au Vieux Berlin
**32 ave. George-V**
**720.88.96**
*M. Jimenez*
*Open until 11:00 P.M. Closed Sat.*
*and Sun. Open terrace. AE, DC, V.*

There is no reason not to applaud Jacques Herbaut for his German cuisine. This one-time student of Jacques Manière prepares the classics from across the Rhine with conviction and talent. His knuckle of pork, with sauerkraut as crisp and acid as you could wish is a masterpiece. The sauerkraut imparts an unexpected lightness even to calf's liver à la Berlinoise, to the fillet of pork with beer and cumin, to coq-au-vin with wine from Baden, and to the other heavyweights of German cooking. Instead of eating in the rich and colossally Berlinish decor of the dining room (where you dine to music), you might prefer the simple, rural inn atmosphere of the bar near the entrance, where you will be served by a radiant Fräulein.
Carte: 140F–160F.

### 13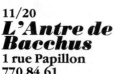
## Chez Vong
**27 rue du Colisée**
**359.77.12**
*M. Vong*
*Open until 11:00 P.M. Closed Sun.*
*Parking at 25 rue de Pontbieu.*
*AE, DC, V.*

While awaiting the opening of his new, larger and more practical restaurant just a few paces from the rue du Colisée, Vong continues in his tranquil Sino-Vietnamese way, although the cuisine is not as original as it once was. The very much deserved success of his sumptuous branch restaurant in Les Halles (rue de la Grande-Truanderie) usurps most of the family's efforts, and this Chez Vong suffers a bit as a result. In any case, the Vietnamese won ton, the steamed chicken, the sautéed abalone with langoustes, the pork with citronella, make a delicious meal.
Carte: 100F–120F. Menu: 60F (serv. incl.).

# 9ème Arr.

### 11/20
## Anarkali
**4 pl.**
**Gustave-Toudouze**
**878.39.84**
*Mme Jilani*
*Dinner only. Open until 12:30*
*A.M. Closed Mon., last 2 weeks in*
*August and during New Year's*
*holidays.*

"We accept only friendly customers," says the owner. If you are unfortunate enough not to fall into this category, you will never know this authentic Punjabi (Northern Indian) cooking, prepared with imagination and subtlety by M. Jilani. It includes tandoori, gobi ghosh (spicy cauliflower and mutton curry), pilau passanda (rice, meats and spices), or moghlaï mutton, with cream, almonds, and herbs. The prices are also friendly on this pleasant, exotic excursion.
Carte: 75F–100F.

### 11/20
## L'Antre de Bacchus
**1 rue Papillon**
**770.84.61**
*M. Lévy*

The drunken little god has entered Philippe Davy's kitchen with a light and delicate touch. He seems to have inspired the delicious escargots in Chablis and fine creamy white wine sauce which accompanies the bavette with écrevisses—a dish which for the past four years has

*Open until 10:00 P.M. Closed Sun. and July 14 to August 15.*
*AE, DC, V.*

been the star attraction on the menu of this intimate and comfortable establishment. We are promised more fish this year, but all of this seems a little too pat. If the likeable owner, Robert Lévy, who worships the client-god, were to take some advice and broaden his repertoire one of these days, it wouldn't hurt our feelings a bit.
Carte: 150F. Menu: 44F (serv. incl.).

14

## *Auberge Landaise*
**23 rue Clauzel**
**878.74.40**
*M. Morin*
*Open until 9:45 P.M. Closed Sun., holidays and during August.*
*Pay parking.*
*V, DC.*

It's not exactly cheerful, this long, neo-rustic corridor that serves as a dining room, with its artificial beams, simulated brick partitions, hick accessories and it's bric-a-brac atmosphere. What a shame! The patronne's welcome is so friendly, the service so alert and agreeable, and the Landes-style cuisine of Chef-Owner Dominique Morin so frank and generous. The thigh of duck with cèpes; the fillet of duck with pepper; the extraordinary thick calf's liver cooked pink and served with exquisite potatoes à cru; the great plate of Landais charcuterie; and the Herculean winter cassoulet, compose several of the sturdiest meals one can find in Paris. Wines include an excellent Cahors. Never a free table, lunch or dinner. Desserts on the whole disappointing.
Carte: 170F.

## 11/20
## *Charlot (Le Roi des Coquillages)*
**81 blvd. de Clichy**
**874.49.64**
*M. Cornic*
*Open until 1:00 A.M. Closed during June, July and August. Pay parking at 11 rue Forest.*
*AE, DC, V.*

There is a happy man who now rules the two Charlot's. (The second is the Merveille des Mers, located nearly opposite.) That happy man is Christian Cornic. So there will be no more fraticidal quarrels, no power struggles, only peaceful waters floating with the most soothing cuisine to be eaten in cozy booths. There are gratin of oysters with Champagne, pike terrine with fillets of turbot, fillets of sole in cider with apples. A wide selection of beautiful seafood.
Carte: 200F and over. Menu: 120F + 15% serv.

## 10/20
## *Chartier*
**7 rue du faubourg Montmartre**
**770.86.29**
*M. Lemaire*
*Open until 9:30 P.M.*

Chartier is definitely one of the last of the cheap Parisian cafés and it has retained its touching century-old decor intact. Last year, we spent 21F including service on a red cabbage salad, roast chicken with french fries, fruit tartlet, a little carafe of red wine, and one espresso. And since we are still alive, we must conclude that, in this age of bills that go out of sight (even in a local café you will easily spend more than 40F for a hasty bite), it is still possible to feed Parisians decently for a derisory sum of money. True, the good Monsieur Lemaire, who owns this institution among cheap restaurants and serves 2,000 meals a day in the rue du fg-Montmartre, and almost as many in the two branches, raises his prices by 6%–7% a year (compared with 15% at the best restaurants). He confesses that he is

happy with "just the crumbs," but a lot of "crumbs" make for a very profitable business. Needless to say, this is not Taillevent, nor even the little local restaurant which you usually frequent. Here you are eating elbow to elbow and swallow each mouthful at top speed so as to free the table for others. But a full-course meal for 25F is something of a feat.
Carte: 25F–30F.

**12/20**

### Chez Chichois

**65 rue de Douai**
**874.80.87**
*M. Chichois*
*Open until 10:30 P.M. Closed Mon. and during July and August.*

Sprightly, vociferous Albert Chiche, nicknamed Chichois, also known as the king of Kémia, is entering his 34th year at the couscous steamer. He is 71 years old, and would not trust anyone else with making his couscous, paella, poisson à l'orientale. Good, rich, homemade deserts round off these generous feasts in a delightful Hispano-Moresque setting.
Carte: 120F.

**12/20**

### La Cloche d'Or

**3 rue Mansart**
**874.48.88**
*Mme Bohbot*
*Open until 3:00 A.M. Closed Sun. Parking at 5 rue Mansart.*
*AE, DC, V.*

For many years, this bell has been ringing through Montmartre around midnight, calling the hungry showbiz people to table. This institution owes everything to the kind Monsieur Marc, who retired two years ago (to go into real estate—don't worry, he's fine). He left the walls covered with photos dedicated to him by the stars (you may well see some of the originals there—older perhaps, but still recognizable). Mme Bohbot has taken a lot of trouble to make it a smooth transition. She has been rewarded by the confidence which all the regular patrons have shown in her. She has done nothing to change the charming, out-dated decor or the immutable selection of dishes. However, the other night we had an experience which, while it does not justify tolling the bell, should at least set off an alarm: a salad of museau of beef, carelessly prepared and badly seasoned; a peculiarly boned and rolled leg of lamb with insipid, undercooked flagolets, and a rather miserable cheese platter. The Beaujolais is still fresh and the service very pleasant.
Carte: 160F. Menus: 69F (at lunchtime). 100F (dinner, wine incl.) + 15% serv.

**12/20**

### Les Diaman-taires

**60 rue La Fayette**
**770.78.14**
*M. Calogirou*
*Open until 10:00 P.M. Closed Mon. evening, Tues. and during August.*

Not many diamond cutters (this is their quarter), but lots of Greeks and Middle Easterners gather in this Spartan canteen of Papa Calogirou. It is Papa himself who puts together the flaky pies with cheese or spinach, the tarama, the stuffed vine leaves. And nothing in his restaurant smacks of the vulgar aggressiveness of the food usually dished out in the ethnic Greek bistros of Paris. Be sure to taste the delicious babaganoutch (eggplant confection), the moussaka (a gratin of eggplant filled with meat), the

keftes (meatballs) and the delicious homemade yogurt while sipping, for example, a nice little red Castello from Crete.
Carte: 100F.

### 13
## Ducs de Bourgogne
**2 place d'Anvers**
**878.35.21**
*M. Mariel*
*Open until 10:00 P.M. Closed Sun.*
*Pay parking.*
*All major credit cards.*

Beneath the beams and the hunting trophies of this warm family restaurant floats the hearty essence of the Burgundian cuisine (coq au vin, eggs en meurette with morels, jambon persillé, tournedos mâconnaise) and some other elaborate dishes in the traditional repertory (a pair of quail with morels and cream, soufflé of young turbot, Beaugé calf's kidneys). But Michel Mariel is not bound by classical culinary dogma; he and Chef Luc Lescot have perfected several less conventional dishes, such as oysters gratinéed au gros-plant served on a bed of mousse of cèpes, a grenadin of tuna with saffron, or rump of rabbit in a cream with basil. These with the others are testimony to their informed search for the freshest produce—all of which comes very dear, especially when the diner succumbs to the temptations of a considerable cellar of fine Burgundies.
Carte: 220F. Menu: 100F, 180F (wine incl.). + 15% serv.

### 12/20
## L'Echiquier
**48 rue Saint-Georges**
**878.46.09**
*M. Pose*
*Open until midnight. Closed Sat.*
*and Sun. (at lunch) and Mon.*
*DC, V.*

Has Patrick Pose's minor success (with which we may have had something to do) gone to his head? We would be sorry if it were so; we had hoped that this good establishment, where the prices are still so reasonable, would continue to welcome its customers good-humoredly and offer them consistent cuisine. But this does not seem to have been the case for some time. Let's not overdramatize though: Patrick Pose is a good cook who likes to choose the best ingredients and to use them elegantly, accordingly to his mood and the season. Among the offerings are barquette of herring, salsify tart, potée of conger, pork with leeks and good patisserie.
Carte: 130F approx. Menu: 62F (serv. incl.).

### 11/20
## Au Gîte d'Armor
**15 rue Le Peletier**
**770.66.25**
*M. Przybyl*
*Open until 10:00 P.M. Closed Sat.,*
*Sun. and August 15–30. Pay*
*parking at rue Drouot.*
*V.*

The seemingly conflicting themes of the menu can be explained by the fact that the owner is a Celt from Brittany, while his wife is also Celtic, but from the Southwest. On the Brittany side, you will find fish and seafood (lisette in Sauvignon, barbue in cider, cockles, smelts, haddock) and the Southwestern side is represented by cassoulets, foie gras and stuffed cabbage. And there is no reason to complain, because in both cases, the cuisine is careful and unpretentious. To round off the meal, there is a good and original selection of homemade deserts, such as charlottes, douillons (or bourdelots), strüdel and pear gratin. The English-style decor is as pleasant as the patronne's welcome.
Carte: 120F.

**12/20**

## Le Grand Café
**4 blvd. des Capucines**
**742.75.77**
*M. Blanc*
*Open 24 hours, year round. Pay*
*parking at 2 rue Meyerbeer.*
*AE, DC, V.*

This Grand Café is open day and night to all of the sounds which echo from the old boulevard life of Paris. Along with l'Alsace of the Champs-Elysées and the Pied de Cochon of the Halles, it belongs to the great Blanc family of restaurateurs who also own the Boucheries Blanc. It could also be taken for a branch of the high seas, by the abundant and vast variety of cooked and raw shellfish, arranged on a refrigerated display (oysters all year round). There is also fresh seafood-stuffed pasta, the grilled bream with beurre blanc, grilled langouste or lobster from the salt-water vivarium. All this is of the best. Less good are the dishes flambéed in whisky or anise, the trout with almonds, etc. The wine list is exceptional, and the decor may be a little bit on the heavy side with all its allusions to the tradition of the old boulevard-cafés.
Carte: 150F. Menu: 88.55F (serv. incl.).

**11/20**

## La Ménara
**8 blvd. de la**
**Madeleine**
**742.06.92**
*M. Filali*
*Open until 1:00 A.M. Closed Sun.*
*AE, DC.*

This gigantic, glittering basement restaurant stands on the site of the bar owned by the famous boxer, the late Georges Carpentier. It is a couscous cellar in the North African style, sumptuously decorated without offending good taste, a none-too-frequent phenomenen. In the evening, a belly dancer undulates lasciviously among the tables, providing added authenticity to the tajines, pastilla, and various types of couscous.
Carte: 100F–150F.

**13**

## Mövenpick-Café des Artistes
**12 blvd. de la**
**Madeleine**
**742.47.93**
*Open daily until 12:30 A.M.*
*AE, DC, V.*

It is difficult to explain and even more so to rate this mixture of restaurants: a sort of "food-bar" and deluxe bistro. Let's say 12/20 for the restaurants and 14/20 for the Café des Artistes at the rear, whose inventive cuisine is making great progress these days (marvelous marinated salmon gravlax); Scottish Angus, beef cooked just pink; émincé of veal, scampi with tomato, Chinese noodles, alluring desserts, little Swiss wines and some fine Bordeaux. In any case, the phenomenal success which attracts everyone in the quarter and even Tout-Paris to this modern and hospitably decorated restaurant, where one is served with zeal and for reasonable prices, is a lesson in Swiss professionalism.
Carte: 150F–200F at Café des Artists; 40F–100F at Mövenpick.

**14**

## Opéra (Café de la Paix)
**Place de l'Opéra**
**742.97.02**
*M. Meyrueis*
*Open until 11:00 P.M. Closed*
*during August*
*All major credit cards.*

Much effort has been expended by Gil Jouanin to revise the dated cuisine that we criticized (with many nuances) last year. If the results are not entirely convincing, one must take into account the problems faced in a decor dedicated to the extravagances of the Second empire. As a result, we feel tempted to call the cuisine nouvelle luxury-hotel cuisine, characterized by useless sophistication (suprême of sea bass périgourdine is a typical example) and at the same time by modern culinary research. Let us list among these preparations the sautée of lamb offal seasoned with basil, the gourmand of chicken à l'étouffée bressane, and the noisette of lamb served with a vegetable crépinette. Desserts are always remarkable (a gratin of fresh fruits amandine), and there's a fine cellar whose bottles are served by a very knowledgeable wine steward. Carte: about 250F.

**13**

## *Pagoda*

**50, rue de Provence**
**874.81.48**
*M. Tan Dinh*
*Open until 10:30 P.M. Closed Sun.*
*(during August). No dogs.*
*V.*

Nothing of note has changed in this fine old Chinese restaurant. Just as well. The menu is too crowded, true, but there are still the shrimp sautéed to perfection, the very nice fried crab claws, the admirable Peking duck (180F for three or four persons and must be ordered 48 hours in advance) whose crispy skin is one of the wonders of the world. Friendly service (one of the waiters will entertain you with his carving—not of the duck, but of paper from which he fashions works of art) and at prices which can be taken in stride, in a decor rich with trumpery.
Carte: 80F–100F. Menu: 32F (serv. incl.).

**12/20**

## *Au Petit Riche*

**25 rue Le Peletier**
**770.68.68**
*M. La grange*
*Open until 12:15 A.M. Closed Sun.*
*and during August Pay parking at*
*pkg. Drouot.*
*V.*

The decor, more than a hundred years old, is still in perfect shape and offers an attractive glance at a bygone era. The cuisine is no less attractive, for there is good home-style cooking with specialties from the banks of the Loire (Touraine). Since the brother of Lameloise (three toques in Chagny) has assumed direction of this gracious old bistro, there has been no diminution of the good old recipes prepared in light fashion by this chef: terrine of young rabbit with aspic, loaf of pike with purée of crayfish, eel matelote, and andouiette vouvrillonne, hot tart. A superb collection of Loire Valley wines to drink here or take out.
Carte: 150F

**11/20**

## *Au Pupillin*

**19 rue**
**Notre-Dame-de-**
**Lorette**
**285.46.06**
*M. Vidonne*
*Open until 1:30 A.M. Closed*
*during August*
*V.*

A single menu served until 1:00 A.M., labeled "a good French meal quickly and courteously served," is an exemplary and civilized reply to the debasing proliferation of fast-food establishments. About 20 francs at the counter and a little more than twice that on the second floor, with a hot tarte with amourettes or mousse of duck liver with grapes, brochettes of leg of lamb with tarragon, calf's head, sauce tartar and, finally, sherbets from Lenôtre and a good chocolate or mint dessert. And some excellent little wines sold by the glass, pitcher, or bottle, including the Syrah cépage, Les Perrières '79 Burgundy, and the astonishing Pupillin, which all by itself justifies the evening.
Carte: 65F. Menu: 40F + 15% serv.

**12/20**
## Le Quercy
**36 rue Condorcet**
**878.30.61**
*M. Simon*
*Open until 9:30 P.M. Closed Sun.*
*and during August.*
*AE, DC, V.*

André Simon, the owner of the Quercy, is launching a vast national survey with which we are happy to cooperate. What André would like to do is form a club to bring together the dozen of Andrés who belong to the thousands of Simons, as proven by the Paris and provincial telephone directory. He has already contacted more than 1,000 Parisian Simons. The others will probably come forward by themselves as soon as they realize that this friendly owner will offer them one of the best cassoulets, as well as a curly endive salad with chicken and lardons, fricassée of cèpes and confit of apples. The decor is medieval in the Quercy style.
Carte: 170F. Menu: 70F (serv. incl.).

**12/20**
## Le Sainton-geais

**62 rue du faubourg**
**Montmartre**
**280.39.92**
*M. Girodot*
*Open until 10:00 P.M. Closed Sat.*
*(at lunch), Sun. and the last 3*
*weeks of August.*

This is one of the very few Paris restaurants which specializes in the cuisine of Aunis and Saintonge. The young owners are just as friendly and frank as the good old dishes of their childhood, generously sprinkled with Charentes wines. There are chaudrée saintongeaise, cagouilles, mouclade, rabbit in Pineau des Charentes, bouilliture d'anguilles, etc.
Carte: 130F–160F. Menu: 64F + 15% serv.

**12/20**
## Savoie-Bretagne
**21 rue Saint-Lazare**
**878.91.94**
*M. Le Grand*
*Open until 9:00 P.M. Closed Sat.*
*evening, Sun. and during August.*

The miserable surroundings are reminiscent neither of Savoy nor of Brittany. Nor does the very limited menu reflect either of these two provinces, with the exception of an escalope montagnarde on the Savoy side, and all the fish prepared in a great, classic style and the greatest accuracy in the cooking time (turbot with julienne vegetables, skate in brown butter) for Brittany. There are also some very fine home-cooked dishes such as the estouffade of beef, which should be enough to recommend this friendly little restaurant to those who like unpretentious cooking at reasonable prices.
Carte: 130F–150F.

**11/20**
## Les Trois Portes

**65 rue La Fayette**
**878.23.04**
*M. Bel*
*Open until 1:00 A.M. Closed Sat.*
*(at lunch) and during August.*
*AE, DC, V.*

Les Trois Portes was a bistro on this site in 1840. One of these eponymous doors opened onto the rue Lafayette, another onto the rue Cadet and the third on the corner angle, right in front of what is today the entrance to the Cadet metro station. Since 1924, the Bel family, father and son, have welcomed a cosmopolitan clientele drawn from three great local establishments—the Grand Orient (Masonic Lodge), the Club des Diamantaires (the Diamond Merchants Club), and the world-famous Folies Bergère. Each enters through the door of his choice. As far as the cuisine is concerned, the menu is classic, unpretentious but sufficiently varied (onion soup, spring vegetable terrine, seafood platter, choucroute, etc). As for the decor, the dining room is lively and bright and was

completely redecorated recently. This is a good place for dinner or lunch, where you won't have to wait too long before getting a table.
Carte: 120F. Menus: 39F, 50F + 15% serv.

13
## Ty-Coz
**35 rue Saint-Georges**
**878.42.95**
*Mme Libois*
*Open until 11:00 P.M. Closed Sun.*

Since the birth of this restaurant a good twenty years back, only fish, shellfish and other seafood have made the menu of Jacqueline Libois. She and her daughter defend the honor of the most classic cuisine (young turbot with beurre nantais; grilled bass; lotte with cider; cotriade (this plate only if ordered in advance and for a minimum of four persons), and the very freshest of oysters—Marennes specials only—clams, hermit and spider crabs, and prawns. A Marquis de Goulaine muscadet.
Carte: 160F–180F.

# 10ème Arr.

**12/20**
## Brasserie Flo
**7 cour des Petites-Ecuries**
**770.13.59**
*M. Bucher*
*Open until 1:30 A.M. Closed during August*
*V.*

This is the "mother" brasserie of the Bucher empire (Julien, Terminus Nord, Vaudeville). It's the only one, moreover, which was and still is a real 1900s brasserie. This explains why it has retained for many years the most faithful, numerous and fashionable clientele around. But that's not the only reason: the cuisine, served in a wonderful setting, is also of remarkable quality for its price, and consists of traditional brasserie offerings such as sauerkraut or fresh foie gras of the house, seafood, salmon with sorrel, and the excellent wines by the pitcher at a very kindly price. The rub is that you must reserve your table ahead of time and show up at the time specified (otherwise, you miss your turn and must wait for another in the crowded bar) and accept the hectic service, but this is all part of the charm of the house.
Carte: about 120F.

13
## Casimir
**6 rue de Belzunce**
**878.32.53**
*M. Pujol*
*Open until 10:00 P.M. Closed Sat. and during September. Open terrace. Parking at 12 rue de Rocroy.*
*AE, DC, V.*

Though this little restaurant has changed owners, the old patron is still in the kitchen. So one still comes here to taste the andouillette with two sauces, the grilled meats, and the old-fashioned desserts, but also the exquisite chiffonade of artichoke bottoms with foie gras, and the pike pâté (it should not be served cold), calf's liver with raspberry vinegar accompanied very well in season by blackberries and finely sliced squash, and veal sweetbreads with girolles (poached in water and not, alas, well drained). The food is all honest, appetizing and carefully prepared. The small fixed-price meals allow you, at a reasonable price, to attack some of the good classics of the house and thus to avoid a check that soars rapidly, even while you drool over some tempting Burgundies. There is an exquisite little Jaboulet-Verschere Rully at 85F. Carte: 200F-plus. Menu: 50F, 85F + 15% serv.

**15**

## Au Chateau-briant
**23 rue de Chabrol**
**824.58.94**
*M. Forno*
*Open until 10:00 P.M. Closed Sun.,*
*Mon. and during August No dogs.*

Should we reproach a restaurateur who takes no heed of criticism, who steers his own course, avoiding reefs and temptations? To be sure, for his obstinacy keeps writers from waxing lyrical or venting their spleen. Well, what to say about the professional passion of this irreproachable chef, about the unfailing kindness of the reception, about the high quality of his products, about the perfection of this generous Franco-Italian cuisine, the marvelous pastas, the grilled scampi, the artichokes à la sicilienne, the foie gras of the house, the sabaglione with Marsala? There is nothing to say; one can only applaud. Superb lithographs and happily crowded tables.
Carte: about 180F.

**10/20**

## Le Curveur
**9 blvd. Denain**
**280.34.10**
*M. Chretiennot*
*Open until 12:30 A.M.*
*DC, V.*

This is one of the very few places in Paris where you will find dishes typical of the La Rochelle area and the province of Aunis, and they should have been located near a more suitable railway station (from this one, you can only go northeast to Amsterdam and Lille). Here is the place to try the mouclade of Aunis, mussels à la Rochelaise, grilled sausages with Pineau-des-Charentes, the local grillons, and (year-round) the excellent oysters from that coast. It's rather pleasant, well cooked and nicely served in pleasant modern surroundings.
Carte: 100F–120F.

**12/20**

## La Grille
**80 rue du Faubourg-Poissonnière**
**770.89.73**
*M. Cullerre*
*Open until 9:30 P.M. Closed Sat.,*
*Sun., holidays, during August and*
*school holidays.*
*DC.*

Yves Cuillère, who is a capable owner-chef, and his charming wife Geneviève, who supervises the wine-red and bottle-green surroundings, are both responsible for the local success of this little restaurant. The menu offers some fresh dishes, all of them basically fish: seafood terrine, scallops in beurre blanc, grilled turbot. The wine is a nice red Menetou which takes up a good proportion of a rather large bill.
Carte: 150F.

**12/20**

## Julien
**16 blvd. du Faubourg-Saint-Denis**
**770.12.06**

The agreeable formula "entrée included" which —along with the astonishing 1890s decor, and its contemporary pop art, almost entirely in its original state—contributed to the success of Julien, succumbs this year to the

*M. Bucher*
*Open until 1:30 A.M.*
*V.*

imperatives of the time. Jean-Paul Bucher is modifying his menu to conform to those of his other brasseries (Flo, Terminus-Nord, Vaudeville). Many dishes are thus common to all four, and the same tested and proved traditional cuisine is very carefully prepared and cleverly modernized. But there remain other dishes that are unique to Julien: the goose cassoulet, the terrine of turbot with saffron, and the fried calf's liver with black currant vinegar. Good wine in carafes.
Carte: 130F–150F.

## 10/20

## Ling Nam
**10 rue de Mazagran**
**770.02.27**
*M. Liang*
*Open until 10:25 P.M.*

It was many years ago in this small, recently renovated Chinese restaurant that we had one of our first French experiences with dim sum. Chef Kar Yiu still seems to be best at preparing these little steamed Cantonese morsels in bamboo baskets which leave you with a fresh taste and a light stomach. Good news: Thomas Liang, the owner, has just had his menu translated into eighteen languages—a good beginning.
Carte: approx. 80F.

## 14
## Louis XIV
**8 blvd. Saint-Denis**
**208.56.56**
*M. Descombes*
*Open until 1:00 A.M. Closed Mon.,*
*Tues. and during July and August*
*Parking at 10 blvd. de Strasbourg.*
*AE, DC, V.*

Legions of gourmets who eat without paying heed to the bill gather each day in this 1935 setting—slightly threadbare despite the reupholstered banquettes—to sit elbow to elbow at cramped tables where they are served hurriedly to their hearts' content—from Thermidor, hollandaise, à l'américaine, Rossini, *i.e.* all that one should carefully avoid on this long (more than 100 offerings) menu, from which we ourselves choose everything that can escape overcooking and oversaucing, for the ingredients are always excellent and absolutely fresh: the oysters and superb shellfish, among which the poached prawn à la nage, the exquisite fritter of small fish, the grilled sole, the scallops á la nage with seaweed, and, in season, roast game, which is the special ornament of this great, sympathetic and ruinous house. Nice Muscadet in pitchers.
Carte: 200F.

## 15 🍴
## Chez Michel
**10 rue de Belzunce**
**878.44.14**
*M. Tounissoux*
*Open until 10:00 P.M. Closed Fri.,*
*Sat. and during August. Parking at*
*12 rue Rocroy.*
*AE, DC.*

It was a great thrill for us four years ago to hear Michel Tounissoux proclaim an about-face in his cuisine: "The nouvelle cuisine, light sauces, products cooked and prepared so as to retain as much as possible their natural taste—this is the only truth, as long as one does not overdo it." But the good Michel has tried so hard not to overdo it that he has gone only halfway, and in preparing the nouvelle cuisine (which also means renewal, ideas, creativity), he serves again this year two or three timidly audacious plates that seduced us two or three years ago: the calf's liver with honey, poached Belon oysters with tarragon, a salad with shellfish. Which certainly does not

mean that this scrupulous perfectionist no longer deserves our admiration: we are aware that he has "rethought" as much as possible (notably, for more precise cooking times and lighter sauces) all the dishes of his first and, as it turns out, only loves. We can only stand in admiration of his veal sweetbreads, vallée d'Auge the godets of stuffed mussels, the médaillons of lobster with Noilly, the veal sweetbreads with morels, the turbot Cardinal, the omelet président Vincent Bourrel, or the crêpes flambéed with Grand Marnier. That's plenty to keep us happy in this comfortable and elegant bistro in the shadow of the church of Saint Vincent de Paul. Fearsome bills, good and great wines, an irresistible little list of liqueurs.
Carte: 200F-plus.

**11/20**

## La Moutardière

**12 ave. Richerand**
**205.96.80**
*M. Dubarry*
*Open until 9:30 P.M. Closed Sat. (at lunch), Sun., Mon. evenings and August 15–31.*
*AE, DC.*

The best of this kind of cuisine is done in old vessels. This truism is justified here in the freshness and variety of the hors d'oeuvres of which you may eat as many as you want, the quality of the main course meats (including entrecôte with mustard or red wine sauce). You may also choose as much as you like from a selection of cheeses, and there are homemade desserts and wine from the cask. In the evening, candlelight provides an intimate atmosphere for these very modestly priced repasts.
Menus: 50F (lunch), 65F (dinner) (wine and serv. incl.).

**13**

## New Port

**79 rue du Faubourg-Saint-Denis**
**246.81.59**
*MM. Martin and Pion*
*Open until midnight. Closed Sat. (at lunch) and Mon.*

The New Port has enjoyed a fashionable clientele ever since it opened last spring on the fishy banks of the Faubourg Saint-Denis. Pierre Martin is well-known in London because of his two restaurants there, Le Suquet and La Croisette, where this one-time bartender from Fouquet's has been host to the cream of the Entente cordiale. It is surprising to discover at the end of this drab street a sort of chromed yacht club, the kind you find at fashionable ports. The waiters are dressed as sailors, and it is (tacitly, to be sure) recommended that diners wear blazers and check their yachts at the door. In Paris as in London, Pierre Martin cleverly offers a single menu, at 130F, comprising a dozen entrées: seafood platter, various delicious feuilletés with shellfish such as crabs, prawns, and seafood salads, fresh crabs, scallops; followed by seven or eight fish, depending upon the market; and, finally, cheese, dessert and coffee. The freshness of the fish is perfection, but above all they are cooked with real talent in light pastry, and the sauces are very well prepared. Too bad the coffee is just as bad as in London tea room.
Carte (at the bar): 170F. Menu: 130F + 15% serv.

## Nicolas
**12 rue de la Fidélité**
**246.84.74**

*M. François*
*Open until 10:30 P.M. Closed Sat.*
*and during August. Parking at 107*
*rue du faubourg-St-Denis.*
*AE, DC, V.*

The street name is not one that exactly inspires revolutionary sentiments. Nor does one encounter in these old-fashioned surroundings reeking of bourgeois morality anything but a down-to-earth, loyal clientele. They are the kind who like to call a spade a spade and a tête de veau a tête de veau. So don't expect anything original or sensational, unless you consider an unfailing allegiance to good ingredients well-prepared all year round to be sensationally original. There is fresh marinated herring, blanquette of veal, sauté of lamb, beef bourguignon, oeufs à la neige. . . . Unfailing, did we say? Maybe we exaggerated. Several of our readers have recently blown the whistle on Nicolas, telling tales of ill-temper and carelessly-prepared dishes. Wherever will we go if Nicolas stops setting the example of perfection? Carte: about 160F.

## 13 ♡
## Le Paillon
**4 cours des**
**Petites-Ecuries**
**523.02.77**

*Open until 11:30 P.M. Closed Sun.,*
*Mon. and during August.*
*AE, DC, V.*

Bourride, tripe à la niçoise, aïolli with cod and ten vegetables, farcis niçois, ravioli with dâube, squash fritters, rabbit with tomato and polenta: a very southern cuisine which brings a ray of sunshine to this cool corner. It's a cuisine, though, that despite its regionalism does not remain immobile. Roger Roux taps out a new menu on his typewriter each day, according to the availability of produce at the market, what is in season, his own mood, and recipes he finds in old family cookbooks. He is a tireless prospector who never ceases to enlarge his repertóire. A rustic decor, a bit faded. Good choice of wines of Provence, and a very warm reception. Carte: 150F.

## 11/20
## Pinocchio
**49 rue d'Enghien**
**770.01.98**

*M. Bruno*
*Open until 10:00 P.M. Closed Sun.,*
*holidays and during August.*
*AE, V.*

Charming family restaurant serving a large, regular clientele. The fresh pasta is prepared by Salvatore Bruno in his tiny kitchen. There is also piccata and bacala (salt cod) à la Sicilienne, polenta and, in winter, bollito misto. Clean and well-kept; generous portions. Service sometimes a little hurried. Carte: 100F.

## 13 ♡
## La P'tite Tonkinoise
**56 rue du Faubourg-**
**Poissonnière**
**246.85.98**

*M. Costa*
*Open until 10:00 P.M. Closed Sun.,*
*Mon. and during August and*
*1st 2 wks. of September.*

This is the only restaurant in Paris (and doubtless in France) serving a Far East cuisine to receive a star in the rival red guide. While it's always a bit behind the times, Michelin thus shows that it knows the genuine article, at least when it's staring them in the face. Henri Costa, an old Vietnam hand who had a French restaurant in Haiphong for ten years, has prepared Vietnamese food for the same length of time in France, first in Bayonne, where we discovered him, and a little later in Paris in this agreeably sedate setting. It is an absolutely original cuisine, expressed in a very short menu and it is entirely dependent upon what is available each day at the market. Henri Costa and his son Michel, who backs him up in the kitchen, will prepare you fritters of fillets of turbot en beignets with sorrel sauce, émincé of beef with braised bamboo shoots, steamed Tonkinese turnovers (banh cuôn), or mackerel with tea. The cooking is precise, the flavors diverting, and the ingredients as fresh as can be. Carte: 120F–150F.

### 12/20

### Terminus-Nord
**23 rue de Dunkerque**
**285.05.15**
*M. Bucher*
*Open until 12:30 A.M. Private dining room for 10.*
*V.*

Old-fashioned cooking, well prepared and served in a rather special setting, and, above all, intelligent. For this you can have confidence in Jean-Paul Bucher. In a clever Belle Époque–Gay Nineties setting, as in the other brasseries in his collection (Flo, Julien, Vaudeville), he offers the same friendly and efficient service and gets the same crowd. It comes to taste the seafood, the Flo foie gras with Riesling, the beef au gros sel, the peasant-style sauerkraut, and even a few "fashionable" plates, all well turned out. Finely chosen wines at tiny prices (30F–40F per liter). Carte: 120F.

# 11ème Arr.

### 13
### L'Armorique
**32 ave. de la République**
**700.08.09**
*M. Guillotte*
*Open until 11:00 P.M.*
*Closed Sun. evening and Mon.*
*Parking at 21 rue Gambey.*
*AE, DC, V.*

The cuisine of this comfortable and substantial house takes the classic-traditional route with a menu that's much too long but with several imaginative stops here and there along the way. Thus you'll find, cheek by jowl with fish soup or grilled sardines, a curious salad of crayfish with fresh kiwi, and an unusual but very successful hot frog leg's sausage with chives. The same thing happens in the fish section, with sole meunière, suprême of bass normande, a navarin with scallops and, flageolets that successfully weds lamb with shellfish. The stew is slightly overcooked, but that is really neither here nor there. We retain the memory of a very bright meal, darkened somewhat by the bill. Carte: 200F.

### 11/20
### Astier
**44 rue J.-P.-Timbaud**
**357.16.35**
*M. Picquart*
*Open until 9:00 P.M. Closed Sat., Sun. and during August.*

A wooden bar counter, on which an apéritif is won or lost at the throw of the dice. 1950's wall paper. Jovial conviviality (a rather affected expression, perhaps), presided over by an attentive, matronly hostess. She is the former owner, who is now holding the hand of her successor, Michel Picquart, who had never set foot in a

kitchen before he bought this bistro. He has not done too badly. There is fresh marinated mackerel, veal soup, île flottante. No unpleasant surprises, but no special ones either. Just a flashback in time and style to a little provincial inn.
Carte: 80F–100F.

### 13

## Cartet
**62, rue de Malte**
**805.17.65**
*Mme Noaille*
*Open until 9:00 P.M. Closed Sat.,*
*Sun. and during August.*

Marie Cartet has hung up her apron after a half century of happy service in the cause of traditional cooking, but she still keeps an eye on the restaurant where Mme Noaille has succeeded her. The cuisine remains strictly the same for the moment and is almost without demerit: an excellent terrine of chicken liver; mackerel with white wine, perfect breaded veal sweetbreads (avoid the heavy sauce), calf's kidneys cooked just right (but flambéed, which is like flambéeing tripe lyonnaise), beautiful morels (served, unhappily, on a piece of bread), copious servings of potatoes, and an admirable lemon tarte. The service appears to have improved, but the prices have not been sitting idle since last year. The Roussette of Bugey is delicious.
Carte: 180F–200F.

### 11/20

## Le Grand Méricourt
**22 rue de la Folie-**
**Méricourt**
**700.43.87**
*M. Berrier*
*Open until 9:45 P.M. Closed Sat.*
*and Sun.*
*V.*

The hunt has been the sole inspiration for the dreary decor of this local bistro. "Personal" reception by the owner, a big, jolly fellow with a charming smile. The cuisine is inconsistent, ranging from relatively decent to extremely bland. On the positive side, there are fresh, well-prepared starters, such as salade d'écrevisses and chiffonade of spinach with mushrooms and chervil. On the negative side, main dishes which seem rather tasteless, heavily-sauced. . . . failures, in fact (veal kidneys, sweetbreads with onions). . . . Just a little effort would save them from disaster; lighter sauces, no more overcooking. That's all. It simply remains for them to put these recommendations into practice.
Carte: 150F.

### 12/20

## Le Péché Mignon
**5 rue Guillaume-**
**Bertrand**
**357.02.51**
*M. Rousseau*
*Open until 10:00 P.M. Closed Sun.*
*and August 15 to September 15.*

An aggressive young chef is trying to make this dreary little restaurant (plywood, orange-colored fabric, but it is going to be redecorated) into one of the best of the local eating places. His culinary efforts are basically successful, thanks to some inspired dishes. Even if the inspiration sometimes comes from others, such as cassolette of escargots with cèpes or blanc de turbot en papillote au beurre rouge. There are a few faults and hesitations here and there, it is true; for instance, crab in sorrel or sweetbreads in coulis of mushrooms. But if we look at the overall performance, taking the location and price level into account (prices are reasonable even including an

excellent red wine from Marsannay), it deserves only encouragement.
Carte: 130F–150F. Menu: 35F (serv. incl.).

14

## Chez Philippe (Auberge Pyrénées-Cévennes)
**106 rue de la Foli-Méricourt**
**357.33.78**
*M. Serbource*
*Open until 10:30 P.M. Closed Sat., Sun. and during August. Parking at 102 rue de la Folie-Méricourt.*

The entrance looks just like that of an exquisite little village café, except that the clientele doesn't wear wooden shoes. "Nothing has changed in my restaurant for fifteen years," boasts Philippe Serbource, and this is true if one considers only the decor, the warmth of the reception, the friendliness of the owner and the waiters. It is less true, let us admit with heavy hearts, when you take a close look at the copiously served food of this old inn. But we are so fond of Philippe that we can no longer keep from telling him that his cassoulet is not what it used to be (what has happened to those miraculous white beans?) and that certain peasant or bourgeois dishes, such as the knuckle of ham with lentils, the boeuf bourguignon with morels, crème au chocolat, reveal a tendency toward heaviness, as if Serbource were confounding rustic with prosaic which, of course, is just the opposite with him. This may not be too alarming; a little laziness, perhaps, or maybe this is the sabatical year? Nothing should prevent you from going to dine here, beneath the beams and the hams, upon his marvelously fresh fish and shellfish, his magnificent foie gras, and the fascinating little wines chosen from the growers.
Carte: 160F.

14

## Le Repaire de Cartouche
**8 blvd. des Filles-du-Calvaire**
**700.25.86**
*M. Pocous*
*Open until 10:00 P.M. Closed Sat., Sun. and July 17 to August 15. Parking at 96 rue Amelot.*
*V.*

Raymond Pocous, a printer fired by a passion for cuisine, has just put this restaurant back on its feet. We had execrable memories of it, but its comeback is assured, thanks to some very good ingredients brought in from the Southwest (confits, foie gras, and a surprisingly good Madiran wine), and thanks even more to an attractive cuisine personalized by young Chef Raphaël Puchois. The calf's tongue with foie gras, the salad with "favorites" of duck (the noble attributes of our web-footed friends), the veal sweetbreads with mussels, the quenelles of wild salmon with a purée of crabs, and a chocolate fondant with coffee sauce—all these dishes herald a talent dedicated to well-controlled originality. Here, then, is an attractive new address (in a quarter that was lacking in good addresses) where prices are very reasonable, the reception and the service warm, and the dark wooden decor restful and agreeable. Very attractive collection of 40 Armagnacs.
Carte: 120F–160F. Menu: 60F + 15% serv.

14

## À Sousceyrac
**35 rue Faidherbe**

Gabriel Asfaux is hard put to hide his pride and joy: The wood-paneled provincial bistro which he has directed for 32 years, succeeding his father, will stay in the family. His

**371.65.30**
*MM. Asfaux*
*Open until 10:00 P.M. Closed Sat.,*
*Sun. and during August. Parking*
*at Motor Garage, rue Jules Vallès.*

two sons—Patrick in the kitchen and Luc in the dining room—seem determined to carry on to the last detail all the traditions of this rock-solid old establishment. And the heritage is not to be taken lightly. To convince yourself of this you need only to decipher—and that's just the word—this long, luxuriant menu in violet ink. You will find delicious terrine of foie gras, timbale of young rabbit and lobster, scallops with Champagne and sorrel, dodinette of guinea hen with morels, veal sweetbread with crayfish, and the true cassoulet quercynois, coffee parfait with chocolate sauce, and ice cream with honey and walnuts. Yes, the Asfaux family demonstrates each day the traditional cuisine need be neither boring nor indigestible when it attains this level in its tastes and flavors. Cheers for the prices, which have scarcely risen this year (although they got off to an early jump previously) and more cheers for the wines that the boss brings up from the cellar each day; they are often truly marvelous!
Carte: 180F–200F.

# 12ème Arr.

**12/20**
## La Connivence
**1 rue de Cotte**
**628.46.17**
*Messieurs Guetta and Trastour*
*Open until 10:30 P.M. Closed Sun.,*
*Mon. and during August.*

A plain and friendly bistro, behind the Aligre market. The decor consists of modern bricks, pink tablecloths, and farily old plates and glasses. The cuisine connives with the rather contrived simplicity. There is filet mignon of veal with rhubarb, pot-au-feu of lotte, magret of duck with peaches and Roquefort soufflé. The lunch menu is a real delight, and so is the Loire Chenin Blanc (25F a bottle). Carte: 80F–100F. Menu (lunch only): 33F (serv. incl.).

**11/20**
## Les Fleurs
**197 ave. Daumesnil**
**343.24.61**
*M. Michel*
*Open until 10:00 P.M. Closed Sun.*
*and during August.*
*AE, DC, V.*

Jean Michel has included dishes on his menu from all of the great regions of France, including his own Berry (with its fine wines). Ham takes you on a trip from the Ardennes in the northeast to Bayonne in the southwest. The theme is continued with andouille from Guémené (Brittany), Troyes andouillette (Champagne district), rillettes from Connerré (Normandy). Nor should we forget other districts such as the Landes, Périgord, and Charolais. The terrines are original (sauvageonne, sansonnet), there is an unusual jarret of veal en meurette and a few exciting fixed-price meat or fish dinners. For instance, there is a dinner consisting of a terrine of merlan with vegetables, broiled salmon in chive sauce, cheeses and homemade tarte.
Carte: 100F. Menu: 70F (wine and serv. incl.).

**12/20**

## Chez Jacques
**62 rue Crozatier**
**343.97.39**
*M. Rebeuf*
*Open until 9:00 P.M. Closed Sat.*
*and Sun.*

It may be a little hard to read Jacques Rebeuf's new menu, but it is full of pleasant surprises. It reveals a nature which has only recently discovered a love for good but unfamiliar wines and excellent ingredients purchased from the best suppliers in Paris or outside it. The charcuterie comes from Besson in Lyon, the salmon from Petrossian, the cheese from Allard, the sherbets from Zagori, etc.). These ingredients are used to produce a very classic but nevertheless individual cuisine, which has recently displayed some inspired touches: the marinated mackerel with Meursault, the fresh quenelles with a coulis of langoustine, the navarin of rabbit with country cider, the andouillette à la ficelle, the veal kidneys cooked in cider vinegar and honey. There are some very good wines at attractive prices.
Carte: 130F.

**13** 🍴

## Marcel
**7 rue Saint-Nicolas**
**343.49.40**
*M. Trottet*
*Open until 9:30 P.M. Closed Sat.*
*(from Easter to September), Sun.*
*and during August.*
*V.*

Fashionable Parisians have not yet learned to venture beyond the Bastille to discover the virtues of this traditional old bistro and its cuisine of not long ago. Aside from the prices, which are very much up to date, nothing is modern, nothing has changed since the 1950s reign of the foster father of the present owner, a man crazy about flowers and Beaujoulais. Still the same banal decor, the same efficient service, the utensils all aligned, and two good bottles—one of red, one of white—set up on the tables: ("Drink as much as you like," and it is good.) But, above all, the best herring with fried potatoes in Paris (the potatoes are a bit too cold), the little mackerel, the pork charcuterie, the dandelions with bacon, beautiful haddock, an excellent calf's head, a tender pot-au-feu, marvelous tripe, streaky bacon with cabbage, oeufs à la neige. All of this in extravagant portions, served to the bon vivants of the neighborhood. This is a generous and endearing museum dedicated to the good old days.
Carte: about 150F. Menu: 80F (serv. incl.).

**12/20**

## Le Morvan
**22 rue Chaligny**
**307.47.66**
*M. Guyard*
*Open until 9:15 P.M. Closed Sat.,*
*Sun. and during August.*

Get there early if you want to eat at lunchtime. It's hard to get even part of a table in this charming bistro with its Morvan regional cooking and its beautifully-carved wood bar. The owner, Denis Guyard, is also from the Morvan region. His chef, Jean-Claude Prieur, is without equal in preparing civet of pork, duck in cucumber and cream, beef estouffade and lapin dijonnaise. The service is superb and they've promised to work on the desserts (homemade ice cream).
Carte: 80F.

**10/20**

## Chez Peppino
**7 rue Rondelet**

Thirty years at the kitchen stove in this pleasantly working-class neighborhood has given the owner, who comes from the Italian Alps, the authority to take a few liberties

**307.38.72**
*M. Callegari*
*Open until 9:00 P.M. Closed Sat.*
*and during September.*

with the Italo-Corsican dishes which make up the (good) basis of her menu. You will thus find furtive and inexpensive joy in chicken cooked in Sylvaner or boeuf au gros sel, as well as in the friendly atmosphere of her attractive bistro.
Carte: 75F. Menu: 28F (serv. incl.).

12/20
## La Petite Alsace
**4 rue Taine**
**343.21.80**
*M. Rosenblatt*
*Open until 10:00 P.M. Closed Sun.*
*evening, Mon. and during August.*
*Pay parking at 42 rue Taine.*
*AE, DC, V.*

The decor is typically Alsatian, rustic and cozy. The waiters wear red vests, and the owner is from the Sundgauve region of southern Alsace. The choucroute may be light—in fact it's one of the best in Paris—but the bill is really heavy! The charcuterie is good, the kouglof is a little heavy and the wines come from the best vintners in Alace (Beyer, Trimbach). This is a nice little spot for provincial cooking and it is well run, but once again, is much too expensive.
Carte: 170F. Menus: 49.80F (wine and serv. incl.), 60F, 90F, 150F + 15% serv.

15
## Au Pressoir
**257 ave. Daumesnil**
**344.38.21**
*M. Séguin*
*Open until 10:30 P.M.*
*Closed Sun., Mon.,*
*15 days in Febuary*
*and 3 wks. in August.*
*Parking at 264 ave. Daumesnil.*
*V.*

The avenue Daumesnil is about as close as you will get to the provinces and still be in Paris. The large and spacious dining room of the Pressoir (wine press), with its tables attractively arranged in a judiciously modern fashion, also evokes the provincial virtues. The cuisine, on the other hand, is marked by a spirit of invention bordering at times on the avant-garde. Let's just say that the muse of the table has placed Henri Séguin (who worked with Andre Guillot at Vieux Marly) in the kitchen. His ragoût of cardoons, artichokes, truffles and Jerusalem artichokes is a small sweet-and-sour masterpiece. On the other hand, we question whether he should strengthen the taste of orange accompanying the calf's kidneys by serving it with a granité which sweetens the meat unnecessarily. The mesclun salad of preserved pig's ear, the marrow pastry with sweet leeks, the baby goat Monsieur Séguin, the fillet of duck in an eggplant pancake, and the exquisite desserts (treacled white cake, warm pear with cinnamon ice cream) are irreproachable. The young and serious waiters would benefit from learning to smile like Mme Seguin, the hostess. The bill is oppressive (220F) with a small grower's Burgundy. An enthusiastic reader writes, "This restaurant is worth three toques!" No, not yet; but certainly two.
Carte: about 200F.

12/20
## Le Quincy
**28 ave Ledru-Rollin**
**628.46.76**
*M. Bosshard*
*Open until 9:30 P.M.*

A sweet little country-style restaurant between the Bastille and the gare de Lyon. The rustic decor is endearing, and the smiling reception of the owner is always accompanied by a "glass of friendship" and a slice of sausage. For the rest, do not expect much. The tendency of the cuisine is

*Closed Sat., Sun. and from
August 15 to September 15.
DC.*

southern, with cassoulet with preserved goose, knuckle of ham, young rabbit with shallots or Dombres quail forestière. Excellent little Syrah growth from the Ardèche to wash it all down.
Carte: 120F.

**11/20**

### Rôtisserie du Plateau de Gravelle
**Bois de Vincennes
2 route du Pesage
368.00.13**
*Messieurs Pompanon and
Geeraerdt
Open until 10:00 P.M. Parking.
AE, DC, V.*

The establishment tries to create the effect of being isolated in the middle of the woods, and viewed from the dining room windows, the Bois de Vincennes looks like a thick forest. Thus, a pleasant restaurant both in summer (when you can dine under the trees in the open air) and in winter, with its rich remodeled Louis XIII-style surroundings. Jacobée, the chef, has succeeded Picard, who has gone into a well-deserved retirement. Essentially, however, this carefully prepared, classic cuisine has not changed. We suggest you try the inclusive menu (even wine, coffee and service are included) which offers a choice nearly equal to the a la carte menu: raw fillet of salmon with dill, lotte and Provence herbs and fresh pasta, Troyes andouillette with mustard. The service is good and the reception friendly.
Carte: 200F. Menu: 145F (wine and serv. incl.).

**11/20**

### La Sardana
**4 rue de Chaligny
343.02.84**
*Mme Font-Puigferrer
Open until 10:30 P.M. Closed Sun.
and August 15–31.
AE, V.*

Although the Pyrenees have long ceased to be an obstacle, Spanish cuisine has never succeeded in establishing itself solidly on the banks of the Seine. However, standing out for once from other mediocre Spanish cuisine, we found this little restaurant which essentially offers the Catalan style of Spanish cooking: bell peppers in oil, genuine gazpacho, grilled rabbit, zarzuela and a delicious huge paella. All this is quite well-prepared and pleasantly served in agreeable, rustic surroundings. The welcome is lively, but the prices are a little demanding—nearly 150F with one bottle of an excellent Rioja, the Sangre de Torro.
Menu: 45F (serv. incl.).

**12/20**

### La Sologne
**164 ave. Daumesnil
307.68.97**
*M. Médard
Open until 10:00 P.M. Closed Mon.
evening and Sun. Parking at
103 rue Claude-Decaen.
V.*

Médard, the owner-chef, who three years ago replaced Jean-Pierre Morot-Gaudry, specializes not so much in what he calls classic cuisine as in super-refined cuisine. The result can be an excess of carefulness. Although a number of his dishes are well-prepared and well-conceived, such as the blancs de seiche with bell peppers, the salad of écrevisse tails with cabbage, the médaillon of lotte à la bourguignonne, the mignon of veal with coulis de morilles, they lack a little spontaneity and verve. The same criticism applies to some of his rich preparations of game—one of the bases of the fine reputation the Médard family makes for itself during the hunting season. The reception and the service have become a little slack, the decor is pleasant.
Carte: 150F.

**12/20**
## Le Train Bleu
**20 blvd. Diderot
(Gare de Lyon -
2nd floor)
343.09.06**
*M. Chazal
Open until 11:00 P.M.
All major credit cards.*

Much has been said about the extravagance of this "official" 1900 decor, with its elaborate woodwork, sculpted ceilings, frescoes and artistic metalwork; we've nothing to add. A few words, however, need to be said about the cuisine. Its general Lyon-Forez (the home territory of Owner Albert Chazal) emphasis becomes more and more marked: leg of lamb forézienne, quenelles with crayfish, salads, gâteau forézien. In autumn there is a fine choice of mushrooms to accompany the meats and fowl, and, year-round, the omnipresent gratin, which here is called forézien, sprinkled cheese, distinguishing it from the gratin dauphinois. Prices shooting up.
Carte: 180F-plus.

**17**
## Au Trou Gascon
**40 rue Taine
344.34.26**
*M. Dutournier
Open until 10:00 P.M. Closed Sat. and Sun. Parking at 103 rue Claude Decaen.
V.*

Without altering in any way the naïve grace of this old bistro, which originally catered to taxi drivers, Alain Dutournier has rejuvenated it. The turn-of-the-century decor is an additional reason to go there to dine upon the subtle marriage of the Parisian and the provincial that makes the Trou Gascon one of those rare places where one has the impression of a perpetual holiday—an inspired cuisine in which are combined the pleasures of traditional Gascony with the subtleties of more modern taste. Dutournier might well have stuck with his admirable Chalosse ham au couteau; his foie gras au naturel; his drip-roasted farm squab; his Landes chickens sautéed with asparagus; his succulent preserved cèpes; and we would still have applauded him. But this adventurer with a radiant smile beneath his handle-bar moustache is not content to tread the beaten path. He is constantly experimenting, inventing, and often his genius produces a masterpiece such as his lobster with ginger, which, alas, appears only rarely on his menu. But even when his genius is not operative, his talents are manifest, sufficiently so that we have decided to bestow upon him a third toque. When you have tasted his ravioli with foie gras and truffles, his fricassée of cheeks of skate with spices, his wild salmon cooked with smoked bacon (what a divine combination!), his minute of red mullet with purslane, or his leg of lamb en rognonnade, you will agree with us. Listing rare wines from nearly forgotten vineyards, Dutournier's wine list is not only one of the most attractive in Paris, but also one of the most intelligent and most lucid. It is presented by a wine steward so in love with his cellar that it seems he must sleep there. Dutournier and several other restaurateurs have superbly furnished a cellar at Port-Marly (Les Toques Gourmandes at 29 bis route de Versailles, 916.11.73), where you can order to your heart's content.
Carte: 200F. Menu (lunch only): 100F (serv. incl.).

# 13ème Arr.

### 12/20
## Les Algues
**66 ave. des Gobelins**
**331.58.22**
*M. Fargeau*
*Open until 10:00 P.M. Closed Sun.*
*eve., Mon. and during August*
*(subject to change).*
*V.*

The pale grandmotherly decor in sleazy-bar pink, brightened with naïve crockery and etched glasses, exudes the faint, numbing charm of a 1920s harbor café, not without its pretty, lamplit appeal in the evening. In short, a pleasant spot, in an area where they're not abundant. The new chef, Patrice Blomet, continues along the same fish-strewn path cleared since the opening by the young Fargeau's, busy, sometimes absentminded owners (such as when they forget to be as cheerful and friendly as you'd hope) and inattentive—our dish of calf's liver and sweetbread with crayfish was scarcely presentable. A few pretty modern salads, and exquisite hot little oysters with a fondue of leeks. An unfortunately generalized tendency for things to be overcooked (fresh pasta, skate with sorrel, salmon with scallops) and sauces which are a bit heavy, though delicate and finely seasoned (something we can't say for the insipid vanilla sauce called on for the chocolate mousses and the charlottes). Very pretty wine list for little and not so little wines, and a remarkable fixed-price meal.
Carte: 130F–150F. Menu: 58F + 15% serv.

### 11/20
## Chez Grand-Mère

**92 rue Broca**
**707.13.58**
*Mme Long*
*Open until 10:00 P.M. Closed*
*during Febuary and July 14 to*
*August 15.*

The decor is the outmoded mode of 1900 (lamp shades with skirts of old lace and similar accessories). The cuisine offers delicious boudin with vinegar, piperade, loin of pork with lentils, fritters with onions, and family desserts (semolina cake, crème au chocolat). Friendly atmosphere.
Carte: about 80F. Menus: 70F, 80F (serv. incl.).

### 12/20
## La Mandragore

**22 rue des Gobelins**
**331.69.01**
*Open until 10:30 P.M. Closed Sat.,*
*Sun. and during August.*
*V.*

A strange name to pick for a restaurant, since the mandrake is an evil-smelling plant used for centuries in witches' brews. The more so, since the young succubus who works at the kitchen stove seemed to us to be as innocuous as she was well-intentioned. She has a Southwestern accent and in her happy little kitchen, which is always filled with laughter and song, she prepares some very interesting dishes. The decor of the small dining room with its stone walls is in keeping with her special cuisine. The restaurant is housed in an old building in the old rue du vieux Gobelin on the banks of the Bièvre, and we wonder why the tables and seats are so low. The menu is definitely fish-oriented. Among its

noteworthy items are an excellent version of bouillabaisse with Mediterranean fish and with aïlloli, and a good seafood terrine. The sea bass in wine was a little overcooked, but the wine sauce served with it was pleasantly light, and there was good raw marinated mackerel (although this good idea was badly executed, as the pieces were too large and tasted strongly of vinegar). The desserts are uninteresting.
Carte: 130F–160F.

**12/20**

## Les Marronniers

**53 bis blvd. Arago**
**707.58.57**
*M. Lorenzatti*
*Open until 11:00 P.M. Closed Sun.*
*and during August.*
*DC, V.*

On pleasant, warm days and evenings, under the chestnut trees of the Boulevard Arago, you might think you were in the country. All year 'round in the cozy surroundings of the small dining room, you will get almost excellent cuisine—providing the bad-tempered chef, who is also the despotic owner, is in good form. He serves gogue angevine (mentioned by Rabelais), charlotte of turbot in beurre blanc or fillet of veal in white mushrooms. If the owner is in a bad mood, all you will be left with is the pale memory of a dull but expensive meal.
Carte: 170F.

**11/20**

## Chez Michèle

**39 rue Daviel**
**580.09.13**
*Mme Bonnigal*
*Open until 10:30 P.M. Closed Sun.*
*AE, V.*

The charming owner, Michelle Bonnigal (note the two l's in her first name), describes it as an old bistro with class. In her kitchen, chef Ikkache prepares all the variations of couscous, whose fiery aftertaste can be extinguished with sherbets by Berthillon. The pitcher of Gamay from Touraine is excellent.
Carte: 90F–100F. Menu: 50F (wine and serv. incl.).

**11/20**

## La Scala

**68 blvd. de l'Hopital**
**337.91.78**
*Mme Brulard*
*Open until 10:30 P.M. Closed Mon.*
*and during August.*

This is a far better place than the one on the opposite side of the street. You will realize this when you take a table at this welcoming bistro whose terrace overlooks the Piété-Salpétrière hospital. Although the decor is dreary Italian, achieved with the aid of the most conventional props, the welcome is delightful, and the service full of smiles. The owner will regale you with a list of her fresh pasta, saltimbocca, osso buco, fried scampi, and zabaglione. In the evening, a bearded singer will serenade you South American style.
Carte: 100F–120F.

**13**

## Les Vieux Métiers de France

**13 blvd. A.-Blanqui**
**588.90.03**

The brand-new, modernistic construction super-imposed upon a neo-Louis XIIIth frontage of plaster medallions and stained glass should not make you jump to the conclusion that everything here is a crude fake. The interior of this extraordinary building is ornamented with elegant stonework and genuine wood. It was installed ten

*M. Moisan*
*Open until 11:00 P.M. Closed Sun.*
*and Mon.*
*V.*

years ago to clad the cold concrete of the superstructure by friends of Michel Moisan, who were members of the Guild of the Tour de France. The cuisine is just as frank. There is the same spirit of truth in pursuit of the best ingredients and the simplest preparations. Dishes include a ragoût of giblets, fresh salmon with chives, navarin of fish, stuffed Belon oysters, duck livers en papillote with cabbage, and a bavarois of wild strawberries. All this is served in these warm, intimate surroundings, with attentive service (the tableware is very attractive). Here, you will spend the best possible evening in the 13ème arrondissement. Customers may visit the impressive cellar which holds 20,000 sleeping bottles.
Carte: 180F. Menus: 160F (serv. incl.).

# 14ème Arr.

14
## Chez Albert
**122 ave. du Maine**
**320.21.69**
*M. Beaumont*
*Open until 10:30 P.M.*
*Closed Mon. and August 9 to 23.*
*Open terrace. Parking.*
*All major credit cards.*

For about fifteen years we have been watching attentively for the slightest change in the offerings of this old bistro, which was for a long time a great restaurant. But no; the scallops and the foie gras with port wine aspic are still there, along with poached lobster with herbs, roast rack of lamb—all as it was so long ago when we felt our first gastronomic stirrings. Though any change would be considered a sure sign of planetary cataclysm by the faithful clientele, we should point out that Marcel and Suzanne Beaumont and their chef of 25 years each day insert a few "suggestions," among which you will find an incomparable calf's head ravigote, grilled bass with chive butter, Marennes oysters with sorrel, or Gâtinais quail en surprise. Let it be hoped that this audacity in no way dampens your enthusiasm for this pleasant restaurant, where the reception is warm, the tables are flowered, the ingredients irreproachable, and the bills high. Attractive Arbois wines are a specialty of the house.
Carte: 200F–250F.

14
## Les Armes de Bretagne
**108 ave. du Maine**
**320.29.50**
*M. Boyer*
*Open until midnight. Closed Sun.*
*evenings, Mon. and July 14 to*
*August 15. Air cond.*
*Attendant parking.*
*All major credit cards.*
*(à la carte only).*

Culinary diplomas have never much impressed us, and we even have an instinctive distrust of cooking "contests." So it is more than Roland Boyer's first places in the Taittinger and Montagné competitions or his placing in the finals of the "Meilleur Ouvrier de France"; it is the terrine of turbot with a mousse of rascasse, the roast lobster with sorrel, the sole with chives, the grouper with pink peppercorns, and the scallops with fresh J.-C. Boucheret pasta which bring us back to his neo-Napoleon III dining room. The Armes de Bretagne is devoted to duck and prepares it in six

different ways, the most successful of which is called "with pink peppercorns" (it's true that Claude Terrail does not hold a patent on it). On the second floor are three agreeable and soundproof salons (for business meals and private receptions) and some attractive fixed-price meals that offer good price-quality ratios.
Carte: 200F–280F. Menu (in the private salons only): 100F, 120F, 160F + 15% serv.

14

## Auberge de l'Argoat
**27 ave. Reille**
**589.17.05**
*M. Goareguer*
*Open until 10:00 P.M. Closed Sun., Mon. and during August. No dogs.*

Everything in this restaurant comes from Brittany, not only the fish and the shellfish, but also the butter, the bread, the eggs and the rustic decor—not to mention the white wine and the owner himself and his passion for the natural and for ecology, which leads him more and more toward a delicate, fresh and modern cuisine. With more than sixteen years of toiling in the fields of tradition (Maxim's, Lasserre, Fouquet's), what an admirable conversion to come today to a terrine of rascasse with grapefruit, for example, or the coral of sea urchins, or exquisite steamed andouillettes with cider, or hot oysters stuffed with crabmeat, or salmon with peach vinegar, or rillettes of mackerel with chives! Finally, after several lean years, success seems to be reaching this house. Aided in the kitchen by his son-in-law Laurent (who is sent to Troisgros for courses) M. Goareguer has been able to devote some of his time to prettying his restaurant which, with flowers, new dishes and, very soon, a terrace, will surely become one of the most agreeable fish restaurants in Paris.
Carte: 150F–180F.

12/20
## Auberge du Centre
**10 rue Delambre**
**326.67.77**
*M. Berthier*
*Open until 10:30 P.M., (until 11:00 P.M. Sat.). Closed Sat. (at lunch), Sun. and during August. V.*

Onion tart, curly endive salad with lardons, eggs en cocotte with cream or en meurette, tourte bourbonnaise, gésiers Périgord, confit of duck, sole meunière. These are some of the traditional dishes on the menu at the pleasant Auberge du Centre (the Centre refers both to the Montparnasse center, as well as to the center of France). However, there are also a few overwhelming dishes whose sauces are heavily laced with alcohol, or which are flambéed right at your table by the patron himself, and which you would do well to avoid.
Carte: 160F.

10/20
## Le Bar à Huîtres
**112 blvd. du Montparnasse**
**320.71.01**
*M. Triadou*
*Open until 2:00 A.M. Closed Mon. Pay parking.*
*AE, V.*

Strategically located at the intersection of boulevard Raspail and boulevard Montparnasse, a step away from three of the best fish restaurants in Paris (Le Duc, Le Dôme, Les Arêtes), this is a spacious and well-lit eating place. The decor, though modern and amusing, in fake nautical style, is perhaps a little overdone, but this bar has a lot going for it. A lot, that is, except for the quality of the food. The shellfish are not first rate . . . some of them are not even second-rate; the fish have been prepared with

laudible effort, but are overcooked (apart from an excellent haddock, which was, however, too salty); the portions are miserly, the service is unprofessional and the wine (obviously a piece of bad luck) was corked. . . . The prices, however, are unrestrained: 260F for a giant seafood platter!
Carte: about 150F (excluding oysters).

### 11/20
### Bougnat Boutique
**16 ave. du Gal-Leclerc**
**543.98.18**
*M. Lebrun*
*Open until 10:30 P.M.*
*V.*

The juxtaposition of Bougnat (coal merchant) and Boutique might give cause for apprehension. Nevertheless, the name belies a delightful eating place (which has not deteriorated under new ownership). There are excellent regional products, such as delicatessen from the Auvergne, farm cheeses, local wines. The simple dishes are most reasonably priced, and there is also a take-out section.
Carte: 80F. Menus: 45F, 62F (serv. incl.).

### 12/20
### Le Bour-bonnais
**29 rue Delambre**
**320.61.73**
*M. Jallet*
*Open until 10:30 P.M. Closed Sun.*

Bourgeois cooking in the tradition of the province of Bourbonnais, as the name proclaims. These are the delicious dishes finely concocted by the young chef of this newly-renovated old establishment: coq au vin, potée bourbonnaise, andouillette braised in Saint-Pourçain wine, and meat tart.
Carte: 120F.

### 11/20
### Café Francais
**17 blvd. Saint-Jacques**
**589.89.80**
*Open until 10:30 P.M. Closed during August. Pay parking (12F half day).*
*AE, DC, V.*

Each year, three or four of the regions of France (cleverly featured in a small newspaper-like brochure) are represented in succession in the vast, excessively ornate banquet suite on the second floor of this establishment. According to the occasion, you will dine in the Beaujolais, Touraine, Basque, Alsatian, or other styles. The menus are all-inclusive, but offer a choice (including a huge buffet of hors d'oeuvres and hot and cold starters). All this may sometimes lack finesse, and the wines, which are supposed to be typical of each region, do not always do them justice. However, despite mounting prices, the Café Français is a good choice for an amusing, informal dinner (there is a piano player every evening except Sunday).
Carte: 160F. Menus: 90F (serv. incl.), 125F, 192F (wine and serv. incl.).

### 13
### La Chaumière des Gourmets
**22 place Denfert-Rochereau**
**321.22.59**

Jean Bequet is one of the most knowledgeable "fish men" of the region; no one knows better how to choose the best or how to modify his menu according to the uncertainties of the market. In his little restaurant across from the catacombs, much less a thatched cottage than a confection, you will surely appreciate as we did his salmon à la manière de Paul Bocuse, the bouillabaisse with aspic, the marmite dieppoise, without forgetting

*Mme Bequet*
*Open until 10:00 P.M. Closed Sat.,*
*Sun., holidays and during August*
*and 1 wk. in winter. Parking at 25*
*rue Boulard.*
*V.*

## 13
## La Chaumière Paysanne
**7 rue Léopold-Robert**
**320.76.55**
*MM. Dupuy and Leclerc*
*Open until 10:00 P.M. Closed Sun.,*
*Mon. (at lunch) and during*
*August. Parking 4F. at 138 bis*
*blvd. du Montparnasse.*
*V.*

## 11/20
## La Coupole
**102 blvd. du**
**Montparnasse**
**320.14.20**
*MM. Fraux and Lafon*
*Open until 2:00 A.M. Parking at*
*118-135 blvd. du Montparnasse.*
*V.*

## 11/20
## La Créole
**122 blvd. du**
**Montparnasse**
**320.62.12**
*Mme Renaudon*
*Open until 11:00 P.M. Closed Sun.*
*and August 15–30. Dinner only.*
*Pay parking.*

## 13
## Le Dôme
**108 blvd. du**
**Montparnasse**
**354.53.61**
*M. Bras*
*Open until 1:00 A.M. Closed Mon.*
*AE, DC, V.*

several good landlubbers' dishes—such as salad of veal sweetbread with turnips and an excellent apple tarte flambéed with Calvados.
Carte: 180F–200F. Menu: 120F (serv. incl.).

Except for several entrées with a more or less modern accent, the cuisine of Jean-Claude Leclerc in his personal style principally honors the great Southwest: escalope of foie gras en papillote, cassoulet with preserved duck, roast magret, Chalosse confits. All this, with an attractive Cahors and the marvelous Christian Constant sherbets contributes, in a somewhat faded rustic decor, to the most serious meal that you are likely to find on the outskirts of Montparnasse.
Carte: 160F.

Another year's reprieve from the developers who are eager to turn La Coupole's magnificent site into a cinema and parking lot. Meanwhile, this old café-restaurant stands like a beached liner in the center of Montparnasse. The clientele is as brilliant as Lipp's and more picturesque. The Othon Friesz's frescoes, in a fog of cigars and plats du jour, underscore the essential mediocrity of the 1925 decor, and the cuisine—an average of more than 500 meals per day—is not as careful as you might like; there's a complacency in the elaborate dishes, but it's better than you might suspect if you stick to the oysters, the seafood and the grills.
Carte: 130F – 150F (perhaps less).

The very traditional Caribbean cuisine (stuffed crab, cod sauce chien, ragout de queues de cochon with red beans, fricassée of kid) is matched by a jolly, warm-hearted atmosphere straight from the French Antilles. The waitresses are pretty and curvaceous and there is singing with guitar accompaniment from punch to coffee.
Carte: about 120F. Menu: 55F (serv. incl.).

Dark woods, engraved glass, intimate corners, the delicate lighting of the great brasseries of yesterday. Just behind the restaurant, on the rue Delambre, a small affiliated fish shop supplies raw material of first-class quality and great diversity. A cuisine of simple and studied refinement: shrimp cooked live with cider, salad of raw haddock, tiny calamari from Marseille sautéed with garlic, poached bass with citronella, perfect oysters and sea urchins, a rich bourride equalled only by the ultra-rich bouillabaisse. Reasonable prices with little wines from Rhône Valley and Provence.
Carte: 130F–150F. Menu: 85F + 15% serv.

**17**

## Le Duc
**243 blvd. Raspail**
**320.96.30**
*MM. Minchelli*
*Open until 10:30 P.M. Closed Sat.,*
*Sun., Mon. and holidays.*

Paul and Jean Minchelli's most remarkable contribution to cuisine has been, without dispute, the invention of the fish. Before them, the fish was unknown; apart from them, no one knows how to prepare it. Anyway, this is what this prodigious cook and that incomparable maître d'hôtel maintain, and it is not far from the truth. This dictum might well be extended to include all else that comes from the sea as well, for where else but in this happy, distinguished restaurant can one discover the true taste of prawn (in warm soup with pasta, sautéed in palm oil "en folie"), lobster (with orange), clams (with thyme, or fresh pasta), oysters (with curry), and many other shellfish? It is also in serving these uncooked (tartare, or else very thinly sliced) or poached, or grilled, or with very little or no sauce, that the Minchelli's prove that seafood is not what it was thought to be, but something much finer, richer in subtle aromas: sole with vinegar, daurade with clams, John Dory with vodka. No meat here—only the sea. And salty (about 250F with some admirably and creatively chosen wines—even chilled red Burgundy with the fish). Carte: about 250F.

**12/20**

## Le Falstaff
**42 rue du**
**Montparnasse**
**326.91.34**
*M. Chaillot*
*Open until 11:00 P.M. Closed Sun.*
*and Mon. (at lunch). Parking 4F*
*at garage at 52 rue du*
*Montparnasse.*
*AE, DC, V.*

A second youth for this very old Montparnasse address, under the able management of M. Chaillot, who spent ten years with Lasserre. However, the chef is the author of a cuisine that is somewhat unimaginative and only timidly Parisian: salad of lotte with avocados, sole with leeks, and calf's kidneys with piñon nuts. Carte: 170F.

**11/20**

## Au Feu Follet
**5 rue**
**Raymond-Losserand**
**322.65.72**
*Mme Bihourd*
*Open until midnight. Closed Sun.*

Odette, whom we know from the rue du Dragon in Saint-Germain-des-Prés, has set up her kitchen only a few hundred yards from the gare Montparnasse. The atmosphere is that of a small prewar bistro, and it appears as if nothing, not even the old-fashioned counter or the green plants has been changed since. Cuisine behind the times, a short menu which nevertheless is ample, considering the closeness of the quarters: quiche with bacon, split pea soup, palette of pork, guinea fowl with cabbage, served in parsimonious portions on small plates (38F + serv.) Home-cooking but bit a perfunctory. Our head of veal was not too tender and the sauce verte was too salty. But there's an excellent Touraine Gamay, served well chilled, and the service is in the image of Odette herself: kind and friendly. Carte: 130F.

## 12/20
### Le Flamboyant
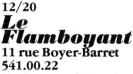

**11 rue Boyer-Barret**
**541.00.22**
*Mme Vanuyzer and M. Lagaville*
*Open until 11:00 P.M. Closed Sun.*
*evenings, Mon., Tues. (at lunch)*
*and during August.*

Betty, the friendly owner-cook, has removed from her menu any dishes which originated in her native Belgium. A pity, because her dishes cooked in beer were amusing and unusual among the eggplant gratin with Caribbean yams, pork with banana, the touffé of shark and other ragouts with sweet potato or coconut milk. However, this has not affected the quality of the above-mentioned (although the quantity leaves something to be desired). These are genuine, well-prepared Caribbean dishes. The sorbets are delicious, and an impressive display of island punches. It is wise to make a reservation.
Carte: 80F–100F. Menu: (Wed., Thurs., Fri. lunch only): 28F (wine and serv. incl.).

## 11/20
### Jardin de la Paresse

**(Restaurant du Parc Montsouris) 20 rue Gazan**
**588.38.52**
*M. Beytout*
*Open until 9:30 P.M. (weekdays*
*during winter), until 10:30 P.M.*
*(weekends during winter), and*
*until midnight (in summer).*
*Closed Sun. evening and Mon.*
*(from October to end of April).*
*Open terrace. Parking.*
*AE, DC, V.*

Seating yourself in this long, greenhouse-like dining room is no less pleasant than being on the terrace shaded by great trees, but the terrace has the advantage of overlooking a playground where your children can frolic between two courses of a clever "little" fixed-price meal (small piece of beef, vegetables, ice cream) designed for the kids. For the adults, a fashionable cuisine—which seems infused with the spirit of the tired service and worn table linen. Very attractive cheeses and Touraine Marionnet Gamay.
Carte: 180F. Menus: 38F for children, serv. incl., 98F (aper., wine, serv. incl.).

## 10/20
### Léni Olympic-Entrepôt
**9 rue François-de-Pressensé**
**541.06.17**
*M. Chevasson*
*Open until midnight. Closed Tues.*
*and Christmas.*

Installed in an old book binding workshop which was also, rumor gleefully has it, where the licentious publications of Paris were pulped, it is the last remaining complex with bookshop, ice cream bar, movie theater and restaurant. You can be served here quite late and inexpensively a dolled-up country cuisine in a strange decor of green plants and steel beams; offerings include white cheese with herbs, sauté of veal with tarragon, chocolate mousse. Many actors, journalists, pretty intellectuals with nervous laughs, youngsters on the make, and mama's boys soberly dressed in yellow undershirts, their hair dyed a subtle electric green, belted with shower hose and with attractive teaball earrings. The cream of Paris, what?
Menu: 70F (serv. incl.).

## 15
### Lous Landès
**157 ave. du Maine**
**543.08.04**
*Mme Descat*
*Open until 10:30 P.M. Closed Sun.*
*evening, Mon. and June 1 to 22.*
*Open terrace.*
*DC, EC, V.*

Georgette Descat won't like us for saying this, but we must tell her anyhow: you shouldn't arrive too early at Lous Landès or you'll miss the pleasure of pushing Jean-Pierre to the piano, where he renders with a pudgy hand his own numbers or else the good old prewar songs. But he is sensitive enough, when he does not "feel" the audience, to return to his pastries, his Bordeaux and Cahors (ah, that

Cahors from chez Gilis!), and his old Armagnacs. As for Georgette, she looks more fulfilled than ever since her restaurant has changed sides of the street, happy that her business has never been so good and that she is freezing to death in her air-conditioned kitchen. She'll share her good mood with several plates of her own invention, such as the marvelous crayfish sautéed with hazelnut oil and wild rice, haddock salad and all of the other fish (don't forget that she sold fish in her youth) that she prepares with a thousand knowing tricks and a thousand unusual flavors. So much for the cuisine of her fancy. But the Landes region is always in the background—farm-cured hams (among the best in Paris), exquisite foie gras, confits that melt in your mouth, magret à la ficelle, and potatoes sarladaise. There's nothing like a Landes meal to drive away the blues, and you will soon be caught up in the fun and confusion of the kitsch paintings and voluptuous bric-a-brac from the Belle Époque, in a most reinvigorating evening, if not the most economic, for you know that, faced with a Farbos '54 or a Poyferré '28, you tend to let yourself go.
Carte: 180F–220F.

14

## Le Moniage Guillaume
**88 rue de la Tombe-Issoire
522.96.15**
*MM. Lecerf*
*Open until 10:30 P.M. Closed Sun.*
*Attendant parking.*
*All major credit cards.*

One of the surest spots in Paris for fish and shellfish. Serge and Bernard Lecerf, with the same team since 1968, never cease to progress in their prosperous, well-lit, comfortable little house. The cuisine is based principally upon an unfailing regularity in the purchase of the products and perfecting (that is to say, simplifying) their cooking. Chef Raymond Archimbeaud is, from this standpoint, one of the great specialists of steam cooking with sea-weed, as is evidenced by his fillet of John Dory with wild nettles, a turbot with blood oranges, and his admirable lobsters and langoustes which are pulled from fish tanks and served, all things considered, at reasonable prices. His short menu stimulates the imagination as well as the appetite (soufflé of three fish, melon cocktail with lobster, terrine of crab and hazelnuts) and even the desserts which, since he studied a few times with Lenôtre, show diversity and high quality. The very remarkable fixed-price meals "based on a fish" (autour d'un poisson) have not gone up in price this year. Service is charming and the good wines expensive.
Carte: 230F. Menu: 110F (wine incl.). + 15% serv.

10/20
## Mon Petit Bar
**7 rue Campagne-Première
320.93.04**
*Mme Teissèdre*
*Open until 9:00 P.M. Closed Sat.,*
*Sun. and during August.*

The clientele is a local gang of old and faithful pals, always anxious to celebrate Yvonne Teissèdre's cooking. Yvonne is an Auvergnate to the tip of her toes, and so is her food: stuffed potaotes, potée, tripoux. The decor is corner-café depressing.
Carte: 80F–100F. Menu: 36F (serv. incl.).

144

## 15
## Chez Provost

**1 rue des Coulmiers**
**539.86.99**
*M. Provost*
*Open until 10:00 P.M. Closed Sat.,*
*Sun., holidays and during August.*
*Parking at 36 rue Friant.*
*AE, V.*

Chez Provost was formerly merely a branch, of one the best charcuteries in Paris. Now the country house-style restaurant has become a really good restaurant on its own, and André Provost a first-class chef. To be sure, on his short menu, which evolves almost daily in response to his ideas and the humors of the market, a good part is devoted to boudin andouillette (the best in world, as we have already written about those served at the Ciboulette, since both are made in the same spot), pig's trotters, and fresh smoked salmon. But he also knows the secret of light sauces, of dishes in which the best ingredients are wed with great happiness. Thus the John Dory en waterzooi, turbot with artichokes, or calf's liver with lime. Attractive wines at approachable prices. The decor is that of a private home, intimate and restful.
Carte: about 170F.

## 10/20
## La Route des Andes

**3 rue Pernety**
**542.87.97**
*Open until midnight. Closed Sun.*
*Dinner only.*

A few specialties from Peru and elsewhere (shrimp Bahia-style, chili con carne, ceviche), served in surroundings that are wildly Andean. The owner, a former newspaper photographer for *l'Express,* has a passion for the exotic.
Carte: about 120F.

## 11/20
## La Route du Château

**36 rue Raymond-Losserand**
**320.09.59**
*M. Perrault*
*Open until 12:30 A.M. Closed Sun.,*
*Mon. (at lunch) and during*
*August.*
*AE.*

This place is not on the route to any châteaux of note, but it is very pleasant in the evening when the neighboring construction work stops and the dust has settled on the nearby building site. This delightful old street-corner bistro, with its etched-glass windows serves home-style cooking to a youngish, rather elegant clientele. Dishes include: rabbit in cider, petit salé with lentils, coquelet with Auvergne blue cheese.
Carte: 100F–130F. Menu: 54F (serv. incl.).

## 12/20
## Le Vallon de Vérone

**53 rue Didot**
**543.18.87**
*Messieurs Constiaux and Dahdah*
*Open until 8:00 P.M. Closed Sun.*
*Parking rue du Moulin-Vert.*
*V.*

Unless the name refers to Verona's famous lovers (there usually are a few here, too), it leaves us perplexed because the cuisine is essentially from the southwest of France. Then there is the "Vallon" (little valley), at the bottom of which the owner-chefs, Daniel and Gérard, seem to simmer their specialties from one year to the next. The dishes include cassoulet, ventre de veau gascon, and turnips with magret of duck. In this former tavern, one eats elbow to elbow (just a little less so now that a new dining room has been opened), but always merrily (the Latin Quarter isn't far away), and everything is evocative of southwestern France—including the desserts (pastis Quercynois) and the wines (Côtes du Marmandais). The prices seem to be climbing rather fast.
Carte: 150F. Menu: 82F (serv. incl.).

**11/20**
### Yakitori
**64 rue du**
**Montparnasse**
**320.27.76**
*M. Funaga*
*Open until 10:30 P.M. Closed Mon.,*
*May 1, August 15, Christmas and*
*December 30 to January 4.*

One of the less traditional of the Japanese restaurants in Paris. For years, the formula has been based entirely on brochettes which are adeptly prepared right in front of you. Since they are the only course, you will need to eat a lot of them in order not to die of hunger and also to be able to sample the twelve to fifteen different spicy, salty or sweet sauces which serve as accompaniments.
Carte: 100F.

**12/20**
### Zeyer
**234 ave. du Maine**
**540.43.88**
*Mme Bras*
*Open until 1:00 A.M. Parking.*

The flowered art deco tiles which Slavik retained when he redecorated the old Zeyer are glorious! It would be premature to say that Paris high society drops in every night, near this unattractive and rather remote intersection. However, so far it has attracted the best of the Porte d'Orléans neighborhood society and the staff takes very good care of them. The menu is enormous and contains a little of everything, which does not mean just anything, for the owner loves to eat, and he keeps a close eye on everything (except the fries). His andouillette is splendid (could it possibly be made by his neighbor Provost?), and so is the côte de boeuf and the bitter chocolate crème. Good Bordeaux served en carafe.
Carte: 110F.

# 15ème Arr.

**11/20**
### L'Aman-guier
**51 rue du Théâtre**
**577.04.01**
*M. Derderian*
*Open until 11:00 P.M.*
*AE, DC, V.*

This former wood and coal merchant's has been transformed, like the other restaurants of the Amanguier chain into an exotic garden. And just like the others, it swarms morning to evening with an economical but food-loving crowd. The service is fast and efficient, the reception very simple. The tables are comfortable and the formula menu is light and well-done, obviously under the management of a young entrepreneur who knows how to plan intelligently. For example, for 39F you can choose between various starters combined with a series of main dishes: salad with aiguillettes of duck, the sander in sorrel and gratin of zucchini. You can add chocolate cake (14F), a pitcher of pleasant sparkling Touraine rosé (25F), and you will nearly have had a really good meal for well under 100F.
Carte: about 80F. Menu: 63F (wine and serv. incl.).

**11/20**

## L'Auberge Fleurie

**34 rue de Vouillé**
**532.88.78**

*M. Rébillard*
*Open until 10:00 P.M. Closed Sat.*
*evening, Sun. and during July.*
*V.*

The pigs' trotters à la Sainte-Menehould which recently won an international award for René Rébillard are the star attraction here. But instead, you may decide to select only the plain broiled pigs' trotters, the kidneys, the filet mignon, or the hot Brittany sausage. The table linen is not always too clean, but the service is kind and motherly. They have a good Côtes de Bourg wine.
Carte: about 120F.

**12/20**

## Auberge de la Tour

**6 rue Desaix**
**306.58.37**

*Open until 10:00 P.M. Closed Sat.*
*(at lunch) and Sun.*
*AE, DC, V.*

The simple decor of this little restaurant consists of fairly mundane but frequently changed paintings and a fascinating collection of football club pennants, found at the bar. There is a lively atmosphere in the evening, by candlelight. This is the place to go for Italian cuisine; its chief merit is that is has left the well-trodden paths, but when interpreting classic dishes (osso buco, minestrone, calf's livers Venetian style, scampi), it does so with much grace. Try the tagliatelle au pistou, taglialini with cèpes, the gnochetti, the Tuscan-style civet of guinea-fowl and the exquisite zabaglione made by the young chef Ivano, formerly with Poccardi. Ask for the Barbera wine to be served slightly chilled.
Carte: 120F.

**14**

## Benkay

**61 quai de Grenelle**
**575.61.62**

*Open until 10:30 P.M. Parking.*
*All major credit cards.*

Chef Komatsu of the Japanese restaurant in the Nikko Hotel is a famous artist and we cannot recommend strongly enough his one-man-show in the vast, well-lit and discreetly Japanese setting where he presides right under your eyes. You may even have to return another time to taste the traditional Alaskan seaweed, the jellyfish, the raw daurade marinated with saké vinegar. Service of the teppanyaki is an authentic Nipponese tradition: on an ultra-modern hot plate Komatsu prepares a cuisine sautéed in oil, while starring in a spectacular in which he is juggler, artist and sculptor all at the same time, before serving the spellbound guests a multitude of meat and fish servings, freshly cooked and exquisite. You will certainly adore this; the same is true of the sashimi tempura and the delicate cold hors d'oeuvres. The portions are honorable for a Japanese restaurant.
Carte: 180F–200F. Menus: 160F, 170F, 180F, 210F and 240F (serv. incl.).

**16**

## Bistro 121

**121 rue de la Convention**
**557.52.90**

*Mmes Moussié*
*Open until 10:30 P.M. Closed Sun.*
*evening, Mon. and from July 14 to*
*August 19. Parking at 124 rue*
*de la Convention.*
*AE, EC, V.*

Before his death, our Jean Moussié invented one last dish, the astonishing fricassée of eels with verjus, as if to leave a testimony to the enthusiasm, the liberty and the talent with which he so strongly influenced post war Parisian cooking. Naturally, with Christine and Monique Moussié and their chef André Jalbert, the Bistro carries on in its elegant frills, surrounded by a chic clientele and with the good cuisine that we have known and loved for so long, at

once traditional and modern: fish à la tahitienne, raw sirloin, duck's liver with verjus, the bass with seaweed, the veal gribîche, chicken with vinegar, and beautiful salads and sherbets. ·
Carte: 220F – 225F. Menu: 220F + 15% serv.

12/20

## *Brasserie du Pont-Mirabeau*

**61 quai de Grenelle**
**575.62.62**
*M. Leclercq*
*Open until 11:00 P.M. Pay parking.*
*AE, DC, V.*

Having seen the brasseries "like they don't make them any more" and the new brasseries being turned out by the dozen, we have here a large, comfortable brasserie on the second of the 31 stories of the hotel Nikko facing the Seine and the headquarters of French Radio. The decor is well-lit, spacious, comfortable and the cuisine is faithful to the brasserie style. The sauerkraut is very good, the broiled meats excellent, and thought is given to the special of the day (rack of lamb, gibelotte dijonnaise). Agreeable wines come from good vintners. Very pleasant service.
Carte: about 130F.

13

## *Le Caroubier*

**8 ave. du Maine**
**548.14.38**
*M. Michel*
*Open until 10:30 P.M. Closed Sun. and during August.*

The friendly owner, Pierre Michel, was the first, several years ago, to put together the real couscous as it is made in North Africa—or, to be exact, it was Mme Michel, whom one does not see but who sends into the dining room of the Caroubier those six varieties of light, well-rolled couscous (the garnishes are, however, often only so-so), not to mention the couscous "for children" or the exquisite sweet Sefaa couscous with cinnamon, almonds and raisins. Even if you order the delicious pastilla with pigeon, the grilled merguez (the *real* ones) then a mutton and prune tajine (a Moroccan dish cooked in a special untensil), you will spend scarcely more than 80F–100F.
Carte: about 100F.

13

## *Les Célébrités*

**61 quai de Grenelle**
**575.62.62**
*M. Leclercq*
*Open until 10:30 P.M. Pay parking.*
*AE, DC, V.*

Although the inimitable restaurant manager, Robuchon, has left to run Jamin, and the chef, Jacky Fréon, has gone to the Nova Park, Nikko's management has not been deterred from its aim of providing great French cuisine. Jacques Sénéchal, formerly of the Tour d'Argent, is now the chef. The meal he served us, soon after his arrival, certainly had no serious defects—salad of sweetbreads with langoustines, young Bresse pigeon en vessie, feuilleté of pears—but it was still based on the menu of his predecessors. We will have to wait to make a really good judgement on the basis of new dishes introduced by Sénéchal. Let us hope that he follows the lead taken by Robuchon, whose inventiveness brought Les Célébrités extremely close to receiving our three-toque award. The service is extraordinarily good, the surroundings facing the Seine are modern, elegant and extremely comfortable.
Carte: 250F. Menu: 250F (serv. incl.).

**12/20**
## *Charly de Bab-El-Oued*
**215 rue de la Croix-Nivert**
**828.76.78**
*M. Driguès*
*Open until midnight.*
*AE, DC, V.*

This jewel in Charly's imperial crown (a new and excellent Charly opened this year at the Porte Maillot) consists of a patio decorated in Persian-Andalusian style, scented with spicy Merguez sausages. You will be served in a cordial, fatherly atmosphere, with all the varieties of brik (4), genuine couscous (8), tajine stews (6), and other North African specialties, such as the delicious soubressade, or even . . . not quite so North African . . . crottin de Chavignol à la Provençale.
Carte: 90F.

**12/20**
## *Clos de la Tour*
**22, rue Falguière**
**322.34.73**
*M. Dalbin*
*Open until 10:30 P.M. Closed Sat.*
*(at lunch), Sun. and during*
*August.*
*AE, DC, V.*

This attractive new bistro has in the last few months risen from the dust of a section pulverized by bulldozers. A young Alsatian who used to work at Outhier and at Haeberlin, M. Dalbin serves a cunning, fairly sophisticated cuisine (civet of Chartreux pork, a flan of chicken with marrow, a lemon mousse with a purée of raspberry), it has the merit of charming a clientele made up of Left Bank movie people whose chic carelessness goes marvelously with the careless chic of the decor.
Carte: 130F–150F.

**13**
## *Le Copreaux*
**15 rue Copreaux**
**306.83.35**
*M. Millon*
*Open until 10:30 P.M. Closed Sat.*
*(at lunch), Sun. and August 15 to*
*September 7 and December 25 to*
*January 3.*
*AE, DC, V.*

Yves Millon, whom you remember from Chiberta, has just opened—without fanfare—this tiny house of flowery and intimate decor. One inspiration was to install Jean-Luc Quatreboeufs (also an old Chiberta hand who afterwards spent two years at the Champs d'Or) in the kitchen. You will taste his marinated scallops on a bed of lamb's lettuce; his salad of duck (magret and skin); his perfect preserved duck's wing with blood; calf's kidneys with mustard seeds, beautifully cooked and served in a very light sauce—delicious—and some ravishing desserts like the exquisite sherbets of the house in their fresh fruit soups. A cuisine which smacks neither of banality nor of bored genius. The reception, the table settings and, above all, the prices are witness to the same careful equilibrium and good taste.
Carte: about 150F. Menu: 60F + 15% serv.

**13**
## *Courrège*
**2 rue de Langeac**
**842.55.26**
*M. Courrège and M. Lampreia*
*Open until 10:30 P.M. Closed Sun.,*
*Mon., Easter and second 2 wks. in*
*August.*
*V.*

An old neighborhood dive (way down at the end, over there, near the porte de Versailles), very attractively refurbished with Napoleon III settees, etched glasse, and large tinted mirrors reflecting green plants that climb toward a ceiling of scaly metal. The moustachioed maître d'hôtel (one would think he came with the decor) and the attractive owner, Michèle Courrège, greet you with smiles that in themselves guarantee your happiness. But the best feature of the evening is the cuisine itself, prepared by José Lampreia. It's exactly what you'd expect

in this baroque and sympathetic setting—generous, modern, carefully prepared and without frills: warm fondant of artichokes with basil; salad of beef pot au feu, stuffed cabbage with lobster, sauté of pork with blood. Always a remarkable little fixed-price meal (entrée, main dish, dessert) with varied offerings, and a cellar of house Côtes-du-Rhône that help moderate the bill.
Carte: 130F–150F. Menu: 60F. + 15% serv.

14

## *Le Croquant*

**28 rue Jean-Maridor**
**558.50.83**

M. Rumen
Open until 10:30 P.M. Closed Sun.,
Mon. and August 15 to
September 1.
AE, DC, V.

Hervé Rumen, who for ten years was the director of Christian Constant, the fine pastry shop on rue du Bac, took over this cute little restaurant of only 22 place settings about a year ago. He prepares a short but attractive menu that reflects the freshness and the rhythm of the seasons of the Southwest. The cuisine is prepared with intelligent lightness: a fricassée of eel with fresh herbs, souris of leg of lamb with bouquets of haricot beans, magrets of duck with preserved young garlic. Also, a few frankly modern offerings such as a delicious mesclun salad with raw beans and new onions, and a lotte with a tarragon fumet (a little salty). And, finally, some exquisite desserts, as one may well imagine. In all, quite reasonable prices for such quality.
Carte: 140F. Menu: 100F (wine and service incl.)

12/20

## *Foo-Lim*

**27 rue Cambronne**
**566.88.89**

M. Tai Han Yun
Open until 11:00 P.M.
AE, V.

The great specialties of owner-chef Tai Han Yun, who has been cooking the gamut of Chinese dishes for 40 years, include, among other spicy and strong-smelling dishes, Szechuan-style daurade and émincé of lamb with chives. However, don't be afraid to venture into the unknown, because this uncompromising cuisine, with classic dishes in Cantonese or Peking styles, deserves to be trusted. Cozy surroundings and a welcome worthy of a great restaurant.
Carte: about 100F. Menu: 42F (serv. incl.).

13

## *La Gauloise*

**59 ave. de**
**La Motte-Picquet**
**734.11.64**

M. Apbécetche
Open until 11:45 P.M. Closed Sat.
and Sun. Open terrace.
V.

The cuisine is based on fish at the frontier between classic and modern, with several very good traditional dishes (fricassée of duck, navarin of lamb), and various more or less new dishes that the chef prepares with a light hand to justify his once having been an apprentice saucier in important houses (Lasserre, Grand Véfour): braised veal sweetbreads with sorrel, aiguillette of duck with honey and sherry vinegar, medaillon of veal with sweet garlic. The decor has been redone, but the provincial charm of this peaceful long dining room has not been ruined.
Carte: 160F–180F.

## 14
## Le Grand Venise
**171 rue de la Convention**
**532.49.71**
*Mlle Lani*
*Open until 11:00 P.M. Closed Sun.,*
*Mon. and from August 5 to*
*September 15. Parking at*
*rue Blomet.*
*AE, DC, EC.*

Officially, Mlle Lani has taken the reins from the hands of her Papa, Angelo, but things remain the same, the warm, family-like reception, the fastidious preparation of the saltimbocca romana, superb and ultra-light ravioli Piedmontaise, the extraordinarily fine lasagna stuffed with seafood cooked just right, fresh red mullet with tomatoes, and an array of original and lip-smacking desserts prepared for these last eight years by the young French chef Jean-Noël Gaudron. The service is always a little slow in getting started, but the plate of fresh crudités placed on the table will help you to await the arrival of your first course in this restaurant which will convince you that Gargantua was Italian and where we thus recommend you arrive with an empty stomach.
Carte: 200F.

## 13
## Long Yuen
**27 ave. du Maine**
**548.62.59**
*M. Chang*
*Open until 10:30 P.M.*
*DC, V.*

It cannot be repeated too often: to taste Chinese restaurant cuisine at its best, you really must order a banquet in advance for six to eight people. Charming young M. Chang excels at this. He will serve you, for example, such unusual dishes as quail with salt and four spices, delicious bouillon of steamed pigeon, scallops in Chinese wine, sole in salted Hunan ham, and of course, Peking-style glazed duck, which is as close as one can get to the original. This does not mean you will be disappointed by the regular menu. On the contrary, the shrimp in Shanghai sauce, sautéed pork with soy paté, fried dumplings, sautéed chicken Szechuan-style (sweet and sour), or sautéed duck with bell peppers will provide the most pleasant meals in this simple but unusual restaurant located in the shadow of the Tour Montparnasse.
Carte: 70F–100F. Menus: 47F (serv. incl.) and about 180F (special order).

## 16 
## Morot-Gaudry
**8 rue de la Cavalerie**
**567.06.95**
*M. Morot-Gaudry*
*Open until 10:15 P.M. Closed Sat.*
*(lunch) and Sun. Open terrace.*
*Attendant parking.*
*V.*

The altitude of his restaurant notwithstanding (on the ninth floor, on a street almost impossible to find—via avenue de Suffren and rue du Laos), Jean-Pierre Morot-Gaudry had some trouble taking off. People criticized the small portions of his business lunches, his bizarre accompaniments, his taste for sweets-savories and for spices. And then, the fog lifted, and Morot was airborne. His wife's charming reception; the modern, warm decor; the delicious flowered terrace from which you can almost touch the Eiffel Tower; and, above all, the quality of an extremely inventive and mastered cuisine (superbly associated with a remarkable wine cellar). The duck liver is one of the best in Paris, the cervelas of crab, the compote of chicken with leek, the calf's head with horseradish, the lotte with crocus pistils, the lamb's tongue with Sauternes, the coffee marquise, the rice cake with ginger, and a few other inventions-to-be merited

another point—and the prices, almost reasonable, a tip of the toque.
Carte: 200F–230F. Menu: 150F serv. incl., 230F (dégustation, wine and serv. incl.)

14

## Napoléon et Chaix
**46 rue Balard**
**554.09.00**
*M. Pousse*
*Open until midnight. Closed Sun.*
*Open terrace.*
*AE, EC, V.*

André Pousse, actor, bicyclist and an old pal from good and bad times, has won his bet. This attractive bistro lost among the Citroën factories, is now a chic stop on the circuit of fashionable Parisians. Even at lunch, businessmen gather to gossip. The warm reception and the clear if sometimes uneven talent of Chef Gerard Magnan are the reasons for this success, despite the pitfalls of finding one's way to this spot so strangely named, (Napoléon Chaix the famous printer to the SNCF, and father of a president of the gourmet Club des Cent). Our favorite dishes are fresh pasta with foie gras, the platter of raw fish, the choucroute with haddock, and the oeufs à la neige. Very amusing little wines.
Carte: 160F–180F. Menu: 80F + 15% serv.

17

## Olympe
**8 rue Nicolas-Charlet**
**734.86.08**
*M. Nahmias*
*Open until midnight. Closed Mon.,*
*dinner only (except Thurs.) from*
*December 22 to January 2 and*
*August 1 to 25. Air cond.*
*AE, V.*

Dominique, a small angular-faced woman with an explosive temper, knows what she is about. She is the daughter of a Corsican lawyer (Corsicans are known for their bad characters) who, one fine day, dropped everything to open a restaurant in the South of France. Possessed by a passion for cuisine and trailing along her husband Albert, a sociology student at the university, she created several years ago in Montparnasse (whence the name Olympe) a tiny restaurant that very quickly began to attract a fashionable clientele. Eventually, restricted by the lack of space, she moved to larger premises on a deserted street, which she decorated according to her taste in art deco style. Not only her faithful customers followed her— a new clientele made up of everybody who is anybody in the entertainment world began to gather each evening in her dining room decorated with the authentic wooden panels of the celebrated *Orient Express* and with several pieces of 1925 furniture. Those who are not part of this illustrious society and who come simply to have a good meal might feel excluded, for Dominique and Albert do tend to pay more attention to their friends than to unknown visitor. This is obviously a false impression, but you might become an habitué yourself after having tasted the exquisite cuisine that this small woman in the white apron prepares herself with untrammeled imagination. Among her successes are the sensational ravioli with broccoli purée, soup with smoked duck, prawn with homemade pasta that is a marvel, pigeon with parsley and shallots, and several crayfish preparations, sautéed or in cream, each more delicious than the other. It remains to be said only that the servings are not always generous and that the prices are severe.
Carte: 250F–300F. Menu: 148F, 240F (serv. incl.).

## 12/20
### Le Petit Mâchon
**123 rue de la Convention**
**554.08.62**
*M. Moussié*
*Open until 10:30 P.M. Closed Sun. evening, Mon. and July 14 to August 19.*

When the home restaurant is good, so are the branches. This is the case for Le Petit Mâchon of Jean-Claude Moussié (his Le Bistrot 121 is just next door), which is entirely devoted to regional cuisine, mainly that of Lyon, whence the name mâchon; (delicatessen-type restaurant, serving at all hours), and that of Quercy. The menu is very tempting from beginning to end, from a salad of sheeps or calf's trotters with chicken livers and hard-boiled eggs, to the hot sausage or the truffled cervelats Lyon with fried potatoes, and the stuffed pig's trotters, the tablier du sapeur, the knuckle of ham with lentils, to the rice gâteau à la crème anglaise.
Carte: about 100F–120F.

## 12/20
### La Petite Bretonnière
**2 rue de Cadix**
**828.34.39**
*Mme Laurens*
*Open until 10:30 P.M. Closed Sat. (at lunch), Sun. and the last 3 weeks of July. Pay parking at 374 rue de Vaugirard.*
*DC.*

The waltz of chefs from one restaurant to another has been embellished this year with a shuffling of restaurant names. The former Planteur restaurant, now La Petite Bretonnière (the Grande Bretonnière is in Boulogne), has a new chef in the kitchenette. Alain Plant, a former partner of Joël Leduc, is courageously trying to restore standards with light and appetizing dishes, most of which have been tested in the Grande Bretonnière, the mother-restaurant in Boulogne. Most of them are part of an inclusive fixed-price menu, an attractive scheme featuring, for instance, feuilleté of plie with fresh thyme. There is a light chocolate charlotte with vanilla sauce. The decor is pink, intimate and snug, although the tables are closely-packed, and the reception by Claudine Laurens is not necessarily friendly and is sometimes plainly unpleasant.
Carte: 150F–170F. Menu: 85F (wine and serv. incl.).

## 11/20
### Pfister
**1 rue du Dr.-Jacquemaire**
**828.51.38**
*M. Pfister*
*Open until 10:00 P.M. Closed Sat. (at lunch), Sun. and during August.*
*AE.*

The service here is so slow that you'll have plenty of time to study the etchings and the intimate, feminine café-au-lait decor. Philippe Pfister's cuisine remains indecisive (the skate salad is too salty and a bit soggy, the rillettes of rouget reek of haddock, the fillets of rascasse are overcooked, the sauces are uncertain). However, nothing is unsalvageably poor: the surroundings are very pleasant, the tables nicely laid, and the clientele rather elegant, especially in the evenings. The prices are reasonable, and the Pfister house red wine (selected by André Paul) is delicious. The desire to do well is obvious.
Carte: 150F. Menu: 75F (serv. incl.).

## 14
### Raajmahal
**192 rue de la Convention**
**533.15.57**
*M. Kassam*

Lit through a glass roof, decorated like a rajah's palace out of Tintin, this long restaurant offers a very fine Northern Indian cuisine, not too heavily spiced, composed mainly of curries, tandooris, marinated meats, chicken, ham hocks, shrimp, lamb, all of them tender and spicey and

Open until 10:30 P.M. Closed Sun. and Mon. (at lunch). AE, DC, V.

grilled over charcoal in earthenware ovens, with the famous basmati rice, which is to our everyday rice what caviar is to salmon roe, and, to drink, either the astonishing yogurt with herbs or simply a good Bordeaux. The prices are quite high, but the progress achieved here since its opening makes one forgive everything, even the service which, while courteous, is a little sleepy. Carte: 150F.

14

## Le Relais de Sèvres
**8-12 rue Louis-Armand 554.95.00**
M. Bertrand
Open until 10:30 P.M. Closed during August. Pay parking.
AE, DC, V.

Sofitel must have realized that its largest hotel should indeed house a restaurant that lives up to the international prestige of the name with a creative, distinguished cuisine at the forefront of the culinary scene. Young Roland Durand, who studied with Troisgros and Lameloise, is well aware of this effort. He offers inventive, fanciful dishes: cervelle de veau aux écrevisses, diced lotte with grapes, pink daurade with garlic, baby rabbit with mint, gratin of red fruit. The decor is charming and intimate, a pleasant contrast to the discouragingly huge size of the hotel. The Club caters to businessmen. Good menu.
Carte: 220F–250F. Menu: 130F (serv. incl.).

10/20

## Au Rendez-Vous des Chauffeurs
**166 blvd. de Grenelle 783.54.38**
M. Gaubert
Open until 10:00 P.M. Closed Sun. and during July. Open terrace.
V.

Each year the prices rise scrupulously and with moderation. The plats du jour remain the same: beef tongue, duck with turnips, navarin or streaky bacon with lentils. M. Gaubert has been preparing all of this for a long time past, and we hope that he will continue to do so for a long time to come.
Carte: 80F. Menu: 34.50F (serv. incl.).

12/20

## La Rôtisserie sur Seine
**8 rue Linois 575.72.29**
M. Funaro
Open until 11:00 P.M. Open terrace. Parking at 12 rue Linois.
All major credit cards.

Across from the Maison de la Radio, which looks like a great round steamship, and in the Beaugrenelle center, which looks just like all the shopping centers in the world, this rôtisserie is run by a chef who for eight years was second chef at Prunier-Duphot. On the spit (rabbit in mustard, chicken with tarragon, stuffed duck) or on the grill (lamb chops with mint, calf's liver à l'anglaise, rib steak). The ingredients are very fresh, the little Côtes-du-Rhône agreeable, and the à la carte prices remarkably good value for money.
Carte: 100F–110F. Menu: 138F (wine and serv. incl.).

12/20

## Aux Senteurs de Provence
**295 rue Lecourbe 557.11.98**

This funny corner bistro only a short way from the porte de Versailles would be the most humdrum restaurant in the neighborhood if it were not for its owner, Jean Gras, a true partisan of the regional cuisine, announced in the restaurant's name. The small rustic dining room will hardly evoke the Mediterranean shores—the menu does

*M. Gras*
*Open until 9:30 P.M. Closed Sun.,*
*Mon. and during August. No dogs.*
*V.*

that. A bourride and aïolli make a happy couple, and the bouillabaisse dear at 80F, is a meal in itself and irreproachable also, fish soup with rouille, served prior to a beautifully fresh fish. Lovely chocolate marquise, and a return to the sunny South with the perfect white Bandol. Agreeable feminine reception, without fuss. Carte: 160F.

**10/20**

## *Tartine*
**34 rue du Laos**
**567.01.92**
*M. Loumic*
*Open until 10:45 P.M. Closed Sat.*
*(at lunch), Sun. and during*
*August. Open terrace.*

In the evenings a boisterous young crowd on its way to a nightclub or coming back from a tennis tournament at Roland-Garros, meets elbow to elbow in this old (1900s) tavern run by an ex-bartender from the Crillon, to swallow a salad of foie gras (canned), some good herring, and a brochette of chicken with lime drowned in sauce. A likeable gratin dauphinois and some refreshing sherbets. Carte: 100F–120F.

**12/20**

## *La Toison d'Or*
**29 rue Castagnary**
**531.52.44**
*M. Antadzé*
*Closed Tues. and July 20 to early*
*September. Reservations required.*

Just open the formidable door to this izba, and the Golden Fleece is yours . . . that is, provided you can convince the temperamental Georgian owner, M. Antadzé, that you're dying to try his specialties along with his heavily-mustachioed friends. The kidney beans with walnuts, mutton goulash, exquisite small grilled lamb's milk cheese and cheesecake are just as good here as in Tiflis. In fact, it's best to give advance notice and come with a few friends. You'll be even better taken care of. Carte: 80F–100F.

**14**

## *Toit de Paris*
**18 ave. de Suffren**
**273.92.00**
*Closed Sun. and during August.*
*Dinner only.*
*All major credit cards.*

Couples waltz and rumba (three out of four women are draped in lamé) to sounds unheard since the 1950s. The essentially American clientele now dines, between spins on the dance floor on authentically French cuisine, in its best and most rejuvenated form: Xavier Grégoire arrives from Senderens by way of Pangaud and a short stopover at La Ciboulette. Superb mullets, rubbed with peppers on a bed of spinach, crayfish in their juice, ragoût of lobster and Bresse chicken (with sweet garlic), remarkable duck's liver (prepared simply, with walnut oil), veal sweetbread escalope with truffles seasoned with parsley (alas, served a bit overcooked) and charlotte of pears (overly gelatinized). The discovery of a cuisine so well controlled (on the whole) in an ambience so resolutely American (as currently understood in our provinces, we need hardly add) with, just opposite, the four iron feet of the Eiffel Tower, constitutes, at this moment in time, one of the most pleasantly exotic of experiences. Pretty wine list, service on a grand scale, in terms of both number and professionalism. And, of course, very high prices. Carte: 240F. Menu: 195F (Champagne and serv. incl.); 230F (dégustation) (serv. incl.)

**12/20**
## Aux Trois Horloges

**73 rue Brancion**
**828.24.08**
*M. Pons*
*Open until 11:00 P.M. Closed Sun.*
*evenings, Mon. and during August.*
*AE, DC, V.*

After having worked here with his parents for more than fifteen years, Bernard-François Pons is now in full command of this warm, bustling, newly-redecorated colonial-style bistro. Although he claims to be starting off in a new direction, the new owner still remains faithful to the traditional recipes of colonial Algeria: his clientele wouldn't tolerate anything else. You'll have no reason to doubt the authenticity of the fresh anchovies in vinegar, the raw or grilled soubressades (they're much better raw), the black sépia served with noodles and garlic, the delicious sardines in scabèche, and, of course, the half-dozen varieties of couscous and the Wednesday barbouche. The atmosphere is always noisy and colorful. Prices are reasonable.
Carte: about 100F.

**12/20**
## Au Trotteur
**103 rue Brancion**
**828.16.73**
*M. Bertron*
*Open until 10:00 P.M. Closed Sat.*
*(at lunch), Sun. and the first 2*
*weeks in August.*
*AE, DC, V.*

One evening, if you happen to follow the donkeys on their way from the Jardin des Plantes to the stables in the former slaughterhouse at Vaugirard, you'll pass M. Brunetière's tiny restaurant, Au Trotteur, which, three or four years ago, won top ranking in the arrondissement (along with Pierre Vedel and the Bistro 121). The cluttered decor of plants and bric-à-brac is charming, and becomes even more so in the evenings with intimate lighting. You'll need all the help you can get to ignore the uninviting district, the cramped tables and the sullen reception and service. This being said, new owner André Bertron's cuisine aspires to lightness and modernity, as evidenced by the way it is described on the menu, but turns out to be rather clumsy. But what you get for your money is acceptable: delicious melon with pastis and fresh mint, ragoût of duckling, too often reheated, with green grapes (which aren't really green at all) accompanied by a nice gratin of zucchini and feuilleté of spinach. For dessert, one of those omnipresent coulis. Dinner is served with a perfect Cahors from Vigouroux. The service—we repeat—is grim.
Carte: about 160F.

**15**
## Pierre Vedel
**50 rue des Morillons**
**828.04.37**
*M. Vedel*
*Open until 10:30 P.M. Closed Sat.,*
*Sun. and from July 15 to August*
*15 and the week between*
*Christmas and New Year's.*
*No dogs.*

Pierre Vedel has won back his 15/20. He lost a toque with perfect sportsmanship, evidently asking himself what motivated this rebuke from Gault and Millau, who had never been miserly with their encouragements. Let's be precise: the loss of the toque resulted from Pierre Vedel's temptation to modernize several of his specialties in order to be "with it." This native of Sète, passionately attached to his home region, is a lot less inspired when he leaves it. Which is not to say that he lacks imagination. He takes liberties with traditional regional recipes, and this is the way we like him when, for example, he adds a dash of sherry vinegar to a fillet of rascasse, or rhubarb à la crème with saffron to white of turbot, or accompanies his escalope of veal sweetbreads with a marvelous mousse of

beets or aiguillettes of duck with a tian of eggplant. All that remains is to obtain a table, and this is not as easy despite his remote location, for the bistro of Pierre Vedel is never empty. The cuisine and the owner's warm welcome are certainly important reasons for this, but take into consideration, too, the bill, since with an émincé of daurade and pimientos in a light court-bouillon aspic, a braised rouelle of veal with preserved lemon, oeufs à la neige with caramel and a half-bottle of a remarkable Minervois, you will spend less than 125F.
Carte: 110F–140F.

**12/20**

**18 ave. de Suffren**
**273.92.00**
*M. Georgiou*
*Open until 11:00 P.M. Pay*
*parking. No dogs.*
*All major credit cards.*

The decor is Western all the way, and the extraordinary grilled T-bones and ribs come directly from the U.S. Chef Michel Dufrenne, who cooked for President Kennedy, also prepares good Santa Fe rissoles with crab, giant crabs à la Vasca, cream of clams with corn, and desserts piled as high with whipped cream as Squaw Valley is with snow. All of this will give you the best possible sample of good regional American cooking.
Carte: 160F–180F. Menu: 118F (serv. incl.).

**12/20**

**47 ave.**
**Raymond-Poincaré**
**727.98.40**
*M. Gadit*
*Open until 11:00 P.M. Closed Sun.*
*AE, DC, V.*

The name of this restaurant gives you a clue to what it does best. The other available dishes, such as the tendron of veal with vegetables or the sautéed sweetbreads, do not quite equal the quality of the good, carefully-grilled meats. Pleasant, modern decor.
Carte: 150F–180F.

**12/20**
### Brasserie
### Stella
**133 ave. Victor-Hugo**
**727.60.54**
*M. Guerlet*
*Open until 2:00 A.M. Closed*
*August. Pay parking at 130 ave.*
*Victor-Hugo.*

The "fashionable 16th" continues to rendezvous in this brasserie without age or decorative charm other what the clientele brings. Very pretty young girls and women in jeans or mink, trail behind them a noisy, picturesque crowd from the quarter. The service is bustling and does not hide either its chagrin or its good humor. And the cuisine? Very dear for a brasserie, but without fault when it sticks to the potée limousine, rabbit with mustard, stuffed cabbage and various other flavorful plates of this kind. A very hot place.
Carte: 110F–120F.

**11/20**
### Au Charbon de Bois
**10 rue Guichard**
**288.77.49**
*Mme Pruneau*
*Open until 10:30 P.M. Closed Sun.*
*and during August.*
*AE, DC.*

A 23-year old chef at the Charbon de Bois? Has Mme Pruneau lost her mind? Don't worry, the amiable Marino has been here for years and cut his teeth on the blanquette, grilled boudin, grilled salmon, grilled côte de boeuf and other such dishes, all pleasantly served (but don't come too late). The Saint-Germain-des-Prés-style decor is nice.
Carte: 110F–120F. Menu: 48F (serv. incl.).

**14**
### Paul Chêne
**123 rue Lauriston**
**727.63.17**
*M. Chêne*
*Open until 10:30 P.M. Closed Sat.,*
*Sun. and during August. Parking*
*at 120 rue Lauriston.*

The decor, the atmosphere, the service are still those of the good old provinces of papa's time, and you couldn't ask for more. The cuisine is not so simple; even though it has a strong whiff of nostalgia reaching as far back as grandma's day, the execution remains adroit and delicate. Good old Paul Chêne, chef—and master chef—as authentic as his old-fashioned daube of beef accompanied by a purée mousseline such as one no longer finds, his poule au pot Henry IV, his brouillade of truffles that Jean Gabin doted on, or his incomparable apple fritters with currant jelly, and all else that he and his chef of fifteen years (and trained right here in this kitchen by Paul Chêne himself) simmer and stir together. Delicious little wines and some very expensive great ones.
Carte: 180F–200F. Menu: 150F (wine and serv. incl.).

**11/20**
### Au Clocher du Village
**8 bis rue Verderet**
**288.35.87**
*Mme Patenôtre*
*Open until 10:00 P.M. Closed Sat.,*
*Sun. and during August.*
*V.*

Robert Parise started out just before World War II under Albert Lebrun, and he's still going strong. The decor of his village-style bistro is delightfully seedy, and Parise's original paintings grace the walls. He'll take you back to the '40s with his escargot de Bourgogne, hot sausage pie, tête de veau ravigote (including the tongue and the brains) and famous kidneys in creme sauce. All of this is not exactly given away, but then, in Passy, what is?
Carte: 120F–130F.

**13**
### Conti
**72 rue Lauriston**
**727.74.67**
*M. Fayet*
*Open until 10:30 P.M. Closed Sat.,*
*Sun. and during August.*

The peculiar decor of this classic of peninsular cuisine is characterized by plastic moldings of a heavy, musty taste that—who knows—might be in vogue tomorrow. The cuisine, since Pascal Fayet (formerly of Paul Chêne and Taillevent) took over, has become better and better. The fresh pasta, notably accompanying seafood, is admirable, and the menu is enriched little by little by remarkable preparations like the assiette de l'artiste (in which one finds among other things a marvelous carpaccio and some tender Parma ham) or the delicious nocciole di agnello (noisettes of lamb). Interesting desserts (zabaglione) and some Italian wines in carafe, not at all displeasing.
Carte: 200F plus.

## 13
## L'Estournel
**1 rue Léo-Delibes**
**553.10.79**
*M. Lo Monaco*
*Open until 10:30 P.M. Closed Sat.,*
*Sun. and during August. Pay*
*parking at garage Magdebourg,*
*1 rue Magdebourg. No large dogs.*
*AE, DC, V.*

The very flower of the Étoile business community enjoys lunches in this round dining room, redone with supreme elegance by Michel Boyer, one of today's best decorators. Chef Henri Boutier displays just as much elegance in his way. Serious care and a spirit of inventiveness go into the preparation of his marinated salmon with coarse salt and black pepper, his feuilleté of leek whites, his veal piccata with ginger, and his bavarois with purée of peaches. In short, exactly the opposite of what you would expect to find in the dreary cuisines of many grand hotels. M. Lo Monaco, director of the Baltimore, must be pleased, we are (but not because of the prices).
Carte: 200F.

## 18
## Faugeron
**52 rue de Longchamp**
**704.24.53**
*M. Faugeron*
*Open until 10:00 P.M.*
*Closed Sat. for lunches*
*(from October to April); all*
*day Sat. (from May to September)*
*and Sun. and during August.*
*No dogs.*

He spent the year quietly perfecting his restaurant and perhaps preparing a new point of departure. Thus in 1981 Henri Faugeron was not heralded as one of the brightest stars in the galaxy of Parisian restaurateurs. But we didn't hear a single adverse word, either. For in his intimate, dimly-lit and attractive restaurant, aided by a most exquisite maîtresse de maison, he offers, in addition to his "classics" (soft-boiled eggs with purée of truffles or fried eggs with parsley, veal sweetbreads cressonnette, young rabbit with salad of artichokes, sautée of lamb with mint) some astonishing and excellent new preparations, such as the lobster or oyster flan; salad of duck with foie gras; salmon with aspic and pepper; bitter chocolate soufflé. All is perfect—even the prices have scarcely risen, and the businessman's menu at 130F is light but generous (for example, artichoke salad, "improvised" fish, roast calf's liver, strawberry feuilleté) and is unbeatable in Paris.
Carte: 250F–280F. Menu: 130F (at lunch only), 220F and 300F (menus-dégustation) plus 15% serv.

## 14
## Le Grand Chinois
**6 ave. de New York**
**723.98.21**
*Mme Tan*
*Open until 11:00 P.M. Closed Mon.*
*and 2 wks. in mid-August.*
*AE, DC.*

Or maybe it should be called La Grande Chinoise, for it is a young woman, Colette Tan (who used to be maître d'hôtel in her father's excellent Pagoda), who has reigned for the past three years over this ultra-Peking, but nevertheless restful and comfortable decor. From the long menu or, infinitely better, by ordering in advance, you will taste a number of light and ingenious dishes, almost all of them reflecting the "nouvelle Chinese cuisine": the hot salad of Chinese cabbage with steamed crab, the crab à la nage épiceé, fried crab claws or the marvelous lacquered chicken whose smooth meat is sandwiched between crispy skin and a quilt of shrimp pâté. Great wines, preferably expensive.
Carte: 130F–150F. Menu: 36F (Serv. incl.).

## 15
## La Grande Cascade
**Bois de Boulogne,**

The fabulous pavilion did not keep its new chef, whose gifts we praised last year, so we start over again with his successor Jean Sabine, newly arrived from La Marée. Plenty of talent and all that it takes to make your guests'

**near the
Longchamps
racetrack
506.33.51**

*M. Menut
Open until 10:30 P.M. Closed
December 20 to January 20;
Lunch only from October 15
to March 15.
AE, DC, EC.*

14

# Île de
# France
**Facing 32 ave. de
New-York
720.22.32**

*M. Benoist
Open until 10:30 P.M. Closed Sat.
(at lunch) and Sun. Parking at
quai Debilly.
All major credit cards.*

17

# Jamin
**(Joël Robuchon)
32 rue du Longchamp
727.12.27**

*M. Robuchon
Open until 10:30 P.M. Closed Sat.,
Sun., and during July. Attendant
parking at 11 bis rue Magdebourg.
All major credit cards.*

eyes pop out in this noble and tasteful decor: an attractive langouste salad, exquisite hot oysters with vegetables, a curious lotte with spinach, superb roast leg of lamb, a panaché of steamed fish, dazzling desserts, remarkably well chosen wines, a terrifying bill. A second toque in any case. Let us hope that it lasts.
Carte: about 300F.

François Benoist's empire stretches from the excellent Buffet de la Gare de Vincennes (Nord) to Chez les Anges (in the 7th arrondissement) and includes this barge which yields nothing to the others. The Île de France, beautifully decorated in colonial style, with Isabelle Benoist's discreet and smiling reception and the faultless service, charms those who come for business lunches or for tête-à-tête dinners. For two years this restaurant has benefited from the proven talents of Bruno Fava, 28, who has studied at Troisgros and other good restaurants. Broken in at Chez Les Anges, he is at liberty here to give free rein to his inspiration. The result is a balanced and tempting menu, enriched each day by what is available at the market: marinade of lotte with exotic fruits, sauté of lobster with Cramant sparkling wine, paumes of veal sweetbreads with basil. A very good wine list on which appear some affordable Bordeaux and small growths.
Carte: about 230F.

He not only turned the Célébrités of the Hôtel Nikko into one of the best hotel-restaurants in the capital, he made it one of the best in France. He demonstrates a real passion for subtle elegance and good ingredients. He prefers the old recipes he picked up on his apprentice's Tour de France. Joël Robuchon, at age 36, has decided to settle down. He broke open his piggy bank and took over the old Jamin that used to be so popular with people who played the ponies back in the '50s.

He brightened up the decor a bit with a slightly contrasting but cheerful harmony of red and green. And, above all, he buckled down to the task of developing a menu that intelligently balances sober sophistication with well-learned rusticity. A mere perusal of the menu is enough to trigger off a violent explosion of your tastebuds; evidence of this smiling chef's consuming passion to do things right. Unless you want to renew acquaintanceship with the modernist tendencies honored at the Célébrités—with such stunning dishes as the poêlée of crayfish with braised veal sweetbreads and vegetables with truffles, the noodles with crayfish and scallops, the hot foie gras with preserved endives, the minute of bass with a seasoned marinière, or the admirable squab en croûte de sel—you'll allow yourself to be tempted by the robust lightness of the rediscoveries.

Such as, for example, an exquisite terrine de col-vert with its miraculous dandelion salad with gizzards, truffles and artichokes; an extremely rare, soft herring roe exquisitely seasoned with capers, accompanied by highly spiced slices of potato; the fresh pasta with crayfish and scallops; the very simple and admirable pig's head with sage; and extraordinary mashed potatoes (it takes some daring!). Not to mention the truly perfect desserts (including a fabulous clafoutis), the rich wine list presented by a competent sommelier, and the thoughtful service. And, since happy tidings never travel alone, we should point out that our luxurious Robuchon doesn't hesitate to offer his rich 16th arrondissement clientele, in addition to his large dégustation fixed-price meal for 210F, a rare one for 110F consisting of, for example, a simmered potagère de veau, an effeuillé of skate with chou pastry, perfectly aged cheeses, and a choice of desserts. Enthusiastic, won-over from the start, we won't waste any more time in awarding Joël Robuchon the third toque he was about to receive at Célébrités. We wavered, wondering just how long he was going to stay at the Hôtel Nikko. Now that he's finally come home to his own home, we don't have to worry that he'll vanish into thin air!
Carte: 300F without trying.

## 13

## Jenny Jacquet
**136 rue de la Pompe**
**727.50.26**
*M. Jacquet*
*Open until 10:00 P.M. Closed*
*Sat. (at lunch), Sun. and*
*during August.*

Freshness, light, originality, invention—don't look for them here in this pale brown petit bourgeois setting. Jenny Jacquet has not touched the dining room he took over from the old Chez Nous, judging it more important to go to work first on the kitchen, which is renewed and modernized, and, particularly on his cuisine, which constitutes one of the most agreeable surprises of the year to come out of this dreary neighborhood. Previously with Chez Augereau (Les Rosiers-sur-Loire) and Lenôtre (whence the hot chiboust with currants and the frozen nougat with candied ginger and pistachio, two very subtle desserts), this quiet native of Saumur offers a menu (renewed every two months) on which almost all the plates bear his personal stamp and his concern for originality without excess. The ravigote of mussels, terrine of squab with vegetable remoulade, bream with fettuccine, fresh salmon with a mushroom purée, a tendron of veal simmered à l'ancienne, saddle of young rabbit with wild mushrooms, all have about them a completely surprising aura of inventiveness. Let us add that the service is prompt and without flaw, that the cellar of Loire wines is irresistible, and that the bill is among the most reasonable for such quality.
Carte: 130F–150F.

## 12/20
## Marius
**82 blvd. Murat**
**651.67.80**

The decor is light and fresh, the reception and service are reproachless, but the seafood cuisine is a bit dated. The bouillabaisse and the pieds et pacquets marseillais, which

*Mme Manuelli*
*Open until 10:30 P.M. Closed Sun.*
*evenings, Mon. and late June to*
*early September.*
*AE, DC, V.*

## 14

## Le Moï
### 7 and 14 rue
### Gustave-Courbet
### 704.95.10
*Mme Oggeri and Rabani*
*Open until 10:30 P.M.*
*Closed Mon. and during August.*
*Pay parking at Victor-Hugo.*

## 13

## Morens
### 10 ave. de New-York
### 723.75.11
*M. Morens*
*Open until 9:45 P.M.*
*Closed Fri. evening, Sat.,*
*from December 24 to January 2*
*and during August.*
*AE, DC, V.*

## 15

## Michel Pasquet
### 59 rue La Fontaine
### 288.50.01
*M. Pasquet*
*Open until 10:45 P.M. Closed Sat.*
*at lunch (in winter), Sat. (in*
*summer), and during August*
*DC, V.*

the owner has been serving since the mid-'30s are this expensive restaurant's major attractions. This year, there have been some really daring innovations, including sole with Roquefort cheese, turbot en papillote with white of leeks, and loup en croûte.
Carte: 200F.

The beautiful Huguette reigns over the new Moï at number 7, and Claude, just across the street, over the old Moï. Each restaurant has its followers; the "new" is more comfortable, the "old" more intimate, but on both sides of the street you will find a delicious, authentic Vietnamese cuisine that makes the chopsticks click. Vietnamese won ton, steamed stuffed crab, grilled pork meatballs, brochettes of beef with citronella, soup with shrimp and tamarind fruit, and caramelized spareribs are the specialties of the house(s) and are also our favorites, perfectly accompanied by the Doisy-Däene or the Lirac of the small but excellent cellar, composed by Claude with unfailing flair.
Carte: about 130F.

A simple, well-executed, rigorously traditional cuisine is the only one that has found its way into Roger Morens' heart in the twenty years that we have known him, and for the last thirteen or fourteen of these he has had at his side a chef of like mind. So we never have the slightest worry when we seat ourselves in the glassed-in winter garden and order with our eyes closed the futots of prawns, the young rabbit with aspic and white Sancerre (from May to September), beef fillet Morens, and the cassoulet with goose toulousain, which remains one of the monuments of Parisian cooking. Carte: 200F.

Michel Pasquet scolds us for not taking all our meals in his restaurant so that we can better follow and report on the effort he is making to improve his cuisine. The truth is that he works like a devil, behind the grim façade on that street without joy, to please and even astonish his clients. A charming candy-pink decor, a friendly reception, distinguished service, but above all a diversified cuisine chock-full of subleties, even with the most humble ingredients: salad of crayfish with preserved duck gizzards, raw haddock with olive oil, warm veal sweetbreads with an artichoke vinaigrette, feuilleté of skate cheeks, salmon with rhubarb, sautéed pigeon with Pomerol, shoulder of lamb with sweet peppers, oeufs à la neige, and chocolate mousse with mint. Two attractive fixed-price meals (businessman's and dégustation). Several original wines at affordable prices. Everything has

converged at the right time for a second toque, a red one, with which we crown this head so admirably deserving of it.
Carte: 180F–220F. Menus: 110F, 170F (serv. incl.).

## 14 Passy-Mandarin
**6 rue Bois-le-Vent**
**288.12.18**
*M. Vong Vai Pui*
*Open until 11:00 P.M. No dogs.*
*V.*

The dining room has been enlarged, the decor retouched, and mighty efforts—some successful—made to bring Passy Vong up to the level of its brother Vong at the Halles. Already, the dim-sum are among the best in Paris (one can buy them to take home from the shop at number 16 of the same street), and the cuisine, where steam cooking is the rule, is very delicate. The chef's scallops, the lamb with ginger, the squab with vegetables, the pork spareribs with seasoned salts make up the exquisite meals that bring an additional point to the large and resourceful Vong family.
Carte: about 120F.

## 13 Pavillon Royal
**Route de Suresnes,**
**Bois de Boulogne**
**500.51.00**
*M. Bryant*
*Open until 10:30 P.M. Closed Sun.*
*evening and Mon. Pay parking.*
*AE, DC, V.*

Beautifully situated facing the trees by the lake, the majestic dining room of this crystal palace makes the perfect spot for an intimate meal for two or a business lunch. Unfortunately, this year we have to say that the superb memory we took with us from a previous meal of lobster salad printanière, crépinettes of baby rabbit with wild mushrooms, and aiguillettes of duck has been somewhat tarnished. To tell the truth, our next meal there was totally disappointing, the food wasn't hot and the sauces were coagulated. An accident? Let's hope so. We have to admit that the Bois de Boulogne restaurant business is heavily dependent on the weather and the seasons, and that large restaurants are difficult to manage. The wines are superb, the coffee marvelous, the cigars fresh and the service is grand.
Carte: 280F–400F. Menus: 159F, 220F + 15% serv.

## 16 Le Petit Bedon
**38 rue Pergolèse**
**500.23.66**
*M. Ignace*
*Open until 10:15 P.M. Closed Sat.,*
*Sun. and during August*
*V.*

Le Petit Bedon—the name evokes a whole era. Wrought-iron, napkins tucked in the collar, cream sauce on the chin, the belt discreetly let out a notch or two after the last glass of brandy. It was also, during the reign of Chef Bernard, one of Paris's best restaurants, before going slowly to pot. Christian Ignace, who took over several months ago, is working to make us forget the sticky period; from now on one ought to speak not of the Petit Bedon but of the Restaurant Ignace. After the inevitable period of adjustment, the young chef is back in the stride that created with Raymond Oliver at the Grand Phoenix, one of Paris's most interesting cuisines. (Oliver should have hung on to Ignace to restore a little brilliance to the Grand Véfour.) The somewhat woebegone decor of the Petit Bedon is not particularly inspiring, but Jean Dive, who succeeded so well with the redecoration of Chiberta, is about to transform it. In any case, there's no reason not to go taste some specialties as delicious as the fresh sautéed duck foie gras with artichokes and grapes with Armagnac, lobster en cocotte with "pure malt" (which reconciles us forever to cooking with whiskey), escalope of bass with tomato, avocado and beurre rouge, the mignon of saddle of lamb with thyme, and its vegetables with basil, the delicious roast Challans duckling with fresh rosemary delicately accented with lime in a sauce with smoked tea, and all the desserts, of which the bitter chocolate granité with aiguillettes of orange and the croquant of peaches in a caramelized feuilleté with spices will satisfy anybody's sweet tooth. Ignace is wisely keeping his prices in line, including those of his wines (there's an excellent Chablis for 70F), and in dropping 170F into the saucer one can surreptitiously let the belt out a notch or two. Carte: 160F–180F.

## 11/20
### Le Petit Victor-Hugo
**143 ave. Victor-Hugo**
**704.57.95**
*Messieurs Biancheri and Vignaud*
*Open until midnight. Closed Sun.*
*Pay parking.*

We fervently beg Messieurs Biancheri and Vignaud to lower the volume of their background music. Otherwise, the clientele will never be heard complimenting the pleasant modern decor enlivened with greenery, the good salad of warm pot-au-feu, the calf's liver in sherry vinegar, and the brandade of salt cod, which are all more to be recommended than the uninteresting broiled meats. There also appear to be some other blind spots, as evidenced by our readers' letters. Good, generous menu. Carte: 130F. Menu: 60F (serv. incl.).

## 18
### Le Pré Catelan
**Route de Suresnes,**
**bois de Boulogne**
**524.55.58**
*M. Lenôtre*
*Open until 10:30 P.M. Closed Sun.*
*evenings and Mon. Open terrace.*
*Parking.*
*V.*

In August, a dreary dinner beneath the chestnut trees, just in front of the ravishing new winter garden; Patrick Lenôtre approaches the table in hope of a compliment, but returns empty-handed and pouting. This rebuff provided the spark. Pushed by Uncle Gaston and encouraged by Aunt Colette, Patrick went to work with a will, tore up the yellowing old menu, and created and perfected twenty . . . thirty new dishes. A miracle, a marvel. Let us hope that this time it will last, for it was four toques that this restaurant was flirting with on our last visit. There were stunning appetizers such as the baked scallops; the potato stuffed with haddock; rich and light tagliatella with salmon, turbot and lobster; delicate scallops and warmed but uncooked clams with a herbed sauce; wild salmon with lightly scrambled eggs with truffles; a fabulous sea urchin soufflé; calf's trotter tenderly stuffed with mushrooms; an airy tarte with calf's sweetbreads and kidney; pink émincé of pigeon on a bed of warm salad made of a forgotten vegetable: the potato, here sumptuous and classic, with a ballottine of sweet-savory pheasant. And there are two desserts that are beyond belief: the soufflé with Calvados, and the souffléed crêpes with burnt almonds. Add to these the majestic decor, the rustling forest all around, the fire in the fireplace of the

Belle Epoque dining room, the distinguished service (friendlier in winter than in summer), the remarkable wines served by princely sommeliers, and you have an earthly paradise.
Carte: about 300F. Menu (business lunches): 140F plus 15% serv.

## 14

## Prunier-Traktir
**16 ave. Victor-Hugo**
**500.89.12**
*M. Barnagaud*
*Open until 10:30 P.M. Closed Mon. and during July. Open terrace. Pay parking at ave. Foch, K entrance.*
*AE, DC, V.*

Always the perfect gentlemen, Claude Barnagaud has not flinched under the lash of our last year's comments. Neither have our readers, which is perhaps greater cause for concern. However, with 14/20 the good old Traktir maintains its standards, and there is no risk of your being disappointed. The specialties created several thousand years ago, such as the turbot Verilhac, the bass à l'angevine, the Boston fillet, haven't disappointed us for a long time, and the beautiful oysters, the mutton trotters poulette, and the eels au vert are charmingly simple; moreover, paintbrushes have refreshed the old place, and the ground floor from 1925 remains the most attractive and best patronized in Paris.
Carte: about 125F.

## 12/20

## Ramponneau
**21 ave. Marceau**
**720.59.51**
*M. Valette*
*Open until 10:15 P.M. Closed during August.*
*AE, V.*

The chef, Claude Debos, has been here for 20 years, so he knows by heart his hot duck livers with grapes, his crêpes maman sarthoise, his lobster Thermidor, his rump of veal with sage, and his chicken with cèpes. There is an occasional innovation—his winter cassoulet and summer sautéed lamb with spring vegetables, to mention the latest. And the prices are steadily rising and rising. . . .
True, the ingredients are excellent and fresh, the portions enormous and the staff extremely gracious. True, also, the terrace of this very pleasant-style inn does have a lot of charm when the sun shines.
Carte: 230F.

## 18

## Guy Savoy
**28 rue Duret**
**500.17.67**
*M. Savoy*
*Open until 11:00 P.M. Closed Sat., Sun., and beginning of January*
*V.*

Let's not lose our heads; above all, let's not swell that of a modest young man who has less than total confidence in himself. But let's say loud and clear that in him Paris possesses the most talented of chefs, with Alain Senderens. Like Senderens, but with humility, Guy Savoy realized that modern cuisine offers the artisan the divine possibility to work as an artist, to create day in and day out, to add what is wanting, to discover what it is that transforms banality into perfection, to revise, to enchant, like a painter who never repeats himself or copies others. His small and lively restaurant is but a stone's throw from one of our offices, and this has permitted us to become very well acquainted with his cuisine—no, not to know it by heart, for it is never the same: Each time it astonishes us anew. But we will not soon forget a veal sweetbread with saffron aspic, a scallop of foie gras with Indian rice, a potage of lobster with leeks, calf's kidneys with shallots, a potée of prawns, red mullet with wild asparagus, salmon trout with parsley butter, a raspberry millefeuille. Nor will we forget the wines, and prompt and paternal service. Carte: 250F–280F. Menu: 190F + 12% serv.

14

## Le Sully d'Auteuil
**78 rue d'Auteuil**
**651.71.18**

*M. Brunetière*
*Open until 10:30 P.M. Closed Sat.*
*(at lunch), Sun. and during August*
*Open terrace.*
*AE, V.*

With much enthusiasm, Michel Brunetière, who this year celebrates his fortieth year in the kitchen, has pulled this little lodge out of its misery and made it one of the best restaurants in the district. A profusion of flowers and plants, a small terrace (a bit noisy), the decor a little heavy but very comfortable, well-mannered clientele, a charming reception and attentive service complement a cuisine that happily weds traditional and modern. Let's forget the salad of smoked goose needlessly encumbered with prawns, and retain the delicious memory of the mélé-mélo of fish with cream of sea urchins and Sauternes, the bass steak with artichoke bottoms, the calf's kidneys with grapes, and several desserts, among which is a marvelous hot flaky apple and raspberry tarte and a spectacular gratin of pears with nougatine. In a corner of the lodge, Michel Brunetière has installed a small grill room (about 80F including wine) and has very attractively arranged his cellar as private dining rooms for receptions. Carte: 150F–180F. Menu: 120F (wine and serv. incl.).

**12/20**

## La Tour Céleste
**66 rue de la Tour**
**503.45.17**

*M. Boo*
*Open until 10:30 P.M. Closed Sat.*
*(at lunch) and during August. Pay*
*parking at 3 rue Scheffer.*
*AE, DC, V.*

Before locking himself up in this celestial tower, Chef Wong worked a lot in restaurants in the Far East, especially in Thailand. He finally decided upon a characteristically Chinese cuisine. We feel he made the right choice, especially when it comes to such excellent and well-made dishes as smoked duck in jasmin tea, leg of lamb Peking-style, sautéed shrimp in spicy sauce, or the spicy Mandarin chicken. Carte: 90F–100F. Menus: 29F, 38F (serv. incl.), 85F + 15% serv.

**12/20**

## La Tour de Chine
**135 ave. de Malakoff**
**500.36.73**

*M. De Yen Chou*
*Open until 11:00 P.M.*
*AE, DC. V.*

The owner of this hostelry discreetly adorned with a few Oriental knick-knacks likes to welcome the customers himself, explain the menu to them and convince them, if necessary of its merits. The place is brightly lit, unlike so many Chinese restaurants. Here, you will be able to taste langouste en sauce, shelled shrimp with pearl onions or delicious fried, salted butterfly shrimp; there is also an unusual sole with ginger and delicious grilled lamb kebobs. Carte: 100F. Menu: 45F (serv. incl.).

## 13

## Tsé Yang

**25 ave.
Pierre-ler-de-Serbie
720.68.02**

*M. Tsé Chu
Open until 11:00 P.M.
All major credit cards.*

Chinese cooks are like magicians: They often disappear in a puff of smoke. This happily is not about to happen at Paris's most luxurious Chinese restaurant, because the chef, M. Kui Yang, is also co-owner with the sprightly M. Chu, who divides his time between the kitchen, and the world of finance, the banks of the Seine and Geneva. All this activity does not prevent his serving you the best (shrimp tails with lime, fillets of Szechwan chicken, duck with five spices, steamed Pekinese dim-sum, rice noodles with pork and shrimp) alongside the most banal (stuffed crab claws, pork with pineapple and squash). But the same could be said of most Chinese restaurants, and this one offers at least the privilege of an extremely refined and sometimes inventive cuisine, as several plates unknown in Canton and Peking demonstrate: the sautéed calf's liver and kidneys, or the fillets of veal sautéed with shallots, which are delicious. The decor of this mandarins palace, with sumptuously set tables and subtle lighting, great Bordeaux, and the affluent clientele all hike the bill much higher than is usual in Chinese restaurants. Despite a menu at 85F, and another at 100F, you won't find hungry students or large families here. But since that's just the way M. Chu wants it, and since the restaurant seems to be doing well, one can say that M. Chu has won a long-shot bet.
Carte: about 230F. Menus: 85F, 150F + 15% serv.

## 10/20

## Van Ming

**7 ave. de Versailles
288.42.42**

*M. Van Ming
Open until 10:30 P.M. Closed Sun.*

The friendly owners of this Vietnamese restaurant, which we have recommended for several years for the steamed dishes, are eager to invite us to a typically Vietnamese lunch prepared by their Saigon cooks. However, as they seem to welcome criticism, we have some for them: this typical meal (sweet and sour soup with tamarind and shrimp, caramelized pork and shrimp, steamed fish) should appear on the menu in red letters, replacing the insipid beef and chicken kebobs. The decor is hybrid.
Carte: 70F–80F. Menu: 40F (wine and serv. incl.).

## 17

## Le Vivarois

**192 ave. Victor-Hugo
504.04.31**

*M. Peyrot
Open until 9:30 P.M. Closed Sat., Sun., and during August Open terrace. No dogs. Parking at 181 ave. Victor-Hugo.*

Having worn out their old Knoll furniture, the Peyrots have redecorated the Vivarois in the uniform of eternity—gray marble. Although it's not wildly merry, it is elegant and clean. On the walls hang violent abstract paintings. The dining room, however, is larger and it is well-lit, and, as far as the garden, ready for a fresh start. As for Claude Peyrot, he pronounces himself clear-headed and ready to march once again toward the culinary glory that he has at once sniffed at and disdained. After a period of uncertainty punctuated by last summer's vacation, his cuisine has once again become inspired, and exquisite with feuilleté of truffles, a soufflé of sea urchin, salmon with green vegetables, poularde with vinegar, the astonishing lamb with a tent of eggplant, black currant mousse, and some marvelous Côtes-du-Rhônes. The prices are also inspired.
Carte: 300F–320F.

## 10/20
### Wall Street
**8 ave. de New-York**
**723.33.52**
*M. Collard*
*Open until 12:15 A.M. Closed Sat.*
*(at lunch) and Sun.*
*AE, DC.*

Wall Street retains a fashionable clientele between (or despite) its mauve curtains (ugh!) and flashy watercolors. About eleven in the evening, the place begins to jump, as actors, television personalities and movie people arrive to sup on salad of gambas, lotte steak with tarragon, and other trifles hastily put together (the Lenôtre desserts are no longer served) from the anemic menu, while attractive press attachés and chief squaws of the movie industry look on to be looked upon. At least one of the fashionable clients goes into the kitchen to prepare his own eggs. Carte: 150F. Menu: 79F + 15% serv.

## 15
### Yan - Le Toit de Passy
**94 ave. Paul-Doumer**
**524.55.37**
*M. Jacquot*
*Open until 10:00 P.M. Closed Sat.*
*(at lunch), Sun. and December 20*
*to January 12. Open terrace.*
*Parking in the building.*
*V.*

There are several differences between the Toit de Passy and the Tour d'Argent. One of them is that here, to get to the elevator, you must wend your way through an automobile show room. Claude Terrail would never have thought of this sort of diversion. But let's not make any more comparisons. Despite this rooftop restaurant's somewhat strange situation and a bad gastronomic reputation—now a thing of the past—Yannick Jacquot has in two years succeeded in achieving two toques, putting together a faithful and contented clientele and transforming very happily his dining room and terrace into a harmonious and very comfortable whole. Here he offers with consistency a very fine, discreetly modern cuisine somewhat in the same spirit as that of Claude Peyrot of Vivarois, where in fact he worked for some time. Perfectly served in grand style are such pleasurable discoveries as feuilleté of haddock with sweet peppers, buisson of crayfish with vinaigrette of truffle, delicious salad of lamb sweetbreads and warm scallops with spinach, plate of lobster with saxifage and turnips, the marvelous sautéed lamb with basil and, finally, a succulent array of desserts, notably a fabulous chocolate and mocha cake. Some good wines, one of them a J.-L. Chave Saint-Joseph at 80F. Also, some dishes to take out. Carte: 200F. Menu: 95F + 15% serv.

# 17ème Arr.

## 11/20
### L'Amanguier
**43 ave. des Ternes**
**380.19.28**
*M. Derderian*
*Open until midnight.*
*AE, DC, V.*

Last-born of the Amanguier chain which at present has three links, all of them rigorously identical as to decor (exotic garden), prices (very light), quality of reception and service, and, to be sure, cuisine. See what we have said about the Amanguier in the 2nd arrondissement. Carte: about 80F. Menu: 63F (wine and serv. incl.).

**11/20**

## Auberge de Recoules d'Aubrac

**150 blvd. Pereire**
**380.20.48**

*M. Lehors*
*Open until 10:30 P.M. Closed Sat.,*
*Sun., holidays and during August.*
*Pay parking 48 rue Laugier.*
*AE, V.*

The flavor of the Aubrac region is as unapparent in the decor as it is in the cooking. However, Pierre Lehors, who runs the dining room side, and Kléber Bonnet, a chef of the old school in the kitchen, both maintain high standards. There is game in season, pot-au-feu and cassoulet in winter, and every day good fish or fresh langoustes from the vivarium.
Carte: 170F.

**14**

## Chez Augusta

**98 rue de Tocqueville**
**763.39.97**

*M. Bareste*
*Open until 9:30 P.M. Closed Sun.,*
*holidays, and August 5 to 25.*
*DC.*

Chez Augusta: in a straightforward, cozy setting, a Marseille-type seafood cuisine which, if not sublime, is a sort of simple perfection. Advised by the petulant hostess or by the active and friendly waiters, you will be regaled with langouste en salade, raw sardines, bouillabaisse with potatoes, bass à la nage, lotte with prawns, and all the beautiful fish of the sea on command. Without forgetting the incomparable pieds et paquets of mutton and the attractive little white wines.
Carte: about 160F.

**11/20**

## Le Ballon des Ternes

**103 ave. des Ternes**
**574.17.98**

*M. Caffin*
*Open until 1:30 A.M.*
*AE, DC, V.*

The name has nothing to do with the big glasses of Beaujolais red that have been drunk for so long in this street corner café. It is a reference to the hot-air balloon in which Léon Gambetta escaped the Prussians in 1870. The Caffin brothers now run the establishment, which has an attractive, period decor, in a good imitation of the classic brasserie style with the accent on fish and seafood. The stars appearing at the Palais des Congrès like to eat here.
Carte: about 120F. Menu: 45F (wine incl.) + 15% serv.

**17**

## La Barrière de Clichy

**2 blvd. de Douamont**
**737.05.18**

*M. Verger*
*Open until 10:00 P.M. Closed Sat.*
*at lunch and Sun.*
*AE, DC, V.*

Only 28 years old, little Chef Schufenecker—timid but bristling with controlled passion—is already a great cuisinier, one who sticks to his stove, inventing and perfecting a cuisine that is always changing, always delicate, always surprising. Claude Verger need have no regrets in having entrusted his beloved restaurant to little "Schuf." The only thing that might trouble M. Verger is the fact that his Barrière is in Clichy, for this (as well as the size of the check) might discourage Parisians from flocking to discover the lobster terrine, the salad of foie gras, roast Brittany pigeon, veal sweetbreads with spinach, the cassolette with oysters and prawns. If so, Parisians would be depriving themselves of much pleasure (and some exquisite wines).
Carte: about 250F.

14

## La Barrière de Neuilly
**275 blvd. Pereire**
**574.33.32**
*M. Verger*
*Open until 11:00 P.M. Open*
*terrace.*
*AE, DC, V.*

Claude Verger's next-to-last restaurant (he has since opened the Barrière des Champs) has finally gotten its act together; our readers no longer complain, and it is certainly due to young Chef Magnard (he trained at Paineau, 17/20, in Questembert), to his simple, light, and imaginative cuisine, made from the finest produce (and also the best butter in Paris), to his crayfish salad, compote of rabbit with aspic, noisettes of Lot lamb, sea trout with beurre blanc, and his light tarts. It is also due to some attractive little wines, a smiling and (but not always) speedy service and, above all, to the remarkable direction by an attractive young woman, Danielle, who is none other than the daughter of our old friend Albert of the late, lamented Bistroquet.
Carte: 180F–200F.

13

## Baumann-Ternes
**64 ave. des Ternes**
**574.16.66**
*Mme Baumann*
*Open until 1:00 A.M. Closed 3 wks.*
*in May and December 24 thru*
*January 3. Open terrace.*
*All major credit cards.*

If you come often to this attractive restaurant-brasserie, decorated by Slavik in a tenderly demented way, you will already know that since last summer the terrace has been enlarged and planted very appealingly. Also, that Guy-Pierre Baumann has not deemed it fit to lengthen his list of eleven choucroute (plus a twelfth served raw with crab, and a thirteenth, no less raw, with salmon and haddock marinated in lime), all of them interesting, delicate and light, after being cooked in the miraculous choucroute "washing machine" of his own invention. As at Baumann-Baltard in the old Halles district, his menu also proposes numerous interesting plates such as the leek salad Adeline and lotte baudroie with bacon and fresh pasta, and some good little Alsatian wines to go with them. Service is prompt and precise.
Carte: 130F–150F. Menu: 129F (serv. incl.).

16

## Le Bernardin
**18 rue Troyon**
**380.40.61**
*M. and Mme Le Coze*
*Open until 11:30 P.M. Closed Sun.,*
*Mon. and during August*
*V.*

Maguy, more attractive than ever, and Gilbert have won their bet. This spacious and attractive restaurant in the Étoile district, quietly and agreeably decorated, is enjoying three times the success of the Petit Bernardin of the Left Bank quais. With an inventive cuisine dedicated entirely to seafood, and subtle sauces blended remarkably well with materials of striking freshness, the Le Cozes have made of the Bernardin in only a few months a must of the neighborhood and of Tout-Paris. You will understand why when, with a dry Doisy-Daëne or a Saint-Véran, you taste the tiny fried squid, the thin slices of raw salmon marinated in finely strained tomato juice, the oysters with truffles or curry, the stuffed scallops, baked prawns, the bass or the red mullet meunière—admirably cooked—the skate with hazelnut butter, the John Dory with white onions, the lobster with basil or, finally, the unusual assortment of shellfish à la nage. Some good ice creams and sherbets.
Carte: 200F–250F.

## Le Beudant
**97 rue des Dames**
**387.11.20**
*M. Gonthier*
*Open until 10:30 P.M. Closed Sat.*
*(at lunch) and Sun. (dates of*
*annual closing not yet fixed).*
*Parking at 2 rue Dulong.*
*AE, DC, V.*

This minuscule restaurant—twenty settings at most—is filled each day by a coterie of gourmets convinced that this is the most unjustly underrated kitchen in Paris. The owner-chef is of the same opinion. As for us, we continue to find his hand light and happy (except when he presents the bill) in the preparation of a salad of mussels with basil, sander and salmon with mousse with chives, veal sweetbreads with sweet garlic, and a gratin of red fruits. For these, we crown him with a toque. Intimate and sensitive decor and smiling service. Very remarkable menu dégustation.
Carte: 180F. Menu: (dégustation): 95F + 15% serv.

## 10/20

## La Bourriche
**18 bis rue**
**Pierre-Demours**
**572.28.51**
*M. Gilbert*
*Open until 10:30 P.M.*
*AE, V.*

An ancient waitress, ancient beams, and neatly arranged rows of ancient customers who come to enjoy very fresh concave Brittany oysters served all year round, and not-so-good scallops which, in August, come from the freezer. Actually, the cuisine needs a few improvements (very poor fish soup and bouillabaisse) and the same applies to the wine list. Very reasonable prices.
Carte: 120F–140F. Menus 30F, 50F (wine incl.) + 15% serv.

## 12/20
## La Braisière
**54 rue Cardinet**
**763.40.37**
*M. Thomas*
*Open until 10:00 P.M. Closed Sat.,*
*Sun. and during August.*
*AE, DC, V.*

A moustachioed giant from the Southwest took over the kitchen and the management of La Braisière. Jacques Thomas has not touched the decor (purple wallpaper, greenery, immaculate white tablecloths and waiters' uniforms), which is more comfortable than lively. He has also inherited his predecessor's habit of presenting his customers with bills big enough for the more prestigious establishments. His new menu might be a little monotonous, but it's not altogether boring, and it contains a few nice dishes, such as the gratin of mussels in celery, the fillet of rougets cooked in wine lees, or the confit of duck wing with braised cabbage. However, the cassoulet is a rather disappointing haricot bean stew devoid of the required smoothness. The wine list is fine, but also expensive, covering nearly the whole range of French wines.
Carte: 200F.

## Le Brazais
**42 blvd. Pereire**
**763.82.17**
*M. Van Lingen*
*Open until 10:00 P.M. Closed Sat.*
*and Sun. Easter to November 1;*
*Sun. November 1 to Easter, and*
*May. Pay parking 28 blvd. Pereire.*
*AE, DC, V.*

Le Brazais has changed neither its decor (comfortable neo-rustic with an other-side-of-the-tracks view of the trees bordering the railway line) nor its owners (cool and only as friendly as necessary). But it has changed its chef, who retains in the cuisine the slight Norman accent it has always had, but enriching and lightening it with purely personal touches. Thus, right beside the magret of duck with cider and apple Calvados sherbet, you will find on

the menu a reasonably priced Brittany lobster, baked with a sauce with basil and fresh tomatoes. As for us, we prefer the very simple fish plates such as the gâteau of whiting cressonière or the sand dab with lettuce hearts. Also the delicate civet of lotte stewed in wine with prunes, or the mushrooms in pastry, among items on a menu that is perhaps too long but is well balanced, with reasonable prices. A good menu and some not too expensive wines of the country.
Carte: 160F.

## 12/20
## Le Cévenol
**14 rue de Thann**
**763.47.42**
*M. Cros*
*Open for lunch only. Closed Sat.,*
*Sun., holidays. Open terrace.*

This is the bistro annex to Guyvonne where Guy Cros for the past year has been offering a hearty and healthful meal at fairly reasonable prices: tongue ravigote, pork with lentils, tripe niçoise, brandade of cod, calf's head sauce gribiche, blanquette, couscous. Very sympathetic in a smiling setting.
Carte: about 100F. Menu: 60F + 15% serv.

## 13
## Le Chalybon
**75 place du**
**Dr.-Félix-Lobligeois**
**627.33.37**
*M. Noel*
*Open until 10:30 P.M. Closed Sun.,*
*Mon. and August. Open terrace.*
*AE, V.*

This restaurant was opened just a year ago behind the Sainte-Marie-des-Batignolles church. Its decor is dark red, matching the color of a wine of long ago (a favorite of Assurbanipal), from which, presumably, the name Chalybon was taken. At any rate, it does not appear on the wine list which is still modest. The young chef Alain Rousset has impressive references (Taillevent, Maxim's, Tour d'Argent) and, despite a few shortcomings due to the newness of the operation, we were left with the impression after our first visit that this is a very good address. We think that will be your impression too, after you have tasted this pleasant, fresh, light cuisine served on attractive dishware. The hot fish terrine with beurre blanc (a bit too salty), émincés of smoked fish with avocado sherbet, langoustine salad with fresh coriander, a marmite of scallops and small fish, duck with lemon, and, above all, the marvelous desserts (charlotte, sherbet millefeuille). This sort of fare will soon fill this seductive restaurant so far off the beaten track. Charming reception and service.
Carte: 160F–180F. Menus: 80F, 160F (serv. incl.).

## 13
## Charly de Bab-El-Oued
**95 blvd. Gouvion-**
**Saint-Cyr**
**574.34.62**
*M. Driguès*
*Open until midnight.*
*All major credit cards.*

An extraordinary Oriental decor, an atmosphere very North African-colonial, and some generous Algerian and Moroccan specialties, successful for the most part. We particularly like the entrées (soubressade and grilled white kidneys, bestelles, merguez, sardines en escabèche, shrimp à l'algèroise), very nice couscous and original tajines prepared with excellent lamb. Superb pastries. Some specialties to take out. Prices quite high.
Carte: 120F–150F.

## 12/20
### Le Congrès
**80 ave. de la Grande-Armée**
**574.17.24**
*M. Joulie*
*Open until 1:30 A.M. Open terrace.*
*All major credit cards.*

Like its name suggests, mood music, air conditioning, attaché-case decor, a cuisine at once "healthful" and quick—everything is designed for the neighboring "Palais" convention hall and the big office buildings. Excellent oysters—winter and summer, fish and meats charcoal grilled, accompanied by good fresh steamed vegetables. One of the best quality-price ratios in the quarter. Service a bit lethargic.
Carte: 100F–120F.

## 13
### La Coquille
**6 rue du Débarcadère**
**574.25.95**
*M. Blache*
*Open until 10:00 P.M. Closed Sun.,*
*Mon., holidays, and from July 27*
*thru to September 3. Parking at 29*
*rue Brunel.*
*V.*

The genial giant Paul Blache would rather close his attractive if slightly tacky bistro than allow people to assume that it was named after a famous brand of frozen food. (It wasn't.) We certainly have no reproach to make after tasting his scallops, cooked au naturel and served on the half-shell. This is one of the two front-line dishes of which his faithful clientele never tire (nor do we), the second being a spectacularly insignificant soufflé with hazelnut praline and kirsch. Day after day, on the other hand, his menu offers grilled stream-caught Scottish salmon (served with dreadfully spongy steamed potatoes), an escalope of sea bass "Escoffier," chicken fricassée with cream and morels, game in season. The products are fresh and attractive (the bill leaves us in no doubt that they are expensive), although at times a bit mistreated during preparation. Beautiful—very beautiful—wine list on which you'll find some excellent vintages; all things considered, they're less expensive than the food. Minimalist portions, horrible coffee, perfect service.
Carte: 200F-plus.

## 12/20
### La Côte de Boeuf
**4 rue Saussier-Leroy**
**227.73.50**
*M. Delmond*
*Open until 10:30 P.M. Closed Sat.,*
*Sun. and during August.*
*AE, DC, V.*

This pleasant local bistro isn't especially attractive or cozy, but that is the last thing Simon Delmond's clients care about. They close their eyes and come to eat his beef (côtes de boeuf à l'os, pavé marchand de vin), game in season, and the delicious bourgeois dishes he serves all year round. These include: duck with turnips, coq au beaujolais, boudin with apples. They may be curiously reminiscent of something; Delmond was a chef saucier at Allard's for twelve years. The Côtes du Rhône is very nice.
Carte: 130F–150F.

## 14
### Ma Cuisine
**18 rue Bayen**
**572.02.19**
*M. Donnard*
*Open until 10:30 P.M. Closed Sat.*
*(at lunch) and Sun.*
*DC, V.*

That decor! Elegant, vague, a bit somber, not particularly jolly prewar. But the cuisine is progressively more sure of itself, presented on an attractive menu that would be somewhat passé if Alain Donnard had not updated the meats in a very simple and intelligent fashion. He was with Dagorno at La Villette and with Chiberta for three years, and knows meats perfectly. You will not be disappointed with his marbré of veal sweetbreads, his roast rack of lamb with garlic cream or his incomparable beef à la ficelle. But taste as well his terrine of artichoke with fresh crab, the roast sander (a triumph), the lotte with a fondue of spinach, and the beautiful desserts (bitter chocolate granité), while regretting, as we did, a certain failure of inspiration in the accompanying vegetables. Service and wine list getting better all the time. Prices too. Carte: 180F.

### 13 Dessirier
**9 place du Mal-Juin**
**227.82.14**
*M. Robinet*
*Open until 12:30 A.M. Closed*
*during August. Parking at 210 rue*
*de Courcelles.*
*AE, V.*

After a long period of dedication to the lonely oyster, the Veillat-Kaufmann-Robinet family is now paying homage with great success to fish and shellfish. Without yielding an inch to the new cuisine, but nevertheless reducing cooking times and buying only first-class produce, this old (but very modern) brasserie is climbing back up the hill. After exquisite "papillon" oysters, we last had a small lobster à la nage, and a turbot hollandaise that we're not ready to forget. Excellent Sancerres and Beaujolais. The bill will grab you too.
Carte: about 200F.

### 15 L'Ecrevisse
**212 bis, blvd. Pereire**
**572.17.60**
*M. de Leyssac*
*Open until 10:00 P.M. Closed Sat.*
*(at lunch), Sun. and during August*
*AE, V.*

About two years ago Christian de Leyssac and his charming wife left their native Lozère to take their chances in Paris. "The little crayfish will become big," we wrote at the time, and we were not wrong. At least this shellfish for which they named their place is not moving backward like a crab. Better still, since our last visit this impassioned chef has defined his talent and perfectly mastered a cuisine at once personal and inventive, to the great joy of Porte Maillot, where there's no lack of competition. A cuisine that rings true, with precise cooking, sauces with exact tastes, extremely fresh ingredients: so much so, in fact, that we see no reason not to add a second toque to the one that this young aristocrat already wears. He will regale you with his crayfish, either in a superb vegetable soup or in a subtle fricassée with Armagnac, unless you prefer the delicate hot oysters with Sancerre or the fillets of sole with Bordeaux. Among the meats, the aiguillettes of duckling with Burgundy, the noisettes of lamb with truffle juice, the calf's liver with sherry vinegar and the stuffed saddle of lamb with pistou. The desserts are on the same lofty level, with a pear soufflé as light as a violin air or the classic but superb profiterolles with chocolate sauce. One last word: The decor is notable for its sobriety and perfect taste, the salmon pink of the walls relieved by attractive paintings. It will cost you about 180F if you can resist the great wines on the list presented by a young and able steward.
Carte: about 180F.

### 14 Epicure 108
**108 rue Cardinet**
**763.50.91**

Thirty settings in a beige-on-silk decor. Discretion reigns. Even in the kitchen, where the cuisine is unequivocally modern and everywhere characterized by the balance and

*M. Brilhac*
*Open until 10:00 P.M. Closed Sat.*
*(in summer), Sun., Mon. (in*
*winter), and August 15 to 30.*
*Parking at 114 rue Cardinet.*
*AE, DC, V.*

perfection of flavors. It is performed by the young chef Alain Denoual, who began his brief career in the grand classic tradition at Maxim's and the Tour d'Argent, but who plans to pursue it (for a long time) in a cuisine stripped to the bone—light, free of residual sauces and constantly refreshed. The entire menu offered by the owner Louis Brilhac is characterized by this search for the perfect tone and degree of subtlety: steamed bass with rhubarb and apples, lotte with wild mushrooms, curried minute of chicken, navarin printanier, and some attractive house desserts (feuilleté with strawberries and honey), Berthillon ice creams and sherbets.
Carte: 150F–170F. Menus: 95F, 125F (serv. incl.).

**12/20**
## L'Etoile du Bonheur
**25 ave. de Wagram**
**755.65.69**
*M. Lau*
*Open until 10:00 P.M.*
*AE, DC, V.*

Located between the Etoile and the Place des Ternes, this large modern restaurant is very well lit, and does not have too many knickknacks except on the menu—but that is just what one comes for. That is, for the Peking or Szechuan dishes, such as fried dumplings, shrimp in oyster sauce, ginger chicken or candied apples with sesame seed. There are also a few Vietnamese dishes and the ingredients are always excellent, subtly cooked and served.
Carte: 100F. Menu: 31F (serv. incl.).

**12/20**
## L'Etoile d'Or
**3 pl. de la**
**Porte-des-Ternes**
**758.12.84**
*M. Houlin*
*Open until 11:00 P.M. Pay parking*
*at 1 pl. Maillot.*
*AE, DC, V.*

The sauces are a little heavy, the cooking times are too approximate, the dishes unnecessarily complicated, and the prices are formidable. The decor is overpoweringly modernist. However, the ingredients are high quality, the service is attentive and there are a few good wines (especially the Croze-Hermitage). The chef, Joël Renty, certainly has talent and inventiveness. Try the salmon tartare, the beuchelle, the fraise de veau with broccoli and the little tartes.
Carte: about 200F. Menu: 145F (serv. incl.).

**13**
## Chez Georges
**273 blvd. Pereire**
**574.31.00**
*M. Mazarguil*
*Open until 10:30 P.M. Closed Sat.*
*and July 28 to August 31. Open*
*terrace. No dogs.*
*V.*

A good classic house, unchanged since Charlemagne, the decor rejuvenated by Slavik and the cuisine by the chef Merle. Diversity among the hors d'oeuvres, but for the main course three plates have been served here throughout written history: streaky bacon with cabbage, beef ribs, and leg of lamb with flageolets, plus a plat-du-jour that is always very good, especially the ragoût of mutton with potatoes and the giant pot-au-feu. Excellent little growers' wines, among them a marvelous Brouilly, of local growths chosen at the vineyards by Roger Mazarguil.
Carte: 160F.

## 12/20
## Chez Gorisse
**84 rue Nollet**
**627.43.05**

*M. Pommerai*
*Open until 10:00 P.M. Closed Sun.*
*and during August. Parking at 14*
*rue de Claireaux.*
*V.*

This restaurant is high on our list of good bourgeois restaurants. Truly, Maman Gorisse (does anyone remember her today?) could find no complaint about the chef who has taken her place at the stove. Actually, his rouelle of veal (Monday), petit salé (Tuesday), pot-au-feu (Wednesday), tête de veau (Thursday), bouillabaisse (Friday), and the hot saucisson, rabbit in mustard and chocolate marquise (served daily) are every bit as good as hers. Ah, what fine weeks filled with such goodness! Carte: 100F. Menu: 70F (wine and serv. incl.).

## 12/20
## Le Grand Veneur
**6 rue Pierre-Demours**
**574.61.58**

*M. Dattas*
*Open until 10:00 P.M. Closed Sat.*
*(at lunch), Sun. and during*
*August. Parking at 20 rue*
*Guersant.*
*AE, DC, V.*

Comfy, old-fashioned, far, far away from Paris—this is a hunting lodge which has a very pre-war feel as far as the decor and everything else is concerned. After fighting for a parking spot in the fields of Monceau, you come in to warm up. While your boots are drying on the hearth and your hounds are rubbing themselves dry on the Gobelins carpets, you will feast on game and venison (if they're not in season, you will have the delights of sole grand veneur, sweetbreads florentine, guinea fowl with morels . . . ). Of course, you have to like that sort of thing! If you do, you will agree that it is not at all badly done and served, regardless of the cost. You may be slightly wounded in the pocketbook, but then that's the least that can happen to a hunter.
Carte: 180F.

## 11/20
## La Grosse Tartine
**91 blvd. Gouvion-Saint-Cyr**
**574.02.77**

*Mme Pilmis*
*Open until 10:15 P.M. Closed in the*
*evenings (Mon., Tues., Thurs.),*
*Sun. and during August*

Jean-Pierre Bloud, the wine merchant whose store-warehouse is just next door, opened this pleasant bistro several years ago. It offers all year long an unchanging menu which doesn't take long to read: seasoned crudités, platter of Franc-Comté or Aveyron charcuteries, beef steak with shallots, a plat-du-jour (such as streaky bacon, pot-au-feu). A good menu is put together from these offerings by Odette Pilmis, the manager. Interesting wines, as one would expect, with several specials each week that are even more interesting (in quarter and half-liter pitchers). In summer, meals may be taken in the small garden-courtyard.
Carte: 90F–100F. Menu: 67F (serv. incl.).

## 14
## Guyvonne
**14 rue de Thann**
**227.25.43**

*M. Cros*
*Open until 9:45 P.M. Closed Sat.,*
*Sun., holidays, from December 24*
*to January 7 and from July 9 to 31.*
*Open terrace.*

The quality of the food and the exactitude of the cooking, both so important in a cuisine of seafood and offal, testify daily to the honesty of Guy Cros. You won't have difficulty in believing this when you visit this quiet, attractively decorated restaurant in the Monceau district. Here you'll taste the loaf of crayfish, the prawns with asparagus, the bass with parsley, skate with green cabbage, tuna with girolles, lambs' trotters with cèpes, or the veal

sweetbreads with black currants. And don't forget his annex next door, the Cévenol.
Carte: 180F–200F.

13

## François Jarasse

**109 ave. de Villiers**
**380.04.06**
*M. Jarasse*
*Open until 10:00 P.M. Closed Sat.*
*(at lunch), Sun., holidays and*
*December 20 to January 8.*

The riverside dwellers of the Place Maréchal-Juin have finally found their way to the good cooking of François Jarasse, which includes feuilleté of mussels, his grenadin of veal with chives, duck with turnips, and, best of all, his delicious deserts including the indescribable feuilleté pears. The hesitant, dull, badly-lit surroundings might arouse serious doubts, as might certain dishes (true, not many) which are completely outmoded (sweetbreads in port) or novelties that are no longer (fillet with green peppercorns, hot chavignol). Excellent vintages, reasonably priced, such as the Provence red Château de la Bégude. Friendly reception by the young Mme Jarasse and attractive 100F menu (including wine, a Gigondas of good quality) that includes foie gras or mussel soup, baby rabbit or lotte in tartar sauce, roast crottin de Chavignol and perfect sherbets.
Carte: about 160F. Menu: 70F, 100F (wine incl.), 130F + 15% serv.

13

## Laudrin

**154 blvd. Pereire**
**380.87.40**
*M. Billaud*
*Open until 10:30 P.M. Closed Sat.*
*(at lunch) and Sun. Parking at 40*
*rue Laugier.*
*V.*

The culinary classicism of Jacques Billaud is equaled only by a fertile imagination that works overtime to think of ways to make you happy; for example, his idea of serving his amazing collection of growers' wines in magnums (you drink as much as you like, paying only for what you drink); or of proposing nine oysters for the price of six; or, once again, of offering an unbeatable fixed-price meal (service, a Métaireau white and a Chinon included) with foie gras, small stuffed scallops, bass with sorrel, stuffed pigs' tails, cheese and hot apple feuilleté. A la carte are the classic seafood preparations and some good hearty plates like miroton à la lyonnaise or the tripe de la Mère Billaud. Delightful reception and service.
Carte: 190F. Menu: 150F (wine and serv. incl.).

## 12/20
## Chez Léon

**32 rue Legendre**
**227.06.82**
*M. Saccaro*
*Open until 9:45 P.M. Closed Sat.*
*evenings, Sun. and during August.*
*Parking at 40–42 rue Legendre.*
*V.*

Dear old Léon. For more than 20 years he has been preparing immutable, irreproachable fare behind his pretty etched glass window. He alternates classic cuisine and home-style cooking. Examples are hot saucisson with potato salad, leg of lamb with flageolets, braised duck with olives, and ile flottante with pralines. The dining room was redecorated last year, but it still is a little bit depressing.
Carte: 130F. Menu: 80F (serv. incl.).

## 12/20
### Maître Pierre

**2 rue Waldeck-Rousseau**
**574.20.28**

*Mme Boetsch*
*Open until 10:15 P.M. Closed Sat.,*
*Sun. and during August. Pay*
*parking at 11 rue*
*Waldeck-Rousseau.*
*AE, DC.*

A haven of soft, supple naugahide in an ocean of concrete. However, our sentimentality toward this local bistro is not justified merely by the cream-colored '30s decor. The good owner, Renée Boetsch, and the cuisine of her Norman chef, Maurice Tanquerel, are also responsible. Maurice shows his talent in his matelote d'anguille normande, poached eggs in feuilleté sauce mousseline, supreme of John Dory with courgettes and the raspberry charlotte.
Carte: 190F. Menu: 150F (wine and serv. incl.).

## 12/20
### Chez La Mère Michel

**5 rue Rennequin**
**763.59.80**

*M. Gaillard*
*Open until 10:30 P.M. Closed Sat.,*
*Sun., holidays and during August.*
*Pay parking at 30 rue Rennequin.*

Bernard Gaillard would never betray, in word or in deed, the spirit of this old bistro where the Mère Michel came as early as 1932 to pour rivers of beurre blanc Nantais over Paris. The great cuisine of the Vendée is still honored in the attractive menu. All the fish and shellfish are cooked in an excellent beurre blanc, and there is also baked ham with hazelnuts, the smoked eel from Brittany, delicious cheeses, and omelette soufflée des Chouans. And to accompany all this, the acidic but amusing little wines of the Vendée vineyards.
Carte: 150F–170F.

## 14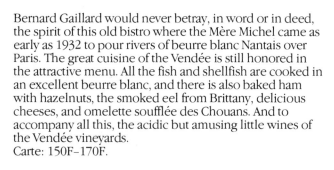
### Paul et France

**27 ave. Niel**
**763.04.24**

*M. Romano*
*Open until 10:30 P.M. Closed Sat.,*
*Sun. and July 15 to August 15.*
*Parking.*
*AE, DC, V.*

Let's not be niggardly in praising the sincerity of the reception, the politeness of the feminine service, the intelligent contribution of the owner-chef Georges Romano (formerly with La Bonne Auberge at Antibes) to the numerous refinements that are part of the meal (appetizers, candied fruits, young wines served in pewter pitchers). A cuisine both rustic and modern, cooked with the precision that is the unmistakable sign of a serious chef. Fricassée of mushrooms, curly lettuce with goose gizzards, sander with a purée of sweet peppers, scallops with a watercress mousse, aiguillette of duck with figs, noisettes of young kid à l'ancienne, chocolate charlotte. The floral decor is not exactly the ace up this restaurant's sleeve.
Carte: 180F. Menu: 100F (wine incl.), 170F + 15% serv.

## 14
### Le Petit Colombier

**42 rue des Acacias**
**380.28.54**

Bernard Fournier has spruced up his bistro of little salons without spoiling its rustic charm. He has lightened the food, using steam cooking to produce several exquisite plates. This real professional has succeeded with his

M. Fournier
*Open until 10:30 P.M. Closed Sun.
(at lunch), Sat. from August 1 to
18 and from December 25 to
January 2.
Parking at 43 rue des Acacias.
V.*

fricassée of fish with wild mushrooms, braised calf's liver paysanne, roast pigeon, fillets of John Dory with sorrel, beautiful meats carved right in the dining room, and his grapefruit tart. Bills are fairly modest for this excellent quality and for the very good wines.
Carte: 180F. Menu: 140F (wine incl.) + 15% serv.

14
## La Petite Auberge
**38 rue Laugier
763.85.51**
*M. Harbonnier
Open until 11:00 P.M. Closed Sun.,
Mon. and during August
Pay parking at 40 rue Laugier.
DC.*

For a long time Léo Harbonnier has successfully followed a policy of moderation and reserve. While many of his colleagues frantically hunt for new and spectacular dishes, Léo remains calm, polishing and perfecting the small number of specialties which he has been serving for twenty years and will go on serving forever. What beautiful work by this honest and scrupulous artisan! His aim is to do today what he did yesterday, but more lightly, more deftly, more elegantly. But we do not advise you to wait twenty years before going to dine upon the eggs Victor Pagès poached in a delicate orange sauce, the young rabbit with figs, the turbot Camille Renault with its exquisite sauce, the salad of scallops Assa, and some very good but simple desserts, such as the millefeuille and apple tart.
Carte: 160F. Menu: 140F + 15% serv.

15
## Pétrus
**12 place du Mal Juin
380.15.95**
*Mme André and M. Berneau
Open until 11:00 P.M. Closed Sun.,
Mon. and during August. Open
terrace. Parking.
All major credit cards.*

A crew of ancient mariners animates this good seafood restaurant. After having created restaurants in the four corners of the world, Mme André and Jean Berneau the owner finally dropped anchor here five years ago, and the young chef Gilbert Dugast came aboard in January 1981. A good restaurant but also one of the most beautiful displays of shellfish in Paris, tended by an oyster-opener *sans pareil.* There are, even in summer, oysters, clams and perhaps sea urchins, which you will eat on the covered terrace or in one of the elegant salons, and several well-conceived, modern plates such as the chiffonnade of seafood, stuffed clams, the bass with sorrel, tartare of daurade, sander with rhubarb, and the astonishing and copious cabbage stuffed with langouste. The wines are interesting, the service zealous, and the bill pretty steep.
Carte: about 200F.

17
## Michel Rostang
**10 rue Gustave-Flaubert
763.40.77**

The beginnings were difficult in this little corner of the 17th, pinched in among four high walls and squashed by the formidable competition of established restaurants. But suddenly this year all that changed; Lady Luck began smiling. Quick to respond, Rostang enlarged the

*M. Rostang*
*Open until 10:00 P.M. Closed Sat.*
*at lunch, Sun., holidays, and July*
*14 to August 17, and 8 days during*
*the winter. Air cond. Parking at 30*
*rue Rennequin.*
*V.*

premises, redecorated, all within a month: lacquered panels, bronze fittings, old engravings and oils, maîtres d'hôtel in dinner jackets—all was ready to receive a Paris that was already waiting in line. Only once or twice a year does a miracle of this kind occur; this time it is Rostang's turn. Perhaps it would be better to wait awhile until all the evidence is in, but if our intuition does not deceive us, this is it. Besides beating the crowd (the dining room is still very small; telephone well in advance for reservations) you will perhaps as well beat a rise in prices. For now, a very good dinner, wine and service included, can cost less than 200F. It is not given away, but it is worth it. The last meal we had there, with both white and red Beaucastel Châteauneuf-du-Pape (both of them marvelous), we feasted on exquisite little raviolis with goat cheese and lobster, raw salmon brushed with oil and served with a big julienne of vegetables, an exceptional small pigeon roast with cabbage, a young steamed Bresse chicken with a light chervil sauce, and superb cakes from a large selection. Michel Rostang and his wife, forever shuttling between kitchen and dining room, will help you order your dinner to celebrate his third toque.
Carte: about 200F. Menu: 95F (at lunch), 220F (dégustation) + 15% serv.

## 12/20
## *La Salle à Manger*
**11 rue de Montenotte**
**380.20.52**
*M. Schmitt*
*Open until 10:30 P.M. Closed Sun.,*
*Mon. evenings and July 14 to*
*August 15.*
*AE, DC, V.*

This is a pleasant restaurant with a discreetly romantic bourgeois decor. The peaceful atmosphere is measured by an attractive clock, and the cuisine by classic dishes on which Patrick Schmitt has left his mark. These include baby rabbit en gelée with tarragon, salade délices (with a good foie gras), civet of chicken, sole with morels, and oeufs à la neige. The sauces are carefully prepared but Danièle Schmitt's welcome is more attentive and friendly than the service.
Carte: 180F. Menu: 108F (serv. incl.).

## 13
## *Le Timgad*
**21 rue Brunel**
**574.23.70**
*Mme Zitout*
*Closed Sun. and during August*
*Parking at 30 place*
*Saint-Ferdinand.*
*DC, V.*

The impressive Oriental-palace decor suggests a Moorish bathroom designed for a movie nabob. Courteous reception, disorienting oriental service, and a successful enough cuisine which prepares brics, tajines, couscous "princier," excellent pastillas (must be ordered in advance), kebabs and stuffed chicken. Excellent wines.
Carte: 150F.

## 11/20
## *Chez Tonton Yang*

The long dining room has been completely refurbished. The bamboo wallpaper, indirect lighting and beautiful red

**11 rue Biot**
**522.36.75**
*Mme Hiu et M. Yang*
*Open until 10:30 P.M. Closed Mon.*

carpeting have replaced a depressing appendix to the dreary street. One no longer has to feel miserable when eating the spicy Southern Chinese cuisine prepared by one of the veteran Chinese cooks in Paris, Monsieur Yang Cheong Shee (revamped spelling). This is sweet and sour cookery which is sometimes a little chancy, but always well-intentioned and inexpensive. Our favorite dishes are scallops in spicy sauce, shrimp with candied nuts, and the sautéed beef with pimiento.
Carte: 80F–100F. Menu: 50F (serv. incl.).

13 

## La Toque
**16 rue de Tocqueville**
**227.97.75**
*M. Joubert*
*Open until 9:30 P.M. Closed Sat.,*
*Sun. and July 14 to August 5*
*V.*

Jacky Joubert had already thrown himself with passion into the nouvelle cuisine for about five years (he was then only 24 or 25) when we discovered him at Le Planteur, a small restaurant in the 15th, which has never recovered from his departure. Chef and owner here for only a short while in this comfortable Toque, he practices a successful cuisine based on the season and the available produce, which is characterized increasingly by his discipline and savoir-faire. You will enjoy his hure of fish with aspic, his feuilleté of lotte with Sauternes, his roast Brittany andouillette with shallots, and his several fresh, well-conceived desserts. Some good little wines, rather expensive, and a perfect Saint-Joseph (72F) which will ease the pain of the bill.
Carte: about 180F. Menu: 65F, 120F (dinner only) (serv. incl.).

14 

## La Truite Vagabonde

**17 rue des Batignolles**
**387.77.80**
*M. Fiocre*
*Open until 10:30 P.M. Closed Sun.*
*and the weekend of August 15.*
*Parking at 10 rue Caroline.*
*AE, DC, V.*

Although his departure was effected with the utmost discretion, a chef such as Emile Musas, who tended the stoves of La Truite Vagabonde ever since it opened 27 years ago, could not leave without being missed. We should hasten to add that Alexandre Fiocre, the shrewd owner, has not lost any of his cool and has passed on the scepter to Gilles Bauden. We are quite sure that although Gilles has been with the restaurant a mere seventeen years, he will try to perpetuate its essential virtues. However, there are already a few telltale signs of cautious innovation which we can only applaud (feuilleté of fines de claire oysters, beignets of scallops with a fresh tomato sauce). Furthermore, the eternally-classic dishes are as magnificent as ever. They include: the fillet of John Dory in saffron on a bed of mushroom duxelle, fillets of sole in coulis of écrevisses, or the noteworthy rack of lamb with potatoes Darfin. The oysters are still excellent all year round, the small tables with the intimate lighting for quiet

tête-à-tête dinners are still there (against a background panorama of snow-covered Alps—you cannot but not like it). The wine list remains superior.
Carte: 180F. Menu: 130F (serv. incl.).

# 18ème Arr.

### 13
## L'Assommoir
**12 rue Girardon**
**264.55.01**
*M. Larue*
*Open until 11:30 P.M. Closed Sun.*
*evening, Mon. and July 14 to*
*August 15. Open terrace.*

Philippe Larue, who was an aspiring actor, welcomes his guests and theater acquaintances with great kindness here on this charming peak of Montmartre. His old working-class bistro has been carefully preserved in its 1900 grocery-bar state with its flowery terrace in front of the Moulin de la Galette. Rather than surrender to the grab-the-tourist-and-feed-him-anything philosophy in service at many of the greasy-spoons of the quarter, he adopted several years ago a frankly homecooked cuisine that has developed today into a happy compromise with the light, modern approach. Although a spécialité recommandée, the cervelas of fish are insipid. We remember, rather, the haddock with saffron sauce, the lotte with curry and ginger, and the good home-baked chocolate fondant. (Saint-Véran white, Jurançon red, Chinon.)
Carte: 130F–150F.

### 10/20
## Le Bateau-Lavoir
**8 rue Garreau**
**606.02.00**
*M. Jallais*
*Open until 10:00 P.M. Closed*
*during June.*

Just a few feet from the Bateau-Lavoir where Picasso lived, an old merchant seaman mans the galley. A nice little menu with, for example, fish soup, rabbit with mustard and chocolate mousse. No reason to drop anchor or fire a 21-gun salute.
Menu: 47F + 12% serv.

### 17
## Beauvilliers
**52 rue Lamarck**
**254.19.50**
*M. Carlier*
*Open until 10:30 P.M. Closed Sun.,*
*Mon. (at lunch), and September 1*
*to 30. Open terrace. No large dogs.*
*V.*

Édouard Carlier has just completed his fourteenth year in this old bakery on the slopes of Montmartre. With exquisite taste he has made it one of the finest salons à manger in Paris, in an admirable profusion of flowers, old engravings, handsome table settings, and all the little things that prepare you for the pleasures of the table. The cuisine seems never to have been better or more inspired.

Stuff your wallet and you will enjoy an exceptional meal with, for example, salad of Brittany lobster on a bed of purslaine, a terrine of girolles with vinaigrette, a turbot with Hermitage wine, the leg of suckling lamb with basil juice, a rich chocolate délice—or, maybe next time, artichoke en chiffonade with crabmeat, fillets of grilled red mullet with pimiento, rogonnade of veal with spinach leaves, and admirable fresh fruit sherbets. Does it make sense to mention all these plates when Edouard Carlier and his chef change their menu each week in accordance with the seasons and their inspiration? Over the years the Beauvilliers has rid its repertory of affectations and complications. The cuisine respects the true flavors of food, is knowledgeably prepared, and is always inventive without being excessive. When the weather is fine, the verdant terrace overlooking the hill creates the sense of a real holiday; as long as the white Saint-Joseph fills the glasses, you'll realize the full pleasure of being alive in Montmarte.
Carte: about 220F–300F.

## La Cerisaie
**108 rue Lepic**
**606.19.29**
*M. Doré*
*Open until midnight. Closed Sun.,*
*Mon. and September 1 to 10.*
*AE, DC, V.*

Gilles Doré, who had been chef at La Ciboulette, about two years ago planted this "cherry orchard" halfway up the slope of Montmartre. He planned things intelligently: first he devised a relaxed decor with a charm altogether remarkable for these parts; most important, he drew up a menu, changed each month, of a brevity no less rare, making it possible to polish each of its offerings with infinite care. It is the cuisine of a wise and inspired technician, with no trace of banality, from the first entrée (mesclun salad with asparagus tips and calf's trotters) to the last dessert (caramel ice cream with nougatine) with, for example, a feuilleté of fish with puréed shallots and beans, a seafood marmite with leeks, émincé of duck à la ficelle, a charlotte au praliné. Small but well chosen cellar. Prices on the whole severe.
Carte: 150F.

## Charlot ler (Merveilles des Mers)
**128 bis blvd. de Clichy**
**522.47.08**
*M. Cornic*
*Open until 1:00 A.M. Closed*
*during July and August*
*Pay parking at 11 rue Forest.*
*AE, DC, V.*

If the serving cart still rolls around the agreeable second-floor dining room to set fire to perfectly good food, it just goes to show that the flambée is not dead and that that is the way that some people still want their meals. But we should inform you that Christian Cornic is one of the few restaurateurs who still goes to the Rungis central market each day to select his produce; the result is that what's on his menu is about as fresh as you can find in Paris. Let yourself be tempted by the oysters, then, or the shellfish, the good fish grilled or simply prepared. You will be completely happy . . . until the bill arrives.
Carte: 230F. Menu: 130F + 15% serv.

13

## Au Clair de la Lune
**9 rue Poulbot**
**258.97.03**

*M. Roussel and Mme Thullier*
*Open until midnight. Closed Sun.*
*and during February school*
*holiday.*
*AE, DC, V.*

Well protected from the tourist circus of the place du Terte just above, this is a very attractive little restaurant where the neo-naive motif of the murals, curtains and the painted wood of the bar gives a spontaneous tone to this agreeable dining room, which is very quiet at midday, but very animated in the evening. The place continues the happy association of Florence Thullier (reception) and her friend Pierrot Roussel (in the kitchen) from their Perroquet vert at the bottom of the hill. The cuisine does not belie the impression of modernism; it relies on first-class products, precise cooking and elegant presentation. You will like the feuilletés of goat's cheese with basil, the haddock with herbs, the turbot with red Chinon, the lamb chops with fresh mint, all accompanied with chilled red Côteaux-du-Lyonnais which make the bill climb like the rue Lepic.
Carte: 180F. Menu: 75F + 15% serv.

15

## Clodenis
**57 rue Caulaincourt**
**606.20.26**

*M. Gentes*
*Open until 10:30 P.M. Closed Sun.,*
*Mon., 3 wks. in August and 2 wks.*
*in February*

With Les Semailles and Beauvilliers, Clodenis is a frontier of the privileged gastronomic region in the northern section of Paris. Less sumptuously elegant than Beauvilliers and with less ultra-nouvelle cuisine than Les Semailles, this attractive bistro is also much less expensive (there's an excellent lunch menu) and not far from being as good. Short menu, inspired cooking—all based on the season and the marketplace: crab salad en chiffonnade, lotte with three purées, sautéed lamb with crayfish, young turbot with ginger, veal sweetbreads with freshly made pasta, sherbets and good Bordeaux. Our readers report that the service is sometimes wanting.
Carte: about 180F. Menu: 80F (serv. incl.).

**12/20**

## La Crémaillère 1900
**15 place du Terte**
**606.58.59**

*Mme Decronumbourg*
*Open until midnight. Closed Mon.,*
*Tues. (at lunch), February 1 to 16*
*and August 9 to 24. Lunch only*
*Fri., Sat., Sun. Open terrace.*
*No large dogs.*
*All major credit cards.*

Would you believe it? An intelligent menu, first-class food, imaginative preparation and reasonable prices—all at the most adulterated spot in the world? A miracle must have guided a young chef from La Marée and another from La Tour d'Argent and Laurent to this funny 1900's brasserie which, with its bower (a protected monument) and its wonderful garden, has become one of the most interesting places on the slope of Montmartre. But it is the freshness of the oysters just taken from their saltwater tank, the savor of the skate salad, the roast rack of lamb with honey, the chartreuse of sole with sorrel à l'aigrelette, and the good traditional desserts that draw the most interest. Will the new owners of this Crémaillère be able to resist the hordes of tourists who assail the unfortunate Butte? They have, at least for the time being, closed their doors to the guided-tour crowd: this took courage on the

place du Tertre. It remains to be seen whether this policy can endure or whether a good brasserie-type cuisine might not be in order.
Carte: 180F. Menu: 120F + 15% serv.

**12/20**

## Chez Frézet
**181 rue Ordener**
**606.64.20**
*M. Frézet*
*Open until 10:00 P.M. Closed Sat.,*
*Sun., during February, school*
*holidays and during August.*
*Parking at 73 rue Danrémont.*

A living legend in loyalty to tradition. M. Frézet could well engrave his menu in bronze or marble. There is compote of rabbit, cassoulet, bouillabaisse, leg of lamb in feuilleté, marmite dieppoise . . . A truly virtuous cuisine to which a clientele that seems hardly to have changed since the restaurant opened pays the most moving respects. Service and prices are friendly.
Carte: 130F.

13

## Les Fusains
**44 rue**
**Joseph-de-Maistre**
**228.03.69**
*M. Mathys*
*Open until midnight. Dinner only.*
*Closed Mon. Open terrace.*
*V.*

The friendly owner-chef, who settled down here recently after a few years with a theater troupe, takes pains to create an imaginative and light cuisine, less prone to the uncertainty and false starts of amateurism of his past. A rather distressing experience last spring, but a very recent pleasant one to make us forget the first; we'll remember the good, fresh sardines en fillets marinated with lime; an exquisite saddle of lamb with red cabbage; and aiguillettes of duck with vinegar and honey, cooked well and full of flavor. Then again there was a rather faded pot-au-feu of crayfish, dreary desserts, and accompanying vegetables which would improve if elevated from their cameo roles. Agreeable, light oak paneling, and very likable atmosphere.
Carte: 160F.

13

## Grand-gousier
**17 ave. Rachel**
**387.66.12**
*M. Vigato*
*Closed Sat., Sun. and during*
*August. Parking at 11 rue Forest.*
*V.*

The Rabelaisian reference in the name of this restaurant, opened only two years ago in this country lane, is only partly appropriate. The soft, pastoral decor, a charming reception, and a distinguished cuisine denote an agreeable rendezvous rather than a Pantagruelian trough. The elegant clientele are attracted by the short, frequently revised menu of Jean-Pierre Vigato, the owner-chef, and they are not deceived. You will agree with them in tasting the terrine of leg of lamb with foie gras, the skate en ravigote with a julienne of vegetables, a panaché of meats with wine lees and, always, lots of tempting desserts (a large plate of bitter chocolate).
Carte: 170F.

## 12/20
### Da Graziano
**83 rue Lepic**
**606.84.77**
*M. Graziano*
*Open until 12:30 A.M. Closed Sun.*
*Open terrace.*

This softly lit setting that the sprightly Graziano devised to attract pretty women, upon whom he dotes, will perhaps attract your own, provided her dress does not clash with the emphatic violet of the settees. The cuisine flies Italian colors, and you will like the San Daniele crêpes; the paglia y fieno pasta (both green and white) with ham, green peas and cream; and the carpaccio. A Tuscan reception and attractive wines from the Boot. Carte: 130F–150F.

## 12/20
### Le Maquis
**69 rue Caulaincourt**
**259.76.07**
*M. Lesage and M. Gentes*
*Open until 10:30 P.M. Closed Sun.,*
*Mon. and during August*
*Open terrace.*

Easy to take, this Maquis: With these prices and this quality, we needn't scratch our heads for something to say about it. Deny Gentes and Claude Lesage of the neighboring Clodenis have opened this attractive, noisy house (the tables are somewhat cramped, but that is part of the formula) where you will be served, for the fixed-price meal, a leek quiche, a sizable helping of mutton stew (a different home-style plate each day). Several francs more will give you access to the fatter menu, where fillets of herring with fried potatoes are to be found beside the knuckle of ham with lentils, and a beef bourguignon beside an osso buco. Some good desserts. Carte: 90F. Menu: 40F (wine and serv. incl.).

## 11/20
### Marie-Louise
**52 rue Championnet**
**606.86.55**
*M. Coillot*
*Open until 10:00 P.M. Closed Sun.,*
*Mon., holidays and late July to*
*early September.*
*DC.*

Everything is in order, which has been the case for the last 20 years. There is not a glimpse of an innovation in this old bistro of yesterday hidden behind the Gare du Nord. Consequently, there is the same generous honesty of the same poultry liver terrine, tête de cochon, côte de veau grand-mère, coq au vin, and homemade clafoutis. And everyone is happy that way. Carte: about 120F. Menu: 60F (serv. incl.).

## 11/20
### Le Petit Marguery
**8 rue Aristide-Bruant**
**264.95.81**
*M. Huin*
*Open until 9:30 P.M. Closed Sun.,*
*Mon. and during September.*

The cook, Jeanne Huin, has been tending the stove of this elegant restaurant for 32 years. Her age has been revealed to us in confidence, so we will not divulge it. However, the youthfulness of this elderly cook will strike you as soon as you taste her fresh marinated herring—the best in Montmartre—her beef bourguignon, her côte de veau à la crème and her fruit tarte. A lot of innocence and a lot of love, that's the secret of this delightful establishment. Carte: 100F, Menus: 28F (serv. incl.), 40F + 15% serv.

**10/20**
## Relais de la Butte
**12 rue Ravignan**
**606.16.18**
*M. Vogel*
*Open until 10:00 P.M. Closed Mon.*
*and during August.*
*AE, DC.*

Richard Vogel abandoned his peaceful sailing up and down the Seine, as captain of a bateau-mouche, to board this attractive, cozy bistro and sail the perilous oceans of Montmartre. He offers a good menu at a reasonable price, including homemade rillettes, pot-au-feu grand-mère and chocolate mousse. Reception and service are pleasant and unpretentious.
Menus: 58F, 88F (serv. incl.).

**17**
## Les Semailles
**3 rue Steinlen**
**606.37.05 and**
**259.93.98**
*M. Jouteux*
*Open until 12:30 A.M. Closed Sun.,*
*Mon. and during July. Dinner*
*only.*
*V.*

The owner being so full of fire himself, it was inevitable that the little restaurant of Jean-Jacques Jouteux would burn down. There followed eight months of inactivity but, finally, all was set right and the Semailles reopened (evenings only), decorated as before in flowery and friendly bourgeois style. But Jouteux is as inflamatory as ever; the white heat of his imagination has created new culinary extravagances: a "soup" with foie gras, turnip millefeuille, compote of asparagus, red mullet with truffled butter, veal sweetbreads with lime blossom (or red radishes). The presentation, inspired by Pointillist art, is extraordinary, the helpings proportioned, the flavors either violently contrasting or completely blended. But what of it? Jouteux wants to leave his mark—already has, in fact—on contemporary cuisine. He has arrived on the scene just at the moment when talent, genius perhaps, can overstep discipline. The chef, in a delirious trance, creates monsters. But he must pass through this stage, and from chrysalis, we are sure, will emerge the most beautiful butterfly in Paris.
Carte: about 300F.

**12/20**
## Tartempion
**15 bis rue du**
**Mont-Cenis**
**606.10.40**
*M. Billon*
*Open until 11:00 P.M. Annual*
*holidays not set. Open terrace.*
*AE, DC.*

A painting by Lorjou celebrating the joys of watermelon among many others, graces the very prettily rejuvenated walls of the former Patachou, a long vine's reach from the place du Tertre. Whole populations of foreign tourists flock here and are pleasantly subjected to stage waiter Angelo's skillfull, insolent wit. Since last autumn, a young chef, Georges Outhier has been at the stoves of this charming establishment where Jean Billon and his wife ensure the uninterrupted reign of good humour. His menu is well done, and all he needs to do is survey its execution a little more closely and he'll finally free himself from the clutches of tourist-and-tin-can cooking: a light millefeuille with haddock (but with its bones, and a far too stiff julienne of leek), overcooked sole sauce vierge, a good fricassée of chicken with raspberry vinegar; grandmother's apple cake, tasteless and floury. A few affordable current wines.
Carte: 130F–150F. Menu: 86F (serv. incl.).

**12/20**

## Au Tournant de la Butte

**46 rue Caulaincourt**
**606.39.86**

*M. Wamber*
*Open until 10:00 P.M. Closed Mon.*
*and during September.*

Summoning all of his courage, chef Maldonado has thrown himself into a few new dishes this year, such as sweetbreads with écrevisses, magret of duck with raspberries, the salmon cutlet in Champagne with spring vegetables. He is to be congratulated for that, even—or should we say especially—if the people of Montmartre (be they residents or visitors) come here only for the fixed-price menu, which offers festive, truly gargantuan meals whose diversity, abundance, and cost (25% higher this year) defy description. But do be sure to have a look at the carte. And when you have finished, ask Michel Wamber to give you a tour of his collection of eaux de vie blanches.
Carte: 110F–130F. Menu: 50F + 15% serv.

**13**

## Le Verger de Montmartre

**37 rue Lemarck**
**252.12.70**

*M. Morazin*
*Open until 11:00 P.M. Closed Sat.*
*(at noon), Sun. Open terrace. No*
*dogs. Parking.*
*V.*

Nothing surprises us less than to see this year's prize for French courtesy awarded to the charming Michel Morazin, who is, in truth, one of the most amiable restaurateurs we know . . . and we have known him a long time. We were the first, five years ago, to discover him in at his stove preparing delicious offerings, and we are delighted to affirm that he has overcome enormous difficulties with his establishment which have not, however, prevented him from serving with a smile the most intelligent of modern cuisines from a minuscule kitchen: émincé of leeks with pink shrimp, warm gâteau of artichokes, paupiette of veal with mussels. A very fine cellar and excellent homemade pastry.
Carte: 180F. Menu: 120F (wine incl.), 165F. (dégustation) + serv.

**11/20**

## Le Wepler

**14 pl. Clichy**
**387.72.64**

*M. Bessière*
*Open until 1:30 A.M. Closed during*
*August.*
*V.*

On this great liner, which sails between Clichy and Montmartre, its lights ablaze until 2:00 in the morning, sample one or the other of the seafood platters which weigh in at around 80F (with six no. 3 Belon oysters, five no. 3 Claire oysters, plus prawns, clams, palourdes, and langoustines). The other is closer to 200F but has eight no. 2 Belon oysters, six no. 2 Claire oysters, six no. 2 special oysters, plus langoustines, prawns, sea urchins, praires and mussels. The wines include Gros-Plant, Muscadet Perle de la Ricochère and Pinot Noir 1978 at moderate prices.
Menu: 98F (serv. incl.).

# 19ème Arr.

**12/20**

## Au Boeuf Couronné
**188 ave. Jean-Jaurès**
**607.89.52**
*Mme Saquy and M. Sagnelonge*
*Open until 10:00 P.M. Closed Sun.*
*Pay parking at marché de la*
*Vilette.*
*AE, DC, V.*

Here, the seductive perfume of the ladies in black (the dozen good-natured waitresses who hurry to serve the beef) is that of tête de veau ravigote, the baked onglet, the pig's feet, the navarin with French beans and a few other memorable delights in generous helpings served in a noisy dining room used for weddings and big dinners. You can abandon yourself to the enjoyment of these large dishes, so generous and unpretentious . . . well, what about this angry reader who declared that her grilled kidneys à l'Américaine were inedible? It must have been an accident.
Carte: about 160F. Menu: 100F (serv. incl.).

**15**

## Au Cochon d'Or
**192 ave. Jean-Jaurès**
**607.23.12**
*M. Ayral*
*Open until 10:00 P.M. Pay*
*parking.*
*AE, DC, V.*

The Cochon d'Or is still on its feet, we hummed the other day when leaving this supreme institution (third generation) of La Villette. The grandiose cultural projects arising from the old site of the Paris stockyards should give a new life to this luxurious old bistro. In the years since the abattoirs moved away, René Ayral has found the time long, which is only more reason to salute his worth for maintaining such high quality in his generous and delicate cuisine. The grilled meats remain the principal attractions, from the simple steak to the Cochon d'Or Special (210F for two persons), and they are always admirable cuts and well cooked. But one finds many other offerings at the Cochon d'Or; for example, an exquisite bass with sorrel, a shellfish salad, a matelote, and we must not forget the unforgettable: the calf's head and some delicious hot desserts. A spectacular wine list.
Carte: 200F–plus.

**12/20**

## Dagorno
**190 ave. Jean-Jaurès**
**607.02.29**
*M. Charmes*
*Open until 10:30 P.M. Closed Sat.*
*Pay parking (7F at 211 ave. Jean*
*Jaurès).*
*AE, DC, V.*

Dagorno used to be one of the best places in the neighborhood when la Villette still had a slaughterhouse. This vast, very dated dining room is still almost as full as in the past with a clientele of voracious carnivores (especially fans of boiled beef à la ficelle) who are sometimes justly seduced into eating the home-smoked fish, the varied and abundant specials of the day, and from September to April, the good seafood. The atmosphere is pleasantly suburban, but the prices are definitely Parisian.
Carte: about 180F.

## 12/20
### Aux Deux Taureaux
**206 ave. Jean-Jaurès**
**607.39.31**
*Mme Tollet-Pélissou*
*Open until 10:30 P.M. Closed Sat.*
*and Sun. evening. Pay parking at*
*211 ave. Jean-Jaurès.*
*AE, DC, V.*

The suburban-cozy Porte de la Villette decor of this restaurant, with its heavily patterned carpet and department store still-lifes, takes both bulls by the horns and tells you unequivocably that there is a place in this former slaughterhouse district where you can have a decent meal, dressed in coat and tie and sporting your best manners. Among the offerings are cervelle with capers, museau ravigote, and pavé "Villette." There is an excellent menu of carefully prepared meats, in the best local tradition, and a few other interesting items such as andouillette, the simple, large grilled sole, and a memorable tête de veau.
Carte: 180F. Menu: 39F (wine and serv. incl.).

## 11/20
### Ferme de la Villette
**184 ave. Jean-Juarès**
**607.77.63**
*M. Charmes*
*Open until midnight. Closed Sun.*
*and during August. Pay parking at*
*211 ave. Jean-Juarès.*
*V.*

What's new down on La Ferme? Nothing, neither a glimmer of a change nor the whiff of an innovation. Justin Charmes, the farmer, is still working hard on the tête de veau, his head bowed over the kidneys flambéed in Armagnac, beavering away at the pig's feet and going full-speed-ahead at the andouillette, the côte de boeuf and pavé Villette. Since the country-style decor is bearable, the reception and service charming, and the heavy meat-eating regulars are on hand to provide local color, everything's working fine. All this has been going for seventeen years, and we are really happy for Justin.
Carte: 130F–150F, Menu: 58F + 15% serv.

## 12/20
### La Mer
**192 ave. Jean-Jaurès**
**208.39.81**
*M. Ayral*
*Open until 10:00 P.M. Open*
*terrace. Pay parking at 211 ave.*
*Jean-Jaurès.*
*All major credit cards.*

This maritime annex to the Cochon d'Or each day serves a full house of peaceful fish eaters who are inseparably attached to the cuisine that bobs comfortably on this calm sea. Each year, Chef Médina serves them the same stuffed mussels, fish soup, grilled red mullet, a marmite dieppoise; and, because it is all fresh, generous, and not badly cooked, they come back for more.
Carte: 170F.

## 11/20
### Le Pavillon du Lac
**Parc des**
**Buttes-Chaumont**
**202.08.97**
*M. Ceccaldi*
*Lunch only. Closed Wed., during*
*August, and 1 week in February.*
*Parking.*

A setting redolent of the dreamer Jean-Jacques Rousseau, but do not insist on solitary walks. This Napolean III-style wilderness setting is displayed before you in such a way as to create an illusion of a picnic in the country. The illusion is intensified by the fare: fresh artichoke hearts with lemon, blanquette of lotte with chervil, and cocotte of Gâtinais rabbit with mustard.
Carte: 170F. Menu: 115F (wine and serv. incl.).

**14**

### Le Petit Pré
**1 rue Bellevue**
**208.92.62**
*M. Vergès*
*Open until 10:00 P.M. Closed Sat.,*
*Sun., holidays.*
*V.*

All the charm of the old Belleville quarter, now disfigured, has found refuge in the sober and charming rustic setting of Christian and Jacqueline Vergès's Petit Pré. The warmth of the reception is from time to time in eclipse, which is too bad, and smiles cannot compensate for the slow service. That also is too bad, even if these faults are accidental, for the cuisine remains enthusiastic, sympathetic, inventive and graceful: wonderful hot duck sausages with a compote of bitter fruit, irresistible vegetable terrine with aspic, delicate veal sweetbreads with pimientos. There are also a few lapses, such as the bland fillet of sander with coriander or desserts that get too complicated (except a superb chocolate mint cake). An intelligent wine list.
Carte: 180F.

**10/20**
### Salons Wéber
**Parc des**
**Buttes-Chaumont,**
**ave. de la Cascade**
**607.58.14**
*M. Valat*
*Lunch only. Closed Wed. and*
*during August. Parking.*

This pavillion in the style of Napoleon III, located in the picturesque setting of the Buttes-Chaumont park, presents an attractive menu in spite of this year's price increase of more than 20%. There is a Bougnat platter, special of the day, and good desserts. The decor and environment add, of course, to the attractions.
Menu: 72F + 15% serv.

# 20ème Arr.

**12/20**
### Aux Becs Fins
**44 blvd. de**
**Ménilmontant**
**797.51.52**
*Mesdames Lefebvre*
*Open until 10:00 P.M. Closed Sun.*
*Parking.*
*AE, V.*

The cuisine of Mesdames Edith and Laurence Lefebvre continues to be reknowned throughout France, while their slate-written menu still follows their whims: oeufs en cocotte, gras-double Lyonnais, cassoulet, bouillabaisse, and frog legs à la Provençale. The terrines are unfailingly good and abundant. However, it is a pity that this cuisine so redolent of good living, yet only a few steps away from the dead in the Père-Lachaise cemetery, continues yearly to distance itself from prices more suitable to the fare it offers (note, however, that a few more modern, delicate dishes are being added to the list).
Carte: about 170F. Menus: 85F (serv. incl.), 120F (wine and serv. incl.).

**11/20**

## Boeuf Gros Sel
**70 rue du Volga**
**373.96.58**
*M. Barthélémy*
*Open until 9:30 P.M. Closed Sat.,*
*Sun., during July and August*

A bit of background: M. Barthélémy is the son of big Léon who, more than twenty years ago, introduced his formula for the famous boeuf gros sel (a beef stew, served with vegetables and coarse salt), preceded by a choice from about a dozen hors d'oeuvres plates and followed by Brie cheese from the farm and fruit tart from the kitchen. What has changed since then? Nothing at all as regards the food or the prices, which remain exemplary. But the endearingly ramshackle decor has succumbed to an unhappy refurbishing in the rustic-hotel style. And Léon is no longer here with his fat mug and his great biceps to single out the snobs and bounce the loud-mouths. Attention: the sympathetic M. Barthélémy has been expropriated. He will transfer his Boeuf and his Gros Sel in 1982 to 30 rue des Maraîchers, same arrondissement. Menu: 47F + 15% serv.

**11/20**

## Mère-Grand
**20 rue Orfila**
**636.03.29**
*M. Heldenbergh*
*Open until 8:30 P.M. Closed Sat.*
*evening, Sun. and during*
*September*

Halfway up Ménilmortant, stamped tablecloth's, paper napkins and the most sincere of traditional cuisines: roast Barbary duck with herbs, crépinette and peas with croûtons, veal sweetbreads with pepper, rabbit with cèpes. A fixed-price meal for 30F, wine and service included, offers a choice among ten entrées and four main dishes, cheese or dessert. Another menu at 40F. Interesting clientele of artisans and neighbors.
Menu: 30F (during the week), 40F (Sat. at lunch, wine and serv. incl.).

**13**

## Relais des Pyrénées
**1 rue du Jourdain**
**636.65.81**
*M. Marty*
*Open until 10:00 P.M. Closed Sat.*
*and during August. Parking at 15*
*rue Frédéric-Lemaitre.*
*AE, DC, EC.*

The clear skies of Pau are evident in the omelet piperade; the paume of veal sweetbreads paloise; garbure; cassoulet. Otherwise, Jean Marty of the Académie Culinaire leans toward the classic crêpe of lobster Duchesse en sabot, calf's kidneys madère, and tournedos périgordin (with a curious nod to the hamburger steak). But he is a remarkable professional, alert and scrupulous, and these qualities have made his remotely located restaurant one of the warmest Basque-Béarnais places in Paris. Delightful reception and service.
Carte: 200F.

# The Banlieue

## BIÈVRES

13
### La Gour-mandière
**à l'Abbaye-aux-Bois,
rue Antoine
019.35.47**
*Mme Valère
Open until 10:30 P.M. Closed Mon.
evening. Open terrace.
AE, DC, V.*

Just a year ago Olivia Valère reopened this long-dormant restaurant, a noble structure that served as an annex for the nuns of Port-Royal, later as a trysting place for notable romantics from Chateaubriand to Lamartine. She installed Lionel Jounault in the kitchen, and it was not long before he showed what he was capable of—that is to say, an absolutely modern cuisine realized with great assurance and taste for his own ideas: terrine of squab with preserved garlic cloves, a scallops en vinaigrette or in a small nage, fricassée with shallots, leg of lamb (cut too thin) with garlic cream, remarkable steamed veal sweetbreads, and a gala array of subtle desserts. Friday and Saturday evenings one can dance to the music of small orchestras, which change from week to week. There's also ping-pong and dining in the garden. A project for next spring: a riding club and some tennis courts.
Carte: 160F. Menu: 100F (serv. incl.).

## BOUGIVAL

17
### La Camélia
**7 quai
Georges-Clemenceau
969.03.02**
*M. Delaveyne
Open until 9:30 P.M. Closed Sun.
evening and Mon. No dogs.
AE, V.*

The departure of his chef must have left Delaveyne, a fantastically gifted chef in his own right, uneasy these past few months. But Delaveyne always bounces back; he reinvents his success. He, the eternal young man, the creator, the inventor without knowing it (in any case, without admitting it), of the nouvelle cuisine, has decided to give his cooking a regional flavor, although for the moment he is still in the Ile de France, which suits the rustic decor of his small house. There is no doubt, however, that his garden terrine, his pigs' trotters, his blanquette of veal, his saddle of veal maraîchère, and his subtle preparations with mushroom, do not resemble anything previously known: Genius must out . . . even over bourgeois convention!
Carte: 250F–300F. Lauréat 1978 de la Table d'Argent.

### 15  Le Coq Hardi

**16 quai Rennequin-Sualem**
**969.01.63**

*M. Van Egroo*
*Open until 10:00 P.M. Closed Wed.*
*and mid-January to mid-February*
*Open terrace.*
*AE, DC, V.*

Apart from the grand classics, such as the incomparable roast Bresse chicken, the veal cutlet with foie gras, the fillet of beef "Delphine Touchard," Jean Van Egroo and his chef Joël Verron propose dishes increasingly daring and modern (maybe even a little too much so), such as a vegetable terrine with kiwis or a seafood cocktail with exotic fish; maybe, also, too "saucy", believing that this marvelous restaurant with hydrangeas all around requires added culinary richness. But taste the lobster soup, the vegetables with crayfish, the sole with artichokes, the daurade with aniseed, the rib en croûte de sel, and you will agree that the old Coq has grown new plumage and spurs. Wines superb; bill superbissimo.
Carte: 350F–380F. Menu: 150F (at lunch, during week, wine incl.), 200F (dégustation) + 15% serv.

# BOULOGNE-BILLANCOURT

### 16 Au Comte du Gascogne

**89 ave. Jean-Baptiste-Clément**
**603.47.27**

*M. Vérane*
*Open until 10:15 P.M. Closed Sat.,*
*Sun., holidays and during August.*
*V.*

With a superb new cuisine, a computer so programmed that even the level of the Armagnac in the bottles can be verified, a beautiful garden of palm trees before him, and his charming wife beside him, Gérard Vérane can be proud of his success. The smooth talker with the gravelly accent has pulled out all the stops, and we can only agree with that Gascon pride when dining upon the light dishes in which his inventive young chef marries the past to the future; the foie gras (with lemon or green peppercorns), the fish brawn, the bavarois of crayfish with melon, a steamed rabbit with mint, magret with basil, a soup of fresh figs, are enchanting—as are all the wines and Armagnacs—but they barely dull the stab of the bill.
Carte: 250F. Menu (dégustation): 170F + 15% service.
Lauréat 1978 de la Table d'Argent.

### 17 Gérard Pangaud

**1 rond-point Rhin-et-Danube**
**605.34.42**

*M. Pangaud*
*Open until 10:30 P.M. Closed Sat.,*
*Sun. and 15 days in August.*
*AE, DC, V.*

The formidable bill (but there is a good and reasonably priced business menu) and the slightly pinched smile of Gérard Pangaud do not always evoke a favorable response from our readers; they must be forgetting the charms of this elegant house, the excellence of the service, and the extraordinary talent of Pangaud and his young lieutenant Stéphane Raimbault. The sautéed foie gras, the salmon brawn dressed in leeks, the turbot with vegetable ravioli, the salmon with watercress, the veal sweetbreads with

truffled artichokes, the pigeon with lobster, and the lamb with coriander, are all there to prove that we are right in awarding three toques to what is incontestably the best restaurant in the suburbs of Paris.
Carte: about 300F. Menu: 135F, 230F + 15% serv.

14

## La Petite Auberge Franc-Comtoise
**86 ave. Jean-Baptiste-Clément**
**605.67.19**
*M. Veysset*
*Open until 10:00 P.M. Closed Sun. and during August.*
*AE, DC, V.*

To tell the truth, it's not necessary at all to be a Boulogne-Billancourt businessman to haunt this Petite Auberge, whose confidence in its modern and regional repertory is increasing. As well, the charming comfortable decor, the irreproachable welcome of Jean-François Veysset and his wife and the attentiveness of the service make this a good address for the evening, peaceful, warm and very provincial, and many Parisians regularly find their way here. In addition to the marvelous Comtois charcuterie which come directly from Arbois, the Morteau jésus with red beans (a fat pork sausage charcoal-cooked with juniper and fir), the potée jurassienne and the hearty cancoillotte, (a cheese from Franche-Comté), the young Jean-Pierre Roy undertakes some original and delicate plates that are frequently renewed: rillettes of eels, a mousse of tomato with crabs, or sole with saffron. The desserts have made some progress (rhubarb charlotte) and the wine list has a stunning collection from the Jura.
Carte: 200F. Menu: 100F + 15% serv.

# CHATEAUFORT

17 

## La Belle Époque
**10 place de la Marie**
**956.21.66**
*M. Peignaud*
*Open until 9:30 P.M. Closed Sat., Sun., from December 22 to January 12 and from August 13 to September 8. Open terrace.*
*AE, DC, V.*

Our friend Michel Piot is right to find the seaweed-steamed lobster "fantastic." We recommended it to you last year, and you will find it again this year at the Belle Époque. Michel Peignaud brings back new ideas and products from each of his frequent Asian trips. Once it was a plate of raw fish Hokkaido-style; another time it was a vegetable ragoût with coriander or a duck with ginger, but never do these discoveries lack succulence. These oriental imports should not obscure the fact that Michel Peignaud is a man of Berri, and his specialties reflect his origin: barboville of duck's thighs, calf's head grand-mère, the suckling lamb à la Façon des bergers, or the delicious caillé goat cheese with Sanciaux. But Michel Peignaud is also crazy about seafood, and you have only to visit his large dining room, which in good weather continues onto a wonderful terrace dominating the green Chevreuse Valley, to taste his terrine of red mullet with a mousse of sea urchins' coral, Brittany oysters with a mousse of

chervil, fried John Dory with spinach, the cassoulet of lotte bream, the cod with garlic and green kidney beans, or the admirable scallops à la nage with mushrooms, followed by delectable desserts of which Michel Peignaud knows the secret: glazed crepes with red fruit, oeufs à la neige, or a peach soup with acacia honey. If there are six of you, you can reserve the small 1900 salon, where you will dine in the midst of the Belle Époque.
Carte: about 250F.

# ENGHIEN

## 16 ♧
## Duc d'Enghien
**at the Casino—3 ave. de Ceinture**
**412.80.00**
*M. Ducis*
*Open unitl 10:30 P.M. Closed August 1 to 17. Open terrace. No dogs. Parking. Cards: DC, V.*

The Casino restaurant has changed its policy, abandoning the resort-like cuisine for more tempting fields. For several months, Alain Passard, who was assistant to Michel Kéréver at the Lion d'Or at Liffré, has been performing miracles in the kitchen, following the direction indicated by Kéréver. The latter has set up a menu (signed by him, in fact) and comes twice a week to supervise its application. Is it the Passard-Kéréver association or the admirable work of this young chef trained in a good kitchen? In any case, we had a meal of absolutely admirable invention, lightness, and balance: superb preserved foie gras with strips truffles on a lettuce leaf seasoned with hazelnut oil, extraordinary Belon oysters en cassolette accompanied by an almost crunchy julienne of endives with zests of lime, goujonnettes of sole with saffron happily freshened with fresh diced tomatoes and intelligently garnished with a fennel flan. Then a masterpiece of mixed flavors: pigeon wing with foie gras and truffles wrapped in a cabbage leaf, steamed, and, finally, an exquisite pear feuilleté—served, alas, stingily with an ultra-light cream. The only false note of this lovely menu-dégustation was a fillet of lamb, insipid despite a fondue of fresh tomatoes. If, in such a cuisine, the balance of tastes and the precision of cooking attain near-perfection, one is apt to be less enthusiastic about the decor: here it's elegance of a somewhat indefinite style conceived by a theater set designer, which in the evenings is unevenly lit and in some places not lit at all. Worse, although the service is rapid, friendly and diligent, the restaurant still lacks a wine steward or at least a maître d'hôtel who understands his wine list.
Carte: 300F. Menu: 120F, 195F + 15% serv.

# LOUVECIENNES

## 13 ♤
## Aux Chandelles
**12 place de l'Eglise**
**969.08.40**

Daylight, even more than candlelight becomes this ravishing restaurant and its large bowered garden. In its simple, cozy second-floor dining room or on the small sunlit terrace with the Marly aquaduct spanning the

*M. Cadot and M. Fontana
Open until 9:30 P.M. Closed Sat.
(at lunch), Sun. evening, Wed.,
during Febuary school holidays
and 3 weeks in July. Open terrace.
DC, V.*

background, you can be sure of a pleasant meal. A close look reveals a personalized cuisine, half-traditional, half-modern, which Guy Fontana prepares with great care from the best food stuffs available daily at the Versailles and Rungis markets. Prove this for yourself with the pig's head with parsley and preserved onions, creamed skate's fin with green peppercorns, leg of young rabbit with an émincé of turnips, or the attractive chocolate feuilleté. Pleasant wines (Bordeaux, Bourgueil, Seyssel, around 50F).
Carte: about 150F.

# MAISONS-LAFITTE

18

## La Vieille Fontaine

**8 ave. Gretry**
**962.01.78**

*Mme. Letourneur and M. Clerc
Open until 10:00 P.M. Closed Sun.
and Mon. Open terrace.
AE, DC, V.*

Restaurant critics have the lamentable habit of bickering over their discoveries. It is understandable, though, that certain of them want at any price to have been the first to uncover the talents of François Clerc, even though, at the time of his first recognition, his cuisine bore no resemblance to what it has since become. Let's say simply that as far as we are concerned, we had the luck to single him out at the precise moment when he changed his style, this self-taught chef entered the enchanted world of new flavors and subtle pleasure. It was a truly extraordinary metamorphosis that, very rapidly placed him at the summit. This completely dedicated amateur became a true professional, and when you think of him, you recall with horror the stupid declarations of certain fuddy-duddy cooks who, blanched by the heat and as rigid as their toques, proclaimed that no one could be a chef who did not have a cooking school diploma. This is the same as stopping Verlaine from writing or Van Gogh from painting on the grounds that they had not formally studied. These quibbles are evidently of no interest at all to the innumerable clientele of the Vieille Fontaine, who are content to find themselves in this attractive nineteenth-century house and to dine, overlooking a small, well-manicured park, upon a cuisine which succeeds in being astonishingly knowledgeable without dabbling or affectation. The aumoniéres of caviar, the steamed Brittany lobster with vegetables, and the hot duck pâté wrapped in a ribbon of macaroni and topped with a truffle sauce— these may all be considered new masterpieces of French cooking. It is sufficient to know, as we do, that François Clerc is never at a loss for new ideas and that a meal at the Vieille Fontaine, nursed over by the adorable Manon Letourneur who treats her guests as beloved children, is each time a new feast, whether one chooses hot oysters with a purée of lobster or calf's kidneys with Chiroubles with blackcurrants cream, the scallops with herbs of Provence, or the leg of suckling lamb with buttered cabbage and tomatoes.
Menu: (dêgustation): 250F + 15% serv. Lauréat 1978 de la Table d'Argent.

# MARLY-LE ROI

14

### Au Roy Soleil
**19 ave. des Combattants**
**958.67.57**
*Open until 9:30 P.M. Closed Sun. evening and Mon. Parking. V.*

It was in this beautiful house that Louis XIV had his laundry done. Today, in summer, in the magnificent surrounding garden, you will have seductive meals that intelligently wed the classical with the modern. The latter is manifested on a small menu of the day or of the market, from which you may choose the hot terrine of sander with leeks, the "laundress's salad" with fillets of smoked goose, lotte with rhubarb compote or the veal sweetbreads with honey vinegar. Very charming service. Carte: 170F–plus.

# MEUDON-BELLEVUE

14 🍄

### Relais des Gardes
**42 ave. du Gal-Gallieni**
**534.11.79**
*M. Oudina*
*Open until 10:00 P.M. Closed Mon. evening, Sat. and during August. Open terrace. Dinner only in garden. Parking. Cards: AE, DC, V.*

This 200-year-old inn has been spruced up, and attractive canvasses now hang on the fresh paint. The old blending with the new is exactly the impression that the cuisine will give you. Prepared here for 33 years by Chef Daniel Bertholom, it is classic cooking that has been relieved of its weight; let's call it "new bourgeois cuisine," the spirit of which shows itself on the daily suggestions section of the menu: pâté of rabbit in fresh herb aspic, steamed John Dory with a purée of crabs, lamb chops with wild mint and a julienne of oranges. The remainder of the menu, prepared by Pierre Oudina, exhibits the same spirit of shrewdness and originality and the same devotion to fresh products simply prepared: fish steamed with seaweed, cotriade des Glénans, grilled lamb kidneys with a purée of garlic. Of course, this use of seasonal food stuffs, this taste for lightness and aversion to the conventional, this spirit of research and perfection, does have a name; it is what we have always called the nouvelle cuisine and it is what Pierre Oudina does with a spontaneity and application that is worth a tip of the toque. Carte: 200F.

# NEUILLY-SUR-SEINE

14 🍄

### Bourrier
**1 place Parmentier**
**624.11.19**
*M. Bourrier*
*Open until 11:00 P.M. Closed Sat., Sun., holidays, 2 wks. at Christmas and 2 wks. in August. V.*

This is a peculiar little building, though warm and provincial, at the rear of which Yves Bourrier prepares his cuisine in plain view of all. You never tire of this restaurant. Filled with curiosity, you push open the door and say, "Let's see what he's making for us today." It is the same question that this off-beat sympathetic chef with an imposing background (Point, Lasserre, Beau-Rivage in Condrieu, Plaza . . .) asks himself each morning at the market. And answers, say, "Hmm . . . fresh cod. Well,

wouldn't that be nice if I steamed it with basil. . . ." No sooner said than demonstrated with a simplicity that hides a clear talent and with a surprising mastery of those twin requisites of good cooking: discreet sauces and precise observance of cooking times. This, at least, is the delicious memory that we have of his hot rabbit pâté, duck salad, fresh pasta with truffles, and his delicate chocolate desserts. While you are here, take advantage of the chance to discover some exquisite Côtes-du-Rhône, at very reasonable prices, for which Bourrier nurses a veritable passion.
Menu: 130F, 160F (serv. incl.).

## 12/20
## *La Caviardise*
**61 ave. du Roule**
**745.70.80**
*M. Sevenet*
*Open until 11:30 P.M. Closed Sat.*
*(at lunch). Pay parking across the street.*
*DC, V.*

An elegant little restaurant with a comfortable setting. A fleeting feminine welcome and a Baltic-Slavic cuisine that is simple and successful: "caviardise" platter (good assortment of smoked fish, tarama, cream of salmon), Baltic herring, crab with tarragon, shashlik, pirogi. Foodstuffs and dishes to take out (salmon, borscht).
Carte: 130F–150F.

## 14
## *Jacqueline Fénix*
**42 ave.**
**Charles-de-Gaulle**
**624.42.61**
*Mme. Fénix*
*Open until 10:00 P.M. Closed Sat.,*
*Sun. and during August.*

What a gorgeous place to eat: flowery, delicate and feminine! A smart clientele to match, mostly male, from the advertising agencies nearby, is greeted by the blond Jacqueline with a sly eye beneath her bangs, is discreetly babied by the personnel, and royally fed by Michel Rubod, a magician of light sauces and of light appetizing cooking. The offerings on this attractive menu do not grow beards. We particularly like the leeks with oil of truffles and chervil served with smoked salmon, the unusual crayfish feuilleté with cucumber, the steamed bass, and exquisite desserts such as the chocolate-nut cake. In the evening, if you feel like blowing a 500 franc bill for two, it is an agreeable refuge for romantic tête-à-tête.
Carte: 200F–plus.

## 11/20
## *La Ferme de la Jatte*
**Ile de la Jatte-**
**197 blvd. Bineau**
**624.69.18**
*M. Siegrist*
*Open until 10:00 P.M. Closed Sat.*
*and Sun. Open terrace. Parking.*
*AE, DC, V.*

This restaurant, an old dairy of the Second Empire, has been functioning under this name since the end of the siege of Paris, during which some old stables were converted to mess halls for the soldiers. M. Siegrist, however, has been here only for the last forty years and has no complaints. A Swiss by birth, he scrupulously maintains the 1925 decor of this charming bistro and especially the unexpected little garden where, in the summer, you will be served boudin with apples, poached haddock with melted butter, or grilled leg of lamb with herbs.
Carte: 130F–150F.

## 13 🔱
### Focly
**8-10 rue Paul-Chatrousse**
**624.43.36**
*M. Lu Suy Hok*
*Open until 10:30 P.M. Closed August 6 to 20.*
*AE, V.*

A true cuisine that is predominantly Chinese; you will find fried won ton in sweet and sour sauce and crab claws in hot sauce. It is not always successful; the lacquered duck is only an approximation of the real thing. But the chef, Mach Quyen, formerly of the Pagoda and an associate in this charming restaurant which is owned by Cambodians, will serve you, as in the old Phnom-Penh days, stuffed shirmp with bananas and the grilled and boned duck Phi-Pha. All of this with inexhaustible smiles and pleasant little wines that are almost a giveaway.
Carte: 100F. Menu: 32F (serv. incl.).

## 12/20
### Les Iles Chausey
**24 rue de Chartres**
**624.48.41**
*M. Montagné*
*Open until 11:30 P.M. Closed Sat. (at lunch) and Sun. Open terrace.*
*V.*

As in the old days on the poop deck of his ship *Les Iles Chausey,* Jean-Pierre Montagné is captain in the kitchen of his pretty green-and-white restaurant. This former naval officer gives two good reasons for his having taken to the stoves: first, because he could do it, since his grandfather Prosper Montangé was one of the old-timers of la grande cuisine; second, because circumstances demanded it of him. With the aid of his chef Michel Caillet, he limits the number of table settings and compensates for the rise in the price of fish by preparing it very simply. All that interests us is the result, and we continue to find here good rillettes of salmon with dill, stuffed tomatoes with fresh crab and shrimp, tartare of grouper, blanquette of veal with basil, and, on Mondays, a delicious landlubbers' cassoulet made according to one of his grandfather's old recipes. A small shop in the annex where until 2:00 A.M. Montagné sells good regional products (andouille, bread with Brie, cider) from his hometown of Vire.
Carte: 170F. Menu: 55F (wine incl.) + 15% serv., 100F (serv. incl.).

## 13 🔱
### Le Mandarin de Neuilly

**148 ave. Charles-de-Gaulle**
**624.11.80**
*M. Lau*
*Open until 10:30 P.M.*

In an old bistro setting with a few indispensable Chinese knickknacks, the talented chef takes you on a whirlwind tour of the principal Chinese gastronomic regions with knowledgeable and lively fashion. All is delicate and fresh, served in a wink, without gimmicks, and it is a true pleasure to dig into the light nems, the shrimp with caramelized nuts, the spicy lamb Szechuan-style, or the roast spareribs. All this happiness is added up in a bill so reasonable that even economy-minded Neuilly residents—and there are some—should remember to come more often.
Carte: about 100F. Menu: 41.10F (serv. incl.).

## 14 🔱
### Le Manoir

**4 rue de l'Eglise**
**624.04.61**
*M. Juveneton*
*Open until 10:00 P.M. Closed Sat., Sun. and August 1 to 24. Dinners only.*
*V.*

Patrick Juveneton has been chef in this traditional restaurant for a long time, and has now become the owner as well. The morose decor has been attractively redone in blue tones, and Juveneton assures us that this is the result of our comments. But we also remarked that his cuisine should lift itself above the perfect execution of simple dishes. We remain convinced that this brilliant chef

would obtain surprising results if he were to harness his craftsmanship and knowledge of foodstuffs to the creative freshness and audacity that must lurk somewhere beneath his toque. While awaiting this event, this explosion, you will certainly not be displeased to be sitting at his attractive, flowered tables, before a strictly seasonal cuisine, whose rigor and confidence assure full pleasure: lotte with green and pink pepper-corns, cassolette of snails with cèpes and nuts, flan of mussels with zucchini, Bress capon. Several tempting Angevin dishes also (a plate of freshwater fish, magret of duck with mushrooms) and a new fixed-price meal which is surely one of the best values for money to be found in Neuilly: an eggplant caponata with toast de poutargue, sander with sorrel, aiguillettes of duck with fruit, and a hot strawberry feuilleté. Good Savennières and red Anjou.
Carte: about 180F. Menu: 120F. (serv. incl.).

## 13
### *Sébillon (Paris Bar)*
**20 ave.**
**Charles-de-Gaulle**
**624.71.31**
*Open until 10:00 P.M. Closed during August.*
*All major credit cards.*

The director sums it up when he says: "Old house, old bourgeois cuisine." To be precise: this is a venerable and busy brasserie two steps from the Porte Maillot, and always a *young* bourgeois cuisine. To tell the truth, if we award Sébillon an additional point this year, it is not because of some new dish (in its case, a new dish would be unnecessary) but to recognize the unalterably high quality of the shellfish, the leg of lamb with haricot beans (the best in Paris), the farm-style dishes, and the fabulous mocha and chocolate éclairs. Such faithfulness to old French values is well worth a toque. Prices get more up-to-date each year, especially this one.
Carte: 140F–160F.

# *ORLY*

## 12/20
### *La Louisiane*
**(Hilton International Orly)**
**687.33.88**
*M. Fournier*
*Open until 11:30 P.M. Closed August 3 to 28. Parking.*
*AE, DC, V.*

It's not easy to find, but don't become discouraged; the place is pleasant and cozy, the pianist on his toes, the young waiters sympatico—and the cuisine not at all bad. Louisiana Creole and Cajun specialties mainly, with an excellent mussel and prawn crêpe (the "hot" sauce accompanying it has, unfortunately, cooled down on its drip across the ocean), a spectacular jambalaya, a very interesting ragoût of gambas, and a good café brûlot (with rum and orange juice). Desserts not so good. Good little wines and great big bills.
Carte: 180F-plus. Menu: 110F (serv. incl.).

## 14 🍴
### *Maxim's*
**Aérogare Orly-Ouest**
**687.16.16**
*M. Lapeyre*
*Open until 10:30 P.M.*
*V.*

No other airport restaurant in the world offers such a magnificent decor (a daring pastiche of Maxim's, rue Royale, but this one is not aging as well), such remarkably smooth service, perfect comfort. We can certainly complain, though, that this is not precisely the cuisine we had expected. Only about a year ago, however, Louis Lapeyre, the new manager, decided to shake things up and to try to escape the yoke of restraints inherent in airport catering. He fired up his excellent chef, Roger Grandin, to polish the formula of the already attractive menu, and to offer new dishes in the Grill as well as in the restaurant. All is not yet perfect, but it shows signs of becoming so. So if you decide to try it, choose the fixed-price meal that offers, for example, salad, escalope of salmon with wild mint, aiguillettes of duckling with bilberries, a cheese platter, melon or currant ice cream. Carte: 250F–280F. (160F–180F in the Grill). Menu: 160F (serv. incl.).

# *PUTEAUX*

15

## *Gasnier*
**7 blvd. Richard-Wallace**
**506.33.63**
*M. Gasnier*
*Open until 9:00 P.M. Closed Sat., Sun., holidays, and June 30 to August 22.*
*V.*

In Hubert Gasnier's house, duck is god: duck liver cold or hot, rillettes of duck, magret of duck grilled with three vegetables, preserved duck (roast with cabbage), cassoulet (where the duck waddles alongside a shoulder of lamb, bacon and sausage—the whole served like religious ritual, ingredient by ingredient, in a very large dish with extraordinarily tender Nord lingot beans). Admirably interpreted and modernized, the cuisine of the Southwest takes pride of place again on the short menu of this knowledgeable cook, with the cold piperade, comme à Hasparren scrambled eggs with truffles, or the blanquette of langouste with Sauternes that his wife and daughter Patricia will serve you (it is essential to telephone for a table; Hubert Gasnier cooks for only twenty persons at most) with all the attention you would expect in the house of a Chevalier de la courtoisie française. Some remarkable old Cahors (all the way back to 1880!).
Carte: 200F.

13

## *L'Hippo-campe*
**2 blvd. Richard-Wallace**
**506.01.37**
*M. Luzé*
*Open until 10:00 P.M. Closed Sat. (at lunch), Sun., Mon. evening and during August.*
*AE, DC, V.*

From the office buildings of the place de la Défense at lunchtime (the evenings are much quieter) a horde of hungry gourmets swarm to this recently opened bistro. The owner of this elegant, dark-brown-colored restaurant is a sturdy man of Nantes, and he has his fish delivered directly from Guilvinec, his oysters from Madec, his shellfish from Erquy; and has them all prepared in a light, modern way by his young chef, Alain Campagne. You will taste his lotte with lardoons, estouffade of turbot with scallops, the petite marmite à la Ty Peurn, and the fine desserts of the day. And you will not be upset to find that all of this is reasonably priced, even with an honest Muscadet of the house.
Carte: 140F–160F.

# RUEIL-MALMAISON

### 13 🍃
### El Chiquito
**126 ave.**
**Paul-Doumer**
**751.00.53**
*Mme. Besson*
*Open until 9:30 P.M. Closed Sat.,*
*Sun. and during August. Open*
*terrace. Parking.*

A very agreeable house only twenty minutes from the Étoile, with a beautiful garden bursting with flowers, a reception no less flowery by the owner Edith Besson, and a frequently changed menu offering mainly fish. Try this year, among the novelties prepared by Serge Bioux, the escalope of fresh salmon with peas, the fillet of sea bass en papillote, the rillettes of daurade, or the salad of warm prawn with vegetables. The produce is perfect, the cooking well mastered, the cellar tempting, and the bill flies high.
Carte: 250F–plus. Menu (dégustation): 210F + 15% serv.

### 12/20
### Relais de Saint-Cucufa
**114 rue du**
**Gal-de-Miribel**
**749.79.05**
*M. Morel*
*Open until 9:30 P.M. Closed Wed.*
*evening and during August. Open*
*terrace. Parking.*
*AE, DC, V.*

It is the opinion of the owner-chef, Marie-Madeleine Morel, that her restaurant is "without pretention." True, but not without its charms. There is a small terrace where on fine days you can dine on fresh fish brought each morning by her husband (a former butcher, he also selects meats expertly), salad of prawn with artichokes, seafood lasagna, plate of three fish (salmon, daurade, turbot). And honest dessert (fruit charlotte), and a pleasant Côtes-de-Bourg (30F) Prices are becoming pretentious.
Carte: 160F.

# SAINT-GERMAIN-EN-LAYE

### 14 🍃
### Cazaude-hore (La Forestière)
**1 ave. du**
**President-Kennedy**
**973.36.60**
*M. Cazaudehore*
*Open until 10:00 P.M. Closed Mon.*
*Open terrace. Parking.*

This house in the forest with its flower garden and its large rustic dining room served only Basque-béarnaise specialties in the old days. It was always the first place we thought of when someone suggested a meal in the country, not too far from Paris, in an agreeable, restful setting. The name of Cazaudehore comes even more easily to mind today. The faithful chef, Jacques Rochard, has taken every possible liberty and then some, with the Basque piperade and chipirones, revolutionary for a chef with a rigorously traditional background. From now on, in addition to these marvelous preserves and foie gras, there'll be all sorts of dishes as the seasons and the chef's imagination dictate. A mosaic of vegetables with a fresh tomato purée, a warm lotte salad with basil, a darne of sander with carrots and butter, émincé of calf's kidneys with Moussy. Service exemplary, reception charming, bills hefty.
Carte: 180F–200F.

# SAINT-OUEN

### 14 🍃
### Chez Serge
**7 blvd. Jean-Jaurès**
**254.06.42**

It took a big heart to turn this rundown café on a busy suburban thoroughfare into a real bistro, full of character, where a crowd jostles every day three deep at the bar,

*Mme. Cancè*
*Closed Sun., holidays. and during*
*August. Lunch only.*
*V.*

washing down sandwiches with Morgon, or at the small tables, packed elbow to elbow in an atmosphere of good humor which is rare these days. The heart belongs to Serge Cancé, and another, just as generous, to his jovial wife Michèle, whose beaming face can be glimpsed from time to time at the serving window. Serge's bistro leads us to believe in the perpetuity of good fellowship in Parisian bistros, although we know that idea to be false since it is non-existent almost anywhere but here. Providentially, you do find exquisite wines (chosen by Serge at the vineyards), and these deserve a trophy. The cuisine is copious, fresh, feminine and not too costly: foie gras with Sauternes aspic, veal with fresh pasta, wild duckling with honey vinegar, and all sorts of traditional items. Carte: 120F.

# SÈVRES

**12/20**
## L'Oursière
**12 ave. de la**
**Division-Leclerc**
**626.66.64**
*M. Perdrix*
*Open until 9:30 P.M. Closed Mon.,*
*Tues. and July 15 to August 20.*
*DC, V.*

The most celebrated heads of Paris once passed beneath the shears of Pierre-Jean Perdrix, but without swelling his own. The barber-turned-restaurateur has his bistro two steps from the Manufacture de Sèvres serving a faithful clientele delighted by the excellent quality at reasonable prices, and a very short menu which is always changing: tomato tart, Perigordine salad, braised tendrons of veal, preserved duck on a bed of choucroute. Carte: 130F.

# VARENNE-ST.-HILAIRE

## La Bretèche
**171 quai de Bonneuil**
**883.38.73**
*M. Lamoureux*
*Open until 9:30 P.M. Closed Mon.,*
*Sun. evening, last wk. of July and*
*during August. Open terrace.*

This pastoral house, across the way from the iron arch of a R.E.R. bridge, carefully hides its charms within a dining room whose only gaiety is what you bring with you. However, from the moment you enter, the smiling kindness of Christiane Lamoureux, the attentive service, the marvelous hundred-year-old ports served as an apèritif, will make you forget the gloomy setting that deprives you even of a view of the river, which flows just outside. The cuisine will cheer you up even more, for Max Lamoureux is one of the most careful chefs we know in the Paris area: He is one of the very few you can find each morning at the Rungis central market, his suppliers are the best provisioners at the market, and all the wines of his attractive cellar are bought personally by him at the vineyards. To this let us add that he and his chef, Morin, who has been with him for ten years, get along like brothers, and you will understand why, each time we leave this restaurant, we have the desire to return. Especially after a meal with a feuilleté of mussels with a fondue of watercress, jambonneau of duck with Pinot,

stewed magret of mullard en pot-au-feu, and some rich classic desserts like macaroons with cream and praline butter.
Carte: 200F. Menu: 90F + 15% serv.

# VERSAILLES

**12/20**
## La Boule d'Or
**25 rue du Mal-Foch**
**950.22.97**
*M. Saillard*
*Open until 10:30 P.M. Closed Sun.*
*evening (except during August)*
*and Mon.*
*AE, DC, V.*

This house is the oldest (1696) of the inns of Versailles. In fact, sitting down to dine here among the antique furniture and the old masters of this refined decor, one almost feels dressed in doublet and breeches. Claude Saillard very cleverly strengthens this impression by devoting a page of his menu to recipes of the period, prettily interpreted: duck en ragoût of Bonnefond (1654), tourte d'herbes of Jacques Pons (1583). (Too bad that the curried mutton with bacon and anchovies of the Princess of Conti is absent, for her attractive portrait hangs here). On the other side of the menu are some Franche-Comté specialties prepared with finesse (trout stuffed à l'arboisienne, scrambled eggs with frog's legs, smoked Luxeuil ham) that this inventive chef strives to renew as often as possible. Prices high.
Carte: 180F–200F. Menu: 95F, 110F (serv. incl.).

13
## Le Potager du Roy
**1 rue du Mal-Joffre**
**950.35.34**
*M. Vié*
*Open until 10:00 P.M. Closed Sun.*
*and Mon.*

When Gérard Vié turned his attention to opening Les Trois Marches (see below), he left his chef Philippe Letourneur here at the Potager du Roy with the mission of serving a good cuisine with the accent on the classic or regional but with a resolutely modern conception, and at reasonable prices. Mission accomplished. On the intelligent and well-balanced menu you will find, according to the season, saddle of hare with bilberries, a cassoulet with sausage, daubes, foie gras both cooked and raw. On the two remarkable menus are to be found marinated raw haddock with chives, delicate terrine of celery with tomato purée, and some magnificent family-style desserts: oeufs à la neige pear with wine. Some good little wines beginning at 30F, and a charming, dark, intimate decor in the small dining rooms.
Carte: 120F. Menu: 75F, 90F + 15% serv.

13
## Le Rescatore
**27 ave. de Saint-Cloud**
**950.23.60**
*M. Bagot*
*Open until 10:00 P.M. Closed Sat.*
*(at lunch) and Sun. Pay parking.*
*AE, V.*

The flag of the *Angélique,* the three-masted schooner of the Marquis des Anges, flies here. If you embark upon this two-decked vessel which was recently repainted and enlarged, (the dining room is on the upper deck), you will find that its captain, Jacques Bagot, in love with the sea and its fish, is also a zealous proponent of a light, inventive and free cuisine. With boundless imagination and a perfect sense of cooking times, Jacques Bagot strives to present each day, on a short and often-revised menu,

the best that the sea can offer. You will enjoy his tartare of fish with essence of herbs, his daurade with lemon, his panaché of lotte and salon with beurre rouge, his châteaubriand with roast oysters and a sorrel cream, and his desserts (a glazed soufflé of exotic fruits). The reasonably priced good little wines do not keep the bill from sailing away. Service is always efficient, and the owner always charming.
Carte: 180F–200F. Menu: 79F (wine incl.) + 15% serv.

## 12/20
### *Trianon Palace*
**1 blvd. de la Reine**
**950.34.12**
*M. Marcus*
*Open until 9:30 P.M. Open terrace.*
*No dogs. Parking.*
*AE, DC, V.*

Don't let yourself be intimidated by the massive arrogance of the fin-de-siècle grand hotel decor, by the pomposity of the salons or the battalion of servitors. If the weather is fine, you can take one of the terrace tables in front of the charming park which abuts upon that of Louis XIV. Thanks to a young chef, Alain Bayle, formerly with Sofitel in Bordeau; you will dine upon a light and tempting cuisine, one which is even a bit fanciful, despite its numerous concessions to hotel tradition; for example, the fillet of turbot with honey and oranges, the mignonnettes of lamb with thyme blossoms, an exquisite salad gourmand, and a duck steak with vinegar (unhappily too tough). The service is of irreproachable discretion and efficiency, the coffee delicious, and the wines far too expensive.
Carte: 250F. Menu: 96F, 130F + 15% serv.

## 17
### *Les Trois Marches*
**3 rue Colbert (place du Château)**
**950.13.21**
*M. Vié*
*Open until 10:00 P.M. Closed Sun. and Mon.*
*All major credit cards.*

Two years after establishing himself in the luxurious hôtel de Gramont, a short distance from the palace, Gérard Vié has found the precise balance. Forget the little lapses that characterized the debut; from now on, in his circle of small dining rooms or in the attractive little garden, served with every attention, you are the Sun King. You will feast upon lasagna with foie gras, sander and frog legs with sweet pepper, oysters in fresh herbs; taste the unexpected flavors of the sherbets; or choose from all sorts of dishes that the febrile mind of Vié has perfected at the last minute. Some little-known wines that are reasonably priced soften the rigors of the bill. On the other hand, the King's suppers that Gérard Vié is planning to organize, with period music and servers in costume, will not be economical.
Carte: 280F–320F.

# VÉSINET (LE)

## 12/20
### *Rossello*
**8 bis ave. Horace-Vernet**
**976.37.50**
*M. Rossello*

This serious and friendly house opens onto a garden where, on fine summer evenings, one is pleasantly served the very painstaking and classic cuisine of owner Georges Rossello: snails sautéed with hazelnuts, hot andouillette Bercy, calf's head ravigote, ballotine of chicken with

*Open until 9:00 P.M. Closed Tues. evening, Wed. and during August. Open terrace. V.*

olives. For nearly half a century these small feasts have been offered here, and no one, certainly not we, has found fault. Prices are high.
Carte: 150F–200F. Menu: 120F (serv. incl.).

# *Where To Give A Reception*

Where is the best place in Paris or within an 80 km radius of the city to celebrate a first communion or have a press reception? Or to invite people for a business luncheon or cocktails? There are public rooms available in all the top Parisian hotels—Hilton, Inter-Continental, George V, P.L.M. Saint-Jacques, Méridien, Sofitel, Ritz, Crillon, Meurice, Grand Hôtel, Bristol, Plaza, Saint James and Albany, and others. However, you may prefer something more unique or intimate, such as a classical reception hall, a cellar, a monument, a suburban castle or a private room in a restaurant. Some ideas:

## *ON A BOAT*

### *Bateaux-Mouches*
**8th arr.**
**Quai de la Conference, pont de l'Alma, Right Bank**
**225.96.10**

You may rent a bateau-mouche for all sorts of events: cocktails, buffets and lunches for 100 to 50 people at 125F to 200F per person. These boats can also be equipped for conventions and meetings.

### *Eiffel-Bretagne*
**7 arr.**
**Port de La Bourdonnais**
**705.00.32**
*Embarcation: Pont d'Iéna, Left Bank. Parking.*

Provided you reserve three months in advance (slightly less in winter), the *Bretagne* will accommodate up to 300 dinner guests for a buffet between 6:30 P.M. and 12:30 A.M., 2½ hours of which are spent cruising up and down the Seine. Rates: 160F per person (includes buffet and service), with a minimum booking of 100 people in the summer (from May to September), 50 in winter. Estimates are available in case you wish to cruise up to Bougival, Conflans or Corbeil.

### *S.S. Nomadic*
**16th arr.**

Entertaining guests on an old boat moored along the banks of the Seine can be a most unusual experience. Yvon Vincent had the ingenious idea of turning the *S.S.*

**Port Debilly**
**723.42.52**

*Nomadic* into a series of reception rooms. The bulky, 70-meter-long boat once ferried passengers to the legendary *Titanic* when she was anchored outside of Cherbourg. Docked within walking distance of the Eiffel Tower, the *Nomadic* can be rented from 4,000F to 8,000F and has rooms designed to accommodate 350 to 700 standing guests and 110 to 480 seated. The vast rooms of the upper deck are particularly charming.

# IN A RECEPTION HALL

### France-Amérique
**8th arr.**
**9-11 ave.**
**Franklin-Roosevelt**
**359.51.00**

France-Amérique offers three rooms (200 square meters) that are richly decked out in Louis XVI style. They are housed in a Second Empire townhouse that is soon to be certified as a historic monument. Rental rates: 4,400F for cocktail parties (until midnight). Catering by Scott; sound systems by Gérard Nouette-Delorme. The modern Franklin room in the basement is also available for receptions up to 200 people. Catering by Angélina.

### Maison des Centraux (Salons Jean Goujon)
**8th arr.**
**rue Jean-Goujon**
**359.52.41**

The Prince of Essling used to own this townhouse, in which you can rent three floors for all sorts of events: lectures, conventions, marathon dances (with ultraviolet lights, spotlights, smoke-machines), wedding receptions and luncheons. The Second Empire Room on the second floor can accommodate 300 to 400 guests. Rates: 300F for a room for 250 guests, from 6:00 P.M. to midnight. Catering by Rosell.

### Palais de Chaillot
**16th arr.**
**Place du Trocadéro**
**505.14.50**

This is the largest reception hall in Paris, and can accommodate 1,000 dinner guests and 3,000 people for cocktails. Catering exclusively by the celebrated firm of Potel and Chabot. Breathtaking views of the Eiffel Tower, the Trocadéro Gardens and the Champs de Mars.

### Pavillon d'Armenon-ville
**16th arr.**
**Allée de Longchamp,**
**Bois de Boulogne**
**747.83.00**

Pavillon d'Armenonville offers six rooms of various sizes and decors (from 50 to 750 square meters). For various kinds of reception there are also the garden and pond, for 50 to 2,000 cocktail guests or 12 to 800 dinner guests (summer only). Cocktail rates for 100 guests are 150F per person (everything included). Available from 5:00 P.M. to 8:00 P.M. or from 6:00 P.M. to 9:00 P.M.

### Pavillon Gabriel
**8th arr.**
**5 ave. Gabriel**
**260.34.90**

This choice location faces the Champs-Elysées Gardens and can accommodate 200 to 2,000 guests (summer only). Owner and caterer: Potel and Chabot. Also featured are lecture rooms, theaters and dinner-shows.

## Pavillon Kléber

16th arr.
7 rue Cimarosa
707.46.22

Located in a charming nineteenth-century townhouse, the Pavillon Kléber includes an inner courtyard (for summer use only) and four rooms to accommodate 30 to 500 guests (in winter) or 1,000 guests with use of the courtyard (in summer). Cocktail receptions for 100 guests, from 6:00 P.M. to 9:30 P.M., costs about 140F per person (room, rental, buffet and service included). Flower arrangements and sound installation extra. From 6:00 P.M. to midnight, the rates are 175F per person.

## Pré Catelan

16th arr.
Bois de Boulogne
524.55.58

Pré Catelan has the most lavish buffets in all of Paris and offers twelve rooms decked out in marble and filled with chandeliers, a greenhouse and a garden terrace, all of which enable you to accommodate 12 to 3,000 guests in the utmost luxury. Conference rooms are also available. Shows and fireworks upon request.

## Résidence du Bois

16th arr.
16 rue Chalgrin
500.50.59

Formerly a Napoleon III-style townhouse, the Residence du Bois features two rooms and a charming inner courtyard. Luncheon rates (60 guests): two rooms 4,000F; two rooms plus courtyard 5,000F.

## Salon de Robech

16th arr.
5 rue
Charles-Lamoureux
553.86.00

This very elegant hotel has three rooms for receptions or dinners, accommodating approximately 350 people each (from 3,000F to 4,000F).

## La Tonnelle de Maillot

17th arr.
89 blvd.
Gouvion-Saint-Cyr
574.86.70

Located right across from the Palais des Congrès. One of the rooms, which can accommodate up to 150 guests, has white walls, green carpeting, wooden beams and paneling. Next door, Jean-Pierre Bloud offers wine and cordials from his Caveau and, upon request, will provide catering and staff. Half-day rentals (1,120F) or longer, available at reduced rates.

# IN A MONUMENT

## Caisse Nationale des Monuments Historiques et des Sites

4th arr.
62 rue
Saint-Antoine
274.22.22
*Closed Sat.*

You may rent any of 40 châteaux or historic mansions throughout France for private receptions, weddings, conventions. In Paris and the metropolitan area, you can become owner of a château for a day: the Conciergerie (18,000F), Maisons-Laffitte Château (2,000F–15,000F), the Orangerie of the Versailles Palace. For more information, inquire at: Service Locations (Rental Office) de la Caisse Nationale des Monuments Historiques et des Sites.

# =====*IN A WINE CELLAR*=====

### Bar de la Table d'Eugénie
**4th arr.**
**27 rue du Petit-Muse**
**272.14.95**

This firm offers two vaulted stone cellars (capacity: 50 to 60 seated, 100 standing). M. Daubin presents you with two alternatives: either you may order a meal from his staff (with 48 hours' notice), served in his wine cellar (80F–150F per person; buffet, 60F–120F per person); or you may organize your own reception with the caterer of your choice. Dancing is allowed until 2:00 A.M.

### Caves de la Tour Eiffel
**16th arr.**
**5 square**
**Charles-Dickens**
**525.63.26**

Inside the Passy Hill, there are several air-conditioned, nineteenth-century vaulted wine cellars that can accommodate up to 300 people (150 for sit-down dinners). The kitchens are specifically designed for catering. Rental is about 4,700F. The cellars feature a wine museum with wax figures illustrating the making of wine, documents pertaining to wine-growing regions, an audiovisual presentation followed by wine-tasting, and a sales outlet for both well-known and rare vintage wines.

# =====*THEY DO EVERYTHING . . .*=====

### Peter Kim
**16th arr.**
**11 bis ave.**
**Victor-Hugo**
**500.89.81**

In effect, Peter Kim will organize virtually anything, from parties to "portable" casino events with baccarat tables, as well as meetings, field trips, public relations events and business trips. Peter Kim will take care of transportation, reservations, hostesses, etc.

### Sextan
**92240 Malakoff -**
**10-14 rue**
**Eugène-Varlin**
**655.10.16**

All it takes is a phone call, and Gérard Nouette-Delorme will light up your garden at night, redecorate your flat for a reception, hire an orchestra or a catering service, set off fireworks, raise tents and lay dance floors.

# Toque Tally

## 19/20

**Archestrate (L')** 7ème

**Taillevant** 8ème

## 18/20

**Faugeron** 15ème
**Marée (La)** 8ème
**Pré Catalan (Le)** 16ème

**Savoy (Guy)** 16ème
**Vieille Fontaine (La)** Maisons-Lafitte

## 17/20

**Barrière de Clichy (La)** 17ème
**Beauvilliers** 18ème
**Belle Époque (La)** Châteaufort
**Camélia (La)** Bougival
**Ciboulette (La)** 4ème
**Dodin-Bouffant** 5ème
**Duc (Le)** 14ème
**Jamin** 16ème
**Lasserre** 8ème

**Olympe** 15ème
**Pangaud (Gérard)** Boulogne-Billancourt
**Rostang (Michel)** 17ème
**Semailles (Les)** 18ème
**Tour d'Argent (La)** 5ème
**Trois Marches (Les)** Versailles
**Trou Gascon (Au)** 12ème
**Vivarois (Le)** 16ème

## 16/20

**Bernardin (Le)** 17ème
**Bistro 121** 15ème
**Bistro d'Hubert (Le)** 1er
**Cagna (Jacques)** 6ème
**Chiberta** 8ème
**Comte du Gascogne (Au)**
    Boulogne-Billancourt
**Crillon (Le)** 8ème
**Duc d'Enghien** Enghien
**Grand Véfour (Le)** 1er

**Laurent** 8ème
**Marcande (Le)** 8ème
**Maxim's** 8ème
**Morot-Gaudry** 15ème
**Pactole (Au)** 5ème
**Petit Bedon (Le)** 16ème
**Petit Montmorency (Au)** 8ème
**Prunier-Madeleine** 1er
**Quai des Ormes (Au)** 5ème

## 15/20

**Allard** 6ème
**Ambroisie (L')** 5ème
**Ami Louis (L')** 3ème
**Barrière Poquelin** 1er

**Besson (Gérard)** 1er
**Bistrot de Paris** 7ème
**Bourdonnais (Le)** 7ème
**Bristol (Le)** 8ème

**Bûcherie (La)** 5ème
**Chateaubriant (Au)** 9ème
**Clodenis** 18ème
**Cochon d'Or (Au)** 19ème
**Coq Hardi (Le)** Bougival
**Dariole de Paris (La)** 8ème
**Ecrevisse (L')** 17ème
**Ferme Saint-Simon (La)** 7ème
**Flamberge (La)** 7ème
**Gasnier** Puteaux
**Grande Cascade (La)** 16ème
**Lamazère** 8ème
**Lord Gourmand (Le)** 8ème

**Lous Landès** 14ème
**Michel (Chez)** 10ème
**Pasquet (Michel)** 16ème
**Petrus** 17ème
**Pressoir (Au)** 12ème
**Princesse** 6ème
**Provost (Chez)** 14ème
**Récamier (Le)** 7ème
**Traiteur (Pierre)** 1er
**Vedel (Pierre)** 15ème
**Vong aux Halles (Chez)** 1er
**Yan-Le Toît de Passy** 16ème

**=14/20=**

**Albert (Chez)** 14ème
**Ambassade d'Auvergne** 3ème
**Anges (Chez les)** 7ème
**Arêtes (Les)** 6ème
**Armes de Bretagne (Les)** 14ème
**Auberge de l'Argoat** 14ème
**Auberge Landaise** 9ème
**Augusta (Chez)** 17ème
**Barrière de Neuilly (La)** 17ème
**Bellecour (Le)** 7ème
**Benkay** 15ème
**Bourrier** Neuilly-sur-Seine
**Cazaudehore** Saint-Germain-en-Laye
**Champs d'Or (Les)** 7ème
**Chardenoux (Le)** 10ème
**Chêne (Paul)** 15ème
**Clovis** 8ème
**Conticini** 7ème
**Croquant (Le)** 15ème
**Delmonico** 2ème
**Edgard (Chez)** 8ème
**Epicure 108** 17ème
**Fénix (Jacqueline)** Neuilly-sur-Seine
**Fontaine aux Carmes (À la)** 7ème
**Franc Pinot (Au)** 4ème
**Galant Verre (Le)** 7ème
**Gourmard** 1er
**Grand Chinois (Le)** 16ème
**Grand Venise (Le)** 15ème
**Guyvonne** 17ème
**Ile de France** 16ème
**Jardin du Printemps (Au)** 8ème
**Joséphine** 6ème
**Ligne (La)** 8ème
**Louis XIV** 10ème
**Ma Cuisine** 17ème

**Main à la Pâte (La)** 1er
**Manoir (Le)** Neuilly-sur-Seine
**Marius et Janette** 8ème
**Maxim's** Orly
**Mercure Galant** 1er
**Moï (Le)** 16ème
**Moniage Guillaume (Le)** 14ème
**Napoléon** 8ème
**Napoléon et Chaix** 15ème
**Opéra** 9ème
**Pantagruel** 7ème
**Passy-Mandarin** 16ème
**Paul et France** 17ème
**Pauline (Chez)** 1er
**Petit Colombier (Le)** 17ème
**Petit Pré (Le)** 19ème
**Petite Auberge (La)** 17ème
**Petite Auberge Franc-Comtoise (La)**
  Boulogne-Billancourt
**Prunier-Traktir** 16ème
**Quai d'Orsay (Au)** 7ème
**Raajmahal** 15ème
**Relais des Gardes** Meudon-Bellevue
**Relais de Sèvres (Le)** 1er
**Repaire de Cartouche (Le)** 10ème
**Ribe (Chez)** 7ème
**Roy Soleil (Au)** Marly-Le Roi
**Royal Monceau** 8ème
**Senonnes (Le)** 5ème
**Serge (Chez)** Saint-Ouen
**Sologne (La)** 7ème
**Sousceyrac (À)** 10ème
**Sully d'Auteuil (Le)** 16ème
**Tan Dinh** 7ème
**Toit de Paris** 15ème
**Truite Vagabonde (La)** 14ème

**Armorique (L')** 11ème
**Assommoir (L')** 18ème
**Atelier Maître Albert** 5ème
**Auberge des Deux Signes** 5ème
**Auberge Perraudin** 2ème
**Baumann-Baltard** 1er
**Baumann-Ternes** 17ème
**Beaudant (Le)** 17ème
**Benoît** 4ème
**Bonaventure (Le)** 7ème
**Bourgogne (La)** 7ème
**Brazais (Le)** 17ème
**Bretèche (La)** Varenne-St-Hilare
**Cannelle (La)** 6ème
**Cartet** 11ème
**Caroubier (Le)** 14ème
**Casimir** 10ème
**Caveau du Palais** 1er
**Célébrities (Les)** 15ème
**Cerisaie (La)** 18ème
**Chalybon (Le)** 17ème
**Champ de Mars (Le)** 7ème
**Chandelles (Aux)** Louveciennes
**Charlot Ier** 18ème
**Charly de Bab-El-Oued** 17ème
**Chat Grippé (Le)** 6ème
**Château de Chine** 8ème
**Chaumière des Gourmets (La)** 14ème
**Chaumière Paysanne (La)** 14ème
**Chiquito (El)** Rueil-Malmaison
**Chope d'Orsay (La)** 7ème
**Clair de la Lune (Au)** 18ème
**Conotier (Le)** 2ème
**Conti** 16ème
**Copenhague et Flora Danica** 8ème
**Copreaux (Le)** 15ème
**Coquille (La)** 17ème
**Corbeille (La)** 2ème
**Courrège** 15ème
**Dauphin (Le)** 7ème
**Délices de Chine (Aux)** 4ème
**Dessirier** 17ème
**Dôme (Le)** 14ème
**Ducs de Bourgogne** 9ème
**Echaudé Saint-Germain (L')** 6ème
**Elyséum (L')** 8ème
**Epicurien (L')** 6ème
**Estournel (L')** 16ème
**Fermette Marbeuf (La)** 8ème
**Focly** Neuilly-sur-Seine
**Fouquet's (Le)** 8ème
**Fusains (Les)** 18ème
**Gaspard de la Nuit** 4ème
**Gauloise (La)** 15ème
**Georges (Chez)** 17ème
**Glénan (Les)** 7ème

**Gourmandière (La)** Bièvres
**Grandgousier** 18ème
**Grandgousier** Bièvres
**Guirlande de Julie (La)** 4ème
**Hippocampe (L')** Puteaux
**Indra** 8ème
**Jacquet (Jenny)** 16ème
**Lapérouse** 6ème
**Laudrin** 17ème
**Lefèbvre** 7ème
**Lipp** 6ème
**Long Yuen** 15ème
**M** 4ème
**Mandarin de Neuilly (Le)**
    Neuilly-sur-Seine
**Marcel** 12ème
**Mareyeur (Le)** 16ème
**Marius (Chez)** 7ème
**Moissonnier** 5ème
**Montecristo** 4ème
**Morens** 16ème
**New Port** 10ème
**Nicolas** 10ème
**Pagoda** 9ème
**Paillon (Le)** 10ème
**Palais Impérial** 2ème
**Palanquin (Le)** 6ème
**Pascal** 13ème
**Pavillon Royal** 16ème
**Pharamond** 1er
**Philippe (Chez)** 11ème
**Photogalerie (La)** 6ème
**Potager du Roy (Le)** Versailles
**Potiers (Les)** 1er
**Pré Carré (Le)** 17ème
**Princes (Les)** 8ème
**P'tite Tonkinoise (La)** 10ème
**Régence-Plaza** 8ème
**Relais Louis XIII** 6ème
**Relais des Pyrénées** 20ème
**Relais Saint-Germain** 7ème
**Rescatore (Le)** Versailles
**Roseaux (Les)** 3ème
**Saharien (Wally)** 5ème
**Savy** 8ème
**Sébillon** Neuilly-sur-Seine
**Séoul (Le)** 8ème
**Tante Madée (Chez)** 6ème
**Taverne des Templiers** 3ème
**Timgad (Le)** 17ème
**Toque (La)** 17ème
**Tour de Jade (La)** 2ème
**Tsé Yang** 16ème
**Tuboeuf (Daniel)** 3ème
**Ty-Coz** 9ème
**Ursins dans le Caviar (Les)** 5ème

Vendôme 1er
Verger de Montmartre (Le) 18ème
Vert Galant 1er
Vieille (Chez la) 1er
Vieux Berlin (Au) 8ème

Vieux Métiers de France (Les) 13ème
Villars Palace (Le) 5ème
Vong (Chez) 8ème
Yakijapo Mitsuko 6ème

# 12/20

Abbyé Constantin (À l') 2ème
Absinthe (L') 1er
Algues (Les) 13ème
Alsace (L') 13ème
André (Chez) 13ème
Annexe du Quai 7ème
Artois (L') 8ème
Attrape-Coeur (L') 6ème
Aubergade (L') 8ème
Auberge du Centre 13ème
Auberge de la Tour 15ème
Beaubourgeois (Le) 4ème
Becs Fins (Aux) 20ème
Bistro d'Isa 6ème
Boeuf Couronné (Au) 19ème
Boeuf sur le Grill (Le) 16ème
Boeuf du Palais Royal (Le) 1er
Boule d'Or (La) Versailles
Boulangerie Saint-Philippe 8ème
Bourbonnais (Le) 14ème
Braisière (La) 17ème
Brasserie Flo 10ème
Brasserie Lutétia 6ème
Brasserie du Pont-Mirabeau 15ème
Brasserie Stella 16ème
Café Terminus 8ème
Caviardise (La) Neuilly-sur-Seine
Cecconi's 8ème
Cévenol (Le) 17ème
Champs-Ze (Les) 8ème
Charly-de-Bab-El-Oued 14ème
Charpentiers (Aux) 6ème
Cherche-Midi (Le) 6ème
Chichois (Chez) 9ème
China Town 8ème
Ciel de Paris (Le) 15ème
Cloche d'Or (La) 9ème
Cochon d'Or (Au) 1er
Coconnas 4ème
Colisée Pagode 8ème
Congrès (Le) 17ème
Connivence (La) 12ème
Côte de Boeuf (La) 17ème
Coupe-Chou (Le) 5ème
Crémaillé 1900 (La) 18ème
Croque au Sel (La) 7ème
Da Graziano 18ème
Dagorno 19ème
Délices Saint-André (Aux) 7ème
Deux Taureaux (Aux) 19ème
Diamantaires (Les) 9ème

Dominique 6ème
Drouant 2ème
Drugstorien (Le) 8ème
Echiquier (L') 9ème
Ecluse (L') 8ème
Escargot-Montorgueil 1er
Etoile du Bonheur (L') 17ème
Etoile d'Or (L') 17ème
Falstaff (Le) 14ème
Ferme Irlandaise (La) 1er
Flamboyant (Le) 14ème
Foo-Lim 15ème
Fourchette en Habit (La) 6ème
Foux (La) 6ème
Francis (Chez) 8ème
Françoise (Chez) 7ème
Frézet (Chez) 18ème
Fusains (Les) 18ème
Garnier 8ème
Globe d'Or (Le) 1er
Gorisse (Chez) 17ème
Gourmet de l'Isle (Au) 4ème
Gramond (Chez) 6ème
Grand Cafe (Le) 9ème
Grand Veneur (Le) 17ème
Grille (La) 10ème
Grosse Horloge (La) 6ème
Guy 6ème
Hippopotamus 8ème
Hulotte (La) 6ème
Iles Chausey (Les) Neuilly-sur-Seine
Iles Philippines (Aux) 5ème
Impérial Select 8ème
Jacques (Chez) 12ème
Jarasse (François) 17ème
Jardins d'Edgard (Les) 8ème
Jenny (Chez) 3ème
Julien 10ème
Julien (Chez) 4ème
Lancaster 8ème
Léon (Chez) 17ème
Lieutenance (Le) 4ème
Locomotive (La) 2ème
Louis XIV 1er
Louisiane (La) Orly
Maison du Caviar (La) 8ème
Maison du Valais (La) 8ème
Maitre Pierre 17ème
Mandragore (La) 13ème
Maquis (Le) 18ème
Marée Verte (La) 5ème

**Marius** 16ème
**Marlotte (La)** 6ème
**Marroniers (Les)** 13ème
**Mer (La)** 19ème
**Mère Michel (Chez la)** 17ème
**Monastère (Le)** 1er
**Morvan (Le)** 12ème
**Muniche (Le)** 6ème
**Ousière (L')** Sevres
**Péché Mignon (Le)** 11ème
**Petit Mâchon (Le)** 15ème
**Petit Riche (Au)** 9ème
**Petit Zinc (Le)** 6ème
**Petite Alsace (La)** 12ème
**Petite Bretonnière (La)** 15ème
**Poêle d'Or (La)** 8ème
**Porte Fausse (La)** 6ème
**Que Hong** 7ème
**Quercy (Le)** 9ème
**Ramponneau** 16ème
**Relais-Plaza** 8ème
**Relais de Saint-Cucufa** Rueil-Malmaison
**René (Chez)** 5ème
**Rosello** Le Vesinet
**Rôtisserie (La)** 6ème
**Rôtisserie du Plateau de Gravelle** 12ème
**Rôtisserie Rivoli** 1er
**Rôtisserie du Seine (La)** 9ème
**Saint-Germain (Le)** 8ème
**Saintongeais (Le)** 9ème
**Salle à Manger (La)** 17ème
**Sardegna (La)** 1er

**Savoie-Bretagne** 9ème
**Senteurs de Provence (Aux)** 15ème
**Solonge (La)** 12ème
**Sybarite (Le)** 6ème
**Tante Louise (Chez)** 8ème
**Tartempion** 18ème
**Terminus-Nord** 10ème
**Than** 7ème
**Toison d'Or (La)** 15ème
**Tong Yen** 8ème
**Tour Céleste (La)** 16ème
**Tour de Chine (La)** 16ème
**Tournant de la Butte (Au)** 18ème
**Toutoune (Chez)** 5ème
**Tourtour (Le)** 4ème
**Traboucayres (Les)** 5ème
**Train Bleu (Le)** 12ème
**Trianon Palace** Versailles
**Trois Horloge (Aux)** 15ème
**Trois Limousins (Les)** 8ème
**Trois Moutons (Les)** 8ème
**Trotteur (Au)** 12ème
**Truffière (La)** 5ème
**Vallée des Bambous (La)** 5ème
**Vallon de Vérone (Le)** 14ème
**Vaudeville (Le)** 2ème
**Vert Bocage (Au)** 7ème
**Vieux Saumur (Au)** 2ème
**Vishnou** 2ème
**Western (Le)** 15ème
**Zeyer** 14ème

# 11/20

**Allen (Joe)** 1er
**Amanguier (L')** 2ème
**Amanguier (L')** 15ème
**Amanguier (L')** 17ème
**Anarkali** 9ème
**Androuet** 8ème
**Antre de Bacchus (L')** 9ème
**Armand (Chez)** 1er
**Assiette du Boeuf (L')** 8ème
**Astier** 11ème
**Athènes** 5ème
**Auberge Fleurie (L')** 15ème
**Auberge de Recoules d'Aubrac** 17ème
**Auberge des Trois Bonheurs** 1er
**Balzar (Le)** 5ème
**Bélier (Le)** 16ème
**Bilboquet (Le)** 6ème
**Bistro de la Gare** 8ème
**Boeuf Gros Sel** 20ème
**Bofinger** 4ème
**Bouchons (Les)** 1er
**Bougnat Boutique** 14ème
**Boutique à Sandwiches (La)** 8ème
**Brasserie de l'Ile Saint-Louis** 4ème

**Brasserie Löwenbraü** 8ème
**Brise-Miche (Le)** 4ème
**Buisson Ardent (Le)** 5ème
**Café Français** 14ème
**Calvet** 6ème
**Charbon de Bois (Au)** 6ème
**Charbon de Bois (Au)** 16ème
**Charlot** 9ème
**Chaumière (La)** 7ème
**Chope d'Alsace (La)** 6ème
**Clocher du Village (Au)** 16ème
**Clovis (Chez)** 1er
**Colombe (La)** 4ème
**Côté Jardin** 1er
**Coupole (La)** 14ème
**Créole (La)** 14ème
**Drugstore des Champs Elysées** 8ème
**Drugstore Saint-Germain** 6ème
**Excuse (L')** 4ème
**Ferme de la Jatte (La)** Neuilly-sur-Seine
**Ferme de la Villette** 19ème
**Feu Follet (Au)** 14ème
**Fins Gourmets (Aux)** 7ème
**Fleurs (Les)** 12ème

Fontaine de Mars (La) 7ème
Gabriel (Chez) 1er
Galan 4ème
Gérard 2ème
Germain 8ème
Gite d'Armôr (Au) 9ème
Grand-Mère (Chez) 13ème
Grand Méricourt (Le) 11ème
Grenier sur l'Eau (Le) 4ème
Grosse Tartine (La) 17ème
Guyomard 1er
Jardin de la Paresse 14ème
Joseph 8ème
Korean Barbecue 6ème
Lac de Côme (Au) 6ème
Lyonnais (Aux) 1er
Maître Paul (Chez) 6ème
Mandarin du Forum 1er
Mange-Tout (Le) 5ème
Marie-Louise 18ème
Mario 5ème
Martin Alma 8ème
Mascareignes (Les) 6ème
Ménara (La) 9ème
Mère-Grand 20ème
Michèle (Chez) 13ème
Montagnard (Le) 6ème
Moutardiere (La) 10ème
Noailles (Les) 1er
Pavillon du Lac (Le) 19ème
Petit Marguery (Le) 18ème
Petit Navire (Le) 5ème
Petit Prince (Le) 5ème

Petit Victor-Hugo (Le) 16ème
Petits Oignons (Aux) 7ème
Pfister 15ème
Pied de Cochon (Au) 1er
Pinocchio 10ème
Polidor 6ème
Port Saint-Bernard 5ème
Porte du Bonheur 1er
Pupillin (Au) 9ème
Righi (Le) 8ème
Rose des Sables (La) 8ème
Route du Château (La) 14ème
Roy Gourmet (Au) 1er
Saint-Amour 2ème
Saint-Germain-de-la-Mer 6ème
Saladière (La) 8ème
Samovar (Le) 1er
Sardana (La) 12ème
Saüdade 1er
Scala (La) 13ème
Soma 8ème
Stresa 8ème
Ta Yen 1er
Tannhauser 2ème
Tartempion 18ème
Tong Shin 5ème
Tonton Yang (Chez) 17ème
Tour de Montlhéry (La) 1er
Trois Portes (Les) 9ème
Verger (Le) 8ème
Welper (Le) 18ème
Yakitori 14ème

# 10/20

Auberge de Jarente 3ème
Auvergnat (L') 8ème
Babkine 7ème
Babylone (Le) 7ème
Ballon des Ternes (Le) 17ème
Baptiste (Le) 5ème
Bar à Huîtres (Le) 14ème
Bateau-Lavoir (Le) 18ème
Bateleurs du Pont Neuf (Les) 1er
Bourriche (La) 12ème
Centre Ville (Le) 10ème
Chartier 9ème
Chiroubles (Le) 7ème
Closerie des Lilas (La) 6ème
Conway's 1er
Curveur (Le) 10ème
Diable des Lombards (Au) 1er
Dragon (Le) 6ème
Enclos du Marais (L') 3ème
Faure (André) 1er

Gallopin 2ème
Goldenberg (Jo) 5ème
Grille (la) 2ème
Léni Olympic-Entrepot 14ème
Ling Nam 10ème
Lozère (La) 6ème
Lucie (Lou Mino) 7ème
Lyonnais du Forum (Le) 1er
Mignonnette du Caviar 8ème
Mon Petit Bar 14ème
Monde des Chimères (Le) 4ème
Moulin du Village (Le) 8ème
Oeillade (L') 7ème
Oenothèque (L') 7ème
Pêcheur (Le) 8ème
Peppino (Chez) 10ème
Petit Niçois (Le) 7ème
Petit Saint-Benoît (Le) 6ème
Petite Chaisse (La) 7ème
Philosophes (Les) 4ème

Pied de Fouet (Au) 7ème
Procope (Le) 6ème
P'tit Gavroche (Le) 4ème
Pub Saint-Germaine-des-Prés 6ème
Raccard (Le) 5ème
Relais Boccador 8ème
Relais de la Butte 18ème
Rendez-vous des Chauffeurs (Au) 15ème
Restaurant des Saints-Pères 6ème
Rose des Prés (La) 6ème

Route des Indes (La) 14ème
Royal Mondétour 1er
Sainlouis (Claude) 6ème
Salons Wéber 19ème
Show Gourmet 8ème
Tartine 15ème
Taverne Descartes (La) 5ème
Trumilou (Le) 5ème
Van Ming 16ème
Wall Street 16ème

## NO RATING

Lucas-Carton 8ème

# Where To Eat What

## HOME-STYLE COOKING

### 1er arr.
Clovis (Chez)
Gabriel (Chez)
Pauline (Chez)
Pharamond
Pied de Cochon
Roy Gourmet (Au)
Royal Mondétour
Tour de Montlhéry
Vert Galant
Vieille (Chez la)

### 2ème arr.
Abbé Constantin (L')
Canotier (Le)
Gérard

### 3ème arr.
Enclos du Marais

### 4ème arr.
Bofinger
Galan

### 5ème arr.
Buisson Ardent
René (Chez)
Taverne Descartes
Toutoune (Chez)

### 6ème arr.
Allard
Bistro d'Isa
Charpentiers (Aux)
Hulotte (La)
Joséphine
Lipp
Marlotte (La)
Pascal
Petit Saint Benoît
Polidor
Procope (Le)
Restaurant des Saints-Pères

### 7ème arr.
Annexe du Quai
Babkine

Babylone (Le)
Boule d'Or (La)
Croque au Sel (Le)
Dauphin (Le)
Fins Gourmets (Aux)
Fontaine de Mars
Petite Chaise (La)
Pied de Fouet
Thoumieux

### 8ème arr.
André (Chez)
Barrière des Champs
Dariole (La)
Pêcheur (Le)
Poêle d'Or (La)
Tante Louise (Chez)

### 9ème arr.
Cloche d'Or (La)

### 10ème arr.
Casimir
Julien
Nicolas

### 11ème arr.
Astier
Cartet
Philippe (Chez)

### 12ème arr.
Marcel

### 13ème arr.
Grand-Mère (Chez)

### 14ème arr.
Café Français
Feu Follet (Le)
Route du Château (La)

### 15ème arr.
Gauloise (La)
Pfister
Rendez-Vous des Chauffeurs

### 16ème arr.
Brasserie Stella
Paul Chêne

### 17ème arr.
Cévenol (Le)
Côte de Bœuf (La)
Georges (Chez)
Gorisse (Chez)
Laudrin
Léon (Chez)

### 18ème arr.
Frézet (Chez)
Maquis (Le)
Marie-Louise
Petit Marguery (Le)
Relais de la Butte

### 19ème arr.
Bœuf Couronné (Au)

### 20ème arr.
Becs Fins (Aux)
Bœuf Gros Sel
Mère-Grand

# REGIONAL CUISINE

(Abbreviations: *Auv.*—of Auvergne; *Bord.*—Bordelaise; *Bourg.*—Bourgunion and of Lyon; *Prov.*—of the Provence; *S.O.*—of the Southwest.)

### 1er arr.
Globe d'Or, S.-O.
Louis XIV, Bourg.
Lyonnais du Forum, Bourg.
Petit Traiteur, S.-O.

### 2ème arr.
Corbeille (La), Bord.
Lyonnais (Aux), Bourg.
Vieux Saumur, S.-O.

### 3ème arr.
Ambassade d'Auvergne, Auv.

### 4ème arr.
Auberge de Jarente, S.-O.
Benoît, Bourg.
Gourmet de l'Ile, Auv.

### 5ème arr.
Auberge des Deux Signes, Auv.
Mange-Tout, Auv.
Moissonnier, Bourg.
Truffière (La) S.-O.

### 6ème arr.
Dragon (Le), S.-O.
Épicurien (L'), S.-O.
Foux (La), Bourg.
Lozère (La), Auv.
Maître-Paul (Chez), Jura
Muniche (Le), S.-O.
Petit Zinc (Le), S.-O.
Porte Fausse (La), Prov.
Sybarite (Le), S.-O.

### 7ème arr.
Anges (Chez les), Bourg.
Bellecour, Bourg.
Bourgogne, Bourg.

### 8ème arr.
Artois (L'), Auv.
Auvergnat 1900 (L'), Auv.
Lamazère, S.-O.
Poularde Landaise, S.-O.
Savy, Auv.

### 9ème arr.
Auberge Landaise, S.-O.
Ducs de Bourgogne, Bourg.
Gite d'Armor (Au), S.-O.
Petit Riche (Au), Loire
Quercy (Le), S.-O.
Saintongeais (Le), Charentes

### 10ème arr.
Curveur (Le), Charentes
Paillon (Le), Prov.
Repaire de Cartouche, S.-O.
Sousceyrac (A), S.-O.

### 12ème arr.
Fleurs (Les)
Morvan (Le), Bourg.

Quincy (Le), S.-O.
Train Bleu (Le), Auv.
Trou Gascon (Au), S.-O.

### 13ème arr.
Marronniers (Les)

### 14ème arr.
Bougnat Boutique, Auv.
Bourbonnais (Le), Auv.
Chaumière Paysanne, S.-O.
Lous Landès, S.-O.
Petit Bar (Mon), Auv.
Vallon de Vérone, S.-O.

### 15ème arr.
Croquant (Le), S.-O.
Petit Machon (Le), Bourg.

### 16ème arr.
Clocher du Village, Bourg.
Auberge de Recoules d'Aubrac, S.-O.

### 17ème arr.
Devinière (La), Loire
Grosse Tartine (La)
Mère Michel (Chez la), Loire

### 20ème arr.
Relais des Pyrénées, S.-O.

# ALSATIAN SPECIALTIES

### 1er arr.
Baumann

### 2ème arr.
Tannhauser

### 3ème arr.
Jenny (Chez)

### 6ème arr.
Brasserie Lutétia
Chope d'Alsace

### 7ème arr.
Fontaine aux Carmes

### 8ème arr.
Alsace (L')
Brasserie Löwenbraü
Napoléon
Vieux Berlin (Au)

### 10ème arr.
Brasserie Flo
Terminus Nord

### 12ème arr.
Petite Alsace (La)

### 15ème arr.
Brasserie du Pont-Mirabeau

### 17ème arr.
Baumann

# SEAFOOD

### 1er arr.
Goumard
Prunier-Madeleine

### 5ème arr.
Marée Verte (La)
Petit Navire (Le)

Senonnes (Le)
Villars Palace

## 6ème arr.
Arêtes (Les)
Calvet
Fourchette en Habit (La)
Grosse Horloge (La)
Saint-Germain de la Mer

## 7ème arr.
Délices de Saint-André
Glénan (Les)
Marius (Chez)

## 8ème arr.
Aubergade (L')
Brasserie Lorraine
Marée (La)
Marius et Janette

## 9ème arr.
Charlot (Le Roi des Coquillages)
Grand Café (Le)
Ty-Coz

## 10ème arr.
Grille (La)
Louis XIV
New Port

## 13ème arr.
Algues (Les)
Mandragore (La)

## 14ème arr.
Auberge de l'Argoat
Bar à Huitres (Le)
Chaumière des Gourmets
Dôme (Le)
Duc (Le)
Moniage Guillaume (Le)

## 15ème arr.
Senteurs de Provence (Aux)

## 16ème arr.
Marius
Prunier-Traktir

## 17ème arr.
Auberge de Recoules d'Aubrac
Augusta (Chez)
Ballon des Ternes (Le)
Bernardin (Le)
Guillaume Tell
Pétrus

## 18ème arr.
Charlot 1er

## 19ème arr.
Mer (La)

# OYSTERS IN SUMMER

## 2ème arr.
Vaudeville (Le)

## 8ème arr.
Francis (Chez)
Garnier

## 9ème arr.
Grand Café (Le)

## 14ème arr.
Dôme (Le)
Duc (Le)

## 17ème arr.
Bernardin (Le)
Bourriche (La)
Congrès (Le)
Pétrus
Truite Vagabonde (La)

## 18ème arr.
Crémaillère 1900 (La)
Wepler (Le)

# STEAKS AND GRILLS

## 1er arr.
Bistro de la Gare
Bœuf du Palais-Royal (Le)
Cochon d'Or (Au)
Pied de Cochon

## 2ème arr.
Assiette au Bœuf (L')
Hippopotamus
Vaudeville (Le)

## THE RESTAURANTS / Where To Eat What

### 3ème arr.
Ami Louis (L')

### 6ème arr.
Assiette au Bœuf (L')
Bilboquet (Le)
Bistro de la Gare
Charbon de Bois
Montagnard (Le)
Rôtisserie (La)
Claude Sainlouis

### 8ème arr.
Assiette au Bœuf (L')
Bistro de la Gare
Champs-Zé (Les)
Hippopotamus
Trémoille (La)
Trois Limousins (Les)
Trois Moutons (Les)

### 9ème arr.
Bistro de la Gare

### 10ème arr.
Moutardière (La)

### 14ème arr.
Assiette au Bœuf (L')
Zeyer

### 15ème arr.
Auberge Fleurie (L')
Bistro 121
Brasserie du Pont-Mirabeau
Rôtisserie sur Seine (La)

### 16ème arr.
Bœuf sur le Grill (Le)
Charbon de Bois (Au)

### 17ème arr.
Congrès (Le)
Côte de Bœuf (La)
Cuisine (Ma)
Georges (Chez)
Hippopotamus
Pré Carré (Le)

### 19ème arr.
Cochon d'Or (Au)
Dagorno
Deux Taureaux (Aux)
Ferme de la Villette

# THE WORLD'S CUISINES

### North African
Caroubier (Le), 15ème arr.
Charly de Bab-el-Oued, 15ème arr.
Charly de Bab-el-Oued, 17ème arr.
Chichois (Chez), 9ème arr.
Ménara (La), 9ème arr.
Michèle (Chez), 13ème arr.
Rose des Sables (La), 8ème arr.
Timgad (Le), 17ème arr.
Trois Horloges (Aux), 15ème arr.
Wally Saharien, 4ème arr.

### American
Allen (Joe), 1er arr.
Conway's, 1er arr.
Western (Le), 15ème arr.

### The Antilles
Créole (La), 14ème arr.
Flamboyant (Le), 14ème arr.
Lucie, 7ème arr.
Mascareignes (Les), 6ème arr.

### Brazilian
Guy, 6ème arr.

### Central European
Jo Goldenberg, 4ème arr.
Toison d'Or, 15ème arr.

### Chinese/Vietnamese
Auberge des Trois Bonheurs, 1er arr.
Château de Chine, 8ème arr.
China Town, 8ème arr.
Colisée Pagode, 8ème arr.
Délices de Chine, 4ème arr.
Délices de Szechuen, 7ème arr.
Étoile du Bonheur, 17ème arr.
Foo-Lim, 15ème arr.
Grand Chinois (Le), 16ème arr.
Impérial Select, 8ème arr.
Jardin du Printemps, 8ème arr.
Long Yuen, 15ème arr.
Ling Nam, 10ème arr.
Mandarin du Forum, 1er arr.
Moi (Le), 16ème arr.
Pagoda, 9ème arr.
Palais Impérial, 2ème arr.
Palanquin (Le), 6ème arr.
Panda (Le), 16ème arr.
Passy-Mandarin, 16ème arr.
P'tite Tonquinoise (La), 10ème arr.
Porte du Bonheur, 1er arr.
Que Huong, 7ème arr.
Rose des Prés, 6ème arr.
Tan Dinh, 7ème arr.
Ta Yen, 1er arr.
Than, 7ème arr.
Tong Shin, 5ème arr.

**Tong Yen**, 8ème arr.
**Tonton Yang (Chez)**, 17ème arr.
**Tour Céleste**, 16ème arr.
**Tour de Chine**, 16ème arr.
**Tour de Jade**, 2ème arr.
**Tsé Yang**, 16ème arr.
**Vallée des Bambous**, 5ème arr.
**Van Ming**, 16ème arr.
**Vong (Chez)**, 1er arr.
**Vong (Chez)**, 8ème arr.

## German
**Tannhauser**, 2ème arr.
**Vieux Berlin (Au)**, 8ème arr.

## Greek
**Athènes**, 6ème arr.
**Diamantaines (Les)**, 9ème arr.

## Indian
**Anarkali**, 9ème arr.
**Indra**, 8ème arr.
**Soma**, 8ème arr.
**Raajmahal**, 15ème arr.
**Vishnou**, 2ème arr.

## Irish
**Ferme Irlandaise (La)**, 1er arr.

## Italian
**Auberge de la Tour**, 15ème arr.
**Chateaubriant (Au)**, 10ème arr.
**Cherche-Midi (Le)**, 6ème arr.
**Conti**, 16ème arr.
**Da Graziano**, 18ème arr.
**Lac de Côme (Au)**, 6ème arr.
**Main à la Pâte**, 1er arr.
**Mario**, 5ème arr.
**Montecristo**, 4ème arr.
**Pinocchio**, 10ème arr.
**Righi (Le)**, 8ème arr.
**Sardegna**, 1er arr.
**Scala (La)**, 13ème arr.
**Stresa**, 8ème arr.

## Japanese
**Benkay**, 15ème arr.
**Iles Philippines**, 5ème arr.
**Korean Barbecue**, 6ème arr.
**Séoul (Le)**, 8ème arr.
**Yakijapo Mitsuko**, 6ème arr.
**Yakitori**, 14ème arr.

## Peruvian
**Route des Andes**, 14ème arr.

## Portuguese
**Saüdade**, 1er arr.

## Russian
**Dominique**, 6ème arr.
**Maison du Caviar**, 8ème arr.
**Mignonnette du Caviar**, 8ème arr.
**Samovar (Le)**, 1er arr.

## Swiss
**Maison du Valais**, 8ème arr.
**Raccard (Le)**, 5ème arr.

# Menu Savvy

The following list contains a good number of cooking terms which may appear on French restaurant menus.

**Aiguillette (of beef):** the top part of beef rump.

**Aïoli or Aïlloli:** a sort of mayonnaise with lots of garlic; also, in the Midi, an entire dish, composed of cod, snails, and vegetables served with aïoli.

**Américaine or Armoricaine:** a sauce with white wine, Cognac, tomatoes, and butter.

**Andouille:** slices of chitterlings in a pig intestine. Usually served cold.

**Andouillette:** chitterlings, served hot.

**A L'Anglaise:** dipped in beaten eggs, and then coated with breadcrumbs.

**Anguille Au Vert:** eels with white wine and about ten green (vert) herbs, served cold.

**Argenteuil:** a soup with asparagus.

**Aurore:** sauce with a small quantity of tomato (named after his mother by Brillat-Savarin).

**Baba:** sponge cake with raisins, soaked with rum or kirsch.

**Ballottine:** boned, stuffed, and rolled cut of meat.

**Bavarois:** thick cream with egg yolks and whipped cream served with fruits and chocolates.

**Béarnaise:** thick sauce made of shallots, tarragon, vinegar, egg yolks, thickened with butter.

**Béchamel:** a sauce of flour and butter with milk.

**Beef Au Gros Sel:** beef, boiled and served with the vegetables with which it was cooked, and coarse salt.

**Belle Dijonnaise (À La):** a dessert with blackcurrants.

**Bercy:** sauce made with shallots, white wine, and butter.

**Beurre Blanc:** sauce of minced shallots reduced in white wine and vinegar, plus whipped butter.

**Beurre D'Escargots:** seasoned butter with shallots, garlic, and parsley.

**Beurre Maitre D'Hôtel:** melted butter with parsley and lemon.

**Beurre Marchand De Vin:** butter with shallots and red wine.

**Beurre De Montpellier:** butter seasoned with herbs, garlic, and anchovies.

**Beurre Noir:** browned butter with vinegar and capers.

**Beurre Noisette:** butter lightly browned.

**Bigarrade:** sauce with orange.

**Billy By:** a soup with mussels—a specialty of Maxim's.

**Bisque (of crayfish, lobster, etc.):** velouté with white wine and cream.

**Blinis:** small, thick wheat flour crêpes with eggs and milk; yeast.

**Bohémienne:** rice with tomatoes and fried onion slices.

**Bombe Glacée:** ice cream made from cream mixed with eggs, plus whipped cream variously flavored; originally ball-shaped (bomb).

**Bordelaise:** fairly thin sauce of shallots, red or white wine, and tarragon.

**Borscht:** consommé with beets and meat; cream served separately; a Russian dish.

**Bouquetière:** artichoke bottoms, carrots, turnips, green beans, peas, and bouquets of cauliflower.

**Bourdaloue (À La):** poached fruit coated in thick cream with vanilla and crushed macaroons; served accompanied by a purée of fruit; many variations. The tarte Bourdaloue is a pear tarte with pastry cream.

**Brandade De Morue:** cod in a purée thickened with oil and milk; usually seasoned with garlic.

## C

**Caille (or Faisan or Perdreau) A La Souvaroff or Souvarov:** quail (or

223

pheasant, or young partridge) in a clay cooker with truffles and foie gras.

**Canard A La Presse:** duck which has been suffocated, and not bled, roasted for a fairly short period; the breast is cut into aiguillettes (slivers); the thighs are served grilled; the carcass is pressed to express juice and blood, to which butter and the pounded duck's liver are added, and, optionally, red wine and Cognac, and then served over the aiguillettes.

**Canard A La Rouennaise:** duck, identical to canard à la presse, but the carcass is stuffed with liver, onions, and bacon.

**Carottes Vichy:** carrots, sliced (optional) and boiled; with butter and parsley.

**Carpe A La Juive:** served cold; carp cut into sections, deboned, and then reassembled; sauce thickened with oil.

**Charcutière:** sauce with onions, white wine, gherkins.

**Charlotte:** dessert of various crèmes and/or fruit molded around lady-fingers.

**Chasseur:** sauce with shallots, white wine, mushrooms.

**Chevreuil:** sauce of vegetable stock, red wine; sometimes currant jelly.

**Choron:** béarnaise sauce with tomato.

**Chou-Fleur A La Polonaise:** cauliflower; poached, breaded, baked.

**Clafoutis:** pastry or pancake with fruit.

**Clamart:** soup with peas.

**Clivet de Lièvre:** hare; a sort of ragoût with red wine, lardoons, and onions; sauce thickened with the animal's blood.

**Colin A La Grenobloise:** hake with butter, capers, and lemon.

**Condé (A La):** poached fruit on rice pudding, covered with fruit syrup.

**Confit:** pork, goose, duck, turkey, or other meat cooked in its own fat, and covered with the fat to seal it.

**Côte De Veau Pojarsky or Pojarski:** minced veal and bread, shaped into a cutlet; breaded and fried.

**Côtelettes De Mouton Champvalon:** mutton chops; baked between layers of potatoes and sautéed onions.

**Cotelette De Saumon Pojarsky or Pojarski:** a mixture of salmon and bread crumbs, shaped into a cutlet; breaded and fried.

**Coulibiac or Koulibiack De Saumon:** a hot tourte made with salmon.

**Crécy:** soup with carrots.

**Crème Chantilly:** whipped cream with powdered sugar.

**Crêpe Suzette:** crêpe stuffed with sweetened butter mixture, Curacao, and juice and zest of mandarin.

**Croquant:** a crunchy petit four.

**Croque-Monsieur:** sandwich baked with Gruyère cheese and ham.

**Croustade:** ragoûts, etc., served in flaky or puff pastries.

**Crudité:** an appetizer usually consisting of raw vegetables.

**Cultivateur:** potage with thin slices of vegetables and bread; (optional) cubes of bacon.

# D

**Dieppoise (A La):** seawater fish cooked in white wine and garnished with mussels.

**Diplomate:** bavarois, generally with chocolate and strawberries in layers, covered in cream with vanilla.

# E

**Emincé:** thinly sliced meat covered with a sauce and reheated.

**Entrecôte Mirabeau:** grilled, topped with anchovy fillets and served with anchovy butter. Garnished with pitted olives.

**Escalope:** slice of meat or fish, flattened slightly, and sautéed.

**Escalope (De Veau) Milanaise:** escalope of veal; breaded, sautéed; garnished with macaroni, tomato, ham, mushrooms.

**Escalope (De Veau) Viennoise:** escalope of veal; breaded, sautéed, served with lemon.

**Escargots A La Bourguignonne:** snails with herbed garlic-butter.

**Escargots A La Chablisienne:** snails, as above, but with white wine.

# F

**Financière:** sauce with Madeira and truffles.

**Florentine:** with spinach.

**Foie De Veau A L'Anglaise:** calf's liver; grilled, with slices of bacon.

**Fondue:** in addition to the well known dishes, where food is cooked in a boiling liquid, it is also a dish with vegetables cooked at length in butter and thus reduced to pulp.

**Forestière:** with sautéed mushrooms and lardoons.

**Foyot:** béarnaise with tomato.
**Frangipane:** pastry cream and chopped almonds; used to fill thick crêpes.

**Galantine:** boned poultry or meat, stuffed and pressed into a symmetrical form. They are cooked in a gelatine broth.
**Génoise (or Génoese):** a sponge cake filled with chocolate, fruits.
**Germiny:** soup with egg yolk, cream, and sorrel.
**Grand Veneur:** sauce with vegetable stock, vinegar, currant jelly, cream.
**Granité:** a type of sherbet, very slightly sweetened.
**Gratin Dauphinois:** a dish consisting of slices of raw potatoes baked with milk, cream (sometimes), and grated Gruyère.
**Gribiche:** cold herbed sauce with hard-boiled egg yolks, oil, and vinegar.
**Gribiche:** mayonnaise with chopped hard-boiled eggs, capers, pickles, and various herbs.

**Haricots Blancs A La Bretonne:** haricot beans with onions browned in butter.
**Hollandaise:** a sort of light béarnaise without shallots or tarragon, but with lemon juice; recipes differ from one "school" to another.
**Homard (and Langouste) À La Parisienne:** lobster and langouste served cold; escalopes placed in the shell; served with mayonnaise.
**Homard (and Langouste) Newburg:** pieces of lobster or langouste; Cognac, Madeira, or sherry; cream.
**Homard (and Langouste) Thermidor:** lobster and langouste split in two lengthwise; wine sauce; gratiné.

**Ile Flottante:** carmelized oeufs à la neige served with crushed, grilled almonds. It can also refer to a biscuit soaked in kirsch and layered with apricot marmalade, covered with crème

chantilly and "floating" in cream with vanilla.

**Joinville:** sauce for fish, with egg yolk, cream, purées of crayfish and shrimp; small diced truffles sometimes added.
**Julienne:** can refer to either a vegetable soup made from a clear consommé, or any shredded foodstuff.

**Lièvre A La Royale:** hare stuffed with foie gras and truffles.

**Macédoine:** raw or cooked mixture of fruit or vegetables served hot or cold.
**Médaillon:** various foodstuffs cut in round or oval medallions.
**A La Madrilène:** clear broth (or other dishes) flavored with tomato juice.
**Maltaise:** hollandaise with juice of a blood orange.
**Marcassin A La Saint-Hubert:** young boar; cutlets roasted in the oven. Stuffing of fat boar meat and meadow mushrooms. Wrapped in caul, with breadcrumbs.
**Merlan En Colère:** whiting, fried; its tail is placed in its mouth.
**Meurette:** sauce with red wine and butter, for freshwater fish and poached eggs.
**Miroton:** stew made with cooked meat and onions.
**Montmorency (À La):** with cherries.
**Mornay:** béchamel plus grated cheese.
**Moules Marinière:** mussels cooked in the shell with white wine, shallots, parsley.
**Moules Poulette:** mussels on the half-shell; sauce poulette.
**Mousseline:** hollandaise, lightened with stiffly beaten egg whites.

*N*

**Nage (A La):** cooked in a seasoned court-bouillon.

**Nantua:** stock from vegetables and crayfish, with white wine and tomato.

**Navarin:** ragout of lamb or mutton with small onions, potatoes, and, optionally, carrots, turnips, peas (and is thus called "à la printaniere").

**Noisettes:** delicate pieces of rib or loin.

**Nougat:** sweet made with roasted almonds and honey.

**Oeufs A La Neige:** small mounds of beaten egg whites poached in milk and served with vanilla-flavored cream.

**Omelette Norvégienne:** sweet souffléed omlette, filled with ice cream.

**Pannequet:** rolled crêpe, with jam.

**Parfait:** ice cream made with eggs and whipped cream, plus any flavor.

**Parisienne:** with leeks and potatoes.

**Parmentier:** with potatoes.

**Paupiettes:** thin slices of meat stuffed with forcemeat and shaped into cork-sized rolls.

**Pauvre Homme:** "poor man's" sauce with onions, vinegar, mustard, tomato.

**Paysanne:** butcher's meat or poultry, usually braised, and garnished with sliced, lightly cooked carrots and turnips, plus onions, bacon, and potatoes.

**Périgueux:** sauce with truffle essence.

**Pigeon En Crapaudine:** pigeon, flattened slightly (the shape is similar to a toad-crapaud) and grilled.

**Piquante:** sauce with shallots, white wine, vinegar, gherkins, fine herbes.

**Pirojki:** small croquettes with cheese or minced game, fish, or vegetables.

**Pochouse:** a matelote made of freshwater fish (especially eel), cooked with white wine; butter thickens the sauce.

**Plombière:** ice cream with vanilla, kirsch, candied fruit, crème chantilly.

**Poiurade:** vegetable stock and vinegar marinade.

**Polenta:** boiled corn semolina plus butter and grated cheese.

**Pommes (De Terre) Allumettes:** potatoes; fried, in matchstick (allumette) form.

**Pommes (De Terre) À L'Anglaise:** potatoes; peeled, then boiled or steamed, served plain.

**Pommes (De Terre) Anna:** pancake made of layers of sliced potatoes, then fried.

**Pommes (De Terre) Boulangère:** potatoes; sliced and baked with onions.

**Pommes (De Terre) Château:** whole, fairly small potatoes sautéed in butter.

**Pommes (De Terre) Chips:** potato chips.

**Pommes (De Terre) Dauphin:** potatoes, grated and cooked as pancakes.

**Pommes (De Terre) Dauphine:** croquettes of potato purée and chou pastry breaded and fried.

**Pommes (De Terre) Duchesse:** potato puréed with egg yolks, glazed with egg and baked.

**Pommes (De Terre) Lyonnaise:** sliced potatoes, sautéed with onions.

**Pommes (De Terre) Macaire:** pulp of potatoes mixed with butter and baked.

**Pommes (De Terre) Mousseline:** puréed potato, with whipped cream.

**Pommes (De Terre) Noisette:** like pommes château, but smaller—the size of big hazelnuts (noisettes).

**Pommes (De Terre) Paille:** potatoes sliced as thin as straw (paille) and fried.

**Pommes (De Terre) Pont-Neuf:** elegant designation for french fries.

**Pommes (De Terre) En Robe De Chambre or Robe Des Champs:** potatoes boiled or baked in their skin.

**Pommes (De Terre) Sarladaise:** potatoes, sliced, cooked in the oven with goose fat, and (optional) truffles.

**Portugaise:** peeled tomatoes cooked down with garlic and onions.

**Poularde Demi-Deuil:** pullet studded with truffles and poached.

**Poulet Basquaise:** chicken with tomatoes and peppercorns.

**Poulette:** velouté with mushrooms (not always), lemon juice, parsley.

**Printanier:** diced carrots or turnips, blanched, with peas and French beans.

**Profiteroles:** small balls of puff pastry filled with custard, chocolate, or whipped cream covered with chocolate or other sauce.

**À La Provencale:** Dishes with tomato and garlic, and sometimes only garlic.

**Purée Argenteuil:** purée of asparagus.

**Purée Clamart:** purée of peas.

**Purée Crécy:** purée of carrots.

**Purée Parmentier:** purée of potatoes.

**Purée Saint-Germain:** purée of split peas or peas.

**Purée Soubise:** purée of onions.
**Purée Vichy:** purée of carrots.

**Ravigote:** white sauce with white wine, vinegar, onion, lemon juice, parsley, shallot butter, fines herbes.
**Rémoulade:** mayonnaise plus capers, onions, parsley, gherkins, and herbs.
**Riz Créole:** rice pilaf with peppers and tomatoes.
**Riz A L'Impératrice:** dessert rice with egg yolks, cream, and candied fruit.
**Riz A L'Indienne:** boiled rice.
**Riz Pilaw or Pilaf:** chopped onions and rice browned in butter, then cooked.
**Rizotto:** rice pilaf with various additions: grated cheese, saffron, tomato.
**Robert:** sauce with onions, white wine, vinegar, mustard.
**Rognons Beaugé:** kidneys, in Bordeaux, with Madeira and mustard (this dish was dedicated to André Beaugé, a singer from Bordeaux who was very famous between the two World Wars). Elsewhere it is subject to variations.
**Rognons Vert Pré:** kidneys, grilled, with butter and parsley, garnished with watercress.
**Rougets A La Nicoise:** mullet, grilled or fried; with tomatoes, anchovy fillets, and black olives.

**Salade Russe:** all sorts of diced vegetables thickened with mayonnaise.
**Savarin:** crown-shaped sponge cake, soaked in flavored syrup and doused with liqueur—rum, kirsch.
**Santé:** with potatoes and sorrel.
**Selle De Veau Matignon:** saddle of veal, baked covered in a thick layer of "matignon" (fondue of vegetables), bacon or ham, and caul.
**Selle De Veau Orloff:** slices of saddle of veal alternating with a purée of onions, mushrooms, and truffles.
**Soissons:** with haricot beans.
**Sole Cardinal:** fillets of sole, poached, with a cream sauce made with crayfish.
**Sole Dugléré:** sole; with tomatoes, parsley, onion, shallots, plus butter and—sometimes—béchamel.
**Sole Marguery:** sole, with white wine, accompanied by mussels and shrimp.
**Sole (or Truite) Meunière:** sole, or trout, dipped in flour and sautéed in butter; parsley, lemon.
**Sorbet:** sherbet; sometimes mixed with frozen Italian meringue.
**Soubise:** béchamel with onion.
**Spätzelli:** noodles made of flour and eggs.
**Spoom:** sherbet with lots of Italian meringue (stiffly beaten egg whites).
**Steak Au Poivre:** pepper steak; steak covered in crushed peppercorns, browned in a frying pan, flambéed with Cognac; sauce deglazed with cream.
**Suprême:** chicken velouté with cream.

**Sabayon:** zabaglione; thin cream of beaten egg yolks and sugar, plus wine or liqueur; served warm.
**Saint-Germain:** purée of split or green peas; croutons.
**Salade "Folle":** the only nouvelle cuisine term widespread in culinary usage; most often made of lightly cooked green beans, foie gras, shellfish.
**Salade Francillon:** mussels, potatoes marinated in Chablis, truffles, hot vinaigrette.
**Salade Lorette:** lamb's lettuce, celery, beets.
**Salade Mimosa:** lettuce with orange and not, as often believed, with crumbled hard-boiled eggs.
**Salade Nicoise:** green beans, tomatoes, potatoes, anchovy fillets, olives, and capers.

**Tartare:** mayonnaise plus hard-boiled egg yolks with onions and chopped chives.
**Tarte Tatin:** with apples, upside down; served hot.
**Tête De Veau En Tortue:** calf's head; see Tortue.
**Tomates A La Provencale:** tomatoes, cut in half, and baked with a sprinkling of parsley and garlic.
**Tortue:** sauce with various herbs, tomato, Madeira; or a consomme of beef, chicken, and turtle, with various herbs, including basil, sage, etc.
**Tournedos Henri IV:** tournedos accompanied by a béarnaise sauce with reduced stock added.
**Tournedos A La Monégasque:** tournedos sautéed in butter, served with a slice of

eggplant, and garnished with a fondue of tomatoes and black olives.

**Tournedos Rossini:** tournedos sautéed in butter; the pan juices are poured over them. Garnished with stuffed tomatoes.

**Truffes Sous La Cendre:** truffles wrapped in oiled paper or aluminum foil, and cooked under ashes; or wrapped in dough and baked; or wrapped in a thin slice of fresh bacon and oiled paper and cooked under ashes.

**Truffes A La Serviette:** truffles cooked with Madeira or Champagne, and presented in a timbale or casserole, in the middle of a folded napkin.

**Truite Au Bleu:** Trout boiled live in water with vinegar; it turns "blue."

**Vacherin:** ice cream in a meringue shell.

**Vallée D'Auge:** sauce with Calvados and cream.

**Veau Marengo:** veal, sautéed in oil with tomatoes, onions, and mushrooms.

**Zingara:** garnish for veal and fowl; white wine, mushrooms, tomato sauce, and ham.

# THE DIVERSIONS

## Joe Allen
1st arr.
**30 rue Pierre-Lescot**
**236.70.13**
*Open until 2:00 A.M.*

This New York-style bar, a replica of Broadway's Joe Allen, with the same checked tablecloths and red brick walls covered with photos, serves all kinds of American drinks. Due to its popularity you may have to wait awhile at the bar before you can sit down to the delicious spareribs and black bean soup. Joe Allen is always packed with pretty girls.

## Bar du Bristol
**8th arr.**
**112 faubourg Saint-Honoré**
**266.91.45**
*Open 11:00 A.M. to 2:00 A.M.*

Michel, the head bartender, has recently been elected vice president of the French Association of Bartenders. We highly recommend you try some of his cocktails such as Nathaly's, which is named after his daughter and contains Grand Marnier, white Martini vermouth, cognac and raspberry brandy. The Arbona has pear brandy, dry vermouth and banana cream. Halligan's is made of Curaçao and sherry; and the Limerzel is a blend of orange, Cuaçao, pear brandy, gin and raspberry brandy.

## Bar du Café de la Paix
**9th arr.**
**place de l'Opéra**
**260.33.50**
*Open noon to 3:00 P.M. and 6:00 P.M. to 10:00 P.M.*

Although the bar may not be as charming and splendidly decorated as the Café de la Paix, it nevertheless offers a superb choice of cocktails selected by Jean Doreau, who is also the head bartender at the Grand Hôtel. His specialties are côté droit, or "right-hand cocktails," which contain orange juice, Dubonnet, Calvados and mandarine brandy; and côté gauche, or "left-hand cocktails," which are a blend of Irish whiskey, Calvados, grenadine syrup and a touch of fresh cream.

## Bar du Concorde-La Fayette (Plein Ciel)
**17th arr.**
**3 place de la Porte-des-Ternes**
**758.12.84**
*Open 11:00 A.M. to 2:00 A.M.*

From its thirty-third floor, the hotel's big windows offer the best view of Paris. You can see the Bois de Boulogne, Mont Valérian and the Arc du Triomphe. The Plein Ciel bar is light, carefully decorated and offers excellent drinks concocted by the inspired and authoritative bartender, Michel. The ground-floor bar, La Fayette, offers more intimacy and is decorated with tin soldiers. A jazz pianist performs there every night starting at 10:00 P.M.

## Bar du Concorde-Saint Lazare (Golden Black)
**8th arr.**
**108 rue Saint-Lazare**
**261.51.20**
*Open 11:00 A.M. to 2:00 A.M.*

Whenever there is an important sports event, like the American Cup or the five-nation tennis tournament, the Golden Black is packed to the rafters with customers. The rest of the year you may sit back and enjoy many of Joel's superb cocktails such as the Good Will, which is made of rye, banana cream, brandy and lemon juice; or the Bloodhound, which contains gin, vermouth and strawberry syrup. The bar is right next to the Bistro 108's superb poolroom.

### Bar du Crillon

**8th arr.**
**10 place de la Concorde**
**296.10.81**
*Open 11:00 A.M. to 12:30 A.M.*

Its agreeably modern but bland decor is being revamped. For the moment, the Bar du Crillon is the perfect place to meet before dinner in the adjacent restaurant. The cocktails are good and the service is impeccable. Ask the bartender to bring you some of those delicious hot feuilletés, along with some Champagne or whiskey.

### Bar du Fouquet's

**8th arr.**
**99 Champs-Élysées**
**723.70.60**
*Open 9:00 A.M. to 1:30 A.M.*

This bar is filled with movie producers, foreigners and rubbernecks off the Champs-Elysées. The bar and its celebrated terrace are always very animated, if not at times downright noisy. The service is fast and efficient, the cocktails are excellent, and the prices outrageous. The Lady's Fouquet cocktail, made with Champagne, Cognac and Imperial mandarine, and the Fouquet's Special (Champagne, Dubonnet, grapefruit juice) are priced at 50F, not including service.

### Bar du George-V

**8th arr.**
**31 ave. George-V**
**723.54.00**
*Open 11:00 A.M. to 2:00 A.M.*

Although the patio is most agreeable, you may prefer to sit at the bar where the devilish Nino will be happy to serve you a bullshot as made in the U.S. (beef broth, vodka and lemon juice with a dash of Worcestershire sauce). An American taste that also suits the French temperament.

### Bar du Grand Hôtel

**9th arr.**
**12 blvd. des Capucines**
**260.33.50**
*Open 11:00 A.M. to midnight.*

Located under the huge arches of the Grand Hôtel lobby, this well-proportioned and attractive watering hole features various levels carpeted in thick dark pile. Jean, a remarkable bartender who has been there 23 years and knows all his customers by name, whips up some excellent cocktails. A pianist performs during the late afternoons.

### Bar de l'Hôtel

**6th arr.**
**13 rue des Beaux-Arts**
**325.27.22**
*Open 6:30 P.M. to 3:00 A.M.*

The pleasant bar and garden are located on the ground floor of a hotel designed by Claude-Nicolas Ledoux, the great eighteenth-century architect. Many young art dealers enjoy coming here to listen to the piano player; in the past, Oscar Wilde (who died here) was one of its most prominent customers.

### Bar du Meurice

**1st arr.**
**228 rue de Rivoli**
**260.38.60**
*Open 11:00 A.M. to 1:00 A.M.*

Pierre, who has been at the Meurice for nearly thirty years, is highly reputed for his Bloody Marys and dry martinis, which will further enhance your appreciation of the bar's beautiful mahogany paneling and comfortable armchairs.

### Bar Anglais (Plaza-Athénée)

**8th arr.**
**25 ave. Montaigne**
**723.78.33**
*Open 11:00 A.M. to 11:30 P.M.*

Located in the hotel's basement, this intimate bar is decorated with splendid mahogany paneling and thick Scottish carpets. The bartender is highly competent and the bar's distinguished international clientele, most of whom are hotel guests and well-dressed, nibble on almonds, mindless of the din, which is apt to be interrupted by the laughter of a beautiful *Brasileria*.

### Bar du Relais-Plaza
8th arr.
**21 ave. Montaigne**
**723.36.46**
*Open 11:00 A.M. to 1:30 A.M.*

The bar, in the Plaza-Athénée hotel, decorated in a prewar transatlantic style, lines elegant Parisiennes, young and less young; rich foreigners; and occasional music lovers who drop in from the Théatre des Champs-Élysées. The admirable Paul Ribrioux has retired, passing the cocktail shaker on to his equally brilliant assistant, Maurice Teyssère, whose excellent concoctions include the Relais-Plaza, which is a combination of orange juice, two shots of apricot juice, brandy and one shot of cognac.

### Bars du Ritz
1st arr.
**15 place Vendôme**
**260.38.30**
*Open 11:00 A.M. to 1:00 A.M.*

As you walk in through the place Vendôme entrance, you'll see the cocktail lounge to your left, lazy in the sun on a fine afternoon. The lounge leads into a peaceful patio that could easily be mistaken for a tea room, and there is nothing particularly charming about its 1930 decor or the classical piano music one hears so much in lounges and bars. The house specialty, Champagne with strawberries or peaches, tastes more like a milkshake; the Pépé Guindi (tequila, brandy and kiwi juice) is slightly too strong, but will enable you to undertake the long march up to a shopping gallery and to two other bars, one of which was recently redecorated. The other is an English bar, also known as the Bar Hemingway, with intimate decor—just the place to establish yourself until 1:00 A.M. closing.

### Bar Romain
9th arr.
**6 rue Caumartin**
**742.98.04**
*Open 11:30 A.M. to 2:00 A.M.*
*Closed Sun.*

Bar Romain is one of the handsomest drinking spots on the Right Bank. In 1905 an unknown Italian artist left fifteen paintings here, all of them depictions of Rome. Many performers featured at the nearby Olympia come here before and after the shows to make the arduous choice from among the gentle M. Papillon's 150 cocktails, made with or without alcohol. The basement, designed by the well-known decorator Slavik, has been done like a Belle Epoque railroad car, and was the first of its kind in Paris. (You can actually hear the train's whistle in the rest rooms. Between noon and 2:00 A.M. the Bar Romain's chef offers an outstanding steak tartare garnished with french fries or lentils vinaigrette.

### Bar du Scribe (Saint-Laurent)
9th arr.
**1 rue Scribe**
**742.03.40**
*Open 10:00 A.M. to midnight.*

A luxurious, comfortable, air-conditioned watering hole, featuring a green lacquered ceiling and light furniture. About all that remains from the Scribe's earlier days are the gorgeous mahogany counter, the padded bar stools and the white leather gondola-style armchairs. Clients include business people from around the world who come here for its quiet, cool atmosphere and its Irish, Canadian and Scotch whiskeys. A different Canadian whiskey cocktail is featured every day.

### Bar du Sheraton (Corail)

All the way at the bottom of the Sheraton tower, the bar is set against the green plants of the surrounding shopping mall. A rather nondescript place, with a smooth piano

# THE DIVERSIONS/Bars

**14th arr.**
**19 rue du**
**Cdt-Mouchotte**
**260.35.11, ext. 60.21**
*Open until 2:00 A.M.*

player who complements the high-priced and equally smooth cocktails prepared by David, the bartender.

## Bar du Westminster
**2nd arr.**
**13 rue de la Paix**
**261.57.46**
*Open 11:00 A.M. to 11:00 P.M.*

A peaceful English-style bar patronized by bankers, jewelers and business people who drop in from the rue de la Paix and the Opéra. The bartender, Raymond, whips up two excellent Campari-based cocktails, the Mona and the Westminster.

## Le Boeuf sur le Toit
**8th arr.**
**34 rue du Colisée**
**359.83.80**
*Open daily from 11:30 P.M., disco until 2:00 A.M.*

Writers, artists, models, designers and gurus come to the busy Boeuf to join the songfest at Bob Vatel's piano. The admirable Aaron Bridges takes over the piano four times a week, from 2:00 P.M. This little red boite was recently done over and the bar extended.

## La Calavados
**8th arr.**
**40 ave.**
**Pierre-ler-de-Serbie**
**359.27.28**

For at least two Républics, the Calavados has been open and serving whiskey while the milkman makes his rounds. The bar still has the same imitation candles which shed a warm red glow on the well-polished, sculptured wood paneling. The atmosphere is always warm and sometimes even hot when there's a big race at Longchamp. Young English people drop in from the neighboring princely hotels to chat with the international aristocracy of tipsy night-crawlers and a few red faced Parisians who hold court in this noctural haven. The clink of their glasses provides a nonsensical counterpoint to the piano music.

## Closerie des Lilas
**6th arr.**
**171 blvd.**
**Montparnasse**
**326.70.50**
*Open 11:00 A.M. to 2:00 A.M.*

It's difficult for a nightspot not to fall prey to the vagaries of fashion. The Closerie des Lilas has solved this quandary by hiring a remarkably gifted old-time piano player, Ivan Meyer, as well as two superb bartenders, Claude and Lionel, who constantly come up with brilliant, new cocktails. Owner Jacqueline Milan and her scion have thus created a place where it's fashionable to drop in for a drink at 1:00 A.M. Their customers include upper-class people, artists, the ultra-chic, arch-snobs and some real characters, who all enjoy strong spirits and memories of the Closerie's past clientele, including Hemingway, Gide, Verlaine and Trotsky.

## La Coupole
**14th arr.**
**102 blvd.**
**Montparnasse**
**320.14.20**
*Open daily until 2:00 A.M.*

La Coupole's bar has been the scene of many "historic" Montparnasse events. This is the place where Louis Aragon fell head over heels in love with Elsa, and during La Coupole's heyday in the '20s, where Bob, the bartender, generously lent his gentle profile to many fine art deco novels.

233

## *Furstemberg*

**6th arr.**
**27 rue de Buci**
**354.79.51**
*Open daily 6:00 P.M. to 3:00 A.M.*

The Furstemberg is comfortably furnished with padded benches, and its cocktails, such as Aquarius, Paradise and Zombi, prepared by Jean-Luc, are all excellent; each costs approximately 35F. The principal attraction of this cellar is the always terrific André Persiany and his two jazz musicians. Sing, laugh and dream, kids.

## *Harry's Bar*

**2nd arr.**
**5 rue Daunou**
**261.71.14**
*Open 10:30 P.M. to 4:00 A.M.*

Although it was the famous American jockey, Tod Sloane, who opened the bar in 1911, it was Harry MacElhone who took over the operation two years later. His son Andy has managed "Sank Roo Doe-noo" ever since his father's death. Harry's has served innumerable generations of boozers, celebrated and glorious. Guynemer hosted a party here for the first American aviators; F. Scott Fitzgerald pondered several of his novels here; Gershwin mentally dreamed of his *American in Paris* hunched over Harry's own Black Velvet and White Lady cocktails; Georges Carpentier took a swing at a bemused Ernest Hemingway; and Antoine Blondin punched a heavy-set English soccer player for having uttered some derisive remarks pertaining to French literature after excessive ingestion of Side Cars (another of Harry's original cocktails). Today customers can choose a drink from Andy's selection of 168 brands of whiskey or from his wide variety of cocktails. Bloody Marys were "coined" here in 1921. Andy himself came up with Blue Lagoon in 1972. Harry's three bartenders, Maurice, Mark and Guy, are as expert at prescribing the correct dosage as they are polite. The superb piano player, Tino Redman, performs daily until 2:00 A.M. in Harry's cellar, maintaining a propitious atmosphere for consumption. Harry's is open every day except Christmas.

## *Piano Club*

**1st arr.**
**12 rue Sainte-Anne**
**296.28.84**
*Open from 11:00 P.M. to 5:00 A.M.*
*Open Sun. midnight to 5:00 A.M.*

This agreeable bar is under the auspices of Ysolde, a former airline hostess. Here you can drink whiskey and eat Pianos, a grilled ham and cheese sandwich, in good company until dawn cracks. The soft music is both live and recorded.

## *Le Sherwood*

**2nd arr.**
**3 rue Daunou**
**261.70.94**
*Open daily until 5:00 A.M.*

All that separates the Sherwood from Harry's Bar is a wall. And a world, especially now that the Sherwood features a cellar decorated in a neo-Queen Anne style and upholstered in green and red tartan. Hungry patrons may order tournedos Florintine and daurade Rossini, while thirsty ones drown their chagrin in whiskey or beer. The bar, which has been decorated in vaguely Victorian style, is pretty dismal despite the presence of a color TV.

## *Suffren (Hilton)*

**15th arr.**
**18 ave de Suffren**
**273.92.00**
*Open 11:00 A.M. to midnight, Sun. to 2:00 A.M.*

Charming, intimate and definitely posh, the Suffren is the most attractive of the Hilton's ground-floor rooms. Jean-Marie, the bartender, will make you one of his Suffrens, containing orange juice, Cointreau, Cognacs and Champagne while you listen to the piano played by Phillipe Bécaud (son of Gilbert).

### Tahonga (P.L.M. Saint-Jacques)
14th arr.
17 blvd. Saint-Jacques
589.89.80

This unusually attractive big bar has comfortable armchairs, subdued lighting, a tropical island decor and captivating island music. The star attraction is the Cuban pianist and singer, Numidia. The house features 45 different cocktails, which include Scorpion, Embuscade, Paul Jones, Admiral Barington and others, all priced at 39F. Pierre, the bartender, recommends you try them all.

### Toit de Paris (Hilton)
15th arr.
18 ave. de Suffren
273.92.00
*Open 6:00 P.M. to 2:00 A.M.*
*Closed Sun.*

Ten floors separate the Cocktail Corner in the Toit de Paris from the Suffren. Recently remodeled, the bar offers a few exotic drinks. Jo Ricotta and his band play "cha-cha-chas."

# Cafés • Brasseries

### Café de la Mosquée
5e. arr.
39 rue Geoffroy-Saint-Hilaire
331.18.14
*Open 10:00 A.M. to 10:00 P.M.*

This establishment offers inexpensive pastries, Turkish coffee, mint tea and barley water to students and tourists who have come to visit the mosque. They are served either in a quiet room next to the Turkish steam bath, on a beautiful white patio with fountains and fig trees, or in a sumptuous lounge where guided tours of the mosque wind up.

### Café de la Paix
9th arr.
12 blvd. des Capucines
260.33.50
*Open daily 10:00 A.M. to 1:00 A.M.*

An integral part of the fine Relais Capucines restaurant, this good fast-service café has the same marvelously restored Opéra decor and is classified as a national landmark. Between 3:00 P.M. and 6:00 P.M. the café serves classic English tea and old-fashioned lemonade.

### La Coupole
14th arr.
102 blvd. du Montparnasse
320.14.20
*Open daily until 2:00 A.M.*

During the 1930s, La Coupole was a mecca for intellectuals and artists like Soutine, Breton, Foujita and Kiki. Today the celebrated frescoes above the café's twelve square columns are about the only reminder of the glory that was. More interesting are the permanent comings-and-goings of long-haired poets, neighborhood merchants, idle intellectuals, Dutch painters, Scandinavian models, spaced-out Ophelias and curiosity seekers from all over the world. And the beers are quite good.

## Les Deux Magots
**6th arr.**
**70 blvd.**
**Saint-Germain**
**548.55.25**
*Open daily 8:00 A.M. to 2: A.M.*

The reputation of Les Deux Magots is built on the fame of its clientele. Rémy de Gourmont, Léautaud and other editors of the weekly *Mercure de France* (1672–1965) were regulars here. They were the ones who spread the rumor that author Alfred Jarry drew a pistol from his pocket and shot a blank through the window; he then turned to a beautiful woman seated across from him and said, "Now that the ice is broken, let's talk." Jean Giraudoux enjoyed the café, as did Sartre, Simone de Beauvoir, Auguste Breton and many, many other luminaries. Today, the café is still expertly managed. The waiters all wear short jackets, vests and long white aprons and serve little pots of excellent coffee on trays. The house carries 25 brands of whiskey, which are presented in bottles, which is unique for a Parisian café. The hot chocolate, however, is no longer the "best in the world," and the ice cream, though generously served, is the manufactured kind. Nevertheless, the Deux Magots is still the most agreeable Parisian terrace café in which to have breakfast in the sun, after 8:00 A.M., facing the bell tower of Saint-Germain-des-Prés.

## Le Flore
**6th arr.**
**172 blvd.**
**Saint-Germain**
**548.55.26**
*Open daily 8:00 A.M. to 2:00 A.M.*

We often wonder if Le Flore's owner still remembers Sartre, Simone de Beauvoir, Camus, Audiberti, the Prévert brothers, the actors, philosophers, filmmakers and others who used to gather around the glowing stove in winter and discuss the advanced ideas that were to make this place famous. The Flore was already well patronized during the Second Empire with the likes of Huysmans and Rémy de Gourmont, as well as by the clique from Action Française which included Maurice Barrès, Paul Bourget and Moréas. Apollinaire founded his "Les Soirées de Paris" revue in this establishment. During the 1950s its owner, Boubal, transformed his first-floor apartment into a bar/lounge which was later taken over by the Reine Blanche, a gay Parisian society that turned it into an international gay center. Today, the Parisian literati still come into the Flore for a drink at 5:00 P.M.

## Lipp
**6th arr.**
**151 blvd.**
**Saint-Germain**
**548.53.91**
*Open 8:00 A.M. to 1:00 A.M.*
*Closed Mon.*

The "emperor" Roger Cazes rules over Lipp's 65 employees, 25 of whom are waiters. Since 1933, when the famous Bouboule retired, Gérard Jaegar has been Lipp's headwaiter. To become a waiter, applicants are thoroughly screened and must present impeccable references. In 1920, Marcellin Cazes bought the establishment from Lippman, an Alsatian whose ambition was to have a "Rhine-styled brasserie" in Paris. Lipp's decor has remained roughly the same, with its superb wooden paneling, copperware, "moleskins" or imitation leather seats, and Fargue ceramics. And it is one of the few Parisian establishments in which something is always happening. Celebrities often turn up here and are warmly greeted by Roger Cazes, who immediately ushers them into a special section on the ground floor. Unknown foreign tourists, however, will have to be content with sitting on the terrace or, worse, upstairs, far from the action. During the quiet morning hours, Lipp's is more relaxed and casual and without excessive fuss patrons may enjoy excellent beer on tap, such as Mutzig light ale or Bavarian dark beer.

## Mollard
**8th arr.**
**115 rue Saint-Lazare**
**387.50.20**
*Open daily until midnight.*

Of all the Parisian brasseries, Mollard is the most sumptuously decorated, with gold-leaf mosaic walls and stained glass windows with delicate flower motifs that are set into incredible inverse cast iron columns. There are also four art nouveau painted ceramic panels by Simas. Two depict the towns of Ville-d'Avray and Trouville; the third is an allegorical theatrical scene; and the fourth, Alsace and Lorraine the way they looked in 1895. Although Mollard is considered a brasserie, its sauerkraut, which is served only on Fridays, Saturdays and Sundays, is very disappointing. The beer, however, is good and the wines, of which there is a good choice, are reasonably priced.

## Le Procope
**6th arr.**
**13 rue de**
**l'Ancienne-Comédie**
**326.99.20**
*Open daily noon to 2:00 A.M.*

In the middle of the afternoon, sometime between lunch and dinner, Le Procope assumes its role as the "oldest café in the world." Coffee is served in the tranquility of its exquisite red walls bathed in the warm glow of crystal chandeliers. It probably tastes exactly like the blend that Francesco Procopio introduced to France in 1685. Portraits of Le Procope's illustrius patrons, Voltaire, Diderot, Danton, Gambetta and Huysmans; Bonaparte's hat, which he forgot in a moment of great haste; and the table where Voltaire fired off a few verses to his archenemy Fréron—all evoke the cafe's glorious past.

## Rhumerie Martini-quaise
**6th arr.**
**166 blvd.**
**Saint-Germain**
**354.28.94**
*Open daily 3:00 P.M. to 3:00 A.M.*

Regardless of the time of day, this is one of the hardest places in Paris to get a table. Even though its clientele is unquestionably upper class, the house punch is as strong as it was during its more proletarian Saint-Germain heyday, immediately post war.

## Le Sélect
**6th arr.**
**99 blvd.**
**du Montparnasse**
**548.38.24**
*Open daily until 2:30 A.M.*

The Sélect offers a Bordeaux, a Côtes-du-Rhône and a Muscadet, as well as a good Sauvignon. There are beer on tap including Carlsberg, Abbaye de Leffe, Spatenbraü and Guinness; and sixteen kinds of bottled beer, the best of which are Belgian. The Sélect's customers also get high contemplating the promising future of local avant-garde artists who patronize the café. Its owner, M. Plegat, loves to recreate the old spirit of Montparnasse, and after 60 years, the Sélect's 1920s decor bears true testimony to a time that was.

### Le Singe Pèlerin

**1st arr.**
**15 rue Montmartre**
**236.07.56**
*Open 4:00 A.M. to 4:30 P.M.*
*Closed Sun.*

This tiny, venerable bistro, decorated in gold, marble, and naive drawings and stoneware, attracts neighborhood merchants who wish to escape from their concrete surroundings. The Singe is dominated by an enamel panel depicting two admirably shaped women. This work is attributed to Eugène Grasset, the great Belle Epoque ornamentalist.

# Drugstores

### Drugstore des Champs-Elysées

**8th arr.**
**133 Champs-Elysées**
**723.54.34**
*Open daily 9:00 A.M. to 2:00 A.M.*

This "drugstore" has been an integral part of the Champs-Elysées scene for nearly twenty years. Customers casually drop in to look at the window displays, listen to the latest reggae records, leaf through a book or buy a Monte-Cristo cigar. Featuring a little bit of everything, the Drugstore has found the perfect gimmick. The large counter has comfortable stools and is so crowded that you'll have to come here at 2:30 P.M. to find a seat. Furthermore, the prices are reasonable. A good hamburger, a glass of rosé and coffee will cost you no more than 40F. The restaurant offers decent food that is perfect before or after a show. Such a meal might include rumpsteak with béarnaise sauce or fillet of beef Mirabeau, preceded by fresh oysters. Children will be delighted with the Drugstore's strawberry sundaes, sweet cristianias and Coca-Cola floats. In other departments you can find books and newspapers, fresh cigars, and last-minute gifts such as various gadgets, transistor radios, calculators, records, video-cassettes, toys, fancy leather goods and jewelry. The fashion department isn't the best, and the recently opened sports department is still sparsely stocked, although you can find a tennis racket, a pair of shorts or a sweater when other shops are closed. The delicatessen offers a wide variety of take-out dishes. The Drugstore also features a pharmacy, a stationery counter, a theater booking outlet and very quiet phone booths.

### Drugstore Matignon

**8th arr.**
**1 ave. Matigon**
**359.38.70**
*Open daily 9:00 A.M. to 2:00 A.M.*

Its soaring success, which has disrupted the normal activities of this otherwise deserted traffic circle, is due to the customer services it offers: movies, books and newspapers, fancy leather goods, perfumes, liquor, gifts, electronics, games, records, tobacco, a video shop, a pharmacy (with a wide selection of medicinal plants such as poppy, couch grass, marjoram, mallow and feverfew), a small gunsmith's shop and a theater ticket outlet. Both the ground-floor snack bar and the bar located on the mezzanine offer mixed salads, a mixed grill and daily specials, as well as desserts such as the gourmandises Publicis, opulent and varied frozen custards. The circular restaurant on the first floor, Le Drugstorien, is done in contemporary decor and features good, classical cuisine. The menu is priced at 75F, 50F, or à la carte at approximately 120F. Dinners are served until 12:30 A.M.

### Drugstore Opéra
**9th arr.**
**6 blvd. des Capucines**
**266.90.27**
*Open daily 9:30 A.M. to 2:00 A.M.*

An average of 20,000 customers walk into this place every day. The Drugstore Opéra has two entrances, one of which is located on the boulevard des Capucines and provides access to the cafeteria and handsome terrace. The other, on the rue Halévy, leads directly into a pastry shop and a well-stocked liquor store. As in other drugstores, you can find nearly anything, including suitcases, shoes, perfumes, gifts, gadgets, toys, books, newspapers, records, groceries, a car rental counter, a film shop, a stationery counter, a pharmacy and a foreign exchange bureau—open daily 10:30 A.M. to 7:20 P.M. and Sundays, noon to 7:50 P.M. But the most amazing thing about this drugstore is its six restaurants that can accommodate 800 people. The ground floor is always so busy that the waitresses hardly ever have time to smile. Its restaurants include La Corbeille with a fixed-price meal at 27F; the Scotch Pub with its intimate decor, ten varieties of cocktails, mixed grill and daily menu at 30F; and Le Boeuf, serving charcoal-broiled beef at 32F. The first-floor restaurants are a pizzeria; the attractive Au Rôtisseur, with a menu at 100F; and Aux Provinciales, with a more elaborate menu and a splendid view of the Opéra.

### Drugstore Saint-Germain
**6th arr.**
**149 blvd. Saint-Germain**
**222.92.50**
*Open daily 8:00 A.M. to 2:00 A.M.*

Slavick decor with a Restoration touch. Beautiful paper store in the basement: everything that's new and lots of comic books. For the rest of it, food, gifts, luggage, gadgets, perfume, the latest hit records, a video shop, selection of humidors, and a pharmacy that's open late.

# *Pubs*

hough modeled very freely after English public ale houses, the first Parisian pubs were established by an Alsatian, M. Probst, who was very fond of English beer. From the moment he asked the then-unknown Slavick to decorate the Winston Churchill and then the London Tavern, scores of honest bistros were seized with

Anglomania and became overnight pubs—to the disgust of many Parisians. The trend is now more or less over, and beer lovers have a large choice of pubs in which to drink their favorite brew.

### Académie de la Bière

**5th arr.**
**88 bis blvd.**
**Port-Royal**
**354.66.65**
*Open 3:30 P.M. to 2:00 A.M.*
*Closed Sun.*

The Académie's non-decor, with its formica tables and ads plastered on the walls is very popular with the young and others who admire beery authenticity. Kids from the neighboring high school come here to sing and swing their mugs. Pierre Marion, who also owns La Gueuze and Manneken Pis, has set up his headquarters here among the bottles of Duvel, Watou, Barmy Stout, Saint-Landelin and Ch'ti beer. There are 150 brands in all, including 10 on tap. The Académie also serves mussels and sandwiches made with delicious Poilâne bread.

### Bar Belge

**17th arr.**
**75 ave. de Saint-Ouen**
**627.41.01**
*Open 3:30 P.M. to 1:00 A.M.*
*Closed Mon.*

A traveler stranded between Pigalle and Saint-Denis will easily recognize this temple of Belgian beer by its small wooden and glass-paneled terrace. The Bar Belge features twenty varieties of Belgian suds, including three kinds of Leffe as well as their Trappist counterparts, and a few exotic beers such as the foamy, bitter Christmas. Ask the waiters to bring you some delicious Flemish sausages and Dutch bread to complement your beer. The owner, Julien Forêt, whose advanced age keeps him from singing, is nevertheless still in charge and makes a splendid appearance in his white and gold striped jacket.

### Cockney Bar

**9th arr.**
**39 blvd. de Clichy**
**874.80.80**
*Open daily noon to 4:00 A.M.*

This pub features John Courage on tap, the most popular English beer on the Continent, as well as Guinness. Patrons can also select a beer from the Cockney's list of 30 other brands, including the estimable Chester Brown and Mary-Ann from Jersey.

### Au Général de La Fayette

**9th arr.**
**52 rue La Fayette**
**770.59.08**
*Open 9:30 A.M. to 3:00 A.M.*
*Closed Sun.*

American expatriates and Parisian habitués love to congregate on the terrace or at the counter of this comfortable Anglo-Belgian bar and drink pints or half-pints of Guinness stout served in mugs with lids. Other ales include two varieties of Mönchshof, Double Diamond, Gueuze, Krieck Saint-Louis, Dub, Leffe and Vézelise. The bar's new owner, M. Planchon, also offers a wide range of beers on tap, including Duvel and Tennent stout.

### London Tavern

**6th arr.**
**3 rue du Sabot**
**548.42.39**
*Open 10:00 A.M. to 2:00 A.M.*

People flock to this pub on Saturday evenings to listen to the excellent jazz musicians who start playing at 10:00 P.M., and to inspect the curious decor of this ancestor of pubdom. Only two beers are served here, Watney's and Heineken.

## Manneken Pis

2nd arr.
4 rue Daunou
742.85.03
*Open noon to 2:00 A.M., Fri., Sat. noon to 4:00 A.M. Closed Sun.*

This tavern features two Belgian-style rooms, one of which features a myriad of elegant glasses and mugs as well as the Manneken Pis statue peering into a large crystal ball. The tavern offers its patrons 130 varieties of beer including Barmy Stout, Saint-Sixtus and Black Bull Stout which are served with rabbit à la Gueuze or gratinéed de Bruges Brugian dishes. This tavern, an offshoot of the Académie, would be a major attraction for the elite of beerdom if it weren't for the presence of the very popular Harry's Bar located across the street.

## Mort Subite

5th arr.
16-20 rue Mouffetard
331.41.48
*Open daily noon to 2:00 A.M.*

M. Puget, the former owner of the Pinte Odéon, took over this establishment with the amiable formula: "beer, jazz and women." This beer-loving man offers a wide selection of bottled brews, as well as fifteen varieties on tap, including Grimbergen, Campbell's and Saint-Léonard. Every evening, Mort Subite rocks with the sounds of Memphis Slim, Bill Coleman and many other fine jazz musicians who perform in the adjoining room.

## La Pinte

6th arr.
13 carrefour de l'Odéon
326.26.15
*Open 6:00 P.M. to 2:00 A.M.*

Posted in its window displays is the long litany of glorious beers—more then 50—that are served on a long tiled counter in this narrow establishment. Its close quarters tend to stimulate conversation, depending on the time of day. From a tiny orchestra pit subdued jazz airs emanate every evening, performed by a pianist or small band.

## Pub Henry VIII

6th arr.
111 rue de Rennes
222.50.94
*Irregular closing hours.*

This small new pub gets very animated in the evenings, when patrons celebrate its English kings and other good works, such as plum pudding and stout, as well as twenty other brands of beer including Scottish ales, Belgian Carolus, German Weissbier, Czech Pilsen and many others.

## Pub Saint-Germain

6th arr.
17 rue de l'Ancienne-Comédie
329.38.70
*Open 24 hours.*

The pub's well-known owner, M. Lacassagne, founder of the Society of Beer Drinkers, lists 250 bottled beers, 10 beers on tap, whiskeys and cocktails including the "lethal" black velvet, which is a blend of Irish stout and Champagne. Service, however, is not the best and the basement "tavern" could use a new coat of paint. The Pub Saint-Germain has three floors.

## Pub Winston-Churchill

16th arr.
5 rue de Presbourg
500.75.35
*Open daily 9:00 A.M. to 2:00 A.M.*

Winnie's place features only one beer, Watney's, and 50 brands of whiskey including 30-year-old Ballantine and 20-year-old J&B, as well as vodka, port and many other beverages. Numerous teas are sold at the pub's Fortnum and Mason counter. Pub Winston-Churchill also serves various English dishes such as leg of mutton with mint, Cambridge sausage, haddock and, on Sundays, steak and Yorkshire pudding, as well as a delicious apple pie.

241

### Taverne de la Bière
**10th arr.**
**15 rue de Dunkerque**
**285.12.93**
*Open 11:00 A.M. to 2:00 A.M.*

With all the frescoes and the other accessories found in typical Belgian or Parisian pubs, taverns and cafés, the Taverne de la Bière isn't particularly attractive. Fortunately, this pub offers a huge selection of beers (200 in all) such as Sanctus, Moinette, Hoegaard, Faxe, Hannen, Tennent, Charybdus and Scylla, that are guaranteed to knock you under the table. The Taverne de la Bière also features delicious choucroute.

### Taverne de Nesle
**6th arr.**
**32 rue Dauphine**
**326.38.36**
*Open daily 7:00 P.M. to sunrise.*

This friendly tavern with its somewhat medieval comforts, is fully furnished with old weapons and beer steins that evoke the great provincial breweries of the past. Its ecumenism is evidenced by a new owner, M. Robi, who earned the "Meilleur Chope (best stein) de Paris" in 1977. His establishment is popular with foreigners who love the barrel-tapped Guinness, tonic barley wine, Trappist-brewed beer, Bavarian Urstoff and Berliner Weisse that are served by German-speaking waiters. There are 160 excellent brands in all, and the house also features a good choucroute.

### Le Trappiste
**1st arr.**
**4 rue Saint-Denis**
**233.08.50**
*Open 8:00 A.M. to 2:00 A.M.*
*Closed Sun.*

This establishment is so vast it could accommodate an entire monastery of pot-bellied Trappist monks. Yet it is still too small to accommodate all the up-to-date dandies who drop in from the new Beaubourg-Halles district. M. Grisoni, its present owner, knows how to lure them into his tavern. He offers 150 brands of beer, among which you'll find Koelsch, Belgian pink and white beers, Black Bull, Stout, Pastor Ale and others. Le Trappiste also serves sauerkraut and a selection of grilled meats.

# Tea Rooms • Quick Lunches

### Angélina
**1st arr.**
**226 rue de Rivoli**
**260.82.00**
*Open daily 9:30 A.M. to 7:00 P.M.*

The pastries depicted on the ceiling, the stucco columns and the six landscapes by Lorrant-Heilbronn recall the tea room's high society days when it was celebrated as Rumpelmayer, one of the high places of modern style. The tea room's marble pedestal tables, however, aren't enough to conceal the ugliness of the Louis XV armchairs upholstered in green imitation leather. Although the waitresses are overworked, they still manage to serve guests piping hot, delicious chocolate. Its smoothness and scent make it the best in Paris, and it is properly served with whipped cream and a glass of ice water. Other

Angélina specialties include excellent Indian and Chinese teas, delicious pastries like the famous Mont-Blanc, the Aga Khan's favorite, which consists of meringue, whipped cream and cream of chestnut. Light meals are served until 2:30 P.M. and include mixed salads at 20F, cold cuts at 30F and a daily special.

## *Auberge In*
**5th arr.**
**34 rue du**
**Cardinal-Lemoine**
**326.43.51**
*Open noon to 2:30 P.M. and 7:00 P.M. to 10:30 P.M. Closed Sun.*

In the days when it was run by the three Padilla brothers, whose customers included students from the nearby schools, a few designers and neighborhood merchants, the Auberge In was the best and liveliest vegetarian restaurant in Paris. The new owner of the chain of Auberge In restaurants presents guests with an orthodox cuisine of talsbouli, vegetable pâtés; large mixed salads with yogurt, coconut and feta cheese; and desserts. The restaurant has rough-hewn arches and bouquets of dried flower that bring to mind the peacefulness of an old house in the south of France. The waiters urge diners to choose only one dish, and as a result, the tab comes out to be about 40F–50F per person.

## *Belusa*
**6th arr.**
**86 rue du**
**Cherche-Midi**
**222.52.58**
*Open noon to 6:00 P.M. Closed Sun.*

Belusa is beautifully decorated with beige walls, red-tiled floors, throw rugs, lace curtains and green plants at the windows. The antique furniture and curios, even the piano, are all for sale in this ten-table restaurant where you can have lunch or tea. Featured on the menu are quiche, leek or salmon tarte, feuilleté of potatoes, a few daily specials such as boudin with potatos, fresh pasta with seafood sauce, and poached eggs Florentine. For dessert, the restaurant offers an exquisite chocolate cake with berry sauce, a good linzertorte, a questionable cheesecake and red currant tourte. A wide choice of teas. The welcome is faint.

## *Bistro d'Hubert*
**1st arr.**
**36 place du**
**Marché-Saint-Honoré**
**296.98.07**
*Open 10:30 A.M. to 6:30 P.M. Closed Sun., Mon.*

Hubert had the ingenious idea of opening a place for those intimidated by fancy, high-priced luncheons. His bistro has two tables in front and ten others in the back room. Featured dishes are all well prepared and inexpensive and include an excellent vegetable pie, easily large enough for two people; a ham salad; salade bouchère with onions or steamed fish; as well as more substantial dishes such as roast chicken with mashed potatoes at 32F, and leg of lamb with gratin dauphinois at 48F. His desserts include caramel custard and chocolate mousse. Local wine is served by the glass at 5F to 10F or by the carafe.

## *Boulangerie Saint-Philippe*
**8th arr.**
**73 ave.**
**Franklin-Roosevelt**

Its unusual and highly eclectic "rustic-modern" decor consists of wooden beams, limestone floor tiles, wall hangings and a navy blue ceiling. The menu, which is written on a blackboard, features an excellent house terrine, mixed salad, grilled meats and all kinds of brochettes. The table setting always includes a tub of fresh butter and a basket of exquisite little rolls. For dessert, the

**359.78.76**
*Open 7:30 A.M. to 7:00 P.M.*
*Closed Sat.*

Boulangerie offers tarte tatin and pastries such as lime tarte, éclairs and noisettines. Good wine is served by the glass (7.50F). Teatime is from 3:00 P.M. on.

**La Boutique à Sandwiches**
**8th arr.**
**12 rue du Colisée**
**359.56.69**
*Open until 12:30 A.M. Restaurant*
*open until 11:00 P.M.*

Patrons who manage to grab a table at this "boutique" will be promptly served a decent hamburger, sirloin, mixed grill, or daily special for approximately 50F. Other featured dishes include weekly specials such as Indian-style stuffed crêpes, Welsh rarebit and ravioli, and yearly specials such as raclette and pickelfleisch, Alsatian-style breast of beef. Pickelfleisch is the establishment's mainstay and it is also prepared to go, hot or cold.

**Chez Julie**
**14th arr.**
**8 rue Jolivet**
**320.70.34**
*Open noon to 3:00 P.M. and*
*4:00 P.M. to 6:30 P.M. Closed Sun.*

This cheerful, noisy tea room/restaurant is highly successful due to its low prices and take-out counter. Its successive rooms are whitewashed and have lace curtains, tiled floors, large tables with country-style tablecloths, white dishware and colorful flowers. Julie specializes in savory pies, like the provençale, which is an exquisite blend of tomatoes and eggplant; or those made with seafood; nuts; white cheese and garlic; leeks; asparagus; or spinach. The salmon pie is tasteless and to be avoided at all costs. A tempting selection of dessert pies is also featured.

**La Ciboulette-Terrasse**
**4th arr.**
**141 rue Saint-Martin**
**271.72.34**
*Open 9:00 A.M. to 7:00 P.M.*
*Closed Sat., Sun.*

Breakfast, lemonade, coffee, beer on tap, a glass of wine and snacks are all served outside on the terrace facing the Centre Pompidou in summer, and in the ground-floor front room during winter. Jean-Pierre Coffe's gourmet restaurant is upstairs. The front room is hung with green plants and decorated with light furniture, and also has a counter that is noisily attended by two waiters clad in black vests and long white aprons. The sandwiches are, indisputably, the best in Paris. Other featured items include warm and savory tartes such as watercress, leek or beet; and fruit tartes, cakes and pastries, all of which are made in the three-star kitchen upstairs.

**Christian Constant**
**7th arr.**
**20 rue du Bac**
**296.53.53**
*Open daily 8:00 A.M. to 8:00 P.M.*

This light and airy tea room, located next to the pastry shop, has nineteen varieties of tea served with acaccia honey or five kinds of sugar, warm brioches and jams, or one of the delicate little pastries of which Christian Constant has the secret.

**Côté Verrière**
**1st arr.**
**6 rue du Jour**
**508.56.56**
*Open noon to 6:00 P.M.*
*Closed Mon.*

Côté Verrière has rugs patterned with coconut matting, wicker chairs, whitewood tables, dried flower bouquets hanging from the walls and ceiling, and cheerful flowered place settings that are also sold on the ground floor. The menu lists five savory dishes under 20F that include a delicious pumpkin soup; eggs with tarragon; a salad with lettuce, mushrooms, carrots and grapefruit; a rather bland potato-carrot feuillete; an exquisite leek tarte with cream; and a few good pastries.

## La Croissanterie

**1st arr.**
**Forum des Halles,**
**4th level,**
**297.48.77**
*And ten other locations.*

If your mouth begins to water at the aroma of pastries and hot croissants, you're probably not far from La Croissanterie. Each day, many hundreds of croissants, pains au chocolat, brioches, raisin rolls and apple turnovers are baked in this tiny shop's ovens. Everything here is delicate and crisp. The croissants are delicious, and you can have a cup of coffee to go with them from the shop's vending machine.

## Daru

**8th arr.**
**19 rue Daru**
**227.23.60**
*Open 9:00 A.M. to 11:00 P.M.*
*Closed Sun., Mon.*

Located at the foot of the Russian Orthodox Church, this agreeable 50-year-old shop was established by a Russian who looks as if he had stepped out of a John Ford movie. Featured fare include Danish smoked salmon, Iranian caviar, koulibiak, vatrouchka, and vodka. The establishment's limited accommodations of one corner bench and some bar stools are offset by very prompt service. Daru is perfect for quick lunches or for dinner before or after a show.

## Dattes et Noix

**3rd arr.**
**4 rue du Parc-Royal**
**887.88.94**
*Open daily 11:00 A.M. to midnight.*

This snack bar is decorated with white tiled floors and counters, whitewashed walls, and attractive turn-of-the-century chairs that are inlaid with date pits! This is a spot for the young "in" crowd, who come here for eggs en cocotte, salads, tarama dishes, tourtes with mushrooms or artichoke bottoms, and delicious desserts. Dattes et Noix is located off the small Parc-Royal square, next to the Carnavalet Museum.

## L'Écluse

**6th arr.**
**15 quai des**
**Grands-Augustins**
**633.58.74**
**8th arr.**
**64 rue Francois-Ier**
**359.77.09**
*Open 11:00 A.M. to 2:00 A.M.*
*Closed Sun.*

Great for after-theater snacks, these two old-fashioned, country-style bistros feature first-rate, fresh homemade foie gras, Italian carpaccio, Parma ham, fillets of smoked goose, salmon, Chavignol crottin cheese served with grapes, scooped Roquefort cheese and an exquisite "grandmother" chocolate cake. Georges Bardawil, L'Écluse's good-natured owner, offers a fine selection of Bordeaux, served by the glass or carafe.

## L'Épicerie Russe

**16th arr.**
**3 rue**
**Gustave-Courbet**
**553.46.46**
*Open noon to 11:00 P.M.*
*Closed Sun., Mon.*

With its pine-green lacquered walls lined with colorful bottles, bowls and boxes, this shop is the sort you'd find in a picturebook. The bar and tables are patronized by locals who come here for salmon, homemade blinis, koulibiak, beef Stroganoff, poppyseed cakes, sachertortes, teas, Alsatian wines and vodkas. The waitresses are all very efficient.

## L'Épicerie Verte

**17th arr.**
**5 rue Saussier-Leroy**
**764.19.68**
*Luncheon served noon to 2:30 P.M.*
*Closed Sat., Sun.*

As of now, we won't venture an opinion on macro-organic foods, as we can't decide whether or not to take this cuisine seriously. L'Épicerie Verte is dedicated to such foods, which it serves as lunch in a simple, agreeable setting of pale green walls, natural wood railings and a profusion of green plants. The restaurant offers many vegetable dishes, soft-boiled eggs with country bread, marvelous sausages—all you can eat for 23F—cream cheese and good fruit tartes. The cakes are terrible. The waitresses are friendly and efficient. Beverages include tea, Hérault wine by the pitcher, cider, beer, fruit juice and infusions.

## Eurydice
**4th arr.**
**10 place des Vosges**
**277.77.99**
*Open noon to 10:00 P.M., Fri. Sat. noon to midnight. Closed Mon., and Tues.*

We discovered the Eurydice under the arcades of the place des Vosges. Jean Marais, who played Orpheus in Cocteau's celebrated work, designed the establishment's business cards. Inside, Eurydice offers a beautiful fresco depicting a bathing party during the 1930s, as well as freshly decorated white ceramic walls, a small blue reflecting pool, and transparent dishware. The absence of curtains, rugs and wall hangings makes conversation very difficult. Eurydice's menu includes Assiette Varsovie (spicy smoked breast of beef, chasseur sausage, chopped chicken liver, Russian gherkins, horseradish and white cheese), Assiette Oslo (smoked fish and blinis), classical salads, various desserts (the best are the chocolate truffons), tea, beer, vodka and wine served by the carafe. The highly efficient service somehow manages to make up for the expensive tab. Eurydice serves brunch on Sundays.

## Fanny Tea

**1st arr.**
**20 place Dauphine**
**325.83.67**
*Open 1:00 P.M. to 7:30 P.M. Closed Mon.*

This friendly, old-fashioned establishment offers magazines and one book of poetry per table for its exclusively female clientele who come here to eat various egg dishes, grilled ham and cheese sandwiches, Roquefort, salmon or tomato tartes and delicious desserts, all of which are served with excellent scented tea. Lunch is served outdoors in summer, facing one of the most beautiful and quiet squares in Paris.

## Fauchon
**8th arr.**
**26 place de la Madeleine**
**742.60.11**
*Open 9:30 A.M. to 6:30 P.M. Closed Sun.*

Though noisy, this is undoubtedly the best self-service cafeteria in Paris. Guests have to stand up while eating their club sandwiches or such dishes as vegetable tourtes, moussaka, tagliatelli, pastries and desserts. Everything here is excellent, well presented, generously apportioned and inexpensively priced. A decent lunch costs between 30F–40F.

## La Feuillade

**1st arr.**
**6 rue de la Petite-Truanderie**
**296.83.02**
*Open noon to 1:00 A.M. Closed Sun.*

This small, country-style tea room/restaurant is a bit too "high-tech" in our opinion, despite its attractive old wall tiles with their vine and grape patterns. La Feuillade specializes in salads and very good daily specials such as beef bourguignon, chicken with cream, and sautéed veal (26F). The desserts are excellent, including the chocolate cake and exotic fruit pies. The service is friendly, and our only regret is that La Feuillade has just ten tables.

## Flora Danica
**8th arr.**
**142 Champs-Elysées**
**359.22.91**
*Open daily noon to 11:00 P.M.*

This agreeable little room, located next to the Danish shop, has an attractive Scandinavian setting with light wooden furniture. The service, however, is very slow despite the fact that the generously apportioned dishes are prepared in view, just behind the counter. They include exquisite pickled herring; smoked salmon, halibut, and eel; shrimp salad; roast beef with onions; fillet of smoked pork; and marinated salmon. The pastries are delicious and served with mountains of fresh whipped cream. Accompanied by one of the best Tuborg on tap to be found in Paris, a meal comes out to about 50F–70F.

### Le Flore en l'Ile
**4th arr.**
**4 quai d'Orléans**
**633.08.36**
*Open daily 11:00 A.M. to 1:45 A.M.*

Located along the banks of the Seine, Le Flore faces the Tournelle bridge and the Tour d'Argent restaurant. Le Flore en l'Ile is Paris's most masculine tea room, decorated in dark brown and beige with wooden ceiling beams. Bathed in music by Vivaldi, guests discuss the past and future of drama and cinema while eating salads with Roquefort, hors d'oeuvres and rumpsteak. Breakfast is served from 11:00 A.M. Le Flore has an additional tea room located at 42 quai d'Orléans (tel. 329.88.27).

### Au Franc Pinot
**4th arr.**
**1 quai de Bourbon**
**329.46.98**
*Open 11:00 A.M. to 3:00 P.M. and 6:00 P.M. to 11:00 P.M. Closed Sun. evenings and Mon.*

For over 300 years, Parisians have enjoyed drinking in this landmark establishment embellished with a delicately ornamented façade and wrought-iron railing. M. Meyruey, its owner, has succeeded in reviving Paris's oldest tavern by offering excellent homemade minced duck rillettes or gâteau with young rabbit as well as a fine selection of local wines served by the glass.

### Ladurée
**8th arr.**
**16 rue Royale**
**260.21.79**
*Open 8:30 A.M. to 7:00 P.M. Closed Sun.*

To the delight of the puffy-cheeked cherubs depicted on Ladurée's ceiling, prosperous middle-aged patrons flock here to enjoy Chinese or Ceylonese tea, croissants, millefeuilles, babas and the exquisitely delicious royals, which are almond biscuits flavored with chocolate or mocha. The atmosphere is posh, and the service is efficient and courteous. Hot meals for about 30F, such as gratin of turbot or chicken with french fries, are served upstairs.

### Le Lieu-Dit
**5th arr.**
**171 rue Saint-Jacques**
**354.83.87**
*Open 12:30 P.M. to 7:00 P.M. Closed Sun., Mon.*

At the entrance you will be greeted by a sweet gray cat. This former glass works has a wood partition that separates the dining area from the reading section in which you'll find a couch, a few coffee tables and lots of books. The dining room is warm and hosted by two young romantic feminists who offer guests an appetizing and diversified menu that includes chicken liver pâté with hazelnuts and poached eggs with watercress. At tea time, Le Lieu-Dit offers hot lemon juice with honey, tea, fresh fruit juice and an exquisite chocolate cake; or, if you prefer, Poilâne bread with semisweet butter and Auvergne ham, served with a glass of wine.

### Les Mille Feuilles
**2nd arr.**
**2 rue Rambuteau**
**278.32.92**
*Open noon to 6:30 P.M. Closed Sun., Mon.*

A big tea room/bookshop is lighted by large bay windows. Under the pink ceiling are fifteen small tables, and bookshelves on which you will find recent editions catalogued according to topics: women, music, history, ethnology, foreign literature, cinema and theater. The establishment is filled with local intellectuals who come here for the delicious Poilâne bread served with horseradish and carrots, celery with Auvergne blue cheese, or old-fashioned jams.

## Un Moment en Plus

**7th arr.**
**1 rue de Varenne**
**222.23.45**
*Open noon to 7:30 P.M., Sat. noon to 7:00 P.M. Closed Sun.*

More a bookshop than a tea room, this establishment has three large wooden tables surrounded by stands filled with books, magazines and comics. Under the superb antique wooden beams patrons can enjoy snacks, orange or chocolate cake and fruit tartes. The banana-rum is particularly good. Un Moment en Plus is less expensive and much quieter than the other neighborhood cafes.

## Muscade

**1st arr.**
**36 rue de Montpensier**
**297.51.36**
*Open noon to 11:00 P.M., Sun. noon to 7:00 P.M.*

Regardless of the weather, don't miss the opportunity to stroll through the Palais-Royal Gardens. The Muscade entrance is located under the arcades. Indoors, the atmosphere is posh with salmon-pink walls and tablecloths, and a spinach-green rug. The equally appetizing menu offers steak tartare, streaky bacon with lentils, grilled steak at 36F, steak with pepper sauce, and tea with assorted pastries. From May through September, the garden terrace is open.

## Olsson's

**1st arr.**
**26 rue de la Reynie**
**233.03.37**
*Open noon to 10:30 P.M. Closed Sun.*

This new Swedish tea room, which is combined with a restaurant and grocery shop, is easily distinguishable by its turquoise façade. It is a warm, friendly establishment with white lacquered wooden floorboards, a spiral staircase, and green plants at the windows and suspended from the mezzanine. Customers include artist types and passersby who drop in to order delicious anchovies à la Svédoise; marinated salmon with dill; caraway seed cheese with figs; or the Baltic dish, a meal in itself consisting of marinated herring, salmon, shrimp, potato salad and eggs. Olsson's also features marvelous cakes with crème fraiche such as the pepparkaka spice cake and chokladkaka, as well as fruit juice, extra-fresh vegetables and a selection of teas.

## Pandora

**2nd arr.**
**24 passage Choiseul**
**297.56.01**
*Open noon to 7:00 P.M. Closed Sat., Sun.*

This charming little tea room is named after an old Ava Gardner movie. The ladies who come here to sip their tea may not be as gorgeous as la Ava but, then again, their main preoccupation is having a bite to eat. The decor is old-fashioned, with its frosted maroon façade, beige and cinnamon lounge, small lamps with pleated shades, pretty picture frames, cane chairs, old-fashioned plates with fruit and flower motifs, silver-plated cutlery and delicate glassware. Pandora's menu offers delicious tartes made with endive, ham or morels; Baltic herring with cream; cucumbers in yogurt and mint; mixed salads; and a large variety of delicious desserts such as lemon tarte, cheesecake, linzertorte, mincemeat pie and brownies. The two attractive young hostesses are very friendly and efficient.

## Plat du Jour
3rd arr.
**60 rue Rambuteau**
**274.46.33**
*Open noon to 9:30 P.M.*
*Closed Sat., Sun.*

The Plat du Jour serves rabbit chasseur, fricasséed turkey, duck stew, calf's head in sauce gribiche, and aiguillette of beef à la mode, all of which are prepared by a charming Irish woman and consumed in a 1930's decor. Delicious desserts include fruit pies and eggs (à la neige).

## Le Potiron
2nd arr.
**16 rue du Roule**
**233.35.68**
*Open noon to 11:00 P.M.*
*Closed Sun.*

Marie-Françoise Clément has decorated her strange-looking loft located next to les Halles in pumpkin colors. Le Potiron is perfect for light meals or for a full dinner, and the menu changes daily. It includes vegetable tartes and pâtés, white cheese with shallots, lamb tartes with garlic sauce, pork with prunes, chicken in lemon juice. Le Potiron also features monthly exhibits of paintings.

## A Priori-Thé
2nd arr.
**35-37 galerie Vivienne**
**297.48.75**
*Open noon to 7:00 P.M.*
*Closed Sun.*

More English than American, this tea room/restaurant, located in the beautiful Vivienne Gallery, was opened by three American food lovers, Polly, Peggy and Bonnie. In one of the nicest locations in the city, it has beige walls, pinewood seats and tables covered with white damask tablecloths and bouquets of freshly cut or dried flowers. While listening to classical music, patrons may have light meals such as vegetable soup with crackers, salad, delicious spinach or leek tarte, meat loaf, and simple American sandwiches with pâté, tomatoes and cucumbers. The excellent desserts are served with crème fraiche and include apple crumble, nut or fig pie, corn muffins with butter and jam, and brownies, the house specialty. The little French wines have been selected by Steven Spurrier.

## La Route du Thé et de la Soie
3rd arr.
**157 rue Saint-Martin**
**271.37.35**
*Open 11:30 A.M. to 7:00 P.M.*
*Closed Mon., Tues.*

Located on the first floor of a little white house, this intimate tea room faces on one side the gigantic pipes of the Beaubourg Center, and on the other a picturesque alley miraculously saved from the clutches of the bulldozers. Its beautiful decor consists of warm, honey-colored walls, old Chinese photos and rattan furniture. Customers may enjoy a cup of tea along with a delicious homemade cheesecake, chocolate charlotte, nutcake, lemon tarte or scones. The luncheon menu offers soft-boiled farm eggs, vegetable tarte, tarama and blinis, and other selections. The service is efficient, and the prices are reasonable.

## Saint-Louis
4th arr.
**81 rue Saint-Louis-en-l'Ile**
**329.81.52**
*Open noon to 8:00 P.M., Sat. and Sun. noon to 11:00 P.M.*

Located on the Ile Saint-Louis' main street, the Saint-Louis is usually filled with tourists and strollers, rather than "islanders." This rustic tea room offers good, simple dishes such as quiche lorraine, Yorkshire ham with spinach, and many more. In the afternoons a variety of 50 kinds of tea is served with scones, caramel-chocolate cake or sherbet.

## Le Satay
5th arr.
**10 rue**

You almost need a machete to get through a tropical forest of rubber plants and dieffenbachias to find an intimate corner where you can refresh yourself with a delicious

**Saint-Julien-le-Pauvre**
**354.31.33**
*Open 4:00 P.M. to 2:00 A.M.*
*Closed Sun.*

cocktail such as the Bamboo, which is passion fruit, lime and vodka; or a Guépard, which is a combination of grapefruit, gin and curaçao. Whereas men prefer the bar, women tend to gather around the tables to enjoy tea and pastries or a marvelous Berthillon sherbet. Dinner is served from 7:30 P.M. and might include escalope of veal with lemon, poultry or crayfish curry, or other diversified dishes.

## W. H. Smith
**1st arr.**
**248 rue de Rivoli**
**260.37.97**
*Open 10:15 A.M. to 6:00 P.M.*
*Closed Sun.*

The best time to try W. H. Smith is between 3:00 P.M. and 4:00 P.M., after the lunch crowd has gone and before the tea crowd comes storming in. Located above the bookshop, this large, charming tea room, with its low ceilings, soft lighting, ochre stucco walls and dark wood paneling, is nearly deserted between rushes, save for a few quiet couples and an occasional British au pair girl. The best seats are located in the back, where you can see the rue de Rivoli through the small panes of the frosted windows. Your best bet is the Darjeeling tea with a slice of lemon pie, or any of the delicious toasts, muffins, scones or pancakes served with salted butter, jam and golden syrup.

**Tartes et**
**Galettes**
**1st arr.**
**Forum des Halles,**
**3rd level**
**233.79.32**
*Open 10:30 A.M. to 8:00 P.M.*
*Closed Sun.*

The Croissanterie inspired its president, Jean-Luc Bret, to open the Tartes et Galettes tea room. It is sparsely decorated in high-tech style with white tiled floors, white tiled walls with fruit and vegetable motifs, and maroon tiled tables and counters. The establishment is patronized by scores of young people who make their selections, pay the cashier, and walk off into the Forum des Halles or sit down to eat feuilletés with leeks, onions, cheese, mushrooms, ham or chicken, as well as fruit tartes and galettes. Beverages include coffee, hot chocolate, fruit juice and milkshakes.

## La Tchaïka
**6th arr.**
**9 rue de l'Eperon**
**354.47.02**
*Open 11:30 A.M. to 7:00 P.M.*
*Closed Sun., Mon.*

La Tchaika is located in the annex of the Maison du Livre Etranger, a foreign bookshop opened during the 1930s on the peaceful rue de l'Eperon. Its simple, charming decor consists of ten tables with red tablecloths. Specialties include zakouskis, tarama, minced liver, Caspian poached eggs, pirogi, spratz, smoked salmon, pressed caviar, and desserts such as vatrouchka and chocolate cake. Everything here is good and inexpensive, approximately 50F, even with a glass of vodka.

**The Tea**
**Caddy**
**5th arr.**
**14 rue**
**Saint-Julien-le-Pauvre**
**354.15.56**
*Open noon to 7:00 P.M.,*
*Sun. 2:00 P.M. to 7:00 P.M.*

Established by an Englishwoman, Miss Kinklin, in 1929, the Tea Caddy is much like a favorite old tweed jacket you can't bear to go without. For the last fifty years, it has lived a peaceful existence under the Saint-Julien-le-Pauvre belfry. The dark paneled lounge is lit by bracket lamps with parchment shades and amber rays of sunlight that seep in through the tinted glass windows. The chairs are rustic, but the tables are small and a little cramped. The Franglais, food is simply prepared and includes bacon and eggs, mushroom omelets, salads, poached eggs on toast, spinach gratin, salade Niçoise, and other standards. Guests help themselves to the delicious desserts such as fruit tarte, linzertorte, chocolate cake, scones, buns and muffins. Beverages include five varieties of coffee, hot chocolate, fresh orange juice, beer, port and Bordeaux. All in all, an amusing blend of two cultures.

### Toraya
**1st arr.**
**10 rue**
**Saint-Florentin**
**260.13.00**
*Open 10:00 A.M. to 7:00 P.M.*
*Closed Sun.*

Toraya (or tiger), a Japanese tea room/pastry shop, has opened behind the place de la Concorde. Its superb black, gray and white setting features only one ornament, a large ceramic tiger, which is the house emblem. Specialties include traditionally prepared yokans or sweet bean noodles; kuzukiri, transparent noodles made from jellied arrowroot with mitsu, a sweet sauce; and green tea.

### Verlet
**1st arr.**
**256 rue Saint-Honoré**
**260.67.39**
*Open noon to 6:30 P.M.*
*Closed Sat., Sun.*

This excellent coffee-roasting house has a few tables where customers may sample a variety of coffees or teas and order croque-monsieurs, toast, sandwiches, Viennese pastries; and birchermuesli, a Swiss granola. Verlet is a hangout for actors from the nearby Théâtre-Français.

### Willi's
**1st arr.**
**13 rue des**
**Petits-Champs**
**261.05.09**
*Open 11:00 A.M. to 10:00 P.M.,*
*Sat. 11:00 A.M. to 4:00 P.M.*
*Closed Sun.*

Mark Williamson serves a few specialties that are highly recommended by his unusual-looking counter assistant, who hails from Texas. These dishes were designed to complement the bar's selection of 100 labels of wine, some of which are sold by the glass. The best dishes are braised oxtail, Yorkshire ham with seasonal vegetables, stewed chicken, pork loin with fennel, cassoulet, roast beef and leg of lamb. Some may prefer sausages or rabbit pâté in aspic, while others will choose spinach or cheese tarte. And everyone will raise a glass to Dolores, the charming and efficient English waitress.

# Wine Bars

It was some ten years ago that the English made a discovery of historic importance: that a bar serving wine could be chic. "Wine bars," which soon took the land of beer and Scotch by storm, inevitably infiltrated Paris, where men also enjoy tasting a little wine along with their ham and cheese at lunchtime. Now it's up to women to open up their own wine bars. No doubt they will.

## Café de la Nouvelle Mairie

**5th arr.**
**19 rue des Fossés-Saint-Jacques**
**326.80.18**
*Open 10:00 A.M. to 8:00 P.M.*
*Closed Sat., Sun.*

Bernard Pontonier, a man who knows all about the wines produced in his native Touraine, has opened a wine bar suitable for young and old alike. His sparkling establishment brings together blue-collar workers, local students and neighborhood VIPs who appreciate the excellent selection of bottles. Included are amazing white wines from the Lyon region, a perfect Gamay, a remarkable Bourgueil from the cellars of Jean Gambier and many more. Bernard Pontonier also serves a delicious selection of sausages and cheeses. His bar is always packed with a cheery crowd at lunchtime.

## Le Chai de l'Abbaye

**6th arr.**
**26 rue de Buci**
**326.68.26**
*Open daily 7:00 A.M. to 4:00 A.M.*

This nondescript café, which is always jammed with the Saint-Germain clique, features far less interesting wines than those served by its former owner.

## Chez Georges

**6th arr.**
**11 rue des Canettes**
**326.79.15**
*Open noon to 2:00 A.M.*
*Closed Sun., Mon.*

This bistro is so popular with Americans, Japanese and other foreigners, that in the evenings you'll hardly ever hear French spoken within its walls. During the daytime, however, it is always teeming with local shop attendants and students from the nearby university who come to sample vintages, which are limited to the Côtes-du-Rhône, Côtes-de-Provence and Beaujolais. Chez Georges so much resembles the classic French bistro, we often wonder why it hasn't been classified as a national landmark. Don't forget to drop in on the cabaret downstairs.

## Chez Serge

**93400 Saint-Ouen—**
**7 blvd. Jean-Jaurès**
**254.06.42**
*Open 7:00 A.M. to 9:00 P.M.*
*Closed Sun.*

This typically suburban bistro is the ideal spot to enjoy a large sandwich and a glass of Morgon. Owner Serge Cancé who was awarded the Meilleur Pot 1976, selects the barrels of Beaujolais himself. His other wines include Sauternes, Savennières and Santenays, as well as a Champagne produced by Legras. Many of these wines may be bought to go. M. Cancé also has a pleasant restaurant of the same name in the 18th arrondissement.

## La Clairière

**9th arr.**
**43 rue Saint-Lazare**
**874.32.94**
*Open 7:00 A.M. to 8:00 P.M.*
*Closed Sat., Sun.*

Robert and Micheline Terret have abandoned their Café Royal at the place des Vosges and have opened La Clairière in the murkier corner of the rue Taitbout. This most recent addition to Parisian wine bars offers a rather cursory selection of house Beaujolais, Brouilly 1979, Juliénas and primeurs. The Beaujolais Villages appears to be the best bet, particularly for the price (3.50F per glass). There are as well a good white Sancerre at 5.50F, a pleasant Côtes-du-Rhône and a vigorous Alsatian Edelzwicker, which is sold by the carafe. Nor to mention a good Muscadet at 21F per half-liter and an estimable Tavel at 28F. A few snacks such as hot or cold sausages, ham, kid and Poilâne bread are also served.

## La Cloche des Halles

**1st arr.**
**28 rue Coquillière**
**236.93.89**
*Open until 10:00 P.M. Closed Sun.*

The bronze bell was once used to signal the closing time of les Halles, the vast produce market that was once located in the center of town. The Cloche's former owner, Gérard Rougier, who was awarded the Meilleur Pot 1973, has handed the business over to Serge Lesage, his old pal and assistant. Lesage has enlarged it to accommodate the increasing number of customers who come here to sample his superb white or rosé Sancerres at 4F per glass, Morgons, Côtes-de-Brouilly and many others. La Cloche also offers delicious baked ham, as well as a decent chicken liver pâté and homemade pastries.

## La Dame Jeanne

**17th arr.**
**69 rue des Dames**
**387.06.94**
*Open noon to 10:00 P.M.*
*Closed Sat., Sun.*

La Dame Jeanne, owned since May 1980 by Christian Flacelière and Michael Smith, serves vintage wines by the glass, thanks to a Bordeaux oenologist who devised an ingenious process for preserving uncorked wine by introducing a small dose of nitrogen into open bottles. La Dame Jeanne, a onetime butcher shop, offers its patrons 35 local and vintage wines including Chateau-Sinard 1973 at 10F, Labégorce-Zédé 1976 at 11F, Yquem 1947 at 110F, Latour 1961 at 130F, a Trapet Chambertin 1973 and a Richebourg 1954. The wine bar has twenty seats grouped around individual tables where guests may eat ham from Lyon and the Cotentin area, mixed salads, delicious cheeses and a daily special, such as guinea fowl with cabbage and duck with preserved turnips. With the exception of vintage wines, bottles may be purchased to go.

## L'Ecluse

**6th arr.**
**15 quai des Grands-Augustins**
**663.58.74**
**8th arr.**
**64 rue Francois-Ier**
**359.77.09**
*Open 11:00 A.M. to 2:00 A.M.*
*Closed Sun.*

Georges Bardawil now has a wine bar as well as his well-known Left Bank bistro. The old-fashioned wine cellar decor of l'Ecluse, as well as its clientele, is roughly the same as that of the bistro. The same is true for his intelligent selection of Bordeaux, from little known châteaux to the greatest vintage wines, all of which may be tasted by the bottle, carafe or glass. We recommend you try his admirable Cheval Blanc, Ducru-Beaucaillou and Haut-Batailley, as well as a substantial snack such as smoked ham, goose rillettes, and crottin Chavignol cheese. After a visit to l'Ecluse, we guarantee you will attain the nirvana of a true lover of Bordeaux.

## Au Grand Comptoir

**1st arr.**
**4 rue Pierre-Lescot**
**233.56.30**
*Open noon to 10:30 P.M.*
*Closed Sat., Sun.*

All that's left of les Halles is the fence surrounding the Forum. Yet, at the Grand Comptoir, you'll still find the friezes, moldings, fauns, caryatids, paneling and polished shields that were once characteristic of les Halles. This old bistro offers excellent Beaujolais and very decent Sancerres and Bordeaux that are served on a long counter by men clad in white wearing bow ties. You may also eat at a table in the restaurant that offers one or two traditional meals that are modestly priced. The patronne often offers a drink on the house to regular clients.

253

## Ma Bourgogne

4th arr.
**19 place des Vosges**
**278.44.64**
*Open until 11:00 P.M. (until
1:00 A.M. in summer).*

The redoubtable inspector Maigret, Georges Simenon's food-loving detective, used to spend a few pages surveying the customers in this charming bistro. He would have been better off sampling the Morgon and Fleurie wines served by this fashionable establishment located under the arcades of the place des Vosges. Ma Bourgogne offers good sausages from Aveyron, the best croque-monsieurs in Paris.

## Jacques Mélac

11th arr.
**42 rue Léon-Frot**
**370.59.27**
*Open 8:30 A.M. to 8:00 P.M., Tues.
to 10:00 P.M. Closed Sun.*

This friendly bistro, with geranium-filled windows, is the port of call for local cabinetmakers. Its owner, a huge young man from Aveyron with a Gallic moustache, offers agreeable estate-produced wines such as Crozes-Hermitage, Gigondas, Fleurie, Côtes-de-Bourg, Saint-Joseph and Chinon, which he buys in barrel, bottles himself, and serves by the glass at 2.60-4.20F. At the bistro counter and a few tables, you will be served excellent Aveyron ham with Poilâne bread for 16F, delicious cheeses such as Saint-Nectaire, and a perfect daily special that may include tripe, streaky bacon with lentils, Lyons sausages and large sausages from Aveyron.

## Aux Négociants (Tricoche)

18th arr.
**27 rue Lambert**
**606.15.11**
*Open 7:00 A.M. to midnight.
Closed Sat., Sun.*

This charming bistro on the outskirts of Montmartre attracts postmen, local artisans and taxi drivers who come here to discuss (inexhaustibly) the Sauvignon and world politics. The Tricoches, who are the nicest café owners in Paris, enjoy serving Burgundies and Bourgueils, along with their delicious country sausages and herb omelets which are simply prepared and inexpensively priced.

## Le Père Tranquille

14th arr.
**30 ave du Maine**
**222.88.12**
*Open 9:00 A.M. to 8:00 P.M.
Closed Sun., Mon.*

The irregular configuration of the avenue du Maine has discouraged a great number of potential clients from entering Jean Nouyrigat's bistro. Those who do walk in are graciously offered a selection of delicious Gamays, Saumurs, Champignys and Muscadets, and then are thoroughly insulted and thrown out of the bistro for no reason whatsoever. Every once in a while, however, M. Nouyrigat will welcome an unfamiliar face and behave like a charming and sensitive host, offering the newcomer a table in his attractive terrace, where they both will sit down and enjoy excellent sausages, delicious cheeses, homemade pâtés and ineffable calf's head.

## Petit Bacchus

6th arr.
**13 rue du
Cherche-Midi**
**544.01.07**

This tiny bistro, across the street from the Poilâne bakery, has all the attributes of a cosy little tea room. At the minuscule counter, Jean-Marie Picard serves wines produced by his friends. We recommend that you accompany them with his dish from Auvergne that consists of ham, rillettes and dried sausage, with a Cantal or goat cheese (60F). Though no food is served on Saturdays, the shop does sell wine.

## *Le Petitou*

**1st arr.**
**17 place Dauphine**
**354.45.95**
*Open noon to 8:30 P.M.*
*Closed Sat.*

Raymonde Martin delights in serving her customers Burgundy, Bordeaux, Cahors, Morgon and Sauvignon wines. Her clientele consists chiefly of public servants from the nearby Ministry of Justice, as well as a few actors and gastronomes who arrive here at dusk. Featured dishes include sausages, cheese crêpes, and pear or apple tartes. Le Petitou has a tiny terrace on what is considered the oldest and most beautiful square in Paris.

## *Le Rallye*

**14th arr.**
**6 rue Daguerre**
**322.57.05**
*Open 9:30 A.M. to 8:30 P.M.*
*Closed Sun., Mon.*

Over the years, Bernard Péret has been credited with serving the city's most consistent and best selection of Beaujolais nouveau. A native of Saint-Urcize, he is also well versed in Pouillys, Sancerres and Sauvignons. He serves his wines at the counter or out on the terrace, along with his marvelous Vivarais sausages and slices of Poilâne bread. His clientele consists of famous painters, journalists, writers, bums and merchants who come in off the exceedingly noisy street. Le Rallye also features a take-out counter.

## *La Royale*

**14th arr.**
**80 rue de**
**l'Amiral-Mouchez**
**588.38.09**
*Open 7:00 A.M. to 8:30 P.M.*
*Closed Sun.*

Roger, a cousin of Bernard Péret (see above), is well known among connoisseurs for his Loire Valley wines for which he was awarded the highly coveted Meilleur Pot 1977. Rabelais, who is invoked at each of these annual ceremonies, could hardly hope to find better wines than those offered at La Royale, which include a Chinon directly brought in from M. Aygalenq's native vineyards, a Vouvray which he appropriately describes as a "taffeta wine" and a perfectly smooth Saumur. These wines are served with slices of Poilâne bread or with a daily special such as sautéed veal.

## *Sancerre*

**7th arr.**
**22 ave. Rapp**
**551.75.91**
*Open 8:00 A.M. to 9:00 P.M., Sat. to 4:00 P.M. Closed Sun.*

Many of this peaceful cafe's steady customers work at three television networks in the nearby Cognac-Jay Studios. Consequently, M. Guillaume has traded in his black-and-white TV for one in color. As indicated by its name, this bistro is known for its Sancerre, and its incomparable nectar, both of which are produced in La Moussière by the owner's predecessor, M. Mellot. The café Sancerre also serves a fresh Chavignol crottin cheese, smoked ham or andouillette.

## *Taverne Henri IV*

**1st arr.**
**13 place du Pont-Neuf**
**354.27.90**
*Open until 3:00 P.M. Closed Sun.*

This former tobacco shop now offers red, white and rosé wines to the judges and police commissioners who drop in from the Palais de Justice and local police station. The bistro is ornamented with a statue of Henri IV and well stocked with Beaujolais, Quart-de-Chaume, Lyon, Jurançon and marvelous Burgundy wines that Robert Cointepas (a 30-year veteran of his business) keeps lovingly in his two-tiered Louis XIII cellars. The tavern features several tables where excellent sausages are served with Poilâne bread. Due to this bistro's popularity, tables are reserved in advance.

## Le Val d'Or

**8th arr.**
**28 ave.**
**Franklin-Roosevelt**
**359.95.81**
*Open 8:00 A.M. to 9:00 P.M.*
*Closed Sun.*

It's been a few years since Gérard Rongier, the affable former owner of the Cloche des Halles, opened this unassuming bistro in this elegant quarter. Among his fine selections of wines, we recommend the delicate Côtes-de-Brouilly at 4F per glass, the respectable Côtes-du-Rhône, and a few lovely Sancerres and Beaujolais. The Côte-de-Nuits 1974 stands out among three great Burgundies and is sold for slightly under 100F per bottle. Although featured dishes have included only a baked ham and a few sausages, daily specials are planned in order to entice the parishioners from the Saint-Philippe church as well as workers from the Champs-Elysées.

## Willi's

**1st arr.**
**13 rue des**
**Petits-Champs**
**261.05.09**
*Open daily 11:00 A.M. to*
*10:00 P.M., Sat. to 4:00 P.M.*
*Closed Sun.*

Born 27 years ago in the shadow of Buckingham Palace, Mark Williamson spent his adolescence in South African vineyards before returning to London to work in the wine cellars of the Connaught Hotel. He then came to Paris where he met his compatriot, Steven Spurrier, who had spent three years in France learning all about wine. And presto! Mark Williamson took over a small nightclub and turned it into a daytime wine bar which is now amply stocked with 99 French wines, not including aperitifs. Naturally, all his wines have been selected by Spurrier and his assistant, Legrand, and include six Côtes-de-Beaune, four Côtes-de-Nuits, 28 Bordeaux, and 20 or so Côtes-du-Rhône. Apart from these bottled wines, Willi's offers a weekly selection of wine by the glass that includes a likeable Jaudeau Muscadet at 7F, a smooth Jurançon at 11F, plus a few Graves such as a Château-Fieuzal 1979 at 13F, and a Château-Giscours Margaux at 16F. To complement their wines, Willi's offers a few daily specials such as oxtail, various sausages, chicken-in-the-pot, and cassoulet, all priced at 30F.

# THE NIGHTLIFE

# THE
# NIGHTLIFE

## STREET SCENES

**S**everal dozen organizations share the thankless task of rescuing the masses of people eager for a taste of our capital's famous nightlife from the boredom of dismal hotel evenings.

One "Enchantment" tour (it was thrust upon us by an agency pursuing success) starts with an unusual assignation: Please meet at nine-thirty sharp, ticket in hand, beneath the fleur-de-lis banner which Joan of Arc flourishes in the middle of place des Pyramides. Every night the Saint, riveted to her pedestal, contemplates more than forty buses taking off for the "hot" streets. For our part, we chose the tour which offered to regale us consecutively with the Petit Balcon, Moulin Rouge and Crescendo. Two Mexican ladies, five Englishwomen, four German women, two indefinable couples and a lone gentlemen, sitting somewhat sheepishly in the back, have already gotten into the bus.

Our guide in turn enters the bus. He's a prepossessing fellow, hardly at all embarrassed by the language barrier. He comes up to fire a cordial, polyglot greeting at each of us and to check our tickets. Then, mike in hand, he makes more or less the following speech, as the joyous convoy starts rolling:

"Good evening, ladies and gentlemen. Allow me to introduce us: our driver, Jacques A., and myself, Jacques B. I wish you an excellent evening. We're going to start off with a cabaret that is very typical of an old section of Paris, the Bastille. It's the Petit Balcon, where you'll see the famous dancing apaches, gigolos and gigolettes. You'll be able to sample a glass of sparkling wine: the Champagne is reserved for our other stops. . . ."

The Petit Balcon's sparkling wine is a rare blend. It leaves deep streaks on the jelly glasses, which barely manage to contain its sulphurous effervescence, and our stomachs remember it long after the evening was over. Now then, however, that's not the real spectacle. This is to be seen, first of all, in that famous passageway where every bus in the world seems to be keeping an appointment. Lined up one after another on the sidewalk, every half-hour they discharge a flood of candidates for the wine, the white wooden tables, sticky benches and the exhibition put on by half a dozen seedy-looking hoods in the pay of the folklore syndicate. The show doesn't last long. A few coarse dances, a lady bonecrusher leading a fat, dumfounded Helvetian onto the dance floor and inviting him to undo her blouse. A pretense at a skit is made amid the general hilarity and it's over, finished; you dodge the apache, and make a dash for the bus . . .

"Did you like apaches, ladies? . . . ah! ah! And now . . . ."

At the Moulin Rouge it's another story. What a setting! This is the real Paris! You are squeezed in at a table for eight next to the dance floor, completely off to one side. You can see next to nothing, but the ruffles fan your cheeks pleasantly each time they go by and you barely avoid being knocked over by all those lovely girls, driven by the lascivious music to shake their generous bosoms beneath our noses, as they head back on stage from the wings.

The Champagne is on the table: two bottles for the eight of us. Which is correct, as far as quantity goes. Three thousand pairs of eyes from the capacity audience converge on the hat of a magician who is conjuring baby chicks out of a spectator's trousers. Which is correct, as far as quality goes. Unfortunately, we must be the only French people astray at the Moulin Rouge, and we miss the better part of the remarks uttered in American from the stage in front of the musicians. Something tells us we didn't miss much. The sparkling wine from the Petit Balcon is furiously upsetting our usual serene objectivity. Be that as it may, the Moulin Rouge really puts on one swell show and at the sumptuous finale, in which a swarm of chorus girls descends from the ceiling in a balloon, releasing big red balloons upon bald heads and white shoulders, our enthusiasm knows no bounds.

We move on to other pleasures.

"You like Moulin Rouge, ladies? . . . ah! ah!"

The bus rolls silently down toward the Seine. Our next and last stop is the Crescendo.

"You've seen the apaches, you've seen the Moulin Rouge and its splendors, but you can't end this Parisian night without sampling the atmosphere of a striptease. . . ."

A few couples are dancing between the tables in the half-light of this cellar filled with blaring music. A velvety American voice calls for silence and whispers magic words into a mike: "And now, the artless, the troubling, the daring, the perverse . . . Nadia Nora! The little bride of your dreams."

The curtain does indeed open on an enchanting young bride in her white gown and train, who immediately sets to work raising our temperatures and throwing her veils one by one onto a fourposter, instantly put to the test with a few solitary, innocent revels. Two other numbers of the same ilk bring our visit to a close, and we regain the bus with a ration of thrills and a store of images for cold winter nights.

Yessir, you can really have a ball in Paris."

Cityrama, 3 place des Pyramides, (tel. 260.30.14). "Paris By Night": (Five options: from 380F to 470F).

# Ballrooms

The following establishments are all living museums, poetic temples in violet and pink, lined with neon and crystal balls. Dance halls that perpetuate a tradition, a past which is thick with Brylcreem and steeped in accordion music. They are the last places in Paris where true dance palace lovers can still have some fun.

## Le Balajo

**11th arr.**
**9 rue de Lappe**
**700.07.87**

*Open afternoons 3:00 P.M. to 7:30 P.M., evenings 9:30 P.M. to 1:00 A.M., Fri. to 2:00 A.M. Sat. ballroom dancing 10:00 P.M. to 4:30 A.M. Tues. afternoon dancing with accordion.*

Emerging like a beam of light from the past, Balajo's enormous neon sign pierces the now dreary nights of the rue de Lappe, where in happier times couples used to waltz amid the aroma of cabbage soup. This old, huge, glorious tango palace has escaped demolition by attracting every single day busloads of foreign tourists bent on discovering the Parisian underworld's most awesome hideouts. At the Balajo, they are rarely disappointed. Casque d'Or and his Pomaded gang are always here, dressed in impeccable costumes. Whistling, with their hands in their pockets, they swagger up and down the wooden planks, eye some *choucroute,* and toss her a carnation. But the moll is most likely hunched over her mint julep and engaged in a tête-à-tête with her companion in one of Bajalo's boxes ornamented with pre-World War I photos of wrestlers. In the balcony decorated with artificial flowers, the silver-moustached musicians strike up a heartrending tango, and the crowd downstairs bursts into applause. The first drink here is 30F.

## La Boule Rouge

**11th arr.**
**8 rue de Lappe**

Since the time it was called the Family Ballroom, nothing has really changed here. One can still hear "Bleus tes yeux, bleu mon amour" (Your Eyes Are Blue, and So Is My Heart), a tune once sung by Mimi Souris, who, according to rumors, is now selling sewing kits in the 18th arrondissement. La Boule Rouge is lively, particularly on certain nights, and highly nostalgic for the elderly lovers of the rue de Lappe who miss the gradual disappearance of the smell of cabbage soup and the strains of accordion music wafting through the streets.

## Chez Gégène

**94340**
**Joinville-le-Pont**
**162 bis quai de Polangis**
**883.29.43**

*Open evenings until midnight, April thru October, Sat. 9:00 P.M. to 2:00 A.M., Sun. 3:00 P.M. to 7:00 P.M.*

Gégène brilliantly evokes Joinville's good old days in this traditional dance hall, with its mint juleps, mechanical piano, "fleabox" and 1850 accordion music. Hand the accordionist 25F, and you're all set to sweat one out. Just be careful not to step on lady's toes, for her muscle-bound companion with the moustache and sideburns may not approve. The meals are not the best, no matter how well the accordionist plays.

## Au Tango

**3rd arr.**
**11-13 rue Au-Maire**
**272.17.78**
*Open daily 2:30 P.M. to 6:30 P.M.,*
*Fri., Sat. 9:00 P.M. to 2:00 A.M.*
*Reduced rates for ladies.*

We've included this daytime establishment (excluding Saturday nights) in the "nightlife" section of this book because daylight can barely get in through its painted little windowpanes. Its decor will send you back to the year 1906, when the tango first appeared in Paris. Its steady customers include Marais artisans with thin moustaches and polka-dot shirts; the Brylcream set, with thick gold rings and trifocal glasses; grinning lover-boys with impeccable teeth; big mamas clad in violent silks; and perfumed pensioners, who have all been coming here for the last 30 years to dance a tango with friends. The best and cheapest setting in Paris.

# *Cabarets*

## Caveau de la Bolée

**6th arr.**
**25 rue de l'Hirondelle**
**354.62.20**
*Open nightly from 9:00 P.M.*
*Showtime: 10:45 P.M.*

What was once a wine cellar for Saint-Germain-des-Prés monks is now a club known for its Gallic songs and med-school humor, a ritual largely attributed to singer Aristide Bruant. Nothing could be more innocent, if you were to consider the laughs generated by Baudelaire, Verlaine and Appollinaire, who once performed here.

## Le Caveau des Oubliettes

**5th arr.**
**11 rue Saint-Julien-le-Pauvre**
**354.94.97**
*Open nightly 9:00 P.M. to 2:00 A.M.*

Within the dungeons of the former Petit-Châtelet prison, wandering, gregarious Bavarians sing old French songs designed to make you drink, laugh and weep. The club is filled with medieval wood paneling and chastity belts, and you are waited on by transvestite troubadors. The Caveau des Oubliettes has been a mainstay of Parisian snobbery for the past 60 years.

## Crazy Horse Saloon

**8th arr.**
**12 ave. George-V**
**723.32.32**
*Open nightly 8:00 P.M. to 2:30 A.M.*
*Showtimes at 9:00 P.M. and*
*11:00 P.M., Fri., Sat. 8:20 P.M.,*
*10:30 P.M., 12:50 A.M.*

The show begins with sixteen gorgeous girls in black leather boots and sequined caps informing you that the "Crazy Horse is beautiful." These abstract bodies, outlined with miraculous lighting and costumed in surrealistically chaste nudity, belong to girls with bizarre names such as Ivy Speculation, Baba Moleskine and Lena Sapajou. This show is as puritanical as they come, and 30 years after it premiered, the Crazy Horse show remains faithful to its "intellectual" naughtiness which prevents it from growing old. There's no doubt that Alain Bernardin has a genius for making striptease into a distinguished middle-class form of entertainment. Thus, the Crazy Horse show is the exact opposite of your typical Parisian striptease. The girls are in effect dressed up by a combination of lighting, music and ingenious choreography. Everything is beautiful, well rehearsed and concise, yet eroticism is wholly lacking. The proof is to be found in the disappointed half-smiles of the audience at the end of the show. What we really object to is that no matter how many times Bernardin replaces his girls, changes the lighting cues or comes up with new and ingenious tricks, we are always left with the impression of having seen the same show, which after all, isn't *that* important since the spectators are rarely the same. Each show costs 250F, excluding service, and entitles customers to two drinks.

## Folies-Bergère
**9th arr.**
**32 rue Richer**
**246.77.11**
*Open from 8:30 P.M. Closed Mon.*

This show is alive and well and features 40 different acts. The fact that it is financially viable is important, for the Folies has spent hundreds of millions of francs to keep it from going under like many other ostrich-plumed bastions of the past, such as Mayol and the Casino de Paris. The Folies-Bergère once featured Mistinguett, Colette, Maurice Chevalier and Josephine Baker. Today you'll see Norma Duval, Bernard Bruce, Nicky Bell and other great talents. Although times have changed, a good time is still to be had by all. Oh, you have to reserve your seats fourteen days in advance.

## Au Lapin Agile
**18th arr.**
**22 rue des Saules**
**606.85.87**
*Open 9:00 P.M. to 2:00 A.M. Closed Mon.*

At the bottom of the butte Montmartre, you'll see a fenced pavilion covered with ivy. This is the first and last of the great Parisian sing-along cabarets. A fifteen-minute wait while the performer winds up his act is enough time to inspect the walls hung with polished copperware and earthenware bowls and knicknacks, all eloquent testimonies to the Lapin's nineteenth-century past. The excellent pianist, Yves Robrecht, the ribald Clothilde, Yves Mathieu, and the eccentric Jean-Pierre Bourdeaux make the Lapin the cherished institution it is and has been since the late nineteenth century. The show is moving, well presented, funny without being coarse, and Gallic without being vulgar. With an inexpensively priced glass of kirsch, nothing should prevent you from spending five hours on an old wooden stool in the noisy setting of a country wedding. Drinks are from 42F.

## Lido
**8th arr.**
**116 bis**
**Champs-Elysées**
**563.11.61**
*Open for dinner/dancing 8:00 P.M. Showtimes: 10:30 P.M., 12:30 A.M.*

At the Lido, past and present shows are one and the same thing, which is to say they are always marvelous, impeccable, diabolically controlled, lavishly tricky and artificially dazzling. Who cares if there are busloads of Japanese tourists, soccer team members and auto dealers in the room? After all, it is dimly lit. Besides, there are also bare-breasted girls appearing out of the ceiling, helicopters battling one another among the stars, typhoons devastating the stage in a stream of foam, stage areas vanishing underground, and dolphins cavorting in a pool. Sets are forever going up and down, turning around, and vanishing in the most elaborate mechanized stage in the world. Then why is it that some people are bored by it all? Because many of these sets are so overdone and infinitely cretinous that many spectators grow instantly tired of seeing them. Thank heaven there are a lot of absolutely perfect traditional numbers performed by jugglers, illusionists, contortionists and acrobats. Only the Lido can offer you that.

## Moulin Rouge

**18th arr.**
**82 blvd. de Clichy**
**606.00.19**
*Open nightly. Dinner at 8:30 P.M., showtimes at 10:00 P.M., midnight.*

The Moulin Rouge is the Lido's outlet in Pigalle. The management is the same, the food is the same, and so are the busloads of tourists. The amount of ostrich feathers is the same, as is the quality of the shows, and the Doris girls' bosoms are every centimeter the equal of those of their Bluebell cousins. Yet the Moulin Rouge is probably the best address of its kind in Paris, if not the world. Since it isn't equipped with the same stunning machinery as the Lido, it features revues that are beautifully choreographed and designed. The memories of Valentin le Désossé, La Goulue, and a crippled genius named Toulouse-Lautrec are duly evoked during the finale when the cast performs a frenetic French cancan that is imitated elsewhere but never equaled.

## Peanuts

**10th arr.**
**51 rue**
**Lucien-Sampaix**
**255.34.22**
*Open 9:00 P.M. to 2:00 A.M. Closed Sun., Mon.*

After touring the United States for seventeen years, Varel and Bailly, two music hall survivors of the postwar period, decided to revamp this former boathouse alongside the Saint-Martin Canal. At night, the youthful enthusiasm is so infectious that people forget to eat their rabbit in mustard sauce and broiled ham with pineapple in order to dance the "best tango in the world" with famous guests. There really isn't any time here to get nostalgic, as the entertainment is excellent and contemporary. Topical costume events are constantly being organized during the evenings, and the winner is awarded with his or her weight in peanuts.

# Discos

## L' Apocalypse

**8th arr.**
**40 rue du Colisée**
**225.11.68**
*Open nightly 10:00 P.M. to 8:00 A.M.*

There's no need to feel apprehensive about the name, for no nuclear catastrophe is about to take place in this disco. Patrick and Graziella Leroy manage this large club whose customers include all kinds of big spenders who usually come here for a nightcap after their nightly rounds at the Keur Samba, the "78," Régine's and the Elysées Matignon, which are all located on the same block.

## Les Bains-Douches

**2nd arr.**
**7 rue du Bourg-l'Abbé**

The old Bains-Douches, or public baths recalled by Proust, is ornamented with a superb 1900 façade and graced by two nymphal torchbearers. There's hardly any point in emphasizing that two years ago this basement

**887.34.40**
*Open 8:30 P.M. to 2:00 A.M. Closed Mon.*

disco was a hangout for branchés, the in crowd. This term, which is now old hat, was used by a young, self-proclaimed underground elite composed of rock musicians and petty socialites whose preoccupations were to single out the squares from the hips in discos such as this one. Of course, everybody wanted to be hip or in to get past the club's watchdog. The criterion was sartorial—someone in drag had a better chance of getting in than a person with a famous name. And, once inside, he would be totally discredited if he hadn't met "so and so." Today, the Bains-Douches is definitely out, and the privilege of getting in belongs to the Palace's Le Privilège club. The Bains-Douches' doors are now wide open to all young people who come here looking for what no longer exists. Nonetheless, the music is resolutely in and well chosen.

## L'Écume des Nuits
**17th arr.**
**1 blvd.**
**Gouvion-Saint-Cyr**
**758.12.30**
*Open nightly from 10:30 P.M.*

Since its reopening, L'Écume des Nuits has managed to stay at the top of the new wave of dancing establishments. Its elegant, fantastic decor, consists of an entirely black-lacquered room reflecting from all angles a gigantic Greek mask with shiny eyes, and a dance floor lit up like an airport landing strip on which a specially equipped DJ's booth creates extraordinary special effects. Those who find the volume too loud can go to an upper tier protected by a glass partition where they will find visiting Near and Far Easterners, chic Parisians, and other beautiful people. L'Écume des Nuits provides inexpensive drinks and courteous service to its chic clientele.

## L'Eléphant Blanc (Club Saint-Hilaire)
**6th arr.**
**24 rue Vavin**
**326.86.38**
*Open 10:30 P.M. to 6:00 A.M. Closed Mon.*

During the '60s, this place was well known for its nightlife. Today, it is a quiet, decent and somewhat exclusive disco, patronized by very proper people. Its main attraction, however, is its lovely dining room/terrace where, on a clear night, patrons may have an excellent meal under the stars in the heart of Montparnasse.

## Keur Samba
**8th arr.**
**79 rue de La Boétie**
**359.03.10**
*Open daily 11:00 P.M. to dawn.*

This is a bastion for those who refuse to go to bed. When all other clubs begin to close, Keur Samba begins to wake up. When the garbage collectors start their rounds, the dance floor is throbbing, Champagne bottles are being noisily uncorked, and night owls are snuggling up against one another in the black-upholstered foyer. Customers include diplomats, dancers, cover girls, stockbrokers, actors and singers (Serge Gainsbourg is always here), dashing young men, sharks, sheep, wolves, chicks, foxes, crazies, North Africans and American tourists. No one really cares about the disappointing exotic decor—the beautiful people are far more interesting. The owner, an austere-looking man whose name is Kane, will carefully look you over at the door. Upon arrival, you will be handed over to his cheerful manager-host, Touré. The house lights are turned up at 9:00 A.M., party is over.

## *Martine's*
**16th arr.**
**Le Pavillon Royal,**
**bois de Boulogne,**
**route de Suresnes**
**500.51.00**
*Open 9:00 P.M. to dawn.*

This is the only club located in the Bois de Boulogne. Sam Bernett's place, formerly named Samantha, is open to the selected few who reside on Neuilly's and la Muette's best avenues. The clientele is somewhat young and always properly, if not elegantly, clad. Once in a while someone like Catherine Deneuve will pop in for a drink. Martine's concept of opening an all-night restaurant serving good and inexpensive food has been successful.

## *Midnight Express*
**92800 Puteaux**
**Les Quatre Temps,**
**La Défense**
**773.54.32**
*Open Mon., Tues., Thurs., Fri. 10:00 P.M. to dawn, Wed., Sat., Sun. 3:00 P.M. to dawn.*

Midnight Express is named after the highly successful film about drug dealing and Turkish prisons. The club, however, has nothing to do with drugs, judging by the fresh and healthy faces of its clientele. The club's entrance is linked to the dance floor by a long neon-lit passageway. The decor is futuristic, and the layout ingeniously arranged on multiple tiers surrounding the dance area. The lighting system is truly extravagant, consisting of sparkling wire netting, stroboscopes synchronized to the beat of the music, and rotating mirrored balls that cast hundreds of patterns onto the dance floor where several roller skaters employed by the club attempt to stimulate a somewhat intimidated public. Free parking is featured at the place de la Patinoire.

## *Le Palace*
**9th arr.**
**8 faubourg**
**Montmartre**
**246.10.87**
*Open from 10:30 P.M. Closed Mon., Tues.*

Many people envy Fabrice Emaer's staying power. After all, three years is a long time for a club to be considered the Empire of the Night. Indeed, considering the huge rock concerts, the tea-dances, afternoon roller skating events, cultural evenings and public tattoo sessions, not only does the Palace have staying power, it has become a permanent fixture. There is a possibility that the nights spent in this huge cauldron are less wild than they used to be, but this remains to be proven. True, the beautiful young men wrapped in fur pelts; the tall young women, naked but for their black turbans; and the sturdy tatooed men with sunglasses, their hair parted in the middle, all seem rather passé. The Palace is worth seeing for its hugeness, extravagant sound system and technical marvels. Two thousand people a night come here to dance, which shows that Emaer must be doing something right.

## *Le "78"*
**8th arr.**
**78 Champs-Élysées**
**359.09.99**
*Open 11:00 P.M. to dawn. Closed Sun.*

Ricardo Anaral's rich experience, stemming from his past ownership of the Papagayo and Crocodilus de Rio nightclubs, has prompted the Brazilian to set up a "super-cool" night spot in what was formerly the gaudy Venetian-kitsch styled Lido. Rather than imitating New York's Studio 54, Amaral has concentrated on making his club a more popular and commercial success. If you were to walk in and befriend the club's three managers, Patrice Calmettes, Michel Garland and Paolo Pilla, you'd be ushered to a table in the "habitué's corner," where you're guaranteed to be seen. In this club a bottle of Champagne costs 500F. The 80F admission entitles customers to one drink.

# Gay Clubs

The addresses listed below are of a peculiar nature. We have included them because, despite your possible prejudices, homosexuals can be very talented. What's more, in these changing times, "gaydom" is now officially recognized. Thus, there is nothing wrong with being gay. And gay establishments, all professionally run, are often unique, amusing and wild.

### L'Ange Bleu
**15th arr.**
**50 blvd. Pasteur**
**322.04.78**
*Open 11:00 P.M. to dawn. Closed Sun.*

Aldo is always at his counter, equipped with a closed-circuit video monitor that allows him to see who is at the door. L'Ange Bleu (The Blue Angel) isn't open to everyone, and only a few gays from good backgrounds, palefaced eccentrics returning from the bois de Boulogne, and silly drag queens will be allowed to enter this cozily decorated bar. With its ten years of uninterrupted business, L'Ange Bleu remains *the* spot for refugees of the night.

### Chez Moune
**9th arr.**
**54 rue Pigalle**
**526.64.64**
*Open nightly 10:00 P.M. to 6:00 A.M.*

The Mounies who run this "chiefly feminine cabaret" will soon have to acknowledge publicly their difficulties in recruiting personnel. The conservative three-piece suits worn by their staff are no longer in vogue among women who prefer women. Chez Moune's main attraction is an international striptease.

### Katmandou
**6th arr.**
**21 rue du**
**Vieux-Colombier**
**548.12.96**
*Open nightly 11:00 P.M. to dawn.*

After having written *Les femmes préfèrent les femmes* and other lesbian tracts, Elula Perrin, an intelligent, funny woman, is currently preparing a novel that will most probably be about women. The half-French, half-Vietnamese woman, who in these books confesses her faith in Sapphos with both gentleness and candor, informs us that she went to school at the Convent des Oiseaux, taught geography at a university and did research for an institute of statistics. Her principal occupation today, along with her associate, Aimée, is running a popular club filled with lovely ladies. The Katmandou is an attractively modern club where women do not sport moustaches and flats like the amazons at Moune's or Le Monocle's. Elula doesn't mind at all conversing with men; therefore, they are always welcome, accompanied by their wives, of course. Providing you get through the door, which is attended by an austere woman named Maryan—we urge men to keep their cool.

### Michou
**18th arr.**
**80 rue des Martyrs**
**606.16.04**
*Open from 9:00 P.M. Closed Mon.*

Michou and his lads have long abandoned their wings and inflatable breasts and now concentrate on more "serious" forms of entertainment. The shows are now well presented, good-natured and often accompanied by amusing songs, composed by Michou and interpreted by his ensemble. A good time is to be had by all.

## Le Monocle
**15th arr.**
**60 blvd.**
**Edgard-Quinet**
**320.89.55**
*Open nightly 11:00 P.M. to 6:00 A.M.*

Le Monocle is patronized by women of a certain age who come to see the striptease and listen to the all-female orchestra. The club created a scandal when it first opened 50 years ago, yet today it appears to be a bit passé.

## Le Sept
**1st arr.**
**7 rue Sainte-Anne**
**296.47.05**
*Open nightly 9:00 P.M. to dawn.*

The upper crust of the gay establishment, wildly elegant and sophisticated, love to be seen accompanied by pretty laughing boys and quivering courtesans in the tinted mirrors of Le Sept's black-lacquered restaurant. The exquisitely courteous staff, dressed in black leather vests, serve a very delicious cuisine. The basement disco opens only after midnight. Guests can dance by themselves, the disco has many mirrors, and the decor is so charmingly fresh it could easily convert anyone who might hold gays in contempt. Le Sept is yet another elegant creation of Fabrice Emaer, the owner of the Palace.

# International

## BRAZIL

## Chica
**2nd arr.**
**6-8 rue Quincampoix**
**887.73.57**
*Open nightly 7:00 P.M. to 2:00 A.M.*

Those who remember the colorful Dzi Croquettes will be delighted to learn that one of them, Reginaldo, has opened a small cabaret-restaurant in the middle of the Halles. The club's whitewashed walls feature a few drawings that depict his native Bahia. The Brazilian meals are as inexpensively priced as the bossa novas performed by the two guitarists are soft. Along with a delicious batida cocktail made with coconut, mango or passionfruit juice, Brazil is but a dance away.

## Chez Félix
**5th arr.**
**23 rue Mouffetard**
**707.68.78**

The club's ground floor features Félix's dinner shows. Downstairs in the enlarged fourteenth-century cellar, his brother, Jean-Claude, supervises the samba dances that go on until dawn. Chez Félix is very much in vogue among Brazilians living in Paris.

## Le Petit Discophage
**5th arr.**
**11 passage du Clos-Bruneau**
**(31-33 rue des Écoles)**

You have to be a contortionist in order to see the stage. And, if you consider how uncomfortable the stools are, and how unfriendly the hosts can be, you might decide to walk right past the club's heavy door. Yet it's well worth putting up with a sore bottom for the show. Le Petit Discophage is the oldest Brazilian club in Paris and well remembered for singers such as Nazare Pereira, Zé Pédro,

**326.31.41**
*Open from 9:00 P.M. Closed Sun.*

### Ze Carioca (Restaurant San Marco)
**8th arr.**
**9 rue du Colisée**
**225.28.71**
*Open 7:30 P.M. to 1:30 A.M.*

Dodo Sampaio, and many others who have performed here. Drinks are priced from 50F.

Although owned by an Italian, this basement club is run by Carmen Faria, a gorgeous Brazilian from the Minas Gerais. Ever since she managed the Cachaça Club in New York, Carmen has always selected the best musicians, whose percussion instruments can resuscitate the dead. Ze Carioca features delicious—and deadly—batida cocktails.

# GREEK • CENTRAL EUROPEAN

### Djuri
**6th arr.**
**6 rue des Canettes**
**326.60.15**
*Open 11:45 P.M. to 1:45 A.M. Closed Mon.*

Heaven only knows how Djuri made his way to Paris twenty years ago and set up his basement club in Saint-Germain. His clients are mostly doctors and psychiatrists who come here to listen to him sing and play songs from the languid puszta, the foggy ghettos of Warsaw, Louisiana plantations, and the vast plateaus of Altiplano. This cheerful man is an accomplished guitar player and is fluent in at least ten languages.

### L'Olympe
**9th arr.**
**15 rue Grange-Batelière**
**824.46.65**
*Open 9:30 P.M. to 4:30 A.M. Closed Fri.*

Onassis and Aznavour were among the immortals who came to this Olympus. Mouskouri, Moustaki and Mercouri used to come here to listen to the sounds of the bouzoukis and forget the slow murder of their exile from Greece. Every night, under the supervision of Jean Vassilis, the guests kick up an energetic sirtaki.

# MEXICAN • PERUVIAN

### El Mariachi
**16th arr.**
**56 rue Galilée**
**720.41.69**
*Open 8:30 P.M. to dawn. Closed Sun.*

El Mariachi is the undisputed center of Paris's Mexican nightlife. Although you are greeted with a fanfare at the door by Los Mariachis, "direct from Mexico," they'll quickly abandon you during the evening, leaving you with two pieces of paper in your hand. The first is an inventory of 40 musical entrées including "Maria Chucheta," "La Noche y Tu," songs "revolucionario," and "romantico," and many more. The second, of course, is the tab.

### L'Escale
**6th arr.**
**15 rue Monsieur-le-Prince**
**354.63.47**
*Open nightly 11:00 P.M. to 4:00 A.M.*

The four Guaranis, who own this little ground-floor night spot, play a variety of instruments such as kenas, samponas, harps and others suitable for folkloric music. Their Peruvian folk songs, however, have long since disappeared, and the performers are now more inclined to sing about the Sainte-Geneviève *sierras* and the Saint-Michel *selva* or jungle. Parisians are more apt to go downstairs and dance to the salsa performed by a Cuban band while tourists and out-of-towners get together upstairs.

# RUSSIAN

## Douchka
**3rd arr.**
**6 rue du**
**Pont-aux-Choux**
**272.17.00**
*Open from 8:00 P.M. Closed Sun.*

The decor is all red and carefully lit, the feminine staff is charming, and some of the tunes played by the pianist and violinist are typically French. Everything here is pleasing, providing you sit at the bar and don't order any of the bland, overpriced food.

## Étoile de Moscou
**8th arr.**
**6 rue**
**Arsène-Houssaye**
**563.63.12**
*Open nightly 9:00 P.M. to dawn.*

We often wonder what Soviet diplomats are doing in this white Russian nightclub. What we *do* know is that if there hadn't been a revolution, the old songs sung in this candle-lit cabaret wouldn't be nearly as heartrending. The performances usually last until dawn, and will make you cry your eyes out and empty your wallets and purses on the table. The pre-show dinners, accompanied by Pali Guestros' vertiginous vibratos, quite good in the shashlik and smoked salmon range. The whole tab comes to 250F, and lots more for those who *must* have caviar and Champagne.

## Karlov
**6th arr.**
**4 rue du**
**Cherche-Midi**
**548.09.79**
*Open 8:30 P.M. to 2:00 A.M. Closed Sun.*

The Karlov has recently been done in black velvet. Some of its customers are of Russian origin, while others, such as Aragon and Serge Gainsbourg, simply come for the music performed by authentic gypsy violinists. A jazz pianist plays during the interlude preceding Ivanovitch, a fascinating character whose balalaika would melt the snows of Siberia.

## Ludmila (Pavillon Russe)
**8th arr.**
**45 rue Francois-Ier**
**720.70.61**
*Open 8:00 P.M. to 1:00 A.M. Closed Sun.*

Each time Ludmila asks her audience, in a tender, muted voice, whether they want to hear a sad or cheerful song, they always answer en masse: "Triste!" Ludmila had sold her Pavillon Russe on the rue Lauriston expecting to retire, but she soon grew so tired of doing nothing that when she was offered La Salamandre, an inactive night spot located at the angle of the rue François-Ier and the rue Pierre-Charron, she dashed over with bearskins, old Russian paintings, a piano and crates of Petrossian caviar. The Grand Dukes can now come out of hiding, for Ludmila is once again among us with her good-natured charm. A great bargain is her luncheon for 120F, including wine and service; but for those who want to hear her sing while eating their caviar blinis and shashlik, the time to come is in the evening.

## Monseigneur
**9th arr.**
**94 rue d'Amsterdam**
**874.23.35**
*Open nightly 9:00 P.M. to dawn.*

People who know how to have fun really enjoy Monseigneur's delirious violinist, the caviar blinis, and its featured international stars. Monseigneur's owner, Mme Andrée, treats celebrities and non-celebs alike— with all the care in the world, providing they're willing to spend a few 500F notes. Monseigneur has a history that dates back to pre-World War I days. And if you shut your eyes and listen to the velvety violins, you can believe that anything is possible.

### Raspoutine
**8th arr.**
**58 rue Bassano**
**720.04.31**
*Open nightly 9:00 P.M. to dawn.*

For those who are suffering from financial anemia, we don't recommend the Raspoutine and its mind-boggling royal crimson decor. Those who can afford to be treated like royalty, on the other hand, will love the deep cushions; velvet drapings; elegant tablecloths and chairs; the glitter of mirrors, candles, torches and elaborate Champagne buckets. Customers are urged to consume Champagne and caviar to help enhance their appreciation of the club's 52 musicians and innumerable "international attractions." In short, "kings and queens for a night" may well wind up driving taxis the following day.

### Le Samovar
**1st arr.**
**14 rue Sauval**
**261.77.79**
*Open from 8:30 P.M. Closed Sun.*

The Samovar's blinis, stuffed cabbage, palmenis and blintchikis don't really evoke the nostalgia for Old Russia, but the slavic airs affected by the club's steady customers make up for the difference. The latter cheerfully sing along and improvise Soviet or czarist tunes on the guitar, depending on how long they have been in exile.

### Shéhérazade
**9th arr.**
**3 rue de Liège**
**874.85.20**
*Open daily, dinner show at 9:00 P.M.*

After 50 years, the Ballets-Russes type of decor still makes an impression. Shéhérazade is a slavic, 1001 nights cavern with arches and columns decked out with drapes and gold leaf. The cuisine as well as the show are far less lavish. There was a time when Farouk and Marlene Dietrich, Rita Hayworth and Peter Sellers came here to sing old Russian songs, pay court to reigning queens decorated in solid gold, and applaud an 80-year-old cymbalist, Nitza Kodolban, who claimed to have performed for Rasputin.

# Jazz

Although Paris has not been a jazz capital for many years, you can still find a good number of jazz spots in the city. What's more, you can obtain weekly information pertaining to jazz events by dialing 325.28.27 at no cost. Many jazz concerts are performed in the spots listed below.

### American Center
*14th arr.*
*261 blvd. Raspail*
*354.99.92*

### Le Connétable
*3th arr.*
*55 rue des Archives*
*277.41.40*
*Open noon to 1:00 A.M. Closed Sun.*

### Le Cardinal Paf
*4th arr.*
*11 rue Saint-Paul*
*272.54.86*
*Open nightly 9:00 P.M. to 2:00 A.M.*

**Birdland**
**6th arr.**
**20 rue Princesse**
**326.97.59**
*Open nightly 10:00 P.M. to*
*5:00 A.M.*

This is a cosy bar for habitués, with no dancing or live music, but you can usually find a seat here when it isn't too crowded. Its chocolate-brown decor is strangely appealing. The taped music is excellent, the drinks are reasonably priced, and the atmosphere is friendly.

**Les Bouchons**
**1st arr.**
**19 rue des Halles**
**233.28.73**
*Open nightly 10:30 P.M. to*
*2:00 A.M.*

This round room, ornamented by two life-sized statues of blacks, features excellent black musicians and superb black singers who perform the greatest of blues repertoires. The cozy bar is decorated as if it belonged to a luxury hotel. This impression is confirmed by a pleasant ground-floor restaurant and by the decorations on its façade. Just two years ago, this place used to be a cork factory.

**Caveau de la Huchette**
**5th arr.**
**5 rue de la Huchette**
**326.65.05**
*Open nightly 9:30 P.M. to*
*2:30 A.M., Sat. and holidays to*
*3:30 A.M.*

This large, gloomy-looking cellar is the last holdout on what was once considered the street of jazz; and the many tourists who cruise up and down the rue de la Huchette haven't altered its musical integrity. The Caveau is often filled to capacity with enthusiastic fans who come to listen to Maxim Saury, Marc Laferrière, Benny Waters and other dixieland performers, and for these events the management lowers the admission fee from 30F to 25F.

**Caveau de la Montagne**
**5th arr.**
**18 rue Descartes**
**354.82.39**
*Open nightly 9:30 P.M. to 3:00 A.M.*

This cellar, pleasantly decorated in royal blue, is designed to resemble America of an earlier age. A huge fireplace serves as a backdrop for light jazz and bebop duos and trios that perform here. Some of the jazz is elaborately improvised and has brought its musicians, such as "Faton" Cahen, a certain amount of fame.

**La Chapelle des Lombards**
**11th arr.**
**19 rue de Lappe**
**357.24.24**
*Open 8:30 P.M. to 11:00 P.M.*
*Closed Sun., Mon.*

The new Chapelle des Lombards is located next to the old Balajo dance hall, in the vaulted cellar of the former Barreaux Verts prison, whose grates have been decorated with artificial flowers. Its austere decor, however, is offset by the enthusiastic fans who come here to listen to relatively unknown musicians such as Bernard Lubat, Michel Portal, Martial Solal and Henri Texier.

**Le Dreher**
**1st arr.**
**1 rue Saint-Denis**
**233.48.44**
*Open nightly 10:00 P.M. to*
*2:30 A.M.*

This cozy basement bar once featured the greatest names in jazz, such as Archie Shepp, Art Taylor, Don Cherry and Chico Hamilton, as well as lesser-known talents like Martial Solal, Maurice Vander and Christian Escoudé. Night after night, the club's booths are packed with migrant semi-professional musicians and fans for whom the admission fee of 50F is relatively inexpensive, considering the quality of the shows, the comfortable atmosphere and the delicious drinks, the first of which is free with the price of admission.

**Le Furstemberg**
**6th arr.**

From the moment the Angelus bell is rung, neighborhood gents follow the path leading to this little, angular and well air-conditioned basement room whose mirrors

**27 rue de Buci**
**354.79.51**
*Open 6:00 P.M. to 3:00 A.M.*

## *Jazz Unité*
**92800 Puteaux**
**Les Quatre Temps, La**
**Défense**
**776.44.26**
*Open 7:00 P.M. to 3:00 A.M.*
*Closed Sun.*

## *La Louisiane*
**2nd arr.**
**176 rue Montmartre**
**508.95.02**
*Open 7:30 P.M. to midnight.*
*Closed Sun.*

## *Le Méridien*
**17th arr.**
**81 blvd.**
**Gouvion-Saint-Cyr**
**758.12.30**
*Open nightly 10:00 P.M. to*
*2:00 A.M.*

## *New Morning*

**10th arr.**
**7-9 rue des**
**Petites-Ecuries**
**745.82.58**
*Showtime at 9:30 P.M.*

## *Le Petit Journal*
**5th arr.**
**71 blvd. Saint-Michel**
**326.28.59**
*Open 8:00 P.M. to 2:30 A.M.*
*Closed Sun.*

reflect the soft leather of its benches, subdued lighting and, depending on the angle, the Napoleonic profile of André Persiany accompanied by two musicians. This eclectic, consistently inspired pianist is, and has always been, the Furstemberg's main attraction.

Jazz fans are incurable. Every night they flock to this giant amphitheater with a decor modeled on New York's jazz discos: comfortable tiers of shell-shaped seats and mushroom-shaped tables, huge marble pillars, subdued neon lights and large bar. Here they will listen to top performers like Archie Shepp, Al Singer and Chris McGregor. At 25F, admission is practically free.

The signs on the walls tout the establishment's creole cuisine. The dishes are basically the same, even though a lot of energy is deployed to induce customers to eat the jambalaya and oysters Rockefeller. But these are not La Louisiane's main attractions. Since 1974, the establishment has been honored with the presence of quality jazz performers such as Christian Morin, Zanini, Maxim Saury and Stéphane Guérault. A dinner here costs 150F, and drinks are priced from 30F.

Tucked between the toilets and the stairs in the gigantic lobby of the Hôtel Méridien, this boîte has a shockingly ugly decor. Still, you can only applaud its featured attraction, a lovable, pot-bellied music hall veteran and accomplished drummer named Moustache. His performances of French-style jazz, suitable for a middle-aged audience, aren't nearly as interesting as when he plays along with a few old friends like Maxim Saury, Al Grey, Eddie Davis, Dorothy Donegan and Lionel Hampton.

Well named, the New Morning reflects the future of Parisian jazz, which over the last two years has been shedding its image of smoke-filled cellars to move into larger, well-ventilated and nicely decorated clubs such as this, where customers can listen to the sounds of the greats such as Dizzy Gillespie, Art Blakey and others. This well-lit night spot is comfortably laid out on two levels.

This friendly, typically Parisian pub offers its customers a little newspaper which is hung on the walls alongside its famous predecessor, *Le Petit Journal.* The music performed here is much appreciated by a good-natured audience that goes wild over dixieland and easy-listening jazz and bebop. After ten years, Le Petit Journal decided to enlarge its basement by tearing down a wall. Next, television monitors were installed in remote corners so that all customers could easily see performers such as Claude Bolling, Sacha Distel, Bill Coleman, Sugar Blue, and less frequently pianist Doctor Feelgood, and the Metropolitan Jazz Band.

### Slow-Club
**1st arr.**
**130 rue de Rivoli**
**233.84.30**
*Open 9:30 P.M. to 2:00 A.M. Closed Sun., Mon.*

Not everyone likes Claude Luter and Maxim Saury's age-old New Orleans jazz, but there will always be sufficient fans to ensure the future of this style of music.

# Private Clubs

### Castel-Princesse
**6th arr.**
**15 rue Princesse**
**326.90.22**

The news this year is that Castel no longer lives at Castel. He has moved to some other location in Paris and has transformed his two floor apartment into a restaurant, lounge, billiard room and sauna, reserved for the 2,000 happy few who have paid their dues to the Club Saint-Germain. Nothing has changed downstairs, including the basement club with its dream girls, the ground-floor bar packed with spirited young men, or Jean's little snack bar across the hall. Castel-Princesse contains Paris's funniest and craziest characters, such as dandies, interminable gossips, writers, hippies, ministers, turbanned hermaphrodites, retired Crazy Horse performers and numerous socialites who, night after night, create happenings of all kinds. To get into the club, you must pass Corinne's inspection at the box office window, which is quite a feat. You can count on a "no" if she doesn't like your looks, so don't insist.

### Elysées Matignon
**8th arr.**
**2 ave. Matignon**
**225.73.13**

You no longer have to fight to get into the Elysées-Matignon as you did during its heyday. Yet admission to this club is more than ever subject to examination by the droll Nicole, whose intransigence is luckily tempered by the presence of her affable sidekick, Bernard. This private club's relative casualness is much appreciated by young applicants who haven't got a membership card or the face of Polanski, Deneuve or Girardot. Everyone here is treated equally by a very nice, little, round, red-bearded host named Jean-Yves Bouvier who used to be at New Jimmy's. Only he will be able to get you a table in the restaurant or direct you to César, the headwaiter, who will seat you at the discotheque's bar. The disco itself, lighted by a very sophisticated system, is run by two DJs who are constantly reproached for their choice of dance music. It is in fact pretty stale, and that's the only complaint you can lodge against this place.

### Le Privé
**8th arr.**
**12 rue de Ponthieu**

Its psychedelic, Far Eastern decor, which was beginning to lose its freshness, has recently been redone in burgundy, which is perfectly suited to its youthful new image. Le

**225.51.70**

Privé's very young customers enjoy dancing to very loud music at all hours of the night. It is thus preferable to put on adolescent airs if you want to get past the young and lovely brunette who guards the door.

## Le Privilège
**2nd arr.**
**1 ter, cité Bergère**
**246.10.87**

The sign recently posted by Fabrice Emaer in the basement of his Palace Disco epitomizes an old demand by his customers: "Give us a spot where we can get together in cozy, home-away-from-home style. We'll even wear real trousers and a tie to get away from the polyester crowd. A place in which you'll turn down the stereo so we can sit comfortably, talk, and have a few drinks with our friends." Fabrice could not remain indifferent to such a legitimate request for very long. He dismantled the skating rink and soundproofed the walls. He then added a fountain, antique vases, frescoes, columns and tragic masks designed to recreate a prewar neoclassic setting. Glenn Miller's music and Frank Sinatra's voice fit in perfectly with the comfortable velvet couches. The moment Maryline, the receptionist, lets you in, your first "privilege" will be to enter through the cité Bergère doorway instead of through the Palace's main entrance. Other privileges include valet parking; a warm greeting by Guy Cuevas-Carrion, a former Palace and Club du Sept DJ; the generous smile of Paquita Paquin, the club's driving force; and maitre d's outfitted by Cerruti. And, remember, should you ever grow tired of the atmosphere, there's a door that leads directly upstairs to the Palace Disco and its vulgar trampling.

## Régine's
**8th arr.**
**49 rue de Ponthieu**
**359.21.13**

Régine knows exactly what she's doing, and realizes that if a nocturnal queen is to preserve her staying power, she should not be seen too often. In fact, Régine is so adept at this, one wonders whether or not she still exists, or whether she has boarded some rocket to the moon or is hiding out in some remote retreat. According to her faithful followers, she is still alive and well and living somewhere between Buenos Aires, Marbella, New York, Monte-Carlo, Santiago and the rue de Ponthieu. Once in a blue moon she will get on stage or publish a self-aggrandizing book in which she is portrayed as an enchantress. She continues to weave her web and spout clichés about her *joie de vivre*. Today Régine's on the rue de Ponthieu has transcended the notion of being merely fashionable. Within its dimly lit and beautiful walls, one encounters both famous and ordinary people, the same to be found at Maxim's, the Ritz or the Tour d'Argent. Providing gentle little Pierrette—who is adorable even when she is being insulted—lets you in without a membership card, you will be very well treated. Régine's dinners are delicious, her customers, nearly always beautiful, are seated next to the bar, which is the in place to be; you'll be able to take in all the perfumes of 1001 nights.

# THE HOTELS

# THE
# HOTELS

**W**e have listed hotels according to classifications of: Luxury, First-Class, Small and Charming, Large and Modern, For Students, Very Discreet, and The Banlieue Some of these hotels are noted with symbols, the official French government classifications (N.N.) ranging from one to four indicating the quality, comfort and price.

There is a service in Paris that can arrange a reservation in any Parisian or French hotel for the same day. For a fee of 6F to 20F, depending on the hotel, Les Hôtesses de Paris can find you a room. They also provide tourist information on Paris or France. All you need to do is drop in at one of the following locations.

## Office de Tourisme de Paris

*8th arr. 127 Champs-Élysées (tel. 723.61.72). Open daily 9:00 A.M. to 10:00 P.M. (to 8:00 P.M. in winter), Sun. 9:00 A.M. to 6:00 P.M.*

## Gare d'Austerlitz

*13th arr. 55 quai d'Austerlitz (tel. 584.91.70). Open 8:00 A.M. to 10:00 P.M. Closed Sun.*

## Gare de l'Est

*10th arr. place du 11-Novembre-1918 (tel. 607.17.73). Open 8:00 A.M. to 1:00 P.M. and 5:00 P.M. to 10:00 P.M. (5:00 P.M. to 8:00 P.M. in winter). Closed Sun.*

## Gare de Lyon

*12th arr. 20 blvd. Diderot (tel. 343.33.24). Open 8:00 A.M. to 1:00 P.M. and 5:00 P.M. to 10:00 P.M. (5:00 P.M. to 8:00 P.M. in winter). Closed Sun.*

## Gare du Nord

*10th arr. 18 rue de Dunkerque (tel. 526.94.82). Open 8:00 A.M. to 10:00 P.M. (8:00 A.M. to 1:00 P.M. in winter). Closed Sun.*

••••
## Bristol
**8th arr.**
**112 faubourg**
**Saint-Honoré**
**266.91.45**
*AE, DC, EC*

By any measure—the elegance of its period furniture and reproductions, comfortable rooms with magnificent bathrooms, luxury suites (50) and the clientele—the Bristol is one of the last authentic (and the most expensive) grand hotels in Paris. The Bristol makes annual improvement, such as the refurbishing of the new

La Résidence wing, which consists of 30 suites with a separate entrance, the creation of ultra-modern conference and meeting rooms, and the installation of a sauna and a small heated pool on the sixth-floor terrace overlooking the roofs of Paris. The hotel recently opened a restaurant over a 2,000-square-meter garden planted above the hotel's private parking lot. The staff is hand-picked and very courteous, and the guests are mostly visiting diplomats and politicians since the Elysées is within walking distance. The hotel is also a favorite haunt of prominent Americans. The Bristol was recently acquired by a German conglomerate based in Baden-Baden.

Air conditioning is in 90 of the 211 rooms, with meeting facilities for ten to 250. Free attendant parking. Rates: from 600F–1,200F, including service; suites 1,650F–2,500F; breakfast 40F; additional child's bed 130F.

**••••**
## Claridge-Bellman
**8th arr.**
**37 rue François-Ier**
**723.90.03**
*AE, DC*

After three long years of remodeling the bar, dining room, kitchens, bathrooms and elevators have been totally rebuilt and modernized. The Bellman hotel resembles a large townhouse and has all the charm of a family home. This impression is heightened by many treasures such as paintings, objets d'art and antique furniture from the now-defunct Claridge Hotel. The hotel has an elegant lobby, lots of wood paneling, a beautiful seventeenth-century tapestry, a Coromandel folding screen, Chinese vases and charming, beautifully decorated, soundproof rooms—marred slightly, alas, by unattractive minibars and TV sets. The hotel has no suites, although it does have corner apartments with two bedrooms, a small vestibule and two bathrooms. There is also a lounge in which breakfast is served, the Relais Bellman restaurant, and an English bar. Its international clientele includes North and South Americans, Germans, and Italian couturiers who usually reserve their rooms well in advance, making it very difficult (as in most luxury hotels) to find a room on the spur of the moment. Public parking is on rue François Ier. Rates: from 450F–528F including service; breakfast 30F; children 96F.

**••••**
## Crillon
**8th arr.**
**10 place de la Concorde**
**296.10.81**
*AE, DC, V*

The last of the Parisian grand hotels to remain authentically French, the Crillon has been undergoing a major face-lift. The rooms, lounges, bar, galleries, restaurant, and even the kitchens have been refurbished under the energetic guidance of the Crillon's director, M. Philippe Roche. The hotel's interior courts, terraces overlooking the great place de la Concorde, lounges, and exquisitely (though often smallish) designed rooms, experienced staff and admirable façade built by the architect Jacques-Ange Gabriel—all convey an aura of tranquil dignity not often found in today's hotels. The newly restored rooms and suites recapture the elegant intimacy of old with Louis XVI furniture, heavy silk curtains, new carpeting, pastel walls, marble bathrooms, wood paneling, unobtrusive minibars, and soundproof windows overlooking the place de la Concorde and rue Boissy-d'Anglas. The walls of the corridors and galleries are covered with luxurious velvet and the carpet is done in matching tones. Future improvements will include a new gallery off the main lobby which will open into a beautiful Louis XV-style court, with large French windows, where guests may dine around a lovely fountain. The bar and restaurant, whose harsh blue-and-green decor conflicts with the general style of the hotel, will also be completely redone. Amid all this change the Crillon's clientele remains much the same: princes, diplomats, rich foreigners, and official government guests (only twelve percent of the guests are French). The Crillon belongs to the Relais et Châteaux chain of hotels. There are 170 rooms (80 with air conditioning) and 31 salons, with meeting facilities for ten to 40. Parking and an underground garage can be found at place de la Concorde. Rates: from 860F–1,075F including service; breakfast 48F; children 126F; fee for dogs.

••••
## *George V*
**8th arr.**
**31 ave. George-V**
**723.54.00**
*All major credit cards*

A few years ago this huge hotel, with its massive continental-style façade, was a white elephant, seemingly doomed to oblivion. Fortunately, the George V has become a shining example of the way a period palace can be successfully resurrected. Rehabilitation of this endangered monument has included remodeling the bar and restaurant (Les Princes) which overlook a delightful patio; totally remodeling the rooms, corridors and lounges; and enhancing the decor with valuable objets d'art such as the admirable Regency clock, Renoir's painting, *Vase de roses,* and hanging tapestries, many of which are Flemish. The staff receives you with exemplary courtesy, room service is attentive and efficient, and the view unencumbered from the hotel's upper floors— which also help make the George V one of the best hotels in the world. The 294 rooms have air conditioning, and meeting facilities are available for ten to 300. Rates: from 702F–978F including service; suites from 1,840F; breakfast 40F; children 100F; dogs 60F.

••••
## *Grand Hôtel*
**9th arr.**
**2 rue Scribe**
**260.33.50**
*All major credit cards*

The old Grand Hôtel has undergone drastic restoration and renovation, from the façade to the Café de la Paix. The most notable change has been the addition of an immense central lobby-patio that for comfort and calm is unmatched by any grand hotel lobby. Finally, the hotel's 600 rooms have been completely redecorated and refurnished in a colorful style. This prototype of the palace-type hotel has in the process lost some of the aura of grandeur, and its faceless, international clientele is not the kind to turn heads. However, its proximity to the Opéra still attracts a few great performers. The Grand Hôtel's staff is extremely courteous. The hotel has combination bedroom-offices for business people, a gymnasium, a sauna, massage services and tanning rooms, as well as two restaurants, Le Ravel and Café de la Paix. Two parking lots, the Paramount and the Caumartin, are both nearby. Air conditioning can be found in ten of the 583 rooms, and meeting facilities are provided for five to 400. Rates: from 570F–690F including service and breakfast; suites from 1,200F; children 100F; dogs 50F.

••••
## Inter-Continental
**1st arr.**
**3 rue de Castiglione**
**260.37.80**
*All major credit cards*

Since this aging luxury hotel, with its classic façades, was bought by a giant American hotel chain in 1968, it has wholly recaptured its glorious reputation and luxurious atmosphere. Fortunately, the hotel's new functional style has not affected its beautiful lounges—designed by Garnier, who also built the Opéra—and three out of seven are classified as historic monuments. Meeting and banquet facilities and multiple modern services are perfectly suited to the business world. Old-time charm and comfort are to be found in the beautiful patio and most of the rooms, including the single bedrooms on the top floor which offer a beautiful view of the Tuileries. The hotel features three restaurants: La Rôtisserie Rivoli, Le Café Tuileries, and Le Bistro. There is air conditioning in the 473 rooms and 27 suites. Meeting facilities for 30 to 100; public parking at the place Vendome. Rates: from 505F–770F including service; breakfast 33F–54F; children under 14 free.

••••
## Lancaster
**8th arr.**
**7 rue de Berri**
**359.90.43**
*AE, EC*

For the last twenty years, the Lancaster has been referred to as a jewel among Parisian hotels. In plain fact, once you've walked past the huge bouquet of flowers in the lobby, you're tempted to think that the hotel's decor in general isn't at all as sophisticated or luxurious as one had imagined. Indeed, the inner garden is in desperate need of reconstruction. The way it appears now is almost rustic, which is pretty ridiculous considering you're only a few feet away from the Champs-Elysées. The rooms and suites are all soundproofed and conventionally decorated. The small dining room overlooks the garden and is perfect for discussing secrets of state. You will be graciously welcomed by a competent and punctual staff. Twenty-three rooms are equipped with air conditioning. Meeting facilities for two to twenty; parking at 6 rue de Berri. Rates: from 530F–805F; suites from 1,380F–2,875F; breakfast 40F; children 172F; dogs 50F.

••••
## La Pérouse

**16th arr.**
**40 rue La Perouse**
**500.83.47**
*All major credit cards*

Formerly the residence of the Allégrier family, owners of the Lucas-Carton restaurant, this small and super deluxe hotel is ideally located near the place de l'Etoile and was entirely remodeled in 1979. Its 36 rooms and suites have been beautifully redecorated with pink and beige curtains, English mahogany furniture, and marble bathrooms. It features an English bar and an agreeable restaurant, L'Astrolabe, which has three bay windows overlooking the rue La Pérouse. The lower level has two lecture halls that can also be used as private lounges. One of them is done in blue Venetian style and can accommodate ten to twelve. The other is wood paneled and resembles the interior of a turn-of-the-century ship's lounge. La Perouse has air conditioning and meeting facilities for ten to 25. Rates: from 560F–1,250F including service; breakfast 32F; children free.

••••
## *Lotti*
**1st arr.**
**7 rue Castiglione**
**260.37.34**
*All major credit cards*

This elegant hotel, with its period furniture, is tolerably conventional and much in vogue with British and Italian aristocrats who enjoy its quiet, excellent service and relatively small dimensions. The hotel's comfortable rooms, however, are rather large and beautifully decorated. The Lotti has only one restaurant. 130 rooms, five with air conditioning, and meeting facilities for up to 26. Rates: from 540F–864F including service and breakfast; children 230F; dogs 69F.

••••
## *Meurice*
**1st arr.**
**228 rue de Rivoli**
**260.38.60**
*All major credit cards*

Over the last few years, this gorgeous hotel facing the Tuileries has undergone many transformations. Air conditioning has been installed, and the bathrooms have been redone in pink marble. Only the suites offer views of the Jardins des Tuileries. One of them, Suite 108, is where General von Choltitz had his office during the German occupation of France, where King Alphonse XIII of Spain stayed during his exile, and where Salvador Dali held his press conferences. Although its general atmosphere isn't very cheerful, the Meurice continues to attract important guests and is still considered one of the best hotels in Paris. It has one restaurant, The Copper Grill, where you may sip tea or cocktails to music from 5:00 P.M. to 9:00 P.M. The parking lot is within walking distance. Meurice has 194 rooms, including 22 suites with air conditioning. Meeting facilities for ten to 50. Rates: from 592F–823F including service; breakfast 45F; children 6 and under free; dogs are paying guests.

••••
## *Nova-Park Elysées*
**8th arr.**
**51 rue Francois-Ier**
**562.63.64**
*AE, DC, EC, V*

According to René Hatt, there should be far better things to do in a hotel than sleep. Naturally, you can manage to get some shut-eye in any of his super deluxe hotels in Zurich, Cairo and New York, but in his brand-new Parisian establishment wealthy clientele from around the world can receive guests in their own private rooms and walk about the terraced gardens; swim in an exotic pool, have a sauna or work out in the gym; dictate business letters to a hired secretary; hold meetings in private office; keep up with Wall Street; play bridge, pool or electronic games; have a very classy lunch prepared by Fréon, the trusty chef; dine at the Paris-Match restaurant; dance during teatime or organize rooftop parties. They may also drink cocktails at a piano-bar, distract themselves with dinner shows, or see a movie projected on the wall of an adjoining building. In short, there's hardly any time left for sleeping. The presidential suite goes for 35,000F a night. Rates: from 1,050F; breakfast 28F.

••••
## Plaza-Athénée
**8th arr.**
**25 ave. Montaigne**
**723.78.33**
*AE, DC, EC*

The Plaza's former director, Paul Bougenaux, realized that by paying, feeding and entertaining his staff well, his guests would be all the happier with the service. Fortunately, his successor, Franco Cozzo, has continued the same policy. As a result, the hotel's employees, down to the youngest elevator boy, are renowned for their discretion, efficiency and politeness. The huge rooms have been entirely remodeled—the ones facing the rue Montaigne are all soundproofed—and the corridors and galleries are redone each year. The clientele consists of people like the Rockefellers, von Karajan, rich Brazilians, and show business celebrities. The hotel features two restaurants, the Régence and the Relais-Plaza. The Plaza has 216 rooms and 37 sitting rooms (with air conditioning) and valet parking. Rates: from 805F-1,783F including service; breakfast 45F; children 143F; dogs 110F.

••••
## Prince de Galles
**8th arr.**
**33 ave. George-V**
**723.55.11**
*All major credit cards*

The Prince de Galles (Prince of Wales) hotel is distinguished by its Empire style and rich draperies and furniture. Many of the rooms have working fireplaces. Also featured are terraces alive with flowers and an agreeable open-air patio surrounded with Ionic, Doric and Corinthian columns. A portion of the patio is used by the hotel's restaurant, Le Panache. 166 rooms and meeting facilities for fifteen to 50. Rates: from 572F–821F including service; breakfast 42F; children over 6,203F; dogs 50F.

••••
## Raphaël
**16th arr.**
**17 ave. Kléber**
**502.16.00**
*AE, DC, V*

The Raphaël is a luxury stopover for image-conscious business clientele, the Raphaël attracts many Italo- to preserve an air of intimacy. The hotel has oriental rugs, marble floors, columns and wood paneling, antique paintings and period furniture. Overall, this is a quiet place with luxurious rooms decorated in all styles— mostly Louis XVI, Empire and Adam. All have modern bathrooms, twin beds and minibars. Apart from its business clientele, the Raphaël attracts many Italo-American movie celebrities. The hotel has its own restaurant. There are 87 rooms and five suites, with meeting facilities for five to 50. Parking is available at 34 rue Lauriston. Rates: from 340F–730F including service and breakfast; suites from 1,350F–1,380F; children 70F; dogs 60F.

••••
## Ritz
**1st arr.**
**15 place Vendôme**
**260.38.30**
*All major credit cards*

If the truth be known, the few ultra-sophisticated 10,000F-per-day suites offered by the world's most luxurious hotel are not exorbitantly priced. The Ritz's other superbly decorated rooms are within the price of the average emir and Texas oil mogul. Even the 71F fee for dogs, excluding meals, isn't that excessive for chic greyhounds or chihuahuas. The much-awaited reopening of the Espadon restaurant will not deter emirs, pampered poodles, dukes and Texans from dining at the Vendôme or, in summer, on the terrace, from listening to the pianist while nibbling on madeleines at tea time. As in the words of the song, Ritz Hotel guests may truly be in paradise. But they won't be able to get their pants pressed after 7:00 P.M. The Ritz features 163 rooms and 42 salons; 71 rooms have air conditioning. There are meeting facilities for up to 60, and underground parking is available at place Vendôme. Rates: from 805F–1,100F; breakfast 42F; children 140F; dogs 71F.

••••
## Royal Monceau
**8th arr.**
**35 ave. Hoche**
**561.98.00**
*AE, DC, EC*

Built in 1930 and located halfway between the Étoile and Monceau Park, this comfortable, practical and stylish hotel is run by highly competent personnel. The rooms that overlook the flowery patio are among the loveliest you'll find in Paris. If you enjoy sleeping late, you'll appreciate the hotel's extraordinary Sunday brunch, served from noon to 3:00 P.M. The Royal Monceau also has a garden restaurant that, despite a short menu, boasts a cuisine far superior to most hotel cooking and is famed for its English-style breakfasts. The 200 rooms are equipped with air conditioning, and meeting facilities are provided for fifteen to 300 people. Rates: from 595F–820F including service and breakfast; children over 6,130F; dogs 60F.

••••
## Saint-James et Albany
**1st arr.**
**202 rue de Rivoli**
**260.31.60**
*All major credit cards*

Ideally located between rue Saint-Honoré and the Tuileries, the Saint-James and Albany Hôtel consists of four buildings encircling the Noailles townhouse, whose eighteenth-century façades have been declared a national landmark. Entirely remodeled in 1979, this residential hotel offers 77 studio apartments, 35 twin bedrooms, 3 suites and 27 duplexes, all with kitchenettes equipped with electric stove, sink, refrigerator and tableware, and offering views of interior courts and gardens. The hotel's contemporary and agreeably functional decor makes the Saint-James and Albany the perfect home-away-from-home for extended stopovers in Paris. There are a few charming studios on the fifth floor, with low ceilings and wooden beams. The two-bedroom apartments located in the new Les Bains wing all face north yet offer splendid views of the garden-floor grocery–delicatessen has all that guests need for a meal in their rooms.
    Guests may also eat at Le Noailles restaurant and its

sunny terrace, at the Bistrot La Fayette cafeteria (open from 7:00 A.M. to 10:30 P.M.) and at the two bars. Saint-James and Albany has a main lobby and three beautiful reception rooms on the ground floor which open into each other and extend into an inner courtyard. Separate entrance on the Saint-Honoré. Meeting facilities are available for ten to 300. Pay parking at 6 rue du 29-Juillet. Rates: from 400F–800F including service; breakfast 30F; children 75F. No pets.

••••
## *Scribe*
**9th arr.**
**1 rue Scribe**
**742.03.40**
*All major credit cards*

The Scribe has reopened its doors after a two-year renovation. Although the Napoleon III façade has remained intact, its lobby, salons, basement dining room and six floors of rooms have been entirely remodeled. While the main lobby and its black marble columns, crystal chandeliers, leather-upholstered couches and sumptuous flower decorations are all superb, its imitation Empire furniture and garish decor leave much to be desired. On the other hand, the hotel's five suites and six duplexes—each with high ceilings, a bedroom with loggia, a combined living/dining/office and a bathroom with a separate "cabinet de toilette"—are all superbly decorated in ochre and China red with Japanese wallpaper, thick carpets, silk draperies and limestone bathrooms. Each of the rooms is equipped with double windows, contemporary and Louis XVI-styled furniture, and color TV and video-cassettes featuring daily films in English. Minibars on request only. The hotel's room service is efficient and available around the clock. The lower level has three convention rooms and a restaurant, Les Muses, with a separate entrance on boulevard des Capucines. A la carte or fixed-price meals cost about 100F, without wine, and are served until 12:30 A.M. Guests get a charming welcome. The 217 rooms have air conditioning, and meeting facilities are available. Public parking can be found at rue Caumartin or valet parking is available. Rates: from 575–825F including service; suites 1,100F-2,500F; duplex from 1,500F; breakfast 35F; children over 12,115F; dogs 80F.

# *First Class*

••••
## *L'Aiglon*
**14th arr.**
**232 blvd. Raspail**
**320.82.42**
*AE, V*

Built in 1925, L'Aiglon offers rooms that overlook the boulevard Edgar-Quinet and the peaceful greenery of the Montparnasse cemetery. The main lobby is decorated with light wood paneling, thick carpets with leafy patterns and comfortable armchairs; there are also three elegant public sitting rooms. The rooms overlooking the inner courtyard are particularly quiet. A minibar is provided in each room. No dining room. A public parking lot is located within walking distance. Rates: from 190F–250F including service; breakfast 17F. No pets.

••••
## *Alexander*
**16th arr.**
**102 ave. Victor-Hugo**
**553.64.65**
*All major credit cards*

This is a quiet, comfortable hotel close to the place Victor-Hugo. It is beautifully decorated in light wood, and has thick carpets and deep, restful armchairs in its three elegant lobbies on the ground floor. The 62 rooms are well equipped and handsomely decorated and furnished. Those on the courtyard are particularly quiet and pleasant. The rooms do not have kitchens, but each has its own minibar. Nearby public parking. Rates: from 275F–385F including service and breakfast; child's bed 70F. No dogs.

•••
## *Alison*
**8th arr.**
**21 rue de Surène**
**265.54.00**
*All major credit cards*

Most guests at the Alison are English and American, whose respective embassies are both close by. Newly decorated in orange, beige and brown, the hotel has modern, functional rooms with double-glazed windows on the street side, a lobby filled with leather-upholstered sofas, and a breakfast room in the vaulted basement. All the marble bathrooms have ceiling stereo speakers. The sixth-floor suite consists of two bedrooms, two bathrooms, a balcony and an alcove for a baby. No restaurant. Rates: from 185F–280F including service; breakfast 17F; children 50F. No pets.

••
## *Ambassade*
**16th arr.**
**79 rue Lauriston**
**553.41.15**
*All major credit cards*

Formerly the Cimarosa mansion, the Ambassade was taken over by the owners of the Victor-Hugo Hotel in February 1980. The 38 entirely remodeled rooms have been decorated with floral wallpaper bordered with friezes, and painted in pink, beige and brown tones. The furniture is all lacquered rattan, and the bathrooms have been done in gray marble with wallpaper that matches the paper in the rooms. The best rooms are Nos. 43 and 45 on the fourth floor, and No. 9 on the ground floor. Parking at 47 rue Lauriston. Rates: from 200F–296F including service; breakfast 18F; children under 4 free. No pets.

••
## *De l'Avenir*
**6th arr.**
**65 rue Madame**
**548.84.54**

This well-kept small hotel, with only 35 rooms, is located right next to the Luxembourg gardens. The owner, Mme Poignant, has remodeled her superb lounge with leather, mahogany and English furniture. Some of her rooms are large and have been carefully decorated, like No. 35, which has an antique armoire and a gorgeous chest of drawers. This fine little neighborhood hotel has no restaurant. Rates: from 67F–174F including service and breakfast; children 30% extra. No pets.

## •••• Baltimore

16th arr.
**88 bis ave. Kleber**
**553.83.33**
*AE, DC*

Under new management for the last three years, this entirely remodeled and greatly enlarged hotel is excellently located for business people, halfway between the Trocadéro and l'Étoile. The Baltimore is attractively furnished with oriental rugs, marble floors, elegant arches and columns, and huge armchairs. In addition to the Copper Bar, the hotel houses an excellent (and expensive) new restaurant, L'Estournel, which has been superbly decorated by Michel Boyer to resemble the interior of a 1937 ocean liner. The Baltimore's basement has six beautiful meeting rooms, of which the largest and most elegant was once the vault of the National Bank of Paris. Rooms are all very comfortable and decorated in the conventional style of the 16th arrondissement. The Baltimore has 119 rooms and meeting facilities for ten to 200. Parking is at 11 bis rue de Magdebourg. Rates: from 420F–540F including service and breakfast. No large pets.

## ••• Caravelle

9th arr.
**68 rue des Martyrs**
**878.43.31**
*All major credit cards*

Located within walking distance of the Butte-Montmartre, the Gare du Nord and the Gare de l'Est, the Caravelle is a quiet, comfortable small hotel with green plants, an aquarium and a large fireplace. Its 33 rooms are all modern, air conditioned and soundproof; they have TVs, minibars and radios. Rates: from 210F–240F including service; breakfast 18F; children 80F; dogs 20F.

## •••• Cayré

7th arr.
**4 blvd. Raspail**
**544.38.88**
*AE, DC, V*

Ever since writer George Bernanos lived here, many other authors and artists have come to stay in this traditional hotel, which was completely remodeled in 1973. Pablo Casals was one of its most prestigious guests. Cayré is conveniently located between Montparnasse and Saint-Germain-des-Prés, but is very quiet. No restaurant. Rates: from 317F–370F including service and breakfast; children 30F; pets 20F.

## ••• Colisée

8th arr.
**6 rue du Colisée**
**359.95.25**
*All major credit cards*

Its three-star award is due to its proximity to the Champs-Élysées and to its top-to-bottom renovations. Reopened in June 1981, the first and third floors have been redone in blue, the second and fourth in green, and the fifth and sixth in beige and brown. The rooms all have beautiful wallpaper, quilted bedspreads, monochromatic draperies and rustic or bamboo furniture. The beds are all set in alcoves. Rooms with numbers ending with an 8 are larger and equipped with daybeds and windowed bathrooms. Those on the top floor have wood-beamed ceilings.

The combined bar/salon features comfortable leather armchairs as well as four breakfast tables. You will be warmly welcomed by M. and Mme Polly. There is parking at rue de Ponthieu. Rates: from 290F–350F including service and breakfast; children 60F; dogs 20F.

••••
## Concorde-Saint-Lazare
**8th arr.**
**108 rue Saint-Lazare**
**261.51.20**
*AE, DC, V*

The largest of Paris railroad station hotels, the Concorde Saint-Lazare has undergone systematic and spectacular renovations over the last few years. Eighty-one rooms were redone in 1981, and Slavik and Sonia Rykiel collaborated in the restoration of the hotel lobby (now floored in Italian marble). The Concorde's highlights, however, are its stunning 1889 lounge, which is a national landmark and is notable for its splendid Bohemian crystal chandeliers, and its ten-table billiard hall, redone in turn-of-the-century decor with raised benches for spectators. Otherwise, the Concorde is a thoroughly up-to-date hotel with the usual amenities such as color TV in most rooms; an American bar, the Golden Black; a restaurant, Café Terminus, decorated like a turn-of-the-century dining car; and the brasserie Bistrot 108. There are 300 rooms and meeting facilities for ten to 50 people. Rates: from 400F–560F including service and breakfast; children under 12 free.

•••
## Étoile
**17th arr.**
**3 rue de l'Étoile**
**380.36.94**
*AE, DC, V*

Very well located between place de l'Étoile and place des Ternes and within walking distance of the Porte Maillot and the salle Pleyel, the Étoile has ultra-modern functional furniture, thick orange carpets, lithos and green plants. Soft music is piped into the ground-floor rooms; lovely etchings are featured in the corridors; and the 25 rooms have beautiful bathrooms and wallpaper. In the hotel's vast lobby there are a few tables for breakfast, a corner bar and a small library. If there isn't any vacancy, ask Mme Garoche to get you a room at the Courcelles Hôtel which she has also managed since 1980. It's slightly larger, and its 42 rooms have been entirely redone and are of the same quality as the Étoile's. Rates from 220F–300F; breakfast 20F.

••••
## Frantel-Windsor
**8th arr.**
**14 rue Beaujon**
**563.04.04**
*All major credit cards*

The Frantel-Windsor is located on a quiet street next to the Champs-Élysées. This austere and massive 1925 building conceals a remarkably comfortable hotel which is constantly being remodeled. Its bright, spacious rooms are equipped with simple and functional furniture, minibars and color TVs. There is room service. The hotel lobby, lounges and Le Clovis restaurant, specializing in nouvelle cuisine, are also modern and comfortable. The

Frantel-Windsor has 135 rooms and meeting facilities for five to 100 people. Rates: from 450F–710F including service; breakfast 30F; children 80F; dogs 30F.

##### ..
## Des Hollandais
**9th arr.**
**16 rue Lamartine**
**878.25.13**

This charming little hotel with 46 rooms is located behind the Grands Boulevards and the Notre-Dame-de-Lorette church. You will be received like a friend and lodged in clean, quiet and comfortable rooms. No restaurant. Rates: from 85F–200F including service; breakfast 12F; children 50% extra.

##### ...
## Kléber
**16th arr.**
**7 rue de Belloy**
**723.80.22**
*AE, DC*

The Kléber is located within walking distance of l'Étoile and Trocadéro. Rooms are modern with beige walls, striped carpets, and curtains and bedspreads with turquoise diamond motifs. Also featured are impeccable tiled bathrooms. The ground floor has a comfortable lounge and bar. The Kléber has one suite on the sixth floor. Parking is 22F at 5 rue de Belloy. Rates: from 300F–480F including service and breakfast; children 40F.

##### ..
## Laumière
**19th arr.**
**4 rue Petit**
**206.10.77**

Located near the Buttes-Chaumont, the Laumière is a good, modern, notably inexpensive little hotel. All rooms are soundproofed. No restaurant. Rates: from 50F–160F including service; breakfast 12F. No pets.

##### ....
## Littré
**6th arr.**
**9 rue Littré**
**544.38.68**
*AE, V*

This classic, comfortable hotel is located near Montparnasse and has warm, soundproof rooms. The lobby and lounge are rather old-fashioned, yet still luxurious. Direct-dial telephone service in all rooms. Public parking at 153 rue de Rennes. Restaurant. There are 100 rooms and meeting facilities for up to 30. Rates: from 320F–370F including service and breakfast. No pets.

##### ....
## Louvre-Concorde
**1st arr.**
**Place André-Malraux**
**261.56.01**
*All major credit cards*

This hotel is superbly located. Across the street are the Palais-Royal gardens and the Tuileries, and faubourg Saint-Honoré. The Louvre is within view and the Opéra and Comédie-Française are around the block. The remodeled rooms offer all the advantages of a large hotel chain, including TV, minibar and 223 soundproof rooms. There is a bar/restaurant. Meeting facilities for ten to 25 people. Rates: from 380F–490F including service and breakfast; children over 12 90F.

••••
## Lutétia-Concorde

6th arr.
**43 blvd. Raspail**
**544.38.10**
*All major credit cards*

The Lutétia is the largest of the old Left Bank hotels. Strategically located near Saint-Germain-des-Prés, the Luxembourg, and Montparnasse, this hotel has remodeled, modern rooms, as well as some with period furniture. Bar/restaurant. Meeting facilities for fifteen to 200. Public parking nearby at Boucicault. Rates: from 380F–490F including service and breakfast; children free; dogs 20F.

••
## Magellan

17th arr.
**17-19 rue**
**Jean-Baptiste-Dumas**
**572.44.51**
*All major credit cards*

A quiet hotel located between the porte Maillot and the porte Champerret. The lounge and breakfast room have just been completely remodeled. Business visitors appreciate the quiet rooms overlooking the garden, automatic clock-radios, direct-dial telephone service, comfortable bathrooms, and the proximity of the place de l'Étoile and peripheral boulevards. No restaurant. Rates: from 178F–240F including service and breakfast; children 80F.

•••
## Massenet (Mapotel)
16th arr.
**5 bis rue Massenet**
**524.43.04**
*All major credit cards*

This excellent hotel, known for its elegant clientele, is located in an ordinary-looking building in the Hameau de Passy. The decor is a little aged but well cared for and discreet (the same could be said of the staff). The lobby and some of the rooms have been newly remodeled. In summer, breakfast is particularly pleasant outside on the flowery patio. No restaurant. Pay parking at 5 rue Nicol. Rates: from 140F–300F including service and breakfast; children 80F. No pets.

•••
## Métropole Opéra

2nd arr.
**2 rue de Gramont**
**296.91.03**
*AE*

Located not far from the Opéra, this agreeable hotel was intelligently remodeled from roof to basement a few years ago. The staff is friendly and distinguished. No restaurant. Public parking at the place de la Bourse. Rates: from 110F–310F including service; breakfast 15F; children 50F; dogs 25F.

•••
## Modern-Hôtel-Lyon

12th arr.
**3 rue Parrot**
**343.41.52**
*AE*

It's easy to fall asleep in this hotel's soundproof rooms. For over 70 years, the same family has continued to run the Modern-Hôtel-Lyon, which is continually being modernized. No restaurant. Rates: from 165F–255F including service; breakfast 16F. No pets.

••••
## Montalem-bert

7th arr.
**3 rue de**
**Montalembert**
**548.68.11**
*EC*

This charming 1930s-style hotel is conveniently located near the Pont Royal, the Tuileries, the Louvre and Saint-Germain-des-Prés, in the heart of a quarter filled with publishers and antique dealers. Over the years its management has subtly renovated the hotel by changing the upholstery and carpets. The bathrooms were all completely redone a few years ago. Montalembert's clients are mostly Americans, Italians, writers, and occasional guests who decide to stay on forever. Sixty-one rooms and meeting facilities for up to 40. Public parking is at rue de Montalembert. Rates: from 180F–380F including service and breakfast; children 60F; dogs 30F–60F.

•••
## Montana-Tuileries
**1st arr.**
**12 rue Saint-Roch**
**260.35.10**
*CB*

Located halfway between the Concorde and the Palais-Royal, this small hotel offers large and attractive rooms that come with entirely remodeled bathrooms. Each floor has a dominant color scheme. The first is salmon pink, the second green and the third rose; the bathrooms in the liveliest rooms are a cheerful raspberry. The fourth floor is blue, the fifth floor is beige, and the sixth is multicolored. The rooms on this floor are somewhat smaller and the bathrooms are tiny, yet No. 70 is truly charming. The ground floor has a huge lobby and a small lounge. No restaurant. Rates: from 190F–280F including service; breakfast 16F. No pets.

•••
## Rennes-Mont-parnasse
**6th arr.**
**151 bis, rue de Rennes**
**548.97.38**
*All major credit cards*

This excellently run hotel has 38 perfectly quiet rooms in front and back. Rooms No. 50 and 40 overlook the Panthéon, and the ground floor lounge leads into a little garden courtyard. The breakfast room in the basement is oppressive. No restaurant. Public parking at 153 rue de Rennes. Rates: from 125F–285F including breakfast and service; children 30% extra; dogs 20F.

••••
## Rond-Point de Longchamp
**16th arr.**
**86 rue de Longchamp**
**505.13.63**
*AE*

Located between the Trocadéro and avenue Victor-Hugo, this hotel has been completely remodeled. The ground floor features an attractive lounge, bar and billiard room decorated in honey-colored wallpaper and featuring comfortable beige leather armchairs. Lounge, bar and paneled billiard room are all air conditioned and green with plants. The hotel has newly decorated modern rooms as well as highly appealing Louis XVI-style ones with four-poster beds, and blue, pink or Nile-green flowered draperies and wallpaper. All 59 rooms have double windows. M. Dumontant, the hotel's director since 1962, will give you a warm welcome. The Belles-Feuilles restaurant, closed Saturdays and Sundays, offers a menu at 85F as well as a buffet dinner on Tuesdays. The restaurant is open to nonresidents for lunch and Tuesday dinners only. Rates: from 280F–350F including service; breakfast 20F.

••••
## Royal Saint-Honoré

This distinguished establishment, located near the Tuileries, offers excellent, comfortable and relatively quiet rooms at very reasonable prices. Most of the bathrooms have been entirely remodeled. The hotel restaurant

289

**1st arr.**
**13 rue d'Alger**
**260.32.79**
*All major credit cards*

features specialties of Southwestern France. Eighty rooms with meeting rooms for up to 30 people. Rates: from 250F–350F including service and breakfast; children under 12 free; dogs 50F.

••••
## San-Régis
**8th arr.**
**12 rue Jean-Goujon**
**359.41.90**

Decorated with antique furniture, paintings and curios, the San-Régis is one of the most chic and luxurious small Parisian hotels. Guests include Lauren Bacall, Raquel Welch, and Gene Kelly, as well as American business moguls and the royal family of Luxembourg. No restaurant. Rates: from 300F–450F including service; suites from 500F–800F; breakfast 25F. No pets.

•••
## Sévigné
**16th arr.**
**6 rue de Belloy**
**720.88.90**
*AE, DC, EC*

The Sévigné has recently been completely remodeled and enlarged. Rooms are spacious, modern and functional, with light-toned walls, harmonious beige and brown colors and balconies on the second and fifth floors. No restaurant. Rates: from 208F–368F, including service and breakfast; children 40F; parking 28F.

••••
## Splendid Étoile
**17th arr.**
**1 bis, ave. Carnot**
**766.41.41**
*AE, DC, V*

This quaint little hotel near the Arc de Triomphe, was completely renovated in 1976. Its spacious and comfortably furnished rooms and bathrooms are very well equipped. The Splendid-Étoile features a charming little lounge, an American bar and an interesting restaurant, Le Pré-Carré. Public parking on avenue Foch. Rates: from 200F–500F including service; breakfast 22F; children 120F.

••••
## Terrass Hôtel (Mapotel)
**18th arr.**
**12 rue Joseph-de-Maistre**
**606.72.85**
*All major credit cards*

Not far from places Clichy, Pigalle and Blanche, the Terrass is an oasis of tranquility and comfort. Far from the clamor and crowds of Montmartre cemetery. Its elevated site offers an unobstructed view of the Panthéon, Invalides, Eiffel Tower and Arc de Triomphe. Since it opened in 1912, the hotel has constantly updated the quality of its rooms. The Terrass has two restaurants, L'Albaron and Le Guerlande, and a garden terrace on the seventh floor, which in summer has a bar. Rates: from 290F–380F including service and breakfast; children under 6 free.

••••
## La Trémoille
**8th arr.**
**14 rue de la Trémoille**
**723.34.20**
*All major credit cards*

La Trémoille is close to the Théâtre des Champs-Elysées, Christian Dior, Ricci, and Scherrer. Entirely renovated two years ago, the Trémoille has 117 comfortable and air conditioned rooms and suites with period furniture, luxurious bathrooms, garden balconies, and grand hotel service. Light meals are served on the premises, yet should you desire a more copious meal, you'll find fine restaurants nearby at the Plaza-Athénée or the George-V, both of which belong to Trusthouse Forre, owners of La Trémoille, so you can charge your meals there. Valet parking. Rates: from 425F–850F including service; breakfast 35F; children free.

### Victor Hugo
**16th arr.**
**19 rue Copernic**
**553.76.01**
*All major credit cards*

Built in 1973, this hotel is conveniently located next to avenue and place Victor Hugo. Its large period rooms are all equipped with color TV, minibars and marble bathrooms. The fourth-floor rooms overlook the Copernic Reservoir, with its greenery, ducks and occasional gulls. The hotel has a number of small English-style lounges, as well as a winter garden for breakfast in the green days of early spring. Good ambience. Meeting rooms for ten to twenty people. Pay parking is located at 47 rue Lauriston. Rates: from 245F–365F including service and breakfast; children under 4 free. No pets.

### Victoria Palace
**6th arr.**
**6 rue Blaise-Desgoffe**
**544.38.16**
*AE*

This little "palace" is located between rue de Rennes and rue de Vaugirard. It offers 113 beautiful Louis XV-style rooms, marble bathrooms and a parking lot with attendant. Restaurant. Conference room and meeting facilities for ten to 30. Pay parking at 8 rue Blaise-Desgoffe. Rates: from 385F–510F including service and breakfast. No pets.

# Charming

Charming little hotels are to the huge sleep shops what bistros are to truck stops. And even if you can sometimes hear your neighbors brushing their teeth or slipping into a pair of stockings, you have the marvelous feeling of not being just a number. That may be the very reason it's so hard to find a room in one of these charming hotels.

### Abbaye Saint-Germain
**6th arr.**
**10 rue Cassette**
**544.38.11**

This ravishing hotel set back from the road was once a convent. The lobby contains stone arches, the bar combines modern couches with antique furniture, and there are two pleasant lounges, one of which leads into an expansive garden surrounded with a trellis fence. The rooms are charming and in excellent taste. Although the top floor features rooms with alcoves and authentic wooden beams, the nicest rooms are to be found on the ground floor, particularly No. 3, which is next to the garden. No restaurant. Guests are warmly greeted. Rates: from 250F–320F including service and breakfast. No pets.

•••
## Angleterre
**6th arr.**
**44 rue Jacob**
**260.34.72**

The building was once the English Embassy—the one that Ben Franklin refused to enter to sign the U.S. Declaration of Independence because it was considered British soil. It makes a lovely hotel—Hemingway once lived here—built around a flowered patio where you can have breakfast during the summer. The rooms and suites have been entirely renovated and are all superb. Some of them are huge and feature high ceilings, wooden beams, large beds and luxurious bathrooms, especially rooms No. 5, decorated with a wisteria motif, and No. 7, done in beige monochrome. The ground floor offers a brand-new bar and a piano lounge. Rates: from 160F–300F including service; breakfast 15F. No pets.

••••
## Atala
**8th arr.**
**10 rue Chateaubriand**
**562.01.62**
*AE, DC*

Located in the heart of the city, this calm, colorful hotel has its rooms grouped around what was once a beautiful secret garden (it now has a heated, enclosed terrace as well). The peaceful Atala has just installed a second elevator and added two new suites. The service is splendid. Rates: from 270F–450F including service; breakfast 18F; children 70F.

•••
## Banville

**17th arr.**
**166 blvd. Berthier**
**755.70.16**

This charming hotel, with its lovely window boxes planted with flowers, is located on a service road off boulevard des Marécheaux, within shouting distance of the Étoile and Porte Maillot. Its owner, Mme Lambert, provides guests with light, cheerful, soundproof rooms with thick carpeting, lovely upholstery, natural or white-lacquered bamboo furniture, an occasional alcove and direct-dial telephone service. The Banville has a breakfast room and charming lounge with comfortable armchairs and a TV. No restaurant. Rates: from 216F–230F including service and breakfast; children 42F; dogs 10F.

•••
## Bergère
**9th arr.**
**34 rue Bergère**
**770.32.40**
*All major credit cards*

This classic hotel, which has been gradually modernized, is extremely quiet, especially if your room faces the little interior garden court with climbing ivy. The 94 rooms are spacious and, though unimaginatively decorated in modern or rustic styles, comfortable. Pay parking can be found at rue Drouot. Rates: from 210F–360F including service and breakfast.

•••
## Bradford
**8th arr.**
**10 rue Saint-Philippe-du-Roule**
**359.24.20**

The Bradford, a small model of serious hotel keeping, is expertly run by M. and Mme Mourot, who go out of their way to please their guests. The rooms are huge and light, meticulously clean and mostly well furnished. The bathrooms are all brand-new. Although the hotel is located right next to faubourg Saint-Honoré and the Champs-Elysées, it is extremely quiet. The lobby is decorated with immense bouquets of flowers, the service is discreet and friendly, and there is a comfortable little Louis XVI-style lounge. No restaurant. Rates: from 230F–280F including service and breakfast. No pets.

## *Chopin*
**9th arr.**
**46 passage Jouffroy**
**770.58.10**

Formerly Hôtel des Familles, the Chopin is located at the end of the quaint passage Jouffroy and is exceptionally quiet. Its mid-nineteenth-century façade is classified as a historical monument; its rooms are small and somewhat dim; the decor is provincial, with white openworked curtains; and the bathrooms are tiny. Some of the rooms have three beds. Breakfast room. No restaurant. Rates: from 121F–202F including service.

## *Colbert*
**5th arr.**
**7 rue de**
**l'Hôtel-Colbert**
**325.85.65**
*AE*

Located in a lovely eighteenth-century residence built around a small patio, the Colbert has small, simply furnished rooms, sixteen of which overlook Notre-Dame. A bar is located in the hotel's large conventional lounge. Although the atmosphere is somewhat chilly, the hotel is very quiet and well located near the Seine and the cathedral. No restaurant. Pay parking at Notre-Dame and rue Lagrange. Rates: from 175F–350F including service; breakfast 15F; children free.

## *Collège de France*
**5th arr.**
**7 rue Thénard**
**326.78.36**

Opened in April 1981, this new hotel is located on a quiet street within walking distance of collèplace Maubert and the Collège de France. The simply decorated rooms are done in light browns or greens. The best ones, on the sixth floor, have wooden beams and paneling and offer a view of Notre-Dame's twin towers. The lounge leads into a small dining room where breakfast is served on brick-red lacquered pedestal tables. No restaurant. Rates: from 150F–185F including service; breakfast 12.50F; children over 5, 60F. No pets.

## *Les Deux Iles*
**4th arr.**
**59 rue**
**Saint-Louis-I'lle**
**326.13.35**

This beautiful seventeenth-century mansion has a lobby furnished in rattan and bamboo, a garden court, and walls upholstered with delicately braided fabric. The small pastel rooms, decorated with colorful, provincial fabrics, are very lively, and bathrooms feature ceramic tiles painted in seventeenth-century style. The hotel's bar is open daily except Sundays, until 1:00 A.M., and the lounge has comfortable couches next to an old fireplace. No restaurant. Rates: from 230F–280F including service; breakfast 20F.

## *Ducs d'Anjou*
**1st arr.**

Located off the delightful little place Sainte-Opportune, an old building has been redone from top to bottom and transformed into this excellent small hotel. The rooms

**1, rue
Sainte-Opportune
236.92.24**

are all quiet and decorated with warm-toned floral wallpaper and thick carpets. Rooms and bathrooms are small but impeccably clean and comfortable. No restaurant. Rates: from 104F–188F including service and breakfast; children, 30% extra.

## Family Hôtel
**1st arr.
35 rue Cambon
261.54.84**

This quiet family hotel is located in what used to be the townhouse of the Count of Brienne, Louis XVI's minister of finance. Ask for room No. 50; it has recently been redecorated and has a view of the Vendôme column. Or No. 41 very popular with Americans who love its nostalgic furniture and seldom leave it vacant. The other rooms that face the street are all soundproofed, so you'll sleep well. Guests are greeted warmly, the staff are very competent, and the rates are very inexpensive considering the neighborhood. Rates: from 110F–180F including service; breakfast 12F.

## Grand Hôtel de Champagne
**1st arr.
17 rue Jean-Lantier
261.50.05**

Tidy, quiet, charming rooms with wooden beams and paneling. Repainting, carpeting and the installation of double windows have just been completed. No restaurant. Rates: from 215F–297F including service and breakfast. No pets.

## Grand Hôtel des Principautés Unies
**6th arr.
42-44 rue de Vaugirard
634.44.90**
*Closed in Aug.*

The rooms are cozily furnished, newly decorated and soundproofed, and provide a view of the Luxembourg Gardens across the street. The staff is remarkably efficient and guests are greeted warmly. No restaurant. Rates: from 181F–211F including service and breakfast. No pets.

## Grand Hôtel de l'Univers
**6th arr.
6 rue Gregoire-de-Tours
329.37.00**
*AE, DC, V*

Located on the Latin Quarter's "hottest" street, this hotel offers small but diversified rooms; the best overlook the courtyard. The hotel has been attractively modernized and is always very tidy. Rates: from 230F–350F, including service and breakfast; children 70F.

## L'Hôtel
**6th arr.
13 rue des Beaux-Arts
325.27.22**

Attributed to eighteenth-century architect Claude-Nicolas Ledoux and originally called the "Love Pavilion," this building became the superb Directoire Hotel. Entirely renovated in 1968, it is now called L'Hôtel. Everything has been done in velvet and brocades, including the elevator and the uniforms worn by the male staff. The top-floor suites overlook the Saint-Germain-des-Prés church. The airconditioned rooms have been decorated with sumptuous fabrics, the bathrooms are Venetian marble, and there is also period furniture and curios. The hotel features a dining room, a bar and a charming winter garden with a fountain and palm trees. Distinguished guests have included Mistinguett and Oscar Wilde (who died here in 1900). Twenty-four-hour room service. Rates: from 400F–1,500F including service; breakfast 35F; children free.

### •••
## Isly
**6th arr.**
**29 rue Jacob**
**329.59.96**

This very beautiful old building has been transformed into a modern, air-conditioned hotel. Rooms are small but comfortable. The most beautiful rooms include No. 33, with palm-leaf wallpaper and green curtains; No. 34 with lovely grey-and-red wallpaper and white furniture; and No. 23, with blue floral wallpaper. A suite is located on the fifth floor. Guests are warmly welcomed by the owner, Mme Hédir. Rates: from 115F–250F including service; breakfast 15F; children 30% extra.

### ••
## Kensington
**7th arr.**
**79 ave. de la**
**Bourdonnais**
**705.74.00**
*AE, V*

The Kensington was completely renovated in 1979 and boasts a white façade, new wallpaper, paintings, geraniums at the windows and impeccable bathrooms. Rooms are small and well equipped, with direct-dial telephones and double windows. The rooms are done in either blue or ochre; the blue rooms are more attractive, with a blend of floral and monochromatic wallpaper, cheerful blue carpets, cotton curtains, white stitched bedcovers and blue-tiled bathrooms. The single bedrooms on the sixth floor are both charming and quiet. There are two suites. All in all, a cheerful, tidy place. The Champ de Mars is just across the street for those who enjoy jogging before breakfast. Guests are warmly greeted by the owner, Mme Mahy. Rates: from 150F–180F including service; breakfast 12F; children 35F. No large pets.

### •••
## Lenox
**7th arr.**
**9 rue de l'Université**
**296.10.95**

This elegantly restored hotel, located halfway between rue du Bac and the rue des Saint-Pères, has small rooms decorated with attractive wallpaper and furniture. The top floor features two duplexes with flowered balconies. The hotel has a bar but no restaurant. Snacks served in rooms until midnight. Rates: from 180F–290F including service; breakfast 16F; children 30% extra; dogs 28F.

### •••
## Lutèce
**4th arr.**
**65 rue**
**Saint-Louis-en-l'Ile**

This handsome converted mansion has Louis XVI-style tiled floors, huge bouquets of flowers, a glowing fireplace and an intimate atmosphere in the lobby and lounge. Rooms have whitewashed walls, wooden beams,

**325.79.76**

brilliantly colored cotton curtains and linen spreads. The impeccable bathrooms are small but modern. The top floor features exquisite rooms done in patchwork and offering splendid views of Parisian rooftops and the distant Panthéon. No restaurant. Rates: from 280F–300F including service; breakfast 20F; children free. No pets.

••••
# *Majestic*
**16th arr.**
**29 rue**
**Dumont-d'Urville**
**500.83.70**
*AE, DC, V*

Formerly a townhouse, the Majestic offers richly furnished rooms and suites in Directoire and Louis XV styles, as well as five modern rooms. We highly recommend the hotel's penthouse which has a landscaped balcony, moire hangings, gilded Louis XV armchairs and a purple carpet. The hotel is extremely quiet, as is the street it's on. Pay parking at avenue Foch. Rates: from 310F–440F including service and breakfast; suites from 520F–865F; children 80F.

••
# *Marais*
**3rd arr.**
**2 bis, rue de**
**Commines**
**887.78.27**
*AE, V*

The Marais makes you feel as if you were in the country, with its red hexagonal floor tiles, wooden beams, and flowers; or else on some tropical island with its bamboo and palm-tree motif wallpaper and white-lacquered furniture. This peaceful, charming hotel has cheerful rooms which are unfortunately a bit cramped. (The bathtubs seem to have been designed for midgets.) The wall coverings are in monochrome cotton, the curtains are striped, and the quilted bedcovers all are checkered. The best rooms are Nos. 12, 32 and 52, which have bathrooms with windows. The first and fifth floors each have two adjoining rooms, ideal for families. Rates: from 145F–220F including service; breakfast 15F; children 30F.

••
# *Les Marronniers*

**6th arr.**
**21 rue Jacob**
**325.30.60**

This peaceful hotel gets its name from the two chestnut trees in the garden. Les Marronniers is entirely decorated in themes from nature. The carpets are ornamented with green leaves; the corridors are embellished with flowers and birds; and on the veranda, where guests may have breakfast during summer, the chandeliers, chairs, tablecloths and tableware are all decorated with grapes, pears, cherries and flowers. The best rooms are located above the garden, although those on the sixth floor are also charming and light and done in rustic wallpaper and fabrics. They offer beautiful views of the Saint-Germain-des-Prés church belfry. Unfortunately, these rooms can get very hot in summer, and you can't see the garden. Whatever your preference, the bathrooms are all perfectly equipped and all the rooms have antique beams and fine oak furniture. The entire building has been declared a national landmark and the superb vaulted cellars in the hotel's basement have been transformed into two comfortable lounges. The staff here are extremely courteous and competent. No restaurant. Meeting rooms for ten to twenty.

Rates: from 145F–250F including
service; breakfast 14F; children 50F.

## Nouvel Hôtel
12th arr.
24 ave. du Bel-Air
343.01.81
*AE, DC, V*

Located on a quiet, tree-lined street within 50 meters of
the place de la Nation, this particularly charming hotel
features a garden patio filled with shrubs and flowers
where guests can have breakfast. The peaceful, simple
rooms have either rustic or modern furniture; bathrooms
are comfortable, but the toilets are oddly primitive. The
best room is No. 9, located on the ground floor next to
the garden. The agreeable little lounge features a piano,
some etchings and a splendid 1920s-style frieze designed
with fruit garlands. The hotel's owner, M. Marillier, is an
excellent host. Rates: from 95F–215F including service;
breakfast 20F. No pets.

## Ouest Hôtel
17th arr.
165 rue de Rome
227.50.29

The Ouest, located within walking distance of the Saint-
Lazare railroad station, is owned by a former sailor from
Normandy, who has decorated room No. 49 in the old
Normandy style. The other rooms are all modern and
have recently been redecorated, while the bathrooms
have been retiled. The thick flower-patterned English
carpets and the double windows in each room make for
quieter nights. Since the hotel is remarkably inexpensive,
we advise you to reserve your rooms at least one week in
advance. No restaurant. Pay parking nearby at 42 rue
Legendre. Rates: from 100F–180F including service;
breakfast 12F; children 30% extra.

## Pas de Calais
6th arr.
59 rue des
Saint-Peres
548.78.74

This late-eighteenth-century residence has been entirely
remodeled and is located between the Grasset
publishing house and a hotel that was inhabited by
Chateaubriand in 1815. The hotel's corridors are
unusually laid out and the rooms are all modern. The
ones facing away from the street are particularly quiet.
Breakfast is served in the garden courtyard. No
restaurant. Public parking is available at Saint-Germain-
des-Prés. Rates: from 225F–285F including service and
breakfast; children 70F; dogs 12F.

## Pavillon
7th arr.
54 rue
Saint-Dominique
551.42.87

*V*

Set back from rue Saint-Dominique at the end of a
flower-filled alley, this small, provincial-style hotel
features windows bright with geraniums and tiny rooms
with floral wallpaper. The best rooms are Nos. 9 and 10.
Avoid No. 20. The Pavillon's amiable new directress,
Mme Dubois, has had the hotel renovated. The garden
court features a few tables for breakfast, weather
permitting. No restaurant. Rates: from 140F–190F
including service; breakfast 12F; children 30F. No dogs.

## ˙˙Perreyve
6th arr.
63 rue Madame
548.35.01

Named after an abbot from the nearby diocese, the Perreyve is located within 50 yards of the Luxembourg Gardens. Completely remodeled in 1980, the hotel has all new and comfortable rooms with white cotton-stitched spreads and small but faultless bathrooms. The colors of the walls vary according to the floors. The second and third floors are decorated with beige and pink flowers, the fourth and fifth are in a delicate salmon pink. The ground floor features a charming, provincial-style lounge decorated with Japanese wallpaper, printed cotton curtains with birds and cherry blossom motifs, arched glass doors, large lamps and flowering plants. Breakfast is served in the lounge. Very competent staff. No restaurant. Rates: from 158F–196F including service. No dogs.

## ˙˙Queen's Hôtel
16th arr.
4 rue Bastien-Lepage
288.89.85

Queen's Hôtel is located near to the rue d'Auteuil and the avenue Mozart. Apart from its lovely white façade, the hotel features narrow yet charming, modern and comfortable rooms that have been tastefully decorated in Indian pink or chestnut brown. No. 23 is the largest and most agreeable room. The hotel has a hushed lobby furnished with velvet couches, and a tiny lounge in which guests can have their breakfast. Excellent hospitality. No restaurant. Parking is 25F at the Garage du Village, 57 bis, ave. Theophile-Gautier. Rates: from 165F–230F including service; breakfast 15F; children 30% extra. No pets.

## ····Regent's Garden
17th arr.
6 rue
Pierre-Demours
574.07.30
AE, DC

Within walking distance of the Étoile and the Champs-Elysées, the hotel lives up to its name with a magnificent, peaceful garden that has fountains, flowers, shaded walks and stone statues. Once the townhouse of Napoleon III's personal physician, the beautiful old building does its discreet best to make you feel at home with all the amenities of a venerable family residence. Its huge rooms, with molded high ceilings, have all been decorated either with handsome rustic or period furniture. The frequently remodeled rooms come with perfectly equipped bathrooms. No restaurant. Rates: from 240F–290F including service and breakfast; children 50F.

## ····Relais Christine

6th arr.
3 rue Christine
326.71.80
AE, DC, V

Located off a particularly quiet street, halfway between Saint-Germain-des-Prés and Notre-Dame, this luxury hotel, with its splendid façade, was a sixteenth-century cloister. Prior to its reopening in January 1980, the hotel underwent exhaustive renovation and has been redecorated with carpets, Japanese wallpaper, and lovely stitched draperies. There is a huge lobby and spacious, comfortable, quiet rooms. The most agreeable ones include six on the ground floor with access to the rectangular lawn, the duplexes and separate-entry suites located on the top floor, and the modern ones that feature beautiful bathrooms with beige-pink marble sinks and tiled floors. Room No. 1 features a stone wall and a heavy sculptured wood door. The hotel's staff is most considerate. Rates: from 400F–500F including service; breakfast 30F; no pets.

••••
## Résidence du Bois
**16th arr.**
**18 rue Chalgrin**
**500.50.59**

This Second Empire townhouse belongs (like the Crillon) to the Relais et Châteaux hotel chain. The large rooms are furnished in varied styles and overlook a lovely garden. The hotel is peaceful and has a very competent staff. Although there is no restaurant, guests may be served light meals in the lounge, in the garden under the shady trees, in summer, and in their rooms at all seasons. Rates: from 345F–740F including service and breakfast; children 30% extra; dogs 50F–120F.

••
## Résidence Étoile-Pereire
**17th arr.**
**146 blvd. Pereire**
**755.60.00**
*Closed first 3 wks. of Aug.*
*All major credit cards*

Its discreet entrance is sometimes mistaken for that of the building next door. But there is no confusion once you're inside. This residence will put you up for one night or one hundred. Rooms are all large and tastefully decorated in turn-of-the-century style. The bathrooms have been entirely remodeled, although three of them still have the old-fashioned claw-foot bathtubs that Americans are mad for. In summer, breakfast is served in the small garden court, where the hotel provides twenty varieties of exotic fruit jams. Children's games include darts and bowling. No restaurant. Rates: from 200F–250F including service and breakfast; children free. No large dogs.

••
## Riboutté-Lafayette
**9th arr.**
**5 rue Riboutté**
**770.62.36**

This small and charming hotel faces rue La Fayette and is located within walking distance of the Opéra, the Bourse, and the big boulevards. Its quiet rooms are small and attractively decorated with floral fabrics and bamboo furniture. Very hospitable staff. No restaurant. Public parking at Montholon Square. Rates: from 140F–198F including service and breakfast; children 20F.

••
## Saint-Louis
**4th arr.**
**75 rue Saint-Louis-en-l'Ile**
**634.04.80**

Guests will be greeted warmly in the lobby, which is decorated with bouquets of roses, wooden beams, antique paintings, polished tiled floors and attractive Louis XIII furniture. The simple yet tasteful rooms have floral curtains and thick carpets, and the ultra-modern bathrooms have been beautifully papered. Some of the fifth-floor rooms have balconies with a splendid view of Ile-Saint-Louis rooftops. Public parking at Pont-Marie. No restaurant. Rates: from 80F–210F including service; breakfast 17F; children 50F; dogs 10F.

•••
## Saint-Simon
**7th arr.**
**14 rue Saint-Simon**
**548.35.66**

Set back from the street, this charming, former townhouse is peacefully situated between two gardens. In 1981, all the rooms, suites and bathrooms were completely remodeled and an elevator was installed in the building. The solid pink, green and blue wallpapers, all different, are patterned with leaves, flowers and garlands. No. 33 is exquisitely done in pink. The best rooms overlook the garden, and Nos. 25 and 26 are over the terrace, though, unfortunately, they offer little privacy. The lounge has many alcoves, wooden beams and period furniture. No restaurant. Rates: from 250F–450F including service; breakfast 20F.

••
## Scandinavia
**6th arr.**
**27 rue de Tournon**
**329.67.20**
*Closed during Aug.*

An enchanting hotel decorated with marvelous Louis XIII furniture and located within walking distance of the Senate and Luxembourg Gardens. The rooms are all differently decorated, in warm tones of deep brown, red and gold, and feature antique paintings and large mirrors. Corridors and bathrooms are done in dark enamel; the hotel is fully carpeted, and many of its rooms feature wooden beams and red or dark green ceilings. The large lobby is accented with rocks and a profusion of green plants. The Scandinavia is both intimate and comfortable. No restaurant. Rates: from 220F–240F including service and breakfast. No dogs.

•••
## Seine
**6th arr.**
**52 rue de Seine**
**634.22.80**
*AE, DC, V*

In the heart of Saint-Germain-des-Prés. The façade, rooms and bathrooms have recently been remodeled; all the rooms facing the street now have double-glazed windows. The English-style lounge has large deep armchairs. No restaurant. Public parking at rue Mazarine. Rates: from 120F–240F including service and breakfast; children 25F; no dogs.

••
## Solférino
**7th arr.**
**91 rue de Lille**
**705.85.54**
*Closed Dec. 20 - Jan. 5*

This hotel features pastel walls, simple yet colorful rooms, an exquisite little lounge, a veranda for breakfast and a multitude of charming curios and objets d'art. Guests are treated warmly in this old-fashioned, relaxed hotel. Public parking is located at rue du Bac or at the Invalides. Rates: from 112F–240F including service and breakfast; children 30% extra. No dogs.

•••
## Suède
**7th arr.**
**31 rue Vaneau**
**705.00.08**
*AE, DC*

The Suède has a large, comfortable Directoire-style lobby. Its pleasantly understated rooms and suites are decorated in creamy whites and gray-blues. The third and upper floors offer a view of the Matignon Gardens. The hotel has its own charming interior garden where guests may have tea or breakfast. Warm hospitality. No restaurant. Rates: from 270F–310F including service and breakfast; children 30% extra. No dogs.

### Varenne
**7th arr.**
**44 rue de Bourgogne**
**551.45.55**
*AE*

In the near-rustic calm of the Invalides quarter, this hotel is constantly undergoing renovations and improvements. This year, direct-dial telephones have been installed in all rooms and the windows facing the street have been soundproofed. The rooms are lovely, the charming little lounge is set with flowers, and the patio is perfect for breakfast during summer. Very courteous staff. Rates: from 185F–290F including service; breakfast 18F; children 45F; dogs 15F.

### Vieux Marais
**4th arr.**
**8 rue du Plâtre**
**278.47.22**
*AE, EC*

This charming hotel, located on rue du Plâtre (the street is named after a thirteenth-century plaster factory on the site), was redone in 1980. Its five floors and 30 rooms are simply decorated with Chinese carpets, floral wallpaper and matching curtains. The bright new bathrooms are impeccably clean. Breakfast is served in the pretty straw-colored lounge. Guests are greeted very warmly by Mme Rumiel and her daughter. No restaurant. Pay parking is at the nearby Hotel-de-Ville. Rates: from 140F–240F including service; breakfast 17F, children 25F. No dogs.

### Welcome Hôtel
**6th arr.**
**66 rue de Seine**
**634.24.80**

The Welcome, at the corner of blvd. Saint-Germain and rue de Seine, has 27 soundproof rooms from the first to fifth floors and three rooms on the sixth floor with wooden beams and high ceilings. The latter are to be avoided when the weather gets hot. The first-floor lounge is old-fashioned and charming. The hotel is under the same management as the Hôtel des Marronniers. Rates: from 145F–185F including service; breakfast 15F. No dogs.

# Large·Modern

### Berthier et Brochant la Tour
**17th arr.**
**163 bis, ave. de Clichy**
**228.40.40**

These twin hotels were built in 1975 and completely redecorated in 1981. They share the same lobby and restaurants. Rooms differ in size, price, even category. Both hotels are done in brilliant and cheerful colors, with thick carpets, attractive lamps and functional furniture; all rooms have a view of either the Eiffel Tower or (with some imagination) of the Sacré-Coeur. Breakfast is available in a self-service cafeteria. The comfort and low prices of both these hotels make up for the poor neighborhood and inconvenient location. On the other hand, parking is free and the Porte-de-Clichy and Brochant métro, and bus are within walking distance. The restaurant, Le Village, offers a 39F menu with hors d'oeuvres and a daily special. Meeting facilities are available for fifteen to 50 people. Rates: The Brochant la Tour is from 155F–170F including service and breakfast. The Berthier is from 170F–190F including service and breakfast.

••••
## Concorde-La Fayette
**17th arr.**
**3 place de la Porte-des-Ternes**
**758.12.84**
*All major credit cards*

This hotel offers a splendid view of the Bois de Boulogne, the Étoile and of Paris in general. The Concorde-La Fayette is huge, featuring a 4,500-seat convention hall and banquet rooms that can accommodate up to 2,000 seated or 4,000 standing: 60 shops, 4 cinemas, 2 discos; and a 1,500-space parking lot. The hotel offers direct shuttle service to Roissy-Charles-de-Gaulle and Orly airports. Its 1,000 rooms—250 of which have been completely redecorated—all have modern amenities, and guests are treated in a friendly fashion, despite the vastness of the hotel. Concorde-La-Fayette features two bars, the Plein Ciel on the thirty-second floor, and La Fayette on the ground floor. There are also three restaurants, the best of which is the Étoile d'Or. Free parking. Rates: from 540F–630F including service and breakfast; children under 12 free.

••••
## Hilton
**15th arr.**
**18 ave. de Suffren**
**273.92.00**
*All major credit cards*

Apart from the redecorated lobby, restaurant and bar, the Hilton has remained roughly the same over the years. The first of the modern hotels built in Paris after the war, the Hilton offers spacious rooms, efficient service, free accommodations for children (regardless of age) who share rooms with their parents, and films on the hotel's closed-circuit color television. Other Hilton amenities include luxury shops such as Hermès and Cartier, a bookshop, a hairdresser (René-Louis Josse) and an Air France ticket office. There are three restaurants: Le Western, Le Coffee Shop, and Le Toit de Paris, the latter with a dance floor open until 2:00 A.M. There are also two bars, the intimate Suffren on the ground floor and the rooftop Cocktail Corner located next to the Toit de Paris. Parking is 25F. Meeting rooms are available for ten to 1,000. Rates: from 500F–700F including service; breakfast 39F; children free.

••••
## Holiday Inn

**15th arr.**
**69 blvd. Victor**
**533.74.63**
*All major credit cards*

This middle-sized hotel offers well-designed, air-conditioned, soundproof and comfortable rooms. Its functional nature and unattractive location hardly make for a charming stay, but it's the ideal spot for business people attending events at the Palais des Expositions which is located across the street at the Porte de Versailles. The hotel has one restaurant, Le Tennessee, one bar, Le Watanga. A car rental agency is located in the lobby. The 90 rooms are air conditioned, and parking is free. Meeting facilities for up to 150.

Rates: from 390F–460F including
service; breakfast 27F; children under 18 free.

## Méridien
**17 arr.**
**81 blvd. Gouvion-**
**Saint-Cyr**
**758.12.30**
*All major credit cards*

The largest among the new Parisian hotels, the Méridien is
conveniently located across the street from the Air France
bus terminal and next to the Porte Maillot convention hall.
The hotel is done in transatlantic style, as evident from its
small rooms—they're custom-made for jumbo-jet
passengers. A cosmopolitan atmosphere is sustained by a
multitude of shops, travel agencies and meeting rooms.
There's also a sauna and gymnasiums. Moustache and his
swinging jazz ensemble are a star attraction for young and
old at Le Patio bar. The hotel also offers three restaurants:
Le Clos Longchamp, Le Yamato and La Maison Beaujolaise,
as well as one coffee shop, L'Arlequin. The 1,027 rooms
are air conditioned. Attendant parking is available at rue
Waldeck-Rousseau. Meeting rooms for 25 to 1,600. Rates:
from 550F–615F including service; breakfast 34F; children
over 12 140F; dogs 30F.

## Nikko de Paris
**15th arr.**
**61 quai de Grenelle**
**575.62.62**
*All major credit cards*

Located in the Front de Seine complex, this Japanese-
owned hotel has a red brick exterior and 32 floors. The
rooms are ultra-modern and decorated in western or
Japanese styles, with large picture windows facing the
pont Mirabeau. The Nikko features a hairdresser, a
Japanese pastry shop, a bookshop, a perfume shop, a
swimming pool, an agreeable panoramic bar
(L'Apollinaire), and three restaurants: the Brasserie du
Pont Mirabeau, the Benkay (authentic Japanese cuisine)
and the excellent Les Célébrités. The 784 rooms are air
conditioned. Parking is 30F per day. Meeting facilities for
up to 400 are provided. Rates: from 400F–530F including
service; breakfast 30F; children until 12 free.

## Paris Sheraton
**14th arr.**
**19 rue du**
**Cdt-Mouchotte**
**260.35.11**
*All major credit cards*

This luxury establishment is a fiefdom of American and
Japanese tourists, conventioneers and business people in
general. Decorated in contemporary good taste, it has
comfortable and pleasant rooms. We only regret that the
ceilings are low and the corridors appear to be endless.
There are two restaurants, La Ruche, featuring fast food;
and Le Montparnasse 25, a gourmet restaurant. There is
also a bar, Le Corail. Meeting rooms will house ten to
1,000 people. Rates: from 500F–550F including service;
breakfast 31F; children under 17 are free.

## P.L.M. Saint-Jacques
**14th arr.**
**17 blvd. Saint-Jacques**

This huge hotel operates very smoothly and provides
tourists and business people from around the world
comfortable, small, well-kept rooms. Four floors were
entirely remodeled in 1979. There are three restaurants,
one of which, the June, serves Japanese food; a piano bar,

**589.89.80**
*All major credit cards*

the Tahonga, where bartender Stéphane mixes 57 varieties of cocktails; a shopping mall; a game club featuring bridge, chess, Scrabble and backgammon; 19 meeting rooms, some of which are huge; a hairdresser; a bank; a cinema and an Air France office—all of which lends the hotel the atmosphere of an airport annex. The management gives rates reduced by 10%–20% during the off-season, as well as additional discounts for couples under 25, families and senior citizens. There are 800 air conditioned rooms and meeting rooms for ten to 1,300 people. Parking is 24F per day. Rates: from 416F–492F including service and breakfast; children 80F.

••••
## Sofitel Bourbon
**7th arr.**
**32 rue Saint-Dominique**
**555.91.80**
*AE, EC, V.*

Located in the heart of the 7th arrondissement, behind the Palais-Bourbon and within walking distance of the Seine and place de la Concorde, this hotel is well designed and of modest proportions. The Sofitel-Bourbon isn't *that* luxurious, nor is it superbly decorated. The small rooms, however, though inadequately soundproofed, are functionally furnished, cheerful, and offer the usual amenities such as air conditioning, direct-dial phones, radios and TVs, and minibars.  Four spacious and luxurious suites have recently been remodeled. Parking is 30F; meeting rooms are available for ten to 40 people. Rates: from 490F–720F including service; breakfast 29F; children under 12 free; dogs 28F.

••••
## Sofitel Paris
**15th arr.**
**8-12 rue Louis-Armand**
**554.95.00**
*All major credit cards*

Located near the Porte de Versailles Palais des Expositions, this is the ideal hotel for business people. It features 35 meeting rooms, ultra-modern equipment, simultaneous interpreters in five languages, closed-circuit television, and a 300-seat cinema. The hotel offers excellent service, and is equipped with exterior bubble-shaped plexiglas elevators, as well as a sauna and gymnasium, heated pool and winter garden. The somewhat narrow rooms are comfortable, modern and offer splendid views of the city. The hotel features two restaurants, Le Relais de Sèvres, and La Poterie; and a piano bar, Le Montgolfier. The 635 rooms have air conditioning, and there is attendant parking in the basement for 25F per day. Meeting facilities for fifteen to 800. Rates: from 450F–680F including service; breakfast 30F; children under 12 free; dogs 30F.

•••
## Suffren La Tour
**15th arr.**
**20 rue Jean-Rey**
**578.61.08**
*All major credit cards*

This large and modern hotel is located near the Seine and the Champ de Mars. The rooms are small but comfortable. There's a restaurant, Le Champ de Mars, an agreeable garden terrace and a disco bar, Le Ragtime. Rates: from 320F–350F including service and breakfast; children free. Free parking.

# *For Students*

The four old and remarkably restored Marais hotels listed below are open to students up to 30 years old, with or without a student ID. The fifth listing is a large modern hotel with a pool and garden, located in the 12th arrondissement. Placed under the aegis of the MIJE (Maisons Internationales de la Jeunesse et des Etudiants, or International Youth Hostels), these hotels offer inexpensive and comfortable rooms at 40F per person; 66F with breakfast and dinner.

## *Centre International de Séjour de Paris (C.I.S.P.)*
12 arr.
**6 ave. Maurice-Ravel**
**343.19.01**

CISP, or the International Center for Sojourning in Paris, has a lobby with bay windows, a 150-square-meter garden, a comfortable cafeteria, scores of meeting rooms, a heated pool and many other amenities often unknown to young visitors in Paris. Opened in 1964, its intent was to assist and provide shelter to young French and foreign tourists, offering them agreeable and practical rooms with one, two or four beds, and dormitories with eight beds per room; also a snack bar, a 200-seat restaurant and vending machines. The whole place is cheerfully decorated, with plenty of green plants. CISP's director, M. Hugues Fraysse, is bent on making his establishment a neighborhood cultural center offering lectures, exhibits, workshops, a library, an auditorium, a photolab and dramatic, cinematographic and musical performances—even political meetings. Despite all these activities, CISP is first and foremost a hotel for young tourists who will find here all the information they need in order to discover and enjoy Paris. There are 63 singles, 30 doubles, 16 rooms with 4 beds, and 4 rooms with 8 beds. Rates: from 36F for one to 102F for two including service and breakfast. No dogs.

## *Fauconnier*
4th arr.
**11 rue du Fauconnier**
**274.23.45**

Ten years ago the City of Paris donated this former seventeenth-century townhouse to MIJE, which has marvelously restored it inside and out. What's more, in upkeep and general cleanliness it's superior to many so called luxury hotels. The Fauconnier is peacefully located behind the Hôtel de Sens which houses the Forney Library. The 29 rooms feature tall windows with transoms that overlook a quiet street and, directly below, a small paved interior courtyard. The bedding is simple and clean, yet the furniture is antique and includes attractive armoires, oak chests, and large rustic tables. Each room has its own sink. Notable throughout are the polished tiled floors, flagstones, wooden floors and rugs, as well as wooden beams, attractive double sets of curtains and cheerful linen wall hangings. Breakfast is served in a vast lobby and visiting groups can get together in the hotel's superb fourteenth-century vaulted cellars. The hotel's La Table d'Hôte restaurant is located at 16 rue du Pont-Louis Philippe. There are 10 doubles, 1 single, 14 with 4 beds and 4 with 6 beds. Rates: from 40F–80F, including service and breakfast. No dogs.

## *Fourcy*
**4th arr.**
**6 rue de Fourcy**
**274.23.45**

The former Charpentier townhouse, built in 1672 for a member of the King's Parliament, underwent many misfortunes before falling into the hands of the MIJE, which is currently supervising its restoration. The former servants' quarters have been remodeled into 43 beautiful new rooms, and the carriage house is going to be transformed into a gorgeous meeting room. A large seventeenth-century stone staircase with wrought-iron handrails leads up to the rooms. They are furnished with lacquered iron beds and antique furniture such as chests and armoires. Each room has its own sink and shower. Young foreigners enjoy the Fourcy for is wooden beams and choice location. The hotel's restaurant, La Table d'Hôte, is located at 16 rue du Pont-Louis-Philippe. There are 15 doubles, 25 with 4 beds, 2 with 6 beds and 1 with 8 beds. Rates: from 40F–80F including service and breakfast. No dogs.

## *Maubuisson*
**4th arr.**
**12 rue des Barres**
**272.72.09**

Formerly a townhouse for mother-superiors of the Royal Abbey of Maubuisson, this attractive seventeenth-century house is as well decorated and charming as the Fauconnier (*see above*). An additional feature is its picturesque and peaceful location right next to the Saint-Gervais church. The 29 whitewashed rooms overlook a splendid view of a tree-lined square. The lobby and lounge feature antique tiled floors. The Maubuisson offers a warm, discreet, family-style atmosphere for young people, aged 18 to 30. Non-students welcome. Nearby parking lot. The hotel's La Table d'Hôte restaurant is located at 16 rue du Pont-Louis-Philippe. Rates: from 40F–80F including service and breakfast. No dogs.

## *François-Miron*
**4th arr.**
**6 rue François-Miron**
**272.72.09**

Many members of the Couperin family of famous organists lived in this building. The Pen Club International took it over, and in 1974 installed ten "student" rooms which are comfortable, simple and clean. The walls have been painted salmon pink, the furniture is modern, and each room has its own sink. A shower and a bathroom are on each floor. Although the neighborhood is charming, it is also somewhat noisy. Nearby parking lot. The hotel's restaurant, La Table d'Hôte, is at 16 rue du Pont-Louis-Philippe. There are 4 doubles, 2 with 3 beds, 4 with 4 beds. Rates: from 40F–80F including service and breakfast. No dogs.

# *Very Discreet*

You can arrive at these hotels with or without luggage, check in at 3:00 P.M. or midnight, and no one will bat an eyelash. You may even walk in, take a one-hour nap, and check out.

### *Champs-Élysées Studios*
**8th arr.**
**97 rue La Boétie**
**359.09.55**

The Spanish/Moorish-style rooms overlook a courtyard and are very peaceful. Those facing the street are not as quiet, yet their large Hollywood-style beds set in a Pompadour-Auriol decor make up for it. The bathrooms are all quite nice. Cold and hot meals on request.

### *City-Hôtel Condorcet*
**9th arr.**
**29 rue Condorcet**
**878.30.72**

Guests check in through the street entrance, check out through an exit into an alley—all to avoid embarrassing encounters. This two-star hotel offers comfortable little suites decorated in Louis XV and 1900 styles. Delicious hot meals are served in the rooms at all hours. The sixth-floor suites offer a fine view of Montmartre.

### *Globe*
**6th arr.**
**15 rue de Quatre-Vents**
**326.35.50**

Habitués refer to it as the "Quatre Vents" or Four Winds. The Globe has a discreet entrance located in the seventeenth-century building which has been completely renovated and decorated in fine flea market wares. Enlivened by a multitude of flowers, the Globe has sixteen little rooms with multicolored linen wall-hangings, wooden beams and personable bathrooms. The management takes pride in laying out petits fours on the bedside tables every night. Rooms are priced at approximately 130F. Parking at 6 rue Lobineau.

### *Pavillon Villejust*
**16th arr.**
**46 rue Paul-Valéry**
**501.71.10**

Saint-Louis' bust, which once reigned over the lobby, has been mysteriously replaced with a bouquet of plastic flowers. The rooms, as well as their boudoirs, however, have retained their rococo frescoes and neo-Louis XV-style furniture. In the time-worn bathrooms, the hot water is sparingly pumped. On the other hand, the elderly lady who answers the door is exquisitely charming, even if you do have to wait a long time. It is important to remember that every Saturday at 6:00 A.M., this dear old lady attends Mass, with the key to the bar in her pocket.

### *Résidence Cardinet*
**17th arr.**
**52 rue Cardinet**
**763.80.91**

Located out on the Monceau Plain, this comfortable townhouse is designed for upper-class gentlemen and their guests. Meals are served on request.

**Villa Caroline**
16th arr.
85 rue de la Pompe
504.67.38

This three-star white house with a well-maintained façade is located across the street from the Janson-de-Sailly high school. Its ten rooms, each at approximately 300F, are ostentatiously decorated in a half-contemporary, half-Napoleon III style with imitation potted plants, thick carpets, comfortable beds covered with imitation fur, shiny cushions, "modern" sculptures, subdued lighting with rheostats, and padded doors. The service is efficient and cold meals can be ordered upon request. The Villa Caroline is one of the best hotels in its category. Parking at avenue George-Mandel.

**Windsor Home**
16th arr.
3 rue Vital
504.49.49

Away from the din of the city, this little white hotel looks very much like a family boardinghouse. Its ten simple rooms are arranged around a garden courtyard whose main attribute is it provincial charm. Meals are served on request. A deposit may be needed. The office is closed on Sundays.

# The Banlieue

Over the last few years, the outskirts of Paris have attracted many modern hotels, most of them located near airports or along highways. Since these hotels generally have much the same advantages and inconveniences, we feel it is sufficient to indicate their mere presence without adding too many comments.

## NORTH
## (plus Bourget and Roissy-Charles-de-Gaulle Airports)

**Holiday Inn Roissy**

95500 Gonesse
54 rue de Paris
988.00.22
*All major credit cards. Rates from*

*280F–310F including service; American buffet breakfast 30F. Children free. Air conditioning. Meeting facilities for up to 400. Restaurant: Western Grill. Garden. Free shuttle service to airports. Free parking.*

•••
# Mercure Orsay

*91 Les-Ulis, Z.A. Courtebeuf
Ave. du Parana
707.63.96
AE, D, V Rates from 200F–220F
including service; breakfast 22F, dogs
30F. Air conditioning. Meeting facilities
for 10 to 100. Garden. Pool, volleyball,
lawn bowling, ping-pong. Restaurant.
Parking.*

•••
# Mercure Saint-Witz

*95470 Saint-Witz
par Surviliers
471.92.03
All major credit cards. Rates from 197F
including service; breakfast 18F,
children 35F; dogs 25F. Air
conditioning. Meeting facilities for up to
150. Garden. Pool and children's
playground. Restaurant. Free shuttle
service to Roissy-Charles-de-Gaulle
airport. Free parking.*

•••
# Novotel
# Aulnay-sous-
# Bois

*93600 Aulnay-sous-Bois
R.N. 370
866.22.97
AE, D, V Rates from 200F–230F
including service; breakfast 22F;
Children under 12 free; dogs 30F.
Meeting facilities for 4 to 150. Garden.
Pool, children's playground, billiards,
ping-pong. Restaurant/bar: Les
Philippines.*

•••
# Novotel
# Cergy-Pontoise

*95000 Cergy
Ave. du Parc
030.39.47
AE, DC, V Rates from 192F–207F
including service; breakfast 20F;
children over 12 35F; dogs 30F. Air
conditioning. Meeting facilities for up to
150. Garden. Pool. Restaurant. Free
parking.*

•••
# Novotel
# Paris-le Bourget

*93150 le Blanc-Mesnil
rue du Pont-Yblon
867.48.88
AE, DC, V Rates from 197F–212F
including service. breakfast 20F;
children over 12 30F. Meeting facilities
for 10 to 200. Garden. Pool. Restaurant:
La Rôtisserie. Shuttle service to Bourget
and Charles-de-Gaulle airports. Free
parking.*

•••
# Novotel Paris-
# Survilliers

*95470 Survilliers-A 1
D 16, Saint-Witz
468.69.80
AE, DC, V Rates from 207F including
service; breakfast 20F; children 25F.
Meeting facilities for up to 50 people.
Garden. Pool. Restaurant. Free parking.*

•••
# Paris Penta Hôtel

*92400 Courbevoie
18 rue Baudin
788.50.51
All major credit cards Rates from
330F–360F including service and
breakfast; children 60F. No large pets.
Meeting facilities for 10 to 100. Pool.
Skating rink and bowling alley located
next door at the Charras Centre
Commercial. Restaurant: l'Atelier. Snack
bar. Free shuttle service to Métro and
Quatre Temps shopping mall. Parking
lot.*

•••
# Sofitel Roissy

*95700 Roissy-en-France
Aéroport Charles-de-Gaulle
862.23.23
All major credit cards. Rates: from
280F–340F including service; breakfast
29F. children under 12 free; dogs 40F.
Meeting facilities for 10 to 300 people.
Pool, sauna, children's playground.
Restaurant: Les Valois. Panoramic bar: Le
Plein Ciel. Pizzeria, cafeteria. Bar: Le
Bourbon, disco on Fri. and Sat. evenings.
Airport shuttle service. Parking lot.*

# SOUTH
## (plus Orly Airport)

## ····
## Frantel Paris-Orly

*94150 Rungis 20
ave. Charles-Lindbergh
687.36.36
All major credit cards Rates from
265F–310F including service; breakfast
23F; children 65F. Dogs 30F. Air
conditioning. Meeting facilities for 10 to
250. Indoor pool and sauna. Beauty
salon. Restaurant: La Rungisserie. Free
shuttle service to Orly Airport 6:00 A.M.
to midnight. Valet parking 17F, or free
parking in front of hotel.*

## ···
## Motel P.L.M. Orly

*94547 Orly
Aérogare
687.23.37
All major credit cards Rates from
200F–225F including service; breakfast
20F, children free. Air conditioning.
Meeting facilities for 5 to 250. Garden.
Restaurant: Le Patio. Free shuttle service
to Orly. Free parking.*

## ····
## Hilton Orly

*94310 Orly
Aérogare d'Orly
687.33.88
All major credit cards Rates from
238F–452F including service; breakfast
34F; children sharing room with parents
free. Air conditioning. Meeting facilities
for up to 200. Restaurant: La Louisiane.
Free airport shuttle. Parking.*

## ···
## Novotel-Créteil-le-Lac

*94000 Créteil
Route de Choisi
207.91.02
AE, DC, V Rates from 202F including
service; breakfast 20F; children free.
dogs, 30F. Air conditioning. Meeting
facilities for 10 to 100. Garden. Pool,
tennis courts, wind surfing on lake.
Restaurant. Free parking.*

## ···
## Holiday Inn Paris-Orly

*94150 Rungis
4 ave. Charles-Lindbergh
687.26.66
AE, DC, V Rates from 245F–310F
including service; breakfast 24F,
Children free. Air conditioning. Meeting
facilities for 5 to 250. Pool. Restaurant.
Free parking.*

## ····
## Novotel Massy-Palaiseau

*92120 Palaiseau
18–20 rue Emile-Baudot
920.84.91
AE, DC, V Rates from 192F including
service; breakfast 20F; children free.
Meeting facilities for up to 250.
Restaurant. Garden. Pool. Restaurant.
Free parking.*

····
# Novotel Saclay

91400 Saclay
Rue Charles-Thomassin
941.81.40
AE, DC, V. Rates: from 197F including
service. Meeting facilities. Garden. Pool,
bowling, tennis, archery, shooting range.
Restaurant: Le Champignon. Free
parking.

····
# Relais des Chartreux

91160 Saulx-les-Chartreux
R.N. 20
909.34.31
AE, DC, V Rates from 180F–200F
including services; breakfast 16F;
children free. Air conditioning. Meeting
facilities up to 225. Garden. Pool, tennis,
bowling. Restaurant: Le Chartreux. Free
parking.

# EAST

····
# Nogentel

94130 Nogent-sur-Marne
8 rue du Port
872.70.00
All major credit cards Rates from
205F–235F including service; breakfast
20F; children over 8 30F; dogs 30F.
Meeting facilities for 15 to 250. Sports
center with Olympic pool, tennis and
other facilities. Restaurant: Le
Panoramic. Public parking across the
street.

···
# Novotel Bagnolet

93170 Bagnolet
1 ave. de la République
360.02.10
All major credit cards Rates from
298F–350F including service; breakfast
22F; children 38F; dogs 35F. Air
conditioning. Meeting facilities for up to
800. Garden. Pool. Restaurant: L'Oeuf et
la Poule. Grill: Le Gallieni. Piano bar: Le
Glamour. Pay parking.

# WEST

···
# Club Méditerranée

92200 Neuilly
58 blvd. Victor-Hugo
758.11.00
AE, V Rates from 395F–475F including
service; breakfast 28F; children under 4
free. Air conditioning. Meeting facilities
for 20 to 140. Restaurant with buffet.
Pay parking.

···
# Hameau de Suresnes

92150 Suresnes
70 ave. Franklin-Roosevelt
506.57.00
AE, CB, DC Rates from 190F including
service; breakfast 23F; children 20F;
dogs 20F. Air conditioning. Garden.
Restaurant: La Ferme du Mont-Valérien.
Parking lot.

# Novotel Orgeval

*78630 Orgeval-R.N. 13*
*975.97.60*
*AE, DC, V Rates from 200F–230F*
*including service; breakfast 22F;*
*children 40F; dogs 30F. Air*
*conditioning. Meeting facilities for 10 to*
*100. Pool, tennis, volleyball, children's*
*playground. Restaurant/grill/bar open*
*until midnight. Parking.*

# Ramada

*78140 Vélizy-Villacoublay*
*22 ave. de l'Europe*
*946.96.98*
*All major credit cards. Rates: from*
*310F–355F including service; breakfast*
*35F; children free. Air conditioning.*
*Meeting facilities for up to 200. Pool.*
*Restaurant: La Diligence. Free parking.*

# THE SHOPS

# THE SHOPS

**P**aris just may have it all: a Saint Laurent for less, an alligator-skin saddle, a Le Corbusier sink, a tattoo artist, a mermaid swimsuit, a chocolate record, caviar knives and a Ferrari-for-a-day. Not to mention the thousands of unusual, useful, amazing, tempting, well-guarded and indispensible addresses. We've listed a few of our favorites.

# Antiques

**F**or some time now Parisian antique dealers have been complaining that they no longer can find anything good. The problem is relative. A foriegner visiting France for the first time is, on the contrary, pleasantly surprised by the abundant selection he sees in the shops of these inconsolable dealers. It does so happen that very valuable objects rarely stay in France, but head rapidly for New York or London. There's still a lot left, though, and it's more than enough to gladden the hearts of lesser collectors or people who simply enjoy beautiful things. A serious problem has nonetheless arisen in France as elsewhere, namely, the proliferation of forgeries, whether of paintings, antique bronzes, furniture or curios. Knowledge and flair are becoming more and more essential to obtain a work of exemplary quality, and, alas, not even the greatest experts are proof against unfortunate errors from time to time. You simply have to be prudent when the price of your prospective purchase goes over a certain figure. How? There's no choice: Either you're a real connoisseur and can risk buying anywhere at all, or you can't trust blindly in your own judgment. In that case there is a golden rule which you absolutely have to follow: Buy only from a real specialist. You may end up paying a little more than if you went into the first second-hand store you laid eyes on (and besides, that's not always true), but you'll have the double guarantee that (1) ninety-nine times out of a hundred the object will be genuine, and (2) if it turns out to be false in spite of everything, the dealer will respect the certificate of authenticity he gave you and won't make any fuss about taking it back.

**T**his is why we prefer to give you only a few good addesses instead of drawing up endless lists of antique dealers. We repeat: these people sometimes make mistakes, but we can guarantee that they practice their profession with a maximum of honesty and scruples. If any of them ever takes it into his head to disobey the laws of business ethics, just let us know. You can be sure he'll be chewing his nails after the "publicity" we'll give him.

Our list is not definitive, of course. Paris has thousands of antique and second-hand stores, and we don't pretend to know them all. There are undoubtedly some excellent stores which we may have missed but, incomplete or not, we'd rather stick with the ones we know.

You can find antique stores almost anywhere in Paris. But there is one privileged section where you can take a most agreeable stroll into the past, even if you don't feel like buying anything. This section is on the Left Bank, between boulevard Saint-Germain and the Seine.

Stroll along boulevard Saint-Germain. Turn left onto rue Bonaparte, then right onto rue Jacob. A little further down this street, to your right, you'll find rue Furstenberg and the enchanting little square of the same name where Delacroix had his studio (open to the public). Walk around the square. The shop windows are full of cute, funny, unusual objects. But watch out: the prices are often steep, since this is a very fashionable spot. It's best to compare and decide later.

Back on rue Jacob, go down it again to your left until you intersect rue Bonaparte, on which you turn right, walk past the Ecole des Beaux Arts and come out onto quai Malaquais and, further to the left, Quai Voltaire, which has some highly renowned antique shops. Now go up rue de Beaune, which is lined with several excellent stores. By taking either rue de Verneuil or rue de l'Université, both to your right, you'll emerge onto rue du Bac, which in turn leads back to boulevard Saint-Germain. If you're not ruined or crawling on your hands and knees by this time, cross boulevard Saint-Germain. On the other side is boulevard Raspail, then rue de Grennelle or rue de la Chaise to your immediate left, where you'll discover some good shops. Finally, when you come to the end of rue de Grennelle, take a left onto rue des Saints-Pères, which you will leave either at boulevard Saint-Germain or in front of the Seine on Quai Malaquais, where other quality antique shops await you.

Some other day you can walk along faubourg Saint-Honoré and rue Saint-Honoré from rue La Boétie to place Vendôme. You'll see some very handsome stores which are likely to intimidate you by their rather solemn appearance. But don't let that fool you. On several different occasions we've noticed that prices here are sometimes lower than in the flea market, and the quality usually much higher. But we wouldn't want to claim this is a fixed rule.

# HAUTE EPOQUE, MIDDLE AGES, RENAISSANCE, LOUIS XVIII

Haute-Epoque furniture is becoming increasingly rare, particularly the bulkier pieces that are often hard to fit into modern apartments. These are being replaced by less cumbersome cabinets, little parsons' tables and small Renaissance chests. Of course, they are all outrageously expensive.

**Hôtel Drouot**
**9th arr.**
**9 rue Drouot**
**246.17.11**

On May 13, 1980, Parisian auctioneers returned to the rue Drouot after having spent four years at the Gare d'Orsay. Entirely rebuilt, this old hotel has become the temple of antiques, comprising sixteen rooms on three floors linked by escalators. As a result, the premises are often jammed by bargain hunters accustomed to inspecting articles prior to auction. The building's so-called eclectic façade is a mishmash of contrasting architectural and ornamental features from the past. Nevertheless, this fanciful building, or stock market of artistic values, will always attract 5,000 to 6,000 daily visitors afflicted by the "Hôtel Disease." Every Friday the *Gazette de l'Hôtel Drouot* (located at 99 rue de Richelieu, 2nd arr., tel. 261.81.78) informs readers of the general trend and results of past sales, and announces forthcoming daily sales. For your information, each sale or purchase entails several additional costs:

As a buyer, you must assume the following: 16% of the auctioned price (up to 6,000F): 11.5% from 6,000F to 20,000F; 10% for 20,000F and up. The easiest way for you to figure out how much an object auctioned off at over 20,000F will cost you is to compute 10% of the highest bid and add 570F. For instance, a desk sold at 40,000F comes out to 40,000F + 4,000F + 570F = 44,570F.

As a seller, you have to assume 5% of the highest bid price. Plus, if necessary, a consultant's fee (3%–6% of the auction price, depending on his or her specialty), as well as all costs pertaining to advertising and catalogue entries. In addition to these varying costs (all pre-established and submitted to the seller), there's a 3% "royalty" levied on the auctioned price for original modern paintings and sculptures signed by living artists, or those who have died within the last 60 years.

Estimates: The appraisal desk in the entrance hall (open Mondays thru Saturdays from 11:00 A.M. to 12:00 noon and from 2:00 P.M. to 6:00 P.M.) is staffed by an official who will appraise any object free of charge. For furniture and other cumbersome objects, free appraisals are given in your home, providing the object is subsequently auctioned off at Drouot.

Reserve prices: After consulting the appraiser, the seller may affix a reserve price on the object, which will oblige the auctioneer to withdraw it in case the highest bid falls short of the designated price. The seller is thus protected from having the object auctioned off at a price he considers insufficient; he is obliged to pay a fee (based proportionally on the value of the object withdrawn to cover the costs of exhibiting and putting on the sale.

Drouot Nord: so that Drouot may devote itself exclusively to bona fide works of art, the Association of Parisian Appraisers established Drouot Nord in September 1981 (located at 64 rue Doudeauville, 18th arrondissement). In its three rooms, ordinary objects like household furniture, sewing machines, refrigerators and TV sets are auctioned off Mondays through Fridays, from 9:00 A.M.

## Jacqueline Boccador
**7th arr.**
**22 rue du Bac**
**260.75.79**
*Closed Mon. morning*

For nearly five hundred years, Jacqueline Boccador's family has devoted itself to art in all its forms. Jacqueline herself, currently associated with Domenico di Cortone, alias "le Boccador," has written books on statuary art and (soon to be published) medieval furniture. She easily imparts her passion for beautiful furniture, statues and tapestries which literally come to life in her shop.

## Charles et Philippe Boucaud
**7th arr.**
**25 rue du Bac**
**261.24.07**

Well-known for their pewter, Philippe Boucaud and his mother Mme Charles Boucaud also feature high-quality Haute Epoque sculptures.

## Gabriel Bresset
**6th arr.**
**197 blvd. Saint-Germain**
**548.18.24**

World-famed specialists in medieval statuary of wood or stone—natural-toned or many-colored. They also feature gothic tapestries that are bought by large museums, furniture and sculpted wood objects (marvelous shellacked or ebony-inlaid cabinets), as well as Medieval and Renaissance objects made of bronze, ivory and enamel. Don't miss the superb vaulted cellars on the quai Voltaire.

## Brimo-Laroussilhe
**7th arr.**
**7 quai Voltaire**
**260.74.72**
*Closed Mon. morning.*
**17th arr.**
**58 rue Jouffroy**
**227.71.28**
*Closed Sat. afternoon.*

This highly esteemed house offers Medieval and Renaissance furniture, sculptures and works of art, as well as a few beautiful archeological items.

## Jean-Claude Edrei
**7th arr.**
**8 rue de Beaune**
**261.28.08**

Chiefly devoted to works from the Haute Epoque, this large and attractive shop is particularly well known for the high quality of its earthenwares and pewter. Also featured are tapestries and a few pieces of furniture.

### Marc Lagrand
7th arr.
25 rue de Bourgone
551.47.16

Lagrand offers remarkable Haute Epoque furniture and a few interesting seventeenth-century items. The Lagrands have been antique dealers since 1890.

### Robert Montagut
7th arr.
15 rue de Lille
260.29.25
*Closed Mon. morning.*

The shop features few items of furniture but lots of paintings, bronze objects, curios and, generally speaking, good-looking, high-quality wares. Robert Montagut, a former pharmacist from Toulouse, took over Claude Marx's shop and has installed a "pharmaceutical history department" next to the Haute Epoque department. Indeed, this is a curious shop.

### Mythes et Légendes
4th arr.
12 rue de Sevigne
272.35.43
*Closed Mon.*

Mythes et Légendes offers medieval and Renaissance furniture and collector's items, some of which are voluminous.

### Perpitch
7th arr.
240 blvd.
Saint-Germain
548.37.67

For nearly 40 years, Antoine Perpitch has been specializing in Flemish and Italian Renaissance, French gothic and medieval statuary works, as well as Louis XIII chairs, high quality round-topped chests, parsons tables, and sixteenth- and seventeenth-century tapestries.

# SEVENTEENTH AND EIGHTEENTH CENTURIES

The seventeenth and eighteenth centuries are important dates for French furniture (Regency, Louis XV, Louis XVI and Directoire). Since many antique dealers specialize in this period, it may be difficult to make a selection.

### Didier Aaron
16th arr.
32 ave.
Raymond-Poincare
727.17.79
*Closed Sat.*

One of Paris' most brilliant selections of inlaid furniture and refined artwork from the golden age of French decorative art, the eighteenth century. Aaron is one of the strongest supporters of the Grand Palais' Biennale of antique dealers.

### Antiquités de Beaune
7th arr.
14 rue de Beaune
261.25.42
*Closed Mon. morning.*

M. Horwitz, who is president of the association that organizes the annual Cinq Jours de l'Objet Extraordinaire, is also an expert in eighteenth-century provincial furniture.

## Aveline
**8th arr.**
**20 rie di Corqie**
**266.60.29**

Though Aveline features few items of furniture, they are all museum quality and, quite appropriately, purchased by some of the world's largest museums. The firm is also known for its highly curious and decorative objects and has recently been offering Pompier paintings from the end of the nineteenth century.

## La Cour de Varenne
**7th arr.**
**42 rue de Varenne**
**544.65.50**
*Closed Mon. morning.*

This truly beautiful store overlooks both the street and an exquisite courtyard where you can still see Mme de Staël's servants' quarters. Park your car and enter the enchanted world (two floors) in which Claude Lévy, his wife and their partner Bernard Steinitz have amassed numerous treasures—including curios, clocks and especially seventeenth- and eighteenth-century furniture, some of which is amazing. Repairs can be made on the premises by an unrivaled artisan using remarkable old tools. All the items here, large and small, are of the best quality and are commensurately expensive.

## Dubreuil
**7th arr.**
**25 quai Voltaire**
**261.24.21**
*Closed Mon.*

At Dubreuil's, which offers a wide selection of somewhat low-key, high quality goods, all period furniture and objects are sold with a guarantee.

## Fabre
**8th arr.**
**19 rue Balzac**
**563.79.17**
*Closed Sat.*

Fabre features seventeenth- and eighteenth-century furniture, artwork and tapestries highly sought after by museums and major collectors.

## Denise Gateau
**7th arr.**
**33 quai Voltaire**
**261.19.92**

This little shop has a high-quality inventory, including eighteenth-century furniture and tapestries sold to an international clientele.

## Kraemer et Cie
**8th arr.**
**43 rue de Monceau**
**563.24.46**

Although Philippe Kraemer is an expert in seventeenth and eighteenth-century French antiques and his customers include museums and the world's most famous collectors of furniture, bronze, and works of art, he is nonetheless very modest. His stunning gallery could pass for a museum.

## Étienne Lévy
**8th arr.**
**178 faubourg Saint-Honoré**
**562.33.47**
*Closed Sat.*

Étienne Lévy, a charming antique dealer for over sixty years, is rightly considered one of Paris's foremost art connoisseurs. An expert in seventeenth and eighteenth-century items, he is particularly interested in furniture characterized by original or unusual features such as mechanical tables and goldstone-inlaid writing blocks. The new store on the ground floor, as well as the seven display rooms on the first floor, constitute a sumptuous museum in which you will regularly find work by eighteenth-century master cabinetmakers such as

Weisweiler, George Jacob and Leleu. There are also other perfectly dazzling objects such as master clocks, rock crystal chandeliers, chiseled works and others all signed.

### Lupu
**8th arr.**
**43 faubourg**
**Saint-Honoré**
**265.93.19**

This rather poorly located shop (between the Elysée and the English embassy) has an eye-catching window display. From skeleton clocks to Louis XV corner cupboards, everything featured is gorgeous, of superb quality and, of course, very expensive.

### Jacques Perrin
**7th arr.**
**3 quai Voltaire**
**260.27.20**
*Closed Mon. morning.*

In this flamboyant contemporary setting of lacquered, anonized aluminum, Jacques Perrin displays the most spectacular eithteenth-century furniture. Included are Boulle chests of drawers, Mazarin desks and other high-quality objects such as Marie Antoinette's exquisite little traveling desk, which he donated to the Versailles Palace.

### Maurice Segoura
**8th arr.**
**20 faubourg**
**Saint-Honoré**
**265.11.03**

As successor to Yvonne de Bremond d'Ars, Maurice Segoura has two stories filled with furniture, artwork and paintings bearing the most famous stamps and prestigious signatures.

### Wanecq
**7th arr.**
**12 rue**
**des Saint-Pères**
**260.83.64**
*Closed Mon. morning.*

Jean Wanecq is a serious specialist in Louis XIV furniture and his store is well-stocked with beautiful cabinets that are currently very much in fashion. Also featured are eighteenth-century objects and furniture, as well as seventeenth- to nineteenth-century paintings.

# DIRECTOIRE, EMPIRE, RESTORATION, CHARLES X

Although slightly in disfavor, Empire furniture, superb and imposing, has its staunch supporters. The Grand Trianon was entirely refurnished in Empire style by André Malraux and the Mobilier National. Since there are few bona fide Empire experts, we list only two of them. On the other hand, the elegant lines of the Directoire and Charles X furniture, in light- or dark-toned wood, are increasingly in vogue today.

### Au Directoire
**7th arr.**
**37 rue de Grenelle**
**222.67.09**
*Open Tues. thru Sat., Mon. by appt. only.*

This shop specializes in late eighteenth-century, early nineteenth-century furniture, though it is currently diversifying into gilded bronze items as well.

### *Fabius Frères*
**8th arr.**
**152 blvd. Haussmann**
**562.39.18**
*Closed Sat.*

Father-and-son Parisian antique dealers since 1867, Fabius Frères numbers museum curators and major collectors among his clients. The firm is noted for its seventeenth- and eighteenth-century Premier Empire and Napoleon IV furniture and works of art. Also, there are unusual period sculptures—including important works by Barye and Carpeaux—and various period paintings suitable for major collections.

### *Nicole Gérard*
**6th arr.**
**28 rue Jacob**
**326.26.43**
*Closed Sat.*

You'll find here very distinguished Restoration furniture in light or dark wood, curios and small paintings, and popular Neapolitan gouaches and pastels. Nicole Gérard is one of the finest experts around.

### *Imbert*
**8th arr.**
**157 faubourg Saint-Honoré**
**563.54.89**
*Closed Sat.*

Though the shop's window is small, you'll nevertheless find a large inventory in the courtyard which distinguishes itself by the high quality of its light-toned wooden furniture, its bronze works and opalines.

### *Mancel-Coti*
**6th arr.**
**42 rue du Bac**
**548.04.34**
*Closed Mon. morning*

You can rely on this venerable shop's Directoire, Consulat and Empire furniture, artworks and porcelains. Its knowledgeable customers have included Prince Murat and the Museum of the Legion of Honor. Closed Saturdays, from May to October.

### *Renoncourt*
**6th arr.**
**1 to 3 rue des Saints-Pères**
**260.75.87**

Renoncourt, an expert in Empire, Restoration and Charles X articles, will only display premium quality objects in his boutique. His light wood and mahogany furniture, clocks, bronzeworks, chandeliers and opalines are all coveted by museums and major collectors.

# *LOUIS-PHILIPPE, NAPOLEON II, TURN OF THE CENTURY*

After a long period of contempt—often justified—for furniture and art objects of the years from 1830 to the end of the century (in other words the Louis-Philippe and Napoleon III styles), mahogany, painted or ivory inlaid furniture, romantic and fussy objects, all command staggering prices. Since rattan and bamboo furniture has made such a comeback, you will be able to find more "Époque" styles at some of the antique dealers.

### *Two Villages and a Court*

In the heart of Paris, in midweek intrepid bargain hunters who can't wait until Saturday to search for things at Saint-Ouen, Montreuil or Porte Didot can always find a more sophisticated fleamarket that is modeled on London's Portobello Road. In addition to the Louvre des Antiquaires, there's the Village Suisse which occupies the corner of l'avenue de la Motte-Picquet and l'avenue de Suffren (near the Champs-de-Mars), where the Swiss Pavilion was located at the 1889 World's Fair. The hundred shops (closed Tuesday and Wednesday) are all professionally decorated and offer quality goods. Those in the know are always there Thursdays at 8:00 A.M. to appraise each shop's weekly "harvest." The eighteen stands at the Cour aux Antiquaires (54 faubourg Saint-Honoré) are closed on Sundays and Monday mornings. The art market's dealerships are all represented in these orderly little shops where you'll find all sorts of Greek and Russian icons, nineteenth- and twentieth-century paintings and engravings, Chinese and European ceramics, silverware and curios. Village Saint-Paul, the last of the lot, opened November 22, 1979, and comprises 60 shops (closed Tuesday and Wednesday). It is housed under the Marais' old ceiling beams. Located between the rue Saint-Paul, the quai des Célestins and the rue Charlemagne, the shops feature Haute Époque and Napoleon III pieces and curios from 1900 to 1925.

## Le Louvre des Antiquaires

Le Louvre des Antiquaires is far more important and distinguished than the Village Suisse and far better organized and presented than the flea market. It is France's, if not the world's most successful sales organization for objets d'art. Among the 250 antique dealers who have set up shop in the Louvre's former stores (three remarkably arranged floors), you are sure to find the greatest names in the art market. All these professionals have been previously screened and will only sell articles they personally guarantee to be authentic, such as art deco pieces, distinguished furniture from the eighteenth century, relatively unknown master paintings, ship models and antique earthenware stamped with unusual names. Everything the collector or amateur has ever dreamed of can be found here at reasonable prices. Le Louvre aux Antiquaires also has a delivery service, a club, exhibit halls, bars and a ravishing restaurant, Le Jardin du Louvre.

## Calvet
**9th arr.**
**10 rue Chauchat**
**770.87.03**

This third generation Calvet is a leading expert in quality furniture crafted under Napoleon III. For the last four to five years, this style of furniture has become very much in demand. Calvet is now the exclusive purveyor to the court of Morocco and the presidency of the Ivory Coast (Calvet formerly held a similar position with Iran).

## Madeleine Castaing
**6th arr.**
**21 rue Bonaparte**

Over twenty years ago, Madeleine Castaing, as a decorator and friend of artists (she patronized Soutine), prompted renewed interest in Napoleon III, colonial, French, Russian and English small-sized furniture,

**354.91.71**
*Closed Mon. morning.*

couches, poufs and curios by getting them out of attics and selling them at outrageous prices. Her huge inventory is stored right here in the neighborhood and some of the furniture desperately needs repair. Madeleine Castaing also commissions carpets and exclusive fabrics.

## Andrée Debar
**1st arr.**
**Louvre des Antiquaires, 2 allée Germain**
**297.28.08**
*Closed Mon.*

Formerly an actress, Andrée Debar is now a leading expert in Second Empire styles. She offers high-quality, expensive furniture and curios. Her shop also features 1900 furniture and objects.

## Lecoules
**9th arr.**
**62 rue Taitbout**
**874.69.69**

This venerable house, selling to collectors from all over the world, offers furniture and chairs made by master cabinet-makers during the second half of the nineteenth century.

## Huguette Rivière
**1st arr.**
**Louvre des Antiquaires, 1 allée Riesener**
**297.28.36**
*Closed Mon.*

One of the best Second Empire specialists, Huguette Rivière features mother-of-pearl-inlaid chairs and other furniture, couches, painted jardinieres, opalines and jewelry.

# AFRICAN, PRECOLOMBIAN, OCEANIA

## Argiles
**6th arr.**
**16 rue Guénégaud**
**633.44.73**
*Closed Mon.*

This beautiful gallery features numerous African objects and statues, including many collectors' items, as well as primitive and Eastern jewelry.

## Arts des Amériques
**6th arr.**
**42 rue de Seine**
**633.18.31**
*Closed Mon. morning*

In this charming little shop you'll find a wide selection of quality Precolombian objects, primarily from Mexico, Costa Rica and Colombia.

**Duperrier**
6th arr.
14 rue
des Beaux-Arts
354.38.64

Robert Duperrier's marvelous and uncommon shop features a mixed bag of objects with a total disregard for origin and period. Next to the large Ibo statues, Baoule masks, Biafra fetishes and Gabonese amulets, there's a superb collection of cowboy and Indian clothes and wares. Also featured are unusual Indonesian artworks.

**Galerie Carrefour**
6th arr.
141 blvd. Raspail
326.58.03

Contrary to other dealers, M. Vérité (his real name) believes that African art is unique and rich enough not to be mixed with pre-columbian and Polynesian works. His extravagant, unlimited and expertly selected medley of African art includes Ibéji, Yorouba, Dan masks, Ibo statues, Ashanti bronzeworks, Sénoufo doors, Akan jewelry, Baoulé statuettes, as well as a few Asian objects. The store also features a sprawling Mediterranean Basin antique department. Wide range of prices.

**Galerie Mermoz**
8th arr.
6 rue Jean-Mermoz
359.82.44

The King of Belgium, Mrs. Pompidou and John Huston come here on a regular basis to purchase the gallery's well-displayed Precolombian works. In 1970, Mermoz was one of the first to display Precolombian Mexican objects.

**Galerie 62 (Garcia)**
15th arr.
Village Suisse
78 ave. de Suffren
783.93.03
*Closed Tues., Wed.*

You'll discover a beautiful selection of primitive African and pre-columbian artworks, as well as other archeological finds, guaranteed authentic.

**Galerie Urubamba**
5th arr.
4 rue de la Bucherie
354.08.24
*Open from 2:00 P.M. to 7:30 P.M.
Closed Mon.*

This fascinating little gallery is the only one to specialize in both South and North American Indian art such as feather head-dresses, weavings, turquoise and silver jewelry, and many other dazzling old and new objects. Individual tribal themes are exhibited two to three times a year.

**Hélène Kamer**
6th arr.
9 quai Malaquais
260.75.91
*Closed Mon. morning.*

Within the red-lacquered walls of this superb and modern store, you'll find a variety of large African, pre-columbian and Polynesian objects very much in vogue with the shop's rich international clientele. Hélène Kamer sponsors annual exhibits with precise themes for which she generally publishes a catalogue.

# ═══ ART NOUVEAU AND DECO ═══

The 1900 Style (still called art nouveau in English, Modern Style, "noodle" or "Metro" in French, and Liberty in Italian) is currently in high demand, a phenomenon carefully engineered fifteen years ago by a few ingenious professionals. All pieces in this style, which often bear the signature of the maker, share consciously languid and evanescent shapes, often based on plant-like or natural forms. They also almost always have a remarkable finish. The top names in furniture are Majorelle, Guimard, Gaillard and de Feure; in vases, Daum and Gallé. Before we can even hope to understand and appreciate the Barbès-Henri II style, we should examine its predecessor, the limitless and beautiful art deco. Unfortunately, there is much confusion with regards to art nouveau, art deco and the "throwback style," Barbès-Henri II, and they are often lumped together and simply termed "retro." Many unscrupulous antique dealers have profited from this confusion by thus labeling their ugly white elephants and foisting them on an unwary public.

**Art Nouveau Art Deco**
7th arr.
**38 rue de Lille**
261.18.90

Luc Choveaux has devoted himself to Belle Époque and Roaring Twenties artwork such as glasses made by Daum and Gallé and furniture made by Gaillard, Gaudi and Ruhlmann. His art department in the shop's basement features Symbolists (Levy-Dhurmier, Schwabe, Ranson, Maurice Chabas, Maxence, Osbert), conventionalists (Bouguereau, Canabel) and a few Surrealists.

**Maria de Beyrie**
6th arr.
**23 rue de Seine**
325.76.15

Very good 1900s-style works (Majorelle, Gallé, Guimard), the top names of the 1930s (Ruhlmann, Dunand, Legrain) and architectural furniture by Le Corbusier and his rivals from the German Bauhaus school. For the last few years, Maria de Beyrie has been bent on re-establishing works by the Viennese "Secession" school of art, particularly those by Joseph Hoffmann, who was one of the forerunners of modern art. After having spent ten years in les Halles, she is currently undertaking, at her new location, a comeback for the 1938 "Hollywood" style and for 1925 European avant-garde "Constructivists."

**Stéphane Deschamps**
6th arr.
**19 rue Guenegaud**
633.58.00
*Open from 2:15 P.M. to 7:00 P.M.*

Salvador Dali, Annie Girardot, Barbra Streisand, Liz Taylor, Yves St. Laurent and many others have come to Stéphane Deschamps to purchase turn-of-the-century sculptures, 1850's academic art, and drawings from the nineteenth and early twentieth centuries. He has just enlarged his store and is now offering, off the courtyard, 1880s furniture and high quality sculptures.

**Martine Domec**
6th arr.
**40 rue Mazarine**
354.92.69
*Open from 2:30 P.M. to 7:30 P.M.*

Although it doesn't feature any collector's items, this shop offers a delightful medley from which you may select small bamboo furniture, 1900 jardinieres, and barbotine plates, as well as other curios.

**Alain Lesieutre**
1st arr.
**Louvre des Antiquaires,
32 allee Riesener
297.28.63**
*Open from 11:00 A.M. to
7:00 P.M. Closed Mon.*

**7th arr.
9 rue de Beaune
261.16.81**
*Open from 3:00 P.M. to 7:00 P.M.
Closed Mon. and Sat.*

This dynamic young man who specializes in art nouveau and art deco will not sell any of his personal collection but will show it to you by appointment. In his corner shop, providing there's a bulge in your wallet, you could easily fill your basket with Galle and Daum vases, Bugatti bronze works, Chiparus statuettes and Oriental works of art. Their steep prices oblige them to be both good and beautiful.

**Félix Marcilhac**
6th arr.
**8 rue Bonaparte
326.47.36**

This remarkable expert, whose clients include the Metropolitan Museum and other well-known museums, always features premium quality art deco furniture and objects. Some of the private collectors who have purchased his Roaring Twenties objects include Catherine Deneuve, Andy Warhol and Alan Jones.

**Rodolphe Perpitch**
7th arr.
**52 rue du Bac
538.24.29**
*Open from 2:00 P.M. to 7:00 P.M.*

Here you'll find ceramics, bronze works, lamps, paste glass, etc. This expert in art nouveau and art deco is equally interested in nineteenth- and twentieth-century paintings.

**Vallois**
1st arr.
**15 rue Saint-Denis
508.40.03**

Some of the most valuable furniture and objects by the best known artists from 1925 to 1930 are included in this shop's collection. Customers include major collectors and fashion designers helplessly in love with this style's highly rational and sophisticated lines.

# ENGLISH

During the last thirty years, there has been a surge of infatuation for English furniture. The abundance of copies that has since cluttered the market demands great caution on the part of the buyer. Genuine English furniture is always very expensive, hard to find and very much in demand, with the exception of pieces from the Edwardian era, which are still reasonably priced.

**Colette Brandicourt**
16th arr.
**54 ave. Victor-Hugo
500.76.16**
*Closed Mon. morning.*

This expert in so-called Jersey earthenware has little furniture, yet you'll find lots of amusing curios (from 50F to 30,000F) such as liner trunks, Victorian cases, cigar boxes, objects depicting sporting events and, of course, earthenware.

## Brocante Store
**6th arr.**
**31 rue Jacob**
**260.24.80**
*Closed Mon. morning*

You'll find here lovely antique furniture as well as a medley of objects, cases, utensils and lamps, all made in England.

## Madeleine Castaing
**6th arr.**
**21 rue Bonaparte**
**354.91.71**

See above, under "Louis Philippe, Napoleon III, turn-of-the-century styles."

## Jean Pierre de Castro
**4th arr.**
**17 and 23 rue des Francs-Bourgeois**
**272.04.00**
*Open 10:30 A.M. to 7:30 P.M.*

This shop features a lovely selection of turn-of-the-century furniture made from Irish or English pine and polished fruitwood. See also under "Unusual Objects and Quality Used Goods."

## Galerie Regency
**7th arr.**
**63 rue du Bac**
**548.33.10**
*Closed Mon. morning*

This shop's enormous selection of objects can be put into three catagories: very good, good, and so-so. You'll find everything you need here to become a genuine English lord or lady at prices that would horrify a Scot! Items include furniture, cases, curios, paintings, and curiosity items. Other exceptional objects from different countries are also available.

## Galerie 13
**7th arr.**
**13 blvd. Raspail**
**548.77.31**
*Closed Mon. Morning*

The gallery offers a variety of furniture, including tables, chests of drawers and other premium quality sideboard-desk combinations. Shellacked boxes and beautiful portraits (including some excellent ones in the naive style) round out the gallery's selection of eighteenth- and nineteenth-century English objects apt to satisfy the typical Parisian Anglophile.

## Christian Groille
**7th arr.**
**64 rue du Bac**
**548.09.38**
*Closed Mon.*

As always, this shop offers charming, light-toned furniture made from Oregon pine which was very fashionable across the Channel during the eighteenth and nineteenth centuries. Unfortunately, it is as costly as mahogany furniture.

## Andrée Higgins
**7th arr.**
**54 rue de l'Université**
**548.75.28**
*Closed Mon.*

Andrée Higgins was one of the first to launch English styles in Paris, selecting her eighteenth and (especially) nineteenth-century furniture with the utmost care. The renewed popularity of Colonial-style furniture accounts for the shop's enticing Chinese-lacquered tables and paneled writing-desks that were fashionable in England at the start of this century. One of the shop's most appealing features is its constantly replenished inventory.

# FAR EAST

The current trend towards Chinese, Japanese, Khmer and Tibetan works of art has become such a phenomenon in London, New York and Paris that their prices have hit the ceiling. What's worse, beautiful wares have become almost impossible to find in Paris. And if bona fide collectors have become somewhat scarce, the average buyer is more interested in decorating (Siamese giltwood, eighteenth-century Chinese works) than in archeology.

### Beurdeley
**7th arr.**
**200 blvd.**
**Saint-Germain**
**548.97.86**
*Closed Mon.*

Not only is Jean-Michel Beurdeley the son of one of the world's foremost experts in Far Eastern art, he is also a world-famed art dealer in his own right. Though he is seldom seen in Paris, his gallery is continuously well-stocked with the best Chinese and Japanese items such as steles, statues and folding screens.

### Robert Burawoy
**4th arr.**
**12 rue Le Regrattier**
**354.67.36**
*Closed Mon.*

The best Japanese masks, weapons and armor in all of Paris. Robert Burawoy an expert in Tibetan paintings.

### Captier
**7th arr.**
**25 rue de Verneuil**
**261.00.57**

This is the least expensive quality shop specializing in ancient Japanese works of art. Bernard Captier is the only Parisian antique dealer to travel to Japan two or three times a year to get nineteenth-century Japanese objects and furniture such as cases and chests of drawers. He has them all restored in Paris where his wife Sylvie then sells them at reasonable prices to knowledgeable dealers and collectors.

### Compagnie de la Chine et des Indes
**8th arr.**
**39 ave de Friedland**
**563.83.28**
*Closed Mon.*

In the shop's three floors you'll find a high-quality selection of Chinese, Khmer and Greco-Buddhist terra-cottas, bronzework, steles, porcelain and celadon, some of which are museum-grade pieces. Small wonder Jean-Pierre Rousset supplies some of the greatest museums in the world.

### Bernard Le Dauphin
**7th arr.**
**21 rue de Grenelle**
**222.89.54**
*Open 2:30 P.M. to 7:00 P.M.*

This shop, which specializes in antique Japanese works, attracts more and more collectors who come for its weapons, masks and armor. Bernard Le Dauphin informs us he has sold a fifteenth-century sword to a French Academician who wears it with his green uniform.

### Ariane Faye
**6th arr.**

The few highly decorative and expensive Far Eastern objects don't deter Ariane's knowledgeable clientele from shopping here. She regularly sponsors exhibits on a

**61 rue
des Saints-Peres
222.14.43**

## Gérard Lévy
**7th arr.
17 rue de Beaune
261.26.55**
*Open 2:00 P.M. to 7:00 P.M.*

## Loo
**8th arr.
48 rue de Courcelles
227.53.15**

## Marco Polo
**7th arr.
210 blvd.
Saint-Germain
548.99.87**
*Closed Mon.*

## Yvonne Moreau-Gobard
**6th arr.
5 rue des
Saints-Peres
260.88.25**

## Myrna Myers
**7th arr.
11 rue de Beaune
261.11.08**
*Open 2:30 P.M. to 6:30 P.M.*

## Perret-Vibert
**8th arr.
170 blvd. Haussmann
562.15.85**
*Closed Mon.*

wide range of themes, such as bamboo Japanese baskets, Chinese ceramics, and marble furniture from Mongolian palaces.

Along with Janine Loo, Beurdeley, Moreau-Gobard and a few others, Gérard Lévy is one of the most reliable experts on Far Eastern arts (China, Japan, Cambodia, Korea and Thailand). In his lovely, entirely redecorated shop you'll encounter the leading collectors of the day. And even though he does cater to museums, you'll still find equally fine objects at affordable prices. M. Lévy is also a leading expert in antique photographs.

Only famous experts or bold amateurs dare enter this gallery styled like a pagoda. It is located in a rococo hotel where Charles Dickens used to stay. Yet Janine Loo is no dragon, and since her father's death in 1957 she continues to extend a warm welcome to those who drop by this intimidating and fabulous museum. Ring her bell, take the elevator and admire her three floors of treasures, which include lacquered folding screens, Hindu temple bas-reliefs, porcelains and curios, Ming vases, Han statuettes and Tang horses. Mme Loo also custom-makes Chinese-styled tables.

This collector of Indian, Nepalese and Tibetan art now also features Hindu art, in which he developed an interest while producing the film adaptation of Kessel's "The Horsemen." This shop is especially worth a visit if you're fond of Indian miniatures.

In a section of Egyptologist Jean Loup Despras' gallery, Yvonne Moreau-Gobard offers a solid choice of Chinese, Indian and Khmer archeological objects.

Even if you're not a collector you won't be able to resist stopping in front of Mme Myer's window displays. Open the door and step into this lovely shop to admire the always remarkable collection of Chinese, Japanese and Korean ceramics, all made between the tenth and eighteenth centuries. The shop also features antique jade and fabrics.

Here you'll find a wide variety of Chinese porcelain, low Japanese and Chinese tables, as well as many high quality decorative objects.

# ISLAMIC ARTS

### Arts de la Perse et de l'Orient
**6th arr.**
**21 quai Malaquais**
**260.72.91**

You'll find Annie Kevorkian's splendid and expertly arranged Islamic ceramics, amid beautiful bronzeworks and miniatures.

### L'Ourika
**6th arr.**
**51 rue de Seine**
**354.57.65**
*Closed Mon.*

The shop features elegantly displayed Islamic and Middle Eastern works of art, as well as lovely old and new south Moroccan and Saharan Berber jewelry.

### Joseph Soustiel
**8th arr.**
**146 blvd. Haussmann**
**562.27.76**
*Closed Sat.*

Since the Shah's fall, Persian artworks have commanded lower prices. The changing winds of politics haven't affected their value, however, and you'll find Persian as well as Middle Eastern miniatures, ceramics, bronzeworks and metalworks. This house, run by Joseph and his equally knowledgeable son Jean, was established over a century ago in Istanbul.

# MEDITERRANEAN STYLES

To be an accomplished expert in this field, you need to know all about archeology, art, history and religion. In a field teeming with imitations, it's difficult to find knowledgeable dealers in archeological items. We came up with the following:

### Galerie Nina Borowski
**7th arr.**
**40 rue du Bac**
**548.61.60**
*Closed Mon. morning.*

This well-informed and charming young woman (who is related to Borowski of Basel) offers various Greek, Roman and Etruscan terra-cotta works of art, including vases and other objects in bronze and marble. Each year she supervises an exhibit of numerous archeological finds where you can unearth pretty little Greek terra-cottas for 3,500F and up.

### Galerie du Sycamore
**6th arr.**
**11 rue des Beaux-Arts**
**633.83.55**
*Closed Mon. morning*

You'll find a high quality, though limited, choice of archeological objects from the Mediterranean Basin.

### Maspero
**8th arr.**
**23 rue du Cirque**
**266.65.90**

Antiques aficionados all congregate at Mme Rusen-Maspero's shop where you'll find Mediterranean Basin objects made prior to the Christian era. The shop specializes in Egyptian archeological finds.

## Simone de Monbrison
**6th arr.**
**22 rue Bonaparte**
**633.13.77**
*Closed Mon.*

Simone de Monbrison's new shop is much larger and better than her former shop. She offers a well-studied and often spectacular collection of attractive high-quality Greek, Estrucan, Egyptian, and Roman art objects.

## Mouseion
**6th arr.**
**48 rue Mazarine**
**326.35.11**
*Closed Mon.*

This charming and expertly arranged shop was recently redone by a woman who once lived in Egypt. It features a few lovely Egyptian and Coptic items, as well as Greek and Roman objects, Khmer Bronze works, icons, and Dogon statuettes.

## Mythes et Légendes
**4th arr.**
**18 pl. des Vosges**
**272.63.26**
*Closed Mon.*

Once a year, Michel Cohen publishes a catalogue of archeological objects from Egypt, Greece, Rome, the Far East, and Precolombian America (complete with certificate of origin) which can be purchased by mail. Of course, it's far better to go to his shop in person to hear stories like the one about the woman who wanted to sell a wooden crucifix and swore it was made in 700 B.C.! Little by little, Mythes et Légendes is publishing *Collector's Guides* on a regular basis. They will also reimburse fickle customers and capricious amateurs without batting an eyelash.

## Orient-Occident
**6th arr.**
**5 rue des Saint-Pères**
**260.77.65**

Not only does Jean-Loup Despras offer the best possible selection of Egyptian art, he is also a bona fide Egyptologist who can decode any inscription off a stele and thereby tell a counterfeit from the real thing.

## A la Reine Margot
**6th arr.**
**7 quai Conti**
**326.62.50**
*Closed Mon. morning.*

Collectors flock from all around the world to see this gallery's remarkable collection of antique glassware. La Reine Margot devotes itself chiefly to archeological finds, sculptures and furniture from the Middle Ages up to the seventeenth century. In collaboration with the Galerie Mythes et Légendes, it has been publishing a wonderful brochure for beginners on such subjects as terra-cottas and antique glassware from the Mediterranean Basin.

# RUSSIAN

## Artel
**6th arr.**
**25 rue Bonaparte**
**354.93.77**
*Closed Mon.*

The shop features Greek and Russian icons. Will do restorations.

## Nikolenko
**7th arr.**
**220 blvd. Saint-Germain**
**548.20.62**
*Closed Mon.*

Foreign museums rave about this expert's thirteenth- and eighteenth-century collection of Russian, Byzantine and Greek icons. He regularly publishes an extremely well-detailed catalogue.

### Popoff
8th arr.
86 faubourg
Saint-Honoré
265.38.44

In this shop across from the Elysée, you'll find paintings, icons, miniature porcelain pieces, and other high quality interesting objects, as well as École Française paintings and drawings, and German and French porcelains.

### A la Vieille Cité
1st arr.
350 rue Saint-Honoré
260.67.16
*Closed Sat.*

Alexander Djanchieff's treasures include beautiful silver, gorgeous icons, Fabergé creations, porcelain, Russian paintings and a collection of elaborate Easter eggs.

# OTHER ANTIQUES

## Bronzes

### Fred Guiraud
16th arr.
9 rue de Belloy
704.33.86
*Closed Sat.*

Original bronze animal sculpture made by leading nineteenth- and twentieth-century sculptors such as Barye, Frémiet, Moigniez, Pompon and Bugatti.

### Kugel
8th arr.
279 rue Saint-Honoré
260.86.23

Kugel offers large-sized works made between the Renaissance and eighteenth-century, suitable for museums and major private collections. It won't cost you anything to drop in and view them.

### Alain Lesieutre
1st arr.
Louvre des
Antiquaires, 32 allee
Riesener
297.28.63
*Open 11:00 A.M. to 7:00 P.M.*
*Closed Mon.*
7th arr.
9 rue de Beaune
261.16.81
*Open 3:00 P.M. to 7:00 P.M.*
*Closed Mon., Sat.*

Fashion-conscious customers come here for the shop's turn-of-the-century bronzeworks made by Bugatti, Rodin, Carpeaux, Barye and other major sculptors.

### Moatti
6th arr.
77 rue des
Saints-Peres
222.91.04
*Closed Mon. morning*

Moatti is for wealthy collectors seeking famous European bronze works made between the Renaissance and eighteenth century.

## Buttons

### Marguerite Fondeur
**8th arr.**
**18 rue d'Anjou**
**265.11.56**
*Open 2:00 P.M. to 6:00 P.M.*

The shop features an incredible selection of old buttons made of silver, porcelain, mother-of-pearl, and strass (paste), hand-engraved and ranging in all styles from Louis XIV to the Belle Époque. They also have military and "period" gentlemen's jacket buttons. This shop is intended for collectors and dandies who wish to individualize their attire with little 1900-styled vest buttons in black untreated glass enhanced with green flowers, or with silver-plated cuff links adorned with engraved ducks or woodcocks. The saleslady has been here for 30 years and is extremely charming.

### Subra
**6th arr.**
**79 blvd.**
**Montparnasse**
**538.74.80**
*Open 11:00 A.M. to 7:00 P.M.*
*Closed Mon.*

Subra offers a wide choice of diversified buttons from all periods.

## Clocks, Watches

### Jean-Baptiste Diette
**8th arr.**
**4 ave. Matignon**
**359.98.90**
*Closed Sat. morning*

His shop features seventeenth- and eighteenth-century clocks, all in perfect working order. L'Élysée used to shop here when General de Gaulle and Georges Pompidou were president.

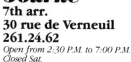

### Michel Journe
**7th arr.**
**30 rue de Verneuil**
**261.24.62**
*Open from 2:30 P.M. to 7:00 P.M.*
*Closed Sat.*

This young and most competent repairman knows everything there is to know about clocks. He also sells antique watches and clocks, mostly intricate ones.

## Curiosities

Highly intriguing objects are to mere curiosity-items what prestigiously stamped furniture is to second-hand furnishings. This heading includes an infinite number of objets d'art that would be impossible to list, such as nautilus shells, Renaissance bronze objects and astrolabes which inevitably wind up on shelves of museums and major private collections accompanied with their requisite certificates of authenticity. The marvelous and undisputed master of "highly intriguing" objects was Nicolas Landau who died in 1979. He was unique in that he knew how to give life to each and every one of his objects.

## Didier Aaron
16th arr.
32 ave.
Raymond-Poincaré
727.17.79
*Closed Sat.*

Paris's elite comes here to purchase Aaron's highly priced decorative items and eighteenth-century furniture which are sumptuous and always in fashion.

## Aveline
8th arr.
20 rue du Cirque
266.60.29

The shop offers a limited selection and has a pronounced taste for extremely rare objects and luxurious antique furniture. Aveline's exorbitant prices do not prevent people from dropping in the shop to give their eyes a treat. Bob Benamou supervises the nineteenth-century art department which offers known and lesser known Pompier and Orientalist painters.

## Le Cabinet de Curiosité
7th arr.
23 rue de Beaune
261.09.57
*Open 11:00 A.M. to 7:30 P.M. Closed Mon. morning.*

Mme Jean Hébert continues to run this shop in the enthusiastic and affable visually pleasing and mentally stimulating objects such as scientific instruments, games, tools and antique woodwork. It is always delightful to find tastefully chosen objects in this exquisite shop.

## Alain Demachy
7th arr.
9 quai Voltaire
261.82.06

In April of 1981, Alain Demachy took over Mme. Camoin's huge gallery that faces the Seine and Palais du Louvre and comprises five exhibit halls on the first floor. Here you will find unique and delicately made seventeenth- to nineteenth-century objects, uncommon furniture, and antique master paintings.

## Jacques Kugel
8th arr.
279 rue Saint-Honoré
260.86.23

Even though he is the top expert in antique gold and silverware, Kugel has further widened his field of activities. His encyclopedic knowledge, flair and financial means have enabled him to constantly renew his eclectic inventory, which he prefers to purchase from individual homes rather than at public auctions. The ornate decor of his shop is enhanced by Georges Geoffroy's sumptuous staircase.

## Moatti
6th arr.
77 rue des Saints-Peres
222.91.04
*Closed Mon. morning.*

This famous antique dealer features in his townhouse a collection of bronze works and refined collectors items.

## Consignments

## Dépôt-Vente de l'Ile de la Jatte

At the foot of the Courbevoie bridge, immortalized 100 years ago in Seurat's painting, *Un Dimanche,* you'll find an old hangar that's open to occasional bargain hunters, professional buyers and sellers, as well as barterers. This

## (V.V.M.)
**9200 Neuilly**
**17 blvd. Vital-Bouhot**
**(Île de la Jatte)**
**637.31.86**
*Open 12:00 noon to 8:00 P.M.*
*Closed Mon.*

pawn-shop format entitles you to display objects you no longer want, providing you pay the biannual subscription of 100F and affix your own price after consulting with the manager, Gérard Vacher. If there's a sale, both you and the buyer must pay the shop-owner a 20 percent commission. If the item does not sell, its price is marked down 10 percent each month. You'll find everything here, from paste glass chandeliers, Louis XVI-Third Republic chairs, attractive Second Empire chromos, to antique kitchen accessories. The store now has its own very in restaurant featuring a daily menu and, on weekend evenings, music.

## Dépôt-Vente de Paris
**20th arr.**
**81 rue de Lagny**
**372.13.91**
*Open 9:30 A.M. to 7:30 P.M.*

This very large shop covers 2,000 square meters and used to be a garage. It features "antiques"—a few authentic, while others actually household appliances. Nevertheless, it is possible to find intriguing art deco sideboards, Brittany armoires and entire bedroom and dining hall sets in the 1920s St. Antoine style.

## Crafts

Today, any piece of carpentry supporting a horizontal and deliberately mis-squared slab of wood is called a "rustic" table. Amateurs are easily fooled by worm holes caused by sugar, gimlets, wet nails and bullet holes or by wood that has been smoked, burnt, veneered and artificially altered. We recommend that you be very cautious, especially when the prices appear to be "out of whack."

## Pierre-G. Bernard
**8th arr.**
**1 rue d'Anjou**
**265.23.83**
*Open daily, Sat. by appt. only.*
*Closed Sun.*

Pierre-G. Bernard is crazy about the evolution of craftsmanship. He collects and sells antique tools as well as everything pertaining to the arts of the table, dining or writing, from Gallo-Roman bronze pans to individual traveling place settings and antique butter and cake molds. He will research anything (including wine-related paraphernalia, his specialty) and come up with the appropriate items and documentation. This multitalented antique dealer is truly an expert on irreplaceable craft documents, tools, antique instruments, scale model machinery, signposts, manuscripts and printed works.

## Robert Guigue
**1st arr.**
**16 rue des Halles**
**233.68.97**
**1st arr.**
**Louvre des Antiquaires,**
**2 allee Mackintosh**
**297.27.55**
*Closed Mon.*

He is one of the top specialists in painted furniture, particularly from the Rhine Valley. The shop also features many reproductions and wall panels and will restore paintings and painted furniture.

## Sonkin
**7th arr.**
**10 rue de Beaune**
**261.27.87**
*Open 2:00 P.M. to 7:00 P.M.*

This charming gallery which smells of wax is located at the former Gray Musketeers' barracks. You'll find here gorgeous rustic antique furniture and "popular art and tradition" objects such as butter molds, salt shakers, cheese trays and goat collars, coveted by French and foreign museums.

## Aliette Texier
**1st arr.**
**39041 quai de l'Horloge**
**354.72.72**
*Closed Mon.*

The shop offers top quality, expensive provincial furniture, as well as a multitude of objects made from wood, copper and wrought-iron used on farms or in homes. To list this collector's latest finds (she was the first to delve into antique folk art) would fill many pages in this book. You'll find everything here, from thirteenth-century trying-planes to Ile-de-France scythe sharpeners. Her increasing number of local customers are always well-off. In her second shop, located at 26 place Dauphine, Aliette Texier exhibits and sells gorgeous American antique quilts.

## Fabrics

## Aux Fils du Temps

**7th arr.**
**33 rue de Grenelle**
**548.14.68**
*Open 2:00 P.M. to 8:00 P.M.*

Marie-Noëlle Sudre has been an antique dealer for a long time, specializing in various-sized antique fabrics from around the world made between the eighteenth century and 1930. In her cave-like shop fabrics are exhibited in threes and fours. Under the spotlights, the fabrics' golden threads shine like treasures against the shop's black walls. For upholstering your set of four armchairs, the shop offers a sea-green Louis XV-styled fabric. Also featured is a Persian wall covering in cotton with golden threads (1.5 meter by 2.5 meter) that costs 6,000F.

## Guns

Many antique dealers who specialize in curios also sell antique weapons, yet none of them are as knowledgeable as the experts listed below. Antique weapons are among the most sought-after collectors' items today, whether an arquebus, a World War I bayonet or a Winchester rifle from the Wild West. Hence, their prices are very high and there's strong chance you'll come across perfect imitations sold as the "real" thing.

## René Johnson

**1st arr.**
**16 quai du Louvre**
**236.56.61**
*Closed Mon. and Sat. afternoon.*

Like his father before him, this astonishing man is an ardent, infallible expert on weapons, gear and medals from all nations. His old store features uniforms worn by soldiers of Napoleon's Old Guard, coats of mail, fifteenth- to seventeenth-century cannons, swords and muskets.

## Charles Marchal

**8th arr.**
**46 rue de Miromesnil**
**265.72.79**
*Closed Sat.*

Charles Marchal is one of France's top experts in collector's weapons, offering maritime objects, medals and tin soldiers.

## Militaria

**4th arr.**
**23 quai aux Fleurs**
**633.66.31**
*Closed Wed.*

This shop features antique weapons, uniforms and military headgear.

### Jewelry

## Les Bijoux Anciens

**7th arr.**
**16 blvd. Raspail**
**548.51.56**
*Closed Mon. (except in December)*

The Sartorios feature a huge selection of beautiful antique jewelry, cameos and wedding rings from the eighteenth century, the Romantic Era, the Belle Époque (Gay Nineties) and the Roaring Twenties, as well as a wide variety of Napoleon III jewelry sets.

## Garland

**2nd arr.**
**13 rue de la Paix**
**261.17.95**
*Closed Sat. in February and August*

Only reluctantly does Minouche sell her uncommon antique jewelry. As the first woman antique dealer in Paris, she has had the privilege of displaying the bracelet Sarah Bernhardt received from the czar of Russia as well as a superb necklace that once belonged to King Farouk. One of her specialties is the *bijou d'amoureux* given to reveal an unavowed passion to the object of your love. These original, charming and delicate jewels date back to the start of the nineteenth century. The shop also features many antique wedding rings which will enable you to offer your loved one a bona fide "family jewel."

## Gillet

**4th arr.**
**19 rue d'Arcole**
**354.00.83**
*Closed Mon.*

Hidden among Notre Dame's souvenir shops, this lovely shop features a large and beautiful selection of romantic rings and antique jewelry priced from 600F.

## Michel Périnet

**2nd arr.**
**26 rue Danielle-Casanova**
**261.49.16**
*Open 1:00 P.M. to 7:00 P.M.*

You'll find here magnificent jewelry in all styles: Charles X, Napoleon III, 1900 (Lalique), art deco (Fouquet, Templier). Though expensive, they make marvelous gifts for the lady of your wildest dreams.

## Sorelle

**6th arr.**
**12 rue de l'Echaude**
**633.59.41**
*Closed Mon. morning*

This charming little shop offers art deco, 1940s and 1950s-styled jewelry made from galalith, lacquered or enameled powder-cases with geometric patterns, raw glass, lamps, vases and other precious curios dating from 1900 to 1930.

## Lamps and Lighting

### Colin-Maillard
**8th arr.**
**11 rue de Miromesnil**
**265.43.62**
*Closed Mon. and Sat. morning.*

An attractive selection of porcelain vases and antique objects (for the most part Far Eastern) that can be made into lamps. Colin-Maillard also custom-makes lampshades.

### Jean Devoluy
**6th arr.**
**3 rue Jacob**
**326.41.55**
*Closed Mon. morning.*

This venerable firm specializes in nineteenth-century French and English lamps and their reproductions.

### Lecoules
**9th arr.**
**62 rue Taitbout**
**874.69.69**

This firm is very well known for its light fixtures crafted by leading artisans of the second half of the nineteenth century. Also featured are furniture and works of art.

### Renoncourt
**6th arr.**
**1 rue des Saints-Pères**
**260.75.87**

This expert in Restoration and Empire lamps also offers admirable nineteenth-century French and Russian chandeliers.

## Mariners' Instruments

### Balmès-Richelieu
**3rd arr.**
**21 place des Vosges**
**887.20.45**

M. Balmès owns some of the best maritime objects in Paris. He also specializes in seventeenth- to nineteenth-century locks and scientific instruments.

### Alain Brieux
**6th arr.**
**48 rue Jacob**
**260.21.98**
*Closed Sat.*

This expert in astrolabes features a variety of objects comprising physical, optical and medical instruments, as well as antique documents pertaining to these topics.

### Le Cabinet de Curiosité
**7th arr.**
**23 rue de Beaune**
**261.09.57**
*Open from 11:00 A.M. to 7:30 P.M. Closed Mon. morning*

You'll discover antique scientific instruments among the unusual collector's items displayed in this charming shop.

## Chambon
**8th arr.**
**44 rue de Miromesnil**
**265.34.98**
*Closed Sat.*

Chambon offers beautiful antique navigational instruments, ship models, seascape paintings, tin soldiers, historic and military memorabilia, as well as other curiosity items.

## Charles Marchal
**8th arr.**
**46 rue de Miromesnil**
**265.72.79**
*Closed Sat.*

Although he is an expert in military and historical memorabilia, Charles Marchal also features maritime objects.

## Roux-Devillas
**6th arr.**
**12 rue Bonaparte**
**354.69.32**
*Closed Mon. morning.*

You'll find in this large and beautiful old-fashioned store a good selection of navigational and optical instruments, as well as antique maps, documents and scientific books.

## Gilbert Suc
**7th arr.**
**30 rue des Saints-Pères**
**548.67.42**

This remarkable antique dealer has a shop right off the courtyard that features thirteenth- to nineteenth-century scientific and navigational objects such as globes, armillary spheres microscopes and sandglasses.

## Mechanical Toys and Dolls

Antique dolls are in high demand and purchasing them is a risky business. Aficionados easily cough up 4,000F for their painted smiles and porcelain eyes. And for those fond of mechanical toys, the Arts et Métiers Museum in Paris, the new and marvelous Neuilly Museum (see "Museums") and the Galea Collection in Monte Carlo are guaranteed to quicken the pulse. Listed below are a few good locations.

## Sophie du Bac
**7th arr.**
**109 rue du Bac**
**548.49.01**

Her doll collection was highly touted in the film *Marie Poupee.* These distinguished little people were nearly all born before 1914 and never sell for less than 1,000F. They come complete with furniture, dishware, and accessories (clothing, hats, umbrellas). Sophie du Bac will also restore antique dolls. The shop features curios and antique jewelry as well.

## Robert Capia
**1st arr.**
**24-26, galerie Véro-Dodat**
**236.25.94**

Collectors universally acknowledge Robert Capia as the leading expert in antique dolls, even though his gallery (founded in 1826 by two butchers Véro and Dodat) is to be found in the most remote passageway in Paris. Capia dolls bear their manufacturers' names (Jumeau, Steiner, Bru, Rohmer, Gaultier. Schmitt) and are equipped with complete wardrobes tucked in individual trunks that make them all the more enticing. The choice of dolls is enormous and the prices are reasonable considering the amount of work involved.

### *La Galerie Pittoresque*
6th arr.
**133 blvd. Raspail**
**548.89.98**
*Open 4:00 P.M. to 8:00 P.M.*

The picturesque nineteenth-century dolls here come in all sizes. You'll see them all on display surrounded by miniature accessories, wardrobes and decorative items made from silver, tortoise shell and ceramic.

### *New Form*
1st arr.
**33 rue Saint-Denis**
**233.37.01**
*Closed Mon.*

Watch out! Only the dolls' *dresses* are authentic, by which we mean they have been tailored from antique snips of fabric by imaginative and dexterous artists who find their designs in period catalogues or in fashion and theatrical engravings. New Form will custom-make all dolls, miniature items and mechanical toys based on photographs or specific themes.

### *Monsieur Renard*
6th arr.
**6 rue de l'Echaudé**
**325.70.72**
*Closed Mon. morning.*

You'll find his personal collection of dolls on the first floor of the store. Alain Renard also sells famous-brand antique dolls in their gorgeous original dresses, as well as quality mechanical toys and antique games. In the adjoining shop, under the "Beau Noir" signpost, you'll discover 1900s curios, rattan or Napoleon III furniture and terra-cotta dogs and statues, all made in Venice at the end of the nineteenth century for the American market and currently enjoying a comeback in popularity.

### *Polichinelle*
18th arr.
**20 rue**
**André-del-Sarte**
**255.85.65**

François Theimer specializes in appraising, restoring, selling and dressing up nineteenth-century dolls made from unglazed porcelain, wax and papier-mâché. These fragile little figures are very expensive (5,000F-80,000F). If they are damaged, the workshop will repair them. The magazine *Polichinelle* is sold by subscription for 100F per year, and doll furniture can be purchased next door at Scaramouche, Polichinelle's twin shop, in which you'll find new and antique dollhouses, furniture and accessories.

### *Minerals and Shells*

### *Boubée*
5th arr.
**97 rue Monge**
**707.01.21**
*Closed Mon. until 3:00 P.M.*

Since 1846, Boubée has offered fossils, precious gems, unusual insects, stuffed animals, skeletons and scientific objects—everything for collectors of all ages.

### *Claude Boullé*
6th arr.
**28 rue Jacob**
**633.01.38**
*Closed Mon. morning.*

André Breton, Roger Caillois and Viera da Silva were all interested in this expert mineralogist's "picture" stones (landscape stones, pictorial stones). His rare collection includes Tuscany limestone, Bristol marble, Oregon jasper and Utah sandstone, all sold in slabs.

### *Michel Cachoux*
6th arr.

Michel Cachoux's shop will always bedazzle visitors. Several months a year he travels to Brazil, the U.S., Madagascar, Central America and the Alps to garner

**29 rue Guénégaud**
**354.52.15**
*Closed Mon.*

## *Deyrolle*
**7th Arrondissement**
**46 rue du Bac**
**222.30.07**

## *Ivana Dimitrie*
**1st arr.**
**36 galerie Montpensier**
**297.47.68**
*Open 1:00 P.M. to 6:30 P.M.*

## *Minéraux et Gemmes*
**8th arr.**
**164 faubourg Saint-Honoré**
**256.32.67**
*Closed Mon.*

## *Perlae*
**17th arr.**
**19 rue de l'Arc-de-Triomphe**
**380.84.47**

mineral treasures. He has just opened a second gallery across the street where you will find more affordable stones.

Salvador Dali comes here for rhinoceros horns. You'll discover a variety of shells, quality minerals, fossils, butterflies, stuffed birds, botanical plates, and other curiosity items from Mother Nature.

This shop is located under the Louis XIV arcades in the Palais Royal gardens and features fossils, cut agate and amethyst stone brooches as well as exotically styled "assembled jewelry."

In this beautiful shop you'll find gorgeous imported minerals, as well as gold and silverplate jewels crafted around unique gemstones.

The store advertises its specialty as "decorative natural objects." It is filled from top to bottom with sea shells and coral, regularly shipped in from West Africa by the store's two partners, Pierre Barbier and Sylvain LeCochenne. You will find delicate decorative items, some of which are inexpensive.

## *Money and Metals*

All numismatists are located within walking distances of the National Library Department of Coins and Metals.

## *Émile Bourgey*
**9th arr.**
**7 rue Drout**
**770.35.18**
*Closed Sat. afternoon*

## *Numisma-tique et Change de Paris*
**2nd arr.**
**3 rue de la Bourse**
**297.53.53**
*Closed Sat. afternoon.*

Along with Vinchon, Émile Bourgey is one of the best-known coin specialists in Paris. Here you'll find, among a wide selection of coins, the portrait of a man you have always loved: Hadrian, whose likeness enhances this gold coin minted between 125 and 128 A.D.

Jean Vinchon keeps his private collection of coins at his rue Richelieu shop. His daughter runs his rue de la Bourse boutique, buying and selling old currency notes, coins and contemporary medals, particularly silver and gold coins which are negotiated in transparent plastic bags sealed under the purchaser's eyes. This guarantees the value of the coins in case you want to bring them back—still sealed—for reimbursement at the current rate.

## Jean Vinchon
2nd arr.
**77 rue de Richelieu**
**297.50.00**
*Closed Sat. afternoon.*

Not only is Jean Vinchon one of the best and most ardent numismatists in the world, he is also one of the first to promote this discipline as a full-scale art form open to all, instead of a hobby or passion reserved only for knowledgeable experts. Although his cosy little shop is usually filled with major collectors arguing over rarely seen coins and medals, he will nevertheless give his entire attention to those who have little money to spend and know nothing about numismatics. By the time they leave his shop, most of them will have become ardent collectors.

## Musical Instruments

## André Bissonnet
3rd arr.
**6 rue du**
**Pas-de-la-Mule**
**887.20.15**
*Open from 2:00 P.M. to 7:30 P.M.*

André Bissonnet is a real character. His brother, Jean Bissonnet, is a famous Parisian butcher, and after spending many years as a butcher himself, he suddenly developed a passion for antique musical instruments (he is also an accomplished musician). He threw in his smock, redecorated his butchershop and made it into one of the most entertaining shops in Paris, where you will discover incredible instruments, some of which are bona fide museum pieces.

## Robert Capia
1st arr.
**24-26, galerie**
**Véro-Dodat**
**236.25.94**

In addition to his antique dolls, Robert Capia also collects ancient phonographs with copper or painted sheet-metal horns. He also sells cylinder phonographs which are in perfect condition (guaranteed by the shop's first-floor workshop), as well as many 78 rpm records which will enable you to listen to Coquelin, Sarah Bernhardt and Caruso.

## Alain Vian
6th arr.
**8 rue**
**Grégoire-de-Tours**
**354.02.69**
*Closed Sat.*

Boris Vian's brother, Alain, a former drummer at the Tabou nightclub, owns this shop where collectors and curious visitors all congregate to see antique string, brass and woodwind instruments. Since these are becoming more and more scarce, Alain Vian now also features music boxes, merry-go-round organs, antique accordions, self-playing violins and antique cameras. His favorite instrument is the Barbarie organ for which he also composes contemporary melodies on perforated sheet music. Alain, who is a secretary general of the Compagnie des Experts, delights in examining all objects brought to his shop.

## Panoramas and Wallpapers

Genuine antique panoramas are expensive and very hard to find. They originated after the French Revolution and are still popular today. Many wallpaper experts also feature gorgeous reproductions.

## Carlhian

**16th arr.**
**6 ave. d'Eylau**
**504.70.80**
*Closed Sat.*

This is the number one shop for well-to-do Parisians, specializing in nineteenth-century panoramas and eighteenth-century woodwork.

## Jean-Louis Chasset

**5th arr.**
**6 rue Saint-Victor**
**326.83.00**
*Closed Mon.*

A few superb antique wallpapers and many reproductions executed in eighteenth- and nineteenth-century methods. Chasset will also restore antique wallpaper, painted sheet metal items, folding screens and billboards mounted on cloth.

## Pewter and Copper

You'll find a magnificent display at the Arts et Traditions Populaires Museum located on the route de Madrid in the 16th arrondissement.

## Charles et Philippe Boucaud

**7th arr.**
**25 rue du Bac**
**261.24.07**

Charles Boucaud died in 1980, but his widow and son Philippe are still the best experts in pewter and 15th- to 19th-century mortars and pestles.

## Photographs

## Aux Fontaine de Niepce et de Daguerre

**18th arr.**
**20 rue André-del-Sarte**
**257.27.13**
*Closed Mon.*

In this spacious and superb museum/store Guy Bomet displays and sells cameras from one of the best collections available. Initially amassed before World War I by his father, Dr. Bomet, the collection has been enlarged by Guy in the last 30 years. Collectors and amateurs alike flock here from all over the world to view and purchase these treasures, which range from the eighteenth-century camera obscura—mother of all cameras—to Chevalier's prism. You'll find nearly 500 incredible cameras as well as daguerreotypes, ambrotypes (positive images on glass plates) and photographs done on enamel and porcelain.

## Gérard Lévy

**7th arr.**
**17 rue de Beaune**
**261.26.55**
*By appt. only.*

Although a specialist in Far Eastern art, Lévy was also one of the first antique photo experts. Many of his highly unusual daguerreotypes and photos have already been purchased by museums, while others have been displayed at the Grand Palais' Second Empire exhibit.

### L'Octant
1st arr.
10 rue du 29-Juillet
260.68.08
1st arr.
5 rue du
Marché-Saint-Honoré
296.35.26
*Open 2:30 P.M. to 7:00 P.M.
Closed Sun. at rue du Marché-
Saint-Honoré location.*

Alain Paviot collects, buys and sells period prints by French photographers and regularly sponsors exhibits based on individual themes or photographers (such as Paris-Paris, Atget).

### Le Photographe
1st arr.
Louvre des
Antiquaires,
3 allee Mackintosh
297.27.57
*Closed Mon.*

Le Photographe features movie stills and photographs only, "prehistoric" and/or difficult to find.

### Photo Verdeau
9th arr.
14-16, passage
Verdeau
770.51.91
*Closed Mon., Sat.*

Jean Latour's timeless window displays will entice you into his 100-year-old shop. Formerly a copy editor, he decided in 1978 to drop everything in order to pursue his costly hobby of collecting historical cameras. Among the different models that range between 700F–1600F, there's the 1890 camera designed by the Parisian optician Darlot and a mahogany English model from 1910. The "detective" model—a large box with plates frequently used by Emile Zola—costs anywhere from 300F–500F for the popular turn-of-the-century model, while earlier models in wood cost 3,000F and more.

#### Porcelains

Popular eighteenth-century stoneware, particularly pharmaceutical items.

### Charles et Philippe Boucaud
7th arr.
25 rue du Bac
261.24.07

### Hélène Fournier-Guérin
6th arr.
25 rue des
Saints-Pères
260.21.81
*Closed Mon. mornings*

This classic boutique offers an expert selection of gorgeous eighteenth-century porcelains and earthenware (Moustiers), as well as Compagnie des Indes porcelain.

### L'Imprévu
6th arr.
21 rue Guénégaud
354.65.09
*Open 2:30 P.M. to 7:00 P.M.*

Lovers of Belle Époque barbotine and stoneware objects will be utterly delighted with this charming shop which offers vases, picturesque plates and every other item worth collecting. L'Imprévu's prices are still affordable.

## Georges Lefebvre

7th arr.
24 rue du Bac
261.18.40

This expert in antique ceramics features sixteenth- to eighteenth-century stoneware, porcelain and sculpture for Parisian society. This 100-year-old firm's customers have included Victor Hugo, Marcel Proust and Georges Feydeau.

## Nicolier

7th arr.
7 quai Voltaire
260.78.63

Since 1908, Nicolier has specialized in ninth- to nineteenth-century stoneware and porcelains, featuring Haute Epoque Chinese porcelain and Iranian pottery, Italian Renaissance majolica (Urbino, Gubbio), vases, trays and statuettes made from European porcelain and stoneware (Delft, Saxe, Rouen, Moustiers, Nevers, Chantilly). All of them are superbly made, in excellent condition and sold with a guarantee.

## Jacqueline Polles

8th arr.
3 rue des Saussaies
265.47.90
*Closed Mon. and Sat. mornings*

Mme Polles offers beautiful seventeenth- and eighteenth-century antique stoneware, Sèvres porcelain and a premium quality set of Chinese ceramics.

## Pierre de Regaini

7th arr.
6 rue de Beaune
261.25.36

Here you will find a vast and lovely selection of French porcelain from the eighteenth and nineteenth centuries, as well as Chinese and European miniatures and snuffboxes, salt shakers, glassware and small collectors' items.

## Vander-meersch

7th arr.
27 quai Voltaire
261.23.10
*Closed Mon.*

This expert in antique ceramics now occupies the ground floor of M. de Villette's townhouse in which Voltaire died. Though limited, his inventory comprises top-quality wares.

## Rugs and Tapestries

Many antique dealers sell antique rugs, yet it is far better to refer to an expert entirely devoted to this form of art.

## Achdjian et Fils

8th arr.
10 rue de Miromesnil
265.89.48

For nearly twenty years this gallery has been specializing in antique rugs woven by Caucasians, Armenians, Chinese and nomadic Turkomans, all sold at competitive prices. Many are museum pieces and have been exhibited in Paris and abroad.

## Roger Bechirian

92200 Neuilly
11 ave. de Madrid
624.53.18

Courts and customs offices have benefited from his expertise. By appointment only, he will show you his collection of Oriental, Far Eastern, Aubusson, and Savonnerie antique rugs. Roger Bechirian has also written an important book on rugs.

## *Benadava*
**8th arr.**
**28 rue de La Boétie**
**266.12.21**

Benadava, formerly located at the rue Royale, has a new store in which he offers rare Middle and Far Eastern rugs exhibited alongside eighteenth-century tapestries woven in Flanders, Aubusson and at the Gobelin Mills.

## *Dario Boccara*
**8th arr.**
**184 faubourg Sáint-Honoré**
**359.84.63**
*Closed Mon. morning.*

Boccara is a leading member of the Compagnie des Experts, whose prestigious firm has attracted an international clientele in search of antique tapestries both sumptuous and rare.

## *Catan*
**8th arr.**
**8 rue d'Anjou**
**266.33.28**
*Closed Sat.*

Josette Catan's friends will regret no longer seeing her in the former Hôtel La Fayette which her husband Victor Catan made into Europe's first antique rug store. Under the current direction of Daniel and Sylvia Catan, this store features a wide selection of rugs from France, Spain, Portugal, the Ukraine, Bessarabia and Tibet. Very appealing—and expensive.

## *Lefortier*
**8th arr.**
**54 faubourg Saint-Honoré**
**265.43.74**
*Closed Sat.*

In this venerable firm, established in 1887, General de Gaulle purchased the tapestry he later offered to King Baudoin and Queen Fabiola of Belgium. You'll find here all kinds of tapestries dating from the fifteenth to the eighteenth century.

## *Meunier-Batifaud*
**7th arr.**
**38 blvd. Raspail**
**548.05.78**
*Closed Mon. morning and Sat.*

A family-owned company since 1863, this shop features tapestries manufactured up to the eighteenth century as well as a few pieces of furniture. Will appraise and repair.

## *Monseigneur l'Ancien (J. Behar)*
**7th arr.**
**24 rue de Beaune**
**261.29.92**
*Closed Sat. morning (and afternoon in the summer).*

This serious little company does not have inflated prices. Its unexceptional wares include well-made antique (Caucasian) and contemporary rugs. Expert restoration service.

## *À la Place Clichy*
**8th arr.**
**93 rue d'Amsterdam**
**526.15.16**
*Closed Mon.*

This well-known store offers carpets, modern French and foreign rugs and remarkable choice of antique rugs from the Middle East, China, Aubusson and Savonnerie.

### Silver and Gold

**Andrieux**
6th arr.
15 rue de Sèvres
548.27.18

This estimable house presents a modern display of beautiful antique gold pieces as well as gold cases and decorative items.

**Pierre Andrieux**
8th arr.
66 faubourg Saint-Honoré
265.62.07

Mme Andrieux sells antique gold as well as a wide variety of silver-plated goods suitable for wedding presents. Lots of silver and silver-plated jewelry too.

**Bacstreet**
7th arr.
1 rue du Bac
261.24.20
*Closed Sat.*

Here you'll find gorgeous and beautifully displayed French and English silverware, most of it from the second half of the nineteenth century, as well as romantic and contemporary jewelry.

**Éléonore**
8th arr.
18 rue de Miromesnil
265.17.81
*Closed Sat.*

This fine shop offers a remarkable choice of eighteenth-century silverware and curios. Also featu:ed is a complete set of documents which will enable you to authenticate French and foreign stamped silverware.

**A l'Épreuve du Temps**

7th arr.
88 rue du Bac
222.11.42
*Closed Mon.*

A l'Epreuve du Temps features charming little antique pieces, small cases, curios and period jewelry—all at reasonable prices.

**Joséphine**
6th arr.
1 rue Bonaparte
326.49.73
*Closed Mon.*

Mme Coulommier is an acknowledged queen of antique gold, a fact she modestly denies. You'll fall head over heels in love with her numerous, tasteful and magnificent items from the eighteenth, nineteenth and twentieth centuries.

**Jacques Kugel**
8th arr.
279 rue Saint-Honoré
260.86.23

Jacques Kugel is France's, and one of the world's, greatest experts in gold and silver, offering princely dishware, regal silverware, paintings, uncommon curios, furniture and chandeliers.

**Au Vieux Paris**

2nd arr.
4 rue de la Paix
261.00.89
*Closed Mon. morning.*

Established in 1849, this is the oldest firm of its kind. Michel Turisk offers tastefully selected antique gold, including gold cases from Louis XV to Napoleon III, watches and splendid objects from the eighteenth, nineteenth and twentieth centuries.

## Tin Soldiers

### Jacques Bittard

**1st arr.**
**34 galerie Montpensier**
*Open 2:30 P.M. to 7:00 P.M.*
*Closed Mon.*

Providing you're willing to wait two to four months, you may purchase a set of Jacques Bittard's handpainted and decorated tin soldiers. His shop offers antique tin soldiers and historical figurines.

### Charles Marchal

**8th arr.**
**46 rue de Miromesnil**
**265.72.79**
*Closed Sat.*

This expert in military works of art features collectors' tin soldiers.

### Soldats d'Antan

**7th arr.**
**12 rue de l'Université**
**260.89.56**

Jean-Pierre Stella ranks first among dealers of antique tin soldiers. He also sells medals and orders of knighthood.

### Vieille France

**1st arr.**
**364 rue Saint-Honoré**
**260.01.57**

This shop features admirable historical figurines and will custom-make ravishing creations. You'll find here the entire series of French kings and many important figures of the *Ancien Régime,* as well as military paintings, medals and Orders of Knighthood.

## Toys and Games

### Robert Capia

**1st arr.**
**24-26 galerie Vero-Dodat**
**236.25.94**

Although Robert Capia sells superb dolls and antique games, he won't sell you his prized tumblers. His innumerable games include backgammon, bone and ivory dominoes, erector sets, charming lithograph magazines, and a few mechanical toys.

### Jacqueline Debay

**16th arr.**
**145 rue de la Pompe**
**727.42.33**

Some of Jacqueline Debay's objects include Chinese chips in ivory or mother-of-pearl, 1925 pin-table football games, pool tables, indoor croquet sets and a delightful choice of fireside games.

### Galerie 13

**6th arr.**
**13 rue Jacob**
**326.99.89**
*Closed Mon. morning.*

This shop features a beautiful and well-planned selection of parlor games to be played by the fireside in winter, as well as French, English and Chinese eighteenth- and nineteenth-century chess sets, gorgeously made backgammon sets with ivory and ebony chips, checkers, dominoes, cards and nineteenth-century inlaid boxes and cases from 200F.

### La Maison de Poupée
**6th arr.**
**40 rue de Vaugirard**
**633.74.05**
*Open from 2:30 P.M. to 7:00 P.M.*

This shop offers charming romantic dolls, accessories and little theatrical sets, but no miniature trains or cars.

### Au Petit Mayet
**6th arr.**
**1 rue Mayet**
**567.68.29**
*Open 2:00 P.M. to 7:00 P.M.*

This shop specializes in cardboard toys such as soldiers, trains, boats and cars.

### Pierre Sieur
**7th arr.**
**3 rue de l'Université**
**260.75.94**
*Closed Mon.*

This dream merchant, whose clients include Paul Claudel, Pablo Neruda, Michel Debré, Ingrid Bergman and Grace of Monaco, features solitary games, cards, puzzles, toy planes and vintage car model sets.

### Ma Tante Zoé
**15th arr.**
**4 rue de la Croix-Nivert**
**567.95.73**
*Open from 3:00 P.M. to 7:00 P.M.*
*Closed Mon.*

This shop offers dolls, games and curiosity items.

### A la Toupie Savante
**5th arr.**
**7 rue Frédéric-Sauton**
**329.37.08**
*Open 2:00 P.M. to 7:00 P.M.*
*Closed Mon.*

Jane Bouvard is a smiling American woman who has recently become a parlor game expert. Her shop features games and antique toys from all over the world, such as backgammon, chess sets, indoor croquet, bowling pins and an extremely varied selection of tops in wood, ivory, bronze, bone, as well as primitive stone tops that are still in use in Polynesia, elaborate gyroscopes, whip and shoe-string tops and simply made teetotems.

## Unusual Trifles

### Air de Chasse
**7th arr.**
**8 rue des Saint-Pères**
**260.25.98**
*Closed Mon. morning.*

Janine Gerhard, also known as "Diana of the rue des Saint-Pères," features everything pertaining to target practice and hunting, such as engravings from the eighteenth, nineteenth and twentieth centuries; curios; bronze animals; and terra-cotta decoys and birds. Her wealthy clients are nearly all hunters.

### Arcana
**3rd arr.**
**83 rue Vieille-du-Temple**
**278.19.22**

Arcana features all sorts of boxes made from leather, papier-mâché and straw or inlaid with different kinds of wood, mother-of-pearl and ivory, as well as cigar boxes, music boxes, pill and powder cases, portable writing blocks, antique painted metal tea, coffee and spice boxes, sewing kits and wine bottle racks. Arcana also features miniatures, poured-glass lamps, pool table lights, pens, inkstands and various flagons.

### Atalante
**92300 Levallois-Perret 23,**
**Edouard-Vaillant**
**737.28.16**

This dark little shop offers all kinds of period French magazines specializing in automobiles, as well as a brilliant selection of European auto parts, particularly radiator grills. M. Bardini loves Ferraris and has amassed all sorts of treasures pertaining to this prestigious car. He also sells collectors' cars and postwar sports cars.

### Atelier 12
**7th arr.**
**12 rue des Saints-Pères**
**260.81.00**
*Closed Mon.*

Here you'll discover painted seashells, modified tortoise shells, ostrich eggs made into lamps. The shop's window displays in themselves are well worth a visit.

### Atelier Mazot-Meyer
**7th arr.**
**32 rue de Verneuil**
**261.08.39**
*Open 3:00 P.M. to 7:00 P.M.*

In this shop's amusing jumble of items (such as bamboo and rattan furniture) you'll find charming, turn-of-the-century earthenware and barbotine dishware, particularly trompe-l'oeil asparagus platters and oyster plates.

### Autrefois
**4th arr.**
**10 rue Ernest-Cresson**
**540.61.63**
*Open from 2:00 P.M. to 7:00 P.M. Closed Mon.*

Here you'll find "sweet nothings" to enhance your life, such as bathroom tables, water pitchers, pedestal tables, rustic items, 1900s dishware, carafes, glassware, lamps and shades, frames, and antique linen.

### Beauté Divine
**6th arr.**
**12 rue Saint-Sulpice**
**326.25.31**
*Closed Mon.*

Beauté Divine, located north of Saint-Sulpice, offers glass and sculpted crystal flasks individually sold, mortars and pestles, unusual boxes, Bakelite powder cases, nail polishers and silver shaving brushes, as well as the loveliest selection of interwar bathroom accessories, all elegantly displayed in a mauve decor.

### Alain Bidegand
**16th arr.**
**9 rue de la Tour**
**520.57.67**
*Closed Mon.*

You'll find an extensive collection of antique boxes and cases in perfect condition (priced from 1500F) such as cigar boxes, glove kits, jewelry cases, perfume kits, cordial boxes and cosmetic kits.

### Jean Pierre de Castro
**4th arr.**
**17 and 23 rue des Francs-Bourgeois**
**272.04.00**
*Open daily 10:30 A.M. to 7:30 P.M. Closed Mon. morning.*

At the No. 17 location, Jean Pierre de Castro features an attractive choice of stripped Scottish pine furniture from the turn of the century. Next door at No. 23, he sells rustic French fruitwood furniture. For the price you paid (one-year guarantee, no obligation), he will repossess purchased goods you no longer want.

## Chez Io
**92200 Neuilly**
**4 rue de l'Eglise**
**745.60.88**
*Open from 3:00 A.M. to 7:30 P.M.*
*Closed Mon.*

Io has always been called Io. Her good friend and neighbor, Damiot, former antique dealer and now curator at the Neuilly Museum, bankrolls her shop. You'll find bizarre and unusual items, including small furniture and curios.

## Colonna
**7th arr.**
**1 quai Voltaire**
**260.22.43**
*Open from 11:00 A.M. to 7:00 P.M. Closed Mon. morning*

Claudine Chatel's tastefully decorated gallery specializes in furniture and various antique items from the Middle East and China. Her beautifully upholstered sofas are as valuable as they are decorative.

## Comoglio
**6th arr.**
**22 rue Jacob**
**354.65.86**
*Closed Mon. morning*

This amazing antique dealer, whose specialty is selling bizarre and unusual items, has had Jean Cocteau, Christian Berard, and numerous TV, movie and stage personalities as customers in his shop. Since 1965, Jacques Lejeune sells and/or rents original decorative items such as woodwork, stained glass, wallpaper, and furniture.

## Dugrenot
**1st arr.**
**18 rue de Montpensier**
**296.02.43**
*Open from 2:00 P.M. to 6:00 P.M. Tues. thru Fri. by appointment only.*

This shop has a predilection for baroque and unusual objects and furniture, some of which are antiques.

## Fanfan la Tulipe
**6th arr.**
**55 rue du Cherche-Midi**
**222.04.20**
*Open 3:00 P.M. to 7:00 P.M.*

André Hollande is a multitalented expert in historical and heraldic memorabilia as well as in tobacco accessories. His wide selection of objects includes the Duchess de Berry's candelabra, a nineteenth-century naive painting, tobacco pouches, Creil dishware, combination walking stick-swords with ornate handles—his specialty—and card games manufactured between the seventeenth century and 1930.

## Galerie Jacques Casanova
**1st arr.**
**25 galerie Montpensier**
**296.23.52**
*Open 12:00 noon to 7:00 P.M.*

The shop features intriguing and often erotic items, witchcraft objects, and an unusual selection of modern drawings and paintings.

## La Mansarde
**1st arr.**
**6 rue des Pyramides**
**260.47.58**

Frédérica, a blonde who dubbed Marilyn Monroe's voice in *Niagara*, counts many artists and bargain-seekers among her loyal clientele. She features turn-of-the-century glassware (flasks. carafes, cups, vases, glasses), porcelain dolls along with their tiny furniture and dishware, shellac-and-horn boxes, fans, figurines, lorgnettes, 1900 neck chains, statuettes, drawings and curios.

## Le Jardin d'Hiver

7th arr.
7 rue de Beaune
261.25.38
*Open from 3:30 P.M. to 7:00 P.M.*

Here you'll find elegant and ornate nineteenth-century Colonial furniture in rattan and bamboo, cushioned Napoleon III chairs, and baroque items such as flower stands, still life paintings, and portraits of children.

## L'Objet Aimé

6th arr.
52 rue Jacob
260.24.46
*Closed Mon. morning.*

This shop offers a choice of curious objects such as dog-shaped tobacco pouches, terra-cotta statuettes, ostrich eggs, bottle or message cases in wood (mahogany), game chests, cigar boxes, specially commissioned furniture, a variety of globes, architectural drafts and ceramics.

## L'Objet Brut

1st arr.
8 rue Mondetour
236.28.90
*Closed Mon. morning*

L'Objet Brut features a myriad of exotic wares, including masks and statuettes, African drums and flutes, Moroccan pottery, Afghan furniture and chests, Javanese puppets and various Indian items.

## Philomène

6th arr.
15 rue Vavin
633.62.01

Antique (1900-1925) jewelry in silver or gold, advertising wares, painted sheet metal boxes, frames and charming turn-of-the-century items like lingerie and lace.

## Yveline

6th arr.
4 rue de Furstenberg
326.56.91

Located at the celebrated place Furstenberg, this charming shop offers international curios and romantic lamps and furniture.

## Walking Sticks

## Lydia Bical

92200 Neuilly
31 rue de Chartres
624.14.30
*Open 3:00 P.M. to 7:30 P.M.*
*Closed Mon.*

At Lydia Bical you'll find hundreds of unusual walking sticks such as military figurines, tin soldiers and Napoleonic memorabilia, all of which span three centuries.

## Madeleine Gély

7th arr.
218 blvd.
Saint-Germain
222.63.35
*Closed Mon.*

Madeleine offers over 400 walking sticks, each more stunning then the next. She also has a fascinating collection of specially modified sticks, such as watch-canes, pipe-canes, cigarette-holder canes, canes designed to gauge the neck and withers of a horse, whiskey canes complete with glass, flask and appropriate cork.

## Philippe de La Querriere

7th arr.
27 rue de Beaune
261.00.84
*Closed Mon. morning.*

The shop offers antique canes, from the simplest models to the most decorative ones with solid gold handles.

## Wood Frames, Mirrors

Their rarity makes them very expensive. You'll find them in the specialized dealerships listed below.

### Georges Bac
**6th arr.**
**37 rue Bonaparte**
**326.82.67**

Georges Bac offers a wide inventory of seventeenth- and eighteenth-century gilded wood frames, consoles and mirrors whose craftsmanship is so fine they are coveted by leading art dealers and museums.

### Marguerite Fondeur
**7th arr.**
**24 rue de Beaune**
**261.25.78**
*Open 2:00 P.M. to 6:00 P.M.*

In Mme Fondeur's shop, established 50 years ago by her parents, you certainly won't find any counterfeit cherubs from Italy or Spain. And if you're bent on purchasing an eighteenth-century gilded wood item or mirror (guaranteed authentic), be prepared to spend a lot of money. The shop also offers genuine seventeenth- and eighteenth-century nongilded furniture and other various objects.

### Lebrun
**8th arr.**
**155 faubourg Saint-Honoré**
**561.14.66**
*Closed Mon.*

Established in 1847, Lebrun features Paris's largest inventory in pier glasses, mirrors, consoles, barometers, sculpted wood and marvelous frames from the fifteenth to eighteenth centuries. The shop is also known for its quality restorations. Parking available.

### Navarro
**6th arr.**
**15 rue Saint-Sulpice**
**633.61.51**
*Closed Mon.*

Navarro sells mirrors, barometers and gilded woodwork from the seventeenth, eighteenth and nineteenth centuries. All items are guaranteed authentic and Navarro will let you try them out in your home before buying.

# Books • Stationery

## RARE AND ORIGINAL EDITIONS

### Les Arcades
**1st arr.**
**8 rue de Castiglione**
**260.62.96**

This shop offers original editions and rare books.

**Robert Cayla**
6th arr.
28 rue Saint-Sulpice
326.48.87

You'll find here large-sized original editions: Maurras, Drieu, Brasillach and other French nationalists from the first half of this century, as well as books by Ferdinand Céline, Blaise Cendrars and Marcel Aymé.

**Francois Chamonal**
9th arr.
40 rue Le Peletier
878.14.41

This store features a remarkable selection of rare books, all reasonably priced. There are also catalogues.

**Honoré Champion**
6th arr.
7 quai Malaquais
326.51.65
*Closed Sat.*

Jeanne Laffitte and Michel Slatkine, the newly appointed directors of this French "temple" of historical lore, are still active editors who publish the bulk of French-language lore as well as a resources collection that lists hard-to-find famous books and outrageously priced first editions.

**Clavreuil**
6th arr.
37 rue
Saint-André-des-Arts
326.71.17
*Closed Mon.*

Clavreuil is one of the best bookstores in Paris. Founded in 1878, this store purchases, appraises and sells modern and rare historical books, among which you'll find a wide selection on Paris, the metropolitan area and French provinces.

**Coulet et Faure**
9th arr.
5 rue Drouot
770.84.87

Coulet et Faure sells rare and romantic books, and large-sized nineteenth-century illustrated works; catalogues are available.

**Eppe**
9th arr.
49 rue de Provence
874.66.68

Marcel Eppe, heir to a long line of antique-book dealers, is considered by his colleagues an intuitive researcher. His store features complete works in general literature and remarkable early nineteenth-century bound editions as well as other books.

**Christian Galantaris**
6th arr.
27 rue de la Seine
354.69.79

By specializing in nineteenth-century illustrators, Christian Galantaris has a limited historical selection of books. He also features rare volumes, top-quality romantic bound editions, literary curios, and large-sized original editions. He is an expert on Balzac.

**Henner**
9th arr.
9 rue Henner
874.60.38
*Closed Mon. and Sat. afternoons.*

Henner offers romantic original editions, sixteenth- to 19th-century illustrated books, literary works, science, and travel books. Catalogues available.

**Paul Jammes**
6th arr.
3 rue Gozlin

This admirable shop features original editions, books written by erudite free-thinkers and Latin poetry from the Renaissance. The son of Paul Jammes, André Jammes is well-known professionally for his seventeenth-century

**326.47.71**
*Closed Mon.*

history of the royal printing office, yet the passion he shares most, along with his daughter, is the history of photography. As a major collector in this field he is considered to be one of the most knowledgeable people in antique photography. French and foreign museums often have recourse to his services.

## Jardin de Flore
**4th arr.**
**24 place des Vosges**
**277.61.90**
*Closed Sat. mornings.*

This specialized gallery-bookshop sells precious art books and re-issues rare and at times unknown illustrated works in limited editions. The works are all finely crafted: The typography is done with separate lettering, the coloring by hand, wood is used for engraving. Fernand Pouillon supervises the collection of architectural books.

## René Kieffer
**6th arr.**
**46 rue de Saint-André-des-Arts**
**326.47.11**
*Closed Sat. in June and July.*

The store offers contemporary and romantic illustrated books, nineteenth- and twentieth-century sewn and bound original editions, and contemporary engravings and illustrations.

## Lardanchet
**8th arr.**
**100 faubourg Saint-Honoré**
**266.68.32**

Most people know this remarkable store for its ground floor, which is devoted to recent editions and art books. The first floor, however, features both an engravings gallery, which is under the direction of Dunoyer de Segonzac's niece, and a rare book department run by Mlle Pralus and M. Meaudre. Here you'll find top bibliophiles from all over the world in search of countless leatherbound books emblazoned with the coat of arms of Mmes de Pompadour and du Barry, Messrs Louvois, Colbert and Choiseul. The large-sized modern illustrated editions include engravings by Lepère, Laboureur and Charles Laborde, as well as paintings by Toulouse-Lautrec, Derain, Dufy, Dunoyer de Segonzac, Matisse, Chirico and Dali.

## Librairie de la Butte aux Cailles
**13th arr.**
**43 rue Bobillot**
**589.05.94**
*Closed Mon.*

Jean-Claude Muet founded the shop in 1974 and Yves Bréon runs it. Together they have totally updated this appealing neighborhood bookstore. Featured authors include Alphonse Boudard (a thirteenth-century writer) and, ever since this shop re-edited his *Brouillard du Pont Tolbiac,* Léo Malet. There are also out-of-print works by Céline and Albert Paraz. As well, you'll find little-known travel journals by authors such as Stevenson and George Sand.

## Librairie Jules Verne
**6th arr.**
**5 rue de l'Odeon**
**326.49.03**

It will take you more than 80 days to read this store's collection of Jules Verne's works. Other books include good turn-of-the-century works and children's books.

### Marc Loliée
7th arr.
40 rue des
Saints-Pères
548.40.19
*Closed Sat.*

Mme. Loliée runs this top quality bookstore known for its original editions, romantic books, and antique and contemporary autographs.

### Nicaise
6th arr.
145 blvd.
Saint-Germain
326.62.38

Nicaise specializes in collectors' books, particularly the Edizione di Dio series. Also featured are Surrealist and Dadaist works, twentieth-century illustrated books, modern engravings and autographs.

### Ribot-Vulin
8th arr.
8 rue de Rome
387.39.46
9th arr.
50 passage Jouffroy
824.98.89
*Closed Sat.*

The rue de Rome bookstore (open Saturdays) is self-service and offers 35 meters of shelves lined with second-hand books. The smaller shop in the lovely passage Jouffroy offers important collected works, fine arts, dictionaries and novels.

### Vrin
5th arr.
71 rue Saint-Jacques
354.70.49

Don't ever judge a book by its cover. The eclectic choice of books in the shop's window does not prevent its manager, who strives to be more than just a competent book dealer, from being one of the best authorities on Alphonse Daudet, Francis Carco, and Joseph Gobineau.

# ENGLISH LANGUAGE

### Albion
4th arr.
13 rue Charles-V
272.50.71

English and American books including history, novels, poetry, drama, general sciences (particularly social sciences), as well as everything you need to learn English! Also featured: science fiction, fantasy literature and all sorts of detective books. The fact that the University of Paris VII has its English Institute across the street accounts for the shop's permanent selection of various second-hand books and for its rental catalogue at unbeatable prices.

### Attica
5th arr.
34 rue des Ecoles
326.09.53
5th arr.
23 rue de Jean-de-
Beauvais
634.16.30
*Closed Mon.*

The rue des Ecoles store specializes in Anglo-American literature and features publications directly imported from the U.S. You'll find the entire gamut of new American literature—in English only. The rue Jean-de-Beauvais shop offers a multitude of English and American methods for teaching English to the French, including books, handbooks, records and cassettes. The lovely saleswoman will let you peruse them while she sips her English tea.

### Brentano's
**2nd arr.**
**37 ave. de l'Opéra**
**261.52.50**

Americans in Paris have been coming here since 1895 for its choice of American, English and French books and magazines. Brentano's is the perfect shop.

### Galignani
**1st arr.**
**224 rue de Rivoli**
**260.76.07**

The oldest of its kind in Continental Europe, this bookstore has always been in the hands of the Galignanis, book dealers from father to son (and from uncle to nephew) for more than 300 years. It features American and English books and paperbacks and will order any new American, English or European work of literature, arts and sciences listed in its periodical catalogue. Allow two to six weeks for delivery.

### Nouveau Quartier Latin
**6th arr.**
**78 blvd. Saint-Michel**
**326.42.70**

The largest available selection of English-language paperbacks and a good selection of art books imported from the U.S. and England. Other categories include graphics, design, architecture, photography and music. The shop's research department is very helpful. Catalogue available.

### Shake-speare and Company
**5th arr.**
**37 rue de la Bûcherie**
*12:00 noon to 12:00 midnight.*

George Whitman owns the largest selection of English second-hand books which you may purchase or peruse in this extraordinary "literary-salon" shop.

### W.H. Smith
**1st arr.**
**248 rue de Rivoli**
**260.37.97**

Among English company's 8,000 English and American titles, you'll find new works, classics, paperbacks, thrillers, science fiction, comic books, schoolbooks, children's books, records and cassettes. The book sections are all clearly marked, so don't expect any help from shop assistants. Sales are held at the end of January and June. During off-hours, it's delightful to read a book upstairs in the tearoom.

# INTERNATIONAL

### Librairie Inter-nationale
**6th arr.**
**141 blvd.**
**Saint-Germain**
**329.38.20**
*Closed Mon. mornings.*

It opened in spring, 1981, and located to the south of the Saint-Germain church, the store features 20,000 books in five languages (English, German, Spanish, Italian and French), all carefully arranged in exquisite scarlet-lacquered wooden shelves. You'll find the bulk of European literature (novels, poetry, philosophy, history and other social sciences). This attractively modern, centrally located shop is definitely a contribution to European unity.

# STATIONERY

### Élysées Stylos Marbeuf
**8th arr.**
**40 rue Marbeuf**
**225.40.49**

Pens were not meant to be lent, even if they do make good gifts. Drop in at Stylos Marbeuf and see the gold mine of felt-tipped pens and fountain pens (with one-year guarantee). M. Darde's highly specialized store features the top French and foreign brands of ballpoints, fountain pens and felt-tipped pens, whatever their design. Fountain pens are definitely back in fashion, especially in gold, which is more flexible and resistant than steel, and blackened steel and lacquer pen caps are very much in demand. Dupont is the only company to use genuine China lacquer, which it guarantees to be authentic.

### Marie Papier
**6th arr.**
**26 rue Vavin**
**326.46.44**
*Closed Mon. mornings.*

Marie's shop features hundreds of sheets of different colored stationery which she attractively displays along the walls according to category: matte, moiré, marbled, embossed, granulated, metal-plated, speckled, lined, checkered, damasked, stencil-printed and gold- or silver-flecked. All paper is individually sold by the sheet from 1F–15F. You'll also find writing paper in 80 colors, sold by the pad with assorted American-sized envelopes and suitable accessories such as ostrich plumes, pen stands, ink (scented, in all colors), notebooks, catalogues, index cards, rotating file cards, filing cabinets and folding desk pads.

### Papier +
**4th arr.**
**9 rue du Pont-Louis-Philippe**
**277.70.49**
*Open 12:00 noon to 7:30 P.M.*
*Closed Mon.*

Ironically, Laurent Tisné, a former publisher, does not carry any printed goods in his shop. Instead, you'll find superb blank-paged books for personal diaries and household budget-keeping, available in seven different formats and with a multitude of covers (from 25F–70F). There are also sumptuous writing paper sold by the weight (25F per pound), catalogues, photo albums (five formats, from 60F–250F) and all sorts of desk-related paraphernalia such as clever little drawing clips, colored sealing wax and monogrammed rubber stamps. In the adjoining outlet, you'll find individual sheets of paper for drawing, engraving and binding.

### Paris-Papiers
**15th arr.**
**54 blvd. Pasteur**
**322.93.60**
*Closed Mon.*

This Montparnasse specialty store features more than 600 kinds of paper and white or colored cardboard displayed in individual sheets, pads or in rolls according to format and thickness. Items for painting and drawing include pencils, felt-tipped pens, charcoal, paintbrushes, pens and oils. Architects, frame-makers, binders, dress designers, interior decorators, publicists, stylists, jacks-of-all-trades, students and many other professionals come here for the great selection of French and foreign brand paper.

# Children

## CLOTHING

### Baby-Dior
8th arr.
28 ave. Montaigne
723.54.44

At Baby Dior you'll find just what you'd expect: beautiful and very expensive garments for very spoiled babies. And to one side, under the alcove, there's a junior shop for the baby's siblings up to age twelve.

### Bonpoint
7th arr.
67 rue de l'Université
551.74.70
16th arr.
64 ave.
Raymond-Poincaré
727.63.63
17th arr.
184 rue de
Courcelles
763.87.49

Bonpoint was the first shop to feature soft, romantic and refined clothing for children. These clothes are simply and elegantly styled, and their fabrics are especially suitable for kids. The elegant and at times luxurious styles have met with great success in many Parisian boutiques. Also featured are fancy dresses and school uniforms. Alterations priced accordingly.

### La Châtelaine
16th arr.
170 ave. Victor-Hugo
727.44.07
*Closed Mon.*

A quality establishment for children from the best neighborhoods. You'll find the nicest layettes in all Paris here. Some of the designs are made exclusively for La Châtelaine by Molli, a Swiss lingerie firm. There are dresses and smocked playsuits that will never go out of style but will be passed down to grandchildren. All this of course costs a fortune. For older children there are classically designed, elegant and well-made clothing which may be tried on at home. Any style can be custom-made from La Châtelaine's own fabric. Biannual sales are at the beginning of January and June. Free home delivery.

### Francoise Ezanno
6th arr.
4 bis, rue du
Cherche-Midi
222.91.87

Formerly named "Pomme Cannelle," this charming blue boutique is for well-behaved children up to ten years old. Garments include flannel or seersucker shorts, kilts, playsuits, overalls and T-shirts, school aprons, exquisitely made swimsuits and cotton knitwear in all colors by Dominique Testu.

### Manby
16th arr.
9 ave. Victor-Hugo
501.66.05

A great place to shop for children's clothes (ages four to eighteen) at the start of the school year. Manby features ultra-classic girls' and boys' clothing, as well as a few dressy garments. P.A.P. Fouks is a new department in the shop for mothers.

## Old England
9th arr.
12 blvd. des
Capucines
743.81.99

On the first floor the store offers a department of traditional English childrenswear, featuring velvet-collared shetland coats (875F for six-year-olds), navy blue classic garbardines (550F), cotton flannel shorts, kilts, sweaters.

## Petit Dom'
8th arr.
18 ave.
Franklin-Roosevelt
225.39.84

This temple dedicated to little "crown-princes and princesses" (1 month through eight years old) features exquisitely made layettes, attractive smock dresses, elegant double-lined English shorts in velvet or flannel and, request, gorgeous English coats with overstitched velvet collars and cuffs. Courteous sales staff.

## Le Petit Faune
6th arr.
33 rue Jacob
260.80.72
*Closed Mon. mornings.*

It's fun to have a large family to dress in this shop's charming clothes. Twins get a ten percent discount. Items include pretty layettes, soft knitted outfits that are machine washable, and a simple yet elegant wardrobe for boys and girls up to age twelve. Alterations are free, except coats. Dressy garments include scalloped, open-worked cotton dresses for baptisms and receptions. The store also has an infants' department featuring exclusive fabrics with easy-to-follow patterns for 50F to 160F, as well as a few maternity dresses priced from 530F.

## La Petite Gaminerie
6th arr.
28 and 32 rue du
Four
548.39.31

These two white shops, with their vaulted ceilings and black façades, located in the center of Saint-Germain-des-Prés, feature a wide variety of clothes in the latest fashion. At the No. 28 location you'll find dresses, shirts and raincoats for children two to six years old, all of which are designed by top designers like Cacharel and Bercher. At the No. 32 location, there are skirts, slacks, blouses and T-shirts for children eight to fifteen years old.

## Scapa of Scotland
6th arr.
71 rue des
Saints-Pères
544.67.52

Smart-looking English and Scottish garments. Although the shop is mainly for adults, it also features clothing for boys and girls from two to sixteen years old. These school-and weekend-styled garments can be worn a long time without wearing out. For girls you'll find twenty traditional Scottish kilts in five solid colors, as well as assorted cotton shirts with scalloped claudine collars. For boys, the shop offers classic trousers, oxford shirts and a wide variety of Scottish ties and bow-ties, as well as V-neck sweaters, cardigans, turtlenecks and vests, all made from lambswool, solid shetland or jacquard. For the summer, the shop features light dresses, seersucker blazers, poplin bousons and delicate striped sweaters. Scapa of Scotland will soon have its own shoe department.

# TOYS

## Ali Baba

**7th arr.**
**29 ave. de Tourville**
**555.10.85**
*Closed Mon., except in November and December.*

Excluding Le Nain Bleu, this is the best and most complete traditional toy store in Paris. Ali Baba's three floors feature a glorious selection of dolls and accessories, miniature collectors' cars, bona fide tin soldiers, scale model trains, and life-sized stuffed animals from 20F to 2,500F. Particularly well-stocked are the model and electric toy departments. Free delivery in Paris.

## Magictoys

**15th arr.**
**Centre Beaugrenelle,**
**16 rue Linois**
**575.58.48**
*Open 10:00 A.M. to 8:00 P.M. Closed Sun.*

Its 1,000 square meters makes it the largest toy store in Paris. Magictoys offers both children and adults everything in its self-service store, from stuffed animals to models. Featured top-brand items include soldier outfits for children, puzzles, dolls, miniatures and educational games. The outdoors department offers inflatable pools, rubber fins, floats, tricycles, scooters, wagons and roller-skates. For children over twelve, Magictoys features a fascinating model department (thirty top brands, including Heller, Italiari, Monogram, Airfix, Tamiya) and dressmaking kits (ten top brands, including Graupner and Robbe).

## Le Monde en Marche

**6th arr.**
**34 rue Dauphine**
**326.66.53**
*Closed Mon.*

Le Monde en Marche is a pioneer in wooden toys and one of the best stores of its kind. Its reasonably priced, fine-quality toys include tops, jumping-jacks, puppets and marionettes from 50F to 130F, music boxes from 90F, Christmas mangers, pyramids from 150F to 500F, and dollhouse furniture.

## Le Nain Bleu

**8th arr.**
**406-410**
**rue Saint-Honoré**
**260.29.01**

This particular dwarf has certainly grown since its birth in 1836 on boulevard des Capucines. Located since 1909 on the rue Saint-Honoré, it has just undergone a series of improvements which have restored it to its original 1909 decor. It is still the most famous toy store in Paris and caters to the whims of little princes, dream merchants and the progeny of all the world's greats. Its three stories of toys far surpass a child's wildest dreams. But all these marvels have given Le Nain Bleu a very expensive reputation, which it does not deserve. Certainly there are rare costly works of art such as the custommade croquet mallets, a doll's sewing room, a gasoline-driven model car for 6,000F, a coal-and-wood-driven train, and even a fabulous Mississippi-style paddle steamer priced at 35,000F. Yet there are many other toys which are no more expensive here than elsewhere, such as the porcelain marionettes dressed in lace, the antique dolls and their furniture, white china tableware in scale, miniature grocery shops, lavish chess sets and the latest scientific games, all of which will undoubtably make you long for the days of short pants and sand boxes. The sales staff are very helpful. Sales are held in January and February, and there's a customer service department that will repair toys and antique games. There is a 5 percent discount for large families and credit-card customers.

### Pain
**9th arr.**
**29 passage Jouffroy**
**770.82.65**
*Closed Mon. mornings.*

This is the most charming toy store in Paris, and because of the nostalgia trend, one of the city's most popular. The marvelous bric-a-brac here is a powerful link to the lush paradise-lost of childhood. You'll find all sorts of replicas of old toys with charming features that owners Jean-Pierre and Françoise Blindermann recreate in their small workshop. The toys include hoops, jump ropes, marionettes, gyroscopes, tops, diabolos and much more. Parents are quite likely to visit this astonishing shop to buy miniature dollhouses, Epinal drawings, old cut-outs and sheet metal toys. On the second floor, you'll find a delightful department of shower gifts, accessories and children's clothing up to age four.

### Sophie du Bac
**7th arr.**
**109 rue du Bac**
**548.49.01**
*Open 12:00 noon to 6:30 P.M.*

Not only does this store feature beautiful antique dolls in excellent condition from the turn of the century, it also carries appropriate accessories and miniature furniture such as tables, chairs, chests of drawers, closets, buffets, jewelry and wardrobes. These refinements easily sell for 400F to 600F, and the dolls cost even more. Sophie du Bac will repair any damage, restore porcelain heads, replace rubber joints, and re-do wigs.

### La Source des Inventions
**10th arr.**
**60 blvd. de Strasbourg**
**206.53.02**

M. Michel, an eminent jack-of-all-trades, is at the source of all these inventions. At the turn of the century, he started inventing all sorts of electric radios and contributed to the development of the telephone bell. To promote his creations, in 1908 he decided to open up a shop where handymen could purchase radios capable of receiving signals from the Eiffel Tower's transmitter. The current owners of this store offer one of the best and largest selections in Paris of remote-control scale model toys. Famous habitués include comedians Roger Pierre and Jean-Marc Thibault, singer Gilbert Bécaud, and actor Bernard Blier.

# Department Stores

Parisian department stores are both exhilarating and charming. They range from hyped-up sales promotions to elegant and sophisticated faubourg Saint-Honoré-style boutiques. Most, of course, are also designed to meet your everyday needs with services such as keys made while you wait, watch repairs, hair styling, banking, bookings (for theater or travel), fur care and storage, wedding gift registration, passport photos; and goods such as jewelry, tennis rackets, lumber, carpets and mirrors. They all sell tableware, housewares, miscellaneous do-it-yourself items, lamps, tools, sportswear, clothing, perfume, fancy leather goods, fabric and furniture. Yet each store has its specialty. For instance, you'll buy clothes at the Galeries Lafayette and Au Printemps, home furnishings at the B.H.V. and Samaritaine. You'll fight the crowds for groceries and refreshments at Au Bon Marché, and you'll purchase linen and gloves at Aux Trois Quartiers.

## Bazar de L'Hôtel de Ville
### (B.H.V.)
*Open 9:00 A.M. to 6:30 P.M.,*
*Wed. to 10:00 P.M.,*
*Sat. to 7:00 P.M.*

B.H.V. is the handyman's dream. Its basement hardware store is one of the largest in Paris. The lock department is the most extensive in France; the garden department features tools, furniture, fences, greenhouses and farm machinery. It also has a complete auto accessories shop. The third floor features everything for the kitchen, including furniture, appliances, utensils, crockery and glassware. The second floor has a good line of accessories for the bath adjacent to the linen and lighting departments. Equally well-stocked are the book, record and sportswear departments (tennis and sailing). As for interior decorating, there is a large choice of name-brand wallpaper and upholstery. A nice surprise is the auto shop featuring radio and seat belt installations, oil change, lubrication, brake adjustments, tuning and tire fitting—if you're lucky, done while you shop.

## Au Bon Marché
### 7th arr.
### 38 rue de Sèvres
### 260.33.45
*Open 9:30 A.M. to 6:45 P.M.*

Despite renovations, this grand old dame of Parisian department stores still has a small-town family atmosphere with nuns and well-dressed matrons going about their shopping. In the basement, Store No. 2 features a huge self-service hardware department where there are never any sales clerks and you're completely on your own. On the first floor, you'll find a large grocery store which, despite its dull supermarket appearance, offers exotic and imported luxury items: Petrossian's salmon, foie gras, fresh pasta, delicatessen items and a wine cellar worth visiting. You'll find antiques on the second floor; they include a nice choice of rustic, Napoleon III and turn-of-the-century objects and furniture. The dining area in the inner court includes a pizzeria, cafeteria and full-menu restaurant. Trois Hiboux Store No. 1 is a children's paradise. Here they can read books at leisure, learn enameling, weaving, clay modeling, basket-making or play music and educational games. The Bon Marché also has the most beautiful collection of oriental rugs in Paris.

# Fnac

**1st arr.**
**Forum: 2nd floor**
**261.81.18**
*Open Tues. to Sat. 10:00 A.M. to 8:00 P.M., Mon. 1:00 P.M. to 8:00 P.M.*

**1st arr.**
**Sport-Forum:**
**3rd floor**
**261.81.18**
*Hours same as above.*

**6th arr.—**
**Montparnasse:**
**136 rue de Rennes**
**544.39.12**
*Open Tues. to Sat. 10:00 A.M. to 8:00 P.M.*

**8th arr.**
**Etoile:**
**26 ave. de Wagram**
**766.52.50**
*Open Tues. to Sat. 10:00 A.M. to 8:00 P.M.*

In addition to its regular clientele, the Fnac now has a membership of 350,000 people who benefit from its various services (discounts on purchases, credit union benefits, theatrical and tour agencies). Through scheduled meetings, seminars and exhibits the Fnac manages to offer many cultural events at very low prices, the former promoting the latter and vice-versa. Though Fnac's prices are more or less the same as its competitors, if not at times steeper, the store's chief attribute is its knowledgeable staff, notably in the photo, audiovisual and sportswear departments, where quality and quantity abound. The Forum des Halles store, which opened in September 1979, specializes in photography, audiovisual equipment, office computers and records. It also has a 250-seat auditorium where you may attend literary debates, children's workshops, super-8 screenings, photo classes and "record-listening" sessions (schedules available at all Fnac outlets). The Fnac-Sport is one of the most complete sporting goods stores in Paris and features excellent hunting, diving, camping and boating departments. The Etoile branch specializes in audiovisual equipment and has a particularly large choice of records. The Montparnasse store features the same items, plus a video department and a remarkable bookshop (120,000 titles). Fnac also maintains several boutiques in metro stations on the R.E.R. line (Sébastopol, Châtelet, Auber, Gare de Lyon.) that sell film, movies and blank cassettes. Film-development service is also available.

# Galeries Lafayette

**9th arr.**
**Haussmann: 40 blvd.**
**Haussmann**
**282.34.56**
**15th arr.**
**Tour Montparnasse,**
**22 rue du Départ**
**538.52.87**
*Open 9:30 A.M. to 6:30 P.M.*

The Galeries Lafayette are at the forefront of fashion. The greats are all here; among them, Mugler, Montana, Castelbajac, Giudicelli, Rykiel, Emmanuelle Khanh, and Popy Moreni (but no V.S. Dorgrers). Everything around you seems to sparkle, but if your wallet is in a state of non-scintillation, move on to Club "20" or Club "30" and your heart will pound less hard. Complete your wardrobe at the appropriate departments: lingerie, perfume, fancy leather goods, shoe and millinery. The Galfa Club is for men, and it's agreeable to find, all under one roof, virtually all brands, sizes and colors of suits, shirts, sweaters and socks. Tableware is represented by the best brands, such as Haviland and Christofle. The interior decorating services will carry out all specifications for your home or office. The high-tech department caters to those who enjoy the 1955 "welfare" look, such as metal-frame beds and rolling chairs. You also eat well at the Galeries Lafayette. The grill is open from 11:00 A.M. to 3:00 P.M. and the cafeteria, open from 10:30 A.M. to 6:00 P.M., is pleasant and faces south towards the opera. Congenial hosts offer country-style buffets, salads, quality meat and desserts. Other services include a twenty-four hour cloakroom (79 rue de Provence), a loading dock (they'll pack your newly acquired bicycle straight into your car), and a charming staff at the travel and show-booking agencies. Parking available.

## Magasins Réunis

**17th arr.**
**30 ave. des Ternes**
**380.20.00**
*Open Tues. to Sat. 9:40 A.M. to 6:30 P.M.*

Magasins Réunis is a large store in the area of Tern
is indispensable to Neuilly and the denizens of the
arrondisement. Its grocery department is well stocked
with teas, coffees, imported delicacies, sweets and
alcoholic beverages. The do-it-yourself department is
useful, and there's a brand-new sports department for
those who enjoy horseback riding, tennis, bicycling,
dancing and jogging. On the third floor there's a tea room,
as well as a "while-you-wait" key and show repair service.
Free delivery for purchases over 1,000F. Parking lot on the
avenue des Ternes.

## Au Printemps

**9th arr.**
**Haussmann: 64 blvd.**
**Haussmann**
**285.22.22**
*Open 9:30 A.M. to 6:30 P.M.*

**12th arr.**
**Nation: 21 cours de**
**Vincennes**
**371.12.41**
*Open 9:30 A.M. to 6:30 P.M., Wed. to 9:00 P.M.*

**13th arr.**
**Italie: Centre**
**Commercial Galaxie,**
**place d'Italie**
**581.11.50**
*Open 10:00 A.M. to 7:30 P.M. Wed. to 9:00 P.M.*

The highlight of the Printemps is the Primavera boutique,
an exhibit of Summerhouse-style articles such as ceramics,
opaline, fabric flowers, bamboo and rattan furniture—a
triumph of charming and lively pastel tones—and a huge
selection of gifts, (the same applies to the Boutique
Noire). Fashion is held in high esteem in this gracious old
store of new trends. In the Nouveau Magasin on the fourth
floor, there's the Rue de la Mode with couturier
boutiques; on the third floor, a women's ready-to-wear
shop; and on the second floor, the trend is geared towards
the youthful, casual look. Score one for the wonderful fur
department (skins and pelts), and another for the wide
selection of lingerie and perfume. Both the toy
department (the largest in Paris) and sound department
deserve attention. The same is true for the lighting and
fancy leather goods departments. Lunch is served in the
charmingly baroque Square du Printemps, although the
cuisine is far below the level of the store's dome, which,
in itself, is worth a visit. An overhead ramp leads straight to
Chez Brummel, specializing in men's ready-to-wear
clothes. Here you'll find a large selection of sweaters and
shirts. They'll tailor the length of your sleeves and sew on
your monogram. Services include a friendly reception at
the travel agency, an animal shelter outlet, a twenty-four-
hour cloakroom (107 rue de Provence) and at-home
interior decorating services. At the Printemps-Nation store,
you'll find a large food department featuring fresh
produce, imported spices, delicatessen items, wine,
pastries and much more.

## La Samaritaine

**1st arr.**
**Pont-Neuf**
**508.33.33**
*Open 9:30 A.M. to 6:30 P.M., Wed. to 10:00 P.M., Sat. to 7:00 P.M.*

At the Samaritaine, nostalgia isn't a trend, it's a way of life.
Items from yesteryear are still going strong: sgt. major
pens, frivolous incense boxes, rat and mouse traps, liquid
brilliantine, hand coffee-grinders. The hosiery department
offers bedjackets complete with bedsocks and nightcaps,
calico granddaddy shirts handwoven in the Vosges. But
you'll also find stylish pajamas, jeans and sandals. Fashion
at the Samaritaine really focuses on work clothes that are
durable and affordable. Le Tout Paris comes here for its
premium quality butchers' smocks, painters' overalls,
maitre d' striped vests or goldsmiths' linen smocks. Home
furnishing departments are both well-stocked and
interesting and feature do-it-yourself goods: paint,

wallpaper, tool rentals, garden equipment, stoves and heaters. There are wide selections in haberdashery and artificial flowers. The "Samar" is the only store featuring a pet department with dogs, cats, fish, birds, chickens and hamsters. You may also have your animal groomed or outfitted with a coat, boots, leash, pethouse or toilet. It's hard to figure out the layout of the four Samaritaine stores, all linked by a common basement. It's even harder to find the parking lot. The elevators are few and tiny and it's better to take the stairs if you're loaded down with packages. The best view of Paris is from Store No. 2 on the tenth floor, but the terrace is closed between October and March. The store also has tearooms, and a cafeteria serving worse food than any army or boarding-school mess.

## Aux Trois Quartiers

1st arr.
17 blvd.
de la Madeleine
260.39.30
*Open 9:00 A.M. to 6:30 P.M.*

First-class all the way, the Trois Quartiers hasn't changed a bit since the time when veiled ladies arrived in carriages to purchase their knickknacks. The stuffy atmosphere and luxurious carpeting makes this very British store different from its competitors. Here you'll find luxury items not glitter, making it more accessible to upper-class matrons than to salesgirls. Clothing here is chic and in good taste (tweed, shetland and cashmere) rather than "new wave" or country. Here you're more likely to find elegant items rather than necessities—no lawn mowers or tools for the handyman. Instead you'll find the best glove department in Paris, fine household linen and a perfumerie as relaxing as a beauty spa. The second floor is entirely dedicated to children, with toys, clothes and furniture. In the basement are household items, and on the fourth floor, a pleasant tearoom, which serves hot dishes during lunch hours. Madelios, the men's shop, is across the street. Parking is available nearby at the Madeleine, which otherwise has nothing special in the line of services.

# *Flowers*

# *ARTIFICIAL FLOWERS*

## Espace Floral

6th arr.
7 rue Mayet
566.76.51
*Closed Mon. morning.*

Catherine Sciacco is a charming "synthesist." In her recently enlarged shop she offers graceful wreaths blending pine boughs and plastic fruit which will make you want to celebrate Christmas every day of the year. She also has mouth-watering clusters of artificial grapes made in Hong Kong, pre-Christmas wreaths made from natural or artificial plants, fabric flower-wreaths mixed with currants, cherries or acorns suitable for table centerpieces, candy- and ribbon-trimmed wreaths, bridal headgear and bouquets, flowering trees and astonishing bouquets which defy both nature and the human eye by their artistic blending of natural, dried and fabric flowers. The Espace Floral also rents artificial bouquets and natural green plants.

## Un Jardin en Plus
**1st arr.**
**44 rue Saint-Denis**
**233.00.68**
**7th arr.**
**224 blvd.**
**Saint-Germain**
**548.25.71**

This is the most opulent winter garden in Paris. Although everything here is artificial, it seems more "natural than nature itself." In this beautiful and vast greenhouse, springtime is eternal. You'll find potted geraniums, primroses, lots of "cut" flowers made of cotton or mixed silks, and all sorts of tropical or temperate-climate green plants, flowering bushes and fruit trees.

## Trousselier
**8th arr.**
**73 blvd. Haussmann**
**265.32.23**

This vast and marvelous establishment has an old-fashioned decor, in which you'll find artfully blended artificial flowers that are paragons of beauty and detail. At the back of the 160-year-old shop, unseen, highly-skilled hands work marvels with Japanese prune trees, marigolds, moss roses and other unusual blooms or country flowers which look more natural than the real thing. Of course, the prices are steep: Garden roses sell from 80F–200F apiece, silk anemones are 18F, and wood-mounted flower-decked trees retail from approximately 650F–2,500F.

# EXOTIC PLANTS

## Bisson
**6th arr.**
**41 rue Dauphine**
**633.84.08**

Alain-Frédéric Bisson offers his own collection of bonsai (six to fifty years old), orchids, mandarin trees, coffee trees, bougainvillea, cacti and potted pine trees (for Christmas). At the opposite end of the courtyard you'll find an everchanging selection of outdoor plants, pots, and containers made from terra cotta or wood. Alain is also a landscape gardener who will, upon request, design, decorate and tend your terrace or balcony.

## E.V.E.
**15th arr.**
**1, 3 and 13 quai**
**de Grenelle**
**578.72.06**

Edouard d'Avdeev does not carry cut flowers. Instead this young horticulturist and sometime-landscape designer sells only potted plants and is on a first-name basis with the most unusual of their species. His love affair with orchids enables him to tell you all about their habits, their tastes and appetites, their repulsion towards tobacco, their unbelievable longevity and their price, which isn't really all *that* expensive. You shouldn't think that orchids are nice little mauve-colored things wrapped up in plastic bags. Edouard's are provocatively healthy, with their grape-like blossoms (the white ones are truly incredible) bursting out of long slender stems, their graceful leaves oblong and glossy. It's easy to walk up and down this dismal section of the quai de Grenelle between the Bir-Hakeim bridge and Front de Seine skyscrapers without even noticing the "EVE" signpost hung over the former garage in which this amazing green-thumbed Russian keeps his plants. Although each plant comes with a booklet telling you how to care for it, Edouard will "follow up" should you encounter any problems. Also featured here are indoor and outdoor plant collections, tropical plants and bonsai. He will also research unusual plants, track down botanical identifications and look after plants during the holidays.

# FLOWER MARKETS

There are only three left in Paris, open daily 9:00 A.M. to 7:00 P.M., except Sunday afternoons and Mondays.

## Marché aux Fleurs de l'Ile de la Cité

• 4th arr.—place Louis-Lépine (quai de Corse)

## Marché de la Madeleine

• 8th arr.—Coté Est de la Madeleine

## Marché des Ternes

• 17th arr.—Place des Ternes

# FRESH FLOWERS

## Arène
16th arr.
4 and 5 rue Mesnil
727.32.19

Karl Dauchy (formerly at Sodéflora ) rules with an iron fist over this fifty-year-old quality firm, which owns two shops facing one another on the rue Mesnil. At the odd-numbered address, there's the flower workshop in which throughout the day and at times all night long, fervent, agile little hands (some of which have been there since the store's inception) busily put together, the most elegant and harmonious bouquets. The flowers can be arranged to suit the decor of your apartment or to complement your table. For instance, they can be put into attractive Italian ceramic or Chinese porcelain vases exclusively designed to enhance them, or arranged in metallic framework and scissor-sculpted to resemble pyramids, animals as a centerpiece. On the even-numbered side of the street, Arène-Plantes offers indoor trees (up to six meters high), potted orchids, bonsai, unusual species of flora and lots of flowering plants. Also, monthly "thematic" sales-exhibits are held featuring, for example, fuchsias (seventy varieties), Ile de France peonies (Sarah Bernhardt, l'Odorante, la Japonaise ), Dutch tulips, cacti and other fragrant flowers. Arène will deliver to your home (for all purchases over 150F) and decorate terraces and gardens from A (as in anemone) to Z (as in zinnia), as well as install lighting, automatic sprinkler systems and greenhouses.

### Lachaume
**8th arr.**
**10 rue Royale**
**260.57.26**

Here you'll find at least twelve dozen beautiful sunset-colored tulips in one vase as well as beautiful green-white lilies in the bud, their fascicules gracefully drooping. At the back of the shop, you'll also see myriads of pale-toned and subtle flowers, ingeniously arranged on both sides of the narrow walkway.

### Maxim's Fleurs
**8th arr.**
**5 rue Royale**
**742.87.10**

Maxim's Fleurs, formerly located at the rue Duras, is now next to Maxim's restaurant. This strange and beautiful shop offers flowers that overflow their art nouveau stands and green-leafed trimmings. You'll also find marvelous moss gardens, sumptuous lilies and extremely rare white or blue amaryllis. Lots of prestigious "terrestrial" or heavenly orchids, which are extremely hard to keep at home. In a word, superb.

### Orève
**16th arr.**
**25 rue de la Pompe**
**503.13.86**

A few very old people will still remember the nurseries and greenhouses M. Orève used to have at the turn of the century. They were located on what is now the avenue Georges Mandel. Today, his grandson, Charles Orève, offers beautifully cut or potted flowers (reasonably priced) in his tiled store adjoining a superb greenhouse. Built in 1911, it is the only commercial greenhouse in Paris and has often been used as a backdrop for films. Here you can rent decorative plants or purchase beautiful flowers, as well as washable, synthetically made green plants suitable for balconies. Customer parking.

### Veyrat
**8th arr.**
**168 blvd. Haussmann**
**562.37.86**

This is a corner shop comprising two superb window displays and an orgy of colors in this otherwise cool and affected portion of the boulevard Haussmann. René Veyrat's flowering plants and bouquets are sold at prices slightly higher than those of other neighborhood florists of lesser quality. Smiling and courteous sales staff.

# Food

## BREADS

### Le Fournil de Pierre
**6th arr. 64**

Le Fournil de Pierre employs the best bakers, who produce all kinds of bread: wheat—in round or triangular loaves—rye, raisin-rye, wholewheat, bran, and butter. All

**rue de Seine**
**634.17.59**
**8th arr.**
**21 rue Vignon**
**265.26.95**
**14th arr.**
**15 rue Daguerre**
*Closed Mon. mornings.*
*Open Sun. afternoons.*

## Haupois
**4th arr.**
**35 rue des Deux-Ponts**
**354.57.59**
*Closed Thurs., Fri. Open Sun.*

## Les Panetons
**5th arr.**
**113 rue Mouffetard**
**707.12.08**
*Open Sun. mornings.*

## La Petite Marquise
**15th arr.**
**91 rue de la**
**Convention**
**554.50.20**
**16th arr.**
**3 pl. Victor-Hugo**
**500.77.36**
*Closed Mon.*

## Poilâne
**1st arr.**
**Forum des Halles,**
**3rd floor**
**297.44.63**
**6th arr.**
**8 rue du Cherche-Midi**
**548.42.59**
**15th arr.**
**87 rue Brancion**
**828.45.90**
**15th arr.**
**49 blvd. de Grenelle**
**579.11.49**
*Closed Mon. at blvd. de Grenelle.*
*Closed Sat. afternoons at*
*rue Brancion.*

are deliciously fragrant, sweet-tasting and will remain fresh for several days. Other goods include an exquisite gâteau de pêcheur or fisherman's cake, a delicious confection of rum-soaked rolls as big as a child's fist filled with nuts and raisins. There are also brioches, croustades, feuilletés, sandwiches on wheat bread filled with excellent Ferme Saint-Hubert cheese and chez Provost charcuteries as well as four daily selections of pizza.

This artisan bakes his bread in the old, traditional manner, making not only the tastiest loaves you'll find on Ile Saint-Louis, but also the best in Paris. Also featured are remarkable cakes.

The decor is simple and cheerful, with cork-lined walls and brick floors that bring to mind the south of France. Les Panetons offers bread of all shapes and kinds, such as large round macro-organic loaves, rye with nuts or raisins, leavened bread, starch-free, sprouted-wheat, poppy seed, caraway seed and many others. There are also tartes made from leeks, onions, or watercress that cost approximately 36F, available in half or quarter portions. Other dainties include apple turnovers at 5F, croquants and large croissants.

La Petite Marquise offers delicious, chemical-free bread— white, rye, whole wheat, egg bread, milk bread, honey bread, raisin bread, and country bread (also known as "persanes"), which consists mainly of crust and costs 4.70F per loaf.

Everyone knows about Poilâne's large wheat rolls. You'll find them displayed on counters in charcuteries, cheese shops and supermarkets, and served in many leading restaurants. They remain fresh long after they're taken out of their wood-heated ovens and are equally delightful toasted. Less well known are Poilâne's exquisite country-style cakes, pies and Viennese pastries. There is always a line thirty meters long in front of the rue du Cherche-Midi shop.

## René Saint-Ouen
**8th arr.**
**111 blvd. Haussmann**
**265.06.25**

It's nearly impossible to list all the different breads offered by this ingenious baker. There is traditional rye, excellent with fish; bread with Brie to accompany pork; bacon bread or hearth cake for aperitifes; wheat bread for cheese; special toasted bread for caviar; French rolls for grilled meats; and the often neglected "split" bread, also known as de deux livres or the two-pounder. Also featured are splendid sculpted breads shaped like animals, bicycles or grape clusters.

# BUTCHERS

## Bell Viandier
**6th arr.**
**25 rue du Vieux-Colombier**
**548.57.83**
*Closed Mon.*

Serge Caillaud is a young butcher who is very much in love with his work. In his old-fashioned shop he sells well-cut premium meats such as Parthenais and Limousine beef. Also featured are pâtés, chitterling sausages and various sorts of paupiettes. His meats are high quality at high prices.

# CAVIAR, SMOKED SALMON

## Comptoir Gourmand (Michel Guérard)
**8th arr.**
**32 place de la Madeleine**
**742.73.51**
*Closed Mon.*

Comptoir Gourmand offers four varieties of salmon; wild Norwegian, dill-scented Norwegian and Scottish, all at 430F per kilo; and Danish at 400F per kilo. The varieties of caviar are Russian oscietra and Iranian, each at 2,900F per kilo.

## Dominique
**6th arr.**
**19 rue Bréa**
**327.08.80**
*Open until 10:30 P.M.*

Should you ever be confronted with an uncontrollable urge for caviar at 10:00 P.M., run in to this little grocery store next to the restaurant and purchase some exquisite Iranian oscietra. You can also stock up on Danish smoked salmon, superb at 360F per kilo; blinis, zakouskis and vodka.

## Fauchon
**8th arr.**
**26 place de la Madeleine**
**742.60.11**
*Closed Mon.*

Fauchon offers extra large-grain Iranian beluga and the ultra-luxurious and difficult-to-find white caviar from the roe of albino sturgeon. There are also sturgeon marrow, imported from the U.S.S.R., and salmon from Scotland and Norway.

## Flora Danica
**8th arr.**
**142 Champs-Elysées**
**359.20.41**
*Open Sun.*

This tiny shop is located on the ground floor of the Maison du Danemark and features remarkable Danish smoked salmon at 380F per kilo, smoked eel and halibut, and canned herring.

## Kaspia
8th arr.
17 place
de la Madeleine
265.33.52
*Open until 1:00 A.M.*

This excellent shop sells its own brand of caviar, which customers are allowed to sample. The firm's own pressed caviar is one of the best in Paris and sells for 175F for 125 grams. Kaspia also features superb whole smoked eel, perfectly smoked wild Norwegian salmon at 380F per kilo and premium quality Russian salmon roe, all of which are offered in the upstairs snack bar.

## Lenôtre
16th arr.
44 rue d'Auteuil
254.52.52
*Open Sun.*

The origins of Lenôtre's superb wild salmon vary according to season. Lenôtre himself smokes the Norwegian and Scottish salmon, while his Danish salmon is smoked in Copenhagen exclusively for him.

## La Maison du Caviar
8th arr.
21 rue
Quentin-Bauchart
723.53.43
*Open every day from 10:00 A.M. to 2:00 A.M.*

This shop features a very good Iranian caviar and salmon from Scotland, Denmark and Norway at 380F per kilo. It is delicate and delightful served on toast or with blinis.

## Petrossian
7th arr.
18 blvd.
de Latour-Maubourg
551.59.73
*Closed Mon.*

Petrossian offers premium quality Russian caviar which is no more expensive than elsewhere. The beluga is 3,120F per kilo. The Norwegian smoked salmon is the best in Paris and sells at 370F per kilo. Free deliveries for purchases over 500F.

## Au Régal
16th arr.
4 rue Nicolo
288.49.15
*Closed Mon.*

For the last five years Irène Benveniste has been running this fine quality firm which offers an Iranian sevruga with fresh and fruity grains that make it the best in Paris at 1,920F per kilo. Her rigorous selection of wild Norwegian salmon is available either smoked at 400F per kilo or marinated at 290F per kilo. Other goods include blinis, koulibiaks and pirogis. Free deliveries for purchases over 150F.

## A la Ville de Pétrograd
8th arr.
13 rue Daru
227.96.55
*Open Sun.*

In this old grocery shop/restaurant, located near the Russian Orthodox Church, you'll find fresh and pressed caviar, smoked salmon, blinis, home-made borscht, and all kinds of Russian specialties.

# CHARCUTERIE

## Battendier
1st arr.
8 rue Coquillière
236.95.50

Established in 1826, Battendier has recently been redone in a beautiful 1930s decor. Since the days when Napoleon III replenished his larder here, Battendier has continued to supply the greatest names in France, including Gambetta, Poincaré, Clemenceau, the Auriol family,

Closed Mon. (Sales outlet at Printemps-Nation, 25 cours de Vincennes, Paris, 12 arrondissement tel. 371.12.41).

## Cerveau
**12th arr.**
**4 rue Marsoulan**
**343.89.57**
*Closed Tues. afternoons and Wed. Open Sun. mornings.*

## Chédeville et Bourdon
**1st arr.**
**12 rue du Marché Saint-Honoré**
**261.11.11**
*Closed Mon.*

## Coesnon
**6th arr.**
**30 rue Dauphine**
**326.56.39**
*Closed Mon.*

## Lenôtre
**16th arr.**
**44 rue d'Auteuil**
**524.52.52**
*Open Sun.*

General de Gaulle and others. Featured foods include andouillette, plain or with herbs at 78F per kilo; boudin; terrines of rabbit, chicken, duck, and veal sweetbreads; salmon pâté; parfait of scallops; ham; and Colmar foie gras available all year long.

M. Cerveau despises "industrial" charcuterie and delights in doing things the old way. He makes his own rillettes, and carefully selects and trims the meats and lard. He cuts his andouillettes by hand, using fresh garlic for garlic sausages and pure butter piecrust for his pâtés encroûte; also superb ham.

In this shop you'll see as many cashiers, butchers and pastrymakers as there are hams hanging from the ceiling. This is a well-known charcuterie where leading Parisian restaurants such as Maxim's, Taillevent, Gérard Pangaud, Laurent, as well as provincial establishments like Le Moulin de Mougins and La Réserve in Beaulieu come to stock up. Featured items include andouillettes, delicius terrines of veal sweetbreads and duck à l'orange, various salads, cooked dishes, good wines and regional specialties.

Without the least hesitation, we believe that Coesnon is the best charcuterie in Paris. It is the most diversified, the most innovative, consistent in quality and freshness and, last but not least, the most reasonably priced, given the high degree of quality. Although the shop is very small, the goods are prepared in large Medieval cellars which are the shop's "laboratory." Coesnon features eighteen varieties of boudins made from apples, grapes, chestnuts, breast of chicken, truffles, veal sweetbreads and many other delicacies; as well as stuffed trotters à l'ancienne; andouilles and andouillettes; ready-to-cook sausages; feuilletés; bream; and unrivalled terrines made from veal sweetbreads, green pepper-corns or fish. He also smokes his own bacon (it's highly regarded by the British colony in Paris), makes his own paupiettes and feuilletés with fresh salmon, pâtés en croûte and onion tartes. Also featured are marvelous terrines made from freshly killed game brought in on Tuesdays before 10:00 A.M. and sold the following day. His appetizers are delicious and he also sells raw foie gras all year long.

An extraordinary choice of charcuterie selected or made by Lenôtre, including terrine of duck with green pepper at 170F per kilo, galantines, white or black boudins sausage and fresh foie gras. Every day Lenôtre offers a different precooked dish which must be ordered 24 hours in advance. A monthly list of dishes is provided in all Lenôtre stores. Delivery is available for a small fee on purchases of 400F and up.

## Provost
**14th arr.**
**128 ave. du**
**Gal-Leclerc**
**539.70.78**
*Closed Mon.*

Provost is one of Paris's leading charcuterie-caterers and an excellent chef in his own right. His two-toque restaurant, which opened in 1976, leads directly to his shop. Except for his cured products, everything he sells is made on the premises, including andouillettes à la ficelle at 64F per kilo; boudins; fresh goose and duck foe gras, 660F and 440F per kilo respectively; smoked or cooked salmon from Scotland in season; and much more. Upon request, he will prepare fresh pike quenelles terrine made from three kinds of fish, rabbit with green pepper or fricasseed chicken with sherry vinegar.

# CHEESES

## Barthélémy
**7th arr.**
**51 rue de Grenelle**
**548.56.75**
*Closed Mon.*

This attractive shop, with its two-toned marble counters, earned its reputation under the management of Mme Forteau. M. Barthélémy, who is considered one of the best cheesesellers in France, has taken over her operation and produces delicious Pussigny Saint-Maure, Salers Cantal, goat cheese and Mont d'Or Vacherin. Other exceptional cheeses include the raw milk Camemberts sold at Harrod's in London, and Ouve Valley raw butter. In the guest register at the rue de Grenelle shop, Giscard d'Estaing noted his reflections about the diversity of cheeses that "make France such an agreeable country to live in, yet so difficult to govern."

## Cantin
**15th arr.**
**2 rue de Lourmel**
**578.70.58**
*Closed Mon.*

Despite his spirited humor and his street urchin behavior, Cantin is considered a leader in his profession. We highly recommend his wide selection of country style cheeses and his excellent butter.

## Carmès
**17th arr.**
**24 rue de Lévis**
**763.88.94**
*Closed Mon. Open Sun. mornings.*

His undisputed talent in aging cheese in his four magnificent cellars has entitled him to the highly coveted agricultural "Croix du Mérite." Carmès, in collaboration with his sons, sells innumerable and remarkably well-made cheeses such as the ash-coated Lucullus, a house specialty; Grand Vatel; and farmers' Cantals; Nectaires and Saint-Maures.

## Créplet-Brussol
**8th arr.**
**17 pl. de la**
**Madeleine**
**265.34.32**
*Closed Mon.*

You'll find over 200 cheeses permanently displayed in this shop that features products from northern France such as Cambai and Avesnes balls, tastefully cured cures nantais, poivre d'âne, époisses au marc and Normandy bouille. There is also English Stilton, Swiss vacherin du Mont d'Or and Italian and Dutch cheeses. Ask M. Lefevre for his cheese calendar. Deliveries are available at a fee of 10F for orders of 80F and up.

## Ferme Saint-Hubert
**8th arr.**
**21 rue Vignon**
**742.79.20**

Located within walking distance of the Madeleine, the shop has a country store ambience with its dark wood shelves, baskets, wicker trays, stoneware bowls and greenery. The charming atmosphere enhances the delicious dairy products marvelously selected by Henry Voy. Featured goods include triple-crème Saint-Hubert, aged Beaufort d'Alpage, farmers' Camemberts, curded white cheese, Auge Valley raw milk and raw butter. To your right as you enter the shop there is a small counter where you may order a cheese plate for 25F. For 35F you may have a hot crottin and a salad and a glass of wine.

## Genève
**16th arr.**
**Galerie Saint-Didier, rue des Belles-Feuilles**
**727.33.60**
**16th arr.**
**16 rue Dufresnoy**
**503.05.47**
**17th arr.**
**11 rue Lebon**
**574.23.45**
*Closed Mon. Open Sun. mornings at rue Dufresnoy and rue Lebon.*

The Genève family has been making and selling cheese since 1789. This excellent firm ages its remarkable Camemberts in its own cellars at the rue Torricelli and offers more than 200 varieties of cheese, including Saint-Cyr Délice, Fourme d'Ambert, farmers' Saint-Nectaire, Reblochon, Maroilles, goat cheese (some marinated in oil), Swiss cheeses and fresh Fontainebleau.

## Lillo
**16th arr.**
**35 rue des Belles-Feuilles**
**727.69.08**
*Closed Mon.*

This charming cheese shop is located within walking distance of the avenue Victor Hugo and features tasty Camemberts, Livarots, Coulommiers and farmer's Reblochons which M. Lillo ages in his own basement cellar. You'll also find goat cheese, farm eggs, white cheese, raw Normandy butter sold in bulk, as well as a superb Charentais butter creamed with the delicate scent of hazelnuts. To your left as you enter the shop you'll see an attractive department featuring cheese-stuffed crèpes, gougères, quiche with Gruyere, Parisian-style gnocchi, Roquefort feuilletés and vatrouchka.

## Maison du Fromage
**7th arr.**
**62 rue de Sèvres**
**734.33.45**

A purveyor to many leading Parisian restaurants such as l'Archestrate, M. Quatrehomme goes out of his way to select his farmers' Livarots, Camemberts, mountain Beauforts, goat cheese, Saint-Nectaire and Grand Bornand Reblochon, Salers Cantal, French and Swiss Vacherin and bulk butter. The Maison du Fromage also features frozen foods by Michel Guérard, as well as a few good wines.

# CHOCOLATES

## Christian Constant
**7th arr.**

Christian Constant imports his beans from Central America, and his chocolates consist of 80 percent ganache which is a blend of chocolate and fats combined

**26 rue du Bac**
**296.53.53**
*Open Sun.*

with fresh cream. He does not use any stabilizing agents, so his candies cannot be preserved for very long and their selection is somewhat limited. He also sells bulk chocolate.

## Dalloyau
**8th arr.**
**101 faubourg**
**Saint-Honoré**
**359.18.10**
*Open Sun.*
**15th arr.**
**69 rue de la**
**Convention**
**577.84.27**
*Closed Mon. Open Sun.*
**15th arr.**
**Centre Beaugrenelle**
**575.59.62**

To our great delight, this confectioner prefers using butter instead of vegetable fats, top brand cordials to synthetic liquor, Italian almonds to those purchased in bulk from unknown origins, and cocoa from Venezuela and Guatemala. Consequently, Dalloyau's chocolates are among the best you'll find in Paris. A featured specialty is his mendiant, or beggar, made of dark chocolate with almonds, raisins, hazelnuts and topped with walnuts, at 180F a kilo.

## Debauve et Gallais
**7th arr.**
**30 rue des**
**Saint-Pères**
**548.54.67**
*Closed Mon. (Open Mon.*
*afternoons in Dec.).*

"Debauve and Gallais, Makers of Fine and Medicinal Chocolates": The inscription on the façade of this honorable firm dates back to 1818, when Sulpice Gallais, a pharmacist by trade, sought to heal people with "cough-relieving and pectoral chocolates, tonic chocolates, carminative chocolates [made with angelica] and analeptic chocolates with salep." Built by two famous architects, Percier and Fontaine, the shop has retained all its charm and has been classified as an historical landmark by the Beaux-Arts. Although the chocolates are no longer "medicinal," they are delicious. Featured are dark chocolates stuffed with pralines, almonds and hazelnuts at 146F per kilo; and, a house specialty, bittersweet dark chocolate crunches at 65F per kilo. Other goods available are praline feuilletés, delicious soft caramels and cream-filled candies.

## Fouquet
**8th arr.**
**22 rue Francois-ler**
**723.30.36**
**9th arr.**
**36 rue Lafitte**
**770.85.00**

This lovely shop sells little round raspberry candies, black currant candies shaped like pillows, violet-flavored candies shaped like violets, and coffee drops shaped like large coffee beans. All are displayed in glass containers and considered by connoisseurs to be the best in the world. Other Fouquet specialties include boxed caramels and walnuts covered with burnt sugar; classic candied fruit or fruit à la Russe rolled in frosted icing, at 200F per kilo; remarkable handmade chocolates, at 200F per kilo including the palets d'or, or bittersweet chocolate kisses; the irresistable old-fashioned caramels individually wrapped in white paper, at 200F per kilo; pralines; Avola drops; flower shaped sugar candy; and much more. All these expensive little candies are made the old-fashioned way on the premises at the rue Lafitte location.

## Godiva
**1st arr.**
**237 rue Saint-Honoré**
**296.30.82**

The famous Belgian chocolates, some of which are made by hand for 170F per kilo. Other locations.

## Hédiard
**8th arr.**
**21 place de la**
**Madeleine**
**266.44.36**

Hédiard has a new chocolate department in addition to the renowned fruit jellies that come in eighteen varieties and sell for 60F per kilo. Other items include frosted candied fruit, and caramel fudge with or without hazelnuts.

## Lenôtre
**16th arr.**
**44 rue d'Auteuil**
**254.52.52**
*Open Sun.*
**16th arr.**
**49-51 ave. Victor-Hugo**
**501.71.71**
*Closed Mon. Open Sun. mornings.*
**17th arr.**
**121 ave. de Wagram**
**924.70.30**
*Closed Mon. Open Sun. mornings.*

The secret of Gaston Lenôtre's superb chocolate is to be found in his ingredients, his marvelous recipes and his workmanship. Whether bitter or sweet, his 30-plus varieties of chocolate, which sell for 190F on up per kilo, are among the best you can find in Paris. The tastefully designed boxes always indicate how long the chocolates can be stored. Other delights include truffles, carmels, all sorts of candies and marrons glacés, or candied chestnuts. Lenôtre's top of-the-line items are his cordial-filled chocolates, at 230F.

## La Maison du Chocolat
**8th arr.**
**225 faubourg**
**Saint-Honoré**
**227.39.44**
*Closed Mon.*

In 1977, Robert Lynxe opened his shop in what was formerly a neighborhood wine cellar. He transformed it into an ultramodern, beautifully decorated "laboratory." Formerly employed at the Marquise de Presle, which at that time was a famous tea room known to have the best chocolate cake in Paris, and later a partner of Gaston Lenôtre, Robert Lynxe is now on his own and offers delicious and expensive chocolate cakes, available with or without truffle mousse filling.

## Tanrade
**9th arr.**
**18 rue Vignon**
**742.26.99**
*Closed Mon.*

From November through February, in their Montrouge workshop, the Tanrades confect what are considered to be the best marrons glacés, or candied chestnuts, in the world. Other delicacies include chocolates, jellied fruit and fifty varieties of candy, including delicious honey drops.

# FOIE GRAS

## Battendier

**1st arr.**
**8 rue Coquillière**
**236.95.50**
*Closed Mon.*
**12th arr.**
**Printemps-Nation,**
**25 cours**
**de Vincennes**
**371.12.41**

Battendier offers an excellent fresh Colmar foie gras, prepared in the Alsatian style, kneaded and shaped like a loaf of bread coated with lard.

## Coesnon

**6th arr.**
**30 rue Dauphine**
**326.56.39**
*Closed Mon.*

All year long, M. Coesnon prepares a splendid goose and duck foie gras. He will also advise you and give you recipes for preparing the raw goose or duck livers he buys in the south of France and sells whole or in escalopes.

## Fauchon

**8th arr.**
**26 place de la**
**Madeleine**
**742.60.11**
*Closed Mon.*

Year-round supplies of the most expensive, top-quality duck foie gras. Paradoxically, the goose foie gras is less expensive than the duck. Also featured is canned, partially cooked foie gras.

## Grand- Mère L'Oye

**9th arr.**
**57 rue de Dunkerque**
**281.33.55**
*Closed Mon.*

Grand-Mère l'Oye features an entire line of goose and duck foie gras which is sold raw, fresh, in terrine, au torchon, à l'ancienne, or in cans, all of which are among the best in Paris and certainly the least expensive, considering their quality. The owner M. Biancarelli also offers a few good wines, truffles, terrines, goose necks stuffed with foie gras, preserved gizzards, fresh or smoked magrets and smoked Norwegian salmon.

## Maxim's de Paris

**8th arr.**
**76 faubourg**
**Saint-Honoré**
**266.10.09**
*Closed Mon.*

Maxim's fresh goose foie gras is prepared by the restaurant and sold in very attractive jars at princely princes.

## Pétrossian

**7th arr.**
**18 blvd. de**
**Latour-Maubourg**
**551.59.73**
*Closed Mon.*

Though especially known for its caviar, Pétrossian also makes and sells its own brand of excellent foie gras made from goose and duck livers.

# GOURMET FOODS

## Comptoir Gourmand (Michel Guérard)

**8th arr.**
**32 place de la Madeleine**
**742.73.51**
*Closed Mon.*

The master of cuisine minceur, has set up shop right between Fauchon and Hédiard on what has become the sacred block of gastronomy. Although Guérard's shop isn't as vast as Fauchon's, nor as polished as Hédiard's, it is very attractive, well lit and well laid out. In short, it is as appealing to the aesthete as to the gourmand. In the shop's limited space you'll find products selected by the master including vintage wine, coffees, teas, jams, honey, spices, truffles, foie gras, gherkins, fruits in vinegar or brandy, and many other specialties. Two of the Comptoir's main attractions are variety and large quantities of take-out food such as zephyr of sole with vegetable purée, asparagus quenelles with crayfish cream, charlotte of lamb, and duck with five herbs. Desserts include almond charlotte with vigneronne pears, chocolate-mint cake and much more. In the preserves department, you'll find stuffed cabbage cake, preserved guinea fowl with wild thyme, cassoulet with three preserves, duck thighs with mandarins, and a selection of frozen foods.

## Paul Corcellet

**2nd arr.**
**46 rue des Petits-Champs**
**296.51.82**
*Closed Mon.*

Ecologists may rejoice that Corcellet's white hunter, who used to comb the Congo in search of pythons, elephant trunks, hippopotamus backs and other exotic delicacies, died recently. Nevertheless, Paul Corcellet, who delights in experimenting with new products, still fills his store with a multitude of marvelous foods. Condiments continue to be his forte and include fruit-based vinegars such as cherry, black currant, raspberry and strawberry; sauces made with vegetables and mangoes; chutneys and mustards, including varieties like Provençale, green pepper, mint, horseradish, tzigane and anise étoilé. Other products include unique brands of Jamaican rum, a delicious passionfruit punch, a small Bordeaux sold under his name, bitter chocolate and mocha-flavored wafers, pure Arabian coffee beans and 60 varieties of jam.

## Faguais

**8th arr.**
**30 rue de La Trémoille**
**720.80.91**

This lovely old shop is well known for its delightful aroma, its affable staff and prodigious line of fine products. Coffee beans are roasted on the premises and the jams and fruit stews—which are made of peaches, raspberries, apricots, peeled plums and other fruits—are all prepared in huge vats in the store's basement kitchen. Other fine products include excellent preserves like whole foie gras au naturel, tripous, duck pâté and confits, all of which are made exclusively for Faguais in Saint-Céré. There are also top-quality oils, twenty varieties of honey, cookies and handmade confections; plus a wide selection of Fortnum and Mason products such as teas, biscuits, piccalilli, chutneys and pickled fruits and vegetables, all of which make Faguais one of the best stores of its kind in Paris.

## Fauchon
**8th arr.**
**26 place de la**
**Madeleine**
**742.60.11**
*Closed Mon.*

A visit to Fauchon is like going to the theater. The sets—the window displays—are extraordinary gardens of fruit and vegetables and old master tableaux of victuals, all of which have been assembled under the instructions of a decorator-chef. The spectacle features 20,000 production numbers, as they say in the trade, including Cambodian green pepper, viande des Grisons, African mangoes, American clam chowder, Mexican chili con carne, English confection, Swiss violet-flavored cachou, Javanese tea, Argentine biscuits, Belgian cinnamon shortbread, Korean ginseng, Indian incense, hundreds of spices and condiments including Singalese curry, nigella, myrtle, artemisia, lemon marinades, and shrimp rougail.

## Fouquet
**8th arr.**
**22 rue Francois-ler**
**723.30.36**
**9th arr.**
**36 rue Lafitte**
**770.85.00**

Among the sweet temptations of this great confectionery (established in 1842), there are delicious Tricastin olive oil and excellent vinegars such as Ile de France, Les Collines, Aux Trois Pèbres and others made from cider, Champagne and sherry, all of which are prepared by Mme Fouquet herself in her 15th arrondissement laboratory. Although she will not disclose her recipes, she suggests how they should be used in salads, mayonnaise and marinades. Other fine products include mustards, all sorts of teas, exquisite pickled fruits and vegetables, and jams. All Fouquet products are very well displayed in jars and glass containers with dark, chocolate-colored lids. The sales ladies are exemplary, the prices exorbitant.

## Hédiard
**1st arr.**
**Forum des Halles,**
**1st floor level**
**297.48.04**
**6th arr.**
**126 rue du Bac**
**544.01.98**
**8th arr.**
**106 blvd. de**
**Courcelles**
**763.32.14**
**8th arr.**
**21 place de la**
**Madeleine**
**266.44.36**
**15th arr.**
**Centre Beaugrenelle,**
**16 rue Linois**
**575.57.50**
**16th arr.**
**70 ave. Paul-Doumer**
**504.51.92**
*Closed Mon. at rue du Bac, blvd.*
*de Courcelles and place de la*
*Madeleine. Closed Mon. mornings*
*at Forum.*

Since 1854, Hédiard has been supplying food to the most delicate palates in Paris. You needn't look elsewhere for three daily meals fit to satisfy the Sun King. For starters, you may choose from over 80 varieties of tea, or one of the house-roasted coffees. You may complete your breakfast with cherry juice nectar, special breakfast jam with only 35 percent sugar content and, to make up for lost calories, almond paste marzipan. For lunch, you may select a Royal Hédiard cassoulet, or a pot-au-feu stuffed cabbage, or a blanquette of veal; or if you prefer, Hédiard offers 30 frozen foods, from sautéed cockerel à la vigneronne to scallops à la Dieppoise. You may wish to enhance their flavor with Hédiard's 88 varieties of spices. At dinnertime, you may ask Hédiard to deliver to your home a duck terrine or a chicken with lemon from Delaveyne of Bougival, whose catering shop is right next door to Hédiard's at the place de la Madeleine. Their prices may be steep, but they're worth the extravagance. Just don't send us the bill.

## Maison de la Truffe

**8th arr.**
**19 place de la Madeleine**
**265.53.22**
*Open daily until 8:00 P.M.*

From November through March, the Maison de la Truffe features the best truffles in Paris. Owner Guy Monier, who took over the operation in 1979, has retained his melodious Tricastin accent and does all he can to keep the prices of truffles down. His other products are also superb, particularly the Périgord goose foie gras, Landes duck foie gras, premium quality charcuteries and the exotic fruit baskets. He also carries excellent Danish smoked salmon and a fine selection of canned goods, such as his own rabbit with aspic or Roger Vergé's artichokes à la Barigoule. The shop has a fabulous wine cellar in which you'll find exceptional wines and liqueurs.

## Maxim's de Paris

**8th arr.**
**76 faubourg Saint-Honoré**
**266.10.09**

Maxim's de Paris, Pierre Cardin's gourmet food department, is located in what was formerly the Charpentier Art Gallery. No wonder the featured products such as mustards, sardines, sherry vinegar and jams sell at nearly the same prices as paintings! Nevertheless, the Norwegian salmon is superb, the Russian caviar delicately fragrant, the duck foie gras excellent and sold in pretty little Maxim containers, the exotic fruits unparalleled, the bitter mocha wafers delicious, and the 1900's decor so sophisticated that you'll have little trouble understanding the products' exorbitant prices.

## Petrossian

**7th arr.**
**18 blvd. de Latour-Maubourg**
**551.59.73**
*Closed Mon.*

Its old green façade, as well as the brilliant disorder that reigns inside the shop, gives Petrossian an Old Russia atmosphere. For over fifty years this Armenian store has been providing Parisians with excellent Russian caviars such as beluga, oscietra and sevruga, which Christian Petrossian selects himself in Astrakhan on the Caspian Sea. Other Petrossian products include Norwegian smoked salmon, which is sold 24 hours after it has been smoked according to a secret process, and is the best salmon you'll ever find in Paris; goose and duck foie gras, in terrine or in loaves, prepared in the Périgord and sold under the Petrossian label; Georgian black tea; excellent jams, particularly the bil-berry; fruit compotes; tianouchki caramels; unique preserves and an excellent selection of wines and brandies, particularly the tinted vodka aged in pear-wood barrels. Petrossian's sales attendants will do their best to assist you with your shopping. At Christmas, you'll easily recognize the store by the long line of people waiting to get in.

# HONEY

## La Maison du Miel

**9th arr.**
**24 rue Vignon**

La Maison du Miel features over 30 varieties of honey, among which you will find French honey from the plains and mountains, such as the precious Vosges. The pine honey was highly recommended for bronchial problems

**742.26.70**

at the start of the century. Imported varieties include Hungarian acacia, Spanish and Mexican orange, and New Zealand and Canadian clover honey. You may sample before making a final purchase.

# ICE CREAM

## Berthillon
**4th arr.**
**31 rue Saint-Louis-en-l'Ile**
**354.31.61**
*Closed Mon., Tues., school holidays, except Christmas. Open Sun.*

The little bistro Hôtel de Bourgogne where, fifteen to sixteen years ago, habitués of l'Ile Saint-Louis came to buy ice cream and sherbets, is now overrun with ice cream addicts from all over Paris. Despite his enormous success, nothing stops M. Berthillon from pursuing his innovative genius in creating new flavors. He has 30, among them: pineapple, cocoa, lichee, candied chestnut which is available from November until Easter, tea, honey, cherry, wild strawberry in season, plum and Armagnac, crunchy pear liquor, strawberry crunch, calvados crunch, kirsch crunch and more. Ice cream is sold by the cone or in containers and may be eaten on the spot (in the afternoon).

## Christian Constant
**7th arr.**
**26 rue du Bac**
**296.53.53**
*Open Sun.*

Christian Constant's ice cream has no coloring or stabilizing agents, only sugar, fresh egg yolks, fresh cream, vanilla, coffee and cocoa, all of which are of premium quality. The fruit pulp used in his sherbets gives them a strong yet delicate taste and includes such flavors as black currant, blueberry, peach, melon, mandarine, lime, pink lemon, Corinthian raisin, kiwi and papaya. His new flavors include honey and pine kernel sherbet; cinnamon-nut, bitter chocolate, and whiskey-raisin ice cream. Other remarkable frozen desserts include a Baccarat biscuit, a combination of strawberry and vanilla sherbets and kirsch-flavored candied cherries, marrons glacé bombes, and black currant sherbet profiteroles.

## Dalloyau
**8th arr.**
**101 faubourg Saint-Honoré**
**359.18.10**
*Open Sun. (Closed Sun. afternoons and Mon. in July and August).*
**15th arr.**
**69 rue de la Convention**
**577.84.27**
*Closed Mon. Open Sun.*

The ice cream and sherbets of this estimable house are remarkable in variety, freshness and presentation. Marvelous frozen desserts include the Roussillon, which is a blend of biscuits, peach sherbet and Cointreau, and is available April through September; the Pont-Aven, a blend of biscuits, pistachio parfait and apricot-raspberry sherbet; and the Sully, a praline, meringue and cognac-raisin parfait. Trompe-l'oeil ice cream decorations may be ordered for a minimum of eight to ten people twenty-four hours in advance, and include frozen fruit dishes, cornucopias, asparagus bunches made of vanilla and pistachio ice cream with English cream, and frosted pineapple served on an éclair.

### Lenôtre
**16th arr.**
**44 rue d'Auteuil**
**524.52.52**
*Open Sun.*

Lenôtre features top quality ice cream and sherbets at 50-58F per liter. Highlights include chestnut-pear sherbet at 58F, Bayadère (a combination of strawberry, pistachio, apricot and cherry extract) at 136F a liter, and Délice, which is a combination of praline ice cream, coffee parfait and coffee beans.

### La Tropicale
**4th arr.**
**4 rue Jean-du-Bellay**
**329.82.79**
**6th arr.**
**128 rue du Cherche-Midi**
**220.79.54**
**13th arr.**
**10 place Pinel**
**583.56.13**
**13th arr.**
**180 blvd. Vincent-Auriol**
**331.42.27**

With La Tropicale's increasing number of Parisian outlets, it is difficult to keep track of each shop's business hours. We therefore recommend you phone them in advance, especially since certain ice creams and sherbets are available only at certain times of the year. Amid the wide range of flavors, sold at reasonable prices, you'll find innumerable specialty ice crams such as date-nut, honey-pine nut, chocolate-mint and banana-sesame; and 17 exotically flavored sherbets low in sugar content and very tasty, such as mango, passionfruit, coconut, guava and ivory nut. There are 20 varieties of classically flavored sherbets such as black currant, mandarin, nectarine, melon, blueberry, damson plum, pear, apricot and blackberry. Eggs based ice creams include coffee, prunes with Armagnac, and candied orange rind.

# FRESH PASTA

### La Maison des Pâtes Fraiches
**9th arr.**
**47 rue Rochechouart**
**526.76.09**
*Closed Mon. mornings.*

The owner of this store, which is housed in a onetime stationary shop, is delighted to assist you in selecting her delicious cannelloni, ravioli, tortellini and other spinach-based pastas.

### Les Milles Pâtes
**4th arr.**
**3 rue du Pont-Louis-Philippe**
**277.99.02**
*Closed Mon. Open Sun.*

Formerly a butcher shop, Les Milles Pâtes is now a delicatessen featuring Paul Corcellet mustards and vinegars; a fine selection of Legrand wines; and Italian, Spanish and French olive oils. Featured pastas include fresh egg-based tagliatelle, fettuccine, spaghetti, green spinach pasta, ravioli (with ricotta, pumpkin, spinach or meat), lasagna and cannelloni. Other goods include Rouergue charcuterie and Parma and San Daniele hams.

### La Table d'Italie
**6th arr.**
**69 rue de Seine**
**354.34.69**
*Closed Mon.*

The ravioli, lasagna, cannelloni and white or green macaroni are all made on the premises and sold fresh with exquisite seasoned sauces.

# PASTRIES

## Brocco
3rd arr.
180 rue du Temple
272.19.81
*Open Sun.*

With its immaculate façade, its vast marble interior, high ceiling and charming little tea room, this is certainly one of Paris's most beautiful pastry shops, offerings include Swiss brioches with almond cream and rum-drenched raisins, templiers (chocolate mousse), mylords (biscuits, meringue and chocolate), framboisines (cookies stuffed with raspberry mousse). There are also rich ice creams such as Créoles chocolate, Vivianes (mocha), and Valencias (Grand-Marnier).

## Christian Constant
7th arr.
26 rue du Bac
296.53.53
*Open Sun.*

Christian Constant is a maker of ice cream, chocolates and confections, catered and tea foods. He is also one of the best pastry chefs in Paris. Nothing is more delicious than his strawberry, kiwi and lemon tartes; his Brésiliens, coffee mousse; or his kalinkas with white cheese and raspberries, (not always available); and his unique freshly made petits fours. His Macao, with bitter chocolate and hazelnuts, and Pont Royal, with biscuits and hazelnut cream, however, have slightly too much alcohol.

## Dalloyau
8th arr.
101 faubourg
Saint-Honoré
359.18.10
*Open Sun. (Closed Sun.*
*afternoons and Mon. during July*
*and August.).*

A large, established house known for the quantity, diversity and high standards of its products. They include ice creams and sherbets, precooked dishes, chocolates, desserts, petits fours and cakes such as opéras, mogadors (a combination of chocolate mousse, raspberry extracts and cookies) cardinals with black currants, and the delicious little arlettes. Other locations.

## Aux Délices
17th arr.
39 ave. de Villiers
763.71.36
*Closed Mon., Tues. Open Sun.*

Aux Délices's large and modern façade conceals the shop's interior old-fashioned decor of dark wood panelling and dessert tables laden with petits fours and confection. The owner, Mme Prié, offers traditional pastries such as marjolaines, noyers, malgaches, succès, polkas, puits d'amour, macaroons—and almond petits fours which may not be as light as we would like them to be but are still a very good value.

## Fauchon
8th arr.
26 place de la
Madeleine
742.60.11

Fauchon features excellent pastries that rank right behind Lenôtre's and Constant's. They include puff pastry fruit tartes, macaroons, mango biscuits, opéras, meringue, chocolate mouse and much more.

## Lenôtre

**16th arr.**
**44 rue d'Auteuil**
**524.52.52**
*Open Sun.*
**16th arr.**
**49-51 ave.**
**Victor-Hugo**
**501.71.71**
**10th arr.**
**121 ave. de Wagram**
**924.70.30**
*Closed Mon. Open Sun. mornings.*

Gaston Lenôtre's versatility tends to make us forget that he is first and foremost a pastry chef. His petits fours, macaroons, shortbread, apple strudel, millefeuilles and tartlets are perfectly exquisite. The same applies to his light and ingenious desserts such as opéras with almonds, coffee mousse and truffles, casinos (rolled biscuits with raspberries and bavaroise with kirsch), pear charlottes, and—his latest invention—passionfruit miroirs.

## Malitourne

**16th arr.**
**30 rue de Chaillot**
**720.52.26**
*Closed Mon. Open Sun. mornings.*

Malitourne, who was once employed by Roger Vergé at the Moulin de Mougins, bakes some exquisite cakes, including Téméraire (made with macaroon cream and Cointreau), the Délice, tartes and fruit-based mousses. His catering department features various terrines and eel rillettes, and special dishes such as poularde with vegetables, civet of lobster and timbale of seafood.

## Millet

**7th arr.**
**103 rue**
**Saint-Dominique**
**551.49.80**
*Closed Mon. Open Sun. mornings.*

A brilliant pastry chef who teaches pastry-making in Tokyo and in Osaka, Millet devotes himself to preparing ultra-light fruit-based confections such as his charlotte with raspberry purée and pears; apricot, peach and cherry mousses in summer; mandarin and apple mousses in winter; and chocolate-based desserts such as his Malgaches and Bûcherons. In all, he features 15 seasonal desserts.

## Le Moule à Gâteau

**5th arr.**
**111 rue Mouffetard**
**331.80.47**
**17th arr.**
**10 rue Poncelet**
**763.06.49**
**18th arr.**
**53 rue des Abbesses**
**264.24.00**
*Closed Mon. Open Sun. mornings.*

This remarkable, five-year-old company sells oven-fresh pastries made from family-style recipes that seem absolutely perfect. Featured items include Linz shortbread (hazelnut pastry and raspberry marmalade), chocolate mamitas, puff pastry pavés, and plum popovers. Slightly more sophisticated are the chocolate charlottes and the cassias which are biscuits with blackcurrant mousse. Everything sold here is simple, delicious, relatively inexpensive and smells of fresh cream and butter. Le Moule à Gâteau also sells good homemade ice cream and sherbets.

## Stohrer

**2nd arr.**
**51 rue Montorgueil**
**233.38.20**
*Open Sun.*

Established in 1730 by one of Louis XV's cooks, Stohrer was celebrated for its babas and savarins in Paudry's 1864 painting entitled Les Renommées. The shop's decor is exquisite and the dainties featured include apple and strawberry pies, noisettines (or hazelnut cake), chocolatines and puits d'amour, all of which smell and taste wonderful.

### Vaudron
17th arr.
4 rue de la Jonquière
627.96.97
*Open Sun.*

Vaudron is best known for its country-style cakes such as shortbread, apple turnovers, lemon tarte and berrichone toute, and for its sophisticated desserts such as Black Forest cake, Saint-Marc cake (caramel biscuits, chocolate mousse and Chantilly cream), truffons (coffee biscuits, mocha bavaroise and truffle) and many more. Other delights include brioches, macaroons and petits fours.

## SNAILS

### La Maison de l'Escargot
15th arr.
79 rue Fondary
575.31.09
*Closed Mon.*

With infinite care Georges Kossorotoff's ten employees scrape, gauge, wash and dry, one by one, more than ten tons of snails a year. This unique Parisian shop specializes in all kinds of escargots, notably the gris, which are shipped in from Dordogne and Haute-Provence and are well-known for their perfumed flavor, and the Bourgogne, which has taken up residence in Savoie ever since winegrowers started spraying the Côte-d'Or vineyards with copper sulphate. These delicious creatures are prepared according to a well-guarded, 75-year-old recipe and sell for 13.50F a dozen and up. You may also purchase them in boxes accompanied by a recipe booklet, both at the rue Fondary shop, and at Printemps-Nation. Or, you may order them by mail.

## WINES

### Jean-Baptiste Besse
5th arr.
48 rue de la Montagne-Sainte-Geneviève
325.35.80
*Closed Mon.*

At 78 years old, Jean-Baptiste Besse is considered one of the most knowledgeable wine dealers in Paris. Should you visit him in his shop on the steep Sainte-Geneviève hill, he will gladly share his passion and philosophy regarding wine. He may even show you his sixteenth-century cellar in which you will see a fabulous and disorderly collection of dusty bottles of the best Sauternes, 50-year-old vintage wines and nineteenth-century ports.

### La Cave de Georges Duboeuf
8th arr.
9 rue Marbeuf
720.71.23
*Closed Mon.*

Ever since Georges Duboeuf opened his wine cellar at the rue Marbeuf, Parisians have flocked there for his Beaujolais, which are among the best in the city. His passion for Beaujolais extends to excellent wines from other regions such as Métaireau Muscadet, Hugel and Trimbach Alsatian whites, and Burgundy wines with prestigious labels such as Vogüe Musigny et Bonnes-Mares, Ramonet Chassagne-Montrachet, Gouges Nuits-Saint-Georges and Delorme Rully. He is currently interested in expanding his selections of Bordeaux. Also featured are good everyday wines. Reasonable prices.

## La Cave d'Hédiard

**8th arr.**
**106 blvd.**
**de Courcelles**
**736.32.14**

Hédiard's exceptional cellar features more than 150,000 bottles, some of which come from the Saint-Émilion area where the company grows and bottles its own wine. Hédiard's customers come here to purchase the shop's great vintages from the best years, and three winemasters assist in selecting wines such as Latour, a choice of eleven vintage years; Haut-Brion, nine vintage years; and lesser known wines such as the marvelous white wine, Pavillon blanc de Margaux, or the extremely expensive Romanée-Conti 1961 at 2,640F a bottle. The foreign wines come from nine different countries. Other Paris locations.

## Edouard Charles

**6th arr.**
**38 rue de Vaugirard**
**354.00.85**
*Closed Mon.*

According to Edouard Charles, "A good Armagnac must be aged at least ten years. After twenty years, it can be considered mature; after thirty years, it becomes charming; and after forty years, very experienced. After that, like man, it often declines." Armagnac is Edouard Charles's passion, and for years now he has been combing the Gascogne countryside and visiting growers in search of the fine flower of them all, the Bas-Armagnac. His shop overlooks the gates to the Jardin du Luxembourg and contains a multitude of top quality brands selected from the Bas-Armagnac area, including 80 varieties from 1939 to 1979. Some of the labels are well known, like Laberdolive or Château de Castaudet, but there are also many unknown labels like Roger Lasseignou's Armagnacs which are ten years old and sealed with wax. Edouard Charles also features cognacs, a wide selection of wines in two superb basement cellars, and a few specialties from southwest France.

## Jean Danflou

**1st arr.**
**36 rue du**
**Mont-Thabor**
**261.51.09**

His small mezzanine shop is known all over the world, and countless celebrities have gotten drunk on his white alcohols such as the beautifully bottled Charles X eaux-de-vies produced under his direct supervision; the Grande Réserve aged kirsch which is 49 percent alcohol, and sells at 160F a bottle with an almost "intellectual" character; the extremely smooth framboisine, which is 48 percent alcohol; the exquisite Exceptionnel Armagnac; and the fabulous Grande Champagne Extra. Jean Danflou has a reception room in which you may sample at no cost his entire gamut of aged brandies whose superior quality justifies their high prices. Also featured are "house" Champagne, and a selection of Burgundies and Bordeaux.

## Lucien Legrand

**2nd arr.**
**1 rue de la Banque**
**260.07.12**
*Closed Mon.*

His waggish wit, kindliness and serenity make him one of Paris's most colorful characters. Nothing in his shop has changed since his parents acquired it in 1919. The jars of chewing gum are still in the same place, the window panes are still lined with copper, and the bottles are still stacked along the same shelves. Even the atmosphere of a time long past seems to be a fixture in this charming old shop. Legrand speaks lovingly of the wines, big and little, that he has bought on his travels. As he says to his customers, "Every wine merchant has his or her preference. I personally like wine that is cheerful, sensuous and not too serious." For these reasons, his cellars are stocked with the largest selection of inexpensive good wines in Paris such as those from the Gard, Tarn and Minervois, as well as a few bottles of Beaujolais. He also carries his own excellent Burgundy.

## L'Oenophile
**12th arr.**
**12 place de la Nation**
**307.98.93**
*Closed Mon. mornings. Open Sun. mornings.*

Over the last five years Michel Renaud has travelled all over France in search of good and great wines which he sells in his charming shop. For those with lots of money to spend, he offers many aged vintage wines from 1970, 1966 and 1961, and a few rare bottles like the Haut-Brion 1953. You'll also find a selection of the best Burgundies from the Côtes-de-Nuits and Côtes-de-Beaune, as well as excellent Cazaubon Armagnacs which are sold to top Parisian restaurants like l'Archestrate and Taillevent.

## Steven Spurrier (Caves de la Madeleine)
**8th arr.**
**25 rue Royale (Cité Berryer)**
**265.92.40**

"My mother," recalls Steven Spurrier, "used to be a food columnist for British newspapers. That's probably where I got my penchant for wine." It took only a few years for this impeccably dressed Englishman to build one of the best wine cellars in Paris. After acquiring his basic knowledge from a wine merchant with whom he worked in London, Steven Spurrier took off to visit vineyards all over France and Europe. This experience helped him hone a palate as sharp as a Sheffield knife and to assemble the extraordinary list of wines in this shop, which he opened in 1971. Nowhere else can so vast a selection be found: 154 "Château" Bordeaux, 138 Burgundy *Crus,* 33 varieties of top label Champagne and the most astonishing collection of Côtes-du-Rhône wines we know—including Côte-Rôtie 78 La Mouline de chez Guigal, Châteaux Rayas 77, and Lirac 78. These wines have a strong personality, characterized by authenticity and naturalness. Whenever someone blames Spurrier for not stocking old vintage wines, he quickly responds by saying that it is up to his clients to assume this patient task. Other featured wines include ten of the best California growths and a small selection of great Italian bottles.

## Au Verger de la Madeleine
**8th arr.**
**4 blvd. Malesherbes**
**265.51.99**

This tiny shop, filled from floor to ceiling with fruits, preserves and bottles, is only the tip of the iceberg. The rest, almost priceless, is in the maze of cellars below, accessible by wheezing elevator. Maurice and Jean-Pierre Legras own one of the best collections of wine in Paris, and it sparks the imagination to see such collectors' items as nineteenth-century Yquems, 1934 white Lafite and the Châteaux Bordeaux from 1970, 1961, 1955, 1949, 1945, 1929 and 1928—which makes Au Verger de la Madeleine a specialty shop for birthday bottles. You'll also find less expensive wines from all over France, including a few curiosities such as the Jasnières, a wine from the Sarthe, the Coulée-de-Serrant and the Château Grillet.

## Beer

### Gambrinus
**4th arr. 13-15 rue des Blancs-Manteaux**
**887.81.92**
*Open until 9:00 P.M. on Wed.*

This former hotelkeeper is so engrossed with beer that he features more than 400 brands from 34 countries in his store's three rooms. They include little-known English beers and ales in cans, such as Samuel Smith's, Worthington E, and Newcastle Brown, which is a favorite of coal miners; and the oldest beer in the world, a white Bavarian brewed at the ancient Weihenstephan Abbey. He also has Swiss beer in five-liter barrels with taps.

# Gifts

### Arcana
**3rd arr.**
**83 rue Vieille-du-Temple**
**278.19.22**

Wall lamps, hanging lamps, lamps in poured glass fringed with pearls, miniature paintings and chromos, inkstands, blotting pads, antique pens, old printing blocks and everything for those obsessed with order—like coffers and boxes for pills, cakes, nails and sewing utensils; and Pandora boxes made of sandalwood, ivory-inlaid wood or papier-mâché.

### Arcasa
**1st arr.**
**219 rue Saint-Honoré**
**260.46.60**

In his large store Patrick Dollfus offers a fine international selection of table gifts and other objects from around the world. In stock are dishware, glassware, place settings, candleholders, trays, smart kitchen utensils, as well as a lovely choice of lamps.

### Bag and Ber
**17th arr.**
**9 ave Niel**
**572.15.04**
*Closed Mon.*

This is a men's giftshop for games players (cards, electronic chess sets and billiards), smokers (pipes and cigar boxes), travelers (Halliburton suitcases, bags, thermoses), casanovas (shaving lotions, mustache combs and Creed perfumes), and pioneers (electronic pocket datebooks and wireless phones). Countless gadgets that make far more interesting gifts than the customary tie.

### Baguès
**16th arr.**
**57 ave. Raymond-Poincaré**
**704.51.00**

After having specialized in artfully made lighting fixtures for over a hundred years, Baguès opened a beautiful shop in 1970 that fits right into this lovely district. The shop's four floors display and sell lamps, furniture, tableware and decorative objects. The wife-to-be will find everything with which to establish her bridal registers by simply walking through the store or by consulting the voluminous catalogue.

## Au Bain Marie
2nd arr.
2 rue du Mail
260.94.55

Aude Clément has an unparalleled knack for finding in basements, attics and flea markets all sorts of domestic objects that were near and dear to our parents and grandparents. Her shelves are lined with artifacts from the 1920s and 1930s as well as some from the turn of the century, such as caviar bowls and knives, lamb chop sleeves, marrow or sauce spoons, menu stands, traveling kits and plate heaters, and also gorgeous restaurant furnishings purchased at hotel and ocean liner auctions (featuring lovely silverware from the *Normandie*). Also featured are individually sold earthenware plates and antique glasses, chromos, engravings and gourmet cookbooks. Nothing here is commonplace or inexpensive.

## Beauté Divine
6th arr.
40 rue Saint-Sulpice
326.25.31
*Closed Mon.*

Here you'll find a most enticing collection of bathroom accessories from the 1930s. Far from being a flea market, Régine de Robien's boutique offers only unflawed or reconditioned objects in a stylish decor.

## Boîtes à Musique
1st arr.
9 rue de Beaujolais
296.55.13

Located in the Palais Royal mall, this little shop specializes in the marvels of mechanized music and offers a large selection of music boxes as simple as painted wooden boxes (60F), and as complex as player pianos and machines equipped with big rollers containing a continuous flow of melodies (up to 8,400F). Also featured are chirping birds, animated scenes under glass domes, and music box stands.

## Boutique Danoise
8th arr.
42 ave. de Friedland
227.02.92

Beautifully displayed classic and contemporary objects, all steeply priced. The store features Scandinavian glassware and white or blue porcelain. Everything is immediately available except the prestigious polychromatic and gold dinner set made by Royal Manufacture of Copenhagen which takes up to four years for delivery. There are also table and kitchen accessories, lazy susans made from natural or inlaid wood, sumptuous rolling tea carts in teak or Brazilian rosewood. Don't miss the beautifully decorated tables at Christmas time.

## La Boutique du Sommeil

1st arr.
Forum des Halles,
2nd floor
297.57.82
16th arr.
24 ave
Pierre-ler-de-Serbie
720.57.36

At the Pierre-ler-de-Serbie location, you'll find just about everything to meet your bedtime needs: Satin, cotton or raw silk sheets, soft-hued lamps; velvety feather beds and cushions; breakfast tables and trays; as well as bedside electric coffee pots; thermoses; and alarm clocks. Next door at No. 26, Sommeilla Annex (tel. 720.52.02) offers nightgowns and 1930s, Hollywood-style pajamas, giant T-shirts, bed socks and nightcaps for sensitive sleepers, and classic English pajamas for classical people.

## Chacun Pour Toi
7th arr.
58 rue de Bourgogne
551.38.48

This shop offers, in a wide price range, individualized gifts for birthdays, anniversaries or weekend hosts, such as engraved glass knife holders, cigarette cases, leather guest registers, playing cards, cushions, plates and embroidered tablecloths.

## La Chaise Longue
6th arr.
8 rue Princesse
329.62.39

This vast and adorable shop offers unusual fantasy objects, such as a huge family toothbrush holder shaped like a toothbrush or soap holders shaped like deck chairs. Though the items aren't really useful, they're whimsical enough. Good low prices.

## Christofle
2nd arr.
31 blvd. des Italiens
265.62.43
6th arr.
93 rue de Seine
325.70.73

This hundred-year-old firm now has, among others, a new shop at the rue de Seine. Your grandmother used to purchase her dinnerware there, and your children will too, once they grow up a little and take their place in the "real world." You'll find in this honorable shop nearly all the ornaments of the typically "good" home, from dinnerware to rosewood cigar humidors.

## Culinarion
6th arr.
99 rue de Rennes
548.94.76
*Closed Mon. mornings.*
9th arr.
9 rue des Mathurins
742.10.38
*Closed Mon.*

In these attractive shops you'll find an impressive amount of well-displayed kitchen utensils that are useful, practical and even pretty. These functional items are often of old-fashioned design and include galvanized or nickel-plated copperware, enameled wrought-iron or steel, stainless steel, wood, white porcelain, stoneware, jugs, and cutlery.

## Dîners en Ville
7th arr.
27 rue de Varenne
222.78.33
*Closed Mon. morning.*

This shop specializes in old-fashioned tableware such as place settings, tea and dessert sets from between 1880 and 1930, as well as glasses, carafes, whiskey flasks and stoneware plates. All these objects are displayed according to function—such as asparagus servers and accessories, egg cups and warmers or tea sets. You'll find in the cool and beautiful vaulted basement a good selection of dishware and contemporary gifts, which, of course, are all related to the table.

## Diptyque
5th arr.
34 blvd.
Saint-Germain
326.45.27
*Closed Mon.*

For the last twenty years this lovely boutique has successfully managed to ignore fads and trends. It offers hundreds of ideas for inexpensive, enticing gifts selected by the owner who gets his wares from England as well as from his native Ireland. High quality crafts include handwoven wool Welsh bedspreads, scented art nouveau lingerie cases and shoebags, Irish wicker, top-name English perfumes (Floris, Mary Chess, Penhaligon's and

391

Trumper), as well as perfume sold under the Diptyque label (eaux de toilette, soaps, potpourris, candles, pomanders and the well-known bath salts). Affable sales staff and charming gift wrap in brightly colored tissue paper.

## Eléphantine

**16th arr.**
**140 ave. Victor-Hugo**
**553.74.40**
*Closed Mon.*

Eléphantine offers Italian terra-cotta in all shapes and sizes, such as huge earthenware garden jugs and flowerpot saucers (glazed on the inside for added water resistance), lamp stands, columns and busts of Roman emperors. Other Italian-made gifts include vases and ceramics, all of which are as dazzlingly white as your favorite yacht.

## La Gadgetière

**1st arr.**
**Forum des Halles,**
**2nd floor**
**297.57.94**
**16th arr.**
**1 rue George-Bizet**
**720.52.20**

Marianne Frey's shop was the first in Paris to feature useless, zany, luxurious—if not downright opulent—gifts. Amazingly enough, these funny-looking objects are in constant demand. They include cigarette cases with automatic switches that open them at pre-set times, smoke-swallowing ashtrays, a "diet conscience" for your refrigerator that preaches to you in English each time you open the refrigerator door, and thousands of other useful and/or cute objects—like the miniature oil well for those who have everything.

## Hermès

**8th arr.**
**24 faubourg**
**Saint-Honoré**
**265.21.60**

World-renowned Hermès is for serious giving. It's justifiably famous for fancy leather goods like the pocket-sized date books, suitcases, gloves and handbags. Everything here is made to last a lifetime. The shop features those famous silk handkerchiefs at 390F (a highlight of the 1950s, they were loosely tied around the straps of handbags), ties, sportswear (this year's collection is larger than ever), furs, jewelry, watches, perfume and countless other objects including magnifying glasses, paper knives, ashtrays of leather or silver-plate. Gifts vary greatly in price, and some are exorbitant. Affable sales staff. Allow one day for beautifully wrapped deliveries.

## David Hicks

**6th arr.**
**12 rue de Tournon**
**326.00.67**

If you're not careful, this famous English designer's shop will delightfully empty your pockets. The simple yet gorgeous items, which in fact are no more expensive here than elsewhere, are shown to their greatest advantage when purchased in groups of at least two or three. The shop features lots of lamps made from ceramic or turned wood, clever American earthenware shaped like fruit or vegetables, pretty octagonal-shaped stoneware plates made in Portugal from a David Hicks design, wool and cashmere plaids in all colors of the rainbow, ceramic or wood ostrich eggs, flowerpot saucers, wicker and flashlights.

## Jansen
**8th arr.**
**9 rue Royale**
**266.51.52**

You'll find gifts on the ground floor. Upstairs is reserved for general decorating items such as furniture, rugs, lighting fixtures made by Jansen and sold at very high prices; as well as wedding register goods like dishware, glassware and silverware. The vast ground floor offers countless superbly displayed curios and practical and/or decorative items. There are antiques (Napoleon III or nineteenth-century English) and antique reproductions, and their prices vary greatly. They include engravings, pyramids, paper knives, boxes, candleholders, objects made from turned wood and silver-plated curios. All in perfect taste.

## Kitchen Bazaar
**15th arr.**
**11 ave. du Maine**
**222.91.17**
*Closed Mon. morning.*

Here you will find countless splendidly presented objects that are both useful and appealing, at prices ranging from 2.50F to 3,500F. They range from innumerable small kitchen utensils to appliances that do everything, as well as multishaped cake molds; pressure cookers; lazy susans for butter, jams and spices; a rolling cart made of (natural or dyed) ash with a folding leaf so you may seat two; hot pads, high-tech metallic shelves; and towels in vibrant colors (Indian pink, bright blue, violet). Also a good selection of cookbooks.

## Maison de Pain d'Epices
**9th arr.**
**35 passage Jouffroy**
**770.51.12**
*Closed Mon. morning.*

This is an outlet for the charming old-fashioned toy shop next door, featuring both antique (glasses, plates, cups, frames, chromos) and recently made objects. Owner Françoise Blindermann specializes in antique painted sheetmetal, publicity posters, decorative cookie boxes and antique wrapping; as well as flour, coffee and cocoa containers and amazing mustard jars, some of which have been reproduced and are sold here and in other stores. You'll also find attractive sweet-stuffs such as jams; aged aperitifs like cherry brandy, marquis (an orange or nut-flavored cordial) or Villeneuve strawberry brandy; as well as all kinds of cake decorations (Happy Birthdays, bathers, brides and grooms) made from sugar or almond paste.

## Maxim's de Paris
**8th arr.**
**76 faubourg Saint-Honoré**
**266.10.09**

This extraordinary store is as mystifying to the Japanese tourist as it is to the blasé Parisian. Just what is sold behind the wax figures in the shop's window display that suggest the grand ways of Chez Maxim's? Chocolates? Caviar? Exotic fruit? Jams? Ashtrays? Bathrobes? The answer is yes!—all of the above, as well as delicious preserves, foie gras, superfine olive oils, household linens, pots and pans, and dishware, all bearing Maxim's emblem and distributed by Pierre Cardin. In effect, this is a showroom for merchants eager to sell products under Maxim's license. It shouldn't stop you, however, from entering the shop. The 1900s setting is marvelous; the sales staff is courteous; and the sardines exorbitantly expensive and—noblesse oblige—the best in the world.

## Must de Cartier

1st arr.
**7 and 23 place Vendôme**
261.55.55
*Closed Mon. morning.*

Everything sold here is a "must"—a Cartier Must. For instance, the famous 1929 triple ring made from gray, yellow and pink gold; or the equally famous Santos watches with flexible and riveted metallic watchbands; all sorts of lighters (1930s design, in enamel or silver-plated); small clocks (Tank, Santos); pens, luggage (cabin kits, "diplomatic" attaché cases); evening bags, wallets and coin purses—all of which are sold at the place Vendôme location as well as in the two Cartier shops (avenue Montaigne, faubourg Saint-Honoré) and in other Cartier-licensed stores.

## Porcelaine

7th arr.
**22 rue de Verneuil**
260.94.36
*Closed Mon. morning.*

You'll find solid Pillivuyt porcelain dishware at affordable prices (approximately 60F) in this charming, attractive shop. The 1930s designs are a bit too busy for everyday use, but they are quite whimsical and perfect for gala dinners. The decorative glassware is charming; the solid bronze candalabra and place settings are far less interesting.

## La Table d'Eugénie

4th arr.
**27 rue du Petit-Musc**
278.19.61
*Closed Mon.*

There's a nice low-priced bistro on the ground floor of a small eighteenth-century hotel which is linked to the shop by a vaulted basement designed to hold receptions and/or exhibits. The shop carries tastefully chosen, ingenious and original objects intended mostly for kitchen or dining room usage: dishware, silverware, numerous place settings, saucepans, double boilers and other stove top equipment. J.J. Daubin, the owner and former Comédie Française actor, offers a discount for theater and movie people.

## Francoise Thibault

6th arr.
**1 rue Jacob**
633.90.67
6th arr.
**1 and 2 rue Bourbon-le-Château**
326.40.23
*Closed Mon.*

This pretty bazaar offers more or less useful and amusing small and large "nothings." For instance, you can recreate Noah's ark with egg-laying puppet-hens, cat cushions, owl paperweights, ceramic doves and painted cork bird decoys. The shop also features lamps, mirrors, enameled boxes and music boxes. At the rue Bourbon shop there's also an attractive choice of painted furniture. Charming sales staff.

## H. G. Thomas

5th arr.
**36 blvd. Saint-Germain**
633.57.50
*Closed Mon.*

H. G. Thomas features hair clippers and silver toothpicks for the ostentatious, digital sphygmomanometers for the anxiety-ridden, jumpropes for bodybuilders, umbrellas designed for lovers, puzzles for the mathematically minded, and boomerangs for the suicidal. There are also kites for people who dream of faraway places, and traveling bags to get them there, well-displayed, affordably priced assortment of men's gifts.

## Valentino Piu

8th arr.

Here you will find Italian-made gifts that are joyful, subtle, superfluous, useful, simple or ostentatious. Since they are one of a kind, they're all the more irresistible. Two new colors (a beautiful Sierra earth-tone and a

**17 to 19 ave.
Montaigne
723.64.17**

bright blue trimmed with gold) have been added to the usual three colors of the Italian flag this year. You'll find them on the round or octagonal ceramic plates displayed on tables alongside glasses decorated with filaments or beads. There are also assorted placemats and tablecloths, candleholders, ashtrays, lamps, as well as ceramic flowerpot holders, heart-shaped boxes, West Indian artifacts and pin trays. Other articles include a few lovely pieces of rattan furniture (king size armchairs, couches, flower stands), household linens and superb printed cotton fabrics with flowered or geometric patterns sold by the meter. Perfectly charming sales staff.

## *Via Domani*
**18th arr.
79 rue Lepic
258.52.09**
*Closed Sat.*

Although the avenue d'Italie is in the 13th arrondissement and the boulevard des Italians is in the 9th, Italian shopkeepers seem to have a particular fondness for the Butte Montmartre and for the shadow cast by the snails of the Moulin de la Galette. Via Domani (situated in Da Graziano restaurant's former location) is a faintly new shop along the steep slopes of the rue Lepic that has been superbly and sparsely designed by the French stylist Geneviève Labro. Displayed among the pale gray walls, slate gray-tiled floor and glass shelves mounted in pink brick, you'll find a collection of objects and furniture by great contemporary Italian designers. Both a showroom and a shop, Via Domani is the exclusive distributor in France of table and household articles designed by Porciani.

# Health· Beauty

## BEAUTY CLINICS

## *Aegina*
**7th arr.
15 rue de Bourgogne
551.65.70**
*Open 10:00 A.M. to 7:30 P.M.
Closed Sat.*

Dr. Emerit's beauty care center is a one-of-a-kind success. Customers (men, women and teenagers) are fastidiously examined and treated in small comfortable booths. The treatments based on sea plankton for acne and fatty skin tissues are extremely effective. The clay-based body beauty mask will make your skin as soft as a baby's.

## *Carita*
**8th arr.
11 faubourg
Saint-Honoré
265.79.00**
*Open 10:00 A.M. to 7:00 P.M.
Closed Mon.*

As of summer 1981, Carita has a new address at the avenue Mozart, with five entirely white treatment rooms overlooking a garden. Hordes of Parisian celebrities bear testimony to the fact that a hairdresser's greatest vocation is livening up the mundane existence of our civilized society. Second to this in importance is the spraying of tonic liquid, cleaning skin, applying makeup, suntanning

**16th arr.**
**36 ave. Mozart**
**520.90.07**
*Open 9:30 A.M. to 7:00 P.M.*
*Closed Mon.*

bodies with ultraviolet beams, European or Japanese massage (shiatsu massage by Sendi) and Chinese pedicures (by Kao). The young attendants clad in white trousers blend well with the maroon decor and assume the tasks of skin care, anti-wrinkle treatments, applying moisturizing masks, hair removal and eyebrow dyeing.

## Clarins
**4th arr.**
**70 rue**
**Saint-Louis-en-l'Ile**
**633.75.44**
*Open 9:30 A.M. to 7:30 P.M., Sat. 11:00 A.M. to 2:00 P.M. Closed Mon.*

**8th arr.**
**35 rue Tronchet**
**265.30.70**
*Open 9:00 A.M. to 7:00 P.M. Closed Sat.*

When you make your first appointment, an "aesthetician" will develop something called your beauty balance sheet without charge and inform you how long it will take before your treatment will produce results. There are three specialties here: excellent lifting molds for the face; "drainotherapy" (aero-rhythm massage) to slim down and harden the body; and, for sagging breasts, exclusively made treatments for firmness, shape and volume. House products here are known for their professionalism and efficiency.

## Maria Galland
**8th arr.**
**9 ave Marceau**
**723.61.10**
*Open 9:00 A.M. to 7:00 P.M.*

Maria Galland's sparkling new establishment covers 250 square meters on avenue Marceau. Her non-violent approach to beauty offers an individualized plan after testing each customer with regard to face, hair, bust and legs. Her principal weapon is a molding mask which, if applied over treatment creams, will marvelously reduce wrinkles and fatty tissue.

## George-V Esthétique
**8th arr.**
**12 ave. George-V**
**723.49.77**
*Staircase D on the 5th floor. Open 9:00 A.M. to 7:00 P.M. Closed Sat.*

This tiny beauty institute caters to the beautiful people under pressure. Miss Bluebell's and the Crazy Horse performers, fashion models, TV hostesses and well-heeled journalists are among her customers. Yet the frenetic succession of appointments (clients are remarkably punctual) seems never to faze the charming Antoinette. While chitchatting, she will remove hair from your legs by applying a pure, pink wax and, if needed, an anesthetizing cream to the sensitive areas. She also offers bleaching of facial fuzz and radical treatment of fatty tissue.

## Guerlain
**6th arr.**
**29 rue de Sèvres**
**222.46.60**
*Open 9:30 A.M. to 6:30 P.M. Closed Mon.*

**8th arr.**
**68 Champs-Elysées**
**359.31.10**
*Open 9:00 A.M. to 6:00 P.M. Closed Sat.*

Tradition and style abound in this venerable Guerlain institution located on the Champs-Elysées right above its perfume and beauty care boutique. It comprises twelve spacious and comfortable treatment booths in which are lavishly administered the classic treatments (cleansing, wrinkle treatment, molding masks, and makeup) which are as effective as those offered in other highly touted establishments. The staff is courteous and always smiling. Superb manicures and two kinds of medicated pedicures.

## Ingrid Millet

**8th arr.**
**54 faubourg Saint-Honoré**
**266.66.20**
*Open 9:00 A.M. to 6:00 P.M.*

In these white, restful treatment rooms decked out with green plants and graced with soft music, you may become instantly younger, thanks to what they call here stabilized cellulary extracts or Pearl of Caviar ampule treatments, which made the firm's reputation. You can also have a healthful saltwater mud-based mask fitted to your body. All kinds of body care, such as massages, reducing treatments, wrinkle treatments, tanning, relaxation, bust firming, hair removal, manicures and pedicures are administered by highly qualified aestheticians who are friendly and have a good sense of humor.

## Payot

**1st arr.**
**10 rue de Castiglione**
**260.32.87**
*Open 9:00 A.M. to 6:30 P.M.*

We expect Payot to be renovating and embellishing its premises, yet at the same of this writing, nothing has occured. The small, ground-level treatment rooms, formerly the "Divina Contessa" Castiglione's townhouse, are as decrepit as ever (the ones facing the street are very noisy). But this does not prevent the use of fine products and the administration of high-quality treatment by professional aestheticians, some of whom have been with Payot since its founding. The house features massages (ask for Georgine), "special institute" masks (some for sensitive and dehydrated skin, others for eradicating wrinkles), and makeup application, (ask for Josée). Unfortunately, there is no manicure, but you'll get good medicated pedicures, passive gymnastics and massages. Subscription rates are available (every sixth treatment is free) and reduced rates for young girls.

## Anna Pegova

**1st arr.**
**346 rue Saint-Honoré**
**260.41.56**
*Open 9:30 A.M. to 6:30 P.M.*
*Closed Sat.*

This is a good beauty institute that treats you with its own products. Anna Pegova's specialty for more than fifty years is peeling, a delicate, costly, yet effective treatment that makes forty-year-old women look ten years younger and seems to cure young people of acne. Anna will also heal sunburn, and eliminate stretch marks, freckles and acne.

# COSMETICS AND PERFUMES

## L'Artisan Parfumeur

**1st arr.**
**5 rue Capucines**
**296.35.13**
**1st arr.**
**350 rue Saint-Honoré**
**296.24.19**
**7th arr.**
**84 bis, rue de Grenelle**
**544.61.57**

Here you just have to be yourself. The perfume craftsman Jean Laporte invites you to become a sorcerer's apprentice and create for yourself or your friends original scents and perfumes. All you need to do is sniff a multitude of little bottles filled with evocatively named essential oils and choose the basic ingredient that most appeals to you—peach, tuberose, jasmine, honeysuckle, verbena, passionfruit, grapefruit, cinnamon, sandalwood, vertiver,—which you may blend accordingly. The result is a perfume with your personal imprint, which may either be applied directly to the skin or used as a room freshener or bath salt. If you dilute your perfume with 90

**16th arr.**
**4 rue Mesnil**
**704.49.31**
*Closed Mon., except at rue des*
*Capucines and rue de Grenelle.*

percent alcohol, you'll have an eau de toilette. Nothing is easier.

## *Dans un Jardin*

**1st arr.**
**1 rue du**
**Marché-Saint-Honoré**
**260.45.14**
**7th arr.**
**80 rue du Bac**
**548.93.75**
*Closed Mon.*
**14th arr.**
**56 rue de la Santé**
**707.47.57**
*Closed Mon. morning.*
**16th arr.**
**26 rue des Sablons**
**442.47.71**
*Closed Mon. Open Sun. morning.*

The refreshing green-and-white decor of the rue du Marché-Saint-Honoré shop was loosely adopted from turn-of-the-century bandstands and has also been used in the firm's other boutiques all over Paris. It is only fitting that this small English band has grown, since it has in one package all the necessary elements with which to succeed: lovely perfume, decor, wrapping and packaging, as well as a clientele of lovely, well-born ladies. Its products include, monogrammed soaps, eaux de toilette, creams, scented lotions, bubble bath, top-drawer bath accessories, dried scented bouquets, jars for night cream and products for men and children. There's also a makeup counter featuring the entire On Stage line of cosmetics for eyes, lips, and cheeks; transparent or matte powders and even phosphorescent ones used by cover girls and other showbusiness people. Personalized makeup applications, advice and trial tests by appointment only.

## *Diptyque*

**5th arr.**
**34 blvd.**
**Saint-Germain**
**326.45.27**
*Closed Mon.*

Here at last you'll find the famous Scotch Water, toilet water that smells like freshly mown hay; it hasn't been available in all of Paris since Chardon d'Ecosse on rue Marignan closed. You'll aslo find other top-name English perfumes like Penhaligon's, Floris, Mary Chess and Trumper. Diptyque has its own exclusive line of soaps, eaux de toilette, bath salts, pomanders, potpourris, scented candles and scented lingerie envelopes. Men will find handsome shaving accessories made of chrome-plated brass such as towel-heaters, shaving brushes, razors, and beard-trimmers.

## *Guerlain*

**1st arr.**
**2 place Vendôme**
**260.68.61**
**6th arr.**
**29 rue de Sèvres**
**222.46.60**
**8th arr.**
**68 Champs-Elysées**
**562.52.57**

Without fear of sounding chauvinistic, we declare unequivocally that Guerlain is the greatest purveyor of perfume in all of Paris, therefore in all the world. Fortunately, the original Pierre-François-Pascal Guerlain (a Picardese purveyor of perfume and vinegar) and his heirs have since 1828 had noses that are perfectly attuned to the finest essential oils. L'Eau Imperiale, created for Empress Eugénie; Jicky, created in 1889; l'Heure Bleue, created in 1912; Mitsouko, created in 1919; and Shalimar, created in 1925, are as successful today as the more recent Chamade, Parure and Nahema.

**16th arr.**
**93 rue de Passy**
**288.41.62**
*Closed Mon. at rue de Sèvres and rue de Passy.*

These perfumes, as well as a whole line of perfumed products, including toilet water, talcs, soaps and bath oils, are sold exclusively in the four Guerlain stores.

## Miss Bamy
**9th arr.**
**3 blvd. Rochechouart**
**878.16.34**
*Closed Mon. morning.*

Afro-style wigs, beauty products for the face and hair, reducing creams for the body, for black men and women.

## Molinard
**8th arr.**
**21 rue Royale**
**265.21.01**

Once a purveyor to Queen Victoria, Molinard continues to sell well-aged eaux de cologne in his rue Royale store: Extra Vieille, Cuir de Russie, Chypre, and the famous Habanita of the Roaring Twenties. You'll also find an entire line of scented products such as spiced or flowery potpourris; handkerchiefs and traveling bags; and lots of beautiful bottles, once made by Lalique and Baccarat, and reproduced in a limited edition. Molinard does not cater to women only, and the store on the first floor will delight the well-groomed man. The line in general favors the first half of the century. There is nothing dazzling here, yet you will find well-designed and attractive objects such as gold or chrome-plated towel heaters, vaporizers, toilet kits and—a luxury for the lazy—shaving trays for the tub. Also available are the Vetiver toilet water and Raffale for men. Prices on the whole are reasonable.

## Roger et Gallet
**8th arr.**
**62 faubourg Saint-Honoré**
**266.45.65**

Our grandparents used to anoint themselves with Jean-Marie Farina eau de cologne. It had then, and still has, the merit of being hardly detectable, yet leaving behind a distinctive clean scent. Fortunately, the soaps of this venerable house are still wrapped in their old-fashioned paper, having survived various trends and emerged victorious against those who found their flowered wrappings and meticulously folded inner wrappers to be anachronistic. The soaps have charming names such as Tea Rose, Violette, Oeillet and Orchidée, which are all sweetly penetrating. You can also find these fine soaps in perfumeries and drugstores.

## Le Saponifère
**1st arr.**
**Forum des Halles,**
**2nd floor**
**297.42.14**
**6th arr.**
**59 rue Bonaparte**
**633.98.43**

No one knows whether soapwort, a pink-petaled plant whose stem and roots contain saponin which makes water much like soap does, is used in any of the numerous soaps sold by Saponifère. It's up to you to decide, knowing that the soaps are made of flowers including briar, heliotrope, gardenia, linden; fruit, including apricot pits, avocados, cucumber; as well as jojoba oil, buttermilk and even goat's milk. There are also candles and incense, men's and women's eaux de toilette, bath oils and salts, various talcs and lotions, towels, and shaving brushes and cups, which round off

**8th arr.**
**rond-point des**
**Champs-Elysées**
**562.38.81**
*Closed Mon. morning.*

this firm's line of bath products. They can be found bubbling all over France from Nancy to Ajaccio, and from Bordeaux to Grenoble. Equally good are the products made by Floris, Crabtree and Evelyn, Village and Creed.

## Discounts

Perfume and beauty care products have always been expensive—if not exorbitant. Chances are that your regular supplier will give you some sort of discount, providing you're a good customer and ask discreetly. Some perfume retailers offer systematic discounts all year long on famous brands, with the exception of those irreducible bastions like Guerlain or Estée Lauder. Otherwise, you may expect 15%, 20% or even 25% discounts off manufacturers' suggested prices. Here are a few other addresses:

### 25% Off

**Michel Swiss**
**2nd arr.**
**16 rue de la Paix**
**261.71.71**

There is no street-level display, so you'll have to climb the stairs to the shop. You'll find the best buys by walking around the three or four sparsely decorated rooms, which are nevertheless equipped with shelves and windows displaying perfumes, scented products, and beauty care ointments for men and women, mostly name brands; Lancôme, Orlane, Rochas, Clarins, Sisley (good for sensitive skin), Jeanne Piaubert, Revlon, Dior, Saint-Laurent, Germaine Monteil and Charles of the Ritz. There are no tags or labels. The friendly, competent sales staff will go over the list of each manufacturer's suggested retail price and mark down 25% (20% for credit card purchases). Other worthwhile departments include: fancy leather goods, top-label scarves from preceding years, ties, cashmere scarves and a good collection of Lacostes, the famous alligator shirts for men, women and children, of which there is always a plentiful selection at the start of each season. There are also jacquard sweaters in wool and acrylic at 25% off.

### 20% Off

**Marionnaud**
•  *78000 Versailles—19 rue des Réservoirs (tel. 953.51.31).*

•  *92140 Clamart—91 ave. Victor-Hugo (tel. 644.75.28). Closed Mon. Open Sun. morning.*

### 15% Off

**Arcadie**
•  *8th arr.—55 rue de l'Arcade (tel. 387.38.28).*

**Athéna**
•  *11th arr.—90 faubourg du Temple (tel. 357.25.66).*

### Camélia
· 9th arr.—13 rue des Martyrs (tel. 878.26.59). Closed Mon.

### Capucines
· 2nd arr.—18 rue des Capucines (tel. 261.08.07).

### Catherine
· 1st arr.—6 rue de Castiglione (tel. 260.81.89).

### Chaland
· 2nd arr.—4 rue Saint-Joseph (tel. 236.47.45). Closed Sat.

### Codip
· 15th arr.—Centre Commercial Maine-Montparnasse (tel. 538.65.07).

### Cosmos
· 16th arr.—2 rue Copernic (tel. 727.72.52) Closed Sat.

### Cyclamen
· 7th arr.—36 rue de Bellechasse (tel. 705.86.46). Closed Sat.

### Elles-Parfums
· 1st arr.—35 rue de Richelieu (tel. 296.02.15). Closed Mon. morning and Sat. afternoon.

### Le Lavandou
· 5th arr.—138 rue Mouffetard (tel. 707.33.71). Closed Mon. Open Sun. morning. 15% off all products. 20% off all purchases above 300F.

### Au Rayon d'Or
· 3rd arr.—178 rue du Temple (tel. 272.32.71).
· 9th arr.—94 rue Saint-Lazare (tel. 874.30.38)..

# HAIR CARE

### Clauderer
**1st arr.**
**26 place Vendôme**
**261.28.01**
**16th arr.**
**55 ave.**
**Théophile-Gautier**
**527.11.67**
**92200 Neuilly**
**113 ave. du Roule**
**624.03.09**

René Furterer's daughters Claudine and Hélène have followed in their father's footsteps and opened their own center for treatment of damaged and receding hair. Their new methods were developed in collaboration with dermatologists, phytotherapists, and biologists. On your first visit to Clauderer, you will be greeted with great politeness by a warmly smiling Hélène, who will check your hair without charge—it takes about fifteen minutes. After you've filled out a questionnaire and she's had time to analyze three strands of hair under a microscope that magnifies them 600 times, she'll give you a diagnosis and tell you what you can expect from a treatment on the premises or at home. At the salon there are five private booths where you will be attended by three young "hair nurses," one hairdresser and an assistant. You may also take the custom-blended products home with precise instructions. While you're there, enjoy the gilded moldings in the waiting room. This is the former home of the Countess de Castiglione. She spent sixteen years here always dressed in black, as a recluse amid veiled mirrors and closed shutters.

## Men's Hair Salons

### Carita

**8th arr.**
**11 faubourg**
**Saint-Honoré**
**265.79.00**
*Open 10:00 A.M. to 7:00 P.M.*
*Closed Mon.*

This Italian-Japanese estabishment has a warm and cozy atmosphere—as well as some of the best men's stylists at one of the best "clip joints" in town. Pierre, with dazzling expertise, cuts some of the most prestigious heads in Paris. Michael concentrates on the well-heeled youth, and the charming Claudine garners with discretion and confessions of Europe's most distinguished corporate presidents. This salon will always be in vogue with all sorts of celebrities who keep coming back for haircuts, facials, manicures and complete hair and body care.

### Césare

**1st arr.**
**6 rue Richepanse**
**260.17.72**
*Open 9:30 A.M. to 6:30 P.M.*
*Closed Mon.*

A place for young movers in the entertainment world and for business types alike. It's a true full-service masculine beauty complex, and you'll step out of it ready to conquer the world. The rooms are spacious with shellacked wood on the ground floor, exposed beams on the first, furnished in white leather armchairs. Of course a phone is always at hand. Every type of hair care is available, including free scalp examinations, hair-enriching treatments (fresh cells, ox marrow, placenta extracts), natural miracle treatment for gray hair, eyebrow-dying, relaxing massages, manicures and medicated pedicures. All this is accompanied by music and broad smiles from Césare, Edouard, Sonia, Linda and others. For desperate cases there are also hair implants on micro-skin, discreetly done in private booths (free tests).

### Henry Courant

**1st arr.**
**5 rue Rouget-de-Lisle**
**260.80.07**
**8th arr.**
**49 ave.**
**Franklin-Roosevelt**
**359.14.40**

In these opulent salons you'll find distinguished politicians, businessmen, academicians and a few stars. This Champs-Elysées-roundabout parlor has been recently redone in good taste, and features refined hair styling specializing in minicurls, natural dyeing and beauty care. The Rouget de Lisle location offers, in addition, a sauna, body massage, medicated pedicure—and air-conditioning in summer.

### Desfossé

**8th arr.**
**19 ave. Matignon**
**359.95.13**
*Open 9:30 A.M. to 6:30 P.M.*
*Closed Mon.*

David de Rothschild, the well-barbered owner; Guillaume Sénécal, the efficient director; a charming decor by Michel Boyer; a select clientele; and perfectly meticulous services: this is Desfossé. You'll get a cut, curling or straightening; dying and bleaching; or full beauty care such as manicure, pedicure, sauna, massage, depilation— performed in comfortable booths with vibrating armchairs to relax your back and legs and a phone to keep you in touch. Full treatment is designed to take three hours including lunch at the bar (equipped with a TV) from which you'll emerge a new man.

### Women's Hair Salons

## Patrick Alès
**8th arr.**
**35-37 ave.**
**Franklin-Roosevelt**
**225.57.49**
*Open 9:00 A.M. to 7:00 P.M.*
*Closed Mon.*

This salon occupies two buildings and is graced with a hanging garden. Its discreet staff are used to dealing with celebrities and remain unruffled by the likes of Mme Pompidou, Jacqueline Onassis and Raquel Welch. Jet setters and show biz luminaries all come here for Romain and his remarkable team: Olga, the masseuse and herbalist; Jean, the short-hair specialist; Denise, who does perms; Roland, who does single-strand frosting; and, of course, the salon's namesake, Patrick Alès, the creator of phytotherathry.

## Alexandre de Paris
**8th arr.**
**3 ave. Matignon**
**225.57.90**
*Open 9:30 A.M. to 6:30 P.M.*

Alexandre, under his new name, Alexandre "de" Paris, now distributes a wide variety of accessories including combs, shaving brushes, hair nets and razors. We will forgive him for going hoity-toity simply because he remains the undisputed crown prince of brilliant hair design. Some of his clients who obviously agree with us are the Countess of Paris, Sophia Loren, Elizabeth Taylor and Romy Schneider. His clientele are among the most celebrated in Paris and include those who marry in June at the church of Saint-Honoré d'Eylau (he specializes in wedding coiffures), or those who want a chignon for opening night at the opera. He has closed his faubourg Saint-Honoré salon and is redecorating the avenue Matignon premises from top to bottom in orange and black art deco with flowery paneling designed by Joy de Rohan Chabot. The staff is pleasant, the comfortable salons face the tree-lined avenue.

## Carita
**8th arr.**
**11 faubourg**
**Saint-Honoré**
**265.79.00**
*Open 10:00 A.M. to 7:00 P.M.*
*Closed Mon.*

This salon is so well known and so prestigious you can address mail simply to "Carita, faubourg Saint-Carita", and it will get there just the same. Along with Alexandre and a few others, Carita has a near-monopoly on the hair design and wigs of Tout-Paris. This great salon has a friendly staff and it isn't the least bit intimidating, even for first anonymous appointment. All sorts of treatments are offered here, including straightening, perms, streaking, split-end treatments, facials, massages, makeup, depilation, manicures and European or Chinese-style pedicures. You will be attended by Christophe, Rosy Carita's nephew, or by a galaxy of star hairdressers whose customers include Isabelle Adjani, Marie-France Pisier and Catherine Deneuve.

## Pierre Darphin
**8th arr.**
**36 ave. Matignon**
**359.61.93**
*Open 8:30 A.M. to 8:00 P.M. Mon.*
*9:00 A.M. to 7:00 P.M.*

Pierre Darphin is the specialist of the modulated cut, which gives you four totally different hair styles with one hair cut. The decor is functional and the staff very pleasant.

## Jean-Louis David

**8th arr.**
**47 rue**
**Pierre-Charron**
**359.75.16**
*Open 10:00 A.M. to 7:00 P.M.*
*Closed Sat.*

Jean-Louis David is one of Paris's most brilliant stylists. Fortunately, in his large and comfortable salons no one imposes a particular look or style on you. Instead your hair is styled flexibly to suit the shape of your face, your silhouette, and your lifestyle. It's expensive, but you'll find slightly more affordable rates in the six Jean-Louis David Diffusion Salons listed below:
· 2nd arr.—27 rue de la Ferronnerie (tel. 296.98.6). Closed Sat.
· 6th arr.—12 rue Bréa (tel. 326.14.89).
· 8th arr.—50 bis, rue Pierre-Charron (tel. 720.90.08). Closed Mon.
· 8th arr.—38 ave. de Wagram (tel. 763.68.91). Closed Mon.
· 16th arr.—50 rue de Passy (tel. 224.63.03).
· 20th arr.—9 cours de Vincennes (tel. 370.51.60). Closed Mon.

## Deluga-Lang

**8th arr.**
**28 rue**
**Boissy-d'Anglas**
**742.86.36**
*Open from 9:30 A.M. To 6:30 P.M.*
*Closed Sat.*

Formerly the site of the famed Boeuf sur le Toit restaurant, this salon has been redone in wood and decorated with plants. Catherine and Jean-Pierre, who were trained by Carita, specialize in layered hairdos that are cropped close to the head. Subtle hair coloring and natural health care are featured.

## Jacques Dessange

**8th arr.**
**37 ave.**
**Franklin-Roosevelt**
**359.31.31**
*Open 9:00 A.M. to 8:00 P.M.*

Jacques Dessange's lovely suite is beautifully decorated and full of green plants. Although the place is as busy as the Metro at rush hour, the services are of the highest quality. The staff is detached yet courteous, and highly sensitive to your needs since the clientele is very beau monde.

## Laurent Gaudefray

**2nd arr.**
**6 rue de la Paix**
**261.18.01**
*Open from 9:00 A.M. to 6:00 P.M.*
*Closed Mon.*

Laurent Gaudefray is a true hairdresser who cuts hair and still uses rollers. He is the champion of evening hair styles and high fashion chignons that are ravishing and sophisticated. He will also design period styles for masquerade balls.

## Harlow

**1st arr.**
**24 rue Saint-Denis**
**233.61.36**
*Open 10:00 A.M. to 7:00 P.M.,*
*Wed. 12:00 noon to 9:00 P.M.*
*Closed Mon.*

**16th arr.**
**64-70 rue**
**du Ranelagh**
**524.04.54**
*Open 9:30 A.M. to 6:30 P.M.,*
*Wed. 12:00 noon to 9:00 P.M.*

The salon for women who hate hairdressers. They love Harlow because at Harlow's, women are loved and pampered. Nearly every aspect of your life is examined before they transform your hair with an expert snip of the scissors. To make certain your hairstyle is harmonious with your life, the staff will evaluate your carriage, your body line and your lifestyle as closely as the features of your face. Instead of a simple wash, cut and blow-dry, a permanent or immaculate frosting to enhance your haircut will make your metamorphosis complete. At Harlow, they also use electric razors which seem to be making a comeback. And you, too, should come back in six weeks for a shower shampoo, a comb-out, or a deft hand fluffed through your hair to completely revitalize your coiffure.

### Katcha

8th arr.
9 rue de Cirque
359.37.31
*Open 9:00 A.M. to 5:30 P.M.
Closed Mon.*

André Katcha is the prototype of the inspired hairdresser. It was he who launched and developed the basics of the new coiffure (precision cuts, blow-drying). First he precision-shapes your hair, then custom-styles it to perfectly frame your face. You won't find any preconceived styles or trendy cuts here—only the finest custom designs. Come by once a month to this balding, 200-pound, sixtyish, utterly charming man who will keep your cut looking its best with a facile snip of the scissors.

### Lawrence

16th arr.
48 rue Copernic
500.66.32
*Open 9:30 A.M. to 6:30 P.M.*

Lawrence is one of the up-and-coming hairstylists, rapidly closing in on the ranks of the greats. He has the talent, the decor (modern with lots of mirrors), and clientele (young lovelies from the best neighborhoods), as well as a friendly staff and a relaxing ambience in his shop. On the ground floor, Jean-Max, Olivia, Jean-Charles, Danièle and Kyo cut and style hair from the tamest locks to the wildest manes, and create alluring styles for evening. Haircare and treatment is done downstairs. Lawrence is now open for men (tel. 500.66.83).

### Look Lemon

16th arr.
9 rue
Gustave-Courbet
704.62.92
*Open from 9:00 A.M. to 7:00 P.M.*

Daniel's clients praise his good nature, his talent and his ability to cut your hair just right to suit your face and personality. Rest assured, a natural look is yours, from Marinette's deft shampoo, to a haircut, a body perm—which adds body and volume to delicate straight hair—or a simple brushing. You'll never walk out of this pleasant salon looking as if you've just been to the hairdresser.

### Jean Marc Maniatis

1st arr.
Forum des Halles,
first level
296.90.95

"Boyish," "wild," "Chinese," "New Lioness"—short or long— are a few of the latest fashions of this talented Greek who has trained a brilliant team of stylists in his methods. The point, chez Maniatis, is not to disguise women, but to transform them according to their individual features. Other locations.

### Mod's Hair

6th arr.
90 rue de Rennes
544.47.02
8th arr.
57 ave. Montaigne
359.06.50

Precision haircuts, super-light frosting, finger-drying and free and casual hairstyles are the highlight of this establishment. Twelve of Mod's hairdressers are employed permanently to do styling for magazines, and you can count on the fingers of one hand the top models who have not passed through their hands. The other stylists, who are also top-notch, concentrate chiefly and with great success on giving you the hairdo that best suits you. The ave. Montaigne shop is more elegant and more expensive. Simone Mahler is the salon's aesthetician.

### Yang International

These comfortable salons have a California elegance and style. Here a team of spirited international stylists will cut, crimp, or tame domestic or foreign heads of unruly

**15th arr.**
**22 ave.**
**de Suffren**
**273.34.28**
**17th arr.**
**Palais des Congres,**
**porte Maillot**
**758.23.36**
*Open from 9:30 A.M. to 7:00 P.M.*
*Closed Mon.*

hair. The four young and talented colorists are fully experienced in the delicate arts of frosting, streaking and lightening. The Pacific Blonde look is a house specialty.

# MAKEUP

## Michel Deruelle
**16th arr.**
**12 ave. Victor-Hugo**
**500.88.76**
*By appt. only.*

For many years Michel Deruelle has discreetly made-up stars of TV and movies, the opera and the Comedie Française, as well as silver screen stars. You too will be able to learn tricks from this magician, who is capable of transforming you into someone else without losing your identity. He will teach you how to apply slight touch-ups, how to blend shadow and highlights, and how to use colors you never before thought suitable for your face. Such a lesson costs money: 300F and more if your interest extends to theater and/or cinema. His high-quality products are no more expensive than other.

## Jean D'Estrées
**8th arr.**
**14 and 5 faubourg Saint-Honoré**
**265.99.67**
*Open 10:00 A.M. to 8:00 P.M.*

When Michel Serrault underwent his metamorphosis in *La Cage Aux Folles,* he came to Jean d'Estrées for help. With thirty years of experince, Jean no longer is sure of how many clients he has had. Fifteen-thousand would be a good guess. You'll find excellent makeup application for day and evening and theatrical makeup and headdresses for dinner or masquerade balls, preceded by full-care treatments such as wrinkle removal, relaxing massage and Estressence energizing care. Makeup advice, along with sketches made by the master, cost 250F; by one of his assistants, 150F. For 20F you may be referred to a student of Jean d'Estrée's reknowned Ecole d'Esthétique who will work under the guidance of a teacher.

# SHAVING

## Kindal
**2nd arr.**
**33 ave. de l'Opéra**
**261.70.78**

For incurable devotees of the straight razor (which we are), there is only one kind suitable for the most exacting chins. It's the one invented nearly eighty years ago by the Swede, Magnus Kindal. This razor, which has shaved all the crowned beards of Europe, has the additional advantage over the modern safety razor of being as sharp as a surgeon's blade, yet safe to use (even early in the morning). The Swedish-made steel blade is thick on one side and extremely thin on the other. Since steel blades cut better when they have a chance to rest (no one knows why), the razor comes with seven blades—one for each day of the week. Of course this razor is a costly marvel, but Kindal blades will last for ten years. For more sensitive chins, there's the Magnus Junior.

## Peter
**8th arr.**
**191 faubourg**
**Saint-Honoré**
**563-88.00**
*Closed Mon. morning.*

Here you'll find razors with solid silver handles for 420F, and Swedish steel hair-tweezers at 72F, as well as specially made kits for beards and moustaches.

# TATTOOS

## Bruno
**18th arr.**
**6 rue**
**Germain-Pilon**
**265.35.59**
*Closed Wed.*

Whether or not you're powerful or downtrodden, from the strong or gentle sex, Bruno will be happy to see you in his shop from 9:00 A.M. to 7:00 P.M. He always breaks for lunch, though, and on Wednesdays he goes fishing. He will use his great talent to tattoo your skin according to your wishes, and the photos on the walls will help you with ideas. He is also very patient. Some works, such as panoramas, are particularly delicate to perform and can take months or even years to execute. At least you won't have wasted your time.

## Etienne
**2nd arr.**
**32 rue Greneta**
**233.50.14**
*Open 2:00 P.M. to 12:00 midnight, and at your home by appt.*
**11th arr.**
**40 rue de la Roquette**
**357.20.95**
*Open 10:00 A.M. to 12:00 noon and 2:00 P.M. to 8:00 P.M.*

There are only two licensed tattoo artists in Paris: Etienne, and, of course, his colleague Bruno over in Pigalle. Etienne's work is quick, careful and painless; his designs are polychromatic; indelible and traditional or specially designed, ornate, symbolic, literal or metaphysical; and suitable for princely or beggarly skin. Of course this form of expression entails all sorts of sociological and pathological scrunity, but this is not our concern. All we want to do is stress his great talent and state that he will tattoo anyone (20 percent of his customers are women) in any nook or cranny of the body, whether it's the bottom of the belly button, between the toes, the palms of the hand, the top of the scalp, under the hairline, inside the mouth, the small of the back, or other areas which he will metamorphosize to create stunning visual illusions. Other services include tattooed freckles, which are more real than the real thing, scar cover-ups and skin recoloring in collaboration with a private clinic.

# TURKISH BATHS

## Hammam du Colisée
**8th arr.**
**17 rue du Colisée**

Hammam du Colisée is submerged in the deep basement of a building near the Champs-Elysées. Amid the pipes and archaic yet fully functioning radiators is the rather small steam room lined with square shaped "altars." In

**225.84.69**
*Open Mon. to Sat. 9:00 A.M.
to 7:00 P.M.*

this oven roasting bodies are stretched out as if they were in medieval torture chambers. As the sweat pours into their eyes, a hail of water droplets falls from the ceiling and reverberates throughout the cavern. In a recessed chamber are seats cut into the cement which form little parlors where you can sit and contemplate the discolored tiles on the walls. This is the small, barbarous kingdom of the jovial M. Brahim, former masseur to the bey of Tunisia. His massage table is now in the hands of a young compatriot who, according to habitues, isn't as good as his predecessor. Small matter; this authentic, Maghreb-styled Turkish bath is truly excellent. And if you think you need a certain perversity or courage to come here, at least you can expect to leave feeling as light as the 50F note you paid to get in.

## Hammam de la Mosquée

**5th arr.**
**39 rue Geoffroy-Saint-Hilaire**
**331.18.14**
*Women: Mon., Thur., Sat.
11:00 A.M. to 6:00 P.M.
Men: Fri., Sun. 11:00 A.M. to
6:00 P.M.*

Properly dressed, in loincloth or tuxedo (everything is allowed), you follow the heat through four increasingly hot chambers attended by odalisques with glistening beards. If you dare go all the way to the last steaming oven, you'll wake up on a mat next to director Si Hamza Boubakeur (master bathkeeper in the face of Allah). You can nurse your indigestion with mint tea while contemplating the cupolas ornamented with Moorish stained glass, the sculpted cedar balconies and the white marble fountain and columns. All this makes Hammam de la Mosquée the most sumptuous Turkish bath house in Paris. The admission fee is an exotic 28F and includes massage. It's difficult to get in on ladies' day due to the large number of matrons bundled up in layers of fat.

## Hammam Saint-Paul

**4th arr.**
**4 rue des Rosiers**
**272.71.82**
*Women: Wed., Fri. 10:00 A.M. to
10:00 P.M.
Men: Thurs., Sat. 10:00 A.M. to
10:00 P.M.
Nudists: Tues. 5:00 P.M. to
10:00 P.M.*

Having pocketed his tip, the grinning cabin attendant will stay by your side until you've entered your mauve compartment with the metal grating on the ceiling. Then he will resume his prowl for customers who are not there for the baths, but for the possibility of an encounter of a more personal nature. It's a known fact that young Romans would only enter the baths accompanied by their tutors. But don't be afraid of taking the narrow staircase down into the diabolic heat of the hamman proper. Once you've pushed open the door, the thick eucalyptus-enriched steam will jolt you (with an instantaneous clearing effect), at the same time almost entirely concealing you from the inquisitive scrutiny of the naked, spot-lighted bodies. All you can do is sit and sweat eternally in this delectable hellhouse, which is as hot and humid as a night in the tropics. The powerful ice-cold water spout, the large tank, improperly called a pool, the room with the relaxing baths, the stationary exercycle, the sauna, the massage tables, the sofas and the reading room are all stages of a journey that is infinitely revitalizing. All along the way, you'll find plenty of scales which allow you to check the gradual slimming down of your physique. The slimming-down process here is relative, judging from the portly clientele. The premises of this very old Turkish bath located in Paris's Jewish district are immaculately clean. You will find many aids to help you relax here. The sweltering price is approximately 50F, not including massage.

# Home

## BATH

### Art et Créations
**8th arr.**
**61 ave.**
**Franklin-Roosevelt**
**225.90.36**
*Closed Mon. morning.*

This store, which specializes in marble, also features, under the Galleria label, Charles Wagner's American collection. You won't find bathtubs here (unless you want one in marble), but there are lots of elegant, handpainted porcelain basins and all types of coordinated accessories, including wallpaper in a dozen designs, soap trays and electrical wall switch plates. There are also gold-plated or marble sink fixtures.

### La Baignoire Délirante
**15th arr.**
**26 rue de Lourmel**
**579.23.19**
*Closed Mon., Wed. and Sat. morning.*

With his pale eyes, angelic smile and flowing beard, he looks just like his compatriot Dostoevski. But his interests lie elsewhere. Serge Valevatch is a plumber zinc maker who is also an antique dealer specializing in hydrotherapy. He is forever criss-crossing Paris in search of unique bath accessories such as rust-colored tubs, delicate sink fixtures, sponge baskets (rigid or flexible, single or double unit), metal towel bars or carafes. He repairs his finds in his basement workshop so you may later have them installed at your home—at a steep price, of course.

### Au Bain de Diane
**8th arr.**
**2 rue de Miromesnil**
**265.29.73**

Michel de Lacour, a former student at l'Ecole des Beaux-Arts, rules over the bathrooms of emirs and diplomats. His rich and often ostentatious creations include double tubs, tubs lined with bronze, luminous-bottomed crystal tubs, sinks carved in marble, multicolored bronze faucets chiseled and hammered by artisans according to seventeenth-century methods and recoated in gold or silver, and bath or poolside statues.

### Beauté Divine
**6th arr.**
**40 rue Saint-Sulpice**
**326.25.31**
*Closed Mon.*

Régine de Robien was the first person in Paris to own a company specializing in bathroom antiques. Régine is quite a woman. She is as vigorous in her search for fine-quality articles as she is in tastefully arranging them on period stands. Her taste leans toward early twentieth-century pieces (from the '30s in particular), which she reconditions and repairs; you'll get an idea of how talented she is by stopping by her shop across from the church. You'll find antique objects like flagons, boxes, bathroom accessories, pharmaceutical jars and enameled vases. You'll also find contemporary pieces such as cotton and linen bath towels, lamps and lighting fixtures and chrome bathroom accessories.

### A l'Épi d'Or
**5th arr.**
**7 rue Saint-Jacques**
**633.08.47**

It used to be a charming bakery. The decor—marble, mirrors and painted glass ceiling—is the same, but instead of finding baked goods, you'll find distinguished turn-of-the-century bathroom accessories made from polished brass, nickel, and turned wood. There are also bracket lamps, towel bars, mirrors, and shelves, as well as sinks from grand hotels, copper bathtubs, and antique bathroom furniture.

# CANDLES

### La Bougerie
**6th arr.**
**3 rue Mazet**
**325.97.57**
**12th arr.**
**146 ave. Daumesnil**
**343.91.91**
*Closed Mon.*

This shop offers candles to enhance any occasion. They are plain and fancy, multicolored, flowered, and scented. Also featured are candleholders and table ornaments.

### Debadier
**6th arr.**
**4 bis rue**
**du Cherche-Midi**
**548.59.55**
*Closed Mon.*

You'll find thousands of candles for all tastes and occasions—rustic, gothic, scented, Mexican, Chinese, sculptured statuettes, floats, handpainted, ones which repel mosquitos, as well as church candles, garden torches, bracket candle lamps and Chinese lanterns. For birthdays, weddings, bar mitzvahs and baptisms, they will engrave your name, date, or whatever you wish on any candle you purchase.

# CARPETS

### Braquenié
2nd arr.
16 rue Vivienne
261.53.94
*Closed Sat.*

This venerable establishment has an inventory of superb and exclusive rug designs from the eighteenth and especially the nineteenth centuries, from which you can order beautiful custom-woven carpets.

### Canovas
6th arr.
6 rue de l'Abbaye
329.91.36

Once you've left the Canovas Fabric Showroom (see below), all you need do is cross the exquisite Place Furstenberg to choose and order a Canovas-designed carpet. Unlike the Fabrics Showroom, this shop is also a sales outlet.

### A la Place Clichy

8th arr.
93 rue d'Amsterdam
526.15.16
*Closed Mon.*

This entirely remodeled and rebuilt establishment is one of the best carpet outlets in Place Clichy, if not in all of Paris. You'll find different-sized carpets made in pure wool or synthetic fibers, as well as a stunning selection of handcrafted contemporary rugs from a myriad of countries, including Portugal, India, China, Sardinia, Spain, Pakistan and Iran. There are also a few antique pieces from the nineteenth century.

# CHINA AND CRYSTAL

### Baccarat
10th arr.
30 bis, rue de Paradis
770.64.30
*Closed Sat.*

Since 1764 Baccarat has been a principal purveyor to czars, kings, presidents and emirs. Using singularly pure crystal (over 30 percent made from lead), Baccarat still manufactures world-renowned designs like the famous Harcourt as well as the more affordable Capri and Don Pélignon models. Also see the museum for its magnificent items and history of crystal.

### Boutique Danoise
8th arr.
42 ave. de Friedland
227.02.92

This shop sells attractive dishware made by the Royal Manufacture of Copenhagen, as well as beautiful contemporary glassware. A word of advice: Read the tags and don't bother the sales staff with your questions. You'll be wasting your time—and theirs.

### Christofle
2nd arr.
31 blvd. des Italiens
265.62.43
6th arr.
93 rue de Seine
325.70.73
8th arr.
12 rue Royale
260.34.07
16th arr.

Along with other fine porcelain, you'll also find the marvelous Claude Monet set sold exclusively by Christofle. It was made by Haviland and Parlon (Limoges) for the opening of the beautiful Claude Monet museum and gardens in Giverny. These plates are snow-white, rimmed with yellow buttercups and periwinkle blue filaments. The plates are in open stock, but should you break one you'll have to wait two months for a replacement. Another Christofle exclusive is the George Sand dinner service by Raynaud (Limoges).

**La Faïence Anglaise**
6th arr.
11 rue du Dragon
222.42.72

Entire place settings, or individual pieces, from 18F to 74F a plate, are offered here, featuring Wedgwood, Masons, Stratford, Laura Ashley, Mill Stream and others.

**Lalique**
8th arr.
11 rue Royale
265.33.70

Established at the start of the century by the silversmith René Lalique, whose name is synonomous with art nouveau, this company has since gained a reputation for being one of the world's foremost crystal manufacturers. Its successive series of designs, such as vases with geometric or flowered motifs, cups, boxes, bottles, flagons, and glass sets will certainly be prominently displayed in future museums of decorative arts. These pieces are a guaranteed investment for the future, given the increasingly high bids the antique Laliques fetch at auction.

**Limoges-Unic**
10th arr.
12 rue de Paradis
770.54.49
10th arr.
58 rue de Paradis
770.61.49
Pary 2 and Vélizy 2.

The No. 12 location features the finest porcelain services by Limoges and Meissen, as well as Baccarat, Saint-Louis, Daum and Laique crystalware and Christofle and Têtard silverware. At the No. 58 location you'll find simpler tableware. Sales are held during the first week in February.

**Madronet Contemporain**
10th arr.
34 rue de Paradis
770.34.59
*Closed Mon.*

Madronet Contemporain has contemporary china, crystal and silverware, particularly the complete Rosenthal collection and Daum raw-glass sculptures (priced from 1,800F–13,200F). Also a few Danish and Italian items.

**Simon**
2nd arr.
36 rue
Etienne-Marcel
233.71.65

This is an old and distinguished firm. For nearly a hundred years, the Simons (father and son) have been purveyors of kitchen and tableware to hotels and restaurants in Paris such as Crillon, Lipp, and l'Escargot Montorgueil; La Goulue in New York; and Ai in Japan. Porcelain, glassware, silverware, stainless steel and woodwork are also sold to the public at trade prices.

## Windsor
**15th arr.**
**Centre Beaugrenelle,**
**16 rue Linois**
**575.74.40**

Windsor has lovely English porcelain dinner services, including Wedgwood, Royal Doulton and bone china. They are all quality goods and can be machine-washed. Margareth Thorogood purchases them directly from the manufacturer. As a result, her wares are 10 percent less expensive than elsewhere in Paris.

### Discounts

## Mont-martre-Verrerie
**9th arr.**
**21 rue Henri-Monnier**
**878.64.63**

Here you'll find strong practical restaurant ware, bistro-style, for tables and kitchens, sold at the same price to the trade and the public. Yearlong sales on certain articles. Good savings for large-sized families. Home deliveries.

## La Porcelaine Blanche
**1st Arr.**
**108 rue Saint-Honore**
**236.90.73**

There are nine of these stores in Paris and more than 70 in France. They sell only white porcelain—particularly their own brand. Prices here are about 15% to 30% less than elsewhere and all stores sell identical wares.

### Your Table In A Flash

## Centre Inter-national des Arts de la table
**10th arr.**
**17 bis, rue de Paradis**
**246.50.50**
*Closed Sat.*

Open in April of 1979, CIAT's five stories comprising 8,600 square meters of floor space are occupied by over 90 French and foreign manufacturers of glassware, crystal, porcelain, earthenware, silverware, household linen, decorative items and contemporary furniture. The center is open to the public from Tuesdays to Thursdays, Mondays and Fridays being for professional dealers only. Note that these are only exhibits, not sales outlets. Part of the ground floor is reserved for traveling exhibits of the manufacturers' latest designs.

# CUTLERY

## Dehillerin
**1st arr.**
**18, rue Coquilliere**
**236.53.13**

Unrivaled for its pantry cutlery.

## Isler
**1st arr.**
**44 rue Coquillière**
**233.20.92**
*Closed Sat.*

Isler has been a leading outlet for Swiss knives since 1933. In this small, old-fashioned boutique you will find, alongside those remarkable Eiffel Tower knives—Swiss-made in stainless steel with Brazilian rosewood handles—all sorts of cutting and slicing kitchen utensils, as well as knife sharpeners for home and professional use. Isler's is a wholesale dealer, but will be friendly to you even if you aren't a professional chef from Lasserre, Ledoyen or Taillevent. Charming multi-bladed Swiss army knives are also featured.

## Kindal
**2nd arr.**
**33 ave. de l'Opéra**
**261.70.78**

In its discreet mahogany-paneled shop, this old and excellent firm presents you with a wide variety of knives for dicing and slicing, for the table, sports, fishing, hunting, and carrying in your pocket. They are all made with ivory, mother-of-pearl, or shellacked wooden handles. There are also cheese slicers and lots of pretty gifts for the table.

## Peter
**8th arr.**
**191 faubourg Saint-Honoré**
**563.88.00**
*Closed Mon. morning.*

Everything that will cut is crafted here in Peter's workshop, including professional cutlery, cutting boards, kitchen knives, sewing kits, deluxe hunting knives, beautiful jackknives, special dishwasher-proof knives, razors and, upon request, admirable reproductions of old designs. There are also lovely classic and contemporary table sets, as well as a fine selection of silver, crystal and china, and commissioned gifts. Courteous staff.

# DECOR

## Boutique Danoise
**8th arr.**
**42 ave. de Friedland**
**227.02.92**

This superb shop is notable not only for its vast size (1,800 square meters) and attractive lighting, but also for its remarkably well presented permanent exhibit of applied Danish artwork. You may browse freely without being bothered by the sales staff. Everything is clearly tagged and free of promotional ballyhoo. The hallmarks of contemporary Scandinavian design, such as balance, line, high quality materials, perfect finish and classical design, can be found in the following departments: dishware, glassware, silverware, lamps, and furniture, the latter particularly elegant in its simplicity.

## Anne Caracciolo
**6th arr.**
**16 rue de l'Université**
**261.22.22**

Anne Caracciolo is a woman of good taste and a decorator by vocation. In this charming shop/gallery she collects and sells turned-wood candlesticks, Chinese and Korean vases and bronzework, rich cashmere shawls, mosaic ashtrays, Napoleon III couches and armchairs, small nineteenth-century furniture and other charming curios. She also has a fine selection of upholstery fabrics. For ten years she has worked under Jacques Grange and now has her own serious staff of fine artisans and an excellent selection of fabrics for upholstering.

## Agnès Comar

**8th arr.**
**7 ave. George-V**
**723.33.85**
*Closed Mon. morning.*

What she has gained in volume of sales, she has lost (a bit) in grace from the days when she was stacking up cushions along the banks of the rue de Seine. Judging by its eye-catching embossed draperies, its white walls spangled with gold, its deep couches and comfortable hassocks you dare not sit down on, the showy beds decked out in overstitched satin and veiled with embroidered muslin, Angès Comar's new shop on the avenue Georges V (just a shout away from YSL) is truly sumptuous. She also has a few attractive gifts.

## Designers Guild

**6th arr.**
**55 rue des Saints-Pères**
**548.90.88**
*Closed Mon. morning.*

This copy of the Trica Guild in London is one of the most exquisite shops in Paris. More than a hundred infinitely matchable fabrics and wallpapers are offered in this warm English home setting. You'll also find carpets; beautiful lamps; and some furniture such as upholstered sofas, coffee tables and rattan armchairs. There are also hassocks, lots of tablecloths, cushions and lampshades made from house fabrics. Fabrics and paper are promptly delivered; note that English measurements are used. Furniture deliveries take four to six weeks.

## Habitat

**1st arr.**
**Forum des Halles, 2nd floor**
**297.51.06**
**15th arr.**
**Centre Maine-Montparnasse, 11 rue de l'Arrivée**
**538.69.90**
**17th arr.**
**35 ave. de Wagram**
**766.25.52**

My Lord! By His Majesty, Terence Conran, this Englishman's habitat is really gorgeous! So gorgeous, in fact, that young French people have become infatuated with this English firm's unending string of stores. There are currently eleven of them in France. What's there to find here? Everything you need to furnish and decorate your home: sofas, tables on casters, lamps, teaspoons, rugs, upholstery fabric, earthenware (supervised by Michel Guérard), iron pots, all of which are conceived in a modern country style at fairly reasonable prices.

## David Hicks

**6th arr.**
**12 rue de Tournon**
**326.00.67**

The harmony and balance typical of England's most famous interior decorator are evident in this pretty shop on the rue du Tournon. Two vast rooms made to look like actual living quarters feature rugs, fabrics, furniture, and practical or decorative objects; they are in perfect taste, luxuriously simple and very expensive.

## Jansen

**8th arr.**
**9 rue Royale**
**266.51.52**

For its centennial, Jansen has got a new president. Without changing its image—the impression that it concentrates on decorating palaces and stately homes—it has added a diversified line of products such as linens, and four entire floors at the rue Royale location open to the public. The ground floor features only gifts, many of them antiques such as nineteenth-century English objects, often unusual, and always decorative at prices ranging from 100F to 5,000F. On the upper floors, in a succession of showrooms, you'll find replicas of antique chairs and woodwork, art deco furniture, Mies van der Rohe armchairs, Eileen Gray pedestal tables, Breuer tables, and contemporary furniture that mixes well with older styles. The shop also features a wide variety of lamps and lighting fixtures as well as a bridal registry department.

### *Maison et Jardin*
**8th arr.**
**38 rue de Courcelles**
**766.93.50**
*Closed Mon. morning*

This rue de Courcelles shop consists of a series of showrooms, some somber, others well-lit and lively, in which are displayed beautiful indoor furniture designed by Jean Dive's study group. We found the dining tables to be the best of the lot. Other shop at 242 bis blvd. Saint-Germain in the 7th arrondissement.

### *Martine Nourissat*
**1st arr.**
**202 rue Saint-Honoré**
**297.50.67**

This Place du Palais Royal store consists of three spacious and well-lit floors that have been tastefully furnished to look like an authentic house, with a strong emphasis on comfort. You may browse freely and make a selection with the assistance of competent and friendly sales people who seem genuinely concerned with your decorating problems and who will help you solve them. Items for sale include soft upholstered couches, custom-made to your specifications, beautiful printed fabrics by either Martine Nourissat or one of the other top manufacturers, assorted carpets, ornate window blinds, lampstands, curios, and commissioned furniture. Home consultation is available. Worthwhile biannual sales whenever Martine Nourissat redecorates the store from top to bottom.

### *Julie Prisca*
**17th arr.**
**12 bis ave.**
**Mac-Mahon**
**380.26.75**
*Closed Mon. morning.*

Julie Prisca has taste, as well as a fondness for fresh colors. She dyes and designs her own fabrics, some in geometric patterns. She also likes lightly veneered wood, and designs her own furniture: notably coffee tables and armchairs, also a soft and beautiful sofa with a back crisscrossed with wooden slats. It's a piece that belongs in the winter garden of a small Florentine palace. You'll also find lovely turned-wood and ceramic lamps and superbly mixed bouquets of dried flowers.

## *FABRICS*

### *Arcasa*
**6th arr.**
**34 rue Bonaparte**
**325.96.25**
*Closed Mon.*

You'll find a thorough selection of the best made French and foreign fabrics, as well as lesser known brands, with an accent on conservative masculine prints and geometric patterns. Arcasa will advise and/or decorate your home with carpet, wall coverings, Venetian blinds, curtains, drapings, bedspreads and sofa coverings.

### *Laura Ashley*
**6th arr.**
**94 rue de Rennes**
**548.43.89**

With one showroom (at 34 rue de Grenelle), three stores and a boutique in the Galeries Lafayette (fifth floor)—not to mention a new mail-order sales department (at 198 avenue du President-Wilson, 93210 La Plaine-Saint Denis, tel. 243.49.25)—Laura Ashley keeps up its headlong growth and

**7th arr.**
**22 rue de Grenelle**
**544.63.04**
*Closed Mon. morning.*

improvement while maintaining the high standards to which it owes its success: low-priced beautifully dyed fabrics in solid colors or discreetly patterned prints.

## The Colefax and Fowler Chintz Shop

**6th arr.**
**2 rue du Furstenberg**
**325.66.64**

In this Parisian branch of the well-known Colefax of London, you'll find all sorts of English chintz, linen in solid colors or printed with large flowery motifs, a variety of wallpaper, some of which is designed to match the fabrics, and those very English, very comfortable chairs.

## Les Décora-trices Gour-mandes

**15th arr.**
**118 rue de Lourmel**
**577.87.60**
*Closed Mon.*

This is a good place for young people who are ready to build their nest. You may browse, ask questions, and get expert advice. You'll find a collection of lively-colored quality fabrics at affordable prices. Upon request, house decorators will make curtains, wall coverings and carpets.

## David Hicks

**6th arr.**
**12, rue de Tournon**
**326.00.67**

David Hicks is devoted above all to fabrics. The firm's huge inventory always includes Tarascon percales, in fresh, lively colors, pastels, and geometric prints, which are not too expensive. There are also more durable, gorgeous, English printed calicos and other high-quality, English-made fabrics that can all be dyed to taste. You'll also find a good selection of lines from the best French and foreign fabric manufacturers, ravishing American printed cottons in particular, as well as Fortuny and Rubelli fabrics.

## Natécru

**2nd arr.**
**39-41 galerie Vivienne**
**260.46.85**
*Closed Mon. morning*

Located in a renovated mall, this conservative but superb store features Patrick Frey's upholstery fabric line. Solid colors only, in natural tones such as white, beige and brown, with a wide selection of piques, velvets, silks, lamés and figured materials.

## Martine Nourissat

**1st arr.**
**202 rue Saint-Honore**
**297.50.67**

In this showroom outlet, fabrics are admirably displayed in simulated home settings incorporating wall coverings, curtains, blinds, couches, and built-in sofas. Some of them, such as the China design (now a classic) and the brand-new Mexican-inspired Leonora have been designed and selected by Martine Nourissat herself.

## Simrane
**6th arr.**
**23 rue Bonaparte**
**345.90.73**

This ravishing little Indian shop alongside the Seine offers exotic handmade Rajasthan printed cotton fabrics that are a marked contrast to the neighboring shops' classic French materials. These superb and exclusive cottons come in fifteen harmonizing patterns. In the beautifully vaulted basement, you'll find hand-embroidered cushions inset with tiny mirrors, as well as a line of table linens, Sheesham folding screens, antique Burmese boxes and Blue Jaipur handpainted doorknobs.

## Sirwy
**6th arr.**
**20 rue de l'Odéon**
**354.03.08**
*Closed Mon.*

Jouy linen and fabric designed from Persian and Indian documents form the end of the eighteenth and beginning of the nineteenth centuries.

## Souleiado
**1st arr.**
**Forum des Halles,**
**2nd floor**
**233.22.14**
*Closed Mon. morning*

With its traditional motifs and refined dyes, Charles Demery's provincial fabrics transcend fashion and are highly suitable for wall coverings, tablecloths, cushions and curtains.

# FURNITURE

## Pierre Cardin Evolution
**8th arr.**
**118 faubourg Saint-Honoré**
**266.24.36**
*Closed Sat.*
**1st arr.**
**2 place due Palais-Royal**
**297.05.00**

We may ruffle a few feathers by saying that contemporary style in France has not inspired any great designers or cabinetmakers. And if today we lack figures like Gallé, Majorelle, Bugatti, Leleu, we at least have a Paul Poiret in the person of Pierre Cardin. You may not appreciate or comprehend the furniture conceived and displayed in his faubourg Saint-Honoré shop, but then, did anybody appreciate Guimard and Mies van der Rohe in their own time? The use of veneers in unusual colors, the extraordinary shapes, the taste for idle luxury, the unexpected materials and techniques, and the limited editions support the statement that this furniture is truly revolutionary, it will never be displayed in supermarkets—the prices will see to that.

## Cassina
**8th arr.**
**168 faubourg Saint-Honoré**
**561.04.17**

This gallery belongs to a famous Milanese cabinetmaker who reproduces prestigious furniture—always contemporary—by Rietveld, Mackintosh and Le Corbusier. Other items include a collection of sofas, chairs, coffee tables and chaise lounges, all of which are very contemporary and sparse, crafted by Italian designers such as Geo Ponti, Gaetano Pesce and Bellini. Prices are steep and you may have to wait four to eight weeks for delivery.

## Castelli
**8th arr.**
**28 rue de Berri**
**359.78.01**

Although it has been a hundred years since the old cabinetmaker Ettore Castelli founded his shop in Bologna, it has only been a few months since the firm bearing his name has hung its shingle over an inlaid, carved-wood temple door in Paris. The Italian firm's superb products are magnificently displayed in the austere premises of its rue de Berri shop. House features include the Angelica White armchair designed by the Dane Paul Khaerholm (1965); Corium straightback chairs by Matteo Grassi; and coffee tables made with glass tops supported by four cubes of marble, travertine or wood. Also featured is luxurious office furniture like the Vertebra line of chairs, mounted on casters, pivoting, adjustable to various heights and capable of incorporating all body movement. There are also conference tables made of koto, an African wood with subtle beige-pink tones, or dark lacquered desks in all sizes, combining wood and leather. All Italian-made.

## Formes Nouvelles
**6th arr.**
**43-45, bd**
**du Montparnasse**
**548.11.65**

These shops sell contemporary, mostly elegant and very comfortable furniture, for the most part reproductions of Le Corbusier, Rietveld and Mackintosh. There are also a few lovely light fixtures. The shop at 168 faubourg Saint-Honoré (8th arr.) specializes in office furniture and furniture for public places. There are clearance sales on remaindered and discontinued furniture. Another location at 22 blvd. Raspail (7th arr.).

## Furnitur - Pierre Sala
**4th arr.**
**56 rue**
**Saint-Louis-en l'Ile**
**633.56.49**
*Open 2:00 P.M. to 7:00 P.M.*

Everybody does a double take or is shocked by the royal blue window display of this Ile St. Louis gallery. Inside the blue, white, and black boutique you'll find an astonishing line of contemporary furniture.

## Grégor
**14th arr.**
**5-7 blvd.**
**Edgar-Quinet**
**320.09.95**
**14th arr.**
**60-80 ave. du Maine**
**260.62.21**

Whether they're square, round, oval or oblong, they all have marble tops—in Carrara white, Greek red, Saint-Laurent black—and wrought-iron legs. They are turn-of-the-century bistro tables, which are constantly being reproduced. Grégor displays them by the dozen, along with their inseparable bentwood bistro chairs in white, black, red, walnut or mahogany, with their cane seats basket-woven or woven in a seashell design.

## Knoll International
**7th arr.**
**268 blvd.**
**Saint-Germain**
**705.74.65**

This big, classy international firm was the first to launch the American Challenge in contemporary furniture. All its furniture and accessories are displayed in decorative arts museums worldwide. Their designers have been the object of biographies and esthetic studies in both trade and general interest magazines. For years these pieces have concentrated on office furniture research in traditional Bauhaus functualism, which, incidentally, has allowed Knoll to conquer the world. His products feature ultimate refinements artistically and technically envisioned by Saarinen, Gae Aulenti and Cini Boeri. Today, Knoll is about to offer in Paris a line of post-modernist furniture, chiefly comprised of couches and tables designed by an architect named D'Urso. It is a line that has been selling successfully in the U.S.

## Manutan
**12th arr.**
**32 bis blvd. Picpus**
**346.12.60**
*Closed Sat.*

For those who appreciate high-tech and its highly abstruse and conceptual furniture geared above all towards industrial use, Manutan has a 425-page catalogue with thousands of products sold on the premises or by mail order, featuring kitchen—(home or restaurant)—sideboards in stainless steel, on casters; dining-hall carts; bookshelves; cabinetmakers' workbenches; and many other objects.

## Mobilier International
**7th arr.**
**8 rue des Saint-Peres**
**260.34.18**

This is one of the largest companies offering furniture and contemporary decor. Permanently on display are Charles Eames' youthful designs, as well as the latest finds by French and foreign designers, such as Pierre Paulin, Michel Boyer and Gerard Gallet. Other locations in the 8th and 11th arr.

## Roche Bobois
**2nd arr.**
**109 blvd. de Sébastopol**
**236.82.55**
**3rd arr.**
**92-98 blvd. de Sébastopol**
**278.10.50**
**7th arr.**
**193 blvd. Saint-Germain**
**222.11.12**

Roche Bobois has the most complete selection of modern home furnishings, from gadgets to opulent couches. These designs are very well made, for big budgets or small, and many can be selected from a catalogue. Generally speaking, the price/quality ratio here is good, but deliveries aren't often delayed. Over the last few years, Roche Bobois has entered the fashion furniture market with its new Provincial stores in which you'll find a wide selection of heavy oak and fruitwood crafted so as to suggest the old days. Although the sales staff isn't always loquacious, you'll find that each piece of furniture is suitably tagged with price, style and type of wood used.

## Garden Furniture

## Barlow Tyrie-Tectona
**14th arr.**
**71 bis rue de Gergovie**
**555.28.24**
*Closed Mon.*

Here you'll find conservative English outdoor furniture superbly made from Burmese teak, the same indestructable wood used both in shipbuilding and street paving a century ago.

## Grégor
**14th arr.**
**5-7 blvd.**
**Edgar-Quinet**
**320.09.95**
**68-80 ave. du Maine**
**260.62.21**

In these shops you'll find only enamel-cast aluminum furniture for summer or winter use in terrace or garden. The furniture is patterned with curved, countercurved, lattice work, scallops and astragals and comes in rococo, neo Louis XV, 1900 and Victorian styles. Also sold by catalogue mail order.

## Un Jardin en Plus
**1st arr.**
**44 rue Saint-Denis**
**233.00.68**
**7th arr.**
**224 blvd.**
**Saint-Germain**
**548.25.71**

Simple or intricately designed, like fine lace, this furniture brings to mind charming colonial verandas and winter gardens of beautiful turn-of-the-century homes. The collection includes sofas, deck chairs, lounge chairs, armchairs, pedestals, and coffee tables, all made from willow, bamboo or rattan, either untreated or shellacked.

## Maison et Jardin
**7th arr.**
**242 bis blvd.**
**Saint-Germain**
**222.06.01**
*Closed Mon. morning*

The furniture here is meant to be used in the garden or terrace from May to September. It is made from resin, wood, rattan or enameled metal. It's solid, elegant, well-made and no more expensive than elsewhere. Each winter, Maison et Jardin rotates it with a display of indoor furniture and decorative items.

# KITCHEN

## La Carpe
**8th arr.**
**14 rue Tronchet**
**742.73.25**
*Closed Mon. morning*

This traditional store has long been known for its extensive line of sturdy articles such as pots and pans, electrical appliances, and other kitchenware.

## Dehillerin
**1st arr.**
**18 rue Coquillière**
**236.53.13**

An elderly fellow we know who would never set foot in his kitchen, a long time ago bought for his darling Clementine, (or was it Constance?), a set of pots made of nickel, a costly investment at the time, meant to be used with care. Does this mean that the Dehillerin firm, which has been supplying top-notch chefs for over 150 years, is truly innovative in offering new copper and nickel-plated cookware? It's hard for us to say. There are saucepans in six sizes; round and oval stewpots in 3 sizes; oval, round or sauté dishes, with handle; oval or round frying pans and stewpots; and utensils made from noble materials—copper and nickel—that have several undeniable advantages despite their high price. The melting point for nickel is 1,450°C, much higher than that of tin, which is only 180°C, and the insides of these pans never need replating. When we asked if they ever have sales they replied, "Of course not. Our wares are above the changing whims of fashion." In fact, you'll find that the marvelous Halles store ground floor and basement are stacked to the rafters with thousands of waffle and kugelhopf irons, frying pans, all sorts of pots, preserving bowls, braising pans, Napoleon III-styled knives and cooking instruments modified by Loubet, all made of cast-iron, copper and tin plate. Unless you arrive when the store opens at 8:00 A.M. and do your shopping before 10:00 A.M. you can forget about courteous treatment or advice.

## Tout pour la Cuisine

**3rd arr.**
**108 rue**
**Vieille-du-Temple**
**887.60.00**
*Closed Mon.*

Tourists find this Marais shop fascinating. Since 1832 it has featured only the finest cookware. The charming Mme Sanoner and her staff will only offer wares that eet their strict standards of high quality. They feature magnificent, though terribly expensive, silverplated copper baking and stew pans that can go directly from the oven to an elegantly laid table. There is also a set of less expensive galvanized copper cookware, 2.5 centimeter thick, which is an absolute must for simmering good dishes. You'll aslo find countless authentic pans made of nickel, stainless steel or enamel. (Did you know that the height of a good pan should be equal to its radius plus one centimeter?) There are more than twenty varieties of stainless cutlery, percolators and pastry tables. The company also holds sales with 12%, 15% or 20% markdowns—clearly indicated by the tags on each item.

# LIGHTING

## Delisle

**3rd arr.**
**4 rue du Parc-Royal**
**272.21.34**
*Closed Sat.*

A pair of Delisle bracket lamps made at the start of this century were mistakenly sold as genuine Louis XV items at a recent auction outside Paris. That should give you an idea of this firm's premium-quality reproductions. Judge for yourself by walking through the exhibit hall at Canillac Hotel, located at the center of the Marais. You'll see nearly 2,000 designs (antique reproductions made only from finely gold-plated bronze or wrought iron), such as chandeliers, bracket lamps, girandoles, candalabra and lanterns. Delisle also specializes in custom projects like the Ecouen Museum, the Palace at Versailles, the Imperial Palace for Foreign Guests in Tokyo, the George V Hotel and the Laurent restaurant.

## Electrorama

**5th arr.**
**11 blvd.**
**Saint-Germain**
**329.31.30**
*Closed Sat.*

Electrorama has a very large selection of all makes of contemporary lamps. Saint-Germain Lumière, which is its own brand, will custom-make special orders. They also have iodic lamps, desk and reading lamps, Scandinavian hanging lamps, Japanese rice paper globes, Murano glass ceiling lamps, decorative lamps, luminous eggs and all kind of spotlights, garden and terrace lights. You'll find expert advice for resolving your lighting problems.

### Renon
**3rd arr.**
**13 rue Payenne**
272.04.15
*Closed Sat.*

Located in the Châtillon Hotel (formerly the Lude Hotel) in the Marais district, this boutique houses one of the most prestigious antique collections of lighting fixtures and ironwork. You'll find here beautiful, costly stylized reproductions of lighting fixtures of various periods. They will restore light fixtures and bronzework.

# LINENS

### Au Bain Marie
**2nd arr.**
**4 rue du Mail**
260.17.78
*Closed Mon.*

Aude Clément has more than one card up her sleeve. For delightful antique table objects, check out her No. 2 rue du Mail shop. For household linen, go next door to No. 4. Her collection consists of organdy, toile, cotton and linen cloths in white, ecru or pastel tones—you won't see any mixed, printed or flower patterns here—which an invisible team of little hands embroider with designs found in early twentieth-century catalogues. Merchandise includes large and small tablecloths, placemats, napkins, sheets and headrests, all of which are scalloped or embroidered in matching or contrasting colors and inset with lace. Goods are reasonably priced; there are also a few beautiful antique linens.

### Sophie Canovas
**6th arr.**
**5 place Furstenberg**
326.89.31

In Sophie Canovas's superb boutique, a dazzling white prevails from the floor and walls to the square paneled glass windows. Fortunately, the light is somewhat softened by venetian blinds. This setting is the perfect showcase for the collection of household linen designed by her husband, Manuel Canovas. You'll find lovely sheets, bedspreads, padded headrests, towels, matching bath towels and floor mats, tablecloths and placemats. Exquisite informal garments include kimonos, tunics and low-heeled slippers. Accessories include laundry bags with watermelon designs, dressing cases and coordinated bathroom accessories with shell prints, pillows and boxes. Both the shop and its sales staff are charming.

### La Châtelaine
**16th arr.**
**170 ave. Victor-Hugo**
727.44.07
*Closed Mon.*

This remarkable shop has a fine collection of classic household linens, such as luxurious sheets made of delicate cotton either printed or embroidered. Even more luxurious are sheets made of linen or natural silk. There are also towels (solid, printed or embroidered) and deluxe handsewn, embroidered tablecloths made of organdy or damask (either white or in colors) that come in all sizes. It's the only place we know that offers white damask linen tablecloths in very large sizes. The hospitality is up to the standards of the house: perfect.

### Colin
**8th arr.**
**10 rue des Saussaies**
265.45.60
*Closed Sat.*

This is a very old shop that sells household linens from another era, which is to say, linens of the highest quality. Their wares include pantry and kitchen linen, butlers' aprons, attendants' jackets and gloves, dish towels; items for the bedroom or table such as large delicate sheets made of pure linen (in white and other colors) and tablecloths, both of which can be custom-made, hand- or machine-sewn, and monogrammed. Equally interesting are the bathrobes, towels and spongy bathroom rugs. There are also classically designed woolen, mohair, camel's hair and cashmere blankets. This is one of Paris's best little establishments.

## *Frette*
**8th arr.**
**48 faubourg Saint-Honoré**
**266.47.70**
*Closed Sat.*

This apartment-boutique, decorated in subtle gray tones, is located on the third floor of a nice building on the faubourg Saint-Honoré. Here is where the great Italian designer exhibits and sells his household linen collection distinguishable by its grape motif, as well as his cashmere, flowered wreaths, satin flowers, violets, motifs. You'll find these designs embroidered in matching colors and designs are used on his terry-cloth towels. You'll also find lace bed ruffles in pink or pale blue linen, and raw silk solid colored sheets.

## *Noël*
**8th arr.**
**90 rue La Boétie**
**359.66.30**

This remarkable firm was established at the end of the last century by the current owner's grandmother. You'll find here the most beautiful tablecloths embroidered with leaves, flowers, fruit or crisscrossed designs, made from the shop's own organdy. There are also embroidered sheets in delicate linen. Don't be startled at the prices. Given the perfection and detail involved, they are totally justified. And if you're good with a needle and thread and have the time and patience, nothing should stop you from purchasing designs, assorted fabric and embroidery hoops. They will supply you with step-by-step directions. It's no easy task, but think of how much you'll save and the satisfaction you'll get from doing it yourself. Noël provides laundry and ironing services for his customers. And at his recently opened "diffusion" department, you'll find household linen at nearly affordable prices.

## *Porthault*
**8th arr.**
**18 ave. Montaigne**
**720.75.25**

This is the most luxurious linen house in town, specializing in beautiful sheets in raw silk or delicate cambric, and embroidered tablecloths in linen or organdy which invariably wind up on Paris's most elegant tables. There is no need to emphasize that the prices here are up to the high standards of the house. Less expensive are the cases made of house fabrics for jewelry, sewing or shoes. Less attractive are the Monet designed lines created for the opening of the Monet Museum in Giverny.

### *Antique Linen*

## *Le Temps Retrouvé*
**1st arr.**
**6 rue Vauvilliers**
**233.66.17**
*Open 1:00 P.M. to 8:00 P.M.*

This may be your place for embroidered or open-worked sheets, beautiful lace or embroidered antique tablecloths. To complement them there are complete place settings in crystal (by Daum), in china (by Vieux Paris or Limoges), in earthenware (by Choisy or Creil), and a few silver pieces such as tea sets and table sets made at the end of the nineteenth century or during the 1930s (some items sold separately). In this tiny shop, filled with furniture and curios, you'll find the charm implicit in its name. Friendly sales staff.

### La Vie en Rose
**6th arr.**
**27 rue de l'Abbé-Grégoire**
**548.85.81**
*Open 2:00 P.M. to 7:00 P.M.*
*Closed Mon.*

This establishment offers a very pretty line of antique linen including ruffled sheets and pillow cases, tablecloths, cushions and charming old-fashioned bedspreads. A specialty is antique handsewn embroidered curtains made from laced or threaded cotton (Milan, Venice, Richelieu, Ténériffe).

### Le Nid de l'Écureuil
**6th arr.**
**25 rue Bonaparte**
**633.98.71**
*Closed Mon. morning*

#### Patchwork Quilts

This shop is an outlet for the California-based Squirrel's Nest Company. Everything here is made in the U.S.A. including multicolored new and antique quilts, printed placemats, pastel patchwork children's bathrobes and those well-known Osh-Kosh overalls in all colors and sizes up to 14 years old.

### Le Rouvray
**5th arr.**
**1 rue Frederic-Sauton**
**325.00.45**
*Closed Mon.*

Diane Armand Delille offers one of the finest lines of genuine U.S.-made antique quilts in Paris. She also provides everything needed to do patchwork, including a large choice of Early American cotton fabric in solid colors or prints, plastic gauges with which to cut fabrics, patterns, quilting needles, sewing needles and instructions.

# NEEDLEWORKS

### Braquenié
**2nd arr.**
**16 rue Vivienne**
**261.53.94**
*Closed Sat.*

Located in the former seventeenth-century Hôtel Colbert de Torcy, this store offers a marvelous line of rugs, tapestries, antique designs and canvases, as well as all kinds of exclusive needlepoint canvases.

### Brocard
**4th arr.**
**1 rue Jacques-Coeur**
**272.16.38**
*Closed Sat.*

For more than 200 years, this distinguished firm has been restoring antique tapestries and embroideries. It also researches tapestries, prepares canvases from antique documents, and sells finely dyed wools and silks.

### Jeux d'Aiguilles
**1st arr.**
**269 rue Saint-Honoré**
**260.22.19**

Everything related to tapestry and embroidery. This fine establishment offers its own designer's handpainted canvases for recovering seats, making tapestries, panels and cushions, as well as designs for embroidering tablecloths and placemats. Princess Grace of Monaco is a regular customer. There are courses in embroidery and tapestry-making.

### Kell's Corner
**7th arr.**
**94 rue de Grenelle**
**544.64.26**
*Closed Mon. morning*

Charming American tapestries with handsewn motifs full of invention and gaiety. They'd be ideal for a child's room or a country house.

### Tapisserie au Point
**1st arr.**
**128 galerie de Valois**
**261.44.41**
*Closed Sat. afternoon.*

Actors from the Théâtre-Français swarm here to buy the firm's superb wools and contemporary or stylized needlepoint canvases. Doing needlepoint is supposedly a remedy for stage fright. Claudine Brunet also reproduces antique tapestries (especially for armchairs) from old and even dilapidated documents.

### Tassinari et Chatel
**2nd arr.**
**26 rue Danielle-Casanova**
**261.74.08**
*Closed Sat.*

The splendidly decked-out sea-green and mauve Queen's chamber at Versaille is credited to Tassinari and Chatel. What's more, they reproduced the fabrics according to their own fabulous documentation of the palaces' original silks. The artisans who have built Tassinari et Chatel's reputation for the last 300 years are, unfortunately, irreplaceable, but they still offer to their discriminating clientele a wide selection of splendid silks and chain-printed moiré fabrics, which give the designs a muted look.

# SILVER

### Christofle
**2nd arr.**
**31 blvd. des Italiens**
**265.62.43**
**6th arr.**
**93 rue de Seine**
**325.70.73**
**8th arr.**
**12 rue Royale**
**260.34.07**
**16th arr.**
**95 rue de Passy**
**654.51.27**
**And Parly 2**
**954.35.40**
*Closed Mon. except at rue Royale and Parly 2.*

This venerable house was established in the 1830s, and 30 years later was appointed purveyor to Napoleon III. At that time it manufactured only silver-plated metal, something quite unique at the time. For generations Christofle products have ornamented bourgeois and imperial tables, either in solid silver which is manufactured at the Saint-Denis factory, or the silver-plated ware manufactured in Yainville, near Rouen. The tableware, escargot forks, fruit knives, butter knives, lobster forks and ice cream spoons come in thirteen varied designs, and we recommend them all, from the simple patterns which include the unadorned Cluny; to the classic eighteenth-century Chinon with its finely threaded trim; as well as the rococo designs such as the Louis XV styled Marly with asymmetric shells and acanthus leaves.

### Odiot
**8th arr.**
**7 place de la Madeleine**
**265.00.95**

Odiot is one of the only firms in the world to stamp four of its designs from dies that date back to before the French Revolution. Odiot custom-makes any piece of solid silver or silver-gilt plate as well as replicas of its own period designs from the eighteenth and nineteenth centuries. There is also a large choice of French and foreign crystal and china that which will elegantly complement any table.

## Peter
**8th arr.**
**191 faubourg**
**Saint-Honoré**
**563.88.00**
*Closed Mon. morning.*

You'll find only elegant tableware here, such as knives and forks made from wrought steel, solid silver or silver plate, mounted with ebony, ivory or stone handles. The silver-plated Domus design, with its colonial nylon handle, was conceived to endure dishwashers. The knife is priced at 166F, the spoon or fork at 182F.

## Puiforcat
**8th arr.**
**131 blvd Hausmann**
**563.10.21**
*Closed Mon.*

This prestigious, premium-quality establishment located on boulevard Haussmann gets its inspiration from the fabulous silver-plate collection amassed by Louis Victor Puiforcat at the end of the nineteenth century most of the collection is now in the Louvre. The staff of silversmiths, chasers, chiselers, engravers and polishers are capable today of reproducing the most beautiful French silverware pieces, regardless of the period. A set of spoons and forks costs about 850F. The art deco set designed by Jean Puiforcat costs 950F.

# WALLPAPER

## Manuel Canovas
**6th arr.**
**7 place Furstenberg**
**325.75.98**

This showroom (no sales here) offers the entire Canovas wallpaper collection, some of which is also available in fabric. Drop in for some good advice and free samples.

## Myriam
**2nd arr.**
**14 rue**
**Etienne-Marcel**
**236.94.67**
*Closed Sat.*

You can't go wrong here, simply because Myriam never features any one brand, preferring instead to select a wide range of the best English, Swedish, American, Italian and French wallpapers at a variety of prices. Always in discriminating good taste.

## Nobilis
**6th arr.**
**32 and 40 rue**
**Bonaparte**
**329.21.50**
*Closed Sat.*

This firm was established during the Roaring Twenties, yet Nobilis' wallpaper and coverings, as well as Suzanne Fontan's upholstery fabrics, are all conservative, unassuming and distinctive. Located between the place St. Germain des Près and the rue Jacob, these two stores and their six window displays are like picture books designed by the top names in interior decorating (Francois Catroux, Andrée Higgins, Jacques Damiot). At the No. 40 rue Bonaparte location, there's a showroom which is open to the public on Saturdays and which overlooks a lovely courtyard. It features panoramic decor, handprinted wallpaper, traditional motifs, and wall coverings made from Korean grass, hemp, and barley-straw. The sales staff is attentively friendly without being bothersome and the articles are splendidly displayed on moveable panels. Large samples are given away without charge.

### *Antique • Panoramic*

**Jean-Louis Chasset**
5th arr.
6 rue Saint-Victor
326.83.00

This antique dealer's hobby is collecting wallpaper from the eighteenth and nineteenth centuries, with or without friezes, and reproducing it exactly from period plates and documents. Although the patterns are gorgeous, the choice is rather limited, but there's a wide range of assorted colors. Given the superior quality of this handmade and very refined work, we find the prices reasonable and often less expensive than some widely distributed popular Japanese wallpapers.

**Mauny**
16th arr.
25 bis, rue Franklin
553.85.20
*Closed Sat.*

This remarkable house specializes in eighteenth-century reproductions or handprinted, panoramic wallpaper and custom-makes various styles—Louis XVI, Empire—that are optionally sold with friezes and trim. End-of-series sales.

# Image • Sound

## HI-FI, T.V., VIDEO

**Paul Beuscher**
4th arr.
23-29 blvd.
Beaumarchais
271.22.11

All the top brands; U.S.-made speakers and amplifiers, as well as sound systems for orchestras, discotheques and private homes.

**Fnac**
4th arr.
Forum des Halles,
2nd floor
261.81.18
*Closed Mon. (Closed Mon. morning at the Forum)*

Inexpensive goods (20-30% less than elsewhere), highly competent salespeople, and a constant interest in state-of-the-art video equipment make the Fnac's various departments the hottest place in town for competent service and the latest technological developments (with an accent on video). For cassettes, you're better off going to the Montparnasse location than selecting them from the Forum-Fnac catalog. Of course, the store features a customer service department. Other locations in the 6th and 8th arr.

**Hi-Fi Vidéo PLG**
8th arr.
2 rue d'Anjou

You'll find custom-made and highly sophisticated stereo, television, and reel-to-reel tape recorders, all designed and implemented to suit your home by Jean-Paul Gastaud and his team. Furniture (housings, frames,

**265.95.23**
*Closed Mon. morning*

## *Hifissimo*
· **5th arr.**
**59 rue**
**Cardinal-Lemoine**
**329.65.13**
**5th arr.**
**99 rue Monge**
**707.21.36**
**6th arr.**
**37 rue Dauphine**
**633.30.60**
*Closed Mon.*

## *Lido-Musique*
**8th arr.**
**68 Champs-Elysées**
**562.30.86**
*Open until 2:00 A.M. and Sunday afternoons.*

## *SVP Vidéo Club*
**8th arr.**
**14 bis, rue de Berri**
**562.65.54**

cabinets) is made from precious woods, altuglas, steel, glass, and enamel. The sound systems all incorporate the latest electronic gadgets, including remote control.

Less expensive! These three shops offer top-brand stereo systems with slight flaws in handling and/or general appearance at marked-down prices. All sold at 35%-60% off with a one-year manufacturer's warrantee for parts and labor.

Although its prices are high, Lido-Musique offers one of the largest video-cassette departments in Paris. Nearly 2,500 titles from which to choose.

This is one of Paris's "video meccas." Not only will owner Sergio Gobbi offer you his video production experience, he'll also offer you advise in filmmaking. His shop features sales and rentals of video-cassettes only.

# *PHOTO*

## *Cipière*
**11th arr.**
**26 blvd.**
**Beaumarchais**
**700.37.25**
*Closed Mon.*

## *Fnac*
**4th arr.**
**Forum des Halles,**
**2nd floor**
**261.81.18**
**6th arr.**
**136 rue de Rennes**
**544.39.12**
**8th arr.**
**26 ave. de Wagram**
**766.52.50**
*Closed Mon. (Closed Mon. morning at the Forum).*

This is a collector's shop in which used goods have been sold or exchanged since 1888. Good wares, good advice, repairs.

You'll find a very good selection of top brands at 20 percent off, plus a 2 percent discount for Fnac members. The customer service department is thoroughly efficient. Also featured are all kinds of equipment for processing and developing film. The Fnac-Étoile store offers free beginners' courses (in groups of eight) for black-and-white and/or color darkroom developing. Some of the Fnac outlets in the Metro offer film, movie cartridges, blank cassetes, and will develop film.

### Optas
**8th arr.**
**71 rue de Rome**
**522.60.37**

For nearly 50 years this curious little shop has been the only one in Paris to sell and rent military optical instruments, including binoculars, compasses, sextants, and even bronze periscopes and binoculars. Most of them are NATO surplus wares. Also featured are fatigues, parachutes and other military attire.

### Photo Mayet

**6th arr.**
**4 rue Mayet**
**567.97.96**
*Closed Mon.*

To your right, upon entering, you'll see Jean-Christophe Doerr, a young professional photographer who develops both black-and-white and old-fashioned sepia-toned prints. To the left, you'll see long shelves jam-packed with antique items such as camera shutters, photographic plates, prismatic machines for drawing, tripods, camera bellows and conically shaped enlarges, and countless other venerable accessories, plus a few magic lanterns, 1890s technical manuals, superb daguerreotypes and other age-old prints.

### Pierre Bris
**93100**
**Montreuil-sous-Bois**
**35 rue de la**
**Mare-a-l'Ane**
**287.13.41**
*By appt. only, until 12:00 midnight.*

Pierre Bris is both founder and president of the Niepce-Lumière Club, a non-profit organization for collectors who research and preserve photographic equipment and cinematographic documents. He also buys, sells and trades cameras, movie cameras, antique projectors, magic lanterns, books and reviews.

### Shop-Photo Mont- parnasse

**14th arr.**
**33 rue du**
**Cdt-Mouchotte**
**320.15.35**
*Closed Mon. morning.*

This gigantic photo-cinema complex is probably the largest in Europe, if not the world. In this 1,700-square-meter space you'll find top-brand products and accessories from Leica, Nikon, Canon, Pentax, Olympus and Minolta. Given this enormous choice, each brand has its individual counter and sales representatives so as not to baffle consumers. The overall prices are the same as at the Fnac. Other departments feature equipment rentals, a well-documented library, second-hand equipment with six months' guarantee, parts and labor, and an open-house photo gallery (with slide and super-8 projections). Black-and-white film takes two hours to develop; color, six hours.

### Vidéo House
**16th arr.**
**178 ave. Victor-Hugo**
**505.97.17**
*Closed Mon. morning. Open Sun. morning.*

In this modern shop you'll find a few popular stereo systems and some state-of-the-art television equipment like video recorders, cinema classics (prices range from 6,000F–20,000F) and laser beam projectors, enabling you to produce TV images on large screens (26,500F).

## RECORDS

### Clémentine
**6th arr.**
**89 blvd. du**

A very large selection of out-of-print and difficult to find records from Europe and the U.S. is available from these former wholesalers who are now import specialists. The

**Montparnasse**
**548.18.35**
*Open daily until 1:00 A.M.*

store is well-stocked, and you may make special orders. They carry all kinds of music except for classical. You'll find a few records on sale, though nothing spectacular, and there are weekly promotions for new releases. The competent and efficient sales staff are more helpful than the posted record charts. The cassettes, video tapes and video-cassettes selection is rather small. Also featured is a ticket sales outlet for large concert events.

## Fnac
**4th arr.**
**Forum des Halles,**
**2nd floor**
**261.81.18**
**6th arr.**
**136, rue de Rennes**
**544.39.12**
**8th arr.**
**26 ave. de Wagram**
**766.52.50**
*Closed Mon. (Closed Mon.*
*morning at the Forum).*

Unless you're looking for an out-of-stock, highly exotic or rare record, you'll find all kinds of records at incredibly low prices in all three Fnac stores—particularly at the Forum des Halles location. All this accounts for the department's weekend rush and packed listening booths, as well as for the chronic unavailability of the relatively competent sales staff. The store also features a concert ticket sales outlet, and a fine selection of cassettes. Membership discounts.

## Les Mondes du Jazz
**1st arr.**
**2 rue de la**
**Petite-Truanderie**
**233.63.42**

Daniel Richard, that marvelously knowledgeable critic, has bought the Lido-Musique jazz collection. Along with his manager, George Wagner, he recently set up shop across the street from the marvelous Pharamond. The somberly elegant shop, predominantly white, accented with black, is brightened by the warm colors of the record covers. Here the jazz lover record collector will be in heaven because of the shop's exclusive jazz selections and the inventory of 10,000 records covering 6,000 categories. The prices are more or less the same as in the Fnac which is next door. Les Mondes du Jazz (the name is taken from a famous André Hodeir song) has set a goal of becoming the most comprehensive outlet for rarities in France. Bizarre records, long forgotten or deemed impossible to find, will be unearthed no matter what it takes! Their racks are already filled with special-request albums from the U.S. and Japan, as well as from other European countries. There are albums from Australia. Some people have a vocation, others an avocation. Thank heaven for the latter.

## Music Action
**6th arr.**
**15 carrefour**
**de l'Odeon**
**326.09.72**

A wide selection of American free-jazz and rock; you may order U.S. records at no extra cost. Also featured are small independent English and American labels. The prices are affordable; there is a remarkable listening booth and a highly competent sales attendant. The sales are well worth a visit.

## Nuggets

**8th arr.**
**30 ave. George-V**
**723.51.14**

This is an electronic media supermarket with turnstiles at the entrance and closed circuit cameras. You will be searched on your way out, but other than that, you're allowed to walk around at leisure, with a basket in your hands and music in your ears (thanks to headphones),

*Closed Mon. morning. Open Fri. until 9:00 P.M.*

among video screens, neon lights, electric games, coin-operated pastry machines, badges, gadgets, and concert tickets, dispatched under the folds of the American flag. The selection of records and cassettes is more or less standard (if not limited) despite the multiple samples featured in each department. You won't be able to listen to cassettes but the sales staff is here to recommend good records and discourage you from buying bad ones.

## Pan
**6th arr.**
**176 blvd.**
**Saint-Germain**
**544.43.95**
*Open 10:00 A.M. to 11:30 P.M. Closed Mon.*

Guy Millètre's admirable selection of records has been recently enhanced with interesting imports and a few re-issues of long-lost great voices. Formerly at the Conservatory (he won a first prize in musicology), he offers highly competent advice. The shop also features stereo systems, video machines and high-quality (and high-priced) TVs. Ten percent discount for students.

## Pannonica
**6th arr.**
**3 rue Racine**
**329.81.39**
*Closed Mon. morning.*

Named after one of Thelonius Monk's most beautiful compositions, this shop, owned by Jacques Charmeteau and Philippe Labrot, offers unexpected treasures, including rare editions, used records and imported LPs for collectors and fervent aficionados of jazz who are perpetually in search of "unfindable" recordings. Bulletins indicate monthly concert events as well as information pertinent to reputedly unavailable records.

## Le Phono-graphe
**9th arr.**
**73 rue Blanche**
**526.22.22**
*Closed Mon.*

It would be unfair to deprive our readers knowledge of the whereabouts of this invaluable shop. It was revealed to us by the music-loving wine-master at the Grand Véfour. Yet, by creating a rush on this place, we realize you may no longer find those fabulous "early" recordings we were able to listen to. In any case, this shop, with its strange outdoor façade and charming listening quarters, features a sufficient number of treasures for everyone. These include exceptional performances (Kristoff, Flagstad), the otherwise unavailable Tristan (von Karajan directs, with Hans Hotter in the leading role) at 45F per LP, as well as other incredible 78 rpm collectors' items, featuring, for instance, Lauritz Melchior.

## Vittoz
**9th arr.**
**26 passage Verdeau**
**523.09.54**
*Open from 3:00 P.M. to 7:00 P.M. Closed Mon.*

Vittoz is one of the oldest record dealers in Paris. Its founder, Leon Vittoz, supposedly sold the very first pressings, along with portable hand-cranked phonographs, in city-sponsored booths at trade fairs along the boulevards during the last fifteen years of the preceding century. Jean-François, the last of the Vittoz line, carries on the tradition out of a sense of loyalty and family pride. Whenever he can find them, he sells old records, as well as Merveilleux toy phonographs, invaluable Mickey-phones, and such like. Jean-François also sells antique records (classical music or miscellanea) which must be handled with care when played on all these funny-looking machines.

# *Menswear*

## *ACTIVEWEAR*

### *Au Petit Matelot*
**16th arr.**
**27 ave. de la Grande-Armee**
**500.15.51**
*Closed Mon. morning.*

We would like to point out to all amateur sailors that this is a good-natured port of call where sails are hoisted quietly, where hunting was meant to be a distinguished sport, and where Saumur is a must for the equestrian. Here you'll find an excellent selection of clothes for all those distinguished sports, from pea jackets to riding coats, from lodens to tweed jackets. In brief, you'll find everything for country outings. The reasonable prices won't drown you either. Happy shore leave!

### *Tunmer*
**8th arr.**
**5 place Saint-Augustin**
**522.75.80**
*Closed Mon. morning.*

Although this quality house deals primarily in sports clothes, for skiing, tennis and riding, it also offers casual wear such as sport jackets, shirts, sweaters and trousers. It's always a pleasure to stroll into this diversified store, and now that an agreement has been signed between Tunmer's and Burberry's, there's a strong chance this store will become simply marvelous. Good prices, agreeable staff.

## *BARGAINS*

### *Biderman*
**3rd arr.**
**114 rue de Turenne**
**277.15.20**

At the very end of an ominous hall, there's a vast warehouse filled with clothes. The salesmen there will cling to your coattails—politely, of course—and try to persuade you to replace everything you're wearing. First-rate-ready-to-wear clothes, some with brands they can't advertise, some end-of-lines whose labels have been removed. A vast selection of suits (390F–990F), among which you may find a three-piece tweed for 750F.

### *Cacharel Stock*
**14th arr.**
**114 rue d'Alésia**
**542.53.04**

It's on the first floor of a large, lively and neatly arranged store. The atmosphere is informal, the music soft. This is where Cacharel displays its own marked-down clothes, 35%-50% off for inventory and end-of-line garments of the previous year. Oxford cotton shirts, 105F. English-styled suits, approximately 600F.

### *Michel Colin*
**18th arr.**
**15 rue de la Fontaine-du-But**

The setting here is very tangy. You climb up a small spiral staircase to the roof and follow a long corridor with hardwood floors to an astonishing collection of jackets and classically designed suits. The highlight of your trip will unquestionably be the store's magnificent fabrics,

**264.14.33**
*Closed Sat. afternoon.*

150 percent British—flannels, tweeds, and cashmeres. And the prices are tearfully moderate: suits from 650F, custom-made 1,200F–1,500F. Also, 40%-45% off other luxury items.Tweed jackets (from 300F–400F), two- and three-piece suits in flannel, tweed and other materials (from about 600F–760F).

## Richard Grand
**1st arr.**
**229 rue Saint-Honoré**
**260.58.73**

Beautiful sweaters and cardigans made from cashmere, mohair and alpaca at particularly appealing prices. Overall, they are 30%-50% less expensive.

## Isphording
**1st arr.**
**10 rue Richepanse**
**296.46.67**
*Closed Sat.*

Cashmere only (but camel hair is soon to come) is sold at wholesale prices (30% cheaper on average) by a designer-manufacturer in a lovely boutique at the end of a hallway in an old building. There are lots of classically designed sweaters including V-necks, turtlenecks, and vests in a choice of twenty colors. Especially lovely are the natural tones in beige-grey and light maroon. Depending on size, figure on spending 400F–500F for the single-knits and 550F–630F for the double knits.

## Stock Ouest
**17th arr.**
**204 blvd. Pereire**
**572.27.42**
*Closed Mon. morning.*

A model-turned-business brain offers Daniel Hechter's last-year ready-to-wear clothes with a 40%-50% average discount. There are also shirts, Saint-Laurent or Saint-Clair (from 100F–130F) and lamb's wool sweaters (140F). All garments are well-displayed on racks or shelves and clearly marked. One dressing room only. Alterations extra. Naturally, no exchanges or returns.

## Marks and Spencer
**9th arr.**
**35 blvd. Haussmann**
**742.42.91**

Hurry! Grab a small steel basket and take the escalator to do your shopping at Marks. Rush over to the sweater department where you'll find classically styled knits in lambswool or cashmere. The Saint-Michael brand is truly unbeatable when it comes to price and variety of color. For those of you who hail from eastern Europe, we recommend the Finnish blousons. You won't be disappointed. Elsewhere, you'll find cookies on sale to go with your afternoon tea. Though this store is as drab as a rainy day in its native London, you'll often see little old ladies whose colorful hats cheer the place up.

## Old England
**9th arr.**
**12 blvd. des Capucines**
**742.81.99**

The gentlemen of Old England gave us a "luverly" treat this year. They polished up their storefront like Her Royal Majesty's yacht, and made the Young Man's Shop in the basement worth visiting once again. It merges well with the store's general ambience, even though they seem to have economized on wood. You feel at home. There's a good selection of clothing. You'll find beautiful maroon linen traveling bags as well as plaids, blankets and a number of attractive belts. The ground floor is still the same, with good-quality English imports in clothes and accessories. If Old England did, in fact, listen to the criticisms we made concerning the basement in our last guide, perhaps it will also listen to our suggestions about the way its salesmen dress. We would like to see some of them in colorful pullovers, others in tweeds and the most conservative in blazers! They should represent Old England style. Perhaps some of the older members will soon be up for a well-earned retirement, thus allowing for a breath of fresh air. Don't leave this place without looking at the famous miracle hair lotion from St. Thomas (West Indies), that calls itself Trebig's Bayrum. *Honi soit qui mal y pense* (Shamed be he who thinks evil of it) Old England is worth more than a trip to London.

# READY-TO-WEAR

## Arnys
**7th arr.**
**14 rue de Sèvres**
**548.76.99**

Jean and Michel Grimbert know how to give Arnys that distinctive British look reminiscent of a time when a Rolls-Royce was truly a Rolls-Royce. You have to admire their window displays, their city and country suits, marvelous jackets in tweed and cashmere, their ties and shirts, pullovers and socks. Upstairs is a gentlemen's department which smells of leather and features tweed and jodhpurs. The Grimberts possibly limit themselves by catering to the 40-year-old male. What's more they also offer women elegant and conservative suits and trousers with the same highly successful Arnys Anglo-French style.

## Berdy
**17th arr.**
**79 ave. des Ternes**
**574.35.13**
**12th arr.**
**86 ave. Ledru-Rollin**
**628.18.24**
*Closed Mon.*

Berdy caters to big men—six to seven feet tall. Nothing extravagant, just good, classically cut clothing and sportswear priced according to your size.

## Berteil
**8th arr.**
**3 place**
**Saint-Augustin**
**265.28.52**

Berteil's taste also is distinctly British. Sport jackets, suits, shirts, ties, and pullovers all smell of heather and briar. If you'd like your blazer enhanced with a coat of arms, dear commodore, all you need do is ask. A very attractive selection at competitive prices. Don't be discouraged by the unattractive exterior.

## Boutique pour Lui
**2nd arr.**
**112 rue de Richelieu**
**296.66.12**

This shop features the best from Saint-Laurent, Guy Dormeuil, Christian Dior and Cerruti. Stockbrokers, insurance men, auctioneers and *le Monde* journalists should be delighted to have this Boutique pour Lui next door to their offices. The affable and efficient M. Walker and his sales staff know full-well what they're doing; the average price is 2,000F. Out of sheer curiosity, go see the magnificent turn-of-the-century dressing rooms and staircase. A fine, classic address.

## Burberry's
**8th arr.**
**8-10 blvd.**
**Malesherbes**
**266.13.01**

Burberry's is synonymous with trenchcoat, and has been since 1914, when Sir Thomas invented this unsurpassed garment with the eternally youthful lines. Burberry's has since grown into a conglomerate featuring a whole line of British goods. We recommend, the straight-line, lightweight cotton raincoats, the reversible garments, woolen or cashmere pullovers, the scarves and plaids, the woolen shirts and kilts. Frankly, we find the workmanship is the least impressive aspect of these garments, and the jackets and suits lack that lighthearted British wink we like so much on the Continent. Reasonably priced, given the superior quality.

## Cacharel
**1st arr.**
**5 place des Victoires**
**233.29.88**

Considerable credit is due Jean Bousquet, who has nursed Cacharel since its birth. He has always collaborated with gifted people with respect to his collections, promotions and shop decor, which is quite unique in this particular line of business. He relied on the great interior decorator Gae Aulenti to design his place des Victoires boutique. The result is a cozy, warm atmosphere with flattering lighting. A one-of-a-kind store where you'll find the entire Cacharel line of shirts, sweaters, ties, pants, jackets and blouses. The choice of colors is perfect, the merchandise the best of Cacharel. We'd be all the more satisfied if the same could be said of the service. Prices are comparatively steep.

## Pierre Cardin
**8th arr.**
**59 faubourg**
**Saint-Honoré**
**266.92.25**

Cardin's latest awaits you here—both the best and the bizarre. The entire line of cardinal elegance is represented, with a rather fine selection of accessories. The young sales staff appear to be warm and candid. The prices are no higher than in other top-name boutiques.

## Cerruti 1881

**8th arr.**
**27 rue Royale**
**265.68.72**

We've always had a soft spot for Nino Cerruti, for his enthusiasm, his professional attitude and his talent. If he makes a miracle now and then, he does it with such sincerity that he can hardly be blamed. His boutique is one of the major men's style shops in Paris. We recommend all his clothes and flannels (though the colors aren't nearly as interesting as they used to be): the super lightweight wools and the cottons (1,950F–2,950F), the sport jackets, sweaters, and cardigans are both classical and forceful. All are superb. Again, we can't recommend the shirts; the collars don't seem right. As a substitute for the classic dinner jacket, you'll find original and amusing evening attire. The window displays tempt you to touch the sumptuous leather goods inside—though the prices are certainly out of reach—and try on the imported hats.

## Christian Dior

**8th arr.**

Christian Dior has a new director for his men's fashion division. We attended the debut of his new collection and saw some very fine designs. It appears that CD Hommes are getting livelier. Beautiful materials are

**30 ave. Montaigne**
**723.54.44**

being used in sweaters, ties and shirts. The shoes are elegant and, on the whole, the clothing is now less stark and more appealing.

## *Em-Manuel*
**8th arr.**
**16 rue La Boétie**
**267.47.26**
**17th arr.**
**30 ave. de la**
**Grande-Armée**
**380.09.30**

Summer in winter: If you're dreaming of sun and plan on celebrating Christmas in Bahia, drop in at Em-Manuel's for a lightweight suit—an elegant must for those tropical heat waves—before you take off. Sunshine prices.

## *Givenchy Gentleman*
**8th arr.**
**8 ave. George-V**
**723.44.40**

It's stating the obvious to say that Hubert de Givenchy is one of fashion's great men; his personality is faithfully reflected in his little boutique. The selection of designs, materials and accessories is scrupulous. Why, then, is it always empty every time we go in? It's a total mystery, for the prices are the same as in comparable boutiques. Well worth a visit.

## *Daniel Hechter*
**1st arr.**
**Forum des Halles,**
**1st floor**
**297.46.31**
**6th arr.**
**blvd. Saint-Germain**
**326.96.36**

Daniel Hechter's style is to be found first and foremost in the design of his various shops. It's a well-known fact that he's a sportsman, and he has adapted his designs to a very casual lifestyle, together with his accessories. Don't forget to look at his overcoats and more functional attire. The prices are competitive, and the staff knows its business in each of the shops.

## *Lanvin 2*
**1st arr.**
**2 rue Cambon**
**260.38.83**

Lanvin 2's spirit is somewhat classic, and its collection rather limited. This year you'll find the complete Lanvin Diffusion collection, and we enjoyed some of the designs offered by M. Victor and his staff. Fine quality at reasonably high prices.

## *Ted Lapidus*
**6th arr.**
**52 rue Bonaparte**
**326.87.84**
**8th arr.**
**Galerie du Claridge**
**359.98.68**

In all of the Lapidus boutiques you'll find the same atmosphere, the same styles and the same accessories, with all their qualities and defects. A few drinks, though, and you won't even notice them. The prices are reasonable. Those who enjoy wearing monogrammed labels will find themselves in paradise, even if their initials aren't T.L. The blazers, safari jackets and suits are all worth seeing, but the ties and shirts are somewhat outdated. Friendly sales staff.

## Marcel Lassance
6th arr.
17 rue du Vieux-Colombier
548.29.28

An open letter to Marcel Lassance: Sir, our compliments for having contributed with tact, taste and discretion to the sartorial transformation of our new President, who, it is true, could hardly have chosen a right-bank tailor. Thus, though you were once the darling of fashion-conscious women, your destiny has now taken another course. Congratulations! We have always had a preference for the Italian and English wares in your store. We love the lightweight raincoats made from water-resistant cotton, the pullovers, the polos, the Italian leathers, the trousers, the casual sport jackets and the well-chosen accessories. All these are far more appealing than your personalized collections, even though they have been improved this season. Your garments are well priced, and your neck-ties far superior to those of Karl Lagerfeld, who has never learned to tie the knot correctly.

## Renoma
16th arr.
129 bis, rue de la Pompe
727.13.79
*Closed Mon. morning.*

You may not like the bazaar-like atmosphere at Renoma, but it's always lively and has a good selection to choose from. Also, Michel and his staff always know how to recommend their merchandise without going overboard. Attractive and well-made windbreakers, sport jackets, raincoats and sweaters. Reasonable prices and, once Michel gets to know you, they're always negotiable.

## Saint-Laurent Rive Gauche
6th arr.
12 place Saint-Sulpice
326.84.40

This is the only men's store that belongs to the great M. Yves himself. Thus, if something bothers you, you can always write him personally. With this out of the way, you'll find that this rather somber shop offers a fine selection of very attractive garments approved by M. Yves. Classically designed suits from 2,300F; custom-made (2nd floor), 7,000F. Fine-looking accessories and a few nice shoes, socks and shirts. If it's lighters or watches you want, you'll find them in the YSL bazaar. Friendly sales staff.

## Sport et Climat
7th arr.
223 blvd. Saint-Germain
548.80.99

If you're dreaming of taking a cruise to Africa or to the South Seas, or planning a safari, this shop, in mid-winter, will provide you with just the right soldier-of-fortune clothing for those hot, hot sands. Tropical prices.

## Sulka
4th arr.
2 rue de Castiglione
260.38.08

Although married to its glorious past, this store is seriously attempting a comeback. Once in a while, you'll find some stunning Italian garments, only to find nothing the following day. They are still too dependent on the Grand Hotel styles. Grand Hotel prices.

## Ungaro
8th arr.
2 ave. Montaigne
723.61.94
*Closed Mon.*

This men's store used to be somewhat deserted until suddenly Emanuel woke up and presented a fine collection of sportswear. Sensible prices, simple yet durable fabrics, with an attractive but limited selection. We hope Ungaro will keep at it. You'll find some less interesting suits.

### Valentino
8th arr.
17 ave. Montaigne
723.64.17

You could walk out of here looking just like the male models in Italy's *Uomo Vogue* magazine. This is not the complete Valentino line, but you'll find some good stuff from it. Steep prices for the limited choice.

## SHIRTS

### Charvet
1st arr.
8 place Vendôme
260.30.70

This is Ali Baba's favorite cave, lined with 4,000 shirts. The richly colored and unique poplin designs are laid out as if they were valuable treasures. M. Colban's critical eye lights up with pleasure every time he absentmindedly strokes a silk shirt. Considering its premium quality and finish, a Charvet shirt is an investment these days. Perfection at any price. You'll also find all sorts of colorful and silky accessories, including handkerchiefs, ascots, briefs, ties and bathrobes. The store is a feast for the eye and well worth a visit, even if the atmosphere is a bit stuffy at times.

### Bernard Gaillet
16th arr.
129 blvd. Murat
288.08.58

Bernard Gaillet's workshop is not all that impressive, but he's delightful. His workshop is behind the boutique and is filled with beautiful fabrics from England, France and Italy. He'll design any collar you like: Italian, Brooks Bros., button-down collars, or Parisian. Everything here is handmade and beautifully finished. Shirts range from 465F to 590F depending on fabric. All it takes is one fitting, a fifteen-day wait, and if you order a dozen shirts, you'll get an extra one free with Bernard Gaillet's warmest thanks.

## SHOES

### Bally
2nd arr.
35 blvd. des Capucines
261.67.34

There are several Bally shops in Paris. We prefer the one on boulevard des Capucines for its Swiss-made shoes, a good investment by today's standards. The store has a tired look, though it's agreeable enough, and Lurçat's tapestry will certainly be a museum piece in the next fifty years. Good quality-to-price ratio.

### Cartier
8th arr.
23 rue des Mathurins
265.25.85

The perfect address for those who love English footwear such as Church and the new classic-cut Piccadilly, Australian kangaroo loafers and shoes from the U.S. Warm reception.

### Carvil
8th arr.
22 rue Royale
260.23.06

Carvil always retains an aura of the golden days of its youth. Even if Mme Rolande is no longer there at the rue Pierre-Charron shop (we miss her smile and warmth), Carvil is still tempting for our feet. Good classical selection and premium quality. Prices fairly steep.

### Robert Clergerie
6th arr.
5 rue du Cherche-Midi
548.75.47
*Closed Mon. morning.*

You don't have to tilt with windmills for a new pair of shoes. The handsome Unic collection awaits you chez Robert. They are durable and elegant. Worth a visit for its prices and friendly staff.

### Charles Jourdan
6th arr.
62 rue de Rennes
548.79.01

This top French shoe manufacturer offers you a great collection of classic designs, good quality boot and, during summer, a remarkable line in linen. All they need to do is bring down the prices for it to be a perfect shop.

### John Lobb-Hermès
8th arr.
24 faubourg
Saint-Honoré
265.24.45

Hermès has joined the world's greatest shoemaker, John Lobb of London. Provided you have the means, you will be greeted on the second floor by M. Dickinson and his staff. The custom-made shoes sell for 5,000F to 6,000F and there is a three-month waiting period. The ready-to-wear shoes sell for approximately 2,000F. You'll find the reputed Hermès loafers in the Hermès-Hommes department. They may well be more expensive than other comparable shoes, but their design is sheer perfection and they last forever.

### Messageries
1st arr.
6 place
Sainte-Opportune
233.80.44

The marvelous solid or two-toned Cole Haan shoes are as worthy of Fred Astaire's feet as yours. You'll feel home on the range in these boots that the Navaro Brothers' make in El Paso, Texas. We also recommend Trickers classically cut English shoes for sensitive feet, as well as the classical American loafers. Prices vary according to exchange rates. A fine address, though at times untidy and in need of a vacumming.

### El Paso Booty
1st arr.
79 rue Saint-Denis
233.42.07

El Paso Booty evokes the wide-open spaces and the opening of the West. You could ride off into the sunset in these boots of ordinary leather, or of ostrich, sharkskin, lizard, antelope or buffalo. Prices vary between 349F–1,800F. Fine labels such as Sanders and Montana are to be found here. Don't forget to look at the accessories. A great place for weekend and holiday cowboys.

### Tanino Crisci
8th arr.
40 rue Francois-ler
723.86.25

After setting up shop in Milan, Rome, Florence, Tokyo and Osaka, Tanino has at long last opened a classically designed shop, rich in leathery scents, in Paris. There is not a large selection, but for boot-lovers they're beautiful. You'll also find boots at 950F that are truly marvelous. *The* address for elegant footwear.

### Weston
8th arr.
114 Champs-Elysées
562.26.47
17th arr.
98 blvd. de
Courcelles
763.18.13

Weston is still one of the great quality shoe merchants and offers one of the best quality-to-price ratios in all of Paris. We are always amazed by the high sheen on the shoes displayed in the windows. You are sure to find your dream shoes here because Weston's large selection is perfect, at a time when traditional footwear is experiencing a comeback. We still prefer the shop on the Champs-Elysées.

# SWEATERS

### Abercombie
6th arr.

No, this isn't the famous old Abercrombie and Fitch outfit. There's an R missing in the name, notice? However, it's

**38 rue du Bac**
**548.48.85**
*Closed Mon. morning.*

amusing to see the Paul Stuart logo all over the shop. You'll find excellent sweaters, socks and shirts here. Abercombie is part of a new generation of boutiques that are well worth visiting.

## Benetton
**2nd arr.**
**28 rue**
**Danielle-Casanova**
**261.16.66**

Here, there, everywhere! A string of shops overflowing with sweaters in the most colorful patterns ever seen. Simple designs include V-necks, crew-necks, turtlenecks, cardigans and polos. The few shirts, trousers and jackets in sporty fabrics match the sweaters. Benettons are truly the best in their field and have easily won-over France with their quiet, but dynamic invasion. Ideal prices. Various locations.

## Hilditch & Key
**1st arr.**
**252 rue de Rivoli**
**260.36.09**

We're astonished the salesmen here haven't got that baffling, snobbish Oxonian English accent appropriate to Her Majesty's diplomats. Their merchandise is certainly top-drawer. Cashmeres in all sizes and styles, camel's hair, alpaca, Ancient Madder silk and Scottish thread are the quality products used by this firm, the most authentic shirtmaker in Paris. And you won't be disappointed by the scarves, ascots and handkerchiefs. A real haven for Anglophiles. The prices are steep but don't miss out on the store's twice-yearly sales.

## Missoni
**6th arr.**
**43 rue du Bac**
**548.38.02**

If you ever dream of being offered a Missoni garment, give your lady-love the above address. It would be insane for you to spend all that money yourself. Let her go broke buying you that unique woolen garment in M. and Mme Missoni's marvelous styles, colors, and prints.

# TAILORS

## André Bardot
**16th arr.**
**19 ave. de la**
**Grande-Armée**
**500.25.02**

M. André Bardot is president of the Syndicated Chamber of Master Tailors of Paris and likes to add that a custom suit lasts at least ten years and that he does everything the way they did it back in the Middle Ages; i.e., by hand. If you would like a tailored suit of armour, dear knight, it will cost you 4,000F–6,000F.

## Marcel Bur
**8th arr.**
**138 faubourg**
**Saint-Honoré**
**359.45.68**

Good old Marcel remains faithful to his miracle fabric, saxbury, in assorted and updated colors. The ambiance of his establishment is that of a good classic designer. He is convincing, affable and knows how to stitch (and double-stitch)! A sexy-looking saxbury costs 3,700F. Don't forget to take a look at the cashmeres on the ground floor.

## Camps de Luca
**8th arr.**
**11 place de la**
**Madeleine**
**265.42.15**

Watch out! This man's dangerous! Yes, this dear old M. Mario de Luca, who rules unchallenged over this honorable house, may very well bewitch you. He is like a Luciano Pavarotti when he sings about his tailoring, his fabrics, his unexcelled workmanship, and the expertise of his workshops. You may very well walk out of his shops with three suits, each costing 7,000F. They're superb. They're Camps de Luca and you'll look great when you show up at La Scala!

## Cifonelli
**8th arr.**
**31 rue Marbeuf**
**225.38.84**
*Closed Sat. afternoon.*

"Give me the ugliest man in the world, the most deformed, a hunchback! I, Arturo, will transform him into a Don Juan." This, apparently, was an anecdote circulating in Rome before Arturo Cifonelli decided to set up shop in Paris. A Cifonelli suit molds to your body: the shoulder line, the collar and the back are tailored for a man-about-town look. These creations are so supple as to make you forget you're wearing them, with the understatement that makes for the elegance. Of course, he uses only the best fabrics. The only thing his boutique lacks is a good Italian interior decorator like Pinto. The carpet is so bright it could blind you. The prices? Oh, 7,000F. Well worth it, if you've got it.

## Courtès
**8th arr.**
**33 rue Marbeuf**
**225.04.81**

Courtès is recommended for large and small paunches. The tailor's shears have been handed down for three generations, and so have the styles. Traditional work in a very traditional setting. Two-piece suits retail for 5,500F. English fabrics.

## Feruch
**8th arr.**
**35 rue Francois-Ier**
**723.46.32**

Even as a child Gilbert had a way with the scissors. As he grew up he remained true to his gift and is certainly now one of the best tailors of his generation. In his combined custom and ready-to-wear shop at the rue François-Ier, he'll fit you to a T and tell you all about it. Gilbert is very talkative, but what talent! Prices from 5,500F.

## Mano-New Market
**8th arr.**
**38 rue de Penthièvre**
**562.07.09**

Mano, the last of the Dinopoulos line, greets you like a prince in his modest, little, boutique. Large sizes are his specialty, and you won't be disappointed (from 4,000F). The same goes for the made-in-England accessories which adorn the shop.

## Opelka Santos
**16th arr.**
**26 ave. Kléber**
**500.68.48**
*Closed Sat. afternoon.*

Formerly called Opelka (after a Viennese), Cumberland (an Englishman) & De Backer (a Dane). The firm has retained the Viennese surname, adding the name of Jose Santos to its sign (a Southerner, no doubt). The newcomer has transformed this pleasant street-level shop on the rue Kléber. M. Alexandre, who presides over the destiny of this honorable firm with a glorious past, has given this young man his chance by making him a full partner of his renowned firm. Beautiful, perfectly cut fabrics. Average prices for a three-piece suit: 6,000–6,500F.

## Paul Portes
**1st arr.**
**rue de Rivoli**
**260.55.34**
*Closed Sat.*

Paul Portes comes from a long line of tailors. The Portes know how to project the gentleman-farmer look, small wonder M. Paul enjoys meeting people amid the foliage of the Jardin des Tuileries. The choice of English fabrics, the quality of work and the classic cut with the Portes touch all contribute to this excellent tailor's smart look. Average price is 6,000F.

### Smalto
**8th arr.**
**44 rue Francois-Ier**
**720.70.63**
**16th arr.**
**5 place Victor-Hugo**
**500.48.64**

The boutique on the second floor of the rue François-Ier is Francesco's kingdom. He is one of the most gifted master-tailors and innovators Paris has ever had. The Smalto style is moderately extravagant good taste. This same style, of course, can be seen in all the ready-to-wear clothes and accessories—including sweaters, shirts, shoes, hats,—even if its Italian appeal is sometimes overdone. In any case, there is a vast selection, and depending on your taste, you should be satisfied in this pleasantly lit, lively boutique, where you are very well received by a highly competent staff.

# Sports

### Boisseau
**8th arr.**
**8 rue Clément-Marot**
**720.68.27**
*Closed Sat. afternoon.*

Boisseau is a lovely shop in a traditional Scottish decor. As indicated on the shop sign, these golf specialists have been selling golfing equipment for fifty years. They have all the top international brands. Putting green (free) and golf lessons (60F apiece) in the basement.

### Boutiques Lacoste
**6th arr.**
**44 rue Saint-Placide**
**222.27.33**
*Closed Mon. morning.*

Here you'll find the entire alligator gamut, from hats to bathrobes and, of course, those famous shirts. Attractive decor. Various locations.

### Equinoxe
**15th arr.**
**173 rue de Vaugirard**
**273.12.45**
**17th arr.**
**70 ave. des Ternes**
**572.18.64**
*Closed Mon.*

You'll find all the clothing necessary for elegant and comfortable sailing. Experienced sailors drop by the Equinoxe for their slickers, great coats, reversible or synthetic fur-lined jackets, pants, boots, caps, gloves and specially made sleeping bags. Wind-surf gear is also available. Efficient customer service department.

### Fnac-Sport
**4th arr.**
**Forum des Halles,**
**3rd floor**
**261.81.18**
*Closed Mon.*

This is one of Paris's most complete sports emporiums, remarkable for its tennis, boating (particularly, wind-surfing), riding, hunting and hiking departments. The store is usually very crowded. Efficient sales staff.

### Gastinne-Renette
**8th arr.**
**39 ave.**
**Franklin-Roosevelt**
**359.77.74**
*Closed Mon.*

This estimable establishment is undergoing transformation to accommodate its growth. Once the renovation's over, superb English and Belgian rifles will be displayed alongside the stock-in-trade firearms. Weekend attire is being brought in and displayed next to the indispensible hunting accessories (leather goods, hats, and all sorts of English and Austrian water-resistant clothing). The combined book and art gallery, as well as the gift department, are also being enlarged. The archery department is expanding, but the bike and moped department is being scrapped. Repair shop and shooting range (target practicing) featured on the premises.

## Go-Sport
**6th arr.**
**45 rue de Rennes**
**544.42.70**
**13th arr.**
**Centre Galaxie,**
**30 ave. d'Italie**
**580.30.05**

The Go-Sport chain has eleven outlets in Paris and in the metropolitan area that offer the same top-brand wares for virtually all sporting activities (tennis, skiing, mountain-climbing, boating, and competitive team sports). Other branches.

## Hermès
**8th arr.**
**24 faubourg**
**Saint-Honoré**
**265.21.60**

A good sixty saddles emerge each month from the faubourg Saint-Honoré workshops. Entirely mounted and handsewn, a racing saddle retails for about 6,500F; custom-made, slightly higher. Regardless of cost, Hermès will custom-make any fantasy you fancy—even alligator-skin saddles, if you wish. In the riding department, which has been superbly decorated in wood and fauve leather upholstery, you'll find fine clothing, all sorts of accessories at various prices (50F and up), and a remarkable leather-conditioning product that will work miracles on your old bookbindings. Hermès also custom-makes the most prestigious jockey caps from exclusive silks. Each design, bearing the name and colors of the owner, has been entered in the house register since the turn of the century.

## Interchasse
**16th arr.**
**12 rue de Presbourg**
**500.04.34**

The darling of Parisian hunters. You go in lured by window displays of animal sculptures or tables laden with the prize of the hunt, and come out with a contract for a week's safari in central Africa. They catch you coming and going. On one side there's an information/reservation desk for world-wide hunting expeditions and, on the other, a ravishing store/bookshop/gallery combining artworks, hunting clothes and gifts. The items here are original and often exclusive, and there are many British imports such as Rowland Ward engraved crystalware, miniature boxes from Bilston and Battersea, James Purdy playing cards, table sets and silverware, Italian porcelain and American-made decoys and hunting knives. Steep prices. Mail-order sales.

## Mettez
**8th arr.**
**16 and 18 blvd.**
**Malesherbes**
**265.33.76**
*Closed Mon. morning.*

Everyone in the world of riding and hunting knows about the exclusive Mettez jacket (in linen, 1,125F; in combined cotton and linen, 770F). Mettez also stocks a fine selection of English clothing (highly durable ripcord jackets, waterproofed oiled-cotton clothing garments) and Austrian (top brands in loden with more than ten styles in assorted colors—around 1,000F each—and jackets and vests in wool).

## Novasport
**17th arr.**
**88 ave. des Ternes**

If you want to go salmon fishing in Norway or grouse hunting in Scotland, Novasport is *the* place for you. Everything you'll need for windy and rainy climates. A very

**574.48.88**
*Closed Mon.*

sensible, good-looking line of clothes and accesorries, at a choice Parisian location. Prices are relatively high, but the quality is tops.

## Au Petit Matelot
**16th arr.**
**27 ave. de la Grande-Armée**
**500.15.51**
*Closed Mon. morning.*

Once housed on the banks of the Ile Saint-Louis, supplier to the Seine's mariners, this house lives up to its 1790 sign and is still a good port in which to find a good peajacket. There are lots of lodens, hunting jackets and raincoats for riding. These clothes, perfect for the ecology-chic, are to be worn on weekend outings and holidays. Everything is in very good taste, and is reasonably priced. Topnotch staff.

## Schilz
**9th arr.**
**30 rue Caumartin**
**266.46.48**
*Closed Mon. morning.*

This venerable establishment was founded in 1815 and has been at its historic rue Caumartin location (both store and workshops) since 1862. Tradition here is part of the stock in trade. For a California collector, Schilz has just reproduced Napoleon III's 1859 parade saddle from original sketches and measurements in the firm's files. Schilz also continues to supply Hoffburg saddles to the famous Spanish Riding School in Vienna. Custom-made saddles retail at an average 4,800F: Also available are dressage, competition and racing saddles that weigh approximately 300 grams. You'll also find partially custom-made Saumur boots as well as fancy leather goods and gifts, and a very cordial sales staff.

## Tunmer
**8th arr.**
**5 place Saint-Augustin**
**522.75.80**
*Closed Mon. morning*

Tunmer features a little bit of everything: large-webbed Prince tennis rackets, Scott ultralight ski boots, golfing gear from beginner's clubs at 695F to the ultimate Ben Hogan and Browning U.S.-made clubs, English rain-resistant riding garments, Barbour clothing for hunting, and equipment for boating. In short, Tunmer has the best and most chic of everthing in the best brands or their own brand, and, generally speaking, excellent weekend outing clothes. Sales are held in the second week of February and July.

# BARGAINS

## Dethy
**4th arr.**
**20 place des Voges**
**272.20.67**
*Closed Mon.*

Dethy features new premium-quality gear such as jackets, shoes and knapsacks for skiing, mountain climbing and camping, as well as brand-new, end-of-line wares and second-hand garments in excellent condition. This tiny but well-stocked boutique is one of the best in Paris. Choice location. Reasonable prices.

## Ski France Distribution
**15th arr.**
**14 rue Letellier**
**577.78.60**
*Closed Mon. morning.*

Everything for skiing, tennis, wind-surfing and cycling, all sold at unbeatable prices: 25%–30% less expensive than in large "volume" stores. Top brands only: Rossignol, Maxell, Kneissel, Fusalp, Donnay, Head, Windsurfer, Raleigh. Other locations.

# Tobacconists

## ═══ CIGARS ═══

### Boutique 22
**16th arr.**
**22 ave. Victor Hugo**
**501.81.41**

For years cigar lovers have been awaiting a messiah in the person of Zino Davidoff. Now it is no longer necessary to travel all the way to Geneva to buy cigars because Davidoff has come to Paris and set up shop right off the place de l'Etoile. The shop's decor of marble, leather and tinted-glass windows offers its privileged customers an ambiance of good taste and unassuming wealth in which to purchase top-brand Havana cigars. In Davidoff's climate-controlled room (70% hygrometry, 18°C temp.), you will be able to select Dom Perignons, double Coronas, Châteaux-Margaux, Davidoff "1000" and No. 2 cigars, as well as the more democratically priced seitas.

### A La Civette
**1st arr.**
**157 rue Saint-Honoré**
**296.04.99**

During the eighteenth century all of Paris bought tobacco at La Civette. Still considered one of France's foremost tobaccostores, La Civette features an entire gamut of goods, from chewing tobacco to the best Havanas. Over 30 years ago, La Civette was the first store in Paris to feature climate-controlled rooms for its cigars. In 1969 the shop's manager, M. Farin, was the first to import Monte-Cristo cigars from Cuba. The store's huge inventory of fresh cigars, as well as its extraordinary selection of tobacco-related goods (over 4,000 pipes), makes it a smoker's mecca.

### Courtial
**10th arr.**
**4 blvd. de Denain**
**281.05.51**

Customers can stock up on Havanas in Courtial's climate-controlled rooms or select cigars from the shop's humidity-controlled vertical glass-enclosed displays. M. Courtial also features tobacco-related goods.

### Drugstore des Champs-Elysées
**8th arr.**
**133 Champs-Elysées**
**723.54.34**

It features a humidity-controlled room for cigars.

### Drugstore Matignon
**8th arr.**
**1 ave. Matignon**
**359.38.70**
*Open everyday from 8:30 A.M. to 2:00 A.M.*

It supplies Laurent, Le Plaza, l'Elysee-Matignon and others with Cuban cigars. Also featured is a humidity-controlled display of "daily" house selections.

446

## Drugstore Opéra
9th arr.
6 blvd. des Capucines
266.90.27

Drugstore Opéra features reliable humidity-controlled cabinets for cigars, as well as Monte-Cristos and Partagas.

## Drugstore Saint-Germain
6th arr.
149 blvd. Saint-Germain
222.92.50
*Open every day from 8:00 A.M. to 2:00 A.M.*

You'll find a wide selection of humidified cigars. Serge Gainsbourg (a French singer) comes here to purchase his Monte-Cristos.

## Lemaire
16th arr.
59 ave. Victor Hugo
500.75.63

M. Blanchat's well-designed rooms can accommodate up to 3,000 boxes of cigars in ideal conditions: 70%–80% humidity and 15–17°C temperature. On arrival, cigars are allowed to "rest" three to four weeks before they are sold. Lemaire features a wide selection of humidors, from plastic containers to sumptuously made cabinets, and a cigar-bank for those who want their cigars deposited for several months. Lemaire is also marketing, nation-wide, its own delectable brand of cigarillos blended with Java, Sumatra and Manilla tobaccos.

## Le Pot à Tabac
8th arr.
28 rue de la Pepinière
522.29.14

Le Pot à Tabac features carefully humidified cigars and Havanas (Monte-Cristos, Davidoff, Quai d'Orsay).

## Au Siamois
8th arr.
4 place de la Madeleine
260.27.69

Charles Ritz, the most uncompromising cigar smoker there ever was, considered Au Siamois to be the best cigar shop in Paris. Today the shop's fine reputation is maintained by M. Aussutre who also sells and repairs pipes.

## Tabac du Dome
14th arr.
108 blvd. de Montparnasse
354.53.63
*Open to 11:30 P.M.*

M. Delpuech's large store features a basement stocked with fresh cigars.

## Tabac George-V
8th arr.
22 ave. George-V
723.44.75

Tabac George-V features humidity-controlled fresh cigars and luxury items for smokers. Sophisticated sales staff.

### Tabac Opéra
9th arr.
8 pl. de l'Opéra
742.46.52

Tabac Opéra features a good selection of cigars and a humidified cigar cabinet.

### La Tabagie
15th arr.
Centre Commercial
Maine-Montparnasse
538.65.18

As purveyor to the Elysée Palace—and consequently to all visiting heads of state—La Tabagie offers the entire line of Havana cigars allowed into the country. This shop displays its merchandise in a highly visible and perfectly air-conditioned vault and features a wide choice of pipes and tobacco.

# SMOKING ACCESSORIES

Leading Parisian jewelers, particularly Cartier, Chaumet and Van Cleef, as well as some distinguished firms such as Christian Dior and Hermès, offer a choice of deluxe accessories, including lighters, cigarette holders, cigarette cases and ashtrays.

### A La Civette
1st arr.
157 rue Saint-Honoré
296.04.99

A remarkable selection of luxury items including top brand pipes, various models of humidors (all sizes), fancy leather goods, pens and watches.

### Denise Corbier
6th arr.
3 rue de l'Odéon
326.03.20
*Closed Wed. and Sat. mornings.*

Some of the items found in the charming little Seita Museum are from Denise Corbier's attractive collection of tobacco pouches and antique pipes. Her shop features antique jewelry, exquisitely made containers and other curios.

### Alfred Dunhill
2nd arr.
15 rue de la Paix
261.57.68

Alfred Dunhill is a shop for men who have about them the aroma of Havana cigars and fine leather, as well as for the occasional courageous female visitor with lots of money to spend on her man. The Paris branch of the famed house of London's Duke Street hasn't changed the mahogany-paneled decor since its turn-of-the-century opening. Last year Dunhill opened a clothing accessories department but has made sure that it doesn't interfere with its primary goal of selling smoking goods. Dunhill pipes made from French and North American briar are among the finest in the world. The light weight and unrivaled quality of their highly polished wood fully justify their unbelievable prices. The round grainy-bowl pipes with ebonite mouthpieces sell at unmentionable prices. The same is true for those truly unique pipes made from calabash (an African gourd that is constantly shaped during its growth and later combined with meerschaum). Dunhill also features innumerable luxurious and expensive lighters in solid silver, gold, lacquered gold (as in the recent ultra-flat "Gemline" series), silver-plate, hand-engraved or jewel-inlaid upon request. There are also French Humidor cigar boxes made from thuya wood combined with milk glass (various sizes include 50, 100, 200 or 300 cigars, from 2,500F) or English boxes lined with cedar or mahogany. Other items displayed include cigar-cutters, amber or shellacked cigarette holders, and beautiful cases made from calf or alligator skin. Last but not least, Dunhill has recently launched two superb eaux de toilette: Classic and the somewhat spicier Blend 30.

## Guyot
**17th arr.**
**7 ave. de Clichy**
**387.70.88**

In what was formerly a dance hall where Fréhel, Damia and Mistinguett made their debuts, you'll find M. Guyot, one of the last pipe-craftsmen in Paris, quietly seated behind his counter repairing and restoring pipes, from elegant nineteenth-century styles to good old everyday pipes. He also sells a variety of artfully crafted pipes in briar and meerschaum. Drop into his shop to see his personal collection of pipes and beautifully crafted knives.

## Lemaire
**16th arr.**
**59 ave. Victor Hugo**
**500.75.63**

Lemaire features luxury smoking accessories such as extraslim cigarette cases, top-brand pocket lighters and hardstone table lighters, as well as a large selection of cigar humidifiers, most of which need only be refueled with water three times a year (from 500F–13,000F—in wood, lacquered amber or china). The shop also has an interesting department of fancy leather goods, pens and quartz watches.

## Sommer
**2nd arr.**
**11 passage des Princes**
**296.99.10**
*Closed Sat.*

Claude Faivret swears that when his celebrated clients tuck one of his fabulous pipes between their lips, they reveal, in a puff of Maryland, Virginia or Gros Cul smoke, the most intimate secrets of soul or state. We are thus inclined to believe in the glorious future of the French pipe in general and in this venerable establishment in particular. Lined in somber antique wood paneling, the shop is crowned with a superb 1805 turret. Famous customers such as George Simenon drop in to purchase pipes from a selection of hundreds of models, some of which can be custom-made.

# Womenswear

## ACCESSORIES

### Canes And Umbrellas

## Antoine
**1st arr.**
**10 ave. de l'Opéra**
**269.01.80**

This is the realm of the walking stick, featuring gold, silver, precious wood, ivory or gem handles, as well as umbrellas and antique riding crops.

**Madeleine Gély**
6th arr.
218 blvd.
Saint-Germain
222.63.35

Discovering rare and unusual canes and umbrellas in this little big store is sheer delight! The salesmen help you discover their treasures with passionate politeness.

### Gloves

**Christian Dior**
8th arr.
32 ave. Montaigne
723.54.44

Christian Dior is quality and elegance. You will find the largest and up-to-date selection at the avenue Montaigne boutique. However, Dior gloves are also sold in most department stores.

**Hermès**
8th arr.
24 faubourg
Saint-Honoré
265.21.60

Always the same selection of really beautiful classic gloves in kid, suede, peccary and ostrich.

**Muriel**
8th arr.
4 rue des Saussaies
265.95.34

Unchanging and traditional, Muriel is a one-of-a-kind boutique. You'll find a huge selection of gloves (18,000 pairs in inventory) for men and women, in lamb's wool, gazelle, antelope, peccary and ostrich. They retail from 150F–390F. All in all, the prices are reasonable, given the superior quality of the skins and finishing. Repairs are free, and you'll find bargains during the sales held in January and June.

### Handbags and Luggage

**Étienne Aigner**
8th arr.
3 faubourg
Saint-Honoré
742.90.27

A luxurious shop where you can dream of world cruises and distant horizons just by standing in front of a 15,000F cabin trunk. There is some beautiful Italian heavyweight hard luggage, in brass-studded leather (1,500F–5,000F), which is very tasteful in every respect except that it bears the house logo. There is also a leather clothing department—boots and jackets for men and women in tones to match the luggage.

**La Bagagerie**
6th arr.
41 rue du Four
548.85.88

This is one of the best names in Paris for bags, purses, folding bags and game bags, which are attractive, chic and not too expensive. They come in kid, deerskin, box calf, linen or lizard. There are also traveling bags and lightweight, practical suitcases. Other locations.

**Bottega Veneta**
16th arr.
48 ave. Victor-Hugo
501.70.58
*Closed Mon. mornings.*

The slogan of this Venetian house is, "Your own initials are enough," in refreshing contrast to so many others. Elegant Morocco leather goods in suble colors—gray, khaki, bordeau, havana, blue—at affordable prices. There are shoulder bags, pocketbooks, purses, and other supple folding bags in braided lamb (the house specialty, from 1,300F) or in crocodile (unpolished and superb, from 1,500F). You'll also find assorted shoes—always flat-heeled,—loafers, pumps and boots. There's a handsome line of baggage in pressed calfskin in various colors, soft or hard suitcases with digital locks (from 3,400F–4,200F), folding suitcases, bags, large "pilot" briefcases, attaché cases and document cases; there's a very attractive one for businesswomen selling at 900F.

## Céline
**6th arr.**
**58 rue de Rennes**
**548.58.55**
**8th arr.**
**24 rue Francoise-Ier**
**720.22.83**
**16th arr.**
**3 ave. Victor-Hugo**
**501.79.41**

Céline's handbags and shoulder bags, like its loafers, are expensive (1,100F–1,700F), but remarkable for the high quality of their skins and exemplary finishing. Handbags by Céline are the ne plus ultra for many Parisiennes and foreigners. They are classic and durable. Either you'll hate their rich-looking gold fasteners or find them superb.

## Chichen-Itza
**1st arr.**
**231 rue Saint-Honoré**
**260.80.16**
*Closed Sat.*

At the end of the courtyard, this excellent artisan custom-makes the design of your choice in any color. In boxcalf he handsews everything, much like a saddlemaker, for 1,500F–2,000F.

## Christian Dior
**8th arr.**
**26 ave. Montaigne**
**723.54.44**

The bags and suitcases in nylon or leather (unfortunately bearing the Christian Dior logo) are displayed next to the shoes. But if you'll go over to 30 avenue Montaigne, you'll find the more luxurious, and exclusive, designs: sumptuous bags in fine English leather, fauve or moss-green (4,800F for a hard suitcase 36 inches long, 2,500F–3,200F for "square-mouth" bags), as well as the prettiest handbags and purses of the collection, which are also the most expensive.

## Fred
**8th arr.**
**8 rue Royale**
**260.30.65**

Under one roof on the rue Royale are Fred's twin boutiques. On the right is the jewelry department; on the left, a complete line of luxurious leather goods, including bags in all shapes and sizes—garment bags, cabin trunks, attaché cases, jewelry cases, suitcases made from three different materials: printed leather, combined printed linen and leather, and combined nylon and leather. A well designed attaché case in embossed leather with digital lock and two partitions, ideal for a one- or two-day trip, costs 3,900F.

## Gucci
**1st arr.**
**350 rue Saint-Honoré**
**296.81.89**
**8th arr.**
**27 faubourg Saint-Honoré**
**296.83.27**

Gucci's leather line is not exactly famous for originality. The classic handbags, made in Florence, are always the same: in box calf and averaging 1,000F. The luggage doesn't vary either: vinyl and leather, with the Gucci signature, with or without the traditional green and red band, are 1,300F–1,600F per case. Semi-soft calfskin cases are 3,150F for the 36-inch size. A set consisting of two hard suitcases (one 30-inch, one 40-inch), a vanity case and a shirt case, all in luxurious wild boar, costs 46,000F for the four pieces (you may buy them separately).

## Hermès
**8th arr.**
**24 faubourg**
**Saint-Honoré**
**265.21.60**

Are the prices here reasonable or completely crazy? Actually, they're both. Check the tags, examine the inner and outer finishings, and think of all the meticulous handwork that goes into cutting, sewing and adjusting the bags and luggage that discreetly bear the Hermès signature on their flaps. If you're still unconvinced, drop into the studio (fourth floor) or the Hermès museum (first floor, by appointment only). Then decide for yourself. Among the handbags, there's the Kelly design (1949) and Constance design (1969), the red Hermès, the grained leather, the linen and leather, and crocodile (green this year) which are always the pride of the house. Although there is much to choose from, the unvarying style and good taste can be a bit boring. An average price is 3,800F (12,000F–15,000F for crocodile). There is a prestigious line of handmade luggage in box calf with reinforced corners (14,000F for a 40-inch suitcase). Current lines are more affordable, made from linen or cowhide or grained calfskin, semi-hard and partially handcrafted (4,450F and 5,300F for the 30-inch suitcase). If you want something really showy, the house will carry out other little requests. For instance, leather coverings for your bicycle saddle or the cockpit of your private jet.

## Lancel
**6th arr.**
**43 rue de Rennes**
**222.94.73**

Lancel has handbags and suitcases, in leather as well as leather and linen, and leather and nylon; all well-designed and at very reasonable prices.

## Morabito
**1st arr.**
**1 place Vendôme**
**260.30.76**

Crocodile—Javanese is the best—is the top skin here and, whatever the price, the best house value. There are beautiful handbags and shoulder bags, with discreet gold-plated clasps (about 9,000F); briefcases, attaché-cases and traveling bags (23,200F), including the sumptuous trunks (71,500F in bordeau or black). The ultimate luxury is an assorted-size shoebox (45-inch by 16-inch, which will hold up to ten pairs of shoes, approximately 58,000F). Elegant and also more affordable are handbags in box calf (1,100F-3,700F) or ostrich (about 6,000F). In the luggage department there's a handsome line of grained leather in gold and maroon, or navy blue and bordeau: 3,300F for a rather heavy, 40-inch hard suitcase with digital lock, which also comes in elephant-print calfskin.

## Renard
**7th arr.**
**3 place du**
**Palais-Bourbon**
**551.77.87**

Beautiful handbags are designed and made here by an authentic saddler, Jean-Pierre. Sometimes the designs are immediately available; if not, you may have to wait fifteen to twenty-one days. These bags are far from expensive, but their durability, superior quality and

*Workshop to the right at the back of the courtyard. Closed Sat. afternoon.*

## Ria Viale

**8th arr.**
**31 ave. Matignon**
**562.04.39**

## Louis Vuitton
**8th arr.**
**78 bis, ave. Marceau**
**720.47.00**
*Closed Sat.*

perfect handsewn finishings will make you forget their price: elephant from 2,400F, ostrich, 2,800F, crocodile 3,500F.

Mme Viale designs and makes timelessly styled, very appealing handbags, which are well-crafted in all their details. They are made of very supple stain-resistant skins, lightly edgestitched and have deluxe clasps. Custom-made or catalogue-ordered.

Those well-disciplined lines of Japanese tourists no longer form in front of Vuitton's doors at the crack of dawn. Since the Japanese can now buy Vuitton at home, the large, bright store on the avenue Marceau is once again the luxuriously agreeable place it was meant to be. Once you're inside—don't forget to smile at the doorman and admire the treasure trunks near the entrance,—a hostess will greet you and escort you from one department to another. Your tour will take you from spectacle cases to wardrobe trunks with their six drawers for linens, hats, ties and gloves (22,000F); to the incredible shoe trunk (designed to house 36 pairs of shoes, each in a separate compartment) created upon request during the inter-war period for the great Lily Pons; and the countless styles of luggage, including soft or hard suitcases (with or without frames), boxes, handbags and satchels in all shapes and sizes and for all uses. They are always of the same material—frequently imitated, yet never equalled—printed linen coated with vinyl, reinforced with *lozine* ribs (it looks like leather, and Vuitton jealously guards the formula); untreated leather for handles and straps; copper for rivets and corners of hard luggage. There are no digital locks, but you may request the same lock for all your luggage and have keys made at any time (each customer has from the start his own registered personal code).

## Hats

## Lanvin
**8th arr.**
**15 faubourg Saint-Honoré**
**265.14.40**

## Motsch
**8th arr.**
**42 ave. George-V**
**723.79.22**
*Closed Mon.*

Ride the elevator to the third floor and you'll see Gelot, the last of the great Parisian hatmakers. His sophisticated taste, his fabrics and his designs will easily convince you to wear either a hat, a cap or toque. As for Lanvin, you'll see it all on your way up to Gelot.

This is the high temple of hattery, in all sizes and styles. Milliner Motsch has beautifully maintained his wooden façade and has captured the aura of a bygone era. What a treat to hop over there and shop for headgear!

## Shoes

## Mario Bologna

Well-made classic shoes have their faithful adherents at this Italian designer's boutique on rue François-Ier,

**8th arr.**
**48 rue Francois-Ier**
**723.87.14**
*Closed Mon. morning.*

where he has been doing business for over ten years (an old-timer among new-wavers). Suede pumps with removable buckles (approximately 700F), sandals and supple calfskin boots. Friendly saleswomen.

## Carel
**2nd arr.**
**41 blvd. des**
**Capucines**
**261.17.85**

Carel features superior quality, classic and elegant shoes and a few trendy designs (400F–850F). Many locations.

## Céline
**6th arr.**
**58 rue de Rennes**
**548.58.55**

Ultra-classic cuts and colors, medium heels and impeccable quality (they're practically indestructable) make Céline's shoes a worthwhile investment. For many Parisiennes, her pumps (750F) and celebrated loafers (450F–750F) are absolute musts. Other locations.

## Tanino Crisci

**8th arr.**
**40 rue Francois-Ier**
**723.86.25**

You'll stride with pride in these flat-heeled beauties. No ridiculous pointy toes or flashy colors here. Instead, you'll find beautiful, sensible shoes, in lightweight kangaroo or calfskin: fringed loafers and 4/5-inch-heeled pumps (in fact, they also come in 2½- and 3½-inch heels). The average price is 690F. There are also handsome box-calf riding boots or, even nicer, mini-calf boots as supple as a glove (2,300F, approximately). All this comes from Italy and is presented to you with a smile . . . and a persuasive accent.

## Christian Dior
**8th arr.**
**26 ave. Montaigne**
**723.54.44**

Following in the shoes of Dior, you pay no attention to the latest styles. This is the realm of pumps and walking shoes (500F–600F), sensible and not very flashy, yet perfectly styled to complement your legs and make walking a pleasure. Nothing here is an attention-getter. To sum it up, these shoes are the true definition of elegance for those no longer twenty. You also find fancy-leather goods—handbags and suitcases—stockings, tights (the prettiest in Paris), belts and umbrellas.

## Durer
**8th arr.**
**28 faubourg**
**Saint-Honoré**
**265.25.76**
**16th arr.**
**94 ave. Victor-Hugo**
**704.70.23**

Durer features beautiful, classic designs, exclusively in kid made by French craftsmen—and expensive (800F–900F).

## France Faver
**6th arr.**

Luxurious and elegant shoes, mostly by Italian designers. Also, low-heeled sandals, pumps, loafers, boots and ankle-boots. The prices, alas!, are as high as the quality of the

**79 rue des Saints-Pères 220.04.29**

shoes. Pumps (450F–700F), loafers (750F), boots (1,400F).

## Free Lance
**1st arr.**
**22 rue Mondétour**
**233.74.70**

Free Lance has flat heels, classic styles and new materials, such as ballet shoes in polished cotton (250F), boots and ankle-boots in aged leather (590F), stitched leather pumps (315F). Pretty and not too expensive.

## Maud Frizon
**6th arr.**
**83 rue des Saints-Pères**
**222.06.93**

Superb, sophisticated, Italian-made shoes for covergirls and rich, smart-looking young women. To match your handbag with your shoes, go next door to No. 79 rue des Saint-Pères.

## Harel
**8th arr.**
**32 ave. George-V**
**720.75.00**
*Closed Sat.*

This master shoemaker's goal is to create beautiful footwear for larger-than-average feet. Elegant pumps in kid, lizard or suede with gold stitching; or "Chanel" sandals or walking shoes which, alas, cost a mint (1,100F, on the average) but will outlast run-of-the mill designs.

## Hémisphères
**16th arr.**
**1-3 blvd. Emile-Augier**
**520.13.75**

From the U.S. come lightweight pompom moccasins (Cardone), solid or two-toned, in box calf or in suede (480F); Astronaut walking shoes (Hawkins) in thick leather with air-cushion soles; and low-heeled cowboy boots (Lucchese). They are made in a variety of colors, in box calf, lizard, antelope or sharkskin (from 1,100F and way up). From France there are beautiful pumps and sandals in box calf or in lizard skin. Although very expensive, they are all of fine quality and durable.

## Charles Jourdan
**1st arr.**
**Forum des Halles, 1st floor**
**297.50.70**
**Various locations**

Everything for every taste, including the best. Good, quality shoes. Approximately 600F for a pair of classic pumps. Many locations.

## Stéphane Kélian
**1st arr.**
**Forum des Halles, 1st floor**
**297.49.02**
**7th arr.**
*Closed Mon. morning at the Forum and rue des Saint-Pères.*

You'll be well-heeled indeed in Stéphane Kélian's footwear. The heels are ingenious, the colors lively (plain or bronze), with lots of braided leather work and pointed toes. They are very expensive for the young people for whom they're obviously intended (about 600F). Other locations.

455

## *Mancini*

**8th arr.**
**20 rue du Boccador**
**720.18.93**
*Closed Sat.*
**16th arr.**
**72 ave. Victor-Hugo**
**500.48.81**

Mancini is very expensive, and very chic: lightweight pumps, sensibly heeled boots and divine sandals (800F), which can be reproduced in kid or fabric and custom-dyed in his Paris studio (two weeks wait, from 1,150F–1,350F).

## *Andréa Pfister*

**1st arr.**
**4 rue Cambon**
**296.55.28**
**6th arr.**
**56 rue du Four**
**548.12.89**

Expensive, elegant shoes made in Italy include classic, hand-stitched pumps with 3½-inch heels and ornamented with bronze buckles and shields (more or less extravagant) and assorted handbags. Loafers, boots and gorgeous, extra-flat ankle-boots, or evening ones with high heels.

## *Mercadal*

**1st arr.**
**3 place des Victoires**
**508.84.44**
**6th arr.**
**70 rue des Saints-Pères**
**222.02.08**

Mercadal has tiptoed into his place in the sun—or, more accurately, in the shadow of the Sun King. He abandoned his boutique-studio in the 20th arrondissement, where models, fashion journalists and young women in the know used to buy shoes for next to nothing. Success has its obligations; his prices have doubled. His designs are still attractive and beautifully displayed. Pointed kid or cobra-skin pumps, in braided leather or cut on the bias, all colors, including bronze, with choice of two or three heels. Also available are flats with santiag heels. Prices average around 500F.

## *Pucci Verdi*

**7th arr.**
**40 rue de Verneuil**
**261.05.59**

Pucci Verdi is a rue de Verneuil Italian shoemaker who is not to be ignored. His white enamel shop, decorated with canary-yellow throw pillows, is like a ray of sunshine in this posh and somber neighborhood. You'll find lovely Italian designs in the latest styles and a rainbow of colors sold at reasonable prices (from 400F and up): fine two-toned kid pumps, flats with bows, ballet shoes in plaited leather or suede, ankle-boots and boots, assorted handbags and belts.

## *Rossetti*

**8th arr.**
**18 rue Royale**
**260.21.39**
**8th arr.**
**54 faubourg Saint-Honoré**
**265.26.60**

The Rossetti brothers, among the top Italians in the shoe business, have opened a store on the faubourg Saint-Honoré decorated in black enamel with mirrors, beige accents and comfy sofas. Without a doubt, the shoes are expensive, yet they are of superior quality, elegant and classic and—strangely enough—comfortable to wear: lovely pumps with moderate heels, in one color or two-toned; ankle-boots as supple as a glove; and delighted flats for walking (600F–700F; in crocodile skin, 1,100F).

## *Sacha*

**2nd arr.**

Teeny-boppers and fashion-conscious young people of both sexes rush over to Sacha at the start of each season

**15 rue de Turbigo**
**233.48.08**
**6th arr.**
**24 rue de Buci**
**354.43.50**

## Walter Steiger

**6th arr.**
**5 rue de Tournon**
**633.01.45**
**8th arr.**
**49, faubourg Saint-Honoré**
**265.96.48**

## Tokio Kumagai

**1st arr.**
**52 rue Croix-des-Petits-Champs**
**236.08.01**

## François Villon

**6th arr.**
**58 rue Bonaparte**
**325.98.36**
**Various locations**
*Closed Mon.*

## Germaine Guérin-Théo

**1st arr.**
**243 rue Saint-Honoré**
**260.08.74**

## John Lobb

**8th arr.**
**24 faubourg Saint-Honoré**
**265.24.45**

to be the first to try on the irresistible new designs; they are imitated everywhere. Boots, ankle-boots, thigh-boots, clergy shoes, ballet slipper, gillies laced with ribbons, Indian moccasins and plastic sandals are wisely sold at prices suitable for the clientele.

Walter Steiger's two boutiques have the same sophisticated decor and pretty window displays. They also both have agreeable sales staffs. They feature luxurious shoes and Italian evening sandals, exorbitantly priced at 1,200F (1,500F for boots and 650F for open-worked flats for flat-heeled sandals). There are a few good classic pumps in delicate kidskin, priced at only 500F.

Tokio Kumagai features fantasy footwear from Spain: funny heels terraced like pagoda roofs or zig-zags; ingenious designs shaped like waves or hearts; shoes with bows or beads in stunning colors. Flats, sandals, pumps (around 500F), both lightweight and a bit wild to make you feel festive to the tips of your toes (hikers, please abstain). Or take a look at the accessories where you'll find genuine knapsacks in supple leather (black, red, khaki or natural), marvelous buys at 550F. The sales staff is extremely courteous in this Japanese designers' new shop a few feet away from the place des Victoires, the hub of snazzy youthful clothes. You'll also find a few shirts, tunics and kimonos, very austere and monkish, in raw silk (550–850F, in a variety of colors).

François Villon has a rather limited collection, but his smart-looking high-heeled sandals (500F–750F) and cavalier boots (forget it if you have large feet or plump calves) are among the most gorgeous in Paris. Always a few pretty "Chanel" sandals (750F). There are also sneakers, bicycle shoes and other laced shoes.

### Custom-Made Shoes

In this narrow, cavernous shop, Mme Théo will help you choose a Germaine-Guérin handbag. In his adjoining studio at the back, her husband, bootmaker and heir to Hellstern, will make you custom-made shoes in assorted styles and colors. Figure on spending 2,500F for the first pair, 2,000F for the following ones, with fittings and a 10- to 15-day waiting period.

The Paris branch of the distinguished English shoemaking dynasty is housed on the second floor at Hermès. There is a three- to six-month waiting period for the first custommade order, less for subsequent orders. They're perfect. Prices reflect the quality of work and the time spent.

### *Bargain Shoes*

## *Bally*
**1st arr.**
**1 rue du Louvre**
**260.22.46**

At the corner of the rue de Rivoli, Bally's two-story shop features permanently reduced prices. It's adjacent to the other shop, whose collection is sold at regular rates. The designs, arranged on vertical displays according to their size, may be somewhat flawed. Tags show both the original and marked-down prices.

## *Chiche*
**1st arr.**
**10 rue du Roule**
**261.78.06**
**8th arr.**
**38 rue de Berri**
**563.49.50**

These attractive boutiques display luxurious designs sold at 50 percent markdowns. They're not really that inexpensive (classic boots: 750F, pumps: 330F, evening sandals: 370F) except when there's a sale—in January and July, or in the 1st arrondissement shop, which offers low-priced, end-of-line shoes (50F–200F). Other branches.

## *Nadège*
**9th arr.**
**25 rue**
**Godot-de-Mauroy**
**742.88.96**
*Closed Mon. morning.*

A clean, agreeable little shop, where superior-quality shoes are sold at lower prices (300F–400F for a pair of pumps, 500F–700F for boots, 200F–250F for multicolored Italian sandals). A good selection of luxury designs, handmade and unlabeled.

### *Umbrellas*

## *Madeleine Gély*
**7th arr.**
**218 blvd.**
**Saint-Germain**
**222.63.35**
*Closed Mon.*

This shop could fit into your lapel pocket. Yet the charming Madeleine Gély weaves her way around this congested space and finds the precise object you're looking for with a flick of the wrist. The liveliest umbrellas are in cotton, with ruffled edges in ravishing colors, from the écrus to the dark mauves, solid or in multicolored patches or with subtle prints. Thank heaven there are no logos or signatures! The most luxurious are made from virgin silk (on request only). Once you've decided on the color and fabric, all you need is a unique handle. For example, the head of a parrot, duck or dog made from sculpted wood. There is also a large selection of walking sticks—both useful (some from the nineteenth century) and decorative, contemporary and antique. Some are collectors' items. There is also a fascinating array of gadget-canes such as watch-canes, pipe-canes, cigarette lighter-canes, whiskey flask-canes, and sword-canes.

# *Cheap Chic*

## *Babs*
**1st arr.**
**34 rue du**
**Marché-Saint-Horné**
**260.07.87**

All the couturiers are represented here, with the exception of Saint-Laurent and Chanel. Suits and dinner dresses from approximately 600F and up. A very large selection of evening dresses, from approximately 750F and up. Alterations take about a week. Other locations.

## Cacharel Stock
14th arr.
114 rue d'Alésia
542.53.04

This great ready-to-wear label has its own sales at 35%–50% off last year's end-of-the-line or remaindered designs. The store is vast and vivid, painted green and navy blue with Cacharel posters on the walls, numerous dressing rooms draped with pearly curtains. The clothing is well-displayed and accessible. Open to all. You can browse at your leisure to soft music.

## Duo 38
8th arr.
38 rue Bassano
723.55.18
*On 6th floor, R. 606. Closed Sat.*

In the spring of 1981, a man from Lyon named Catin, a leading silk merchant and supplier to the haute couture, fell head over heels in love with a dancer named Elysée. This extravagant affair did not prove to be Catin's folly, however, because the line of ready-to-wear clothes he named after Elysée is sold without middlemen and hype (hence, at unbeatable prices) from the sixth floor of a modern building near the Champs-Elysée. Duo 38 is a small studio-boutique where each item is carefully arranged in a plastic garment bag. There are shirtdresses in crêpe de Chine, scalloped silk or discreetly printed designs. Some are classically cut and ravishing. The more daring ones are less attractive, in our opinion (from 270F to 450F). There are a few outfits and shirtdesses in heavier silk (800F–900F). Bermudas and shantung tapered pants (400F–500F) and full ruffled skirts in black taffeta (400F). No dressing rooms, but many mirrors. Silky smooth hospitality throughout.

## Emmanuelle Khanh
1st arr.
6 rue Pierre-Lescot
233.51.62

There are no steet-level window displays, and the shop is on the second floor to the right. There are no dressing rooms either, so you'll have to find a corner to change in, and few saleswomen, so be sure to put everything back in its place. Last year's designs are sold with a 40% markdown.

## Richard Grand
1st arr.
229 rue Saint-Honoré
260.58.73

You'll be surprised at the incredibly wide range of sweaters (particularly for men), which, considering their quality, are among the finest and least expensive in all of Paris. There are luxurious alpaca sweaters and cardigans, solid or finely striped in ravishing colors for 600F, which is 30% to 50% less than what they go for in the larger stores on the West Side. You'll also find sweater sets and vests, handknit and open-worked in wool and in silk as well as cashmeres in all sizes and colors (from 250F up). The secret here is that all the knitwear comes directly from the firm's workshops. No one gets nervous if you try on one item after another.

## Miss Griffes
8th arr.
19 rue de Penthievre
265.10.00
*Closed Sat.*

High fashion and courturier-boutique designs only— evening dresses, silk outfits. Alterations are possible. There is also a fur department. Clearance sales in January and June.

## I.D. Club
**8th arr.**
**146 Champs-Elysées**
**562.51.81**

I.D. club on the mezzanine; It consists of two small and not terribly appealing rooms which are jam-packed. The dresses, coats, shirts, and knitted outfits have been hastily hung up and parked together like sardines. Some designer labels include: Castelbajac, Givenchy, Valentino (Miss V), Saint-Laurent (Diffusuon), Tarlazzi and others. The prices are very low (50% to 75% discounts on the whole), for clothes—not always in their prime—from the preceding season. There are also shoes and boots. You need a good eye and lots of perserverance to unearth a good deal before professional bargain-hunters make off with the best.

## Isphording
**1st arr.**
**rue Richepanse**
**296.46.67**
*Closed Sat.*

Isphording is cashmere minus the middleman. At the end of the hall of an old building there's a shop devoted more to decor than selling sweaters, in which you'll find beige upholstery and cork-lined panels, red linen curtains, clusters of dried flowers, engravings, bowls of candy and, finally, French sweaters in cashmere only. They are arranged on wooden shelves in beautiful red cardboard boxes. There are five sizes and five styles, including crew-necks, V-necks, turtlenecks—sleeveless and long-sleeved. Twenty colors, including beige-gray and maroon and a beautiful red, as well as natural tones that are solid or heathered.

## Anna Lowe
**8th arr.**
**35 ave. Matignon**
**359.96.61**
*Closed Sat. morning.*

Established in 1935, this was the first store to feature discount high-fashion garments. It has an attractive selection of designer clothing—high fashion and couturier boutiques. Alterations are possible.

## Mendès (Yves Saint-Laurent)
**9th arr.**
**65 rue Montmartre**
**263.83.32**
*First floor. Closed Sat. afternoon.*

This is the place to go for the previous season's Saint-Laurents: the winter ones from January 15 on, the summer ones from July 1st on. Also, there's a selection of last year's skirts, blazers, overcoats and shirts, and also a few dressy dresses and evening gowns, which are always in style. Yves Saint-Laurent is by far the most conservative of our couturiers—which is obvious from his boutique collection. It is all hung within reach, with the size, original label and price (wholesale with a 50% markdown) inscribed in red pencil on the tags. Don't expect any advice from the saleswomen; you're to help yourself. There are no dressing rooms, though there are mirrors everywhere. No exchanges or alterations, but there is a large selection of standard sizes (7 to 11) and styles in perfect condition. You'll also be asked firmly—and for good reason—to hang up the clothes you're not going to take so they won't get wrinkled. On the first floor there are marked down garments from the Yves Saint-Laurent Diffusion Collection, which are always far less expensive and include knits, T-shirts, skirts and slacks.

## Jean-Louis Scherrer
**12th arr.**
**29 ave. Ledru-Rollin**
**343.58.34**
*Closed Tues., Wed., Fri.*

Behind the black-trimmed façade you'll find *the* boutique of marked-down garments. You may browse leisurely and try on numerous garments from last season. There are two dressing rooms. Alterations are at additional cost. Good-natured and friendly sales staff. A silk dress retails for from 800F to 1,500F; a woolen coat, 900F to 1,500F.

## Stock Austerlitz (Hechter)
**13th arr.**
**16 blvd. de l'Hôpital**
**707.88.44**
*Closed Mon. morning.*

Less expensive Hechter designs are on sale here in a huge boutique-warehouse facing the Austerlitz railroad station. Skirts, blazers, coats, gabardine or synthetic ciré raincoats, marked down 30%, 40% or 50% off their original prices.

## Stock Ouest
**17th arr.**
**204 blvd. Periere**
**572.27.42**
*Closed Mon. morning*

A former fashion model, with a renewed interest in lower-priced garments, has opened a boutique on boulevard Periere, next to the little train. The store is divided into two parts: on one side, the Jacadi collection for children; on the other, unlabeled items for their parents. The women's selections are somewhat limited compared to the men's, but you'll always find tapered pants in flannel or corduroy (110F-130F), shirts in printed silk (165F-190F), cotton polyester blend (110F), and last season's ready-to-wear clothes, when they're available, at 40% to 50% off the original price. All this is well displayed on racks of shelves and the prices are clearly tagged. One dressing room. All sales final.

## Les Trouvailles
**15th arr.**
**55 rue de la Convention**
**578.21.95**
*Closed Mon.*

Here you'll find top-brand clothing, minus the designer's label, sold at 50% off the initial price. Some items aren't too far behind the latest fashion boutiques. Sales at the beginning of January and at the end of June.

## AND (with 30% to 50% discounts):

### Pierre d'Alby
· *2nd arr.—60 rue de Richelieu*
*295.65.42*

### Franck Olivier
· *15th arr.—6 rue Frémicourt*
*579.65.74*

### Micmac
· *17th arr.—13 rue Laugier 662.58.19*

### Philippe Salvet
· *14th arr.—122 rue d'Alésia*
*541.24.12*

# COUTURIERS

## *All the top names listed without comment:*

### Pierre Balmain
· *8th arr.—44 rue Francois-Ier*
*720.35.34*

### Pierre Cardin
· *8th arr.—27 ave. Marigny 266.92.25*

### Carven
· *8th arr.—6 Rond-Point-des-Champs-Elysées 255.66.50*

### Cerruti
· *8th arr.—15 place de la Madeleine*
*742.10.78*

### Chanel
· *8th arr.—31 rue Cambon 261.54.55*

### Courrèges
· *8th arr.—40 rue Francois-Ier*
*261.52.03*

### Christian Dior
· *8th arr.—30 ave. Montaigne*
*723.54.44*

### Louis Féraud
· *8th arr.—88 faubourg Saint-Honoré*
*260.08.08*

### Givenchy
· *8th arr.—3, ave. George-V 723.81.36*

### Grès
· *2nd arr.—1 rue de la Paix 261.58.15*

### Lanvin
· *8th arr.—22 faubourg Saint-Honoré*
*265.27.21*

### Ted Lapidus
· *8th arr.—37 ave. Pierre-Ier-de-Serbie*
*720.69.33*

### Guy Laroche
· *8th arr.—29 ave. Montaigne*
*723.78.72*

### Hanae Mori
· *8th arr.—17 ave. Montaigne*
*723.52.03*

### Jean Patou
· *8th arr.—7 rue Saint-Florentin*
*260.36.10*

### Per Spook
· *8th arr.—30 ave. George-V 723.78.08*

### Nina Ricci
· *8th arr.—17 rue Francois-Ier*
*256.88.11*

### Yves Saint-Laurent
· *16th arr.—5 ave Marceau 723.72.71*

### Jean-Louis Scherrer
· *8th arr.—51 ave. Montaigne*
*359.55.39*

### Torrente
· *8th arr.—9 faubourg Saint-Honoré*
*266.14.14*

### Emanuel Ungaro
· *8th arr.—2 ave. Montaigne 723.61.94*

### Philippe Venet
· *8th arr.—62 rue Francois-Ier*
*225.33.63*

# ETHNIC AND TRENDY

## Berlingot
**1st arr.**
**3 rue Berger.**

Berlingot is big on nostalgia: very nice shirts in black or cream lace—the prettiest ones decorate the walls—lots of skirts in bleached cotton or imitation silk, casual afternoon dresses in rayon, and in black silk or pearl embroidered for evening. Sheepskin jackets and gray Astrakhan overcoats.

## Creeks
**6th arr.**
**155 rue de Rennes**
**548.26.36**

A monumental imposing gold and silver mermaid overlooks the staircase as you enter—straight from a Cecil B. deMille movie. Then you'll find yourself in three stories of gleefully delirious clothes, all self-service. From the first floor on up, you'll find old-fashioned stiletto heels or satin ballet shoes; pegged or straight pants (ten different brands); loads of T-shirts, and jackets made from linen, suede or leather—masculine and broad-shouldered for girls, fringed for boys (about 300–1200F). And, of course, the indispensable accessories: belts, key chains, and all types of gadgets. The gimmick works well: this former neighborhood movie house is crowded all day long. As chummy as a hoedown with everybody trying on clothes in the same booth.

## La Nacelle
**1st arr.**
**12 rue Pierre-Lescot**
**508.54.19**

This boutique is a former dairy, redecorated in pastels by a Slavic designer. Christina Bukowska presents festive, soft-looking clothes at moderate prices: silk T-shirts, dungarees in delicate wool (350F), sweaters in terry velvet or alpaca, embroidered petticoats for those who want to dress like cool young babas.

## Les Orientales
**16th arr.**
**140 ave. Victor-Hugo**
**533.01.20**
*Closed Mon. morning.*

The city has been invaded by eagles and dragons. No longer is it necessary for those who dwell in the impersonal 16th arrondissement to rush off to les Halles to dress up in Kansai's clothes. *Les Orientales* have jammed all, or practically all, of this renowned Japanese designer's production line into a tiny space. Logo T-shirts in shattering colors, pants, sweaters and blousons sumptuously embroidered with spectacular Japanese patterns, accessories. Arresting attire to be worn with arrogance and a bit of snobbery.

## Elisabeth de Senneville
**1st arr.**
**1 rue de Turbigo**
**236.63.03**

Where there was once a former wholesale butcher shop lined with beef quarters, there is now—in the sparest of settings—futuristic clothing. It's well-designed and partly practical using avant-garde materials such as fluorescent plastic, photo-magazine black-and-white prints, sweatshirts and mini-skirts (400F), and nonwoven Ty-wek, disposable after five to six washings.

## Taffetas et Moleskin
**6th arr.**
**12 rue de l'Eperon**
**326.91.80**

A rock-and-roll hairdo, teased or brillantined and combed back, is a must here if you plan on wearing these taffetas, tulle evening gowns, soft-hued strapless bras, cotton-checked dresses, pipestem trousers and dazzling, scintillating bronze jackets.

## Trucks
**92200 Neuilly**
**24 rue Madeleine-Michelis**
**745.45.44**
*Closed Mon. morning.*

An American flag, a multicolored mannequin, a sign at the entrance flashing "day-and-night auto exit" indicate what it's all about. You make your way to the parking lot by a steep and slippery ramp. Lofty porticos, huge trestles and a quick brush of white paint were enough to transform this place into a wild, funny and provocative clothes garage, signed Fiorucci. These are clothes you'll see on night-owls at the Palace or Bains-Douches. Narrow trousers for 140F upwards; solid-color jeans, striped or star-studded and in black satin or pink glacé cotton, all tastes and styles; classical, deep decolletés; one-shouldered T-shirts (or with straps); miniskirts and strapless dresses in jersey. And, of course, the accessories.

# FURS

## A la Cour du Danemark
**8th arr.**
**3 rue Tronchet**
**265.35.88**
*Closed Sat. from January thru end of September.*

Established in 1880 by a Dane—hence its name—La Cour has abandoned the courtly faubourg Saint-Honoré and is now installed at the foot of the Madeleine (2nd floor). Faithful cutomers from the Ile St. Louis, from the west of Paris and the entire province, have followed it to buy classically cut, superbly custom-made furs and a small selection of ready-to-wear items.

## Christian Dior
**8th arr.**
**30 ave. Montaigne**
**723.54.44**

The furs are among the finest in Paris, sumptuous and expensive. What else would you expect? Oh yes, some good deals during the clearance sales.

## Revillon
**8th arr.**
**42 rue La Boétie**
**561.98.98**

The quality of the furs, the designs, the finishing are beyond reproach and are exactly what you'd expect from this great house. The large dressing rooms are pleasant and the salons are superb. You can admire yourself from all angles and check the line and fall of the coats. The sales staff are intelligent and polite, but cool if they suspect you're wasting their time. Of course, Revillon will pick up your furs at home during the first days of spring and store them in the cooler (free the first year), clean them and bring them back to you with the first northerly breeze. Are they expensive? Naturally. Let's just say that the prices are justified. At the Revillon boutique located at 44 rue du Dragon, 6th arrondissement (tel. 222.38.91) and also at the rue La Boétie, there are also sporty furs, leather, wool, pelts and mink coats from 14,000F.

# JEWELRY

*All the big names, without commentary . . .*

## Boucheron
· *1st arr.—26 place Vendôme 261.58.16. Closed Sat., except October, November, December.*

## Bulgari
· *8th arr.—27 ave. Montaigne 723.89.89*

## Cartier
· *2nd arr.—13 rue de la Paix 261.58.56 · 8th arr.—12 ave. Montaigne 720.06.73 · 8th arr.—23 faubourg Saint-Honoré Saint-Honoré 265.79.81. Closed Sat. except October 1 thru December 31 and from April 1 to June 30. (And "Boutique," "S de Cartier" and "Must")*

## Chaumet
· *1st arr.—12 place Vendôme 260.32.82. Closed Sat. in July, August, September. (And "Les Arcades" and "Les Temporelles")*

## Gerard
· *8th arr.—8 ave. Montaigne 723.70.00. Closed Sat., except in December*

## Mauboussin
· *1st arr.—20 place Vendôme 260.44.93. Closed Sat. June 1 thru mid-September*

## Mellerio dits Mellers
· *2nd arr.—9 rue de la Paix 261.57.53. Closed Sat. August, September*

## Van Cleef et Arpels
· *1st arr.—22 place Vendôme 261.58.58. Closed Sat. except in October, November, December, May June.*

## And:

### René Bouvin
**1st arr.**
**4 ave. de l'Opéra**
**296.01.38**
*Closed Sat.*

Unlike most leading jewelers, Bouvin hasn't got a street-level shop, so you must climb the stairs. You'll find superbly crafted, extremely elaborate and expensive creations immediately recognizable by Boivin's signature and style. You may also have your own stones set or reset, which will bring them back to life.

### Jean Dinh Van
**2nd arr.**
**7 rue de la Paix**
**261.66.21**
*Closed Sat.*

Jean Dinh Van has meticulously crafted jewelry in her shop's beautiful 1930s setting. Her designs make use of gold and precious gems; gold and pearls (black or white); and particularly those famous gold chains, perfect in their simplicity, yet highly distinctive (1,300F and way up).

### Fred
**8th arr.**

Brilliants, emeralds, rubies, sapphires (cabochons or faceted) are combined with yellow gold for the formal look. For those sporty outings, a Force 10 collection of

465

**6 rue Royale**
**260.30.65**

rings, bangle bracelets, key chains and cuff links, in shrouded white gold or surrounded in yellow gold. There is a good selection of watches, some of which (exclusive and spectacular) have visible movements. Friendly sales staff.

### Ilias Lalaounis
**1st arr.**
**364 rue Saint-Honoré**
**261.55.65**

Beautiful gold jewelry-sculptures await you here: necklaces, pendants, bracelets and rings inspired by ancient Greece. And a few reasonably-priced little pieces (rings from 1,000F and up).

### Poiray Boutique
**2nd arr.**
**8 rue de la Paix**
**261.70.58**
*Closed Mon. and Sat. mornings.*

The expensive jewelry is featured next door. Here you may empty your pockets little more slowly by collecting the relatively less costly little rings (2,000F and up). Of course, they are so much prettier worn in twos, threes or fours. There are also beautiful engagement rings with a marquise (diamond, sapphire, ruby or emerald), or "barrel-shaped" rings with a Byzantine motif, and so forth. If you dream of rivers, Poiray offers—so to speak—a mini-river of diamonds or other stones no more than 4/5 of an inch wide.

### Tecla
**2nd arr.**
**2 rue de la Paix**
**261.03.29**

You'll find nothing at this shop—established in 1910—but cultured pearl necklaces, long neck chains, rings, earrings and bracelets, usually matched with brilliant or vividly colored precious or semi-precious stones. If your old string of pearls no longer delights you, Tecla will give it some bounce by restringing it with gold cabochons or pairing it with a string of coral pearls (there's a lovely variety called peau d'ange which is a pale pink), jade or lapis lazuli.

### Jean Vendôme
**1st arr.**
**352 rue Saint-Honoré**
**260.88.34**

It's easy to see why Jean Vendôme's jewelry has been shown at all the leading international exhibitions—and why he is mentioned in Larousse, just like Julien Green, Roger Caillois and Maurice Schuman, whose French Academy swords he engraved. This expert in gemology offers a wide variety of precious stones and minerals in his felt-lined boutique. Next to the costly creations and jewelry-sculptures, you'll find original costume jewelry at reasonable prices.

### Costume

### Anémone (La Porte Bleue)
**1st arr.**
**Forum des Halles,**

The finest in costume jewelry, designed by a real artist of the rue de la Paix, François Herail from chez Poiray. There are collections of marbles made of wood, glass or papier-mâché, passementeries or gilded metallic pieces of impressive volume; iridescent, baroque, sometimes wild, always attention-grabbers; these trendy ornaments are

**2nd floor
297.52.16
1st arr.
235 rue Saint-Honoré
296.44.85**

splendid, and should be worn as if you were modeling them—without a care in the world and with your held held high. As for their price, no need to lift your head too high; they usually do not exceed 300F.

## Exactement Fauve
**6th arr.
5 rue Princesse
325.00.09**

Daytime fantasies for every taste and pocketbook await you at Exactement Fauve, in the form of bird-shaped earrings (25F–45F), dainty little stickpins and brooches (10F–30F), and ravishing little glass necklaces (45F). Slightly more expensive are the feathered or silk-flowered headbands (265F), American masks (200F) and a few older pieces (450F–1,000F).

## Fabrice
**6th arr.
26, 33 and 54, rue Bonaparte
336.57.95**
*Closed Mon. morning and Sat. at No. 26. Closed Mon. morning at No. 33.*

The two little even-numbered shops (on opposite sides of the boulevard Saint-Germain) sell beautiful fantasy necklaces and bracelets made of wood, scale, ivory, elephant hair, gilded metal, sea shells and combined skeins of silk. They are flashy and irresistible, with prices that range from 40F to 1,200F. There is also more conservative gold jewelry—delicate chains, rings, earrings—that you'll wear for years to come. Across the street at the No. 33 boutique, you'll find ravishingly funny turbans and hats, umbrellas, Hollywood-type sunglasses, pouches and jewelry cases.

## Gallery
**6th arr.
8 rue du Cherche-Midi
544.60.66**
*Closed Mon.*

Pinned on the four transparent plastic sheets that hang from ceiling to floor you'll find fascinating contemporary art jewelry, hand-crafted by American artists in bizarre materials such as silicone or acrylic sprayed onto silver- or gold-plated leaves to give a frosted appearance to bracelets (250F–400F); burnt steel for geometrically-shaped earrings; and even titanium (used in missiles), heated in order to get stunning "moon" tones; earrings (about 1,200F) and long Japanese chopsticks to adorn your hair (1,200F for two).

## Ken Lane
**1st arr.
14 rue de Castiglione
260.69.56**

You can wear one of Ken Lane's superb imitations amid connoisseurs of the real stuff without fear of being discovered. For example, try his imitation Bulgari, a heavy-gauge "gold" chain set with colorful cabochons (necklace 400F–600F), assorted matching bracelets, (300F). Other reasonably priced fantasia include "pearl" chokers made from multicolored silk threads.

## Pulcinella
**9th arr.
10 rue Vignon
742.57.23**

Lovely gold or gold-plated jewelry, as well as pieces made from ivory, shell, coral and elephant hair are to be found next to the atomizers and antique brushes, turn-of-the-century lamps and beautiful patchwork quilts. A charming boutique.

## Bargains . . .

## Burma

**1st arr.**
**15 blvd. de la**
**Madeleine**
**261.11.63**
**2nd arr.**
**16 rue de la Paix**
**261.60.64**
**8th arr.**
**72 faubourg**
**Saint-Honoré**
**265.44.90**

"I would like a Bulgari necklace and the latest Cartier earrings." It's the sort of request you'll only overhear at Burma's. And you'll have to admit that these simulated jewels are perfect copies of pieces that would cost you an arm and a leg. Both their quality and finish are truly remarkable. Figure 1,000F and up for the "Bulgari" 400F–600F for truly beautiful earrings in "ruby," "diamond" and "gold," or stainless steel and "gold." If you prefer, you may choose a "diamond solitaire." However, once you've washed your hands, don't expect it to maintain that eternal glitter. If you can't find what you're looking for at one of the Burma shops, simply try another one. The boutiques' suppliers aren't always the same, and the clientele is also quite varied.

## Oxéda

**1st arr.**
**390 rue Saint-Honoré**
**260.27.57**

Oxéda features used jewelry, antique and contemporary, some of which sport top names like van Cleef, Cartier and Bucheron. You'll often find good bargains. If you want to get rid of some of your old jewelry, you might try to sell it here, but get an estimate. Oxéda does not appraise jewelry and, besides, his price is unlikely to be the same as yours; don't forget that unsigned gold items such as chains, bracelets and rings are appraised by the weight of unwrought gold.

## Troc de Bijoux

**6th arr.**
**3 rue Coëtlogon**
**548.93.54**
*Closed Wed.*

Perhaps you have treasures you'd like to get rid of so you can pick up some new ones. Cartier watches, van Cleef rings, family heirlooms or couturier jewels are gauged, weighed and appraised according to the going price of gold and the jeweler's signature, then sold, with your approval, on consignment. You can make up to 70 percent of the sales price (50 percent for items worth less than 1,000F), and if your items don't sell in six months you must pick them up. Gold chains, pendants and bracelets are sold according to their weight down to the gram. Fine selection of slightly flawed earrings.

# LARGER SIZES

Some big stores have specialty departments featuring larger sizes. Galeries Lafayette (third floor) has classic models and sizes up to 22; Le Printemps has a rather limited selection, with sizes up to 18; La Samaritaine has a noteworthy department with skirts, blazers and dresses that are classic and affordable; C & A has low-priced designs up to size 18. Here are a few quality firms that specialize in large sizes.

## Alexandra
**16th arr.**
**97 rue de Longchamp**
**553.60.68**
*Closed Mon.*

Dresses from 700F and up and solid, well-tailored slimming outfits. From sizes 13 to 15. Cruise-wear collection from December 15th onwards.

## Auteuil
**8th arr.**
**76 Champs-Elysées**
**562.29.72**
*Closed мon. morning at rue de Passy.*

An enormous selection of clothes for all tastes. Suits, dresses, coats, up to size 18. The classic designs are the more appealing. Other locations.

## Gerlane
**6th arr.**
**133 rue de Sèvres**
**734.66.93**
*Closed Mon. morning.*

Youthful, stylish dresses and outfits, not inexpensive. Sizes 12 to 18. Free alterations. Home deliveries.

# LINGERIE

## Laura Ashley
**6th arr.**
**94, rue de Rennes**
**548.43.89**
*Closed Mon. morning.*

Simply designed, attractive, long nightgowns, in cotton with round necks or with pointed collars. Others with long sleeves, trimmed in lace or ruffles, have a granny gown appearance. From 200F. Many are solid white, a few others printed in delicate pastels. Other locations.

## Cadolle
**1st arr.**
**14 rue Cambon**
**260.94.94**

Hermine Cadolle, who was a Parisian corsetmaker in 1889, deserves to be immortalized. Why? She invented the brassiere. Today Alice Cadolle, her great-great-grandaughter, who keeps up, so to speak, the reputation of this outstanding invention and of the firm to which Parisiennes have remained faithful from generation to generation. Custom designs, which are magnificent, are on the third floor. Ready-to-wear and more youthful designs are on the ground floor.

## Candide
**8th arr.**
**4 rue de Miromesnil**
**265.80.55**

Candide always enjoys showing off her lingerie to devoted clients. She is aided by a smiling and courteous sales staff, who are always willing to pull out box after box of beautiful nightgowns in raw silk inset with lace (approximately 1,200F) or in crépon (solid or printed), straight-lined, with accordian pleats (450F), or flared with large collars (650F). Assorted bed cushions, cotton negligées, or knitted mohair are also available. All of it is handcrafted and can be custom-tailored for a small fee and a three- to four-week wait.

## Charley
**8th arr.**
**14 faubourg**
**Saint-Honoré**
**874.15.31**

The windows are modest and the decor is nothing special. You can pass in front ten times without noticing it. Yet Charley's lingerie is among the most enticing and, comparitively speaking, least expensive in Paris. The first-floor shop has delectable nightgowns made of cotton crépon with squared, smocked, embroidered or pleated yokes (from 300F and up). Negligées start at 450F. In silk there are fluid and sophisticated designs in black georgette crêpe with delicate straps appliquéd with colorful satin pastilles (1,380F), or champagne silk-satin inset with lace (1,100F). There are also designs for little girls. And for those who like to entertain more formally, there are beautiful black crêpe de chine or flashy red satin hostess dresses (2,800F).

## Christian Dior
**8th arr.**
**30 ave. Montaigne**
**723.54.44**

The very attractive designs by Dior (nightgowns, negligées, panties and tights) are also available in most department stores and specialty shops.

## Les Nuits d'Elodie
**17th arr.**
**1 bis, ave. Mac-Mahon**
**755.68.95**
*Closed Mon.*

Heavenly nightwear, guaranteed to give you sweet dreams. Negligées and long nightgowns in satin inset with lace or in crêpe de Chine, are breathtaking. The same goes for the prices (1,100F–10,000F). Equally exquisite underwear.

## Princess Mary
**1st arr.**
**205 rue Saint-Honoré**
**260.70.37**

Established in 1923, this boutique is named after King George VI's sister, who purchased her silk stockings here. When winter rolls around, come in and stock up on Zimmerlis, Swiss undergarments which are expensive yet the finest in the world—in wool or in silk. You'll also find Swiss Hanro with Scottish stitching.

## Nina Ricci
**8th arr.**
**39 ave. Montaigne**
**723.78.88**

Elegant nightwear, the prettiest imaginable: translucent negligées; long romantic nightgowns—in cambric or in cotton voile—or Hollywood-style, in crêpe de chine or satin—1,500F–3,000F and up. Exorbitantly priced, yet very appearling.

## Sabbia Rosa
**6th arr.**
**71-73, rue des Saints-Péres**
**548.88.37**

Sabbia Rosa's styles are better suited to voluptuous women than slender shapes. The latter, however, shouldn't go without these exquisite and expensive satin-silk undergarments, handsewn and embroidered. The shop will also make men dream. After all, who are better judges of size and fit?

# MATERNITY

## Balloon

6th arr.
70 rue Bonaparte
633.45.79
9th arr.
26 rue des Mathurins
742.17.62
*Closed Mon.*

Some plump women who aren't at all pregnant buy their dresses here; the designs are attractive and very becoming. Full or high-waisted dresses, solid or flowered, with puff sleeves; overalls; pants outfits; evening dresses. Average price is 600F. Also, there are accessories and a large selection of shower gifts. Other locations.

## Pluss

6th arr.
42 rue du
Cherche-Midi
548.33.63
*Closed Mon. morning.*

High-waisted dresses, each one prettier than the next, in zephyr (throughout the year), solid silk or Liberty prints (wool or cotton), finely ribbed or hand smocked: culotte dresses with straps; and a nice selection of pants. They can all be custom-made within a week, and retailored to size after you've given birth.

# READY-TO-WEAR

## Agnès B

1st arr.
3 rue du Jour
233.04.13
6th arr.
13 rue Michelet
633.70.20

Youthful, chic and not too expensive. With music playing in the background, trying on the clothes is child's play at Angès B. Facing Saint-Eustache's Gate, the shop's two large rooms are linked by a spiral staircase lined with shelves filled with neatly arranged T-shirts. It's useless to ask a salesgirl for assistance—they're adorable, but obviously not there to help you. It's difficult to leave, however, without buying four or five superbly cut cotton T-shirts (solid or striped), cotton or black lamb's wool pants (tapered or straight), one of an assortment of blazers, a long linen sweater which can also be worn as a short dress, or a lamé miniskirt with a pleated flounce.

## France Andrevie

1st arr.
2 place des Victoires
233.17.45

She is one of the new innovators of the place des Victoires; offering a limited yet original choice of clothes that are well-defined, cut and finished. These garments are guaranteed not to wind up in the attic or at the bottom of the closet at the end of the season.

## Apostrophe

6th arr.
54 rue Bonaparte
329.08.38
16th arr.
11 bis, ave.
Victor-Hugo
501.81.05

Apostrophe styled are both sophisticated and casual: dresses, tunics, skirts or trousers to mix and match with a variety of tops; fine cuts, exciting fabrics, chiefly silk and synthetic, at affordable prices. The salesgirls are incredibly attractive. Free alterations.

## Giorgio Armani

6th arr.
31 rue du Four
354.87.98

This leading Italian designer has chosen gray, black and white as the austere backdrop for his line. The decor is offset by camel and beige tones and tempered by the beauty of the fabrics. There are soft and supple tweeds, flannels, jersey and silky gabardine for pants, skirts and bermuda-short outfits, gray shirts in satin-silk closed at the neck by a simple catch. Well-crafted, ingenious cuts, with just the right amount of elegance and nonchalance. Unfortunately, Italian elegance and style are very costly. You'll find several nice handbags in the accessories department.

## Arnys

7th arr.
14 rue de Sèvres
548.76.99

One out of ten windows is reserved for women, and there's a small alcove at the back of the store where the Grimbert brothers give a short and stunning demonstration of their talents as designers of elegant sportswear. Numerous well-cut suits in the best masculine fabrics: subtle, light tweeds, flannels, corduroys, printed velvets as soft as a glove. Vests, skirts (straight or flared) and trousers may be purchased separately. Lovely shirts in crêpe de chine, at affordable prices, and exorbitantly priced double-knit English cashmeres. The sales staff are polite; alterations are free.

## Laura Ashley

6th arr.
94 rue de Rennes
548.43.89
7th arr.
66 rue des
Saints-Pères
544.15.96
*Closed Mon. morning.*

Laura Ashley is known for romantic white cotton blouses like the ones Lady Diana wore before she was married; also for short cotton dresses, overalls, batik bathing suits, and long smock-dresses with straps or high waist bands, in flowery cottons. Young girls during the 1970s were already wearing them at their debuts. Pregnant with their first, they continued to wear them for holiday garden parties. There is a small collection of wedding gowns trimmed with satin in worsted cotton or taffeta at reasonable prices. Other locations.

## Loris Azzaro

8th arr.
65 faubourg
Saint-Honoré
266.92.06

Scintillating, seductive and superb, Loris Azzaro's evening gowns will make you the belle of the ball. The same applies to his elegantly simple dinner dresses. Prices range between 2,500 and 14,000F.

## Balenciaga

8th arr.
10 ave. George-V
723.40.88

Balenciaga caters—very successfully—to women who are no longer twenty and don't care to hide the fact. Good woolen and alpaca suits with kick-pleat skirts and double-breasted jackets trimmed with velvet (3,500F), tailored silk shirt dresses. The staff are courteous. Alterations provided.

## Benetton

6th arr.
61 rue de Rennes
544.15.86
8th arr.
8 rue Tronchet

Here is a spirited collection of pullovers (V-necked, sleeved or sleeveless), jackets in wool or wool-angora mix, and scarves that go like candy at a children's party and have the clear, lively colors of lollipops. If you're not a stickler for quality—the clothes will fall apart before you tire of them!—you'd better stock up since they aren't very

**266.63.77**
**15th arr.**
**53 rue du Commerce**
**577.98.82**

expensive; a sweater will cost you 180F, a 3/4 vest goes for 300F. Don't skimp—these skirts (200F), trousers, T-shirts, tams, scarves and assorted tights are truly irresistable. The list of this Italian designer's boutiques and outlets in Paris and the surrounding area is too long to list.

## Anne-Marie Beretta

**6th arr.**
**24 rue Saint-Sulpice**
**326.99.30**
*Closed Mon. morning.*

Advantages: her lovely city-styled hunting jackets (1,200F–1,400F), knickers, trousers, beautifully cut raincoats, superb capes (3,400F for the cashmere ones lined with leather), all in a somewhat masculine but alluring style. Disadvantage: the haughty indifference of the saleswomen, who seem to disdain vulgar commerce.

## Berteil

**8th arr.**
**3 place Saint-Augustin**
**265.28.52**
*Closed Mon. morning.*

There's always a fragrance of heather and lavender in this good store where you'll find English-styled blazers in shetland, tweed, or flannel; quality pleated skirts or culottes; good-looking, well-cut shirts in threaded poplin; and durable loafers that are great for walking. Berteil's classic styles will last forever. The staff will treat you with exemplary politeness.

## Laura Biagiotti

**1st arr.**
**29 rue Cambon**
**261.52.66**

Yet another *Italiana* in Paris. La Biagiotti has set up shop next door to Chanel in a boutique apartment, decorated in white from ceiling to floor, where you can enjoyably lose yourself for an entire afternoon among huge taupe-colored cushions. The cashmere dresses are lovely and expensive (3,600F), as are the cashmere coats—single-lined, fringed, buttonless 5,500F—in which you can wrap yourself up as in a Scottish shawl. Woollen suits of solid skirts and print jackets are sold together with a printed silk shirt (4,700F) and there are smart-looking silk dresses (3,500F), sharkskin bags and luggage, conspicuously branded L.B.

## Cacharel

**1st arr.**
**Forum des Halles, 1st floor**
**297.45.80**
**6th arr.**
**165 rue de Rennes**
**548.96.77**
**8th arr.**
**74 Champs-Elysées**
**563.23.09**

The store is obsessed with Cacharel's perfume, Anais, Anais. Huge promotional photos reflect ad nauseum off the store's enameled walls and huge mirrors. Even so, it's easy to breeze through the rue Tronchet store among shirts with Mao-type or fine muslin collars in solid or flower-print cottons; stevedore and jacquard pullovers. Sweaters are embroidered with pearls; and straight, pleated or slit skirts are priced at approximately 400F; blazers at 680F, and suits at 1,200F. Their choice of colors isn't very exciting with the exception of the superb Cacharel bright reds. Regular items at reasonable prices.

## Pierre Cardin

**7th arr.**
**185 blvd.**
**Saint-Germain**
**548.62.46**

Of the three locations, the one at avenue Marigny is the high-fashion shop selling several very beautiful and very expensive garments that are copies of designs for the collection and mostly custom-made. The boulevard Saint-Germain store, focusing on ready-to-wear clothes, is simpler and more affordable. The faubourg Saint-Honoré

**8th arr.**
**27, ave. Marigny**
**266.92.25**

shop specializes in sportswear: a few skirts and suits at reasonable prices and many sweaters, T-shirts and knit dresses.

**1st arr.**
**31 place du**
**Marché-Saint-Honoré**
**260.78.40**

You want to dress up as a village lass or a shepherdess? Jean-Charles de Castelbajac is just the place for you, offering long vests with reversible collars and hoods; wide Pyrénées-styled woollen coats with or without beige/gold leather trim (2,000F to 3,000F); fringed ponchos; sack-dresses; bermuda shorts (530F) and tunics (1,100F) made from muslin or off-white angora; parkas and down vests.

## *Cerutti*
**8th arr.**
**15 place de la**
**Madeleine**
**742.10.78**
**16th arr.**
**37 ave. Victor-Hugo**
**505.73.13**
*Closed Mon. morning.*

No one could be more strait-laced than Cerutti. Nothing outrageous or costumey, here so don't expect any surprises in his pleasantly well-lit and designed stores. Suits (2,200F), blazers, pants, bermuda shorts and tuxedos impeccably well-cut and made from fine fabrics (tweed, flannel or linen) in classic tones of beige, black, gray, navy blue and red. To leaven this severity are accessories with a touch of fantasy: shirts and silk hankies, jewelry, belts, handbags, very pretty flat-heeled shoes or, if you prefer, fine high-heels. The month of December features the cruise-wear collection. Sales are at the beginning of January and in July. A warm reception is assured throughout the year.

## *Chanel*
**1st arr.**
**31 rue Cambon**
**261.54.55**

Does it make any sense when you're under forty to dress as if you were ten years older? Or vice versa? Or to spend lots of money for the privilege of a Chanel label? Chances are it does, judging by the rue Cambon shop's unmitigated success and by the fact that little Chanels are selling faster than hotcakes (hot to say petits fours). You have to rush over at the beginning of the season to make sure you can get your style and size. Nothing in the world matches Chanel's elegance and subtlety—straight jackets and skirts, soft wool lined with overstitched silk trapunto giving it an unmatched line and suppleness. Price here is irrelevant. And remember, these items are to be worn with assorted blouses and an entire array of accessories: chains and jewelry; two-toned, sling-back pumps; handbags—marvelously Chanel with leather-lined jersey exteriors, complete with inside pockets and refined gold-plated chain—cost a fortune. But to hell with pinching pennies; a coat made of Chanel jersey is so lightweight and warm to wear. It costs as much as a suit yet is less expensive than mink. It would be wrong not to mention the extremely courteous sales staff and their unlimited patience.

## *Le Clan*
**1st arr.**
**20 rue Cambon**

Le Clan features quality sportswear, reasonably priced and from excellent sources, including Scottish cashmere sweaters (500F) and kilts in fifteen different tartans,

**260.07.51**
*Closed Mon. morning.*

Shetland fair isle handmade knitwear, Tyrolean lodens and worsted wool jackets. You'll also find French skirts, blouses, and Lacoste shirts. Nice garments for men too.

## Cocon
**1st arr.**
**255 rue Saint-Honoré**
**260.08.63**
**6th arr.**
**22 rue du**
**Vieux-Colombier**
**548.55.04**

The sign reads "silk only," and that's all there is, at unusually good prices. Crêpe de chine shirts in 30 lively assorted colors at 450F come in all sizes and styles with lace, military, button-down, ruffled, low-cut or open collars, short and long sleeves, etc. Also, loose-fitting pants, double-breasted jackets. Other locations.

## Courrèges
**8th arr.**
**40 rue Francois-Ier**
**261.52.03**
**8th arr.**
**46 faubourg**
**Saint-Honore**
**265.37.75**
**16th arr.**
**50 ave. Victor-Hugo**
**553.70.18**

Indifferent to changing times, Courrèges always dresses you in pastels or children's garments: overalls, short skirts, T-shirts, blouses. Whether it's checked cotton or poplin lined with terrycloth, nothing is more appropriate for making sand-castles during your vacation. If you're a grownup in your thirties, check our Courrèges's winter collection. You'll find relatively inexpensive, well-tailored conservative outfits in navy, beige and white that are very slimming and not too dear. But for heaven's sake, get rid of the Courrèges monogram!

## Christian Dior
**8th arr.**
**26-32, ave.**
**Montaigne**
**723.54.44**

You can spend an entire day here without getting bored. You may walk through the salons and adjacent boutiques like a wealthy foreigner visiting Paris—no one will bother you and you won't have to spend a cent. Even if you only want to look at or touch the beautiful wares, the saleswomen are always smiling and well-disposed. On the other hand, you may also spend tens of thousands of francs at a moment's notice. Home furnishings, men's wear, fancy leather goods, jewelry, scarves, linen, perfume and beauty products are all on the ground floor at the 32 avenue Montaigne store. On the first floor you'll find hats, lavish furs and the widest variety of ready-to-wear clothes for all ages and all occasions. The dinner and evening gowns are especially beautiful. At another entry, though still at the No. 32 address, you'll find elegant sportswear, assorted knitwear in wool or mohair, sporty skirts and trousers, and the cruise-wear collection. In the alcove is Dior Junior for children up to 14 years old. The No. 28 address consists of two shops: Baby-Dior (deluxe baby outfits and shower gifts) and the linen department: bathrobes, swimsuits and beach towels. At the No. 26 address: shoes, tights, handbags and luggage, the latter disfigured by the CD label. The hospitality is overwhelmingly warm, and the services—alterations, wrapping and deliveries—are up to the standards of this truly grand company. You'll find a small selection of the overall collection at the 12 rue Boissy d'Anglas outlet, 8th arrondissement, tel. 265.52.24.

## Dorothée Bis

**1st arr.**
**Forum des Halles,**
**1st floor**
**296.40.70**
**6th arr.**
**33 rue de Sèvres**
**222.00.45**

Dorothée Bis features jersey cottons for summer, knitted wools for winter, and sparkling, multicolored and casual outfits that can be matched or worn with nearly anything depending on your mood and/or the climate. Her shop offers trousers (about 500F), large raglan-sleeved sweaters (600F–800F), loose-fitting dresses with cowl necks (880F), tights, socks, scarves and assorted gloves, as well as the entire Doro-tennis collection in terrycloth, cotton and jersey.

## Erès

**8th arr.**
**2 rue Tronchet**
**742.24.55**

A year-round collection of vacation wear for every climate, lively and not too expensive, with coordinates that are infinitely adaptable, particularly the pretty beach and outdoor dinner outfits. Winter city-styled garments include coats, raincoats, and silk outfits. There's a charming little lingerie counter on the first floor. The various styles are youthful and pretty, the likeable saleswomen never imposing.

## Louis Féraud

**6th arr.**
**47 rue Bonaparte**
**326.82.99**
**8th arr.**
**88 faubourg**
**Saint-Honoré**
**265.27.29**

A dazzling showcase opposite the Elysée. The service is deplorable, but the clothes—on the whole very appealing and original—are sorted out on various racks at your fingertips. Quilted silk pant suits (3,600F); muslin wool skirt suits (3,700F) and assorted silk shirts, classically-styled suits, and other more exciting styles in loden with embroidery (approximately 2,000F). A few gold lamé evening garments.

## Franck et Fils

**16th arr.**
**80 rue de Passy**
**647.86.00**

A monument of the 16th arrondissement. Neither terribly expensive nor very cheap, Franck has everything suitable for women from 17 to 77. The ready-to-wear department is a bit conventional, but the accessories are numerous: linen, shoes, gloves, handbags, hats, perfume, whimsical jewelry, and an up-to-date department for young women on the ground floor, as well as a new and attractive jogging department.

## Galatée

**16th arr.**
**73 rue de Passy**
**527.90.28**
*Closed Mon. morning.*

This tiny shop specializes in knitwear at unbeatable prices, including dresses and coats in wool, angora and nylon, (the latter at 250F), and countless sweaters (under 150F) in a variety of twenty or more colors. You'll also find Gaston Jaunet's ready-to-wear outifts. Their Rive Gauche outlet, Odéa, is located at 12 rue de L'Odéon (tel. 329.60.15).

## Paul de Galvert

**8th arr.**
**350 rue Saint-Honoré**
**260.67.38**
*Closed Sat.*

At the end of the court in what used to be Joséphine de Beauharnais' stables, Paul de Galvert exhibits his latest attire. You'll find shirts, superb knitted overcoats, mohair dresses, pea jackets, cashmere sweaters and vests (collection designs and separates are marked down all year), at reasonable prices and in a wide range of sizes (up to 18). A cashmere jacket goes for about 600F.

## Tan Giudicelli

6th arr.
13 rue de Tournon
329.08.13

Tan Giudicelli has consolidated his two outlets and has installed their distinctly different collections in this one boutique. Here is high fashion, at its best with cocktail, or silk-velvet and enhanced with appliquéd spangles and handstitched embroidery. These little masterworks of custom-made refinement and sophistication are rarely affordable, yet you may find an occasional crepe design for 2,000F to 3,000F. The ready-to-wear designs are both elegant and exquisitely feminine: long woolen jackets (around 1,300F), skirts (straight or full with wasp-waists, 500F–800F), shirts (400F–1,000F), jersey ensembles and attractive accessories. The staff is charming.

## Givenchy

8th arr.
3, ave. George-V
723.81.36
16th arr.
66, ave. Victor-Hugo
500.80.41
*Closed Sat.*

The beautiful boutique on the avenue Georges-V presents a designer collection that is in the firm's own workshops in the same building. Unfortunately, these unusually elegant designs are ruinously expensive; overcoats and suits, 4,500F; the luscious cocktail dresses or evening gowns which, if necessary, can be altered, range from 6,000F to 10,000F. The few boutique outfits aren't nearly as luxurious but they are somewhat more affordable.

## Daniel Hechter

1st arr.
Forum des Halles,
1st floor
297.46.31

You'll find the same traditionally sporty garments in all Daniel Hechter boutiques as the ones featured behind Daniel Hechter's lovely, dark façade: trousers, skirts, blazers, shirts—on the whole, well-cut, youthful, relatively inexpensive and easy to wear, whether in town or on vacation. Many locations.

## Hémi- sphères

16th arr.
1-3 blvd.
Emile-Augier
520.13.75
17th arr.
22 ave. de la
Grande-Armée
755.61.86

Hémisphères is the last word in international sportswear. From England classic Burberrys, superb Aquascutum frocks, frock jackets and dinner jackets—the cashmere will cost you an arm and a leg, but the woolen ones are reasonably priced. You'll also find plaids, kilts and tartans, and a whole gamut of cashmere. From the U.S. jeans, the latest in hosiery (relatively inexpensive), gold-buttoned blazers, loafers, cowboy boots, Gore-Tex parkas, down vests trimmed with or entirely made of leather. From Austria short woolen jackets in thirteen colors, and sumptuous sweaters and vests in soft alpaca (800F–1,300F). From Spain genuine knapsacks either in raw leather (1,200F) or calfskin (about 660F). And, finally, from France sumptuous silk-satin shirts, raw leather handbags and lizard-skin pumps, all skillfully treated and of indisputable quality. The prices are as exorbitant as the shop is exciting.

## Jaeger

8th arr.
3-5 faubourg
Saint-Honoré
265.22.46

A lot of cash has flowed through the registers since 1880, when the good Dr. Jaeger, advocated the use of natural animal fiber in clothing to promote better health. Wool (tweed, flannel), cashmere and camel's hair are the featured highlights in this large store, a subsidiary of the redoubtable Jaeger of London. Chic and good taste are built in.

**Gaston Jaunet**
1st arr.
**Forum des Halles,
3rd floor
297.46.08**
8th arr.
**40 rue Francois-ler
723.64.54**

Classic, well-tailored and attractive for all (young and not so young alike), Gaston Jaunet's designs are comparatively inexpensive given its choice location; Combined-fabric shirtdresses (the woolen ones are approximately 700F); fine classic suits in tweed, velvet and houndstooth are easily matchable: for each jacket there's an assortment of either a straight skirt, a pair of trousers or knickers (815F to 1,200F a piece); several gorgeous overcoats (100F to 1,400F); and lots of attractive wash-and-wear imitation silk shirts (260F to 450F). Free alterations. Smiling helpful saleswomen.

**Kenzo (Jungle Jap)**
1st arr.
**3 place des Victoires
236.56.86**

Three cheers for the breathtaking window display! The immense ground floor is done in light-toned wood and studded with mirrors and support beams. Nobody gets pushed around at Kenzo's and it's easy to park yourself there for an afternoon. Hardly a saleswoman in sight, and if you see one, she seems determined not to sell you anything. Lots of designs, however: long ones, short ones, short-short ones; in cotton, wool, jacquard; with lots of ruffles on skirts, collars, cuffs, straight pants; in combined fabrics and outrageous prints. In brief, these are whimsical garments rather than everyday clothes and, for that matter, quite expensive for the young people for whom they are intended (750F for a miniskirt, 1,500F for jackets with embroidered yokes). Lots of pretty accessories such as boots, ankle boots and flats at reasonable prices.

**Emmanuelle Khanh**
6th arr.
**2 rue de Tournon
633.41.03**

Emmanuelle Khanh has exquisitely feminine transparent silk and cotton voiles for the summer, woolen crêpes and flannels for winter, embroidery for all seasons. The styles are somewhat casual and the colors very subdued.

**Aux Laines Écossaises**
7th arr.
**181 blvd.
Saint-Germain
548.53.41**
*Closed Mon. morning.*

With sublime disregard for trends, this excellent shop remains, conservative and provincial. Handsome sweaters in cashmere, lambswool and shetland (far less expensive).

**Lanvin**
8th arr.
**22 faubourg
Saint-Honoré
265.14.40**

The ground floor boasts attractive accessories—silk scarves, shawls, jewelry, handbags (unfortunately monogrammed)—as well as mass market designs, some of which are without interest except for their labels, others interestingly chic with a distinct classicism (velvet-collared flannel suits 2,100F, silk shirts 900F). On the 1st floor you'll find ready-to-wear clothing tailored in Lanvin's own studios, hence more expensive and high fashion: dinner, cocktail and evening dresses and attractive daytime outfits; the coordinated skirt/vest poncho outfit made from wool and alpaca plus a silk shirt, retails at 5,700F (though you may purchase each item separately).

## Ted Lapidus

1st arr.
**Forum des Halles,
1st floor
296.45.32
Various locations**

Ted Lapidus offers very contemporary decor, arresting window displays and casual saleswomen. The classic and fanciful designs are repeated in a variety of colors and fabrics and are youthful, lively and reasonably priced (blazers 850F, skirts 400F–700F). Amusing accessories include T-shirts, gilt-edged sneakers, pastel-toned felt hats, romantic hooded capes, Hollywood-style sunglasses and kitsch jewelry.

## Guy Laroche

**Various locations**

The least expensive of the high-fashion boutiques. Nothing very original, although the ready-to-wear clothing is classic, well-defined and smart.

## Leo Marciano

1st arr.
**21 rue Cambon
260.02.66
8th arr.
19 rue Francois-Ier
720.74.76**

A limited selection of designs—blazers with three gold buttons, straight or finely pleated skirts, light woolen or crêpe de chine shirts, bordeau and beige monochromes. Everything can be marvelously coordinated, especially if you're bent on classic, discreet clothing. In the same line of colors there are durable outfits made from Alcantara (blousons, vests, skirts, pants) and carefree imitation suede—the same fabric used on pool tables. Alterations. Other locations.

## Marie Martine

6th arr.
**8 rue de Sèvres
222.18.44
8th arr.
50 faubourg
Saint-Honoré
265.68.22**

For those over thirty and willing to pay the price, the style here is definitely upper middle-class. The Left Bank shop, focusing on classic chic clothes, does not necessarily cater to Parisians. Imitation little Chanels, easy to wear and lacking only the Chanel monogram (jacket, skirt and blouse, approximately 500F; same price for the skirt and straight coat); elegant dresses (6,000F); a large collection of evening gowns (6,000F to 11,000F); and fur-lined cloaks at a variety of prices. All designs may be tailored to your specifications in the firm's workshop—no additional charge, with one or two fittings and a two- or three-week wait. Agreeable sales staff. At the faubourg Saint-Honoré location designs tend to be more sophisticated and showier, yet are not necessarily better. Free alterations. You'll find a more casual outlet at Marie Martine Weekend, located at 78 rue des Saint-Pères (tel. 222.43.00).

## Mettez

8th arr.
**16-18 blvd.
Malesherbes
265.33.76**
*Closed Mon. morning.*

Mettez in noted for its superb linen jackets, Austrian lodens and sweaters, classically British raincoats, and for all its hunting and riding clothes, which defy the vagaries of style and time and constitute the true elegance of country weekend outings. Relatively expensive, but you'll have forgotten the price in twenty years.

## Micmac

1st arr.
**Forum des Halles,
1st floor
296.91.44
6th arr.**

The clothes here, made quickly and well, are not too expensive. Fine selection of skirts, jackets and shirts—well-cut though sometimes hastily finished—and delightful T-shirts and coordinated sweaters. The summer cotton dresses are charming and colorful and have the advantage of being shown early in the season. Likeable saleswomen. Free alterations.

## Missoni
7th arr.
43 rue du Bac
548.38.02
*Closed Mon. morning.*

The Missoni boutique lives up to its logo and is both conservative and sumptuous. It features jersey dresses and outifts made of silk (around 3,000F) or wool; superb reversible overcoats—one side in knitted mohair, the other in tweed, silk or nylon (4,600F–5,600F)—and jackets and vests in subtle colors. If the Italian elegance appears restrained, the prices here, unfortunately, are not. Agreeable staff and, amazingly, large dressing rooms.

## Issey Miyake
7th arr.
201 blvd.
Saint-Germain
548.10.44

Original, easy-to-wear and casual, this Japanese stylist's designs are intended for tall women. The shop features broadshouldered jackets in silk and wool, short cotton skirts, narrow-waisted slips in muslin or silk, baggy trousers, flowing handwoven linen tunics, little tops in open-worked cotton with delicate straps, and superb poplin raincoats. Smiling sales staff.

## Hanae Mori
8th arr.
17-19 ave. Montaigne
723.52.03

The shop, adjacent to the fashion firm, is so well hidden at the end of the blind alley alongside the Théâtre des Champs-Elysées that you'll walk right past it ten times before you see it. The window display is unassuming, but push open the great oak door and you will be enthusiastically welcomed. There's a limited choice of skirts and straight-collared short jackets (approximately 3,000F), silk shirts (1,600F), velvet outfits with jacket's piped in gold thread (3,500F), silk dress shirts (2,800F), striking cocktail and evening garments (from 4,000F upwards).

## Thierry Mugler
2nd arr.
10 place des Victoires
260.06.37

You must have guts, a sense of humor and good looks to dress at France's latest and most phantasmagorical young designer's. These arresting get-ups—superwoman, hotel bellhop or streetwalker—are captives of Thierry's basement lair, an iridescent cavern with sea-green mosaics, poured glass adorned with gold filaments and boulders from a Wagnerian opera. Other outlets include the Au Printemps and Galeries Lafayette department stores.

## Les Nuits d'Elodie
17th arr.
1 bis, ave.
Mac-Mahon
755.68.95
*Closed Mon.*

The silver and plum art deco façade, plus the wild satin panties displayed in the windows, give you an idea of the extravagant delights you'll find chez Elodie. Inside there is silk, nothing but silk: 1930s and 1940s-styled blouses, dresses and pajamas for cocktail, dinner or casino outings, outrageously sophisticated negligées and nightgowns. All that you could dream of finding—carefully wrapped in tissue paper—as you unpack your suitcase as the Palace Hotel in Monte Carlo.

## Old England
9th arr.
12 blvd. des
Capucines
742.81.99

Old England is a store in which you'll find down-home English chic: beautiful coats in fine camel's hair (about 3,200F) and English cashmere (5,000F), the latter Italian cut. Fine tweed, flannel and corduroy suits (1,200F–2,000F), kilts, vests, blousons, shirts, weekend outfits. Although the saleswomen aren't all young, they're professional and polite. On the ground floor, you'll find cashmere sweater sets, in all colors, as ruinous as the rest.

## Lucienne Phillips

8th arr.
9 blvd. Malesherbes
265.10.53
*Closed Mon.*

At last, a really different boutique. It's not so much the white and green prairie decor, which is cosy, but the originality of its super-feminine designs which are enticing and easy to wear, at complete odds with the dictates of Parisian and trans-Alpine innovators. Not surprisingly, these designs arrive directly from London, and Lucienne Phillips carries the same garments here that are sold in her Knightsbridge shop. They are the work of young English designer-stylists: Jean Muir, who was the first to win renown this side of the Channel; Penny Green; Bruce Oldfield; Caroline Charles; Gina Fratini, despite her last name a true peaches-and-cream Brit; and Joseph Conran, son of Terence Conran of Habitat fame. No tweeds or cashmere—you'll find these across the street at Burberry's—but many smart, sophisticated outfits.

## Georges Rech

6th arr.
54 rue Bonaparte
326.84.11

These designs are easy to wear, classically cheerful and well-displayed in an agreeable decor. The saleswomen are attractive and pleasant. Dresses priced between 600F and 900F.

## Renata

8th arr.
17 rue
Saint-Florentin
260.11.69
*Closed Mon.*

She's more of a lingerière than a couturière, but what talent! You'll find nothing more graceful than her round-collared blouses or little tops with delicate straps made from hand-embroidered crêpe de chine in white or subtle pastels, 700F and up. Equally delicate and fluid are the gorgeous silk crêpe single-lined suits and discreet claudine-collared print dresses. Other dresses with wide décolletés come with assorted coats. Lovely work, moderate prices.

## Renoma

1st arr.
Forum de Halles,
1st floor
297.47.33
16th arr.
129 bis, rue de la
Pompe
727.13.79

Renoma has by far the best-looking window displays in the 16th arrondissement. Mannequins of both sexes, dressed in the house's finest, fetchingly display the chez Renoma style of casual well-being. The blazers; the suits coordinated with pants or skirts in cotton, linen, flannel or tweed; the cotton shirts and blousons are roughly the same from one collection to another, yet are undeniably appealing and durable. A few attractive styles of footwear, and big sweaters. And it isn't taboo to buy clothes in the men's department. The garments there are practically all unisex. Personable sales staff.

## Nina Ricci

8th arr.
39 ave. Montaigne
723.78.88

This superb suite of salons in harmonious beige offers many temptations within easy reach of your fingertips, if not your wallet. Fortunately Ricci's saleswomen are attentive and expert counselors who help you make sensible decisions. This is a vast universe of window displays filled with true-to-life mannequins dressed in unquestionable taste. The objects you may covet are arranged according to price. First, the accessories: scarves, belts, handbags (the evening ones are irresistible); then the knitwear, alpaca or linen jackets, cashmere ponchos, cotton or wool jersey outfits; next the gifts, jewelry, renowned perfume, fine house linen at relatively reasonable prices; the ready-to-wear clothes and lingerie including conservative suits from 3,500F, lots of smart silk dresses from 3,000F-4,500F, shirts both classic and elegant, dashing and often sumptuous evening gowns. Finally, the furs. Cloaks lined with opossum, 400F; lovely sea otter and mink, 35,000F.

## Roger et Gallet
**8th arr.**
**62 faubourg Saint-Honoré**
**266.45.65**

In contrast to the couturiers who launched lines of perfume in order to make ends meet, this old and distinguished firm, renowned for its eaux de cologne and delicate soaps, decided not long ago to reverse the process and go into the clothing business. The boutique specializes in well-cut, classic outfits; skirts and trousers; sweaters in cashmere for winter and linen for summer; easy-to-wear raincoats; and lots of accessories.

## Sonia Rykiel
**6th arr.**
**6 rue de Grenelle**
**222.43.22**
**8th arr.**
**70 faubourg Saint-Honoré**
**265.20.81**

She has been called the Chanel of the '80s; she has been selected as one of the ten most elegant women in the world; she designed the superb, shadowy new shop on the faubourg Saint-Honoré, and created a new perfume called 7th Sense. She's known to the very tips of her red hair as the beautiful Sonia, who is so photogenic that she shows off her own designs in fashion magazines more effectively than the top models. Whatever your reasons, you cannot remain indifferent to her flowing skirts, cuffed trousers (approximately 600F) made in jersey, linen or cotton for summer; her soft velvet sweatshirts or assorted woolen and angora sweaters, in solid colors or striped, with décolleté or classically cut, characterized by that little something that makes it a Rykiel; and her mohair jackets that are as warm as fur. Once you've tried them, you can't do without them. One thing leads to another and can take you all the way to the subtly colored scarves, tams, gloves and handbags.

## Saint-Laurent Rive Gauche
**6th arr.**
**6 place Saint-Sulpice**
**329.43.00**
**8th arr.**
**12-14 rond-point des Champs-Elysées**
**562.00.23**
**8th arr.**
**38 faubourg Saint-Honoré**
**265.74.59**
**16th arr.**

You can't go wrong with Yves Saint-Laurent. Like Chanel, but in a totally different vein, Yves collections follow and resemble one another. But we won't speak ironically about the steadfastness with which YSL reiterates a formula that has shown exemplary qualities for the last ten years; A formula based on solid concepts, impeccable cuts, superior quality fabrics, perfect finish, classic colors and subtle harmonies. The faithful can spot the distinctive YSL details more accurately than an oenologist can date a vintage wine. There are always the same skirts, straight, pleated, wraparound, or full and gathered, made from velvet, flannel and gabardine, with summer varieties in poplin or cotton, the same severe and full-shouldered blazers in tweed or gabardine; the same short braided jackets in velvet, silk or down-lined; the same tapered pants, marvelous on long legs; and always the same finely printed fuzzy wool or charming little silk dresses; as well as solid color or printed shirts. These outfits are

**7 ave. Victor-Hugo**
**500.64.64**

truly unrivaled. In short, these designs are ideal in that they never go out of style—if you'll exclude the North African variables—and are durable. Expensive? You bet! 1,800F–3,700F for a blazer, 900F–1,200F for a shirt or skirt—yet reasonable considering the bonus of being perfectly well-dressed for any occasion. If your style is up to the standards of the house, the reception is warm and persuasive; if not, they'll keep you at arm's length.

## Jean-Louis Scherrer

**6th arr.**
**31 rue de Tournon**
**354.49.07**
**8th arr.**
**51 ave. Montaigne**
**359.55.39**
**8th arr.**
**90 faubourg Saint-Honoré**
**265.70.96**
**16th arr.**
**14 ave Victor-Hugo**
**501.71.53**

The avenue Montaigne boutique is more intimidating than the others, but it offers far more styles in all sizes as well as the temptation to take a leisurely look at the grand couture collection at Scherrer's next door. Besides, the saleswomen will give you nothing but good advice. Along with beautiful suits and classic shirts, Scherrer has the most gorgeous silk dresses in brilliant colors and prints; and shirtdresses that are ultra-sophisticated, ingeniously cut and truly elegant. For less money you can always acquire the Scherrer look by searching through the marked-down garments at the other end of Paris (29, avenue Ledru-Rollin, 12th arrondissement, tel. 353.58.35), where you'll find the previous season's designs.

## Sara Shelburne

**1st arr.**
**10 rue du Cygne**
**233.74.40**

Sara Shelburne's charm and verve, in addition to her enticing and always very feminine collection, may induce you to commit a thousand follies. The dressy sportswear, and especially the dinner, cocktail and evening gowns—simple or wildly sophisticated—can be made to order very quickly, at no extra cost, and delivered to your home. Exclusive fabrics: jersey cottons and wools, synthetic silks so delightful they can be mistaken for the real thing. Prices range from 1,500F–2,000F.

## Per Spook

**8th arr.**
**18 ave. George-V**
**723.00.19**

The couturier who came in from the cold has a huge new boutique that isn't at all intimidating. The saleswomen are polite but not pushy; the clothes delightfully displayed, well-tagged and moderately priced. The daytime designs, easy to wear and not too flashy, include suits with straight round-collared jackets (2,000F–2,800F); classic silk shirts (750F and up); quilted jackets (approximately 1,600F); and straight woolen or silk dresses. For the evening, lovely velvet outfits, cocktail or evening dresses in black spangles, silk, lamé, muslin and plush velvet (approximately 4,000F).

## Torrente

**6th arr.**
**2 rue de Sevres**
**222.90.50**
**8th arr.**
**9 faubourg Saint-Honoré**

In this contemporary setting, you'll find classic faubourg St. Honoré designs, executed in Torrente's own workshops. These well-cut quality fabrics are not, on the whole, stratospherically priced. Attractive shoe department, exclusively made-for-Torrente by Mercadel. The collections are always displayed in the delightful basement garden parlor at the faubourg St. Honoré location. Winter collections in September and October,

**266.14.14**
**16th arr.**
**6 ave. Victor-Hugo**
**501.66.80**

summer collections in February and March.

## Tunmer
**8th arr.**
**5 pl. Saint-Augustine**
**522.75.80**
*Closed Mon. morning*

An excellent establishment whose primary focus—riding, tennis, skiing and sailing wear—will include from now on city-styled sportswear. Attractive weekend, casual or everyday attire in seersucker, Madras, quilted cotton, flannel and ribbed velvet. Attractive and of good quality. Steep but fair prices.

## Emanuel Ungaro
**8th arr.**
**2 ave. Montaigne**
**723.61.94**
**8th arr.**
**25 faubourg Saint-Honoré**
**266.45.70**

The avenue Montaigne shop, housed in the high-fashion building, has the largest and best selection of designs. You'll miss the dazzling, kinetic prints and the graphic strokes lovingly carried out by Emanuel Ungaro and Sonia Knap a few seasons back, though you may prefer the flowery motifs and subdued tones of today. Without a doubt the harmonies are both subtle and elaborate, though sometimes camouflaging the line of the clothes. Stratospheric prices.

## Valentino
**8th arr.**
**17-19 ave. Montaigne**
**723.64.61**

Valentino is a distraction from the lovely ladies who frequent the Théâtre des Champs-Elysées. Window-shopping, you'll find all of Italy's seductiveness, elegance and élan. Among the classical designs, though, there are also more flamboyant ones: you'll find black pearl-satin suits with skirt or bermuda shorts (5,000F, approximately, slightly less in houndstooth); and black, gold or silver lamé evening sweaters with ostrich feather collars (2,500F). The Miss V collection is discreet and more reasonably priced.

## Victoire
**2nd arr.**
**10-12 place des Victoires**
**508.53.29**
**8th arr.**
**38 rue Francois-Ier**
**723.89.81**

Victoire is the fashion editors' favorite house. Two shops and two women managers. Depending on your taste, you'll choose either the picturesque and congenial jumble at the place des Victoires—where you may shamelessly ransack the shelves and unhook the dresses—or the formal and well-arranged shop at the rue François-Ier. In both, you'll find designs by the top names in ready-to-wear clothes, such as Beretta, Lison Bonfils, Tarlazz, Enrico Coveri, Montana, Rech and others. Clothing yourself from head to toe is child's play, providing you're willing to pay the price. Casually chic, classic attire and a few enticing extravaganzas for the evening: dresses in spangled voile, jersey or in lace, from 1,000–4,000F. In the adjacent boutique at No. 10 place des Victoires, there are large and superb cloth carry-alls in taupe, black or red, which you'll be tempted to fill with holiday dresses, quilted jackets, jacquard cardigans, cotton skirts and accessories, both fun and attractive.

# SUEDE AND LEATHER

## Daim-Style
2nd arr.
**8 place des Victoires**
260.95.13

All the designs are made in this studio-store before your eyes, and the affable owner has the patience of a saint. Well-cut designs, very much in vogue without being too avant-garde. Full-shouldered leather jackets (1,500F–2,200F), skirts, jumpers, coats (2,400F–3,800F).

## Japa
1st arr.
**3 rue de la
Ferronnerie**
260.95.25
*Closed Mon. morning.*

There are lots of leather goods in this shop, which also distributes Yamamoto and Kanzai products. Exclusive designs in ten colors: skirts (700F), blousons (1,000–1,500F); and if you can't find that red blouson of your dreams, you can always have it custom made.

## Merenlender
8th arr.
**3 faubourg
Saint-Honoré**
265.12.36
*Closed Sat.*

Don't go searching for his boutique; both the studio and the salons are located on the third floor. But if you seek it out, you will find superb coats (suede or leather); cloaks made from leather, poplin or silk lined with fur; leather jackets and blousons that this tailor couturier makes to order (the fittings are done in cloth) in extremely supple materials. There is also a department for custom-made furs. M. Merenlender is the official supplier to various high-fashion firms; he also does alterations, cleaning and general upkeep of leather and fur garments, even if they are not his.

# SWIMWEAR

You'll find a few swimsuit designs in most couturier-boutiques, and, of course, these are large selections in all department stores. Buy them early: Once the sun is out, they'll melt before your eyes.

## Christian Dior
8th arr.
**28 ave. Montaigne**
723.54.44

*The* place to come if you're about to spend a few days aboard a princely yacht or beside some tycoon's pool. Dior bathing garments, such as velour bathrobes, attractive terry beach dresses or bath towels, are a serious investment. More reasonably priced are the swimsuits (approximately 350F). However, here as at any Dior outlet, you've got to be careful: the sophisticated glibness of the sales staff may make you oblivious to the prices.

## Erès
8th arr.
**2 rue Tronchet 5**
742.24.55

Every December we await the new collection of swimsuits with the same impatience and, truthfully, we are seldom disappointed. Here there are itsy-bitsy, two-piece suits with adjustable tops and bottoms that retail separately for 150F each; the superbly sophisticated one-piece suits which will (un)dress you beyond perfection are 350F. There is also enticing and relatively expensive assorted beach or after-beach attire, in terrycloth, jersey or cotton voile.

### Réard
1st arr.
9 ave. de l'Opéra
297.40.50

In 1946 he created the bikini (the registered trademark and common noun can be found in the Larousse Dictionary). Then he designed the chameleon swimsuit which changes colors in ten seconds; and the Gutenberg, whose embossed text imprints itself on sand; and, finally, the swimsuit of the year 2000—the Rhodoïd. In short, there are all kinds of styles designed to accent your best features and camouflage others. They are all partially custom-tailored in exclusive fabrics. There is also a line of city clothes in leather so delicate that it is as versatile as fabric and comes in lots of pretty colors.

# Where To Find

## AN APARTMENT, A HOUSE

### Denis Chevalier
8th arr.
103 blvd. Haussmann
265.22.57
*Closed Sat.*

This alert real estate broker will help you find what you're looking for, even if you don't know yourself. He will also advise you how best to sell your property.

### Inter-Urbis
8th arr.
1 rue Mollien
563.17.77

Inter-Urbis rents well-furnished apartments whose owners are occasionally out of town for two to three months. Rates: about 2,500F a month for studios, 3,500F a month for one bedroom. Tenants are required to present first-rate guarantees and references. Inter-Urbis will also rent your own apartment for short periods.

## AV EQUIPMENT

### Domaine de la Vidéo
9th arr.
73 rue de la Victoire
874.32.49

Domaine de la Vidéo rents and sells video-cassettes. An annual subscription of 500F entitles you to rent a movie for three days at 35F, or one week for 50F, without a deposit. Without a subscription the cost is 50F for three days, 75F for one week, plus a 500F deposit. Video projectors rent for 400F (weekends), plus a 6,000F deposit.

### Ghilbert
**16th arr.**
**62 rue**
**Chardon-Lagache**
**288.36.46**

Ghilbert will rent by the day, week or month all movie equipment, projectors, sound-video gear (cameras, projectors, receivers), with or without technician. There are special rates for longterm usage. They pick up and deliver equipment on request. This reliable house will always offer you the best advice.

### Shop-Photo Mont-parnasse
**14th arr.**
**33 rue du**
**Cdt-Mouchette**
**320.15.35**

This store rents cameras, movie cameras, projectors, tape-recorders, video projectors, etc., along with accessories. Technician supplied upon request.

# A BICYCLE

### La Maison du Vélo
**10th arr.**
**8 rue de Belzunce**
**281.24.72**

La Maison du Vélo will rent bicycles equipped with five to ten speeds, for from 25F per day to 300F per month, plus a 200F deposit. The firm also has a small bookshop with maps, books and periodicals, and can advise you on long-distance bike treks.

### Paris-Véo
**5th arr.**
**2 rue du Fer-à-Moulin**
**337.59.22**

Paris-Vélo rents bicycles at 30F a day, 180F a month, or at an annual rate that includes a maintenance contract. Bikes equipped for long distances are slightly more expensive at 45F for 24 hours, 60F for weekends and 260F per month, including third-party insurance, plus a 200F deposit. Home delivery upon request. On weekends and holidays, Paris-Vélo has rental outlets at the Bois de Vincennes, Porte-Jaune intersection and avenue de Nogent.

# BOAT

### Bateaux Parisiens
**7th arr.**
**port de La Bourdonnais**
**705.50.00**
*Departure from d'Iena bridge, Left Bank. Parking.*

You may rent these boats from 9:30 A.M. to 9:15 P.M. for groups of twenty passengers or more. Cost: 10F per person for a one-hour excursion (from 7:30 P.M. to 10:30 P.M. 15F per person, depending on age). Reservations must be made 24 hours in advance.

# A BUS

### Autocars-Services
**13th arr.**
**52 blvd. Masséna**
**583.38.29**

Autocars-Services rents 16- to 60-seat buses, some of which are equipped with air-conditioning and sleeping units.

# A CAMPER

### Car-Away
92400 Coubevoie
60 rue de Caen
334.15.81

Car-Away rents three different models of campers to accommodate three to six passengers. Foreigners need an international driver's license. Weekly rates: 1,900F off-season, 3,550F peak season (includes free 100 km. per day). Weekend rates: from 1,000F (first 500 km. free). All rates include insurance (full coverage) and international assistance.

### Dreamcar
92130
Issy-les-Moulineaux
6 ave du Bas-Meudon
736.01.75
*Closed Sat. afternoon.*

Dreamcar will rent variously sized campers for three to five passengers for excursions and short trips. Weekly off-season rates: 1,600F–2,000F (includes first 100 km. per day); peak season: 3,430F–4,290F (free mileage), plus 2,500F deposit (refundable upon return).

# A CAR

### Avis
7th arr.
5 rue Bixio
550.32.31
*As well as other stations in Paris.*

A Renault 5 rents for 109.37F per day, plus 1.22F per km.; a family-size Peugeot 504, 149.35F per day, plus 2.82F per km. Reserve cars 48 hours in advance. Flat rates for holidays and weekends.

### C.I.F.A.
15th arr.
80-82 blvd. Garibaldi
567.35.24

C.I.F.A. features late-model Peugeots and will deliver to your home during regular working hours. A Peugeot 504 costs 164F per day, plus 2.10F per km. There are outlets all over France and abroad. Chauffeur on request.

### Citer
12th arr.
4 blvd. de la Bastille
579.06.60
*Closed Sat.*

Citer features Citroëns only. GS: 102F per day, plus 1.20F per km. Visa: 92F per day, plus .90F per km.

### Europcar
645.21.25 local
reservations
(France).
664.10.04 out-of-
country reservations.

A Renault 5 GTL rents for 94.08F per day, plus .99F per km. A Renault 20 TX (with automatic transmission): 176.40F per day, plus 2.12F per km. Above rates include taxes. Flat rates for unlimited mileage and/or lengthy usage.

### Hertz
15th arr.
Hôtel Holiday Inn,
73 blvd. Victor
533.29.29

Renault 5, Ford Fiesta and Peugeot 104: 116.50F per day, plus 1.30F per km.

### Mattei Automobile
12th arr.
205 rue de Bercy
346.11.50
12th arr.
108 blvd. Diderot
628.27.50

Rentals by the day or longer. Renault 5 GTL: 94.08 per day, plus .78F per km. Renault 20 TS: 137.59F per day, plus 1.29F per km. All daily rates based on 24 hours. Weekend rentals from Friday, 5:00 P.M. to Monday 9:00 A.M., the same as two-day rates. Rentals for more than six days are at a decreased rate. Other locations.

# =A CHAUFFERED LIMOUSINE=

## Britannique Location
**60 rue Violet**
**575.04.52**
*Open daily, 24 hours.*

Like a lord or an excellency, you too can ride around in a late-model Rolls Royce Silver Shadow II, with or without chauffeur (bilingual on request). Only it will cost you. Rates: 1,300F per day, plus 560F per km. Rentals by the day, half-day or longer.

## Compagnie des Limousines
**92200 Neuilly**
**16 blvd. Vital-Bouhot**
**637.39.33**

This company rents de luxe limousines (Daimler, Rolls Royce, DS Président) equipped with bar, stereo, telephone, newspaper and chauffeur. The cost: 900F entitles you to four hours of luxury (the first 40 km. are free). Great for Friday night rush hour at the place de la Concorde, or for whenever the Métro is on strike.

## Bernard Durand
**92200 Neuilly**
**2 bis, rue de l'Eglise**
**624.37.27**

Bernard Durand rents luxury sedans with distinguished-looking bilingual chauffeurs. Ideal for business or pleasure trips and excursions. Rentals by the half day, day, week, month or longer. A Peugeot 604 rents for 452F from 9:00 A.M. to 1:00 P.M., including 35 km. in Paris.

## Fast International
**16th arr.**
**42 ave. d'Iéna**
**723.88.92**
*Open daily 9:00 A.M. to 7:00 P.M.*

For "important" clients. Rates: from 9:00 A.M. to 6:00 P.M., 2,470F (includes 85 km.). Evening rates (8:00 P.M. to 1:00 A.M.): 2,023F. A ride out to Orly Airport costs 494F, to Charles-de-Gaulle Airport: 565F. Fast International also has secretaries, interpreters, office rental brokers and worldwide reservation service.

## Murdoch Associés
**8th arr.**
**30 ave.**
**Pierre-Ier-de-Serbie**
**720.08.57**
**16th arr.**
**59 ave. Marceau**
**720.63.28**

This reliable firm specializes in renting Rolls Royces with competent (and bilingual) chauffeurs. A Silver Shadow (15 hours, 150 km.) costs 3,175F. Will also rent by the hour.

# ==AN ENTERTAINER ==

## Les Baladins du Crépuscule
**6th arr.**
**169 rue de Rennes**
**544.68.81**

A simple phone call is all it takes for this association to send an operetta singer, a clown, a guitarist, a mime, a puppeteer, a storyteller, a folk-singing group or a gypsy band to your home—all of whom are guaranteed to brighten your day. Les Baladins du Crépuscule hires only professional artists who can be viewed on video-cassettes by prospective clients. Figure on spending at least 1,411F for a show in your home. The company will also install sound and lighting equipment.

# *AN EVENING GOWN*

### *Eugénie Boiserie*
**9th arr.**
**32, rue Vignon**
**742.43.71**
*Closed Mon.*

Eugénie Boiserie will put you into a faubourg Saint-Honoré-styled evening gown or cocktail dress in silk, taffeta or lace. Average rental rate: 400F (Friday to Tuesday), plus a 500F deposit; sizes 9-13.

### *Troc de Truc*
**8th arr.**
**37 rue du Colisée**
**562.08.00**
*Open 2:00 P.M. to 7:30 P.M.*

For an impromptu evening out, Troc de Truc features can supply an evening gown for 300F (48 hours).

# *FURNITURE*

### *L.A.C.M.*
**15th arr.**
**127 rue du Cherche-Midi**
**734.80.58**

Linen is not included in the bed rental rates. For single, 170F per month (includes frame and mattress); for a double, 190F. Same-day bed-repair service.

### *Gaétan Lanzani*
**17th arr.**
**19 rue Basfori**
**379.00.74**
*Closed Sat.*

You can rent a Louis XVI chest-of-drawers or a Regency sideboard by the day or longer (1-4 days: 8% of value plus tax; 2 weeks: 10% of value plus tax). Lanzani also makes, sells and restores all sorts of period furniture and woodwork.

### *Ruby & Cie*
**16th arr.**
**11 rue Chanez**
**651.39.27**

You'll find everything in contemporary or "period styles" with which to furnish your apartment (furniture, linen, dishware, washing machine, etc.). Bed rentals: single, 164.60F per month; double, 188.10F per month.

# *A HELICOPTER*

For an air tour around Paris, transporting a VIP, a publicity stunt, aerial photography, a transfer of funds, or even an aerial leaflet-dropping operation, call one of the two following companies which feature Ecureuil and Alouette II helicopters. 2,350–3,300F an hour, depending on vehicle. See also *The Sights.*

### *Héli-France*
· *15th arr.—Héliport de Paris, 4 ave. de la Porte-de-Sèvres 557.53.67*

### *Hélicap*
· *15th arr.—Héliport de Paris, 4 ave. de la Porte-de-Sèvres 554.12.55*

# A HOT-AIR BALLOON

### Club d'Intervention Aerostatique (Librairie Roux-Devillas)
**6th arr.**
**12 rue Bonaparte**
**354.69.32**

For in-flight baptisms, you can rent a two-passenger hot-air balloon by the hour for 500F per person; or for a party or wedding reception you can rent a larger-sized model (you'll need a lawn 50-by-50 meters for takeoff) in which guests and newlyweds can soar 50 meters into the air and land 200 meters away. Rates: 4,000F for the first hour, 900F each hour thereafter. On request, fireworks can be set off from the balloon.

# A MOPED

### Autothèque
**2nd arr.**
**80 rue Montmartre**
**236.87.90**
*Closed Sat.*

Will rent mopeds and bicycles. Moped rental rates: 50F per day; 250F per week, plus 1,000F deposit. Insurance included.

# AN OFFICE

### Centre Commercial et Industriel
**20th arr.**
**5, 7 bis et 8, rue de Lesseps**
**371.49.69**

This distinguished firm specializes in renting office space from 470F per month. Will also furnish billing addresses (from 105F per month) and answering services, and set up offices in Paris for regionally based companies. Free legal advice.

### Ibos
**16th arr.**
**15 ave. Victor-Hugo**
**502.18.00**

Ibos offers all the conveniences a visiting businessperson needs from an office. Furnished offices (16 to 30 square meters) are rented by the half-day, day (from 435F) or month (5,292F) with conference rooms (882F), telex machines, telephotographic machines and multilingual secretarial services.

# OFFICE EQUIPMENT

### Locomac
**92600 Asnières**
**4 rue Louis-Armand**
**790.65.24**

Locomac rents calculators, typewriters and photocopiers for a one-month minimum. An electric typewriter costs 235.20F month.

### Satas
**17th arr.**
**90 ave. de Wagram**
**763.96.81**
**92111 Clichy**
**107 rue**
**Henri-Barbusse**
**270.85.40**

Satas rents all sorts of machines (27 models) for folding, sealing, opening and stamping letters and parcels.

# A PLANE

### Air Affaires Inter-national
**93350 Le Bourget**
**Aéroport, Zone Nord**
**837.39.35**

Various (five to ten passenger) planes for business trips, all departing from Le Bourget. Daily basic rates range from 1,750F–2,750F. There's an additional rate of 500F–800F for each additional landing. Price based on length of flight from 3,000F–7,000F, plus 7% tax (national flights only).

### Euralair
**93350 Le Bourget**
**Aéroport du Bourget**
**838.92.73**

Successful business people depend on this firm, which features 24-hour service in France and abroad. Their prices must be considered in the light of the time you save doing business. Minimum rental: 9,400F per day for a Learjet 25 (much, much more for a Mirage 10 or 20).

# A POOL BY NIGHT

### Piscine de l'Étoile
**17th arr.**
**32, rue de Tilsitt**
**380.50.99**

For aquatic night owls, midnight swimmers and those who don't like to share their pools. Rates: 400F per hour, from 10:00 P.M. on. Reservations by phone, before 4:00 P.M.

# RECEPTION EQUIPMENT

Rental costs in themselves are expensive, not to mention the additional cost of delivery. If you hire a caterer, he or she will move often than not offer to supply you will all the necessary equipment. It won't cost you a cent more and eliminates a lot of worry. Should you decide to rent equipment separately, call one of the specialty firms listed below, preferably one month prior to your reception. (More notice needed during December or May to June). You will be given rental rates and terms as well as an illustrated catalogue which you may consult at leisure. Upon request, an expert will come to your home and advise you as to what will be needed and how things should be set up. Experience shows that renting all the equipment for a moderately sized reception comes out to about 100F per person (not counting food, etc.).

### Belloir et Jallot
6th arr.
4 rue de Cité
326.64.11

B. & J. are the greatest, most extravagant party organizers, and can be counted on to come up with the wildest and most beautiful decorations imaginable.

### Blin
78000 Versailles
37 rue Carnot
953.10.16

Blin has been hosting parties since the Second Empire. You may collect and return the decorations yourself.

### Catillon
8th arr.
14 faubourg
Saint-Honoré
265.20.93
15th arr.
58 rue de l'Eglise
557.51.60

Founded in 1832, this remarkable firm has high yet justifiable prices. It will take care of the sound equipment and lighting and will decorate all of the reception rooms.

### Rosell
1st arr.
3 rue d'Alger
260.40.93

You may rent all the necessary equipment for your party or reception without being obliged to use the excellent catering department.

# SKIS AND CAMPING EQUIPMENT

### Dethy
4th arr.
20 place des Vosges
272.20.67
*Closed Mon.*

This cluttered shop is the most valuable place in Paris for renting skis, ski boots, clothes and equipment for camping. All goods are exchangeable. Rental rates: skis (10F–18F per day), ski boots (5F per day), steel-framed tents for four people (300F–400F per month), baggage-trailers (616 lbs., 440F per month).

# A STEREO

Paul-Louis Gastaud, an expert in custom-made stereo systems, rents equipment (indoor and outdoor) for

**8th arr.**
**2 rue d'Anjou**
**265.95.23**
*Closed Mon. morning.*

parties and receptions. His equipment includes generators, tape-recorders and a five-hour tape for dancing, or a psychedelic stereo system with a luminous organ, laser beam, bubble-machine, disc-jockey and technician. Rates: 20,000F and more. Reserve at least one month in advance.

# A TELEVISION

## Locatel
**8th arr.**
**52 Champs-Elysées**
**758.12.00**

Locatel has 37 stores in Paris and in the metropolitan area. TV installation, delivery, maintenance and repair service are all free. Rates: color TV, 147F per month for one-year rental. Locatel rents video-projectors (220F per month, two-year contract) and movie video-cassettes (50F, three days).

# A TRAIN

## S.N.C.F.
**10th arr.**
**162 rue Saint-Martin**
**202.50.20**

Why rent a train? If you have a lot of guests, why not? Simply phone the SNCF two months in advance and they will send someone to your home to give you a free etimate. Many options are possible: 1st-class car (54 seats), 2nd-class car (80 seats), dining-car, disco-car, sleeping-car. Incidentally, a 2nd-class car, rented from Paris to Quimper, costs 17,500F.

# A TRUCK, A VAN

## Avis
**92100 Boulogne**
**78 ave. Pierre-Grenier**
**609.04.30**
*And other locations in Paris.*

A Peugeot J9 rents for 253F per day, plus 1.12F per km.

## Hertz
**92400 Courbevoie**
**44 rue Emile-**
**Deschanel**
**270.91.07**

A Peugeot J7 pick-up rents for 222F per day (Mon.-Fri.) plus 1.05F per km. plus 39F for full insurance coverage; weekends, 340F (150 km. per day free).

## Mattei Automobile
**12th arr.**
**205 rue de Bercy**
**346.11.50**

Utility vehicles rented by the day or longer. Good rates. Many locations.

# A TUXEDO

### Au Cor de Chasse
**6th arr.**
**40 rue de Buci**
**326.51.89**

Three-day rental (5 days for weekends): tuxedo (250F–300F), tails or dinner-jacket (300F–400F), top hat (50F–60F); deposit, (800F).

### Jean-Jacques
**6th arr.**
**36 rue de Buci**
**354.25.56**

Jean-Jacques has been renting garments, since 1867, and his prices are still very reasonable. Dinner-jackets: 260F (dark gray) and 300F (light gray); tuxedos: 190F; jackets: 280F.

# Where To Find
# . . . Emergency

# AN AU-PAIR

It is impossible for us to list all the advantages and disadvantages inherent in an au-pair arrangement. In brief, a young girl au-pair isn't necessarily pretty, nor industrious, nor patient with children. To compensate her for five hours of work each day, you will have to provide board and lodging and pay her an allowance, anywhere from 650F–800F a month. On the other hand, if she is industrious and honest, you can only benefit from her presence around the house. Many organizations sponsor girls from Germany, Scandinavia, North and South America for a fee of 150F–600F. For best results, inquire one to two months in advance.

### Accueil Familial des Jeunes Etrangers
• *6th arr.—23 rue du Cherche-Midi 222.50.34. Open 10:00 A.M. to 4:00 P.M. Closed Sat. afternoon.*
  *This serious and competent organization sponsors au pair girls from around the world.*

### Alliance Francaise
• *6th arr.—34 rue de Fleurus 544.38.28, ext. 61. Open 1:30 P.M. to 6:00 P.M. Closed Sat.*
  *All nationalities.*

### L'Arche
· 15th arr.—7 rue de Bargue
273.34.39. Closed Sat.
All nationalities.

### Entraide Allemande
· 8th arr.—42 ave. George-V 720.22.85.
Closed Sat.
German and Austrian.

### Foyer Porta
· 17th arr.—14 rue Pierre-Demours
572.18.66. Closed Sat.
German.

### Inter Séjours
· 9th arr.—4 rue de Parme 280.09.38.
Closed Sat.
English.

### Mission Catholique Hollandaise
· 17th arr.—39 rue du Docteur-Heulin
627.49.02. Closed Sat.
Dutch.

### Relations Internationales
· 9th arr.—100 rue Saint-Lazare
551.85.50. Closed Sat.
English, Australian and American.

# A BABYSITTER

He or she will look after your child throughout the day, evening or night, at home or in your hotel and, if you're lucky, will even accompany you during holidays to Perros-Guirec or Saint-Jean-de-Luz. The price: 13F–20F an hour, plus 20F–30F a day (agency fee). These are the rates applied by Nurse Service, whose staff is extremely competent.

### Institut Catholique
· 6th arr.—21 rue d'Assas 548.31.70.
14F an hour. No agency fee.

### Kid Service
· 1st arr.—17 rue Molière 296.04.16.

### Ludéric
· 16th arr.—11, rue Pétrarque
553.93.93.
14F an hour for a babysitter, plus yearly subscription fee of 380F.

### Nurse Service
· 17th arr.—33 rue Fortuny 622.26.22.

# A BODYGUARD

### Century
**8th arr.**
**102 Champs-Elysées**
**562.62.62**

Century hires out well-trained bodyguards with guaranteed clean police records. They also have guard dogs. Intimate protection is assured day and/or night, regardless of your lifestyle, needs and travels. Depending on the risk factor, bodyguard rates range from 82F–176F an hour (70–117F for a watchdog). For nights, add 20 percent.

## Ludéric
**16th arr.**
**11, rue Pétrarque**
**553.93.93**
*Closed Sat.*

Not only will Ludéric dispatch its staff to serve you dinner; look after the kids; come up with ideas for your business; organize your meetings, travels and receptions; and purchase your firewood and groceries; it will also look after your personal protection. This agency features German shepherds (plus trainers) for 60F an hour or a security guard (armed, upon request) with a radio-equipped car. Estimates available.

# A CHAUFFEUR

## Allô-Chauffeur
**10th arr.**
**12 place**
**Jacques-Bonsergent**
**205.96.96**

Allô-Chauffeur recommends that you phone 24 hours ahead for all-day service (or in the morning for afternoon service) in order to retain an "executive" chauffeur (bilingual upon request). Minimum 4-hour rates: 61.35F an hour, plus 25% evenings and double on Sundays.

## Chauffeurs-Service
**6th arr.**
**132 rue d'Assas**
**326.71.98**

All it takes is a phone call (day or night) to retain a chauffeur for a half day, full day or 24 hours. Rates are as follows: daytime (8 hrs. maximum): 423.30F (65.85F each additional hour; 92.60F after 10:00 P.M.); time-and-a-half on Sundays.

# A CLEANING COMPANY

## Jammes
**10th arr.**
**3 rue de la Fidélité**
**246.32.48**

Whenever you need your invaluable art works carefully cleaned, your antique furniture expertly polished, your carpets shampooed, your floor waxed or your apartment cleaned from top to bottom, give M. Jammes a call. He will come to your home and make an estimate of whatever there is to be done. He will carry out the task himself, or, if necessary, call in his crew. All in all, his rates are reasonable: 750F per day to clean a six-room apartment (with a crew of four).

# A CLEANING LADY

If you still can't find someone to clean your home after asking your concierge or neighborhood storekeeper, or if your ad in the *Figaro* has not met with success, don't give up without first consulting the Bumidom or church-sponsored agencies. The latter are located for the most part in the 16th arrondissement and are the most efficient. They don't ask for a commission and will dispatch cleaning ladies to all Parisian districts.

### Bumidom

· *4th arr.—7 rue Crillon 277.60.20.
Open Mon. to Fri. 9:00 A.M. to 6:00 P.M.*

*Bumidom's staff is either from the
West Indies or the Reunion Islands. They
can be hired with or without board (20F
an hour). For daily chores, phone 24
hours in advance; for live-in domestic
servants, phone one week in advance.*

### Eglise de l'Assomption

· *16th arr.—88 rue de l'Assomption
224.41.50. Open Mon. and Thurs.
afternoon.*

### Église Espagnole

· *16th arr.—51 rue de la Pompe
504.23.57. Open Mon. to Fri. 2:00 P.M.
to 5:00 P.M.*

### Mission Catholique Vietnamienne

· *14th arr.—15 rue Boissonnade
633.14.79. Everyday 9:00 A.M. to 12:00
noon and 2:00 P.M. to 5:00 P.M.*

### Nôtre-Dame de Grâce de Passy

· *16th arr.—4 rue de l'Annonciation
525.76.32. Open Fri. afternoon.*

## A CRAFTSMAN

### Artisan-Service
**720.91.91**
*Closed Sat.*

This free service is offered to you by the Paris Chamber of
Trades. A mere phone call will get you the name and
address of a professional located near your home.

## A DELIVERY MAN

### Allô-Fret
**655.88.80**

Within half an hour, you'll have a delivery man with his
truck at your front door (load: 1,500 kg.; volume: 9 cubic
meters). Rates as per contract or according to meter. Initial
fare: 69.38F, 3.41F per km. in Paris, 5.76F in metropolitan
area; 24.70 each 1/4 hour (standing fare or for loading).

### Allô-Transport
**274.20.40**

Allô-Transport will deliver anything from chocolate boxes
to grand pianos, in Paris or in the metropolitan area.

### G 7 Fret
**93400 Saint-Ouen
52 rue Eugéne-Berthoud
257.33.44**
*Open daily 7:00 A.M. to 10:00 P.M.*

Within two hours, G 7 Fret will dispatch a delivery man
and truck to your home. Rates: 142F per hour (including
mileage) for all deliveries in Paris. Sundays, call 24 hours
in advance (189F per hour).

## DOMESTIC HELP

### Maison Service

Maison Service dispatches cleaning ladies, chambermaids,
cooks, laundry workers, babysitters and nurses, all on a

**16th arr.**
**10 rue Mesnil**
**553.62.30**
*Closed Sat.*

4-hour minimum basis: 220F for cleaning ladies and 238F–292F for laundry workers and cooks.

# AN ELECTRICIAN

**A.S.**
**Dépannage**
**553.94.44**

Same-day repair service of household appliances, plumbing electricity, TVs. Rates: 115F per 1/4 hour, plus 115F transportation.

# AN EVERYTHING COMPANY

**Ludéric**
**16th arr.**
**11 rue Pétrarque**
**553.93.93**
*Closed Sat.*

They will serve you dinners, watch your children, scout out new ideas to start your own enterprise; organize everything for your meetings or seminars, trips with a theme, and receptions of all kinds; deliver your wood, do your errands and take charge of your personal security.

# A FIX-IT MAN

These companies are instantly available to unclog your bathtub; repair your front door lock; replace your fuses; tow your broken-down car, or fix just about anything.

**Pépin-**
**Service**
**16th arr.**
**1 rue des Bauches**
**520.36.13**

This firm offers a 24-hour repair service for plumbing, heating, electricity, furniture, household applicances, TVs, locks, etc. Rates: 100F an hour, plus 88F for transportation. For service on holidays and at night, call 527.34.67 (50% extra).

**S.O.S.**
**Dépannage**
**5th arr.**
**7 rue Linné**
**707.99.99**

The 24-hour service includes repairing locks, plumbing, electricity, heating, windows, etc. Will tow cars. Daily rates: 34F per 1/4 hours, plus 135F for transportation. Night rates (8:00 P.M.–7:00 A.M.), Sundays and holidays: 42F per 1/4 hour. S.O.S. will also do odd jobs such as painting houses and repairing furniture. Estimates available.

# A GASMAN

**Adam**
**Service**
**357.64.33**
*Closed Sat.*

Repair rates range from 153F for radiators and waterheaters to 188F for boilers.

**Dépannage-**
**Gaz**
**887.61.72**

Same day or within-24-hours repair service for gas applicances, except kitchen stoves. Rates: 150F–250F for boilers, 150F for radiators and 180F for water heaters. Three-month warrantee on all repairs.

# THE IMPOSSIBLE

**Ludéric**
**16th arr.**
**rue Petrarque**
**553.93.93**
*Closed Sat.*

If suddenly, at 2:00 P.M., you decide to throw a party, Ludéric will purchase your groceries and prepare the meal by 6:00 P.M. Guaranteed! Also see under "An Everything Company."

**Madame**
**Service**
**17th arr.**
**76 rue Lemercier**
**228.15.30**
*Closed Sat.*

Madame Service will supply you with an "additional" dinner guest, a fourth member for contract bridge, a Swiss citizen to witness your City Hall marriage, an Arab-speaking barker, a stuffed lion.

# A LOCKSMITH

**Cleflash**
**13th arr.**
**180 ave. de Choisy**
**589.90.50**
**15th arr.**
**162 blvd. de Grenelle**
**783.33.18**
*Closed Sat.*

There's no need to get into a flap if you lose your car keys while you're making your rounds. Cleflash will tow your car to its garage and supply you with a new pair of keys within two or three hours (hourly rates: 120F). Will reproduce all keys.

# A MESSENGER

Whether you need a package delivered to the other side of Paris, or a letter that must be immediately mailed, or a simple delivery, just call one of the following moped messenger services (max. 24 lbs.). The nearer your location, the cheaper the rates and the faster the delivery.

**Allô-**
**Courses**
**9th arr.**
**8 rue Blanche**
**281.44.44**
*Closed Sat.*

All deliveries made by moped or motorcycle in Paris and metropolitan areas. Rates: 54F an earrand (50 errands, 1,680F).

## Courses Service
**12th arr.**
**16-18 rue Abel**
**344.67.35**
*Closed Sat. afternoon.*

Errands by moped: 53F per errand (decreasing subscription rates: min. 26.40F). Errands by truck or pickup: 93F, 134F, or 145F per hour (min. 2 hours) depending on vehicle. Nights, double rate. Service available within the hour.

# A NURSE

## La Boueé
**8th arr.**
**114 Champs-Elysées**
**359.74.60**
*Closed Sat.*

For an annual fee of 250F, this mutual aid organization will promptly dispatch a nurse at an hourly wage of 20F (min. 4 hours) plus transportation. All-night rates, 220F–230F; monthly rates, 3,600F–4,000F. They will also dispatch a governess (for home or children) with or without board.

# A PLUMBER

## Allô Plombiers
**15th arr.**
**40 rue des Volontaires**
**734.04.73**

Daily rates: 60F per hour, plus 60F for transportation.

## Boget
**11th arr.**
**8 passage de Ménilmontant**
**357.38.02**

Repairs within 48 hours. Rates: 65F per hour, plus 65F transportation.

# A STEREO REPAIRMAN

## Hifiavie
**18th arr.**
**17-19 rue Lambert**
**255.01.63**
*Closed Mon.*

Hifiavie will dispatch a technician to examine and repair your stereo. Major repairs are done in the shop. With a three-month warrantee and home delivery. Rates: 141F per hour for major repairs, 129F per hour for simple repairs.

# A TV REPAIRMAN

## S.O.S. Télé
**306.41.23**

Rates: 178F for B&W TVs, 198F for color TVs, plus parts.

**Télé-Secours**
15th arr.
142-144, rue de
Théâtre
579.68.91

Télé-Secours has same day or within-24-hours repair service. Rates: 165F (metropolitan area, 188F), including transportation and labor. Major repairs are done in the shop.

# ═A TYPEWRITER REPAIRMAN═

**Le Matérial de Bureau**
92600 Asnières
4 rue Louis-Armand
790.84.69
*Closed Sat.*

Le Matérial de Bureau features 24-hour service. Rates: 76F per hour, plus 76F transportation. Major repairs done in shop (estimates available). Will loan replacement machines on request.

# Where To Learn

## ═CONFECTIONERY═

**Marguerite Lapierre**
7th arr.
122 rue du Bac,
1st floor
222.39.31

Or how to make confections at home using rudimentary utensils. You'll need a marble block, however, and Marguerite Lapierre will see that you get one. Three-level courses offered by this astonishing sugar-spinning sculptress are held on Mondays and Fridays. The cost is 350F for four two-hour sessions.

## ═CUISINE═

**Le Bistro d'Hubert**
1st arr.
36 place du Marché-Saint-Honoré
260.03.00

It's a rare chef indeed who'll share his recipes and secrets with you; Hubert is the only restaurant owner in Paris to have had this good idea. As he says, "I don't teach people how to cook, I teach them my recipes." They include petit navarin de pêche (fish stew) cooked in basil and anise, escalopes de foie gras with fresh onions, paupiettes de sole with langoustine braised in cider. Chef Hubert offers you a shortcut to the 2 toques rating. Courses are held in a professionally equipped kitchen, and your masterworks are then consumed in the restaurant's dining room. The minimum 3 sessions cost 1,500F (2,800F for 6).

Expensive, yet well worth it, for his selection of ingredients and menus are exceptional. Courses are held Tuesdays through Fridays, from 3:30 P.M.–5:30 P.M.

## Marie-Blanche de Broglie
7th arr.
18 ave. de la
Motte-Picquet
551.36.34

Formerly a hard-working student at the Cordon Bleu, Marie-Blanche de Broglie now teaches at her Normandy castle in summer, and in her Parisian kitchen during the rest of the year when she isn't off and running around the world evangelizing French gastronomy (in three languages). She teaches current cuisine that consists of complete, seasonal and simple menus for those who have little time to cook. Courses are held Monday and Friday mornings from 10:30 A.M. to 1:00 P.M. in groups of six, after which lunch is served. Participants prepare their own dishes and decide on the menu for the following session (1 lesson, 200F; 6 lessons, 1,060F). Mlle Broglie also shows you how to prepare a complete menu and assemble the needed ingredient. (Tuesdays and Thursdays, from 2:30 P.M.–4:30 P.M.; 1 lesson, 90F; 6 lessons, 180F). Her dishes include chaud-froid of poultry, melon surprise, eggplant gratin, glazed duck with cherries, pear pies, mousse of foie gras, veal knuckles with carrots, and honey-flavored ice cream. A recent feature are M. Rabourdin's French wine courses (6, 2-hour sessions) in which you can taste six regional wines per session (1 session, 170F; 6 sessions, 920F). Other courses include the art of being a host(ess)—how to prepare and decorate a bufffet, how to arrange flowers—as well as haute cuisine (classes under Chef Laffon which are held on Tuesdays, from 10:30 A.M. to 2:00 P.M.) followed by a luncheon (1 session, 320F; 4 sessions, 1,200F).

## Le Cordon Bleu
7th arr.
24 rue du
Champs-de-Mars
555.02.77

Established in 1895, this celebrated school has been enthusiastically run by Mme Brassart since 1945. She designed the three well-equipped kitchen-classrooms that used to be shops along the rue du Champs-de-Mars. Mme Brassard believes that her students should have a solid foundation before aspiring to stars and toques. Courses at the Cordon Bleu last a minimum 6 weeks and cost 4,200F–4,650F, depending on the level, with 2 practical courses and 3 demonstration-classes per week. The compulsory smock, apron and three dish towels are sold at the school. Practical courses for 10 to 12 students are taught by a former chef from the Petit Marguery and last two hours each. Students prepare a complete menu which is later eaten for lunch. Mme Brassard highly recommends the demonstration-classes (75F for 1, 800F for 12). The lengthier courses are usually for foreigners who want the Cordon Bleu diploma before opening restaurants back home. The demonstration-classes (maximum 50 students) allow for tasting and last 2 hours (mirrors are affixed to the ceiling for a better view). The Cordon Bleu also offers 4-week summer courses (3,000F–4,000F, depending on how many courses you take) and courses in flower arranging and table setting.

## La Cuisine d'Erna

**16th arr.**
**43 rue Copernic**
**500.39.00**

Erna Jacquillat is from Lyon, and her cooking reflects her heritage. After a few years in California, where she first taught cooking, she returned to Paris and, combining her large kitchen with her white and cheerful dining hall, opened up the cooking school. There's a beautiful round walnut table, indoor plants, a working counter in sandstone and brick, two stoves (gas and electric) and quantities of serious equipment such as heavy-bottomed pans and electric appliances. The idea is to prepare a complete menu (hors-d'oeuvre, entrée and dessert) which is sampled immediately afterward. Once you're seated, you're treated as a guest (there's no need to clean up!). Classes consist of 6 to 7 students and are held twice a week: Tuesdays, from 7:30 P.M. to 10:00 P.M., with dinner; Thursdays, from 10:00 A.M. to 1:00 P.M. with lunch. Her cuisine is generous and rather rich. Featured dishes include pullet with coarse salt, squab in garlic, sardines stuffed with spinach and mint, terrines, butters (blanc or monté), lukewarm sole salad, gratin dauphinois, veal sweetbreads in puff pastry, eggs scrambled with sea urchin, desserts and confections. A former student of Marguerite Lapierre's, Mlle Jacquillat will also teach you how to make chocolate truffles and colorful sugar pastries, this course costs 2,000F (6 sessions).

## Les Loges de la Cuisine

**6th arr.**
**8 rue de Nevers**
**633.60.42**

Housed in a vaulted basement, Katherine Bouret's classroom is as well equipped as the Cordon Bleu's or La Varenne's. Each of her students (6 per course) gets his or her own stove and oven and may tote the masterpieces home. For foreigners who can't take their blanquette of veal to their hotel rooms, she organizes luncheons and daily visits to les Halles and culinary specialty shops. For 1,500F you get 4 practical classes and meals, plus an afternoon outing. Katherine Bouret is self-taught, although she has always enjoyed cooking. She has perfected her teaching in three years. Her cuisine is very feminine, earnest, simmering with ideas, quite unsophisticated. Her menus include ducklings prepared with three varieties of peppers, goose conserves (preparation, conservation and application), chaud-froid of poultry, Mauritanian sole, rabbit with mustard. A special course is available for the preparation of foie gras (450F). Otherwise, courses cost 272F apiece and are held every day from 2:30 P.M. to 5:00 P.M. A monthly subscription to 6 sessions costs 1,365F. Also featured are children's courses on Wednesdays from 2:30 P.M. to 5:00 P.M. (60F per class, 500F per trimester)— who knows, your child may turn out to be a chef!

## Le Pot-au-Feu

**1st arr.**
**14 rue Duphot**
**260.00.94**

Established in 1893, right behind the Madeleine, the Pot-au-Feu is the oldest school of cuisine in Paris. It is also accredited by the university as a technical high school. Open Mondays thru Fridays, from 9:00 A.M. to 12:00 noon and 3:00 P.M. to 6:00 P.M., the Pot-au-Feu is designed for students who intend to take the C.A.P. (Practical Training Certificate) exams. Hence its classic menus, which include chicken sauce chasseur, veal stew à la Marengo, sauce à la Duglère. No nouvelle cuisine is featured at the school. The installations are not the best: 20 students have to share the same few utensils and two gas stoves. The tuition, however, is quite reasonable (1,500F per month, for 5 weekly classes). Adult classes are held on Wednesdays, Thursday evenings and Saturday mornings and feature specialties from famous Parisian restaurants (750F per month for 3 weekly classes; 90F per class). Everything prepared on the premises is subsequently eaten, and students take turns doing the dishes.

## Anne Roberts
**9th arr.**
**19 rue de Milan**
**526.85.09**

Since the days of Mary Queen of Scots, some of the world's greatest connoisseurs of French cooking have been the Scots. You'll get the idea at Anne Roberts's school of fine cuisine, next to the Gare Saint-Lazare. This charming, blue-eyed Scot offers 7 courses in French cuisine in her little apple-green kitchen: traditional cuisine (8 classes), nouvelle cuisine (8 classes inspired from Guérard's cuisine minceur pastry-making (6 classes), regional cuisine (8 classes), vegetable (4 classes), fish (4 classes) and buffet preparations. For the moment, all her customers are foreigners (Americans, Indians, Vietnamese). The utensils aren't very sophisticated and there isn't too much room, yet the atmosphere is friendly. And you can chat and eat your own meals on a rooftop terrace overlooking Paris. Each course costs 90F.

## La Varenne
**7th arr.**
**34 rue Saint-Dominique**
**705.10.16**

L'Ecole de Cuisine La Varenne is located in a former bistro between the Invalides and the National Assembly. Its founder-director, English-born Anne Willan, lived in the U.S., where she was a noted food editor. She writes and travels widely, and her customers are mostly foreigners (American, Australian, Canadian, English, Japanese). The lessons are given in French by French chefs, but all commentaries are made in English by translators or La Varenne's cheerful associate director, American-born Gregory Usher. The prestigious school offers traditional French cuisine (beef à la mode, lobster à l'Américaine), nouvelle cuisine and regional specialties (cassoulet, bouillabaisse). On Tuesdays, demonstrations are given by famous chefs like Gérard Pangaud and Antoine Bouterin (Le Quai d'Orsay), Jean-Michel Bedier (Chiberta) and Michel Comby (Lucas-Carton), all of whom prepare entire menus in front of 50 students. You are to take notes and ask questions. Written recipes are then given you for you to take home. Each class (80F) lasts 2-1/2 hours, after which you may sample the food. Practical courses are given by the house chef and director of cuisine, Fernand Chambrette from 9:00 A.M. to 1:30 P.M. or from 5:30 P.M.–9:00 P.M. and include wine and lunch or dinner. The ten students are divided into teams of two to three people who have their own stove, oven and necessary equipment (students are not required to wash dishes). La Varenne offers several formats: a 6-week series (4 practical courses + 5 demonstrations) costs 13,000F–15,000F, depending on level; a 1-week "visitor's" series costs 2,400F; a 1-week summer course costs 2,685F for pastry-making, nouvelle cuisine or delicatessen dishes.

# WINES

## Académie du Vin
**8th arr.**
**Cité Berryer—**
**25 rue Royale**
**265.09.82**
*Closed Sat.*

This institution was founded by Patricia Gallagher and Steven Spurrier in a building that belongs to the Caves de la Madeleine, which is next door. Spurrier, an Englishman, is a widely acknowledged authority on French wine. A few cleverly taught courses in this school's serious though informal atmosphere will give you a clear idea about the intricacies involved in wine-tasting. Suitable cheese is served along with the wine. And, upon graduation, you will stand out at all Parisian dinners with your newly acquired knowledge in wine! Courses cost 550F–850F for 6 2-hour sessions a week, from 7:00 P.M. to 9:00 P.M. A weekly course in English is available during the summer from 11:00 A.M. to 1:00 P.M.

## Association Française de Dégustation et d'Oenologie
**17th arr.**
**69 rue des Dames**
**387.06.94**

Drinking them is the only way to get to know wines, especially if you can compare them under the watchful eye of a connoisseur like the association's president, Christian C. Flacelière. Here you can take 8, 4-hour courses on Wednesdays, from 8:00 P.M. to 12:00 midnight, in groups of 15 maximum. Each course provides you with information on wine: vineyards, vines, geology, oenology; wine-tasting, how and what to look for in tasting and smelling wine; and a dinner during which you learn how to order the appropriate wines for your meal. Price: 1,800F (includes 8 dinners).

## Découverte de Votre Vin
**14th arr.**
**4 rue Didiot**
**543.46.84**

Can wine really be taught in the same fashion as bookbinding and engraving? The answer is yes, thanks to the Découverte de Votre Vin workshop (sponsored by the ADAC and Paris City Hall) and to young Alain Ségelle, a wine master in a traditional restaurant—and a technical consultant on wines. In 4, 2-hour sessions, he will teach you everything about vineyards: the vines, exposure, regions, soil, size, the biological cycle of wines and fermentation principles). After which, glass in hand, you will learn how to identify the colors and aromas of wine. Finally, you will learn how to taste them. Four weeks of wine-tasting will enable you to identify and appreciate well-known and lesser-known French wines. Additional topics covered during courses include glassware, wine serving, wine and meal combinations, setting up wine cellars and purchasing wine. Courses are reasonably priced—roughly the same as a good bottle of wine: 30F for enrolling in the ADAC (27 quai de la Tournelle, 5th arrondissement, tel. 326.13.54), plus 50F for the wine workshop. Four 2-hour sessions, Mondays from 6:00 P.M. to 9:00 P.M. and Saturdays, from 3:30 P.M.–5:30 P.M.

# THE SIGHTS

**O**verdemanding tourists shouldn't bother reading the following pages. They'll be far better off examining the *Guide Bleu* or Michelin's *Guide Vert*. Since we have no intention of outdoing those works, we prefer to list relatively unknown Parisian delights.

# *Airways*

"Altitude, 660 meters; cruising speed, 200 km/hr." The helicopter has just left the Issy-les-Moulineaux landing strip and already Paris seems very small, its peripheral turnpikes resembling country lanes. The pilot follows the Seine, then veers in the direction of the Manufacture de Sèvres and the Saint-Cloud Woods without ever changing the craft's altitude. You follow the auto-route and come to the Versailles château, gardens and pools. The helicopter then swings around and begins to head back, offering a view of the Longchamp Hippodrome, Roland-Garros and the Parc des Princes. Crossing over the Seine, the craft begins its descent. You've just completed a ten-minute ride in a craft with picture windows offering incredible views of Paris and its surroundings. Two companies, Hélicap and Héli-France, offer three separate 10- to 30-minute excursions *around* Paris (flying over Paris is prohibited). Prices are as follows: Château Versailles 180F, La Défense skyscrapers 120F, the complete tour of Paris 320F, and the Loire River châteaux 9,000F, maximum 5 passengers.

## *Héli-France*
*15th arr. — Héliport de Paris, 4 ave. de la Porte-de-Sèvres (tel. 557.53.67).*

## *Hélicap*
*15th arr. — Héliport de Paris, 4 ave. de la Porte-de-Sèvres (tel. 554.12.55).*

# Cemeteries

We see nothing morbid in listing Parisian cemeteries. Rather, we consider these "gardens for the dead," with their green spaces and dramatic trees, to be among the liveliest spots in Paris in which to take a walk.

### Cimetière d'Auteuil
**16th arr.**
**57 rue Claude-Lorrain**
**651.20.83**

This charming little cemetery was planned in 1793 by a philanthropist whose wish was to "put together some trees so as to ornament the plain." Enlarged over the years, this cemetery contains the tombs of the Countess de Boufflers, Mme Helvetius, Hubert Robert, Gavarni, Gounod and many others.

### Cimetière de Belleville
**20th arr.**
**40 rue du Télégraphe**
**636.66.23**

More than 128 meters above sea level, this plot of land is the closest you'll get (in Paris, anyway) to heaven. Claude Chappe came here to experiment with his tachygraphic machine (an early form of shorthand), which was later used to record the victorious battles of the Republic, the first of which was at Valmy. We beseech you not to leave the cemetery without visiting the grave of Jules Caillaux (1862–1916), the founder of the Paternal Union of Flowers and Feathers.

### Cimetière de Charonne
**20th arr.**
**place Saint-Blaise**
**371.40.66**

This exquisite little necropolis is the only one in Paris to have its own church (excluding the tiny cemetery of the Calvaire de Montmartre). You'll find here the graves of André Malraux's two sons who were killed in an auto accident. The largest tomb (eight meters wide) belongs to Bèque, French patriot, poet, philosopher and, supposedly, Robespierre's secretary. You'll see a life-sized statue of him standing on top of a stone slab and holding a rose, the symbol of the French Socialist Party.

### Cimetière de Montmartre
**18th arr.**
**20 ave. Rachel**
**387.62.24**

The countless tombs of literati make this cemetery the biggest outdoor academy in the world. Mme Récamier, one of its inhabitants, could never have dreamed of holding a more brilliant and eclectic salon with the likes of Stendhal, Heinrich Heine, Dumas fils and his heroine, Alphonsine Plessis (a.k.a. Marie Duplessis or Camille), Théophile Gautier and Sacha Guitry in attendance. You'll also see Charcot's grave and the marble headstone of Greuze, a celebrated artist who "painted virtue, beauty and innocence, thereby honoring his paintbrush." Don't leave without visiting the bronze reclining figure of Cavaignac, one of Rude's masterpieces.

## Cimetière Mont-parnasse

14th arr.
3 blvd. Edgar-Quinet
326.68.52

Here, too, as you stroll along the cemetery's rectilinear walkways, you'll come across some of the most illustrious names in French literature, art, history and science. Montparnasse's 36 acres of graves include those of Huysmans, François Coppée (next to the eighteenth-century Charité Mill), Théodore de Banville, Sainte-Beuve, Leconte de Lisle, Léon-Paul Fargue, Guy de Maupassant and Charles Baudelaire. Is it by chance that Vincent d'Indy's grave is right next to Saint-Saëns? Or that Alfred Dreyfus's tomb is next to his attorney's? Fortuitous or not, the names go on and on, with Soutine, Fantin-Latour, Othon Friesz, César Franck, Emmanuel Chabrier, Rude, Houdon, Bourdelle, Sartre. Many of the monuments are picturesque, like the tall white stone with a bare-shouldered young girl attempting to draw a rose (a students' tribute to their teacher), or the extravagant mausoleum depicting Mme Pigeon who, armed with her husband's lamp, is trying to brighten up the universe.

## Cimetière de Passy

16th arr.
2 rue Cdt-Schloesing
727.51.42

Whereas the Père-Lachaise cemetery is known for its Empire heroes and the Montparnasse cemetery for its nineteenth-century celebrities, Passy unites famous figures of the twentieth century. An example is Marie Bashkirtseff, the young poet who died at the age of 24 and who wrote the celebrated *Journal,* delighting the French with her mysticism. She rests in an enormous pseudo-Byzantine chapel decked out with photographs, paintings and busts. A few steps away, you'll discover a grotto with the remains of the great African art dealer, Paul Guillaume. A little bit further, at the intersection of the place du Trocadéro and the avenue Paul-Doumer, you'll find an unassuming white slab with the name of Jean Giraudoux. In the same vicinity, you'll discover the graves of Tristan Bernard, the Comte de Las Cases (Napoleon's companion in exile) and the pianist Yves Nat, housed in a horrible millstone grotto. At the Cimetière de Passy, you'll find an entire series of turn-of-the-century neo-Roman, neo-Byzantine and neo-Gothic chapels.

## Cimetière du Père-Lachaise

20th arr.
16 rue du Repos
370.70.33

You may find it exhausting to visit this gigantic cemetery filled with celebrities. To many tourists, Père-Lachaise has become a funerary museum for the arts. Yet once you've satisfied your curiosity by visiting Oscar Wilde's tomb, you may find it interesting to know that from the top of the hill, a few feet away from the Federated Wall, the young Louis XIV watched the battle waged between Turenne and Condé.

## Cimetière Picpus

12th arr.

This tiny, secret, country-styled cemetery is hidden behind the elevated walls of the rue de Picpus convent, next to a garden of flowers and vegetables. Nothing in this serene and green oasis evokes history and

**35 rue de Picpus**
**346.80.39**

bloodshed, yet this is the site of two huge collective graves of victims guillotined between 1793 and 1794 on what is now called the place des Nations. Although most of these people were commoners, there were also many victims from the greatest families in France. Under the Empire, their descendants purchased the land and made it into a private cemetery. Thus, amid a small grove of trees, you'll see the two historical collective graves and, next to them, 50 tombs in what is considered to be the most exclusive cemetery in France. Aristocratic names like Montmorency, Lévis, Mortemart, Noailles, Rohan, Talleyrand, Montalembert and Polignac. You'll find Old Glory planted atop General Lafayette's tomb. It was the only American flag to have waved in France during the 1940-44 German occupation.

# Churches

Of course, we won't recommend all of the capital's churches. But there are many lesser known places of worship that still contain memorable or beautiful treasures and relics. They stand in tranquil contrast to many more famous churches that are being debauched by blatantly visible electronic gear, irritating audiovisual presentations and souvenir stands.

**Les Billettes**
**4th arr.**
**22 rue des Archives**

The remnants of a charming little fifteenth-century cloister, the last of its kind in Paris. This Lutheran temple, formerly a fourteenth-century convent, also features two interesting Baroque canvases.

**Cathédrale Saint-Alexandre Nevsky**
**8th arr.**
**12 rue Daru**
**227.37.34**

Built in the Napoleon III style (also known as Byzantine-Moscovite), the cathedral is continuously undergoing restoration. It is the oldest Orthodox church in Paris and the one most attended by White Russians. The mass is majestically conducted and the hymns are beautifully sung. The crypt is superb.

**Chapelle du Collège des Irlandais**
**5th arr.**
**17 rue des Carmes**

A dilapidated though charming façade between two rather ugly-looking buildings conceals beautiful little chapels. This is the actual site of the Collège des Lombards, in which Saint Ignatius Loyola sojourned.

## Le Minaret de la Mouffe
**5th arr.**
**1 rue Daubenton**
*Closed Fri.*

You'll be stunned by the immaculate whiteness of this vast and harmonious Moorish-styled mosque with its soaring minarets and cupolas. Its many notable features include colorful gardens and patios trimmed with delicate plants, pink- and white-marble fountains, countless courtyards and corridors lined with friezes and mosaics, sculpted cedar ceilings, stained-glass windows, copperware and admirable mihrabs. . . . Our only regret is that the guided tours are far too brief. The mosque has its own *medersa* (an institute for studing the Koran) whose rector is considered a patriarch to Muslim residing in the western world. During Ramadan, you'll see innumerable followers clad in robes, jeans and three-piece suits in front of the huge portal which is strung with lights.

## Port-Royal
**14th arr.**
**119 blvd. de Port-Royal**

Pascal would stroll up and down its cloister, which served as a prison during the French Revolution. Mother Superior Angélique Arnaud is buried under the slabs of the chapel's choir stalls.

## Sainte-Elisabeth
**3rd arr.**
**195 rue du Temple.**

This church contains beautiful works of art such as a hundred sixteenth-century bas-reliefs from the Saint-Vaast in Arras Abbey and magnificent fifteenth-century panels from Spain and Italy. Marie de Medici layed down its cornerstone in 1628.

## Saint-Germain-l'Auxerrois

**1st arr.**
**2 place du Louvre.**

The bells of this famous church rang out during the Saint Bartholomew Massacre. Inside, you'll discover an admirable gilt wood triptych which is easily comparable to the one in Toledo, Spain. Lebrun designed the magnificent sculptured benches facing the chapel which contains Queen Marie-Amélie's prie-dieu and a badly lit dark wood Flemish retable. The church's stucco walls have been redone in white, and although the master carillonneur is now retired, you can still hear the bells on Wednesdays at 6:00 p.m.

## Saint-Germain-de-Charonne
**20th arr.**
**4 place Saint-Blaise.**

This church, which you would normally find in a village, was constructed in the eleventh century and rebuilt 400 years later. It is the only one in Paris to have its own cemetery.

## Saint-Gervais-Saint-Protais
**4th arr.**
**place Saint-Gervais.**

Salomon de Brosse most probably designed the church's imposing classic façade. According to Voltaire, one glimpse of it was enough for anyone to believe in God. The eight members of the Couperin family who played the organ between 1656-1826 have all contributed to this church's fame.

## Saint-Leu-Saint-Gilles

**1st arr.**

This fourteenth-century church has undergone many transformations over the centuries and contains some notable works of art, such as Jean Bullant's sixteenth-

**92 bis, rue
Saint-Denis.**

century marble depiction of Saint Anne and the Virgin
Mary or, in the manner of Philippe de Champaigne, *The
Marriage of St. Catherine* by an artist of the Perugian
school. Other paintings include Simon Vouet's *Nativity*
and an untitled work by Georges de La Tour.

## Saint-Louis-en-l'Ile

**4th arr.
19 bis, rue
Saint-Louis-en-l'Ile.**

More museum than church, Saint-Louis-en-l'Ile features
innumerable works of art, including eight painted panels
from the sixteenth-century Flemish school of art, *The
Virgin's Death* by the Rhenish school, *Emmaüs'
Disciples* by Titian's brother, an exquisite little painting
from Fra Angelica's school, lovely medieval
embroideries, wooden statues from Italy, Germany and
France. Of the church's original furnishings, only the
statues of Saint Genevieve and the Virgin Mary remain.
During the French Revolution, they were disguised as the
goddesses of Reason and Freedom. Saint-Louis-en-l'Ile
represents the dominant style during the reign of
Louis XIV.

## Sainte-Marguerite

**11th arr.
36 rue Saint-Bernard**

The Ames du Purgatoire chapel in this church lined with
astonishing trompe-l'oeil grisaille by the Italian Brunetti
(1765) is one of the most remarkable and least known in
Paris. Its sculptured works are resplendent. The floor is
made of gravestones, beneath which are burial vaults
where repose, among others, Vaucanson, the eighteenth-
century mechanical genius. In the church's charming
little cemetery, you'll find a grave overgrown with weeds
that is presumed to be Louis XVII's.

## Saint-Médard

**5th arr.
39 rue Daubenton.**

This stunning little rustic church was completely redone
at the same time that its magnificent sixteenth-century
triptych was restored. The superb and colorful nave
features numerous admirable French paintings. The one
depicting Christ appears to have been done by Philippe
de Champaigne.

## Saint-Nicolas-des-Champs

**5th arr.
254 rue Saint-Martin.**

Parisians may not know it, but the interior of this church
is extremely interesting. You'll discover a superb
fourteenth-century altarpiece depicting the life of Christ,
as well as a seventeenth-century reredos containing two
of Simon Vouet's best paintings. Also featured is a
painting by Frans Pourbus which depicts the king of
France kneeling in front of the Virgin Mary surrounded
by sympathetic figures. The exquisite Renaissance
southern gate leads to a picturesque house decorated
with a seventeenth-century sundial.

## Saint-Nicolas-du-Chardonnet

**5th arr.
39 blvd. Saint-Germain.**

This church was rebuilt by Charles Le Brun in the
seventeenth century and houses the Le Brun family
chapel which contains the superbly made tomb of his
mother. Also featured are magnificent paintings such as
Pieter Brueghel the younger's *Crucifixion. The
Annunciation* from the sixteenth-century Flemish

school, Le Brun's *The Martyrdom of Saint John* and many other beautiful works by Nicolas Coypel and Jean and André Restout. The first chapel contains Corot's *Baptism of Christ*. Recently all of the paintings, copperware and bronzework have been immaculately restored, cleaned and polished.

### Saint-Pierre-de-Montmartre
**18th arr.**
**2 rue du Mont-Cenis.**

Most tourists have been to the Sacré-Coeur but ignore the existence of this charming Roman-styled church. Its ogival vault dates back to 1147, making it the oldest one in Paris, and its illustrated capitals are extremely beautiful. The columns may have been part of the original temple of Mercury which was located here, although many contend that they date back to the Merovingian era (A.D. 500-751).

### Saint-Serge
**14th Arr.**
**93 rue de Crimée.**

Among the ten Russian churches in Paris, the most sumptuous and most famous is the Cathédrale Saint-Alexandre Nevskey, known for its stunning choir. Yet, hidden in a garden at 93 rue de Crimée, there is a curious-looking wooden church called Saint-Serge which will make you think you're in Russia.

### Séminaire des Carmes
**6th arr.**
**70 rue de Vaugirard.**

Beyond the magnificent trees rises the cupola of the Saint-Joseph-des-Carmes Chapel. The first dome to have been built in Paris, it features some beautiful seventeenth-century trompe-l'oeil. Its charmingly provincial garden is where the September Massacre occurred in 1792 during the French Revolution.

### La Sorbonne
**5th arr.**
**place de la Sorbonne.**

This is the site of Richelieu's magnificent white marble tomb, designed by Le Brun and built by Girardon. The dome's medallions are by Philippe de Champaigne. Visitors must check in at the rectorship of l'Académie de Paris, 47 rue des Ecoles, 5th arrondissement.

# Educational Tours

Although Paris is steeped in history, and there are plenty of tours to refresh your schoolroom memories, we have listed a few that we think are worthwhile. These learning experiences are great for children of any age!

## Catacombes

**14th arr.**
**2 place**
**Denfert-Rochereau**
**321.58.00**
*Open every Sat. July 1 thru October 15; open 1st and 3rd Sat. October 16 thru June 30. Tours at 2:00 p.m. Fee: 7F.*

In Gallo-Roman times the catacombs were used as a stone quarry. At the end of the eighteenth century the site became a mass grave for thousands of innocents who were the victims of religious persecution. The caverns were first opened to the public in 1861, when the noted photographer Nadar—who photographed the leading men and women of his time—chose this location to demonstrate the use of artificial (galvanic) light for taking photographs.

## Égouts de Paris

**8th arr.**
**Entry across from 93 quai d'Orsay**
**705.10.29**
*Open Mon., Wed., last Sat. of the month (except days preceding and following holidays) 2:00 p.m. to 5:00 p.m. Fee: 6F.*

The sewers of Paris are a huge and winding underground network, 1,800 kilometers long, designed by Eugène Belgrand in 1860. The tour begins under the place de la Résistance and includes a guided walk, an audiovisual narration and a museum visit.

## Musée du Louvre

**1st arr.**
**cour du Carrousel**
**260.39.26**

Countless activities are offered here to both adults and children (see also in "Museums"). There are courses, visits to halls normally closed to the public, lectures, and so forth. And should you become a member of the Society of Friends of the Louvre (located at the Pavillon de Marsan, 107 rue de Rivoli, 1st floor—tel. 260.70.64), you'll receive many benefits such as free admission to the Louvre and Jeu de Paume Museum, a 50 percent discount for all national museums and certain lectures, free admission to temporary exhibits, and reduced-rate subscriptions to the *Revue de Louvre* and *Musées de France.*

## Paris et son Histoire

**9th arr.**
**82 rue Taitbout**
**874.60.00**

This association offers combined tours and lectures throughout the year. On Sundays, from March to October, bus lecture-tour excursions are offered to l'Ile de France. Membership is 85F. Benefits include a monthly bulletin of events mailed to your home, as well as reduced rates for all kinds of cultural events.

## Promenades et Conférences de Paris

**1st arr.**
**62 rue J.-J. Rousseau**
**233.01.53**

Ask Michèle-Mathilde Hager for her program of walking tours of Paris (Wednesday outings are designed for children). Tours feature locations of artisans, famous merchants and historical monuments, and some of the lectures are accompanied by slides and films. All-day excursions include literary themes such as Balzac in Touraine, George Sand in Nohant, Proust in Illiers and Flaubert in Normandy. Pay an annual membership fee or 20F per visit.

**R.A.T.P.**
6th arr.
53 quai des
Grands-Augustins
346.42.03
8th arr.
place de la
Madeleine (next to
the flower market)
265.31.18

Serving as a retailer for France-Tourisme, the "Régie" sponsors numerous afternoon excursions enabling you to discover Paris and regional sites (Givernay, Epernay, Vaux-le-Vicomte) at relatively low prices (74F–125F). It also features two-day excursions to London or Amsterdam (respectively 748F and 771F and one-day trips within France (Mont-Saint-Michel, Morvan, etc.) or abroad (Holland, Belgium, Luxembourg). All excursions are very well narrated. For information, tickets and reservations, see the two addresses listed above. All departures are from the place de la Madeleine.

# *Galleries*

## *CONTEMPORARY ART*

Most contemporary art galleries are in one of three districts. The 8th arrondissement houses most of the big dealers who followed in Paul Guillaume's footsteps and gathered here during the interwar period (1918-1939). The Left Bank (6th and 7th arrondissements) houses mostly younger dealers from the 1950s, some of whom have become very important. The third district is Beaubourg (3rd and 4th arrondissements). Since the opening of the Centre Georges Pompidou, it has become the new hub for modern art dealers.

### *Right Bank*

**Artcurial**
8th arr.
9 ave. Matignon
256.70.70
*Closed Mon.*

How can a large firm such as L'Oréal patronize the arts? Simple—by selecting a number of famous artists (Sonia Delaunay, de Chirico, Étienne-Martin, Agam, Arman, Berrocal) and displaying their work on several floors. The works are then edited, reduced, and reproduced in limited editions. The somewhat confusing layout of the rooms often detracts from the quality of the works, yet exhibits of this type are proliferating and acquiring a style of their own (one which we criticized in the last edition of our Guide). However, the importance given to Étienne-Martin and the wise selections of recent exhibits, which included Marquet's work from his "Boeuf Sur le Toit" days, have made us change our minds. The library is an undisputed success in which you'll find everything about art.

## Galerie Ariel
**8th arr.**
**140 blvd. Haussmann**
**562.13.09**
*Closed Mon.*

For the last twenty years, J. Pollak has been the flagwaver for artists of his generation (those born between 1919 and 1929) such as Appel, Debré, Destarac, Doucet, Gillet, Lindstrom, Marfaing, Mihailovitch, Tabuchi, Weidemann, Anthoons and Subira-Puig. He is very determined to defend Paris's art market against the "glutted" market in New York.

## Galerie Louis Carré et Cie
**8th arr.**
**10 ave. de Messine**
**562.57.07**
*Closed Sat.*

Reopened in 1980 by the founder's grandson, this gallery remains faithful to the great names of its past: Villon, Gromaire, R. Delaunay, Dufy.

## Galerie Jeanne Castel
**8th arr.**
**3 rue du Cirque**
**359.71.24**
*Closed Sat.*

Among yesterday's glorious names in art you'll find here Fautrier and Derain, as well as the memory of Jeanne Castel, who was responsible for making the pre-World War I avant-garde famous.

## Galerie Iris Clert, Le Carat
**92200 Neuilly**
**19 rue Madeleine-Michelis**
**745.66.30**
*Closed Mon.*

It's been a long time since Iris Clert was located on the faubourg St. Honoré. Though she is now the leading art dealer in Neuilly, she really doesn't "belong" anywhere geographically (or artistically, for that matter), judging by the variety of avant-garde artists she features, like Adzak, Barbu, Stevenson, Uriburu, and architect C. Parent.

## Galerie Paul Facchetti
**8th arr.**
**20 ave. de Friedland**
**563.80.26**
*Closed Mon., Sat.*

Facchetti is no longer located on the Left Bank and will receive you only by appointment on Tuesdays and Fridays. Next to the lyrical abstracts he displayed during the 1950s at his rue de Lille and rue des Saint-Pères galleries, he now offers some new "metaphysical and poetical" paintings by Nevelson, Hundertwasser, Bernard Schultze and others.

## Galerie Mathias Fels
**8th arr.**
**138 blvd. Haussmann**
**562.21.34**
*Closed Mon. morning.*

Despite the smallness of his gallery, we owe him a lot for displaying artworks of the 1970s by Arman, Fontana, Hains, Klasen, Rancillac, Rotella, Spoërri and Télémaque.

**Galerie Maurice Garnier**
8th arr.
6 ave. Matignon
225.61.65
*Closed Mon.*

Since 1948, Maurice Garnier (along with Messrs. Drouant and David) has dedicated himself to postwar figurative artists like Mianux, Jansen, Aizpiri and Rosnay. In collaboration with Emmanuel David, he is now devoting himself exclusively to Bernard Buffet, for whom he has held yearly exhibits in February and March since 1947.

**Galerie Henriette Gomès**
8th arr.
6 rue du Cirque
225.42.49
*Closed Mon.*

She used to handle Fautrier and Brauner in times when they were considered less commercially viable, and now handles Hélion and other young artists like Yves Lévêque.

**Galerie Louise Leiris**
8th arr.
47 rue de Monceau
563.28.85
*Closed Mon.*

This high temple of contemporary art (its founder, Kahnweiler, bought Picasso's *Demoiselles d'Avignon* in 1907) has always been a major outlet for Picasso, Beaudin, Masson, Léger and Laurens.

**Galerie Maeght**
9th arr.
13 et 14 rue de Téhéran
563.13.19
*Closed Sat.*

This may well be the most famous of the postwar modern art galleries. Its importance has grown along with its publishing house, its outlets in Barcelona and in Zurich, its office in New York, and the Maeght Foundation in Saint-Paul-de-Vence (in the south of France), which is one of the world's best museums of contemporary art. Aimé Maeght hobnobbed with the best painters of three generations, including Braque, Chagall, Miro, Bram van Velde, Calder, Giacometti, Tapiès, Pol Bury, Riopelle, Ubac, Alechinsky; and, among the younger artists, Adami, Arakawa, Titus-Carmel and Garache.

**Galerie Hervé Odermatt**
8th arr.
85 bis, faubourg Saint-Honoré
266.92.58

It's located in what used to be the New York-based Knoedler Gallery. The paintings represent the new figurative movement in art, particularly the works by Velickovic and Weisbuch.

**Daniel Malingue**
8th arr.
26 ave. Matignon
266.60.33
*Closed Mon. morning.*

This young dealer is attempting something new and interesting. Twice a year he holds a prestigious exhibit of statues and paintings by top artists of the twentieth and late-nineteenth centuries. These works are owned by private collectors who wish to sell them. Basing his prices on public auctions, Malingue publishes (at his own costs) a full-color catalogue, takes a 10 percent commission on all sales, and assumes all other costs pertaining to transportation, photographs and insurance. All in all, a very good deal.

## Left Bank

### Galerie Berggruen
**7th arr.**
**70 rue de l'Université**
**222.02.12**

For nearly thirty years this gallery has been selling, exhibiting and publishing the best engravings in postwar art. Artists include Klee, Kandinsky, Chagall, Max Ernst, Appel, and Baj. It also organizes three to four important exhibits each year, publishing incomparable monographs for each event by Léger, Morandi, Folon and others.

### Galerie Claude Bernard
**6th arr.**
**5 rue des Beaux-Arts**
**326.97.07**
*Closed Mon.*

Claude Bernard Haeim is one of the largest dealers among the postwar second generation. He has introduced his countrymen to some of its younger masters, such as Marfaing, Maryan and Segui, as well as San Szafran, the admirable pastel artist, and Ipousteguy, the singular sculptor. Other older and more accepted masters include Francis Bacon, Balthus and Estève. He also continues to maintain, if not revive, the memory of artists like Léger, Laurens, Giacometti, Bourdelle and Rodin for Tout-Paris amateurs.

### Galerie Isy Brachot
**6th arr.**
**35 rue Guénégaud**
**354.22.40**
*Closed Mon.*

From beyond the borders of France, and out of this world: the Belgian view of surrealism, and the surrealistic view of the human body. Artists include Delvaux, Magritte, Labisse, Dado, Yuba, Gina Pane and Rustin.

### Galerie Jean Briance
**6th arr.**
**35 rue Guenegaud**
**354.22.40**
*Closed Mon.*

This gallery specializes in a certain form of contemporary figurative painting, particularly those of the Panique group (O. Olivier, Topor). There are also French colorists (Samuel Buri), surrealists (Courmes), and expressionists (Czaspski).

### Galerie Jeanne Bucher
**6th arr.**
**53 rue de Seine**
**326.22.32**
*Closed Mon. afternoon.*

Here Jaeger continues the tradition of the Jeanne Bucher Gallery on boulevard Montparnasse. You'll find drawings by Nicolas de Staël, who was first encouraged by Bucher, as well as paintings by young artists (particularly Nallard) who are bent on preserving the "professional side" of western art. You'll also find a near-monopoly of two of the most creative artists in the world: the Portuguese Vieira da Silva (paintings) and the American Louise Nevelson (sculptures). Jaeger's displays also include works by Szenes, Bissière, Moser, Jorn, Aguayo, Flechemuller, Amado and Tobey.

### Galerie Chardin

**6th arr.**
**36 rue de Seine**
**326.99.38**

It's director, Jacques Ratier, remains faithful to the poetic realism of artists influenced by Jacques Villon. Permanent exhibits include works by Paul Charlot, Claude Schurr, Mouly and Jean Marzelle.

## Galerie Colette Creuzevault

**6th arr.**
**58 rue Mazarine**
**326.67.85**
*Open from 2:30 P.M. to 6:30 P.M.*
*Closed Mon.*

In this small gallery, Colette Creuzevault picks up where she left off fifteen years ago at her ave. Matignon gallery. Displays include works by Cesar, G. Richier, Niki de Saint-Phalle, and Laurens.

## Galerie Jacques Damase

**7th arr.**
**61 rue de Varenne**
**705.55.04**
*Closed Sat.*

At 17½, he was the youngest publisher in the world. His 30 years of art publishing have recently been the subject of an exhibit at the Centre Pompidou. For the last fifteen years, Jacques Damase has devoted himself to the glory of Robert and Sonia Delaney, for whom he's the exclusive agent. Other shows include works by Gilioli, Uriburu, J. P. Raynaud, Calder, Man Ray, and (unfortunately) Arno Breker.

## Galerie Nina Dausset
**7th arr.**
**16 rue de Lille**
**297.41.07**
*Closed Mon.*

Having dealt for a long time with "stylized" and "historical" works, Nina Dausset has now returned to the fold of contemporary art, displaying two of the best new figurative artists, Seguy and Recalcati.

## Galerie le Dessin

**6th arr.**
**27 rue Guénégaud**
**633.04.66**
*Closed Mon.*

This was one of the first galleries to exhibit paper artwork, which has since become an accepted medium. Claire Burrus features both well-known artists (Samuel Buri, Cueco, Alan Davie, Degottex, B. Dufour, Jean Voss) and those of lesser fame (H. Bordas, F. Chaillet, M. Paszko, A.M. Pécheur and F. Martin).

## Galerie la Demeure
**6th arr.**
**26 rue Mazarine**
**634.14.62**
*Closed Mon. morning.*

The name of Denise Majorel, founder-manager of this gallery (which is back in the limelight), cannot be disassociated from Jean Lurcat and contemporary tapestry. He owes a lot to her for his fabulous rise to fame following World War II. Denise Majorel continues to promote tapestries made by Saint Saens, Lagrange, Prassinos, Dom Robert and, of course, Lurcat.

## Galerie du Dragon
**6 arr.**
**19 rue du Dragon**
**548.24.19**
*Closed Mon.*

Max Clarac-Seron took over Nina Dausset's gallery on the rue du Dragon and has lost no time in exhibiting works by several leading young artists like Velickovic and Cremonini.

## Galerie Lucien Durand

**6th arr.**
**19 rue Mazarine**
**326.25.35**
*Closed Mon.*

For the last 25 years, Lucien Durand has been coming up with new talent and organizing debut exhibits for young artists who then quickly rise to fame (from Cesar to Dimitrienko).

## Galerie Karl Flinker

6 arr.
**25 rue de Tournon**
**325.18.73**
*Closed Mon.*

After closing his first gallery on the rue du Bac, Karl Flinker temporarily dropped out of sight. Now back in business at the rue de Tournon, the only artist he still features from his former gallery is Jenkins. He now features drawings and new figurative works by Martial Raysse, Arroyo, Aillaud, Gafgen, Moninot, Pichler and Peng. Also displayed are several twentieth century classics like Kandinski, Klee, Yves Klein, Magnelli and, especially, Jean Helion.

## Galerie la Hune

6th arr.
**14 rue de l'Abbaye**
**325.69.25**
*Closed Mon. morning.*

From its postwar beginnings, this gallery has remained a high temple of the graphic arts. Its recent move to the rue de l'Abbaye has given it far more space. The gallery organizes art-event exhibits and displays engravings, lithographs and illustrated books by Ecole de Paris artists.

## Galerie Albert Loeb

6th arr.
**10 rue des Beaux-Arts**
**633.06.87**
*Closed Mon.*

Like his father Pierre, whose contributions to art were the subject of a 1979 retrospective at the Modern Art Museum of Paris, Albert Loeb (after a long stay in the U.S.) has now opened his second gallery. You'll find, displayed among those of other young recruits, works by sculptors like Dodeigne and Jeanclos, and paintings by the Columbians, Caballero and Cuartas, the Japanese Mitsuuchi and the Cuban Wilfredo Lam.

## Galerie Adrien Maeght

7th arr.
**42 and 46 rue du Bac**
**548.45.15**
*Closed Mon.*

The son of Aimé and Marguerite Maeght now has a new gallery next to the Maeght publishing house. Located off the Samuel Bernard Hotel courtyard (46 rue du Bac), it features young artists found in other galleries as well (Poli, Kasen, Kuroda, Pelloille, Télémaque and Voss).

## Galerie André-François Petit

7th arr.
**196 blvd. Saint-Germain**
**544.64.83**
*Closed Mon.*

Tanguy, Dali, Brauner and other Surrealist masters occupy the place of honor in this gallery, along with a few hyper-realists. Worth noting are P.A. Gette's splendid doorknobs, which bear witness to the gallery's continued high standards under the fine management of Alexandre Iolas.

## Galerie Plantin-Blondel

6th arr.
**33 rue de Seine**
**633.82.41**
*Open 12:00 noon to 7:00 P.M.*
*Closed Mon.*

Plantin and Blondel started this gallery after the famous Luxembourg (in which they were partners) was forced to close. Featured are startling works from the Roaring Twenties which had been forgotten but which are slowly being brought back to prominence (such as, Tamara de Lempicka's works).

### *Galerie Regards*
**7th arr.**
**40 rue de l'Université**
**261.10.22**
*Open 2:30 P.M. to 7:00 P.M.*
*Closed Mon.*

Regards is permanently and primarily interested in "hot" French abstracts from the 1950s, such as Fichet, Guitet, Hosiasson, Debré, Sorg, Tourliére, Serpan and Zack.

### *Galerie Stadler*
**6th arr.**
**51 rue de Seine**
**326.91.10**
*Closed Mon.*

Rodolphe Stadler has introduced some of today's most creative artists such as Saura, Serpan and Delay. We are also grateful to him for having noticed the evolution of the French body art and foreign avant-gardes (from the U.S., Italy and Spain). Featured artists include Saura, Damian, Rainer, Luthi, N. Bluhm, and some older ones like Tapiés and Mathieu.

### *Galerie Denise René*
**7th arr.**
**196 blvd.**
**Saint-Germain**
**222.77.57**

Since 1944, Denise René has been a friend, supporter and flag-waver of op(tical) art. These works have been displayed at the rue Boetie (across from the Centre Pompidou), in New York, as well as in other Northern European galleries, all thanks to Denise René, who has earned the nickname of "Our Lady of the Cold Abstracts."

### *Galerie Nane Stern*
**7th arr.**
**25 ave. de Tourville**
**705.08.46**
*Open from 3:30 P.M. to 8:30 P.M.*
*Closed Mon.*

Though geographically apart from her colleagues, Pierre Loeb's former collaborator, Nane Stern, devotes herself to abstract painters such as Ivackovic, Kallos, and Romanthier.

### *Galerie Strombont*
**6th arr.**
**4 rue des Beaux-Arts**
**354.52.19**
*Closed Mon.*

This recently opened gallery promotes turn-of-the-century Pompier and Symbolist paintings and digs up little-known facts about nineteenth-century art.

### *Le Point Cardinal*
**6th arr.**
**3 rue Jacob**
**354.32.08**
*Closed Mon.*

This gallery is always filled with the same artwork it so ardently defends. Works displayed include Henri Michaux, Cardenas, Viseux, Sima, Claude Georges, Louis Pons and others.

### *Beaubourg (Pompidou Museum) area*

### *Galerie Bama*
**4th arr.**
**7 rue Quincampoix**
**277.38.87**
*Open from 2:30 P.M. to 7:00 P.M.*
*Closed Mon.*

Crossing the Seine hasn't changed the gallery at all. It still belongs to the Fluxus Group.

## Galerie Beaubourg

**4th arr.**
**23 rue du Renard**
**271.20.50**
*Closed Mon.*

Patrice Trigano has gone his own way, leaving Pierre and Marianne Nahon in charge of the Galerie Beaubourg at the rue Pierre au Lard, which the three started in 1973. You'll find all sorts of different artists here: Schneider, Wols, Mathieu, Degotte, as well as Erro, Schlosser, Taule, and Dufour. Also displayed are works by Villegle, Chacallis, Fassiano, Messagiez, Cesar, Arman, Fahri, and Barelier. The bookshop has gotten a bit too big for the gallery, and though it's no different from others in the neighborhood, it is very popular with artists and visitors.

## Galerie Alain Blondel

**4th arr.**
**43 rue de**
**Montmorency**
**277.63.60**
*Open 2:00 P.M. to 7:00 P.M.*
*Closed Mon.*

Born of the ashes of the now defunct Luxembourg Gallery, the Galerie Alain Blondel features several early twentieth-century works (now considered classics) and large canvases from the 1930's. You'll also see some stunning trompe l'oeils by Yvel and Bruno Schmeltz.

## Galerie Durand-Dessert

**4th arr.**
**43 rue de**
**Montmorency**
**277.63.60**
*Open 2:00 P.M. to 7:00 P.M.*
*Closed Mon.*

Since 1975 Liliane and Michel Durant-Dessert's ambition has been to get out of Parisian and American art by playing the European card. Their gallery features—for the first time in Paris—works by Richter, Ruthenbeck and Hans Haache, plus French works by Garouste and Micha Laury.

## Galerie Jean Fournier

**4th arr.**
**44 rue Quincampoix**
**277.32.31**
*Closed Mon.*

Jean Fournier is the ideal art dealer. His early abstract displays in 1955 now belong to the annals of art history. He recently gave up his rue du Bac gallery to move into newer and larger quarters near the Beaubourg. Jean Fournier is always available for showing and discussing his selections, such as works by the two abstract artists, Hantaï and Degottex, whom he defended for so long. American artists include Sam Francis, Joan Mitchell and Bishop. You'll also see works by Viallat, leader of the Support Surface movement, and other equally talented artists of the same generation such as P. Buraglio, J.P. Raynaud and C. Bonnefoi.

## Galerie Alain Codin

**4tn arr.**
**28 bis blvd. de**
**Sebastopol**
**271.83.65**
*Open from 2:00 P.M. to 7:00 P.M.*
*Closed Mon.*

This gallery is geared towards contemporary sculpture research, or rather, ways of integrating sculpture with today's architecture and drawings. The owner is a young architect who enjoys organizing dance, musical, and poetry events in his gallery.

## Galerie Daniel Templon
**3rd arr.**
**30 rue Beaubourg**
**272.14.10**
*Closed Mon.*

This gallery, the first one to have moved into the Beaubourg neighborhood in 1972, is modeled after New York's SoHo galleries. Daniel Templon was the first in France to launch conceptual art, language art, and a good portion of the Support Surface movement artworks. You'll also often find works by Ben and LeGac. Templon's current effort is collecting artistic movements from the May 1968 political upheaval. At the time, his gallery was one of the busiest in St. Germain des Près. Also featured are major works by American and French abstract artists like Olivier Debre.

## Galerie de France
**4th arr.**
**50 to 52 rue de la Verrerie**
**274.38.00**
*Closed Mon.*

First established during the Second World War on rue Boétie, this gallery moved to the faubourg Saint-Honoré in 1950. Under the management of Myriam Prévot and Gildo Caputo, it supported a large number of very good artists whose works are still being displayed today: J. Gonzalez, Prassinos, Le Moal, Manessier, Poliakoff, Hartung, Soulages and Zao Wou-Ki. It also owns and exhibits works by Maryan, Bergman, Dotremont, Jacobsen, Le Moal and Tamayo. Since Myriam Prévot's death in 1977, Gildo Caputo has taken on a few young abstract artists who had already been exhibited in Left Bank galleries: Meurice, Péricaud, Pincemin.

## Galerie Gillespie-Laage-Salomon
**3rd arr.**
**24 rue Beaubourg**
**278.11.71**
*Closed Mon.*

This gallery belongs to a young American woman who established it in 1977. The gallery features works by J. Shapiro, A. Messager, J. Johns, J. P. Raynaud, Beuys, Fulton, Baselitz, Lupertz, Penck and Joseph.

## Galerie Yvon Lambert
**3rd arr.**
**5 rue du Grenier-Saint-Lazare**
**271.09.33**
*Closed Mon.*

Lambert continues the pioneering work it had begun on the Left Bank and features works by Lewitt, Twombly, Dibbets, Oppenheim and Christo, all of whom have become internationally famous.

## Galerie Baudoin Lebon
**4th arr.**
**36 rue des Archives**
**272.09.10**

Although the gallery was redecorated in 1980, the style is still the same. You'll find the same sense of humor (the invitations, as always, are illegible); the same high-quality paintings; and the same good choices from Cornell to avant-garde artists.

# OLD PAINTINGS AND DRAWINGS

We have no intention of listing all the important dealers. We'll just name a few of them, big and small, who sell old paintings, including those from the nineteenth century. Should you have any qualms about purchasing something "just anywhere" or wielding an expert flashlight (it will reveal crude touch-ups by illuminating the added coats of paint), rest assured that you can ask any one of these dealers for assistance.

**Didier Aaron**
16th arr.
32 ave.
Raymond-Poincaré
727.17.79
*Closed Sat.*

This famous antique dealer offers fine exhibits of paintings and old drawings (seventeenth, eighteenth and nineteenth century), all displayed in his Parisian townhouse.

**Atlantis**
6th arr.
33 rue de Seine
326.89.62

The charming Marie Jane Garoche specializes in lesser-known quality artists from the end of the nineteenth and beginning of the twentieth century.

**Aubry**
6th arr.
2 rue des Beaux-Arts
326.27.27

In this reputable firm owned by Claude Aubry you're liable to encounter a few works by Gericault, as well as other turn-of-the-century masters.

**Brame et Lorenceau**
8th arr.
68 blvd. Malesherbes
522.16.89
*Closed Sat.*

Mostly paintings done between 1820 and 1920 by Corot, Théodore Rousseau, Daubigny, Degas, Pissarro and Picasso, as well as drawings by Toulouse-Lautrec. Its customers usually have taste and money, or represent U.S. or French museums.

**Paule Cailac**
6th arr.
13 rue de Seine
326.98.88
*Open 2:30 P.M. to 7:00 P.M.*
*Closed Mon.*

Fine drawings from 1830 to present.

**Cailleux**
8th arr.
136, faubourg
Saint-Honoré
359.25.24

"My business is to sell, but my pleasure is to exhibit," are words you'll often hear from this distinguished seventeenth-century specialist. His realm is filled with brocades, overstuffed chairs and an air of nonchalance, and features works by Fragonard, Watteau, Boucher, Lancret and Hubert Robert.

## O. C. Champion
**92200 Neuilly**
**76 rue**
**Pauline-Borghese**
**747.41.67**
*By appointment only.*

This recently opened gallery has adopted a modern formula well-known since ancient times—eclectism. Paintings run the gamut from the Renaissance to the nineteenth century.

## Coligny
**1st arr.**
**138 rue Saint-Honoré**
**260.21.51**
*Open 2:00 P.M. to 7:30 P.M.*
*Closed Mon.*

Enlightened amateurs will find a reasonably priced, eclectic selection of paintings and, particularly, drawings from the nineteenth century.

## J. Fischer–C. Kiener

**7th arr.**
**46 rue de Verneuil**
**261.17.82**
*Closed Mon.*

These experts in nineteenth-century paintings, sculptures and, particularly, French drawings, have moved to the other side of the street. Where they offer two annual exhibits and feature architectural drawings.

## Galerie du Fleuve
**6th arr.**
**6 rue de Seine**
**326.08.96**
*Open from 2:30 P.M. to 7:00 P.M.*
*Closed Mon.*

Jacqueline Dubaut-Bellonte, daughter of the famous aviator, has amassed a tasteful selection of canvases and drawings by neoclassic and romantic masters, big and small.

## Hahn
**8th arr.**
**36 rue de Berri**
**563.45.34**

Hahn specializes in Italian "large scale" artwork from the seventeenth and eighteenth centuries (which doesn't mean they're necessarily the best). Since 1980, the premises have been enlarged, allowing for biannual exhibits of excellent, albeit forgotten, works by artists such as Jacques Gamelin or Philoppoteaux.

## François Heim

**8th arr.**
**15 ave. Matignon**
**225.22.38**
*Closed Sat.*

François Heim has a gallery in London as well as this one in Paris. He exhibits all kinds of work from seventeenth- and eighteenth-century art movements, plus a few beautiful neoclassical and old master's works. He also organizes magnificent exhibitions on a regular basis. Among contemporary French art dealers, he is considered a leading connoisseur of old master paintings. Until recently he would only sell to major collectors or to museums, but now offers affordable paintings to private buyers without compromising quality.

## Heim-Gairac

**6th arr.**
**13 rue de Seine**
**326.57.50**

Here you'll find paintings and antique drawings from primitives to works by the Barbizon School.

## Leegenhoek
**16th arr.**
**96 ave. Kléber**
**553.89.82**

In his low-key, second-story gallery, this Flemish expert offers Dutch landscapes by Brueghel, Cranach and others. This world-renowned specialist is considered to be the best restorer in Paris, but will only work on his own pieces or those belonging to museums and foundations when they need critical attention.

## Marumo
**1st arr.**
**243 rue Saint-Honoré**
**260.08.66**

Marumo offers a wide choice of quality paintings from the nineteenth century (Barbizon School) as well as a few modern paintings.

## Moatti
**6th arr.**
**77 rue des Saints-Peres**
**222.91.04**
*Closed Mon. morning.*

In his townhouse decorated with sculptures and collectors' items, Moatti has recently opened a lovely gallery of antique drawings.

## Resche
**6th arr.**
**20 rue de Seine**
**329.44.03**

Resche offers constantly replenished selections of good nineteenth century canvases, from Neoclassics to Symbolists. Other items sold here include prewar and interwar "art photos," old department-store catalogues, antique children's books, as well as the Argus des Cartes Postales publication, the *Cartophilia Guide* (featuring postcard dealers and clubs) and other kinds of albums comprising postcards and very old photographs.

## Michel Segoura
**7th arr.**
**11 quai Voltaire**
**261.19.23**
*Closed Mon.*

This attractive gallery, owned by Michel Segoura (son of Maurice Segoura, the great faubourg Saint-Honoré furniture dealer), offers good Flemish and Dutch paintings from the seventeenth century. Both the choice and the quality of these works are excellent.

## Tanagra
**8th arr.**
**61 faubourg Saint-Honoré**
**265.89.07**
*Open 3:00 P.M. to 7:00 P.M.*
*Closed Sat.*

In the courtyard at the corner of rue du Cirque, amidst prestigious eighteenth-century furniture by Aveline (see: "Antiques"), Bob Benamou (formerly located near les Halles) offers a selection of lyrical and ostentatious creations by those masters of perfectionism, the practitioners of turn-of-the-century Pompierism. This work contrasts sharply with the decadent spiritualism of symbolists like Wagner, Verlaine and Mallarmé.

# POSTCARDS

Although postcards have only recently become collectors' items, they are already big business. The most important Paris dealers are listed below.

## Fildier Cartophilie
**4th arr.**
**4 blvd. Morland**
**272.09.64**
*Open 2:30 P.M. to 6:30 P.M.*
*Closed Tues., Thurs.*

André Fildier has always been an attentive and ardent collector, judging by his fascinating series that cover all bases. Other items sold here include pre-1914 and interwar "art photos," old department-store catalogues, antique children's books, as well as the Argus des Cartes Postales publication, the *Guide Cartophilia* (featuring postcard dealers and clubs) and other kinds of albums comprising postcards and very old photographs.

## A l'Image du Grenier sur l'Eau
**4th arr.**
**45 rue des Francs-Bourgeois**
**271.02.31**
*Open 2:30 P.M. to 7:00 P.M., Wed.*
*11:00 A.M. to 9:00 P.M.*

This shop stocks regional postcards (including most of France's cities and villages), fantasy cards, illustrated cards, current-events cards; as well as albums, filing equipment and modern card editions. Excellent selections, charming sales staff.

## Jehanno
**1st arr.**
**6 rue Bailleul**
**260.93.68**
*Open 3:00 P.M. to 7:00 P.M., Wed.*
*until 9:00 P.M.*

Amid the muddle of chromos, drawings, programs and calendars, Jean-François Jehanno will show you his limitless collection of postcards of every genre.

## Edouard Pecourt
**2nd arr.**
**58 bis rue du Louvre**
**407.06.75**
*Open from 3:00 P.M. to 7:00 P.M.*
*Closed Mon.*

This shop features a good selection of postcards, like the editions of the first illustrated postcard featuring the Eiffel Tower. The shop also specializes in old records.

# POSTERS

Posters, created by an artist for a special event, are both symbols of an era and a means for you to obtain works of art at lower prices. Be careful not to confuse original posters, made in limited editions by a silkscreen process, with reproductions, which are simply photographs of the originals. Should you be unsure, use a magnifying glass to inspect the work. On a reproduction you can see the "screen" on the photographic paper.

## Berggruen
**7th arr.**
**70 rue de l'Université**
**222.55.22**

A beautiful selection of posters by the best artists of our time.

## Ciné Images
7th arr.
**68 rue de Babylone**
**551.27.50**

An enthusiastic young man runs this shop dedicated to the "seventh art." It is located right across the street from the Pagoda cinema. Amateurs come here to purchase fairly old posters as well as Robert Bresson's photographs.

## Documents
6th arr.
**53 rue de Seine**
**354.50.68**
*Closed Mon.*

In 1957, when Michel Romand started selling the marvelous poster collection amassed by his great-grandfather, M. Sagot, all the traditional shops along the rue de Seine expressed their contempt. Nevertheless, the trend he launched became a fashion. Everyone, especially Americans, continues to buy these superb original posters—all of them lithographs—made between 1875 and 1930 by Chéret, Toulouse-Lautrec, Grasset, Berthon, Mucha, Cappiello and Steinlen.

## Galerie Jean-Louis Fivel
6th arr.
**20 rue Serpente**
**633.64.21**
*Open 2:00 P.M. to 7:00 P.M.*
*Closed Mon.*

This poster specialist sells to museums and collectors all over the world. The best selections are from the U.S., particularly the circus posters, whose popular turn-of-the-century designs bring to mind Georges Seurat.

## A l'Imagerie
5th arr.
**9 rue Dante**
**325.18.66**

This shop features one of the largest selections of French and foreign antique publicity posters in all of Paris. You'll also find numerous original Epinal plates (1900 to 1930), Japanese engravings, antique and modern games and drawings, and curios such as tags, menus and 1925 greeting cards. The shop sponsors four exhibitions each year.

# PRINTS

## Artcurial
8th arr.
**9 ave. Matignon**
**256.70.70**
*Closed Mon.*

This store sells and exhibits engravings and paintings by twentieth-century French and foreign masters. It also distributes lithographs and "mechanical" reproductions (posters) of artistic works, and retails functional objects (rugs, tableware, jewelry). Artcurial has revolutionized the Parisian art market by selling decorative work mass-produced from master stencils by contemporary artists such as Berrocal, Agam and Pomodoro.

## Huguette Berès

7th arr.
25 quai Voltaire
261.27.91

In a lovely setting of antique wood paneling, Huguette Berès offers elegant displays of Japanese drawings and engravings done by great old masters. The shop also features a collection of French work from the nineteenth and twentieth centuries.

## Berggruen

7th arr.
70 rue de l'Université
222.55.22

Original contemporary engravings by Klee, Picasso, Miro, Dali, Chagall and Folon. See also under "Poster" and "Contemporary Art Galleries."

## Bouquinerie de l'Institut

6th arr.
3 quai Malaquais
326.63.49

This shop offers original engravings by Bonnard, Renoir, Dufy, Rouault, Braque, Chagall, Miro, Laboureur, Picasso and twentieth-century masters of the Ecole de Paris. Also featured are illustrated books and posters.

## Carna- valette

3rd arr.
2 rue des
Francs-Bourgeois
272.91.92
*Closed Tues.*

Carnavalette offers books on Paris, as well as original, good quality, affordable engravings. Charming sales staff.

## Chalco- graphie

1st arr.
Musée du Louvre,
place du Carrousel,
entrance at porte
Denon, 2nd floor
260.39.26, ext. 36.45

This 300-year-old institution is unique. In its care are 14,000 engraving plates of great artists. Thus each engraving executed by the Chalcographie is an original. Most are sold by special order in limited editions, so as not to wear out the copper plates. Prices range from 20F–500F.

## Alain Digard

4th arr.
15 rue de lay Reynie
887.41.13

This shop commissions and distributes "little-known" paintings and engravings. As a special feature for 1981, it commissioned dinner plates by Salvadore Dali entitled "Gala's Meals," all numbered, signed and decorated with a matrimonial theme.

## Galerie Guiot

8th arr.
18 ave. Matignon
266.65.84

This store features a permanent exhibition of figurative artwork by Caillard, Cathelin, Desnoyer, Despierre, Kuwahara, Roland Oudot, Sarthou and Savary, as well as a remarkable selection of engravings and lithographs by Ciry, Carzou, Miro, Ortega, Picasso and others.

## Galerie des Peintres Graveurs

6th arr.
159 bis blvd. du
Montparnasse
326.62.29
*Closed Mon.*

Jacques Frapier deals in high-quality graphic works and original lithographs (figurative art), from Impressionists to modern-day artists. Following in the footsteps of his father, he also commissions original engravings from contemporary artists and organizes two or three yearly exhibitions in Paris.

### *François Girand*
6th arr.
**76 rue de Seine**
**325.10.33**

Here you'll spend hours inspecting boxes filled with etchings and engravings. This attractive shop, newly redecorated with stone slabs and wooden beams, features lovely old maps, atlases, regional maps, city panoramic views, hunting scene reproductions, birds, flowers, and more.

### *La Hune*
6th arr.
**14 rue de l'Abbaye**
**325.69.25**
*Closed Mon. morning.*

This shop is an extension of the lovely boulevard St. Germain bookshop. It features engravings, matrices, and illustrated original publications.

### *Louise Leiris*
8th arr.
**47 rue Monceau**
**563.28.85**

Next to its modern sculptures and paintings, Leiris offers a wide range of engravings by contemporary artists, particularly those from the Kahnweiler "stable."

### *La Lithographie*
8th arr.
**31 ave. Matignon**
**266.34.42**
*Closed Mon. morning.*

Mostly lithographs (both abstract and figurative) by École de Paris artists like Sonia Delaunay, Chagall, Estève, Lanskoy, Roland Oudot and Terechkovitch. The fact that the store's manager, Mme France Bennys, is a member of the Syndicated Chamber of Engravers will insure you against counterfeit prints.

### *Louis Loeb-Larocque*
9th arr.
**36 rue Le Pelletier**
**878.11.18**
*Closed Sat.*

The shop offers geographic maps and panoramic views of cities all over the world; atlases; picture books; illustrated books from the fifteenth, sixteenth and seventeenth centuries; and engravings depicting various trades. You'll also find a wide selection of today's much-sought-after French regional works.

### *Fernand Martinez*
6th arr.
**97 rue de Seine**
**633.08.12**

Fernand Martinez offers illustrated books, original engravings, city views from the preceding century, and old geographic maps.

### *Gaston Mas*
9th arr.
**48 rue La Fayette**
**824.77.77**
*Closed Mon.*

This old, dark and inviting shop specializes in portraits and antique engravings (history, topography).

### *Janette Ostier*
3rd arr.
**26 pl. des Vosges**
**887.28.57**
*Open from 2:00 P.M. to 7:00 P.M.*
*Closed Mon.*

You'll find lots of high quality Japanese engravings here, along with other Japanese artwork with which Janette Ostier continues to charm collectors.

531

## Paul Prouté
**6th arr.**
**74 rue de Seine**
**326.89.80**
*Closed Mon.*

In January 1981, one of Paris's greatest art dealers died at the age of 94, a few days after his memoirs, *An Old Engravings Dealer Tells All,* came out in bookshops. His son Hubert has taken over the family business, which includes hundreds of thousands of engravings from the fifteenth century to the present. There are also original antique and modern drawings which are filed according to theme, period and style. Although major artwork may be very expensive, this unique shop also features charming little items that cost remarkably little.

## Robert Prouté
**6th arr.**
**12 rue de Seine**
**326.93.22**
*Closed Mon.*

Mrs. Robert Prouté manages this longstanding firm, which has fewer selections than Paul Prouté's but is of the same high quality. Featured is a wide selection of engravings from all periods.

## Michel R.G.
**5th arr.**
**17 quai Saint-Michel**
**354.77.75**

This firmly established house offers a medley of posters designed by young engravers, as well as a wide range of period engravings.

## Rouillon (Galerie J.P.R.)
**6th arr.**
**27 rue de Seine**
**326.73.00**
*Closed Mon.*

In this charming, old-fashioned boutique you'll find high-quality decorative engravings.

## Paul Roulleau
**1st arr.**
**108 rue Saint-Honoré**
**233.49.52**
*By appt. only.*

House specialties include military engravings and books.

## Maurice Rousseau
**9th arr.**
**42 rue La Fayette**
**770.84.50**

Established in 1862, the gallery is run by Denise Rousseau, a court-appointed expert and a descendant of four generations of Rousseaus. It is remarkable for conservative prices and for the quality and selections of French and English original prints from the nineteenth and twentieth centuries.

## Sagot-Le Garrec
**6th arr.**
**24 rue du Four**
**326.43.38**
*Closed Mon. morning.*

This modern and hospitable gallery has just celebrated its centennial. For over thirty years it has been run by Jean-Claude Romand, President of the Syndicated Chamber of Engravers and great-grandson of the firm's founder, Edmond Sagot. The gallery features original nineteenth- and twentieth-century drawings and prints, and an unusual collection of figurative work from Goya to contemporary artists. Beautiful exhibitions are held here each year, like Villon's in 1978 and Vallotton and Daumier in 1979 and 1980.

### Sartoni-Cerveau
**5th arr.**
**13 quai Saint-Michel**
**354.75.73**
*Open 10:00 A.M. to 7:00 P.M.*

The gallery stocks antique prints, such as old maps, sporting scenes, flowers, birds, horses and racing themes, and maritime engravings. The large selection of prints is priced from 30F–4,000F. The famous chef, Claude Terrail, drops in to consult the gastronomy department.

# Gardens

Not included below are the many acres of the best-known woods and green areas of Paris (Vincennes Woods, Bois de Boulogne, Luxembourg Gardens, Monceau and Montsouris parks, Buttes-Chaumont are some). The following list consists of lesser-known but particularly agreeable gardens and parks.

### Jardin Albert-Kahn
**91100 Boulogne**
**9 quai du 4-Septembre and 1 rue des Abondances**
**603.31.83**
*Open 9:00 A.M. to 12:30 P.M. and 2:00 P.M. to 6:00 P.M. in March, April, October November; from 2:00 P.M. to 7:00 P.M. May thru September. Fee: 2F*

The City of Paris acquired these gardens from a rich diamond merchant who had had them landscaped according to his fancy. Of course, there was no traffic at the turn of the century. The area features a Japanese garden, a Vosge forest, a rock garden, a French-styled park, a small lake bordered with trees, and a beautiful English garden. The last weeks of spring are the best time for a visit.

### Jardin Fleuriste de Paris
**16th arr.**
**3 ave. de la Porte-d'Auteuil**
**651.71.20**
*Open 10:00 A.M. to 6:00 P.M., to 5:00 P.M. in winters. Fee: 1.50F–2.50F.*

As the city's most important conservatory, this garden supplies floral decorations for official receptions. The Jardin Fleuriste exhibits azaleas (April 15-30) and chrysanthemums (October 15-31), and has a hundred marvelous greenhouses in which you'll discover tropical and exotic plants. There is also a French-styled garden and an arboretum.

### Jardins du Musée Rodin
**7th arr.**
**77 rue de Varenne**
**705.01.34**
*Open 10:00 A.M. to 5:00 P.M., to 6:00 P.M. April 1 thru September 30. Closed Tues. Fee: 7F.*

Two thousand rosebushes adorn the French-styled gardens of the marvelous hôtel Biron where Rodin used to live. Forever musing among the flowers is his celebrated *The Thinker*.

## Jardin des Plantes

**5th arr.**
**Entrances: rue Buffon, rue Cuvier and place Valhubert**
**336.14.41**
*Gardens open 7:00 A.M. to sunset. Museums open 1:30 P.M. to 5:00 P.M., to 6:00 P.M. in summer. Closed Tues. Fee: 7F*

The Sun King's once-glorious botanical gardens, with their 10,000 specimens and association with the flower of French Science (Buffon, Lamarck, Lavoisier), were allowed to deteriorate so badly that many of the buildings had to be razed. However, thanks largely to the efforts of crusading journalists, the tide has turned. Parisians have again begun to show up en masse along the charming labyrinth's shaded walks, inspecting the rare species of trees, the sea lions' pool, and the grounds where children used to play and chess tournaments were held; the Jardin d'Hiver (winter garden) filled with the fragrance of countless plants from cold climates; and, last but not least, the huge greenhouse with its dizzying jungle of plants and rows of cacti. Today herbal botanists are again working enthusiastically over the seasonal beds of plants, and the public marvels at the entirely mauve-colored Judas tree, the aromas of the botanical garden and the huge Lebanese cedar brought back by Jussieu and considered, by Bouvard and Pécuchet (two characters from a Flaubert novel) to be nature's tree of knowledge. Considerable (though insufficient) funds are currently being spent to renovate both the greenhouse and the museums of mineralogy and paleontology. A vast zoological museum, to house one of the world's older and more complete collections of stuffed specimens, is scheduled for construction in the near future. Ironically, as a result of all these projects, the Jardin's central walkways may well be fenced off for the next six years.

## Parc de Bagatelle

**16th arr.**
**Bois de Boulogne**
**624.67.00**
*Open 6:30 A.M. to 8:00 P.M. in summer, 9:00 A.M. to 5:00 P.M. in winter. Fee: 1.80F (3F in April for flower exhibits, in June for rose exhibits).*

The main gate to the park is near the intersection of the allée de la Reine-Marguerite and the allée de Longchamp. You may also use the smaller entrance located on the route de Sèvres in Neuilly, across from the playground. This incomparable, 48-acre park was landscaped in 1775 by the famous English designer Blackie at the request of the Count d'Artois, the future Charles X. It boasts marvelous rose gardens, bushes, explosions of tulips, narcissus and hyacinths in spring, and enchanting blossoms of clematis, water lilies and late spring iris. The park also has a small eighteenth-century palace and an orangery which features temporary exhibits of paintings and photographs. Busts of poets and romantic novelists are sprinkled here and there among the flower beds and ivy-covered walls. There is also an open-air tea room.

## Parc Floral de Paris

**12th arr.**
**esplanade du Château de Vincennes, bois de Vincennes**
**374.60.49**

This 56-acre park was opened in 1969 to host the Festival of Flowers. It was designed in contemporary style, complete with concrete pavilions and monumental sculptures by Calder, Agam, Penalba and Stahly. An enclosed walkway leads to a greenhouse featuring orange trees, mimosa and camellias. Well worth visiting are the aquatic plant gardens (1,200 square meters of lotuses) July to October, the pine grove (7 acres of rhododendrons and azaleas) May to June, and the tri-annual exhibits held in the park's pavilions. Orchids are shown at the end of

*Open 9:30 A.M. to 5:30 P.M., to 6:00 P.M. or 8:00 P.M. in spring and summer. Fee: 2.80F (5.60F Sun.).*

February, camelias in March and dahlias in September. On Sundays, from April to October, the park is filled with shows by musicians, clowns and jugglers.

# Hospitals

Really, we're feeling fine! . . . We'd just like to point out that certain Parisian hospitals are among the city's notable landmarks.

### L'Hôpital Saint-Louis
**10th arr.
2 place du Dr.
Alfred-Fournier**

Built by Villefaux, it is an admirable example of Louis XIII style, despite its critical condition.

### La Salpêtrière
**13th arr.
47 blvd. de l'Hôpital**

This hospital is a huge ensemble of buildings that was originally an arsenal. It was built by Le Vau and Liberal Bruant, and Bossuet and Bourdaloue once preached in its chapel.

### Le-Val-de-Grâce
**5th arr.
1 place
Alphonse Laveran**

Currently used as a military hospital, it ranks among Paris's finest seventeenth-century buildings. François Mansart designed the church and, at the age of seven, Louis XIV laid its cornerstone.

# Museums

It's for lack of space, not enthusiasm, that we've had to limit ourselves from listing all the marvelous Parisian museums. We do offer you, however, an eclectic collection of monuments (some big, some small) that we find particularly fascinating.

### Collections Albert-Kahn

**92100 Boulogne**

This museum houses the complete 1910–1931 photographic and cinematographic collection amassed by the philanthropist Albert Kahn and called by him Archives

**10 quai du
4-Septembre
604.52.80**
*By appt. only.*

of the Planet. This formidable project includes 72,000 colored photographic plates and thousands of yards of film pertaining to geography, environment, architecture, culture, art, religion and daily life in Europe, Africa and Asia, plus black-and-white movies related to World War I, political events of the day and social policies. A systematic classification of the material is currently underway and all research is on an appointment-only basis. Temporary exhibits are announced on billboards.

## Historial de Montmartre
**18th arr.
11 rue Poulbot
606.78.92**
*Open everyday from 9:00 A.M. to 6:00 P.M. from Easter to November 11th. Rest of year, Wed., Sat., Sun. only. Fee: 12F (8F children)*

In this wonderfully picturesque setting, you'll discover "la butte" Montmartre through wax figures of well-known personalities. The museum's shop (which periodically exhibits young artists without charging them a fee) offers such art supplies as canvases, frames, easels, oil paints, pastels, etc.

## Las Vegas Muséum
**3rd arr. 23 rue Beaubourg
274.77.21**
*Open 11:00 A.M. to 7:00 P.M., Fri. to 10:00 P.M.*

Founded in 1981 by collector Jean-Claude Baudot, well-known for his excellent Muscat wine from Rivesaltes, Vegas features 150 amusement machines, half of which are Early American and European, the other half from the late 1930s. The collection includes muscular-strength gauges, zodiac horoscope dispensers, one-armed bandits (some have survived the Prohibition Era), electric shock dispensers, small mechanical wall cabinets that discharge coins or chips. Particularly noteworthy is the vertical roulette wheel that once belonged to the famous bordello at the place des Ternes.

## Maison de Balzac
**16th arr. 47 rue Raynouard
224.56.38**
*Open 10:00 A.M. to 5:45 P.M. Closed Mon. Fee: 7F.*

It was in this adorable eighteenth-century pavilion and equally charming garden that Balzac lived from 1840–1847 and wrote the last chapters of the *Comédie Humaine.* Balzaciana include documents, portraits, caricatures and personal effects, as well as a short audiovisual commentary on his life. Be sure to see the rue Berton behind the museum. It's the only remaining "country lane" in Paris where lovers come to kiss.

## Maison de Victor-Hugo
**4th arr. 6 place des Vosges 272.16.65**
*Open 10:00 A.M. to 7:40 P.M. Closed Mon., holidays. Fee: 7F.*

Victor Hugo did not actually live in this building, the former Hôtel Rohan-Guéméné; and all his furniture was sold when he was banished in 1851. Nevertheless, the museum exhibits many worthwhile mementos of the master, including portraits, busts (there's one by Rodin), a romantic and masterful portrait of Juliette Drouet by Champmartin, Hugo's architectural sketches pertaining to his Hauteville House in Guernesey, and his dreamy collection of travel drawings from the Rhine River Valley, Switzerland, Belgium and France. There are 350 of these in all, each one more bizarre and fascinating than the next. Recent acquisitions include numerous family portraits and manuscripts. The Hugo library and the museum's print room are open by appointment only.

## Manufacture des Gobelins

**13th arr.**
**42 ave. des Gobelins**
**570.12.60**
*Open Wed., Thurs., Fri. 2:00 P.M. to 3:30 P.M. Fee: 6F.*

This imposing building built in 1912 is surrounded by beautiful, charmingly provincial old homes. The warper's workshops at the Gobelins, Beauvais and Savonnerie national mills are open to visitors.

## Musée Adam-Mickiewicz

**4th arr.**
**6 quai d'Orléans**
**354.35.61**
*Open Thurs. 3:00 P.M. to 6:00 P.M. By appt. only.*

The life and times of the Polish poet, his work and his relationships with the great romantic French authors are all illustrated and brought to life in this museum. Visit the Chopin sitting room where you'll come across musical manuscripts, portraits and J. B. Clesinger's death mask of the famous musician. The museum also features paintings from the nineteenth and early twentieth centuries by Polish artists who either visited or lived in Paris.

## Musée de l'Affiche

**10th arr.**
**18 rue de Paradis**
**824.50.04**
*Open 12:00 noon to 6:00 P.M. Closed Mon., Tues. Fee: 7F.*

The prosperous Boulenger ceramics firm owned this building and used it as a warehouse until February 1978, when the "second" poster museum in the world (the first is in Warsaw) was installed behind its multicolored Renaissance façade. The 50,000 well-kept and often-exhibited documents represent the entire collection of the Union Centrale des Arts Décoratifs. Included are works by bona fide artists such as Toulouse-Lautrec and Bonnard, who devoted some of their time to "lithographic advertising." There are also movie posters that are currently worth a fortune. Retail goods (like Mars beer and Isigny cider) are beautifully publicized with ravishing, late eighteenth-century images. Wholesale products appear in masterfully crafted, turn-of-the-century works like the Menier chocolate ad (with the little girl) by Bouisset (1897), the Vingeanne milk ad by Steinlen, the comical Nectar and Glouglou Nicolas ad by Dranzy, the Saint-Raphaël aperitif ad by Loupot and, last but not least, the enormous bull's head in the Kub beef bouillon ad by Cappiello (1931). Many interesting exhibitions are held each year, such as the 1981 series of circus posters and Austrian poster art.

## Musée de l'Air et de l'Espace

**93350 Le Bourget**
**Aéroport du Bourget**
**837.01.73**
*Open 10:00 A.M. to 5:00 P.M., to 6:00 P.M. May 1st thru Sept 30; Sat., Sun. and holidays open 10:00 A.M. to 12:00 noon and 2:00 P.M. to 5:00 P.M. or 6:00 P.M. Closed Tues. Fee: 8F.*

The exquisite if cluttered Meudon museum is now closed. However, all the vehicles in which human beings have flown or attempted to fly are currently being restored in Meudon before they are moved to the Musée de l'Air et de l'Espace, scheduled to open in 1983 in Le Bourget. These flying machines include 1783 hot-air balloons, World War I planes, Clément Ader's Avion 3, Lilienthal's glider, Wilbur Wright's airplane and Santos Dumont's Demoiselle. For the moment, there are five large exhibit halls devoted to the aeronautics industry between 1919–1939, World War II planes, French planes from 1945 until today, the French Air Force and light aviation.

### Musée de l'Arc de Triomphe

**8th arr.**
**Place Charles-de-Gaulle**
**380.31.31**
*Open from 10:00 A.M. to 6:00 P.M. (5:00 P.M. in the winter). Fee: 9F.*

The elevator doesn't always work properly and you'll probably have to climb the Arc's 230 steps to visit the large room which passes for the museum. Equipped with an audiovisual presentation, it features documents, archives, photographs and paintings that pertain to the Arc de Triomphe's history.

### Musée de L'Armée

**7th arr.**
**Hôtel des Invalides**
**555.97.30**
*Open 10:00 A.M. to 6:00 P.M., 5:00 P.M. in winter. Fee: 9F.*

The museum's history section contains curiosa such as the cannonball that killed Turenne and Napoleon's gray dinner jacket. You'll also find some of the world's best collections of armor and weapons. Over the last few years the museum has been extensively renovated. Free movies relating to World War I and II are shown every afternoon from 2:00 P.M. on. Other sections include a library, a print room, a photo gallery and the Emperor's tomb (open until 7:00 P.M. in June, July and August).

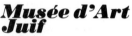

### Musée d'Art Juif

**18th arr.**
**42 rue des Saules**
**257.84.15**
*Open Tues., Thrus., Sun. 3:00 P.M. to 6:00 P.M. (and Fri., Sat. during expositions). Closed holidays and during September. Fee: 4F.*

Founded in 1949, the museum is located on the third floor of the Montmartre Jewish Center. The premises have been recently renovated and feature an ample selection of Jewish art, a collection of scale model Synagogues, ritual items, sculptures, drawings, contemporary engravings and popular Jewish works from Europe and North Africa.

### Musée d'Art Moderne de la Ville de Paris

**16th arr.**
**11 ave. du Président-Wilson**
**723.61.27**
*Open 10:00 A.M. to 5:30 P.M., Wed. to 8:30 P.M. Closed Mon. Fee: 9F.*

This 21-year-old museum is housed in the eastern wing (off the place de l'Alma) of the Palais de Tokyo. Its rich art collection contains works from the turn-of-the-century (Fauvism) to today (Cinetism). Other works include Raoul Dufy's renowned *Electricity Fairy* and Matisse's admirable painting *Danse,* as well as works by Derain, Modigliani, Rouault, Utrillo, Gromaire, Lurçat, Fautrier, and others. The ground floor (quai Wilson entrance) has been divided into "six diversified circuits" specifically designed to house temporary exhibitions. The museum also has a special section called l'ARC (Animation, Research and Confrontations) in which you'll find temporary exhibitions as well as poetry readings, musical performances and workshops. To get to the recently inaugurated New York Concert Hall, enter at 15 quai de New York.

### Musée des Arts Africains et Océaniens

**12th arr.**
**293 ave. Daumesnil**
**343.14.54**

It's rare to find affable museum keepers who are willing to dispense additional advice should the pamphlets handed out at the entrance prove insufficient. If it weren't for their help, you wouldn't be as enthusiastic about the mysteries of black African, Maghreb and Oceanic arts and civilizations depicted in this museum's sculptures, jewelry, pottery, weapons, furniture, rugs and

*Open from 9:45 A.M. to noon and 1:30 P.M. to 5:15 P.M. Closed Tues. Fee: 7F (Sun. 3.5F)*

embroideries. This "palace," with its huge bas-relief on the façade, was built for the 1931 Colonial Exposition. Be sure to see the Ruhlman furniture which belonged to the French minister of colonies, Paul Reynaud, and is exhibited in a corner hall on the ground floor. There's also a beautiful tropical aquarium in the basement.

## Musée des Arts Décoratifs

**1st arr.**
**107 rue de Rivoli**
**260.32.14**
*Open 10:00 A.M. to noon and 2:00 P.M. to 5:00 P.M. Closed Mon., Tues. Fee: 5F.*

You'll find a complete panorama of French homes from the Middle Ages to 1900, as well as rich collections of paintings, sculptures, furniture, tapestries and ceramics, in addition to Middle Eastern and Far Eastern works of art donated by Dubuffet. This museum is currently undergoing important renovations and only the Medieval, Renaissance, nineteenth-century and technical halls are open to the public. Its entire six floors are scheduled for completion in the fall of 1983. The museum is closed at lunchtime, but you're welcome to browse through the library's books on the ground floor next to the gardens. There are many intriguing illustrated tomes pertaining to furniture, woodwork, passementeries and other decorative techniques. You may also consult the National Center for Information and Documentation on Arts and Crafts (open from 12:30 P.M. to 5:30 P.M.) for all questions pertaining to schools and instruction, administrative problems, workshops and current status of artisans. The museum's catalogue lists 10,000 names in geographic and alphabetical order. For children aged from 5 to 12, the museum offers guided tours and conferences (slides and movies) on Wednesdays at 2:30 P.M.

## Musée Bouilhet-Christofle

**93200 Saint-Denis**
**112 rue**
**Ambroise-Croizat**
**820.61.23**
*Open from 9:00 A.M. to 1:00 P.M. and 2:00 P.M. to 6:00 P.M. Closed Sat., Sun. and holidays. Free. By appointment only.*

Once you get to the sea-green waters of the canal, you'll see a red factory partly covered with ivy. The museum will then be to your left, through the monumental gate. Amid the shrewd antique goldware reproductions, you'll find exquisite and authentic antique pieces (Louis XIV ewers, Louis XV bridal bowls, Empire powder cases) as well as the finest Christofle products from the Louis-Philippe era to the present. You'll also see a series of diverse designs from the second half of the nineteenth century, such as the Paiva bidet created at the request of a mysterious admirer, Christofle art nouveau creations, sumptuous art deco objects designed by Sue, Mare, Groult, and Follot, and "Expo 1937" designs, including beautiful objects crafted by that unappreciated Dane, Fjerdinstad. Among the countless place settings there is an enormous display of spoons for stewed fruit, jam, fresh fruit, sugar, pastries, strawberries, desserts, salt, mustard, pickles, oysters, sardines, petit-fours, soup, and so on.

## Musée Bourdelle

**15th arr. 16 rue**
**Antoine-Bourdelle**

Bourdelle lived here until his death in 1929. In 1948 the sculptor's wife presented the City of Paris with his sculptures, original casts, paintings, gouaches and watercolors, as well as the furniture, tools and plants from

**548.67.27**
*Open 10:00 A.M. to 5:40 P.M.*
*Closed Mon. Fee: 7F.*

his workshop. It's best to visit the museum in spring when the trees are in bloom. Exhibits include Bourdelle's Heracles, his study for the Monument to Alvear (based on the one in Buenos Aires), his dying Centaur and Sappho. In 1978 the museum acquired Bourdelle's love letters.

## *Musée Bricard de la Serrure*

3rd arr.
**1 rue de la Perle**
**277.79.62**
*Open 10:00 A.M. to 12:00 noon and 2:00 P.M. to 5:00 P.M. Closed Mon., Tues., holidays and during August. Fee: 5F.*

The well-known lock company inaugurated this interesting little museum in September 1976. Featured objects include a lock collection, keys, door knockers and such from Roman times to the present. One of its latest acquisitions is a chest that once belonged to the Marquis de Sade.

## *Musée du Cabinet des Medailles et Antiques*

2nd arr.
**58 rue de Richelieu**
**261.82.83**
*Open everyday from noon to 5:00 P.M. Fee: 6F.*

Reopened in 1981, this museum offers a selection of archeological treasures on loan from the National Library. Included are large cameos, objects belonging to the Berthouville family, and, from Childeric's tomb, Dagobert's throne, Louis d'Orleans' collection of medals, extremely rare coins, antiques, and, of course, various medals.

## *Musée Carnavalet*

3rd arr.
**23 rue de Sévigné**
**272.21.13**
*Open 10:00 A.M. to 5:40 P.M.*
*Closed Mon. Fee: 9F.*

Much of Paris' history is recalled at the Musée Carnavalet. The museum's collections are housed in a very attractive sixteenth-century hotel, the center of which is enhanced by a garden lined with finely sculpted shrubs and surrounded by flower beds. Currently displayed works of art date from the end of the sixteenth century to the present and include antique signposts, district topographical charts, scale models of monuments, woodwork, furniture and many other objects. The museum recently opened a salon featuring works by François Boucher and fellow artists such as Fragonard. Many of the museum's rooms display paintings of Parisian views, portraits, social and historical scenery. There are also sixteenth-century rooms located on the ground floor.

## *Musée Cernuschi*

8th arr.
**7 ave. Vélasquez**
**563.50.75**
*Entrance at 111 blvd. Malesherbes. Open 10:00 A.M. to 5:30 P.M. Closed Mon., holidays. Fee: 7F (free on Sun.).*

Unknown to most Parisians, this museum houses an admirably displayed Chinese and Japanese art collection which includes antique bronze works, an astonishing series of terra-cotta funeral statuettes, and a fifth-century sitting bodhisattva.

## Musée des Collections Historiques de la Préfecture de Police

5th arr.
**1 bis rue des Carmes**
**329.21.57 poste, 336**
*Open from 2:00 P.M. to 5:00 P.M.*
*Wed. and Thurs. only. Free.*

This museum was founded in 1909 by Lepine, then Chief Commissioner of the Paris police. It was located at the quai des Orfevres Police Archives building until 1975, when it was transfered to the modern 5th Arrondissement Police headquarters. The museum contains interesting documents pertaining to the Parisian police from the sixteenth century on: wax-sealed letters, collections of weapons, and documents on major historical crimes. Detailed documents pertaining to morés, however, are still locked up at the quai des Orfevres.

## Musée de la Chasse et de la Nature

3rd arr.
**60 rue des Archives**
**272.86.43**
*Open 10:00 A.M. to 6:00 P.M., to*
*5:00 P.M. October 1 thru March 31.*
*Closed Tues., holidays. Fee: 8F.*

Located in the middle of the Marais district, this museum is housed in the Guénégaud Hotel built by François Mansart in 1654. Its three floors of exhibits include admirable weapons, trophies and paintings by Oudry, Rubens, Chardin, de Dreux and others. There's a lovely collection of works by François Desportes, Louis XIV's court-appointed artist in charge of depicting hunts. His work includes studies of hunting dogs and animals against landscapes. The museum is a guaranteed treat for children of all ages.

## Musée du Cinéma Henri-Langlois

16th arr.
**Palais de Chaillot,**
**place du Trocadéro**
**553.74.39**
*Tours at 10:00 A.M., 11:15 A.M.,*
*12:15 P.M., 2:30 P.M., 3:30 P.M.*
*and 4:30 P.M. Closed Mon.*
*Fee 10F.*

The evolution of cinema is covered from its very inception (magic lanterns, Robertson's photographic plates, Turkish and Balinese shadow boxes, Louis Lumière's 1895 movie camera) to the French New Wave. Also featured are technical wares, scripts, films, costumes, sets, posters, photos and memorabilia. Guided tours include film screenings.

## Musée Clémenceau

16th arr.
**8 rue Franklin**
**520.53.41**
*Open 2:00 P.M. to 5:00 P.M.*
*Closed Mon., Wed., Fri. Fee: 5F.*

In the unassuming house where Georges Clémenceau spent the final years of his incredible life, there are thousands of his daily effects including his shaving brush, tiny Rodin caryatids, and many other mementoes of the "Tiger's" hours of victory and defeat.

## Musée de Cluny

5th arr.
**6 place Paul-Painlevé**
**325.62.00**
*Open 9:45 A.M. to 12:30 P.M. and*
*2:00 P.M. to 5:15 P.M. Closed Tues.*
*Fee: 6F.*

This museum is housed in the magnificent manor that once belonged to the abbots of Cluny. Its 27 halls feature Gallo-Roman and Medieval works of art such as the statues of the apostles from Sainte-Chapelle, and master tapestries like the *Dame à la Licorne* and *La Vie Seigneurale*. If you visit the museum's flamboyant Gothic chapel, you'll see the early thirteenth-century, double-faced Limousin cross acquired in 1978. The Musée de Cluny has amassed 20,000 works of art over the last 30 years and keeps them in its vaults. Fortunately, some of them are gradually being unearthed for display. The museum's Renaissance collections, which were put into safekeeping after World War II, will soon be displayed at the Château d'Ecouen's Renaissance Museum in the Val d'Oise.

### Musée Cognacq-Jay
2nd arr.
25 blvd. des Capucines
742.94.71
*Open 10:00 A.M. to 5:40 P.M. Closed Mon. Fee: 7F.*

Since this museum is never really crowded, you'll have the time to browse at leisure through its three stories dedicated to seventeenth- and eighteenth-century art. Formerly a townhouse, the museum features works like Rembrandt's *Anesse de Balaam,* Tiepolo's *Festin de Cléopâtre,* Fragonard's *Perrette et le Pot au Lait* and pastels by Maurice Quentin La Tour. You'll also discover an exceptional collection of tobacco pouches, small gold boxes and cases, enamels and gems amassed by the Samaritaine's founder, as well as a unique set of Meissen porcelain statuettes.

### Musée de la Contrefaçon
16th arr.
16 rue de la Faisanderie
501.51.11
*Open 8:30 A.M. to 5:00 P.M. Closed Sat., Sun.*

Here you will find a thousand-and-one illegal counterfeit items, such as counterfeit wines from Narbonne sold by the Gauls in 200 B.C., "Meinier" (instead of Menier) chocolates, "Perrenod" (instead of Pernod) and many counterfeit perfumes. These displays are all housed in an eighteenth-century townhouse which is itself a sham, since it was built in 1900.

### Musée Delacroix
6th arr.
6 rue de Furstenberg
354.04.87
*Open 9:45 A.M. to 5:15 P.M. Closed Tues. Fee: 5F.*

This small museum, located at the top of a dark staircase, is the apartment-studio where Delacroix lived until his death in 1863. Constantly renewed displays include the artist's personal belongings, letters, paintings, drawings and sketches. The studio is on the same level as the charming, romantic garden. The Eugène Delacroix Society of Friends regularly sponsors various exhibits such as "Delacroix and his Parisian Environment," "Delacroix and Riesener" and "Delacroix and Paul Huet."

### Musée d'Ennery
16th arr.
59 ave. Foch
553.57.96
*Open Sun. 1:00 P.M. to 4:00 P.M. in September thru March and 1:00 P.M. to 5:00 P.M. in April thru July. Closed during August.*

D'Ennery bequeathed his Second Empire townhouse to the French government, along with his collections of animal statues, furniture, figurines and other testimonial objects pertaining to Chinese and Japanese religions and cultures from the seventeenth to nineteenth centuries. Included is a beautiful collection of netsukes and a lovely series of elaborate buttons from Japan.

### Musée Français de l'Holographie
4th arr.
4 rue Beaubourg
277.15.12
*Open daily from 11:00 A.M. to 7:00 P.M. Closed Tues. Fee: 15F.*

By looking through a transparent cylinder, you'll see from any angle, realistic, three-dimensional people, considerably reduced in size, of course. Holography was invented by an English physicist, Dennis Gabor, after World War II. It is defined as a "registration and restitution process that allows for three-dimensional images, due to the properties of coherent lighting, i.e., lasers." This small basement museum is located across from the Georges Pompidou Center and was doubtlessly created to promote holography since it's the only one of its kind in France. Over one hundred holographs are featured here, including the Englishman Nick Phillips' "Elliot the Dragon" and the Italian Ruggero Maggi's "Space-bound for Easter Island."

## Musée Français de la Photographie

**91570 Bièvres**
**78 rue de Paris**
**941.10.60**
*Open 10:00 A.M. to noon and 2:00 P.M. to 6:00 P.M. Fee: 6F.*

The windows of this large nineteenth century building overlook a park immortalized in Victor Hugo's *Autumn Leaves.* The museum, which covers the entire technical evolution of photography, started with a collection of objects belonging to M. Fage and his son. Three stories of glass-encased displays reveal an abundance of original documents that retrace the history of photography, from eighteenth-century darkrooms and Niepce's 1816 discovery, to the present day. The museum features an impressive permanent display of antique cameras and a constantly renewed collection of antique and modern photographs related to all sorts of disciplines.

## Musée Grévin

**9th arr.**
**10 blvd. Montmarte**
**770.85.05**
*Open 2:00 P.M. to 7:00 P.M., Sun., holidays and school holidays. 1:00 P.M. to 8:00 P.M. Fee: 20f, children 14f.*
*Forum de Halles, 1st floor (tel. 261.28.50). Open 11:00 A.M. to 10:00 P.M. Sun., holidays 1:00 P.M. to 8:00 P.M. Fee: 22F, children 16F.*

Musée Grévin, with its delirious decor and mind-boggling lights, is the last refuge of popular surrealistic art and receives 600,000 visitors a year. Rediscovered by Parisians after World War II, it celebrates its' 100th anniversary in 1982. Giscard d'Estaing has been shamelessly replaced by Mitterand and his minister, Rocard. Sadat, Begin, Reagan and Pope John Paul II are all under glass. You'll discover recreated historical scenes as good as the ones made in Hollywood with figures like Charlemagne, Roland, François I, and Louis XIV, or marvelous sets depicting international theater and ballet. This exciting museum also features a *Palais des Mirages* and a *Cabinet Fantastique.* Since 1979 the Grévin has had an outlet at the Forum des Halles which recreates the Parisian Belle Époque. It contains twenty animated sets that feature Victor Hugo towards the end of his life, Verlaine at Procope, Pasteur in his laboratory, Jules Verne in a *20,000 Leagues Under the Sea* setting, Parisian boulevards, Montmartre, Charles Worth and Paul Poiret, the 1900 World's Fair, Sarah Bernhardt performing Cleopatra, and Coquelin in the role of Cyrano. Also, there is Emile Reynaud's Optical Theater (praxinoscope) like the model he managed in Montmartre from 1892–1900. You'll see a projection of "Pauvre Pierrot," an early ancestor of today's cartoons.

## Musée Guimet

**16th arr.**
**6 place d'Iéna**
**723.61.65**
*Open 9:45 A.M. to noon and 1:30 P.M. to 5:15 P.M. Closed Tues. Fee: 7F.*

The Musée Guimet houses the National Museum's Department of Asian Arts and exhibits three floors of Eastern, Central and Far Eastern art. The ground floor displays Tibetan and Southeast Asian works: Khmer art from Cambodia, Cham art from central Vietnam, Thai art, Burmese art and Indonesian art from Bali and Java. On the first floor there is Chinese and Indian art, including Chinese funeral statuettes donated by Robert Rousset, as well as antique works of art from Pakistan and Afghanistan. The second floor features art from Japan, Korea, Sinkiang, and the Michel Calmann 1977 donation of Chinese ceramics that includes sixth- to thirteenth-century Souei, Tang and Song pottery and porcelains. In 1980 the museum acquired the Grandidier collection of fourteenth- to eighteenth-century Ming and Tsing porcelains. The museum has an annex at 19 avenue d'Iéna which exhibits a collection of Japanese Buddhist icons.

## Musée Gustave-Moreau

**9th arr.**
**14 rue**
**La Rochefoucauld**
**874.38.50**
*Open 10:00 A.M. to 1:00 P.M. and 2:00 P.M. to 5:00 P.M. Closed Mon., Tues. Fee: 7F.*

Back when Gustave Moreau's Museum was deserted, André Breton was the only one to defend this artist, who is best known for having taught Matisse and Rouault, among other fauves. Part of the renewed interest in Moreau is due to the recent revival of symbolism (thanks to Philippe Julian) and the recent nostalgia trend. His work offers a general outlook on turn-of-the-century tastes by blending the neo-Renaissance "goldsmith" style of the German Nazarene school of art (modified by the Anglo-Saxon pre-Raphaelites) with studies in pure painting that adumbrate the coming of lyrical abstracts.

## Musée Jean-Jacques Henner

**17th arr.**
**43 ave. de Villiers**
**763.42.73**
*Open from 2:00 P.M. to 5:00 P.M. Closed Mon. Fee: 7F.*

Jean-Jacques Henner was referred to as "the Alsatian painter of the French school" by his fellow artists during the Franco-Russian War in 1870. Today it's still hard to believe that French nationalists like Gambetta integrated Henner's works to further their own goals, and that they declared as "officially French" his Florentine "sfumato-styled" portraits popularized earlier by the Parmesan Correge. Degas, whose origins were Italian, called him a "two-bit Leonardo" and accused him of "smoking" too much while painting children. These "smokey" portraits and many others are very well displayed and accompanied by audio-visual narrations. All in all, you will get a clear idea of the confusion that reigned at the end of the nineteenth century by viewing works created by one of its major interpreters.

## Musée de l'Histoire de France—Archives Nationales

**3rd arr.**
**60 rue**
**des Francs-Bourgeois**
**277.11.30 ext. 21.78**
*Open 2:00 P.M. to 5:00 P.M. Closed Tues. Fee: 4F.*

The Museum of French History is housed in the admirable eighteenth-century Soubise townhouse and contains documents and autographs. The first hall (formerly the guards' chamber), hung with remarkable tapestries, has been renovated and features a permanent display of 71 important relics dating from Merovingian times (note the papyrus signed by King Dagobert) to the Second World War (such as Jean Moulin's 1940 memo to the minister of the interior). Also featured are major documents such as the Edict of Nantes, the Declaration of the Rights of Man, Louis XIV's and Napoleon's testaments. The other halls, sumptuously decorated by Germain Boffrand for the Princess de Soubise, house a permanent collection relating to the French Revolution, as well as temporary exhibits (one to two years) dealing with the Ancien Regime and the nineteenth century. Free guided tours for students can be arranged by calling the educational department (tel. 277.11.30, ext. 22.62).

### Muséum d'Histoire Naturelle
**5th arr.**
**57 rue Cuvier**
**336.14.41**
*At the Jardin des Plantes.*
*Open 1:30 P.M. to 5:00 P.M.*
*Fee: 10F–12F, depending on gallery*

There was a lot of hand-wringing over the condition of the Jardin des Plantes. People got so involved in this decaying garden-museum that things finally took a turn for the better. The museum's admirable exhibits began drawing hundreds of thousands of visitors (250,000 yearly for the "Natural History of Sexuality"). Huge renovations were carried out in the zoology deparment; the decrepit aviaries were overhauled; and the menagerie buildings rebuilt. You'll discover the fabulous herbarium's 600,000 items, the insect and butterfly collection, marvelous gems and jewels amassed by the last of the Bourbons in the Mineralogy Hall, the alpine garden, tropical greenhouses, the labyrinth, goldfish, and children laughing and playing. Indeed, there's everything here to make it any Parisian's favorite spot.

### Musée de l'Histoire de la Médecine
**6th arr.**
**12 rue de l'Ecole-de-Médecine**
**329.21.77**
*Open Wed. and Fri. only 2:00 P.M. to 6:00 P.M. Closed university holidays.*

An important collection of medical objects and instruments, as well as seventeenth- to nineteenth-century portraits, manuscripts and medals of doctors and surgeons.

### Musée Historique du Domaine National de Saint-Cloud
**92210 Saint-Cloud**
**Parc de Saint-Cloud**
**602.70.01**
*Open on Wed., Sat., Sun., holidays 2:00 P.M. to 6:00 P.M.*

This charming, little-known museum, opened in 1975, is located in the Saint-Cloud Park's guard house. Its purpose is to recount the history of the park and of the château which burnt down in 1871 (ask a warden for the audiovisual narration). By crossing the park, you may visit Gambetta's house which has been recently made into a museum.

### Musée de l'Homme
**16th arr.**
**Palais de Chaillot, place du Trocadéro**
**505.70.60**
*Open 10:00 A.M. to 5:00 P.M. Closed Tues., holidays. Fee: 10F.*

The North American Indian Hall has recently been refurbished, and the halls featuring Asian and African collections are also ready to reopen. Indeed, renovations and reopenings seem to be the rule here. Nonetheless, this organization founded to "research and teach social sciences" retains a staff of specialists for all disciplines and features a wide range of astonishing displays from all over the world, notably Dogon masks, Dahomey bronzework, huge sculpted heads from Easter Island, Jivaro shrunken heads, Greenland kayaks and, of course, the legendary Hottentot Venus. A series of lectures is held every Wednesday at 8:30 P.M. and costs 12F. The Society of Friends of the Musée de l'Homme organizes trips to private collections both in France and abroad.

## Musée Instrumental du Conservatoire National Supérieur de Musique

**8th arr.**
**14 rue de Madrid**
**292.15.20**
*Open 2:00 P.M. to 6:00 P.M.*
*Closed Sun., Mon., Tues. Fee: 6F.*

Berlioz used to be curator of this museum, which has just acquired 700 musical pieces amassed a century later by his successor, Geneviève Thibault de Chambure, who died in 1975. The works have since been catalogued by Mme Bran-Ricci and integrated into the 3,000-piece collection pertaining to European instrumental music from the Renaissance to the present time. Featured instruments include bagpipes, guitars (one of the lacquered ones belonged to Louis XV's daughter), harpsichords (which virtuosis are welcome to play), violins (Stradivarius) and pianos (one of which belonged to Chopin). Don't leave without viewing the serinette, a small mechanical blowing device designed to teach birds how to sing.

## Musée Jacquemart-André

**8th arr.**
**158 blvd. Haussmann**
**562.39.94**
*Open 1:30 P.M. to 5:30 P.M.*
*Closed Mon., Tues. Fee: 8F.*

Rich and austere, this museum reflects the style and taste of the creative Jacquemart family. Paradoxically, Parisians rediscovered the museum after its curatorship was entrusted to the eminently frivolous artist, Jean-Gabriel Domergue, who sponsored huge temporary exhibitions. The curatorship now belongs to Lydie Huyghe, who has hired skillful decorators to display the museum's collections. On the ground floor of this beautifully furnished building, you'll discover works by Fragonard, Mantegna, Rembrandt, Rubens, Uccello and Watteau. Beneath Tiepolo's huge fresco (formerly at the Villa Contarini), you'll admire Della Robbia's terra-cottas and Donatello's bronzes.

## Musée du Jeu de Paume

**1st arr.**
**Garden of the Tuileries**
**260.12.07**
*Open 9:45 A.M. to 5:15 P.M.*
*Closed Tues. Fee: 7F*
*(3.50F on Sun.).*

The largest collection of French paintings from the second half of the nineteenth century hangs here, beautifully displayed. It includes Impressionist works by Cézanne, Degas, Manet, Monet, Pissaro, Sisley, as well as such predecessors as Corot and successors like Gauguin, Seurat, Signac and Van Gogh. Other works encompass paintings by Helleu, the young Degas' *Sémiramis,* the aging Manet's *Combat de Taureaux* as well as a portrait of his parents. Also, Boudin's *Le Port du Hâvre,* Renoir's *Danse à la Ville,* Pissaro's *Maison de la Folie Eragny,* Guillaumin's *La Pointe de la Beaumette* and Jongking's *Patineurs.* The museum supplies visitors with maps and organizes guided tours at 3:00 P.M. in English on Fridays and in French on Saturdays.

## Musée de la Légion d'Honneur et des Ordres de Chevalerie

**7th arr.**
**2 rue de Bellechasse**
**555.95.16**
*Open from 2:00 P.M. to 5:00 P.M.*
*Closed Mon. Fee: 6F.*

The clearly defined audio-visual tour allows visitors to learn about French and foreign orders and medals throughout history. In 1978 the museum acquired a beautiful collection of porcelains emblazoned with distinguished Russian orders that once belonged to Empress Catherine II. In 1979, it acquired Napoleon's Legion of Honor necklace (also worn by Napoleon III) designed by Biennais and donated to the Museum by Prince Napoleon. The museum has its own theater and organizes guided tours.

## Musée du Louvre

**1st arr.**
**Place du Carrousel**
**260.39.26**
*Open 9:45 A.M. to 5:00 P.M.*
*(to 6:30 P.M. for the main section).*
*Closed Tues., holidays. Free on Sun.*

The Louvre, the nation's greatest single collection, has 224 halls and one huge *Grande Galerie,* 422 meters of wall space, 3 million visitors a year (80 percent foreign in summer, 60 percent in winter and fall) and 400,000 catalogued works of art of which some 500 are usually on loan to other French and foreign museums. We do not remotely have the space to do justice to this awesome treasure trove. Instead, we urge you to consult in detail specialized books like the *Guide Bleu,* for instance. An even better idea is to join the Society of Friends of the Louvre (107 rue de Rivoli, 1st fl., tel. 260.70.64), an organization that offers its members free admission, invitations to exhibitions, educational trips and lectures. We also highly recommend the temporary exhibits displayed in the Galerie de Flore (second floor) consisting of works held under the aegis of the Department of Paintings but in the Louvre's temporary safekeeping. Alongside these works there are complementary exhibitions of sketches that will allow you to understand the historical climate in which the masterworks were painted. Among recent acquisitions and donations, you'll discover Goya's portrait of the Marquise de Santa Cruz, Malatesta's portrait by Piero Della Francesca, Saint Irene weeping for Saint Sebastian by Georges de la Tour, and the Sancy diamond of the Crown Jewel collection, which was repurchased by the French government at a very high price. In its Flore Pavilion, the Cabinet des Dessins (Hall of Drawings) displays a huge number of constantly changing items such as charcoals, red chalks, silver pen tips, pencil leads, Conté crayons, China ink drawings and watercolors. The Cabinet's 90,000 items have been recently enlarged by 104 Mignard drawings and one work by Degas (*Modistes*). Only the watercolors are permanently displayed.

## Musée de la Machine à Écrire

**91560 Crosne**
**place de la Mairie**
**948.42.58**
*Open Wed., Sat., Sun. 2:00 P.M. to*
*6:00 P.M.*

The museum of typewriters is located across the street from city hall, at the end of an old building which might have been a schoolhouse. Claude Pichon inaugurated it in 1975 to consummate his 20-year passion for collecting the machines. Formerly a stockbroker in metals, this man from Tours is considered one of the world's top typewriter experts. His 300-piece collection features 100 conventional machines, such as the 1884 model with piano-like wooden keys, the world's earliest typewriter (the latest ones are from 1930). Other spectacular products include a Japanese model invented during the 1910s with 4,000 barely legible ideograms, the 1906 Pigier stenography machine, the first electrical typewriter made in 1912 which was later commercialized in the 1930s, the forerunner of IBM's "ball" mounted on a curious-looking 1920s German machine, typewriters for the blind like the 1885 duograph (made of mahogany and bronze) which miraculously escaped the Bazaar de la Charité blaze 12 years later, an American "junior" pocket-sized typewriter and a mother-of-pearl-inlaid Remington whose body is adorned with multicolored filaments. Another intriguing object is the arithometer, an adding machine for banks designed by Thomas de Colmar during Louis-Philippe's reign.

## Musée de la Marine

**16th arr.**
**Palais de Chaillot,**
**place du Trocadéro**
**553.31.70**
*Open 10:00 A.M. to 6:00 P.M.*
*Closed Tues. Fee: 8F.*

The world's largest maritime collection is constantly invaded by noisy, enthusiastic kids who touch everything in sight. They may remain indifferent to the magnificent series of Vernet paintings, Les Ports de France, yet they go crazy over the antique and modern navigational instruments, the cannons, the sidearms, the old maps (recently displayed together in a new room) and the marvelous and innumerable scale model ships. On the second Sunday of each month, from 11:00 A.M. on, children can watch model-makers restore model ships. Each year, the museum sponsors retrospectives of maritime paintings and exhibitions on special themes. Guided tours on written request only (1:30 P.M.). The auditorium features films on galleys, whale hunting, and other subjects.

## Musée Marmottan

**16th arr.**
**2 rue Louis-Boilly**
**224.07.02**
*Open 10:00 A.M. to 6:00 P.M.*
*Closed Mon. Fee: 10F.*

The Marmottan Museum is located between the Bois de Boulogne and the Ranelagh Gardens. Formerly a collector's residence, it was donated to the Academy of Fine Arts. Featured are First Empire furniture, objects and paintings, an admirable series of tapestries made during Louis XII's reign and a new hall housing the Wildenstein collection of miniatures. This strange museum's greatest attraction is its extraordinary collection of Impressionist paintings (Donop de Monchy's donation and Michel Monet's bequest), including 165 works by Claude Monet, 80 of which are oils including *Le Pont de L'Europe, Impression*. Additional works by Berthe, Morisot, Sisley, Renoir, Pissaro and Jonking make the Musée Marmottan the second largest Impressionist museum in Paris, after the Jeu de Paume.

## Musée de la Mode et du Costume

**16th arr.**
**Palais Galliéra, 10 ave.**
**Pierre-Ier-de-Serbie**
**720.85.23**
*Open 10:00 A.M. to 5:40 P.M.*
*Closed Mon. Fee: 9F.*

Established in 1956, this museum features the Musée Carnavalet collections and wardrobes that once belonged to Mme de Galéa and other elegantly dressed women of La Belle Epoque, such as the Countesses Greffulhe and Castellane, the Duchess of Talleyrand and Princess Murat. There are 4,000 costumes and over 25,000 articles depicting fashions for men, women and children from 1735–1981. These collections are displayed in a series of exhibits with various themes, such as "Post-War High Fashion" (1977), "Nadar and Fashion" (1978), "Children's Fashion" (1979), "Hats" (1980).

## Musée de la Monnaie

**6th arr.**
**11 quai de Conti**
**329.12.48**

Created under Charles X, this museum is now located in the Hotel des Monnaies. It is one of the most gorgeous buildings from the reign of Louis XVI and is still in perfect condition. The court of honor and many of the salons are well worth a visit in themselves. The museum

*Open from 11:00 A.M. to 5:00 P.M. Closed Sat., Sun., and national holidays. Free.*

## Musée de Montmartre

**18th arr.**

**17 rue Saint-Vincent**

**606.61.11**

*Open from 2:30 P.M. to 5:30 P.M. (Sun. from 11:00 A.M. to 5:30 P.M.). Fee: 5F.*

## Musée des Monuments Français

**16th arr.**

**Palais de Chaillot, place du Trocadéro**

**727.35.74**

*Open 9:45 A.M. to 12:30 P.M. and 2:00 P.M. to 5:15 P.M. Closed Tues. Fee: 7F.*

## Musée de la Musique Mécanique

**3rd arr.**

**13 rue Brantôme, quartier de l'Horloge**

**278.49.16**

*Open 11:00 A.M. to 7:00 P.M. Closed Tues. Fee: 10F.*

## Musée National d'Art Moderne Centre Georges Pompidou

**4th arr.**

**120 rue Saint-Martin**

**277.12.33**

*Open noon to 10:00 P.M., Sat., Sun. 10:00 A.M. to 10:00 P.M. Closed Tues. Fee: 9F.*

displays coins and medals from ancient times to the present, as well as portraits of medal designers, medal models, drawings, studies, manuscripts and books pertaining to coin-making techniques, coin printers, and screw-presses. Temporary exhibits are held as well.

This museum is housed in a beautiful seventeenth-century townhouse surrounded by two charming gardens and the last vineyard in Paris. Here you will find interesting works and memorabilia pertaining to famous Montmartre denizens such as Steinlen, Willette, Poulbot, Gustave Charpentier, MacOrlan, and Dorgeles. There are also famous Toulouse-Lautrec posters and a stunning collection of Clignancourt porcelain. One of the museum's smaller rooms is dedicated to the Commune de Montmartre. Temporary exhibits.

You'll find some of the most famous French monuments in this imposing, well-lit and fascinating museum. These reproductions and models evoke thirteenth- to nineteenth-century sculptures. Medieval murals and French monumental art as a whole, including capitals, tombs and portraits. An audiovisual tour provides a comprehensive understanding of these works.

This museum features Burburry's Barbary Organ and the ingenious pianola for which Debussy and Stravinski composed "specific works," as well as cylinder music boxes, perforated records, harmoniums and other organs with pipes and mobile reed-stops, miniature pianos, violins, sitars, saxophones, trumpets—all mechanized, and, in certain cases, automatic. Some even function with compressed air, like the art deco jazz exhibit which features a life-sized mannequin of the well-known bagpipe player Fredo Gardoni and his little Martinique drum player. At least a hundred marvelous music machines in perfect condition.

The museum's latest acquisitions include post-World War I paintings by Kirchner, Gris and Malevitch, interwar paintings by Magritte (*Le Double Secret,* 1928) and Matisse (*Le Rêve*) and post-World War II paintings by Jackson Pollock, Matta and Giacometti. The museum has recently been enlarged and its display areas are better adapted for large sized works of art. Recent works by young artists are to be found on the fourth floor.

**Musée National des Arts et Traditions Populaires**
16th arr.
6 route de
Mahatma-Gandhi
747.69.80
*Open from 10:00 A.M. to 5:15 P.M. Closed Tues. Fee: 7F.*

Created in 1968, these galleries proved interesting only to researchers and scientists. A new cultural wing, however, was opened to the public in June, 1975 and has made this museum far more accessible to the layman. Popular art objects from the pre-industrial era are clearly and simply exhibited, each in its own socio-ecological context (artisans' workshops, regional interiors, etc.). The museum's temporary exhibits (two to three yearly) are among Paris' most remarkable cultural contributions ("Man and His Body in Traditional Society"). In conjunction with the C.N.R.S., the museum's laboratory does research on French cultural heritage that is later published in prestigious books such as *L'Architecture Rurale Française, Recits et Contes Populaires, Le Mobilier Traditionnel Français,* and *Sources Regionales.*

**Musée National de Céramiques**
92310 Sevres
Grande Rue
534.99.05
*Open from 9:30 A.M. to noon and from 1:30 P.M. to 5:15 P.M. Closed Tues. Fee: 6F (3F on Sun.).*

Sèvres bridge, to your right. The factory occupies a section of the park of St. Cloud, the name of a nearby town in which the first French porcelain workshops were built under Louis XIV. The factory itself was constructed 50 years later, along with a smaller one which now houses the museum. By 1800 the factory was turning out round plates and platters for Napoleon and, subsequently, the Bourbons. In 1824 the initial museum was opened under the heading "Céramique et Vitrique," and in 1876 the museum was housed in its present building along the Seine where it continues to display the factory's wares. Currently, it is reclassifying its documents so the antique pieces will stand out more in the evolution of terra cotta crafts. Since 1979, eight halls on the ground floor have been devoted to the "developing ceramic industry linked to the rebirth of civilization in the Mediterranean basin from the eighth and ninth centuries up until the seventeenth century," after which there was a sudden interest in fine China porcelain. Geographically speaking, the museum's layout tends to confront contemporary works (to the left) with Middle Eastern works. Nothing has been moved around on the first floor, which features works from the Renaissance to the nineteenth century: Nevers earthenware (Hall 1), Delft stoneware (Halls 2, 3 and 4) and others, including those from the Far East (Halls 5, 6 and 7); the Vincennes factory, which paved the way for the one in Sèvres, is featured in Hall 9. The three remaining halls display, chronologically, very well chosen nineteenth-century French and German products which can also be found in the museum's entrance hall. To the right, on your way out, you'll find the sales outlet for the Manufacture Nationale de Porcelaine de Sèvres, which displays constantly changed items. All of them have been conceived and crafted in intermediate workshops which, unfortunately, are closed to the public.

## Musée National des Techniques

**3rd arr.**
**270 rue Saint-Martin**
**271.24.14**
*Open noon to 5:45 P.M.*
*Closed Sun., holidays. Fee: 6F.*

An important exhibition of 8,000 authentic objects that trace the evolution of science and technology from the seventeenth century up to the present. Housed in the buildings that once belonged to the Saint-Martin-des-Champs priory, this collection presents original historical pieces such as Pascal's adding machine, Jacquard's loom, Mouchot's sun-powered oven, Ader's airplane, Amédée Bollée's steam-powered car, the Lumière brothers' camera and a fine collection of antique clocks and mechanical toys. Numerous animated scale models demonstrate how the machines work.

## Musée de Neuilly

**92200 Neuilly**
**12 rue du Centre**
**747.86.84**
*Open 2:30 P.M. to 4:30 P.M.*
*Closed Tues., holidays. Fee: 8F.*

A marvelous assemblage of nineteenth-century mechanical toys, all with original parts, in perfect working order and beautifully restored to their original appearance. Jacques Damiot, the museum's curator and principal donor, often demonstrates these marvels himself at 3:00 P.M. His knowledge and unrelenting energy have made him one of the world's foremost authorities in this field. The mechanical wonders include an exquisite nude snake-charmer, Saint Cecilia, who flaps her wings while playing the harp, a cow who lifts up its muzzle, and the moon smoking a cigar whose ashen crescent Pierrot intends to string up and play. You'll also discover a poet standing on top of a chair; his heart-rending sighs develop into a flood of tears, making it a particularly moving exhibit piece. On the same floor, you'll also find articles belonging to famous women: Elvire Popesco's hat from *Nina,* Marie-Antoinette's green corset, Marie Curie's autograph, as well as interwar photographs of leading European divas.

## Musée Nissim-de-Camonde

**8th arr.**
**63 rue de Monceau**
**563.26.32**
*Open from 10:00 A.M. to noon*
*and from 2:00 P.M. to 5:00 P.M.*
*Closed Mon., Tues., and national*
*holidays. Fee: 8F.*

Located on the Monceau plain, this museum is housed in a beautiful townhouse, which was fashioned after an eighteenth-century Parisian hotel. You'll find paintings by Drouais, Cudry, and Vigee-Lebrun, along with a few other lovely works by eighteenth-century artists, including cabinet-makers.

## Musée de Notre Dame de Paris

**4th arr.**
**10 rue du**
**Cloître-Notre-Dame**
**325.42.92**
*Open Sat. and Sun. only 2:30 P.M.*
*to 6:00 P.M. Closed during July,*
*August. Fee: 5F.*

The museum features paintings, engravings, documents and objects pertaining to the cathedral's history, including holy treasures and relics.

## Musée de l'Opera
**9th arr.**
**1 pl. Charles-Garnier**
**742.07.02**
*Open from 10:00 A.M. to 5:00 P.M. Closed Sun.*

This long and dismal museum evokes the world of ballet and music without fanfare. Featured displays include scale model sets, costumes, drawings, famous artists' memorabilia and a collection from the Ballets Russes.

## Musée du Petit Palais
**8th arr.**
**Ave. Winston-Churchill**
**265.12.73**
*Open 10:00 A.M. to 5:40 P.M. Closed Mon. Fee: 9F (free on Sun.).*

Though very well endowed, the Palais des Beaux-Arts de la Ville de Paris has no intention of competing with the Louvre in art and archeology. Nonetheless, it offers a fabulous cross section of art, from works of ancient Egypt to French Impressionism. Stressing quality rather than quantity, the cleverly lit and exquisitely colored halls feature works by Courbet, Redon, Corot, Manet, Vuillard, as well as a remarkable collection of seventeenth-century Dutch and Flemish works. A lesser-known section of the museum displays the Tuck donation of eighteenth-century furniture, tapestries and objects. You'll discover antique Egyptian, Roman and Etruscan objects and works of art from the Middle Ages to the Renaissance. There are also temporary exhibitions.

## Musée des Plans-Reliefs
**7th arr.**
**Hôtel des Invalides**
**705.11.07**
*Open 10:00 A.M. to 12:30 P.M. and 2:00 P.M. to 6:00 P.M., to 5:00 P.M. in winter. Closed Sun. morning, Tues. Fee: 9F.*

The Musée des Plans-Reliefs features an impressive collection of scale model (1/600) fortresses commissioned by Napoleon and Vauban (Grenoble, Metz, Mont-Saint-Michel), as well as items pertaining to the history of French urbanism.

## Musée Postal— Maison de la Poste et de la Philatelie
**15th arr.**
**34 blvd. de Vaugirard**
**320.15.30**
*Open 10:00 A.M. to 5:00 P.M. Closed Thurs. Fee: 5F.*

Unless they're stamp collectors, Parisians ignore this cleverly conceived museum. They would do well to spend a few hours in its fifteen exhibit halls, which occupy five floors of a modern building across from the Montparnasse railroad station. They could learn about the history of communications, from "terra-cotta" letters (circa 2500 B.C.) to present-day stamped envelopes. The tour begins on the fifth floor, which features an audiovisual presentation. The first eight halls are dedicated to post office history, the next five to stamp-collecting, and the last two to modern-day postal services and automatic letter-sorting machines. The ground floor offers temporary exhibits, as well as a sales outlet for newly issued stamps.

## Musée Rodin

Jean Cocteau once lived in this magnificent Régence-styled townhouse surrounded by ravishing gardens. Rodin's works are displayed in the main courtyard, the

**7th arr.**
**Hôtel Biron,**
**77 rue de Varenne**
**705.01.34**
*Open 10:00 A.M. to 5:00 P.M., to*
*6:00 P.M. April 1 thru September 30*
*Closed Tues. Fee: 7F.*

park and in the mansion itself, while his moldings, sketches and drawings are all in the museum's annex in Meudon (19 avenue Auguste Rodin).

## Observa-<br>toire de<br>Paris

**14th arr.**
**61 ave.**
**de l'Observatoire**
**320.12.10**
*Open at 12:30 P.M. the first Sat. in*
*each month, by written*
*appointment only. Free guided*
*tour.*

In this temple devoted to time and space, generations of researchers have left their portraits and bizarre-looking instruments (astronomical clocks, sundials, sextants, lenses) for the public to view. In the Observatoire's basement, you can see the talking clock with its recently rejuvenated voice. At the time of this writing, and for an indefinite period, some of the museum's collections are closed to the public.

## Palais de la<br>Découverte

**8th arr.**
**Ave. Franklin-**
**Roosevelt**
**359.16.65**
*Open 10:00 A.M. to 6:00 P.M.*
*Closed Mon. Fee: 5F (13F includes*
*planetarium).*

This "exploratorium" features major scientific discoveries. Although many experiments are carried out by attendants, you can also activate some of the machines yourself. In 1980, a new hall was opened and dedicated to electricity and nuclear energy. The museum also has a cinema, a library and a planetarium that features marvelous astrological projections. Every Saturday at 3:00 P.M. the museum organizes lectures (8f), as well as free beginners' courses in astronomy, physics, geosciences, etc., during the week at 6:00 P.M. or 9:00 P.M. Also featured is a monthly publication entitled *Revue du Palais de la Découverte.* It also features temporary exhibits.

## Palais de<br>Tokyo

**16th arr.**
**13 ave. du**
**President-Wilson**
**723.36.53**
*Open from 9:45 A.M. to 5:15 P.M.*
*Closed Tues. Fee: 7F.*

Formerly the site of both the French National Museum of Modern Art and the Parisian Museum of Modern Art, the Palais de Tokyo is no longer called the Palais de New York (baptized as such during World War II). The bulk of its national collections were transferred in 1977 to the Centre George Pompidou and what is left are private donations. Thus, the Palais de Tokyo is really an "outlet" for the National Museum of Modern Art. Permanently featured works include jewelry, Georges Rouault's *Sainte Face* and *Christ aux Outrages,* Georges Braque's *Le Duo, A Tire d'Ailes,* and a few of his sculptures, including *Tete de Cheval* (1943). Other works include sculptor Laurens' drawings and bronze work, Dunoyer de Segonzac's engravings and paintings (including *Baigneurs*—1922), and major works by Surrealist Victor Brauner, some of which have been painted with wax. These permanently displayed works will soon be incorporated into the new Orsay Museum.

In the Wilson gallery (located in the upper-half of the ground floor), you'll find post-Impressionist works by

Seurat, Signac, and other Pointillists like Gauguin of the Pont-Aven school; Symbolists with mystical tendencies like those of the Nabis school, including Bonnard, Vuillard, and Denis; and several representations of art nouveau (decorators, sculptors, and poster designers). Access to the Musée d'Art et d'Essai is on the ground floor. Inaugurated in 1978, it exhibits specific topics, geographic themes and particular styles. These complex paintings are usually from the Louvre, as well as from other public collections, and their juxtaposition with related self-explanatory documents make this museum distinctly different from the others.

# *Waterways*

Parisians and visitors alike can gain some clearer perspective of our lovely city by getting into the flow of things. Nothing parallels the peace, tranquillity and outright beauty of a restful boat ride around the capital.

## THE SEINE

### Bateaux-Mouches

**8th arr.**
**quai de la Conférence, pont de l'Alma, Right Bank**
**225.96.10**

*Tours last approx. 1-1/4 hrs. Depart every 30 min. from 10:00 A.M. to noon, Fee: 10F; and from 2:00 P.M. to 7:00 P.M., Fee: 15F. Evening tours at 9:00, 9:30, 10:00, 10:30, Fee: 15F. Lunch at 1:00 P.M., Fee: 125F. Dinner at 8:30 P.M., Fee: 250F (every day except Mon.; reservations necessary.) Buffet every evening at 9:00 P.M.*

Whenever Parisians cross the Seine, they ridicule the tourists jam-packed into these modern aquatic coaches. How silly! The best way to rediscover the City of Lights is to take an excursion at the beginning or end of the day when the light in Paris is at its most beautiful. At noon and in the evening, you can take in the view while eating a meal, which isn't altogether that bad or expensive considering the cruise. And when the Louvre and Pont-Neuf bridges are lit up at night, it's amazing how easily you'll forget your troubles.

### Bateaux Parisiens

**7th arr.**
**Port de la Bourdonnais**
**705.50.00**

Departures: pont d'Iéna, Left Bank. Tours last approx. 1 hr. Depart every 30 min. from 10:00 A.M. to 5:00 P.M. From April to October every 20 min. from 9:30 A.M. to 10:30 P.M.; Fee: 15F, children 7:00 P.M. to 10:00 P.M. daily in summer and on Sat. in winter, Fee: 20F.

### Vedettes du Pont-Neuf
**1st arr.**
**Pont-Neuf, square du Vert-Galant**
**663.98.38**

Tours last 1 hr. Depart at 10:30 A.M., 11:15 A.M. and 12:00 noon, then every 30 min. from 1:30 P.M. to 6:00 P.M. Evening cruises depart 9:00 P.M. and 11:30 P.M. Every evening May 1 thru October 15; Fee: 15F by day; 20F by night), Children under 10 8F and 10F, respectively.

# THE CANALS

### La Patache
**9th arr.**
**by Quiztour,**
**19 rue d'Athènes**
**874.75.30**
*Reservations by phone 24 hrs. in advance (for week-ends, 1 wk. in advance). Closed Mon., holidays April 1 thru November 4. Depart 9:00 A.M. at 15 quai Anatole-France, 7th arr.; arrive 12:30 P.M. at Bassin de la Villette. Afternoon depart. 2:00 P.M. at corner of quai de la Loire and ave. Jean-Juarès, 19th arr., in front of Les Palmiers Cafe; Arrive 5:00 P.M. at quai Anatole-France. Fee: Half-day 70F; children 6–12 45F, under 6 free.*

The Patache is proudly moored alongside the renovated quai beneath the d'Orsay Station. This 12-meter-long catamaran, which is as flat as a board, has been outfitted with a strange green-and-white house designed to shelter passengers. Every day, La Patache goes up the Seine, then heads for the Saint-Martin Canal. En route, you'll see the Vert-Galant; the Cité's moorings with a dozen or so residential barges; Sainte-Chapelle's spiral; and Notre Dame's rose window. Once you pass Ile Saint-Louis, the boat veers to the left and settles into the first lock. Everyone bids good morning to François; the gates are then locked and the water in the sluice begins to rise. That's it! You've now left a classic and refined setting and are entering the popular and industrial side of Paris. Napoleon I built this 4.5-kilometer canal which links the Seine to the Bassin de la Villette. Its 9 locks allow for a 26-meter difference in water level. Once past the Bastille basin, the boat enters an amazing vaulted tunnel two kilometers long with tow paths on either side that go in the same direction as the boulevards Richard Lenoir and Jules Ferry. This strange and narrow thoroughfare is lit up by distant openings that give it the appearance of a catacomb. Slowly the journey continues through swing-bridges and sluice-gates from the past, isolated lock installations hidden amid the trees, their attendants sitting in the doorways of ivy-covered houses, people streaming over the Baltard-era iron footbridges, . . . "atmosphere, atmosphere," as Arletty pointed out to Louis Jouvet in the famous film, *Hotel du Nord*. And in just three hours, La Patache arrives at the Bassin de la Villette.

# Zoos • Parks

Paris can become a playground for children and adults alike when you take time out from the museuming, eating, walking, touring and shopping to see how youthful Parisians spend their Sundays. These touches of nature give life and freshness to our oh-so-civilized city.

## *Aquarium du Trocadéro*

**16th arr.**
**ave. Albert-de-Mun**
**723.62.95**
*Open 10:00 A.M. to 5:30 P.M., to 6:30 P.M. May 15 thru September 30. Fee: 3F, children 1.50F.*

These cavernous tanks in the Trocadéro Park house a variety of native French river and pond fish that are endangered species.

## *Aquarium Tropical Musée National des Arts Africans et Océaniens*
**12th arr.**
**293 ave. Daumesnil**
**343.14.54**
*Open 9:45 A.M. to 12:00 noon and 1:30 P.M. to 5:15 P.M. Fee: 7F, children free (3.50F on Sun.).*

More than 20,000 live goldfish, 600 kilograms of saltwater fish, 1 ton of meat, 3 tons of vegetables and fresh fruit, 150 liters of worms. This is what guests of this gigantic aquarium eat each year. In the various sized tanks, the largest of which contains 20,000 liters, you'll see an incredible show of tropical species like sting-rays, sea turtles, giant frogs and all kinds of strange creatures including electric eels, catfish, sucker fish, butterfly fish, and clown fish. An excellent map guides you from the tropical freshwater fish to the Nile River crocodiles, Japanese carp and many other spectacularly colored fish, reptiles and amphibians.

## *Jardin d'Acclimatation*

**16th arr.**
**Bois de Boulogne, porte des Sablons**
**624.10.80**
*Open 10:00 A.M. to 6:00 P.M., to 7:00 P.M. in summer. Fee: 3.50F.*

An intrepid little train (children will simply love it) picks up its passengers at 2 P.M. at the L'Orée du Bois station located near the Porte Maillot. The price, including admission to the Bois, is very reasonable. The train runs past the playground area, which is free and looks a bit rundown, the Punch and Judy show, the hall of mirrors, whose reflections will once and for all alter the image kids have of their parents. Next to nothing (approximately 3F) will get you into the hall of mirrors where you'll bump your head and break your glasses. And since it costs money to really have fun, the enchanted river ride, the camel and pony rides, the go-kart and bumper car, the roller coaster and other marvelously entertaining machines will relieve you of 50F per child, not counting the cotton candy. It's wiser to let the big children off at the roller skating rink and take the little ones to see the bears, the birds languishing in their cages or the impudent monkeys. You can even initiate them into country life at the stone-and-wood farmhouse. Its four tiny buildings will transform little city-dwellers into pig and goat farmers. The adjoining Museum of Arts and Folk Traditions offers children's entertainment such as plays, fairy tales, poetry readings, narrated concerts and studio drawing, as well as films and lecture-exhibits at the Musée en Herbe. Lunch is available at the Bird Pavilion; a decent menu is served for 52F. There is also a special dietician's plate for children at 27F.

## Jardin des Plantes

**5th arr.**
**Entrances at rue Buffon, rue Censier, place Valhubert**
**336.14.41**
*Menagerie and Vivarium open 9:00 A.M. to 5:00 P.M., to 6:00 P.M. in summer. Fee: 10F.*

Their tiny cages can only save these miserable-looking animals from the fate of their predecessors who died gloriously for France during the seige of Paris in 1871. To be specific, they were devoured by the same people who cheered the arrival of the first giraffe fifty years earlier. In the same spirit, it is rumored that the park's population of stray cats is served to the snakes, reptiles, big cats, monkeys and predatory birds. Nevertheless, all these animals are housed in quaint Second Empire pavilions, long since scheduled to be renovated. Whatever you do, do not leave without visiting the strange-looking insects in the vivarium, or checking out the non-stop antics of the bears and apes. Also worth a visit are the mineralogical exhibits with fascinating gems; the entomological exhibit which features some of the world's oldest insect species; the paleontological exhibit with all sorts of skeletons of dinosaurs, whales; and, above all, the botanical marvels dispersed throughout the park.

## Parc de St. Cloud

**92210 Saint-Cloud**
**602.70.01**
*Open 7:00 A.M. to 9:00 P.M., to 10:00 P.M. May to September. Fee: 4F per vehicle, pedestrians free.*

From 9:00 A.M. to 7:00 P.M. you can rent a bicycle for 13F per hour, bicycles built for two, three or four; *rosalies,* a pedal cars built for two who pedal and one who rides for 40F per hour; or a *rosaquatre,*—built for four who pedal and two who ride, which will allow you and your family to discover this park's beautiful and often-overlooked spots. Once you've seen the giant waterfall, visit the Lanterne. Its 94-meter-high terrace offers a lovely panoramic view of Paris.

## Parc Zoologique et de Loisirs de Thoiry

**78770 Thoiry**
**Château de Thoiry**
**16/3/487.40.67**
*Open 9:30 A.M. to 5:00 P.M., to 6:30 P.M. April 1 thru October 31. Fee: 34F, children 20F. Reduced rates for groups of 25 or more.*

You'll ride in enclosed cars in this "African" reserve which is home to lions, elephants, American black bears and numerous other exotic animals. Be sure to walk through the French gardens, the vivarium, the monkey island and, of course, the château which houses the archives and where you get a cafeteria lunch. Children may take advantage of a free picnic, games and various other activities. There are more than a million visitors here each year, which means that on Sunday the roads leading to Thoiry are as crowded as those leading to the Opéra.

## Parc Zoologique de Paris

**12th arr.**
**53 ave. de Saint-Maurice, Bois de Vincennes**
**343.84.95**
*Open 9:00 A.M. to 5:30 P.M., to 6:00 P.M. in summer. Fee: 15F, students 10F.*

This huge zoo, opened to the public in 1934, houses 115 species and 1,100 animals from mammals to birds. Some of the animals are extremely rare, such as the bongos (central African antelopes), Eld deer, tapir, giant panda and Andean flamingoes. The animals are permitted to move freely about the enclosures which approximate their natural habitats.

## Zoo Jean-Richard
**60440 Nanteuil-le-Haudouin—Ermenonville**
**4/454.00.28**
*Open 1:30 P.M. to 5:00 P.M. March and October thru November 11; 10:00 A.M. to 6:00 P.M. April thru September. Fee: 11F, children 6F.*

Located at the edge of a forest, this zoo features lions, gorillas and sealions, the latter offering a show at 5F for adults and 3F for children. By bus, take the Courriers de l'Ile-de-France line which departs from the Fort d'Aubervilliers bus station (tel. 838.20.25).

# THE BASICS

A check guarantee card from an American bank makes check cashing a breeze in Paris. So . . . don't leave home without one! Banks also have the best exchange rates.

  Same day mail service? Impossible! Not at all! Pneumatic tube, or "pneu," mail service, whooshes letters to any part of Paris in no time flat for a very small fee.

In both commercial and residential buildings the hallway lighting systems are often manually operated. Just to one side of the entrance, in a conspicuous place on each landing or near the elevator, you'll find a light switch that is automatically timed to give you from one to three minutes of light. Also, in order to enter and exit many buildings, you must press a buzzer located to one side of the front door. This system developed in the days when it was necessary to ring for the concierge to gain entrance to or leave a building.

  Paris is a well-planned, well-designed city divided into 20 arrondissements, or neighborhoods. Almost all addresses automatically include arrondissement number and often the closest metro stop as well. The best way to orient yourself is to immediately purchase a little book called *Paris Par Arrondissement*. It's available in all bookstores and includes a comprehensive map of Paris and an easily comprehensible metro map.

The French number the floors of their buildings differently than we do. The entry-level floor is always the *rez-de-chaussée,* the following floor is the first floor, the next the second, and so on.

The last metro on all lines leaves the terminal at midnight.

Ushers at movie theaters, sporting events, ballets and concerts expect to be tipped, and can be vengeful if you fail to do so.

Tipping correctly is important, but over-tipping is certainly not necessary. When you are out to eat, be sure to check the bottom of the menu. If it says *service compris,* it means that the tip is included in the price of the meal. In recognition of outstanding service, you can leave the odd change as well.

Public telephones can be tricky. Here are a few helpful hints. In most cafes, restaurants or bars you will need a *jeton* or token to use the phone. You may purchase one from the cashier or waiter. Beware the phone button! You only push this when your call has gone through and your party answers. It deposits the jeton and activates the phone. Many an unsuspecting foreigner thinks this device is the coin return. Street-side phone booths use coins; instructions coins; instructions are usually printed on the phone. Central post offices are the best places to find public phones that are always in order. They also have complete long distance services, which many public phones do not.

Matches are not free in France. They may be purchased at tobacconists and at cafes. No wonder the disposable lighter was invented here!

# Night Owls . . .

## BAKERY GOODS

### Boulangerie de l'Ancienne-Comédie

*6th arr. 10 rue de l'Ancienne-Comé die (tel. 326.89.72). Open 1:30 A.M. to 8:00 P.M. Closed Sun.*

# BOOKS

## Bourrelier

*6th arr. 101 blvd. du Montparnasse (tel. 326.75.33). Open nightly until midnight.*
   French and foreign newspaper.

## La Hune

*6th arr. 170 blvd. Saint-Germain (tel. 548.35.85). Open Mon. to Fri. until midnight.*
   Literature, contemporary art, photo, film.

## Le Marché Saint-André

*6th arr. 40 rue Saint-André—des-Arts (tel. 326.16.03). Open nightly until midnight*
   Fine arts, bargain books, paperbacks.

## Mattéi-Leroy

*18th arr. 40 blvd. de Clichy (tel. 264.95.70). Open nightly until midnight.*
   Science fiction, comics, detective novels.

## Shakespeare and Company

*5th arr. 37 rue de la Bûcherie. Open nightly until midnight.*
   Books in English.

# A CAR MECHANIC

## Automarché

*(tel. 371.74.18).*

## G 7 Dépannage

*(tel. 257.33.44 from 7:00 A.M. to 10:00 P.M.; 731.72.37 from 10:00 P.M. to 7:00 A.M.).*

# A FIXIT MAN

## Pépin-Service

*(tel. 527.34.67)*

## S.O.S. Dépannage

*(tel. 707.99.99).*

# FLOWERS

## Zozo

*1st arr. 21 rue Pierre-Lescot (tel. 508.93.94). Open 10:00 A.M. to midnight (to 7:00 P.M. on Sun.).*

# A POST OFFICE

## Paris R.P.
*1st arr. 52 rue du Louvre (tel. 233.71.60).*
   *The largest post office in France, and the only one open 24 hours, every day of the year.*

# RECORDS AND TAPES

## Champs Disques
*8th arr. 84 Champs-Elysées (tel. 562.65.46). Open until 1:30 A.M., Sun. until 8:00 P.M.*

## Fidélito
*5th arr. 12 rue de la Sorbonne (tel. 326.93.88). Open daily until 10:00 P.M. Closed Sun.*

## Clémentine
*6th arr. 89 blvd. Montparnasse (tel. 548.18.35). Open daily until 1:00 A.M.*

# TOBACCO

## Le Diplomate
*9th arr. 19 blvd. Rochechouart (tel. 878.03.85). Open daily until 1:00 A.M.*

## Le Voltaire
*7th arr. 27 quai Voltaire (tel. 261.17.49). Open until midnight (until 8:00 P.M. Mon.).*

## La Favorite
*6th arr. 3 blvd. Saint-Michel (tel. 364.08.02). Open until 3:30 A.M. (until 6:00 A.M. Sat., Sun.).*

## Le Week-End
*8th arr. —3 rue Washington (tel. 563.45.49). Open daily until 2:00 A.M.*

## Royal-Opéra
*1st arr. 19–21 ave. de l'Opéra (tel. 260.32.08). Open daily until 1:00 A.M.*

## JUST ABOUT ANYTHING INCLUDING NEWSPAPERS

Drugstores have deluxe groceries, precooked dishes, wine, books, newspapers, gifts, gadgets, records, tapes, tobacco, pharmacy. In Neuilly, food, books and newspapers only. Open daily until 2:00 A.M. *6th arr. 149 blvd. Saint-Germain (tel. 222.92.50). 8th arr. 133 Champs-Élysées (tel. 723.54.34). 8th arr. 1 ave. Matignon (tel. 359.38.70). 9th arr. 6 blvd. des Capucines (tel. 266.90.27). 92200 Neuilly—14 place du Marché (tel. 745.46.85).*

# Shopping Around

Don't get stuck juggling your grocery store purchases in your bare hands. When you go grocery shopping, be sure to bring your own bag, because Parisian markets don't use paper bags. The customer is expected to supply his or her own tote, carry-all or string bag to transport purchases. These may be bought in hardware stores, houseware stores, kitchenware stores and department stores. Or bring your own tote from home!

In some markets, particularly the larger ones, a clerk will help you select your various purchases. The clerk will then put your groceries aside and give you a bill which you take to a cashier. The cashier will give you a receipt which you bring back to the clerk who then gives you your groceries.

Although fewer and fewer stores follow the old tradition, many places of business close from noon to 2:00 P.M. for a civilized lunch hour. These stores are usually open until 7:00 P.M. or later.

Some shops feature duty-free items and you may purchase all kinds of goods at excellent savings. Check with the concierge of major hotels or the phone book for duty-free shop listings. Because you are taking goods out of the country as a foreigner, you may be exempt from paying VAT (value added tax) which is comparable to our sales tax. Don't be afraid to ask.

# Side Trips

The kings of France have always had two wives: their queens and Paris. And, with perfect constancy, they betrayed both of them; their wives with mistresses, and Paris with the slightest excuse for leaving the capitol. We would never suggest that you leave your wife, but in turn, we encourage you to flee from Paris at least once to discover the marvelous homes that belonged to our kings.

### Château de Versailles
**60 km from Paris**
*Open daily, 9:00 A.M. to 5:30 P.M., except Sun. and holidays.*

Clearly the most spectacular home is the Château de Versailles, which merits an entire day-long visit (reserve ahead for lunch at Les Trois Marches). Guidebooks can help you discover the Hall of Mirrors, the king's and queen's chambers (completely restored and decorated in their original styles), the private apartments and the ravishing Royal Opéra. But you won't need a guide to stroll through the park (illuminated fountains at night on the first and third Sundays of the month, from May through September, starting at 5:30 P.M.) and to visit the Grand and Petit Trianons.

### Château de Fontaine-bleau
**60 km from Paris**
*Open daily except Tues., 9:45 A.M. to 12:30 P.M. and 2:00 P.M. to 5:15 P.M.*

The Château de Fontainebleau was the home to many, notably François Ier, Marie Antoinette, and Napoleon Ier. The ornate ceilings, covered with Renaissance frescoes, and the furniture representing different historical epochs give the palace a rare artistic quality.

### Château de Chantilly
**40 km from Paris**
*Open daily 10:30 A.M. to 6:00 P.M. except Tues.*

The Château de Chantilly is particularly interesting for the beauty of its park, the richness of its museum (works by Clouet, Jean Fouquet and Raphaël), and the beauty of its immense stables—an eighteenth-century masterpiece.

### Saint-Germain-en-Laye
**Paris Banlieue**
*Open daily 10:00 A.M. to 5:00 P.M., except Tues.*

Louis XIV was born here. There is a magnificent park and an extraordinary museum of Gallic and Roman antiquities. And if that's not enough, at the portals of Paris you'll find the ruins of the Château de Sèvres, destroyed by the Revolution of 1789. Nearby you can visit the Musée National de Céramique to see the works from the celebrated Sèvres porcelain factory, open daily except Tuesday, 9:30 A.M. to 5:15 P.M.

### Giverny
**60 km from Paris**
*Open daily 10:00 A.M. to noon and 2:00 P.M. to 6:00 P.M., except Sun.*

Although no king lived here, it's an absolute must to go to Giverny to visit the home of Claude Monet, prince of the Impressionists, and his garden, which is a dream-like jewel.

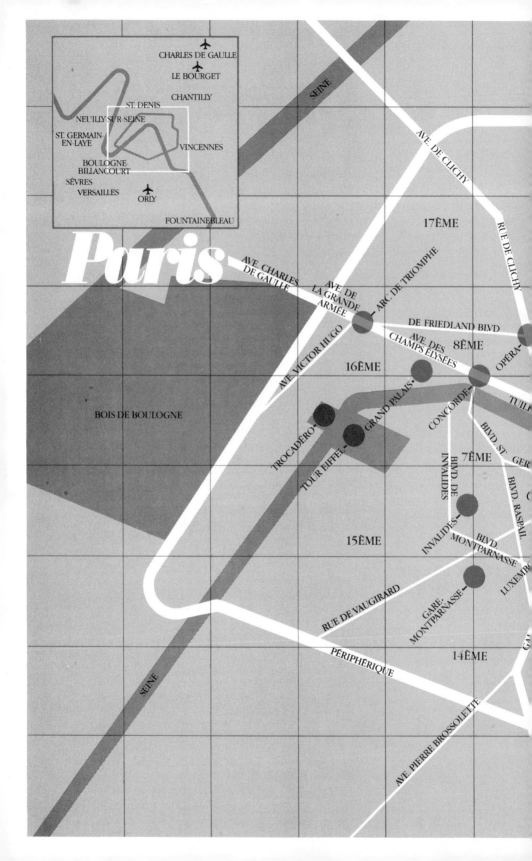

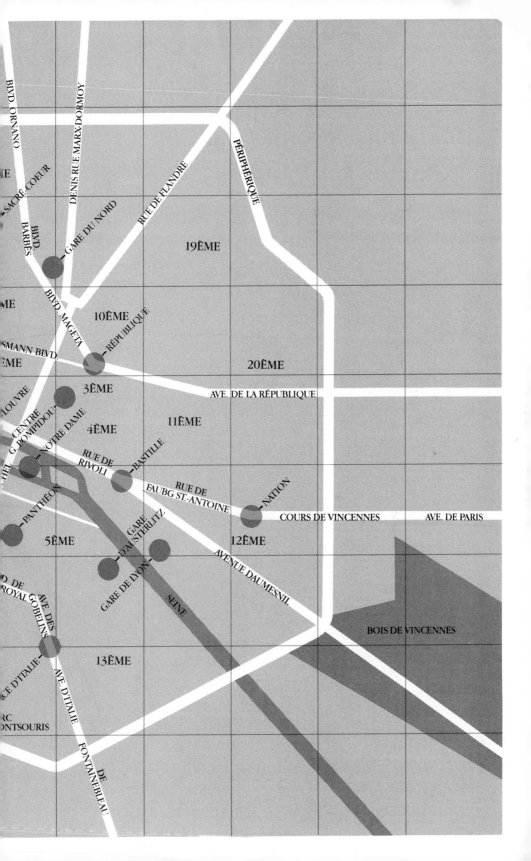

# THE INDEX

# THE INDEX

# D

# G

# H

**P**